The A to X of Alternative Music

The A to X of Alternative Music

Steve Taylor

continuum
LONDON • NEW YORK

CONTINUUM

The Tower Building, 11 York Road, London SE1 7NX

15 East 26th Street, New York, NY 10010

British Library Cataloguing-in-Publication Data

A catalogue record for this book is available from the British Library.

ISBN PB: 0-8264-7396-2

Typeset by Aarontype Limited, Easton, Bristol

Printed and bound by Antony Rowe, Chippenham, Wiltshire

List of Photographs

Foreword

Michael Stipe, REM

Before it became just another category, 'Alternative' was . . . it was attitude.

I bought the Patti Smith record 'Horses' the day that it came out – and at age 15 I decided to be in a band. At that time Patti Smith, Television, Blondie, the Ramones and the Talking Heads in the US, and, in the UK, Wire, Generation X, Japan, Captain Sensible, the Slits, and of course the Sex Pistols and the Clash – they all represented something very powerful to me. They all set the stage for Alternative.

When we started REM, Alternative was exactly what rock'n'roll and punk rock were supposed to be, which was an attitude and an approach to what was clearly at that point a business. Around the same time, there were Black Flag, the Replacements, X, the Rain Parade, the Dream Syndicate, U2, Hüsker Dü, Sonic Youth – and later the Pixies and Jane's Addiction. We all had that attitude. It was about how to move through those sharkey waters without being consumed by the business aspects of having a band, putting out records, having them distributed and being able to play to your fans.

'Alternative' was a word that was a good description of bands like my band, but it became, over time, just another category. And then, of course, it became the mainstream and became as myopic as the thing it was supposedly alternative to. Which is sad. But that's how everything runs its course. It sets the stage for the 'next' wave, the next fringe movement, the next surprise and shake-up. It is the cycle and that is how it works.

The word Alternative still resonates with me personally. Alternative, in its true definition, describes all of my favourite music, all the groups or performers I love, writers that I still go to as a music fan to find inspiration and to pull out the more competitive side of *me* as a songwriter. If Björk or Thom Yorke and Radiohead or Bono and U2 do something that's great, then I get my neck up and I want to do something that's equally great. They raise the bar and I have to jump it. The same with Patti Smith, Grant Lee Phillips, Q-Tip, Courtney Love, Polly Harvey . . . you get the drift, yeah? Conor Oberst, Pharrell and Chad, Will Oldham, Fischerspooner, Dub Taylor, Jarvis Cocker, Peaches, Andy Lemaster . . .

Key for Instruments

b	bass	p	piano	
br	brass	pedal steel	pedal steel guitar	
c	computer	perc	percussion	
cl	clarinet	prog	programming	
cor	cornet	samp	sampler	
d	drums	steel g	steel guitar	
d-m	drum machine	sx	saxophone	
eng	engineer	syn	synthesizer	
fl	flute	tr	trumpet	
g	guitar	t-sx	tenor-saxophone	
hm	harmonica	t-t	turntables	
k	keyboards	v	vocals	
mand	mandolin	vib	vibraphone	
mar	maracas	vn	violin	
o	organ	w-w	wah-wah guitar	
os	oscillator			

The reference to 'First team' in each entry provides details of the most effective line-up of a band's career, and not the original or current personnel. In most cases this will correspond to the album listed under 'What to buy first'. So now you know.

And In My Defence:

This collection might get you annoyed. I hope so anyway. It's not the usual list of same old same olds gathered together in a handy reference encyclopaedia, once again confirming how easy it is to categorize music by haircut and trouser dimension. The artists you're expecting to be here ... well they're not.

Each of the artists gathered here has made a difference. They have all helped shape the popular music we are hearing today, even the bad stuff. When it was their turn, they considered the options and decided to go against prevailing trends and make music in a different way. As a consequence it sounded different, had a different message and ultimately built a different audience. The artists in this book were the leaders of the once new scenes that have since fed into the various mainstreams we have today.

Of course, if it was up to the major record labels that in 2003, once again controlled vast tracts of the industry infrastructure responsible for producing music, we would still have just the one mainstream: pop. A return to a pre-1965 pop world would mean smaller marketing budgets, decreased levels of production (the last two decades have in fact, tended towards over-production) and, most importantly, a customer base which does not need constantly updating as its members constantly adapt their tastes in response to new cultural forms of music, new alternatives. Before 1965 the pop audience was just a bunch of kids.

The term 'pop' came into being with the success of the Beatles, who brought into focus a style of music that had exploded youth consciousness in 1956 with the landing on planet earth of 'Elvis Presley and the Teenagers'. They might as well have come from outer space because both singer and the targeted new audience shook up western society big time. Entertainment took on a new significance and, with rock'n'roll music, a new sector of society could be communicated with, directly and as a mass group. Cinema had its stars and television was just about everywhere, but neither was as direct as rock'n'roll which appealed on a visc-

eral, physical level and demanded the full attention of its new fans.

It took just over a year for corporate America to get a handle on rock'n'roll. By the summer of 1957, Elvis was signed to RCA as a recording artist and to Paramount as a film actor, and a new set of teen idols was being groomed to serve the needs of a brand new money-spinning opportunity. It was then that the first split in the teen market occurred: there were those who spent time and money checking out new releases by the original rock and rollers, and those who were happy to let the manufactured stuff wash over them. To run with the first crowd meant listening to late-night specialist radio shows (Radio Luxembourg in the UK) and going to independent music stores. For everyone else, everything was pre-packaged, a team of writers operating out of the Brill Building in New York wrote songs specifically aimed at the model teen-ager and entrepreneurs like Don Kirshner and Berry Gordy, who had their own team of writers and produccers, knocked the stuff out production-line style. The writers and producers were good though; they knew that teenagers needed to connect with the pop they were producing, and so they tried to get inside the mind of a typical teenager whenever they wrote and produced 'the new' pop music.

In Britain, Lonnie Donegan showed the way in terms of DIY music and the first generation of rock'n'roll fans started forming their own bands. When the Beatles exploded internationally at the beginning of 1964, the template for pop music that we have been using ever since was set. It had to appeal directly, either emotionally or physically, and the signs of its manufacture as a product with mass appeal had to remain hidden while the audience focused on just how great life was, surrounded by pop.

From 1963 to 1967 the British beat groups inspired by the Beatles, the established rock'n'roll stars, and the soul-pop perfected by the Motown label effectively satiated all demand for pop music in most parts of the developed world. There was one mainstream of pop music and it fed into other more specialist areas. Mods, rockers, and those teenagers that showed no allegiance to either group were happy with their musical lot, and if they wanted to explore other styles as they left their teenage years behind them, there were other ready made specialist mainstreams for them to look into – blues, jazz, folk, rhythm and blues, country etc.

It was America that broke first. Without the teen subcultures that Britain had, teenagers had less to keep them interested in the established mainstream. Many formed their own bands as a way of creating some excitement. There was new electric equipment available, and so garage-rock scenes began sprouting up across the country. Older styles were explored by excited young musicians, keen to break rules in jazz, rhythm and blues, and folk. It was the start of the break-up. Things fell apart, the centre could not hold.

The oldest artists included in this book date from this time. All were inspired by the directness and inherent honesty of otherwise manufactured music, but felt that they needed to do it a different way if they, and their audience of peers, were going to get their kicks and throw off the teenage tag which had served its purpose well up to that point, but was holding back a new vibrant form of music that could be taken to a wider and more nuanced audience. When Bob Dylan plugged in at Newport he pinned his banner to pop and left folk behind. As far as he was concerned, pop was the way forward and folk was just going to be one part of it.

After 1965 pop music became more difficult to predict, and more expensive to make, and it ate into the established markets for other specialist music types too. It was crucial for the major companies controlling the industry that they get a handle on it all and stay in control. Diversification was the key strategy and the first split was between pop and rock. Albums were encouraged instead of singles. They cost more to produce, but the financial rewards were far greater. A new 'mainstream' was born, based on a conception of popular music as an art-form separate from the cynical machinations and tyranny of commercialism – and it generated a f**k load of cash. Later on when art-rock reached its nadir and imploded into a black hole of wizard hats, extended codas and 24-track tape, to be

replaced by the leaner, feistier, more relevant punk scene, another new 'mainstream' came into being. This time, the major labels were not initially involved; they left it to a new set of independent companies which, in order to ensure that music never got so pompous, conceited and downright out of touch with real culture again, established a set of working practices that outlawed any music that didn't stand for something. It was a different mainstream that by the end of the eighties was out of touch with real culture, and sounding just a little bit pompous and conceited. In the UK, rave culture took the indie scene by surprise and pissed off the major labels who had just bought up or done licensing deals with a stack of indie labels who were supposed to be in touch with the kids on the street. Of course, the kids had left the street and headed to a field near the M25 to succumb to the tyranny of the groove. Guitar music was apparently dead.

In the US it soldiered on magnificently. The underground went overground in 1991 when Nirvana released their *Nevermind* album and ushered in the 'alternative decade'. That's right, the word that I've chosen to describe the artists in this book had become an official generic term, not just to describe a type of music, but a whole friggin' decade's worth of the stuff. Another new 'mainstream' to add to the others, the final victory of a music industry which has been trying to get pop music back into some semblance of order since 1965. By referring to artists as alternative, the industry has conspired to make it definable and marketable as a commodity, and one which is designed to fit in with a specific taste or lifestyle choice, the bastards.

So how do we reclaim it, make it mean something? Everybody's part of one mainstream or another, so how do we get beyond the reality that everything is for sale, a marketable product with a target audience? What makes something truly alternative despite its inevitable connections with the commercial world? The new definition of alternative is an old idea repasted onto a new word. It plays on a concept of authenticity, that anyone playing real instruments and writing their own songs is authentic and original. But the music and the way it's played is nothing to do with it. Alternative isn't something fixed, it is constantly changing. We can't know what alternative is until we know what it is an alternative to, and we can't know what that is until the alternative shows us. Capice?

Try reading that last sentence again. I'll give you a few moments. Catch up when you're ready.

It's easier to establish who was alternative in the past because we can trace trajectories of influence, locate the point at which something changed. If you analyse the changes and the working practices that led to them, you find out that the artist in question was taking a leap into the unknown. They were not just avoiding the mainstream, they were avoiding the official opposition to the mainstream too. In fact they were avoiding all established musical, cultural or political positions and were operating on instinct, spurred on by a sense of change that came from the people and culture around them.

Manufactured pop is not intended for continued consumption, it's throwaway, designed to connect with a mass audience for a few weeks, maybe months and then when culture moves on, it can be discarded or held forever in purgatory as a 'golden oldie'. Alternative is more targeted, the maker has a particular type of listener in mind when they write and record their songs – someone like them, from the same era with similar experiences and tastes. Ultimately, this music has more chance of having lasting significance because it is based in reality, not fantasy target types that don't actually exist as individuals.

The reality is that there are songwriters, musicians and producers who have done their own thing and had an impact that is still felt today in terms of music, the music industry and key social structures. Crucially, these artists didn't care too much about mainstreams and alternatives, and that's the clincher. They were not driven by commercial imperatives, and they weren't in it for the cultural or social prestige that comes with being different (and successful). They didn't do it for the money and they didn't do it for the reputation. Of course, they made money (most of them) and they have the reputation (some of them) but the driving factor that connects all of the artists here listed is their clarity of intent.

Tony Wilson, the co-founder of Factory Records, describes how Ian Curtis of Joy Division had to write and perform – there was no freedom of choice involved, the songs were in him and they had to come out. There are others like Frank Zappa who felt a

need to draw attention to some of popular music's more ridiculous aspects; John Lydon and the Sex Pistols are credited with a similar plan. It's not true of course. McLaren may tell it like that, but Lydon – the voice and soul of the group – maintains that the Sex Pistols were a staunchly working-class group that simply stated their sense of disenfranchisement through their music. Afrika Bambaataa, the organizer of hip-hop into a philosophy as well as a postmodern free-for-all, was driven by a utopian vision of inter-racial harmony. Ian MacKaye of Minor Threat and founder of Dischord Records was on the same page as Greg Ginn of Black Flag and Jello Biafra of the Dead Kennedys in wanting to establish a new independent music industry that brought opportunities to small town USA, and was imbued with a 'straight-edge' moral philosophy.

Bands like Hüsker Dü made sure that hardcore punk and the American underground scene developed its sensitive side and started a trajectory that led to the breakthrough of Nirvana in 1991. Sonic Youth took up the spirit of experimentation rife in New York during the CBGBs[1] punk heyday and created a new sound for the guitar which launched various textural adventurers. Meanwhile, Prince picked up on the valuable work done by Sly Stone and George Clinton in reconfiguring black identity within popular music, and PJ Harvey followed Patti Smith in challenging the female stereotype in music and a much wider social context. Indie music got the groove as baggy broke in Manchester and the Stone Roses, the Happy Mondays and Primal Scream made music for cultures to blend to. Music-makers in Europe, Asia, Africa, Australasia and South America all did their bit to bring local music to international attention and are listed here too.

The sense of purpose is the key thing, but it's not necessarily about being oppositional or fiercely independent, or making a blow for art in popular music. In fact, self-conscious art-ism is frowned upon in the *A to X of Alternative Music*. Politics isn't a necessary guarantee of getting in either. Everything's political, everything you do, everything you don't do. Anti-capitalist approaches to music are always instructive, and certainly Crass and Billy Bragg have given it a good go, but as Rage Against The Machine guitarist Tom Morello has pointed out, record companies, manufacturers and distributors are the means of getting a message out to a wider public and without them, you might as well not bother, if real change is what you're after.

A key issue is the notion of independence in an industry which is more now than ever, wrapped up and in the control of major entertainment corporations. Not since the days before rock'n'roll has so much been owned by so few, even if it's all licensing deals and 'tight-loose' economics, to give the impression of independence. New artists are signed as alternative artists, or signed and then manufactured as alternative artists. For some years now it's been a genre recognized throughout the industry, and lately it has divided into sub-generic categories complete with their own record labels, dedicated television music channels and sponsorship deals with sporting products, clothes and small dolls which are apparently necessary to connect with the music. Sorry kids, but there's not a lot of recent stuff in here, it just doesn't qualify.

That said, being signed to a major and playing the marketing game does not rule out inclusion here. It's consistency that counts, and besides, getting the message across and connecting is one of the criteria that counts. Selling out is a state of mind. There are plenty of sell-outs in here if the usual accusations are applied. The earliest artist entry is for Bob Dylan who sold out the folkies at Newport in 1965 by going electric. The Velvet Underground sold out rock'n'roll when they let Andy Warhol turn them into part of his art, playing behind dancers and obscured by lights during the Exploding Plastic Inevitable shows. Scritti Politti sold out the British indie scene when they went pop. Hüsker Dü sold out the underground when they signed a deal with Warners. And the Daisy Age crews sold out rap when they remembered Bambaataa's fifth element of hip-hop – the 'knowledge' of black cultural history – which was being undermined by a new nihilist form of rap that played directly into the hands of corporate America. As I said, selling out is a state of mind.

The music-makers in this book have all done things that bucked the trend of the moment. Their alternative credentials are marked by a refusal to go with the flow, and their inclusion is based on the lasting significance of that refusal. The type of music they were making at the time is irrelevant; the existence of lots of little

mainstreams, constantly mutating and coalescing at any one time has ensured lots of alternative scenes operating against them, hence, there are artists included who are noted for their country, folk, soul, jazz, hip-hop, jungle and techno music as well as the usual assortment of punks, post-punks, psychedelics, shamblers, metallers, art-rockers, lo-fis, goths and krautrockers.

Regardless of style, alternative artists are only classed as such if they retain roots in the tradition of popular music. Alternative classical, jazz and avant-garde artists are not included (no Cage, Coltrane, Coleman, Davis, Sun-Ra, Reich). Similarly, artists who are deemed to have worked independently of a prevailing alternative sensibility or culture of feeling are not in either. This does not mean artists who have purposely clashed with ongoing alternative trends – they are most valuable; but rather those artists who are uninterested in current trends to the extent that their work does not connect with the alternative sensibility or spirit of the times, or any time later on (no Newman, Cohen, Morrison). Some artists are not included because they have not maintained a consistency of purpose, and others are only discussed within the confines of their relevant output which may only be one album. Other artists with more extensive entries tend to have developed and adapted their work at crucial points during their career.

The criteria for inclusion in the *A to X of Alternative Music* is as follows:

Working It – the artist will have based their career on a set of organizational and recording procedures that enables them to retain their voice and overall sense of purpose. Commercial imperatives will not have overly influenced their decision-making process and there will be no completely damning evidence of self-conscious arty behaviour or tendency towards cross-generic and cultural bandwagon-jumping, aka 'the Sting syndrome'.

It – the artist will have avoided 'blank parody', in other words they will have consistently challenged the basic set-up of sounds, structure, textures and rhythms in their work, either pursuing a specific aesthetic over a long period (Sonic Youth) or experimenting with new set-ups on an album by album basis (the

Fall). Words will push the boundaries of what is accepted practice in popular music and will be written from a particular perspective and about topics rarely dealt with.

Getting It Across – the artist will have connected with the alternative sensibility of their own era, or since with a newer generation of admirers. Ronald Sukenick has rightly pointed out that 'you become a commodity as soon as you start trying to sell your work … the product becomes your trademark, and you become its brand name. In other words, it's you in your market identity, your "image" … Since you're doomed to commodification you might as well start paying attention to the way you're sold.'[2] Although the artist cannot guarantee how they will be perceived they can make efforts to ensure that they send out a consistent message (performance, videos, publicity) that is in line with their overall sense of purpose and aims.

In addition to this, artists who have clearly influenced later styles or ways of doing things are more likely to be included along with those who have headed up a scene and in so doing have established a connection with a new audience.

Unfortunately there is no room for the originators within the field of popular music, partly because they have been written about at length elsewhere but also more pertinently, because as I have indicated earlier on, they represent a period when there was an evolving consensus of what popular music meant to a youth audience at that time. It is only with the emergence of a new role for pop music and a new audience demanding something more, that music like other aspects of sixties society began to develop an alter-ego, the alternative, which was mass-culturally driven and therefore populist and not associated only with the avant-garde. But just so I don't get too many complaining letters, there follows a brief summary of certain key contributions that prepared the ground for the subsequent growth of alternative music.

Elvis Presley
Invented popular music. He wasn't the first to put country and rhythm and blues together but, with an amazing band who played as raw as some of the early

punk bands, he brought black music to the attention of most of the developed world.

Little Richard
The true king of rock'n'roll? Little Richard made raw shouty songs propelled by relentless hard piano playing. His voice and theatrical stage show were virtually copied by James Brown and he was an inspiration to Otis Redding and Jimi Hendrix. He never left independent label Specialty, staying for the duration of his rock'n'roll career.

Buddy Holly
The first complete pop artist. He wrote, performed and produced his own material, devised the classic band set-up of lead and rhythm guitar, bass and drums, and didn't see any issue with pop stars wearing glasses. He intellectualized pop.

Lonnie Donegan
The first truly independent artist and lo-fi originator to boot. Donegan showed a generation of British kids that rock'n'roll was something that could be done with household furniture. Skiffle didn't last long though as those with guitars who could play properly began hooking up with other proper musicians to form more sophisticated bands. A lot of washboard players hit the scrapheap in 1962.

The Beatles
Part of the first wave of pop groups that gigged relentlessly notably adopting offensive and antagonistic stagecraft while in Hamburg. They wrote their own songs, promoted working-class culture and inspired garage-rock in America. 'I Feel Fine' in 1965 featured feedback guitar, 'Daytripper' had obscene lyrics and the 1966 album *Revolver* changed the way instruments were recorded and albums were made.

The Rolling Stones
The band that put rhythm and blues into a pop band set-up and consequently made it that much rawer. Jagger's original vocal on first single 'Come On' was deemed unfit for release by label Decca. The band's long hair and combative attitude when interviewed became an archetype for cool. They're abandonment

of flower power in favour of realist narratives documenting revolution and rioting set the scene for the decade to come.

The Kinks

'You Really Got Me' may well be the first heavy rock riff following Dave Davies' amp-slashing. By 1965 Ray Davies had come into his own as a songwriter, knocking out social commentaries with lashings of irony. When the world went to San Francisco for real or metaphorically, the Kinks stayed home and recorded the more parochial *Village Green Preservation Society*, echoes of which can be heard in the songs of Paul Weller, Morrissey and Damon Albarn.

The Who

Another R&B band, but one that connected with its audience at a directly cultural level, particularly in songs like 'My Generation' with Daltrey's vocal references to uppers leading the way in the druggie sixties. The mod movement was a mass youth culture by 1965 and although the Who reflected that, it was with the early psychedelic underground and the fallout culture of the skinheads who were into ska and later, northern soul, that alternative culture was born in the UK.

The Kingsmen

One from the American garage band era inspired by the Beatles and advances in technology that brought along the electric bass, organs and fuzz-tone guitar effects. Their rough-and-ready classic 'Louie Louie' was the pinnacle of the new rock sound that would later inspire the Doors, MC5 and the Stooges.

James Brown

Following years as a Little Richard copyist and soul crooner, Brown got on the good foot in 1965 with his transformation into funk which brought rock elements into black music and began to change the perception of black singers and musicians.

The Beach Boys

With *Pet Sounds* in 1966 Brian Wilson created what is widely regarded as the perfect studio album, a production which was painstakingly achieved with obsessive attention to detail, and which launched studio fetishism for the next two decades. As a songwriter, musician, arranger and producer, Wilson blurred the boundaries between the roles and his stay at home policy when the Beach Boys toured emphasized his commitment to recorded music in the first instance.

By 1966 popular music was established as an artform and a money-spinning business opportunity. With Dylan's revolutionary act at Newport, a new sensibility was inspired among those fans that supported him against the old folkies. Dylan's new people were beat group inspired garage bands who played Beatles-inspired raw rock'n'roll that carried with it an air of amateurism and psychedelic experimentalism. In the UK the mass mod culture was slowly dissipating and a new set of music fans emerged as an alternative. As in America, these first alternatives were beginning to seek out underground clubs where they could experience the new psychedelia too.

And that's the starting point.

Beginning with Dylan and the first psychedelic bands, the *A to X of Alternative Music* contains the two hundred most important alternative artists to have emerged in the last four decades. OK, I know that there are some great artists missing, most of my favourite bands are not in either, but this is not about great music, it's about important music.

It's time to get controversial.

A

A CERTAIN RATIO

A Certain Ratio were signed to Factory Records. In fact, they were only the second band to be signed to the label which, along with Rough Trade, was an early champion of the artist's freedom of expression. This meant realistic deals that gave the bands some financial assistance with the basics but allowed them to remain essentially independent and free to develop their music however they wanted. This was certainly true for A Certain Ratio, a band who pioneered their own mix of funk, jazz and northern soul on a label that was establishing itself as a haven for bands like Joy Division and Durutti Column who connected with the clear and concise attitude of punk but developed new musical ways of exploring complex emotions and ideas. A Certain Ratio were punk too. They had a specific agenda and were out there to confront accepted rules and values. It's just that they didn't dig the same records, and had no intention of conforming to what was already becoming an agreed set of influences. 'It's naff to us. All that stuff. We are a funk band, truly ... Parliament, Funkadelic, Earth Wind and Fire, those are our roots. Not Iggy fucking Pop or the Velvet Underground.'

Simon Topping, Martin Moscrop, Peter Terrel and Jeremy Kerr got their kicks on the northern soul scene that flourished around north Manchester during the seventies centring on all-nighters at clubs like the Twisted Wheel.[3] The scene lived on well into the eighties and was a crucial part of the musical and cultural development of Ian Brown and Mani from the Stone Roses and Paul Ryder of the Happy Mondays amongst others. Before Manchester transformed itself into 'Madchester', northern soul was the official hedonist response to a series of winters (and summers) of discontent. Joy Division set the discontent to music, creating a brutal, honest, snug-fitting homological soundtrack. A Certain Ratio did the same but made it possible to dance the blues away at the same time.

Their first single, 'All Night Party' was followed in 1980 by the monster groove of 'Shack Up', a cover of an international club favourite reinterpreted through a harsh, Manchester post-punk groove. It's an inspirational slab of electro-funk punctuated by angry guitar stabs, seven minutes of hedonistic celebration and harsh reality perfectly reflected by the line 'We can sleep together but we can't live together'. Live, the band was all wah-wahs and trumpets, and as such confounded notions of punk wherever they toured. A Factory gig in Derby with Joy Division ended in a riot after an angry member of the audience threw a glass of beer at the band. Even their comrades at Factory Records were sometimes concerned at their apparent jazz tendencies, but the band had a spirit of independence that was particularly infectious for people like Factory co-owner, Tony Wilson, and that alone was enough to allay such fears.

The album *To Each*...recorded in New Jersey in the country where hip-hop was the new street music – the new punk – was engineered by Factory's in-house producer Martin Hannett. Peter Terrel's tape-loop work combines with an even tighter band sound held together by the precision drumming by Donald Johnson and points the way to a series of EPs and 12″ releases that are best described as cold funk. Check 'Knife Slits Water' for a highly danceable account of night-time urban violence.

By 1982 the band had lost Topping and Terrel, and drummer Johnson was pushing the band in a more commercial jazz direction. After one more album they left Factory, but their legacy remained in the design and sounds emanating from the Hacienda club,[4] opened by Factory, and the birth of New Order in 1982. It's about time that A Certain Ratio got pasted onto that unofficial Manchester timeline that seems to run from Joy Division to New Order and ultimately to the Happy Mondays. A Certain Ratio freed the beat in independent music and began the process of democratization at the cutting-edge. They're in.

First team: Simon Topping (v, tr), Jeremy Kerr (b), Peter Terrel (g, tape), Martin Moscrop (g, tr), Donald Johnson (d)

Place, time, scene: Manchester 1978. A Certain Ratio combined the punk and northern soul cultures of Manchester in the late seventies. Cabaret Voltaire in Sheffield, the Pop Group in Bristol and Gang Of Four in Leeds were similarly inspired by post-punk opportunities for breaking a few rules and ended up inspiring a slew of American bands, the mainstream new romantic movement and a whole bunch of indie kids who began to realize that it was okay to make meaningful artistic music that you could also dance to. By the end of the decade no-one was questioning the idea.

What to buy first: *To Each* 1981

And then: *Sextet* 1982

In retrospect: *The Old And The New* 1986

AC/DC

It's 1973. The last great Rolling Stones album is a year old, Led Zeppelin are experimenting with reggae and soul, there's trouble in the camp of the dark lords as Ozzy hits the bottle, and Free have just called it a day. Classic rock was doing itself in, and punk was still at least two years away. If it was going to survive the onslaught, it needed new life and that was exactly what it got. At the same time that garage punks like the Saints and Radio Birdman were setting up shop, AC/DC, working from a similar agenda that included the Stooges but placed the emphasis firmly on the classic rockers of yore, began a career that is as faultless as it is reiterative. Such is the focus and strength of their sound, they have managed to replace one of the greatest rock vocalists of the last thirty or so years without missing a riff. AC/DC have learned from the occasional mistakes of their heroes that progression doesn't necessarily mean messing with the content. You don't have to invent a new language every time you want to say something to someone; it's being listened to and being believed that's paramount. AC/DC will probably go on forever because of precisely this fact.

AC/DC were already a band on the cusp of something new when they played their debut New Year's Eve gig at the Hard Rock Cafe in Sydney in 1973. Malcolm Young had effectively trained his band to play rock-punk; straight and loose. He had spent a lot of time with his brother George Young in the studio helping him produce a variety of artists and had learned that he didn't like things too complicated. Malcolm was no prog-rocker, he preferred the deed done live with the minimum of multi-tracking. Early line-ups centred around the twin guitar attack of the Young brothers, Angus in particular using the early gigs as an opportunity to pin down his musical and performance technique, which Dave Lewis writing for *Sounds* later described as 'frenzied schoolboy lunacy ... making Chuck Berry's duck-walk look like a paraplegic's hobble and oozing sweat, snot and slime like some grotesque human sponge being savagely squeezed by the intensity of his own guitar-playing.'[5] His school uniform, worn as a one-off joke in an earlier band became indicative of AC/DC's lack of pretension in a time when bands took themselves far too seriously.

Bon Scott was brought in as vocalist in 1974. He was a mate of their brother George who knew him from his days in the Easybeats. While George and Harry Vanda were having an international hit with 'Friday On My Mind', Scott had been in a pop band called the Valentines. That wasn't what got him into AC/DC though. Malcolm and Angus had initial reservations about his age but their attitude changed when they discovered that he had spent the early seventies drinking, getting laid and doing stir. The fact that the 29 year-old was a fellow Australian import from Scotland sealed it. After a night of karaoke Chuck Berry, Free and the Stones, Bon was in and Dave Evans, the original AC/DC vocalist, was out. It was a key decision.

Scott gave the band its definition. His vocals were scrawled like graffiti over the top of a solid rock backing. The subject matter was lewd and funny, topical and personal – songs about being a rock'n'roll singer most of the time, with a tendency to draw on the running motif of the male genital region and its functions. There's 'Big Balls', '(She's Got) The Jack' and of course, the considered treatise on Freudian identification theory, 'She's Got Balls'. OK so there's nothing advocating the twin punk concerns of anarchy or nihilism but 'Problem Child' – 'what I want I stash, what I don't I smash' – offers a similar sentiment. When AC/DC visited the UK for the first time in 1976 they were supported by Richard Hell's band the Heartbreakers and appeared on Tony Wilson's TV show *So It Goes*, and it seemed that the punk sensibility existing just below the band's surface was clearly apparent to those in the know. It happened in the US as well, where they played several dates with glam-punks the Dictators and, most bizarre of all, in Holland where AC/DC were even included in a series of bubblegum cards collecting together 'Punk, the New Wave'. The band themselves have never claimed to be anything other than a rock band but then how many punkers said that. That was always the problem with punk. It was against categorization; real punks didn't want to be called punks. They identified such pigeon-holing as the first step to corporate mediocrity and they were proved right in the long run. Listening back now it's clear that most 'punk' bands were pretty much straight rock anyway. As the expression goes, apply mathematical principles to a non-mathematical concept and see what result you get. Or for American readers, do the fucking math!

There were six studio albums between 1975 and 1980. *High Voltage* and *Dirty Deeds Done Dirt Cheap* were big in Oz and had a boogie and blues feel that sounded great in the sunshine, but it's with *Let There Be Rock* and live one, *If You Want Blood You've Got It*, that they really manage to capture the raw and heavy spirit of AC/DC. Like other hard rock bands Motorhead and Iron Maiden, the live album is always an essential purchase. The threat of being dropped by their label meant they were forced to slick it up for the next one, and *Highway To Hell* was produced by the present Mr Shania Twain, Mutt Lange. Still, he did a good job. With the exception of *Back In Black* which followed it, there has never been a more satisfactory mix of raw power and FM sensibility. Radio stations loved it. Not that the subject matter was toned down though. Scott's still at it. 'Touch Too Much' is out and out porn and it's not clear that 'Beating Around The Bush' is entirely concerned with the difficulties of communication in a failing relationship. The title track with its big riff, insistent drumming and rhythmic vocals is prototype Beastie Boys, and maybe it's stating the obvious but 'If You Want Blood (You've Got It)' . . . rocks.

Highway To Hell was released in the summer of 1979 by which point the line-up of the band had tragically changed. On February 20th Bon Scott was checked into King's College Hospital London. DOA. He had drunk himself to death the night before watching new wave bands at the Music Machine in Camden. The band carried on with new front-man, geordie Brian Johnson, a vocalist who Scott had often praised as an influence, and a new album, *Back In Black*, a tribute to their friend which opened with the sombre tolling of 'Hell's Bells'. 'You Shook Me All Night Long' was an international hit and the title track remains a staple of rock, goth and indie club nights the world over. *Back In Black* defined their approach into the eighties and beyond. It was perfect, definitive, an international mega-seller that existed in a hard rock, studio-tanned genre all of its own, a style that required no alternative. No-one would dare.

First team: Malcolm Young (g), Angus Young (g), Bon Scott (v), Phil Rudd (d), Mark Evans (b)

Place, time, scene: Sydney 1973. AC/DC were the band that put together garage punk with heavy metal and sex-crazed rock. They got it so right that UK punks and US glams took them to their hearts at a time when self-styled rock bands were perceived as musical dinosaurs. Their influence is universal, but it's worth pointing out that Black Flag's rock album *Slip It In* and the low-slung loose grunge of Green River and Mudhoney seem to draw on a little of the old DC aesthetic.

What to buy first: *Highway To Hell* 1979

And then: *High Voltage* (UK/US release) 1975, *Dirty Deeds Done Dirt Cheap* 1976, *Let There Be Rock* 1977, *Back In Black* 1980

ADVERTS

The Adverts were one of the first bands formed in the wake of the Sex Pistols. Tim Smith had read about the band in the *NME* and made the trip from Devon where he was studying to see them play in London. It was the summer of '76. Checking out the Clash, Siouxsie and the Banshees and the Damned too, he was inspired to give it a go himself. Punk philosophy in action right there.

Changing his name to TV Smith and bringing in his friend from college Gaye (Advert), together with

9

Air

Howard Pickup and Lorry Driver, he formed the Adverts. After an alarmingly short period of practice, the Adverts made their debut at the Roxy[6] in January 1977 and within a few weeks had been spotted by Brian James of the Damned and signed to Stiff Records, the second band signed to the label, which is acknowledged as the blueprint for the like-minded artists and entrepreneurs that set up in their wake. The band were key to punk's dissemination around the UK. They toured everywhere banging out songs with motivational messages advertised by Mark Perry's inspired slogan, 'here's one chord, here's another ... now go form a band'. The fact that the Adverts were on *Top Of The Pops* by the summer of 1977, complete with female bassist Gaye Advert, further emphasized that anyone could do it.

Also important was TV Smith's approach to writing, which was always more objective than the force of personality that went along with the lyrical outpourings of Rotten, Strummer and even Weller. He was engaged in a kind of reportage, informing the kids and the powers that be of the new culture and the new music in town. Songs like 'One Chord Wonders', 'Bored Teenagers' and 'New Day Dawning' on their debut album *Crossing The Red Sea With The Adverts* capture the mood of the time, notably the sense of optimism that is often missing from generic assessments of the punk generation that focus on its negativity and nihilism. Asked in recent interviews, Smith always takes time to emphasize just how much fun punk was, and that comes through in a song like 'Gary Gilmore's Eyes', horrific, ethically complex subject matter, but

strangely uplifting thanks to a rabble-rousing chorus. Mind you, the vocals might give you the willies. British punk-rock at its best, and a reliable insight into what the scene was really about before the revisionist cultural historians got involved.

First team: TV Smith (v, g), Gaye Advert (b, v), Howard Pickup (g), Lorry Driver (d)

Place, time, scene: London 1977. The Adverts took punk all over the UK inspiring new bands in their wake. The central message was that anyone could do this, music was secondary. TV Smith has since embarked on a solo career writing and performing less highly-charged social commentaries with an acoustic guitar.

What to buy first: *Crossing the Red Sea with the Adverts* 1978

In retrospect: *The Best Of The Adverts* 1999

AIR

When Air released *Moon Safari* in early 1998 it was hailed as the crowning achievement of the 'French Touch', the realization of everything that French house and hip-hop had been working towards since the late eighties when DJ Laurent Garnier left the Hacienda nightclub in Manchester and set up his own club nights in Paris. From that starting point, French dance music got a new lease of life, and after a decade of trying, finally rid itself of the spectre of Europop. In 1991 MC Solaar put out his debut album (*Qui Sème le Vent Recolte le Tempo*) assisted by the production team of Boombass and Zdar. This pair later began recording their own material as Cassius but not before Zdar had teamed up with Etienne de Crecy in Motorbass to release the highly influential *Pansoul* album on their own Solid label. De Crecy also masterminded the development of long-serving scenesters Alex Gopher, Daft Punk and, wait for it, Air. There's certainly a case to be made for a whole scene going on in Paris but it's important not to lose track of the music when coming up with what appears to be a neat little creative subculture. True, Jean-Benoit Dun-ckel and Nicolas Godin did attend the same college as Etienne De Crecy and formed a band called Orange with Alex Gopher, but while dance culture may have had some influence, it's not central to their musical project.

Orange was a fairly traditional set-up of guitars, bass, drums and keyboards. They were an indie band. You had to listen closely to realize that Dunckel and Godin were experimenting with classical modes of playing, and it's that subtlety that has carried forward to Air today. Philosophically they can relate to Mirwais' punk and folk experiments during the 1980s, particularly his time in France's premier punk band Taxi Driver, and this is complemented by a love of music by Brian Eno, Soft Machine and Pink Floyd. It could even be argued that their approach to composition continues a tradition of 'musique concrete', a form of electronic music in France begun by Pierre Henry, the instigator of sampling, back in the 1950s, and developed by industrial bands like Cabaret Voltaire and Throbbing Gristle, who used tape manipulation and looping skills to create montages of sound. Hip-hop artists have followed suit, and the Dust Brothers and Beck are the most recent exponents of built music. The thing is, Air are just as keen to play melodies and incorporate folk styles into their music so that it sounds futuristic and unreal, traditional and organic all at once. It's a balance that requires patience and skill. Playing live is not top of their agenda; composers first, producers second and performers third is a mantra repeated in interviews.

Their debut single 'Modular Mix' was released at the end of 1995, co-produced by De Crecy and issued on the Solid label. It's now available on *Premiers Symptomes* alongside seven other early EP tracks which demonstrate Air's knack for making the kind of music that never actually existed in the sixties but sounds like it should have done. There's an array of old keyboards and some impressive cameo solos scattered across the collection. The final track, 'Brakes On', is a corker. Heavy chugging basslines, pastoral acoustic guitar, 'Penny Lane' trumpet, high end-synth solos, an array of samples and any number of whooshes and splooshes. When *Moon Safari* followed in 1998 it brought Air and the burgeoning French scene to an international audience. The relentlessly beautiful 'La Femme D'Argent' gives way to the mathematically precise pop of 'Sexy Boy' and by the third track, 'All I Need', it's clear that Air have taken pop music to the next level. The track puts together the fragile honesty of Beth Hirsch's folky vocal and acoustic guitar, with cold, considered, contrived electronica – the two sides

of the long fought authenticity debate settled once and for all. The acoustic real and the electronic hyperreal perfectly synthesized at last. The Chemical Brothers had tried it with Beth Orton a couple of years before ('Alive Alone'). A good effort yes, but on *Moon Safari*, Air nailed it.

First team: Jean-Benoit Dunckel (k), Nicolas Godin (k, b, g, v)

Place, time, scene: Paris 1995. Air emerged out of a French scene which had been developing since the late eighties, and together with Daft Punk and Cassius removed the stigma that had surrounded French music internationally, namely the refusal of the international music industry to recognize anything but Europop or classical music. Certainly the internationalism of mainly instrumental dance music has opened up the trade routes but Air have gone beyond such electronic facelessness and have forced record companies to consider other forms too.

What to buy first: *Moon Safari* 1998

And then: *Premiers Symptomes* 1998

ALTERNATIVE TV

Alternative TV were led by Mark Perry, the founder of punk fanzine, *Sniffin' Glue*, a publication set up primarily so that he could spread the gospel of his favourite band the Ramones. Of course, other bands got the occasional mention too, even if they did not, in Perry's opinion, quite match up to his heroes. The Sex Pistols were reviewed in Issue 3 and got 'slagged off' because it was thought that there were too many posers in the audience. The circulation reached 15,000 and then Perry jacked it in, mainly because he was getting disillusioned with punk as it stood. He was particularly disillusioned by all that business of the Clash signing with CBS and felt that it was time to give his own band a proper shot.

His main sparring partner was record store owner Alex Fergusson. Together they came up with their first single 'Love Lies Limp' which was given away as a flexi-disc with an edition of *Sniffin' Glue*. (The mind boggles as to what price a copy of one of those flexis might make today.) The single was raw and direct with the word 'fuck' prominently displayed in the first verse. It also incorporated a reggae beat, which confirmed Perry's cultural awareness of the club-based punk culture and the fact that DJs like Don Letts required something to stick on between the Voidoids and Lee 'Scratch' Perry. EMI soon came calling to do a deal, which is surprising considering all that hassle they had had with the Sex Pistols. There was a studio session with producer Mickey Most, but his bad report back concerning the swearing and the subject matter of the songs, coupled with Perry's anti-corporate stance, put the mockers on any kind of deal. An album eventually came out on Deptford Records, and remains an intriguing enigma. Jools Holland's light jazzy keyboard is the first thing heard on the album, followed by a Frank Zappa cover. There is a selection of early Alterantive TV singles, some live, some studio, and even a little dub. It all demonstrates that Mark Perry's idea of punk was idealistic and individual. Under no circumstances should it be bound by rules, musical or otherwise. And for that reason . . .

First team: Mark Perry (v, g), Alex Fergusson (g) John Towe (d), Tyrone Thomas (b)

Place, time, scene: London 1977. Along with bands like the Ruts and of course, the Clash, Alternative TV pioneered reggae rhythms in punk and then moved on to redefine the musical rules probably inspiring a whole host of post-punk bands. The *Sniffin' Glue* fanzine remains a cultural artefact of some significance.

What to buy first: *The Image Has Cracked* 1978

AMERICAN MUSIC CLUB

Mark Eitzel is the main songwriter, vocalist and, for the most part, the guitarist with American Music Club. Back in 1994, just before the release of the band's seventh and final album, he gave his opinion of why his band had never really caught on: 'I'm ballyhooed a lot in foreign press and yet I still don't seem to fulfill the aspirations. We don't play like really weird rock, we don't play really sensational kind of anything, we're just kind of blah. So people hear that we're great from outside and they go, "well, they suck". It's too neo-MOR.'[7]

Eitzel was born in San Francisco but spent his early childhood in Taiwan, his teenage years in Southampton in the UK and his drinking years in Columbus, Ohio. It was in Columbus in 1978 that he formed his first punk band, the Naked Skinnies, and then three years later, in San Francisco, American Music Club with Danny Pearson, Tim Mooney and guitarist Vudi. Eitzel's vocal ability to make his words resonate truth can make American Music Club a heavy listening experience at times. The words are usually deeply personal and are set to a variety of musical styles ranging from country and folk to rock and punk, chosen carefully to convey and offset Eitzel's narrative. Critics love it, and on more than one occasion he's been called the songwriter of his generation. The problem is just that he and his band have consistently failed to connect with the generation in question.

The first album, *The Restless Stranger*, was released in 1986 just as the independent guitar scene was making the transistion to the big leagues. Hüsker Dü and REM were poised to go worldwide with their powerful and literate amalgamation of post-punk attitude and traditional songcraft, and even independent labels like SST, Dischord, Alternative Tentacles and Wax Trax were becoming established as a successful craft industry. American Music Club didn't have a deal with a major or a fashionable minor, and the situation wasn't helped by Eitzel's sporadic quitting and excessive drinking. In fact, alcohol is a recurring, perhaps cathartic motif in Eitzel's lyrics, and this first-person honesty is a feature of most of his writing even if the context is sometimes pretty surreal.

On the band's 1993 major label debut, *Mercury*, Eitzel reflects on his own role and qualities as a songwriter and singer through the medium of a conversation with Johnny Mathis who asks 'Why do you say everything as if you were a thief, like what you've stolen has no value, what you preach is far from belief?' Heavy stuff, and deeply personal, an eloquent, self-critique of the like rarely found in popular music. The very reason why Mark Eitzel is required listening, both as a solo artist and especially with American Music Club.

First team: Mark Eitzel (v, g), Vudi (g), Danny Pearson (b), Tim Mooney (d), Bruce Kaphan (steel g)

Place, time, scene: San Francisco 1983. Beginning like most other bands of the late seventies, as a punk band, American Music Club, were amongst the first post-punk bands to embrace more traditional styles while Eitzel's lyrics became increasingly personal and sophisticated. Thom Yorke of Radiohead is one of a relatively small but dedicated number of inspired fans.

What to buy first: *Mercury* 1993

And then: *California* 1988, *Everclear* 1991

APHEX TWIN

If popular music had never happened, virtually every artist in this book would never have existed. There would be no mainstream or even a music industry to rail against. It's a difficult thing to imagine, like imagining no possessions — I wonder if you can? Music would still be split into two separate worlds: on one hand, the local travelling folk musician circulating news, songs and dance pieces from town to town, and on the other the salaried singers and instrumentalists, the foremost musicians of the day, schooled and expert in the work of genius composers. If popular music had never happened, in either of the above scenarios, Richard James would still get a gig.

Setting off on his musical journey at the same time as Derrick May was creating techno music in Detroit and Sonic Youth were melding high art with base, populist noisy rock'n'roll in New York, the Aphex Twin was creating difficult and beautiful dance music and rhythmic danceable art at home in deepest Cornwall. By the beginning of the nineties, he had built himself two distinct audiences. There were the dancers of course, and the new breed of non-dancing dance specialists, who, if stereotypes are to be believed, stroke their chins and nod their heads instead. Aphex Twin was the rave scene's genius leader, and is deified by trancers, junglists and technoheads alike. With his independent working practices and mythical, reclusive identity he is the rarest of creatures, a musician seemingly untainted by 'the man'.

Like the great innovators of dub and hip-hop, King Tubby and Grandmaster Flash, Richard James builds his own instruments, specifically synthesizers and samplers, but where they were working with existing tracks to come up with something different, James uses his technical abilities to create sounds from scratch. He has explained in interviews that he has the ability to control his own sleep patterns, napping for short periods in order to gain inspiration for new dream-induced sounds. On waking, he attempts to recreate these sounds on equipment that is specially adapted and adaptable to his requirements. This means having access to samplers that allow him absolute control over the speed and resonance of his musical building blocks. The result is free-form electronic music that is freed from the digitized perfectly-spaced beats and which has warmth and personality. His inspiration was probably the electronic work of Kraftwerk, but James' ambition was not to embrace the precision of electronic technology; he was more interested in undermining that precision. In short, James is an innovator in the purest sense, and remarkably he seems to have done it on his own.

Dating from his teenage years, hidden away in a small Cornish village, his prolific early work has gradually seeped out on a series of albums since 1992, when his personal project found itself in demand by a new subculture developing outside of London, which was in need of faster and faster beats and mind-addling bleeps. The album *Selected Ambient Works 85–92* released on Sheffield's industrial and ambient music label, Warp, collects together his music-making from noodle-doodling early teens onwards. His take on electronica is not as cold and mechanical as earlier material by Kraftwerk and his ambient is not as laboured as the experimental Eno work, which disconnected the acclaimed non-musician from his rock audience. He combines synthesizer washes with more traditional analogue keyboard sounds and underpins the whole thing with gentle, dub-meets-breakbeat rhythms. 'Heliosphan' is majestic and 'Ptolemy' is dark and hard, hinting at some of the loud, heavy stuff that would crop up later on. Overall it's a fairly gentle ambient album which, in contrast to Eno's interpretation of the term as music for living — in the background, fitting in with the rhythms of everyday life — challenges the listener with its unexpected beats and alien sounds.

A further compilation album, *Classics*, shows how his music transfers from studio to outdoor rave. There are two versions of 'Digeridoo', the second one recorded live at an event in Cornwall at the height of the scene and the liveness of the purely electronic experience is tangible, even without the sound of the crowd. By the time he was working in real time, releasing albums of music straight after he had recorded them, his albums started to take on a more cohesive sound. *Richard D. James Album* is his most terrifying concoction, with weird stop-start beats, white noise and tough melodies, and *Drukqs* is notable because of his ability to switch between acid house, techno, jungle and sad little piano pieces at will. The two singles 'Come To Daddy' and especially the R&B inflected 'Windowlicker', which came in-between the two albums, are his most accessible pop moments. They even got some mainstream media exposure, which for just a moment must have made all those dance music producers, super-club DJs and a whole industry of corporately-funded labels that operate a production-line approach to body music, feel just that bit inadequate and maybe, in some cases, a little guilty that they had succumbed to the tyranny of the corporate beat.

It's helpful that people get to hear him from time to time and the opportunities are certainly there for the taking. With numerous releases to his and other names, Richard D James aka the Aphex Twin or depending on when you catch him AFX, Polygon Window, Caustic Window or Dice Man – is a one-man multi-faceted genre which nobody truly knows or understands. Well, not that they can adequately describe in earth language anyway.

Place, time, scene: Cornwall 1985. Inspired by dub and electronic music, Richard James quietly got on with his music far away from the traditional hubs of the music industry. By the beginning of the 1990s his legendary status had grown and his music fitted the new demand for Detroit techno music firing the rave scene. Throughout the nineties he has continued to experiment with sonic texture and rhythm and he has clearly had an effect on bands as diverse as Underworld and Radiohead.

What to buy first: *Selected Ambient Works 85–92* 1994

And then: *Richard D. James Album* 1996, *Drukqs* 2001

AR KANE

When operating as AR Kane, Alex Ayuli and Rudi Tambala were London eastenders who specialized in blurring out songs using a variety of strategies including free-form jazz, feedback and electronics. By the time they had put out their debut album, called *69* in 1988, AR Kane had been signed to three of the key British independent record labels of the period, One Little Indian, 4AD and Rough Trade.

Their time at 4AD included a collaboration with labelmates Colourbox and DJs Dave Dorrell and C J Mackintosh on the groundbreaking single 'Pump Up The Volume'. Alex and Rudi were the A and one of the Rs making up the acronym M/A/R/R/S. The guitar sound that sounds a bit like a metal sphere being held against a lathe is down to AR Kane, and any of the bits best described as dreamy would be theirs too. Inspired by the US and UK noise scenes, free-form playing and the progressive folk-rock of Robert Wyatt, AR Kane operated in that area which was totally original in the mid-eighties, at the junction between the independent sector (alongside bands like My Bloody Valentine) and the evolving ambient scene, which tapped into rave culture. The Orb were formed in 1988, the same year that AR Kane released their debut album and the KLF released their ambient masterpiece *Chill Out* shortly after that, although neither went with the onslaught of guitars that AR Kane specialized in. That was left to Mogwai to perfect ten years later.

As Ayuli puts it 'We were a force of ideas. We helped to get rid of stereotypes. In the '80s black men were doing soul, reggae or rap, not psychedelic dream-rock. We opened doors for bands to be more experimental.' For those whose hobby is tracking down the untrackable, begin with *69* and move onto *i*. A lot of what has happened since will suddenly make sense.

First team: Rudi Tambala (k, prog, g), Alex Ayuli (k, prog, g)

Place, time, scene: London 1986. AR Kane combined the pastoral elements of progressive folk-rock with free-form jazz and the textural experiments of bands like Sonic Youth and the Cocteau Twins. Their own experimentation with form has influenced aspects of rock, hip-hop and dance production and might be seen as a forerunner of those post-rock bands like Mogwai who specialize in building tension and release into their music.

What to buy first: *69* 1988

And then: *i* 1989

In retrospect: *Americana* 1990

ARAB STRAP

Maybe it was because Aiden Moffat and Malcolm Middleton couldn't find anyone else in Falkirk who knew about music made by the likes of Slint and Smog that they ended up working as a duo. Aiden provided the mumbled word narrative and drums, Malcolm looked after everything else. The back-catalogue of albums, all except one released on the Delgados-curated Chemikal Underground label, follow a lo-fi production aesthetic and are musically eclectic. The subject matter is whatever's going on in Moffat's life at the time, which tends to mean endless references to his girlfriend and sex, not that the two are always linked you understand.

If you listen to 'General Plea To A Girlfriend' on the first Arab Strap album *The Week Never Starts Around Here* you get a sense of what Moffat's early drum' n'voice experiments in his Falkirk bedroom must have sounded like, not dissimilar to Robert Johnson's primi-tive blues much earlier in the century. It's followed on the album by the single 'The First Big Weekend' which remains Arab Strap's definitive tale of urban nihilism. The lyrics take us through the events of a typical weekend. Starting with the Thursday night canteen quiz, its off to the nightclub and back to Morag's for drink on Friday; Saturday begins with drinking at 10am, drunken oblivion and failure to wake up in time for the football. A hungover train journey home segues into Saturday night at John's indie disco, more drink, a nocturnal excursion to the park and then a Sunday afternoon drinking and watching *The Simpsons*. In the lyrics Moffat explains that the episode in question is particularly poignant, the central message being 'love always ends in tragedy except of course for Marge and Homer'. And that is pretty much what Arab Strap do. They tell it like it is, occasionally they make life sound tragic and every now and again they raise a smile – 'I thought she was quite pretty until last night when Martin informed me that in fact she had been a pig'.

Listening to Arab Strap, it's difficult to know whether or not the stories Moffat tells are the centrepiece which Middleton enhances and contextualizes with his music – the sort of thing beat poets like Jack Kerouac used to get up to with jazz cats in the fifties – or if the two are on separate musical trajectories altogether. It'd be nice to think that it's the latter but

Arab Strap

sometimes the songs are so brilliantly organized that that whole image of couldn't give a shit amateurism just won't wash. 'Hey Fever' from the *Girls Of Summer* EP deals with love, break-up and getting wasted via a slow-building groove that culminates in the best summer sing-a-long chorus of recent years. From elation to heartbreak and coming to terms with it all by getting high with friends all in the space of five minutes, and it just doesn't get any more romantic than 'I used my best shampoo on my pubes just in case'.

On most of Arab Strap's songs Middleton provides different musical textures that signpost the spatial and temporal changes of Moffat's story-telling, and he can do light or dark depending on the mood required. *Philophobia*, the duo's second album, had plenty of the latter. The first song, 'Packs Of Three' relates a tale of unsafe sexual infidelity and getting tested for STDs before moving on to a series of scenarios detailing disintegrating relationships and past indiscretions and secretions. It's horrible, dirty and compelling. Middleton's playing is suitably downbeat and there's a feeling of claustrophobia brought on by the need to concentrate to hear what Moffat is saying that makes Arab Strap a truly unique and interactive listening experience. Once you've lived through *Philophobia* try 'Trippy', the epic 13 minute B-side to their 1998 single 'Here We Go', which does a night out on acid, and is nothing like the Jefferson Airplane. Not a white rabbit in sight, just paranoia, writhing and spewing up bile. Hey kids, do some drugs, why don't you?

Arab Strap, along with Mogwai, Belle and Sebastian and the Delgados are the sound of young Scotland, if only the rest of the world could boast such focused quality.

First team: Aiden Moffat (v, d), Malcolm Middleton (g, b, k, d)

Place, time, scene: Falkirk 1996. Like other bands associated with the Chemikal Underground label, Arab Strap took their inspiration from pre-grunge American bands experimenting with sound and a more direct mode of address. The term lo-fi is most often bandied around to describe their approach, but the truth and honesty apparent in their music makes such a term woefully inadequate.

What to buy first: *The Week Never Starts Round Here* 1996

And then: *The Girls Of Summer* EP 1996, *Philophobia* 1998, *The Red Thread* 2000

ASIAN DUB FOUNDATION

In the summer of '96 there was a lull in the great Blur/Oasis wars. Neither band would be back until 1997, and Pulp and Radiohead were indisposed too. An infrastructure was in place but was not being used. Bis found themselves on *Top Of The Pops* without a record deal, Super Furry Animals performed 'Something 4 The Weekend' on the Richard and Judy morning TV show *This Morning* and Asian Dub Foundation secured a British record deal. It was a good summer, and about time that a band which represented real Great Britain got to be heard.

In their sound and working practice, Asian Dub Foundation have consistently drawn attention to possibilities and potential that the wider music industry would rather ignore. The band was formed at a Community Music and Technology workshop in Farringdon, London. Bassist Dr Das was a lecturer, DJ Pandit G helped out with the technical stuff and rapper Deeder Zaman was one of the students. Together, they set up a sound system, which developed into a live-performance project, given an extra edge when guitarist and trainee lecturer Chandrasonic got involved too.

From the start they were playing anti-racist gatherings and writing overtly political songs. The *Facts And Fictions* album, released in 1995, sets the agenda 'We ain't ethnic, exotic or eclectic, the only "e" we use is electric.' Since then they have set the record straight on British colonialism as told from an Asian perspective. On *Rafi's Revenge* 'Naxalite' is inspired by a peasants' revolt in Bengal, 'Assassin' is the story of one man's avengement of the 1919 Amritsar Massacre, and the much publicized 'Free Satpal Ram', a protest song that drew attention to ongoing British injustice and institutionalized racism.

The music is built on computer screens out of bass and guitar parts, rhythms, loops and samples, but with space to improvize on stage. Chandrasonic's guitar technique varies but his trademark sound is inspired by single-string sitar style. At other times he adopts a more traditional style but explains that the guitar should be thought of as an extension to the amp, it's the tool used to alter the noise, not an end in itself.

The in-depth knowledge of programming technology and beats amongst all the band members makes for an impressive cross-section of dub, ragga, jungle, hip-hop and rock, which is best experienced live. Failing that, via their second album *Rafi's Revenge* released in 1998, which followed up a tour with Primal Scream that at last got them noticed in Britain. It's a rerecorded version of an album first released in France in 1996 where Asian Dub Foundation have a significant fan base. Respect for the band also extends to eastern Europe, Brazil and in particular Cuba, where their perceived dedication to the community ethic is far more important to the record-buying public than star status. It's embarrassing really, that Asian Dub Foundation could only get distribution outside of Britain at exactly the same time that the music industry was cleaning up on retro rock/pop and nostalgia for all things post-colonial. Sure, there was some good Brit pop and rock, some of it's here in the book, but there was an awful lot of crap that didn't connect with anything real at all. By contrast, Asian Dub Foundation have always kept it real, and their legacy is just around the corner. They've made sure of that. How many other bands can you name that have set up their own higher and further education validated music and sound production courses to train the next generation. Check www.asiandubfoundation.com for details.

First team: Dr Das (b), Chandrasonic (g), Deeder Zaman (v), DJ Pandit G (t-t), Sun-J (k)

Place, time, scene: London 1993. Asian Dub Foundation combined the sound-system dub punk of Adrian Sherwood's On-U-Sound collective with aspects of hip-hop and bhangra to create something unique. Bradford-based band Fun Da-Mental led by former Southern Death Cult drummer Propa-Gandhi had pioneered the mix of hip-hop and Asian styles, but Asian Dub Foundation rocked it live. Other bands like Black Star Liner and Sona Fariq have benefited from ADF's musical and cultural groundbreaking.

What to buy first: *Rafi's Revenge* 1998

And then: *Community Music* 2000

AT THE DRIVE-IN

There were a couple of albums and several EPs before At The Drive-In finally got round to releasing the album that finally put into context everything released in the name of nu-metal, emo and whatever the current term is for non-confrontational corporately-funded pop-punk. The key thing is that *Relationship Of Command* was a forward-looking album that only relied on its influences up to a point, and unlike its nu-metal contemporaries, did not steal the musical signifiers of hip-hop and the lyrics and visual presentation of gangster rap, to reel in an impressionable young audience. At The Drive-In, like the Deftones, were one of depressingly few nu-metal/punk bands given a high profile platform to voice relevant concerns and deal with issues, rather than conform to post-ironic sexism and generic Californian fun-and-sun-rock-video motifs. And for an entire career they managed to avoid the adoption of a bald-headed, fat slob, tattooed-up bass-player. Not even for laughs.

Growing up in El Paso, on the border of Mexico and Texas, the five members of At The Drive-In really had to dig around to find the music they wanted to listen to. Classic rock radio ignored the local scene and the local youth culture so the only way to hear mid-eighties punk-influenced bands like Operation Ivy and Bad Religion written about in skater magazines was to go and see them play live. Omar Rodriguez, Cedric Bixter and Jim Ward were high school buddies who hung with the skate punk set and realized at a formative age that they were not living the multi-cultural American Dream. It was a crucial motivational factor. By the ages of eighteen, they were out touring and over the next five years they regularly spent months at a time away from their home base, barely subsisting while they played hard to small crowds. Their breakthrough record was 1997's *In Casino Out* which brought the band to the attention of a major label scrum for bands to replace the dying grunge scene. At The Drive-In were happy to sign with a major who seemed to offer more long-term support while the fashionable established indie labels obsessed over latest, well . . . fashions.

Relationship Of Command is equal measures sunny Californian rock and heavy Seattle grunge brought together by a form of sectional song construction, developed by emo bands like Fugazi in the nineties. Drummer Tony has explained that his favourite part of being in At The Drive-In is constructing and holding together songs that can change speed, style and rhythm several times in the course of as little as two and a half minutes. Cedric's lyrics are custom-made to fit. He's got the space and time to speak his words during the grotesque satire of 'Invalid Litter Dept.', but then for 'One Armed Scissor' he shouts them out at warp speed. It's wordy stuff, and pretty surreal at times – try 'this gravity is a quadriplegic horse and carriage'. But the thing that Cedric is particularly good at is all that rhyming and poetic alliteration that sounds so good spat out over the top of a fast and loud band, beating the crap out of their instruments. Getting Iggy Pop in to sing 'temper, tampered, temperature' confirmed that At The Drive-In were a band to be reckoned with. It's just unfortunate that they split soon after the album's release. Job done, I guess.

First team: Cedric Bixter (v), Omar Rodriguez (g), Jim Ward (g), Paul Hinojos (b), Tony Hajjar (d)

Place, time, scene: El Paso, Texas 1995. At The Drive-In were inspired by post-hardcore emo music. The music and lyrics are suitably complex but the energy of the nu-metal and 'nu-punk' is also detectable in their delivery, making them sound, at times, like a harder Fugazi, an artier Korn and a more intelligent Green Day all rolled into one.

What to buy first: *Relationship Of Command* 2000

And then: *In Casino Out* 1997

AZTEC CAMERA

A writer for *Sounds* magazine put his finger on it. He realized that the 16 year old Roddy Frame wrote 'like a girl'. It was an observation that led to Frame's band Aztec Camera being dubbed 'wimp rock'. Songs dealing with the complicated issues of love and relationships suggested that Frame was a hopeless romantic. They were also remarkably mature and optimistic and, when accompanied by flamenco-inflected jazz guitar, latin rhythms and even the odd handclap and finger-click, it was also clear that the teenager – who should have been impressing his friends with new wave, electronica, maybe even a new take on rock – was instead,

flicking the v's at the accepted cool of the music industry and the kids that bought into it. Together with fellow Scots, Orange Juice, and a band on the other side of the world called the Go-Betweens, Aztec Camera were there at the beginning of a new approach to traditional song-driven pop music that in some ways made it seem like punk had never happened, but which, in terms of independent working practice and oppositional attitude, actually holds its own as a fully-fledged alternative.

Like Grant McLennan in the Go-Betweens, Roddy Frame's love affair with pop music began with the tingling feeling he got when he heard that bit in 'Space Oddity' when Bowie sings 'This is Major Tom to ground control'. That chord, that key change, it's exactly the sort of feeling anyone with a working tingle system gets when listening to most of the tracks on Aztec Camera's debut album *High Land Hard Rain*. Released in 1983, its roots lie in northern soul, Scottish country and western radio, and the quiet songs on the first Velvet Underground album. At 16, Frame had already played the working-men's clubs for a couple of years and clearly prioritized the more traditional folk and contemporary pop that connected with his socially-diverse live audience, consisting of everything from young children to pensioners, than the increasingly clichéd in-yer-face punk performances then doing the rounds across the UK.

He had been a punk himself, playing hard and loud in the Forensics, and had followed that by a stint sounding like Joy Division in a band called Neutral Blue, but it was when he teamed up with Campbell Owens and David Mulholland that he found his niche. When Alan Horne of Postcard Records heard Aztec Camera songs like 'We Could Send Letters', 'Just Like Gold' and 'Mattress Of Wires', the band were immediately signed up alongside Orange Juice, Josef K and the Go-Betweens on the label that uncompromisingly advertised itself as 'the only true punk label, we don't do new wave!'.

The new pop of Postcard Records lasted just over a year and Aztec Camera only ever released two singles on the label. Their debut album, *High Land Hard Rain* was released through Rough Trade, confirming a change of direction and image for the previously avant-garde label that specialized in industrial, punk and reggae. It could also be read as a further attempt to democratize the music industry, still retaining the DIY aspect of the punk ethos, but doing away with a newly established puritanism which dictated that independent music should, of necessity, be hard listening. In interviews, Frame seemed intent on a wilful teenage contrariness when discussing musical influences and politics, as if embarassed by the apparent connections between independent music and left-wing politics and musical elitism. It was demonstrated in his decision to let Mark Knopfler of Dire Straits produce *Knife*, the second album, at that point, Knopfler was the antithesis of all things independent. The fact that it was the poorest Aztec Camera album might well confirm that Knopfler should not have got involved, but it's the attitude that counts. The third album *Love* was a classic of blue-eyed white-boy soul music, again not a thing to normally brag about, but withhold judgement until you've heard it.

Frame doesn't allow style or fashion to compromise the quality of his songs. There's jazz, latin, folk and an overwhelming sense of pop accessibility on *High Land Hard Rain*, and that's the genius, because many of the songs are barbed and cynical at times. 'Walk Out To Winter' and 'The Boy Wonders' address the death of punk and a social spirit worn down by apathy: 'Faces of Strummer that fell from your wall and nothing was left where they hung'. 'Oblivious' has that line about not being lonely, just being alone and 'Down The Dip', which ends the album, doubles as a paean to Roddy's local pub The Diplomat and existential recognition that life is one long journey downhill. Of course, the fact, revealed in the lyric, that he has someone to share his night out and future life with is just the kind of optimism in the face of adversity that nihilist old punk never really got a handle on.

By the time he was writing grown-up (ha!) songs like 'How Men Are', 'Killermont Street', 'Good Morning Britain' and 'Spanish Horses' ('and her eyes, like Spanish horses danced alive as language died'), there was a strong case to be made for Frame as lyricist of his generation. *Stray*, *Dreamland* and *Frestonia* are all excellent albums. But of course, with the exception of one single, the glorious summer 'soul-seller' 'Somewhere In My Heart', Aztec Camera never really broke through into the mainstream. Their songs and their sound – all that melody, those hooks and exuberant performances – were well, too pop, and everybody knows that, since about 1975, that stuff just doesn't cut it in the Top 40. Proper perfect pop – the new alternative?

First team: Roddy Frame (v, g), Campbell Owens (b), Dave Mulholland (d)

Place, time, scene: East Kilbride 1980. Along with Orange Juice, Aztec Camera were on a mission to make music that was not bound by the unspoken stylistic rules of new wave. Frame's lyrics were both cutting and cynical yet contained a sense of optimism. The tweepop and shambling scene of the mid-late eighties and, more recently, Travis, have more than a little Aztec Camera in them.

What to buy first: *High Land Hard Rain* 1983

And then: *Dreamland* 1993, *Love* 1987

In retrospect: *The Best Of Aztec Camera* 2001

B

ERIC B AND RAKIM

By 1987, hip-hop was establishing itself as the new American music. The Beastie Boys and Run DMC were getting their teeth into some substantial international touring, Public Enemy had released their debut album and were in the process of setting up an unofficial school for rap excellence in their studios in Brooklyn, and elements of the new style were being mashed up with the independent scene and the club scene, particularly in London where the perfect blend of house, post-punk and hip-hop had been perfected by M/A/R/R/S. Unfortunately something had been lost in the translation to the mainstream, and it was only when Eric B and Rakim arrived on the scene that a wider audience finally got to hear hip-hop as it was meant to sound. Eric B reinstated the DJ and the art of live mixing. He re-enacted Grandmaster Flash and his adventures on the Wheels of Steel, and together with an MC who was willing to share the limelight and drop concise, powerful rhymes into the breaks instead of talk all over them, they showed that hip-hop, at its core, was about knowing the music, keeping the beats, perfecting the rhymes and movin' the crowd.

Eric B was a multi-instrumentalist who had foregone the guitar, piano and trumpet for the Technics 1200 and the patronage of Marley Marl in 1985. His colleague, Rakim, was a fellow Manhattan resident who before he could sing, had adopted a sing-speak style that is the very definition of the rap art. He was also a musician, who played saxophone and was a fan of John Coltrane; his rapping – cool, laid-back and multi-textured – is a direct result of his jazz influences.

The album *Paid In Full* shows off Eric B's massive record collection and introduces the remarkable voice of Rakim, so rich and powerful and prone to distortion due to its depth, that it needed to be recorded with microphones normally used for bass drums. Listen to 'I Know You Got Soul' – 'it's been a long time, I shouldn't have left you' – and it's like the bass drum is doing the rhyming. It's the coolest and darkest sound in popular music and it's set against a backdrop of the lightest Motown pop, courtesy of the Jackson 5's 'I Want You Back', the smooth soul of Dennis Edwards' 'Don't Look Any Further' and the ubiquitous JBs, funk lieutenants to the godfather of soul himelf, James Brown. The whole thing is in key and looped to perfection, a masterclass in technique for the next wave of hip-hop producers. Not that everything sounded slick and slaved over. That little touch of the spinning vinyl during the Jackson 5 break, which makes the track appear to slip, is crucial, and demonstrates Eric B's mastery of lo-fi turntablism, always recorded live in one take just like Rakim's vocals, which have proved just as influential. According to Rakim, Marley Marl who produced two of

the tracks on the first album, was always on at him to put more energy into the rhyming, to get angry, but Rakim sounded more sinister when he controlled his emotion, something not lost on the likes of Snoop Dogg and Tupac.

In Britain their track 'I Know You Got Soul' was raided and sampled for 'Pump Up The Volume' and by 1987 Coldcut got the duo in the charts with their remix of 'Paid In Full'. By that point the duo had released *Follow The Leader*, a harder street-rap album to follow up the party vibe of its predecessor. The hits stopped at that point as hip-hop went gangster and the visuals took over. Like Rakim says 'I think it's the content man. It's like battlin' back in the day, MC's was trying to really dismantle a rapper and show him how slick he was with his words. Now it's more like "I'll shoot you, I'll kill you." That's not really nothing exciting man. You know we heard it before, we seen it on TV but back in the day we was thinkin' of better and wittier ways to say "Yo I'll rip your arm off your body." We found better ways to say it man and I think that's the difference man.'[8]

First team: Eric B (DJ), Rakim (MC)

Place, time, scene: New York 1985. When Grandmaster Flash made the switch to the studio and Afrika Bambaataa got the electro bug, the live art of turntable mixing of sounds and rhythms disappeared from recorded music, and took a secondary role as backing for the rapper up front. This meant simpler, more consistent beats, often worked out in a studio. Eric B and Rakim, whose voice was as good as having another instrument, resurrected the original relationship between DJ and MC, where both had something to say and said it regardless of current fashions and clichéd image-making.

What to buy first: *Paid In Full* 1987

And then: *Follow The Leader* 1988

BABES IN TOYLAND

Kat Bjelland's take on feminism did not require positive discrimination in a world of men, especially when it simply meant the introduction of yet another female stereotype. For Bjelland, feminism meant having the freedom to do whatever she wanted to do, regardless of cultural or musical restrictions.

Courtney Love reckons that Kat Bjelland was the best female guitarist of them all, and a pretty good songwriter as well for that matter. Her opinion is based on two months together with Bjelland and Jennifer Finch in a San Francisco-based band called Sugar Baby Doll. They played two gigs, one in someone's front room, and then according to Love, all three of them 'dumbed themselves down to get primal in order to get famous'. Love went on to form Hole, Finch put together L7 and Bjelland moved to Minneapolis where she started another all-female trio, Babes In Toyland.

Musically, the band reflected the current mood for melodic hardcore with screamed vocals and Bjelland's violent attacks on her beloved Rickenbacker guitar. Bjelland would always claim that being a female band meant adopting a different rhythmic approach to the men, exactly the sort of comment that undermined and angered certain feminists, and set the tone for a scene which, it was said, was female-oriented but not necessarily feminist. Later on, it got dubbed Riot Grrrl, and high-profile tours with Sonic Youth and Faith No More, a headline performance at Lollapalooza[9] and the Courtney Love connection, meant that Babes In Toyland became identified as its original perpetrators, much to Bjelland's annoyance. The debut *Spanking Machine*, released in 1990, was notable for Bjelland's primal scream and unsettling lyrics. It also bore little resemblance to the loose grunge prevalent at the time, being a lot rawer like early garage punk.

The second album, *To Mother*, was more varied, opening with the ranting 'Catatonic' and closing with the soothing 'Quiet Room'. It was clearly good enough to get them a major label deal for their third album, *Fontanelle*, produced by Lee Ranaldo of Sonic Youth. It remains their most powerful and assured album, the one that blew away their more one-dimensional contemporaries. 'Bruise Violet' is a thinly veiled attack on Courtney, and from there the album proceeds, with songs dealing with the specifics of a violent relationship and an attempted rape. For the remainder of the album the subject matter takes in lust, drugs and heartbreak, but Bjelland never allows the lyrics to become gratuitous; her words are always honest and

vivid, and all the more unsettling because they never seem clichéd.

There have been two more albums, *Painkiller* and the undervalued *Nemesisters*, and the band is still a going concern, having played several British tours since. Bjelland has also found time to develop her other band, Katastrophe Wife, and most recently has given motherhood a shot, which, in case you were wondering is both female-oriented and feminist.

First team: Kat Bjelland (v, g), Lori Barbero (d), Maureen Herman (b)

Place, time, scene: Minneapolis 1989. A band inspired by the opportunities opened up by the growing success of the independent post-punk rock scene. Bjelland's background and 'little girl' look got her band tagged as a forerunner of Riot Grrrl along with Hole and L7, later encompassing Bikini Kill and UK band Huggy Bear. Babes In Toyland tried to play down the connections, concerned that their real message was being ignored for the sake of stereotyping. Always had more in common with Throwing Muses, really.

What to buy first: *Fontanelle* 1992

And then: *Spanking Machine* 1990

BAD BRAINS

There's not a lot of Bad Brains back-catalogue out there. The albums you can get hold of capture the band in the later stage of their short career. It's a shame because Bad Brains were quite obviously a one-off. They began as a funk and jazz fusion band sometime in 1977, but within a few months and having played just the one gig, calling themselves Mind Power, they went punk rock. The catalyst, according to vocalist HR, was the Sex Pistols' *Never Mind The Bollocks* album. Nothing surprising about that, the band lapped up the attitude but considered the music too slow, and as a result promptly invented speedcore.

In fact, Bad Brains might well have been the first hardcore punk band on the east coast. When they supported the Damned at the Bayou in their native Washington DC in mid-1979, both Henry Rollins, later of Black Flag, and Ian MacKaye, who would form Minor Threat, were in the audience. There, they would have witnessed a band of two halves:

Bad Brains the extreme hardcore band, and Bad Brains the pure reggae band. *New York Rocker* magazine summed it up as 'the perfect one-two punch in a live show: just at the point your heart might stop pumping comes a skanking bass line to delight head and feet simultaneously'. It was similar to those Clash and Ruts gigs in London, but just that more extreme, and all of this coming from an all black line-up. A UK gig might have been the making of the band but they never made it out of Heathrow Airport in 1979 when they came over to London at the Damned's request. Work permits might have been a good idea.

Back in the US they tried to do their thing independently, organizing their own tours and support bands, and there was a Bad Brains record label and compilation album of other hardcore bands planned which never materialized. They may have even broken through with their cassette-only release debut album and the continued interest in their early singles 'Pay To Cum' and 'Big Takeover', but blew it by defecating in their own doorway. They began to express homophobic views in interviews and demonstrated little respect for a growing gay hardcore scene in San Francisco. The cod-Caribbean accent and patois that HR adopted didn't help either.

It's a pity because the first album is a clash of two expertly realized styles. The hardcore is tight as, driven at full tilt by the drums of Earl Hudson and the whirling guitar of Dr Know, while bassist Darryl Jennifer comes into his own on the reggae tracks. 'I Love I Jah' and 'Leaving Babylon' represent some of the best art made in the name of Rastafarianism. They followed it with the Rik Ocasek produced *Rock For Light*, more of the same, just a bit slicker, and the full-on rock of *I Against I*, a powerful, heavy album which lost out as the essentially-liberal hardcore community that had initially supported the band moved on. Henry Rollins was talking democracy and the independent scene was made up of powerful but sensitive rock bands. Many didn't bother with the album because by that point HR was perceived as a purveyor of bad-vibe lyrics, driven by fundamentalist political and religious beliefs. Dr Know's guitar-playing is awesome and remained so on the next few albums but the vitality and the focus had gone. During the nineties, Bad Brains were just another rock band. To quote Mr Gump, shit happens.

First team: Paul 'HR' Hudson (v), Dr Know (g), Darryl Jennifer (b), Earl Hudson (d)

Place, time, scene: Washington DC 1978. Bad Brains were the key east-coast hardcore punk band which most American hardcore and post-punk bands cite as a major influence. They were up there doing fast, energized music before Black Flag, Minor Threat and the Dead Kennedys, while the central role of reggae in their set connected them to the London punk scene, even if this aspect of their sound didn't necessarily make its way into American independent music.

What to buy first: *Bad Brains* 1979

And then: *I Against I* 1986

In retrospect: *Banned In DC: Bad Brains Greatest Riffs* 2003

BAD RELIGION

Bad Religion put out their first record on their own Epitaph label at the same time that Robbie Fields set up Posh Boy Records to release records by Social Distortion, Agent Orange, TSOL and Redd Kross. It was 1980 and what with the success of fellow Californians Black Flag with their SST label and Rodney Bingenheimer's punk-rock radio show, there was a whole So-Cal scene developing. Bad Religion were the best of the bunch. Bringing in piano and keyboards to augment more sophisticated song arrangements and lyrics, they made hardcore melodic. Operation Ivy, the Offspring and Green Day formed in their wake and, almost a quarter of a decade after it was initiated, Epitaph Records is still going strong, the longest-lasting independent label of the post-punk era. Bad Religion are as near as damn it, originators of the mega unit-shifting overground punk that exists in ubiquity as this book goes to press. Let's say that, in principle, they've done a good thing.

Rodney On The ROQ was a crucial radio show. Greg Graffin explains in his cyber-autobiography that the punk music he heard on the show 'was heartfelt and desperate. It spoke of the suffering that comes from the pressure to conform, and the burden that is placed on us by those in power, and the celebration of belonging to a community of powerless misfits.'[10] By the end of 1980, at the age of 15, Graffin and his misfit friends were being played on *Rodney On The ROQ*. They were pretty poor at this stage but Brett Gurewitz, the other songwriter in Bad Religion, had got the funding for a debut EP from his father and musical excellence didn't matter back then. By 1982, with drummer Peter Finestone on board, Bad Religion had practiced and gigged, and become a very good punk band, perfecting a melodic hardcore sound matched with intelligent and considered socio-politically aware lyrics.

The debut album *How Could Hell Be Any Worse* was anti-militaristic, anti-corporate and critical of repressive institutional practice in general. Not many hardcore bands were dealing with the concept of 'oligarchy' at that point and the vocabulary was impressive too – 'No longer will young Christian Americans hedonistically indulge in masochistic submission to rhythmic music, for with your monetary support there is no end to what we can achieve in this country.' The second mini-album *Into The Unknown*, released a year later, used keyboards to develop the band's sound. It didn't sit well with purists at the time who could hear elements of retro Paisley rock and even British New Romantic pop, but the album gets better with every listen, and certainly influenced what Redd Kross were doing across town at the same time. In fact, original Redd Kross guitarist, Greg Hetson, was drafted into the band to replace Brett Gurewitz while he battled with drink and drug addiction, but by the third album he had returned and *Suffer* was definitive Bad Religion. The songs, written individually by Gurewitz and Graffin were hard, fast and clinical yet always manage to cram complex lyrics and unusual guitar breaks and hooks into sub 2.5 minute blast-outs. *No Control* and *Against The Grain* continue the onslaught of speedy but pretty punk, and are notable for Graffin's vocal gymnastics and articulate lyrics dealing with political and social issues (as you would expect from a man with a Ph.D. in biology from Cornell University).

By this point Epitaph had notched up big selling albums by L7 and NOFX, and had signed local band, the Offspring. Their 1994 album *Smash* was the point at which Epitaph hit pay dirt and Gurewitz left the band to concentrate on running the label. The melodic punk that Bad Religion had perfected began its ascent into the mainstream where it would eventually nestle alongside hip-hop and metal as one third of the official non-mainstream youth culture musical hegemony at the end of the decade.

First team: Greg Graffin (v), Brett Gurewitz (g), Greg Hetson (g) Jay Bentley (b), Pete Finestone (d)

Place, time, scene: Los Angeles 1980. Bad Religion brought melody and sophistication to hardcore without sacrificing the power and the energy. They outlasted most of the other So-Cal bands and set in train the rise of melodic punk into the mainstream through their influential musical approach and Brett Gurevitz' work for the Epitaph label.

What to buy first: *Suffer* 1988

And then: *Into The Unknown* 1983, *No Control* 1989

In retrospect: *80–85* 1991, *All Ages* 1995

BADLY DRAWN BOY

Badly Drawn Boy is a multi-instrumentalist and self-trained studio technician who, like Prince, Beck and producer Dave Fridmann before, records, arranges and mixes sound to evoke strong feelings in the listener. Initially working from his bedroom with cheap technology, Damon Gough came into his own when he got free rein of a recording studio. Having studied jazz and classical music, for him the divide between mainstream and alternative, authentic and manufactured music, is irrelevant. In many ways, musical styles associated with the various independent scenes have become just as institutionalized and rulebound as commercial pop. He is one of a number of independent artists who continue to adopt an ethical working practice but will not allow themselves to be confined by a narrow description of what their music should sound like.

Damon Gough loves pop music. When asked in a BBC poll to select his favourite British number one hit single, he chose 'You're The One That I Want' from the soundtrack to *Grease*. He explained that it reminded him of a happy period in his life. It was more to do with the feeling it evoked rather than any musical or social significance the song might have had. His own songs have been criticized for being too much about beauty and not enough about truth, an empty series of postmodern texts that sound great and are neatly ironic but ultimately mean nothing. It's that old one about authenticity meaning simplicity and straightforwardness. He probably doesn't help matters by citing Dylan and Springsteen as his heroes and influences. That just encourages the comparison. Badly Drawn Boy presents himself as an affable buffoon, a weirdy-beardy in a beanie hat who struggles to get his stage show right – a hapless amateur who needs months of studio-time to craft his musical follies. But as Simon Frith points out, Badly Drawn Boy is the authentic article. He is trained in jazz and band arrangement and, like Springsteen, he writes 'songs that capture the way we all read great ideas into small incidents and metaphors'. Frith should know; he's the foremost British academic authority on popular music and its attendant culture, and the bloke who heads up the panel that awards the annual Mercury Music Prize which Badly Drawn Boy won with his debut album in 2000.

The overnight success was a while coming though. Drawing on his college-trained knowledge and expertise in a variety of different styles ranging from folk and country to jazz and rock, most of which he arranges and plays himself. He initially made recordings at home in Bolton with a four-track mixer before offering himself a record deal with Twisted Nerve, a label set up in partnership with Manchester DJ and graphic designer Andy Votel in 1997. Initially the plan was to release 500 copies of the debut Badly Drawn Boy 7″ single, but the label has since helped the Doves, Mum and Dad, and Alfie launch careers with varying degrees of success. *The Hour Of Bewilderbeast*, when it finally emerged, was a *White Album* of an album, taking in an array of styles right from the start. The opening track, 'The Shining', begins as an arrangement for string and brass held together by strummed acoustic guitar and a simple piano motif, before transforming into a full-on rock finish driven by huge drums and weird vibraphone. Once inside the album, the sonic trip is mesmerizing and on more than one occasion, deeply profound. Gough has a knack for writing a clever metaphoric lyric – 'Take a left, a sharp left and another left, meet on the corner, we'll start again'. 'You Were Right' on the second album, *Have You Fed The Fish?*, has him reflecting on the nights that he heard about the

deaths of four musical icons, Sinatra, Jeff Buckley, Kurt Cobain and John Lennon adding 'That was a lot of nights and that was a lot of lives'. Somehow, it's tragic but it's left up to you to decide why. There's something about a Badly Drawn Boy record that grabs you firmly by the emotions, provoking joy, sadness and all the other stuff in-between. The music may occasionally be pastiche, it might sound familiar, but that's why it evokes such strong feelings at times. Importantly though, Badly Drawn Boy avoids the blank parody associated with doing what is expected of him. He is neither slick pop or difficult rebel, neither the cynical performer nor the heartfelt artist. There are categories for artists and niche markets for their work, and Badly Drawn Boy does not fit exclusively into any one of them. Badly Drawn Boy makes pop music that sounds familiar (as pop music should do), but isn't really. And that's what it's all about, in a nutshell.

Place, time, scene: Bolton 1997. Badly Drawn Boy's first releases coincided with the emergence of new artists like Scott 4 and the Beta Band whose incorporation of hip-hop sampling techniques and lackadaisical presentation was a refreshing change from the insular and organized Britpop scene. Beck was certainly an influence, but in Badly Drawn Boy's case, his musical training and love of pop music also came into play. With apparently non-mainstream music becoming more generic and targeted at specific large niche markets, Damon Gough's new alternative pop may prove to be a significant influence, if not musically then in terms of its attitude, in the next few years.

What to buy first: *The Hour Of Bewilderbeast* 1999

And then: *Have You Fed The Fish?* 2002

AFRIKA BAMBAATAA

Bambaataa's role in the development of popular music is pivotal. His refusal to define music as black or white cut to the core of music industry tradition. Acknowledging that block parties and rapping had emerged out of black cultural practice, he made it his mission to make what he dubbed 'hip-hop', democratic and non-racist. From the records he played, to the incorporation of white European electronic styles into his studio work and the tie-in with punk, he walked it like he talked it. His popularization of the Roland 808 drum machine and the sampler simultaneously killed off the manual skill of turntable manipulation and opened up a key aspect of hip-hop – finding beats and looping them – to other musical forms and artists throughout the eighties and nineties. Bambaataa has tended to collaborate on musical projects over the years and as a result does not have a particularly consistent back-catalogue of music available that demonstrates his creative progression, but it is as an icon and originator that his legacy should be judged. An elder-statesman of hip-hop who regularly interjects to 'keep it real'.

Bambaataa Aasim grew up in the Bronx Projects. His name was actually Kevin but an historic Zulu name probably commanded more respect in such a tough neighbourhood. As a youth he was a gang-banging warlord, but he got his head turned around at high school. He began reading more African literature and playing sax and trumpet. He formed the Zulu Nation, a spiritual collective that drew upon the principles of several established world religions and set them to music. In fact, by the age of 14 he had a philosophy, a following and an impressive record collection. Inspired by Jamaican DJ Kool Herc's 'merry-go-rounds', house parties held in various locations in New York, where Herc kept crowds dancing non-stop by mixing records together using two turntables, Bambaataa began organizing his own parties. He competed against the likes of Grandmaster Flash in hour-long sessions, earning the title 'Master of Records' not just because of the amount of records he had, but because he also had a wide-ranging knowledge of styles. This went hand-in-hand with his universalist Zulu Nation philosophy, and an approach to mixing that was also 'colourless' and unconcerned with musical boundaries. Bambaataa began referring to the culture surrounding DJs, MCs, graffiti-writers and B-boys as hip-hop, and today still emphasizes that hip-hop is made up of the four elements underpinned by the fifth element: knowledge. Flash and local celebrity rapper Fab Five Freddy both joined the Zulu Nation, and Bambaataa's notoriety got him invited to DJ at punk venues at the end of the seventies, often returning the compliment by booking punk and rock bands to jam at his parties.

In 1979, the Soulsonic Force was created, consisting of around 20 rappers, B-boys, DJs and graffiti artists led by Bambaataa. They made their first recordings in 1980 leading to a deal with Tom Silverman's Tommy Boy record label in 1981. The deal brought together Bambaataa with producer Arthur Baker and led to a studio meeting with electronic pop-artist John Robie. With all three interested in electronic music, particularly Bambaataa's ongoing love affair with Kraftwerk's oxymoronic minimalist epic *Trans-Europe Express,* work was started on *Planet Rock,* a new style dubbed 'electro funk' at its completion. It's the template for all interesting dance music made since, especially techno forms and anything involving samples. It is also quite a spooky listen with its cold electronics and odd robotic vocals, matched with a slowed-down disco rhythm – the first dance record that you don't have to dance to, to fully appreciate. Released in 1982 just at the point where hip-hop was shifting emphasis from the DJ to the rapper, and cutting-edge music audiences were getting a handle on what the new style was, Bambaataa had breezed in and complicated it all again. As the track gradually worked its way around the world, it took with it the potential of new technology. The Roland 808 was clearly far more effective than the beat-boxes that DJs like Flash had been using, and the concept of sampling became a reality for musicians and producers the world over with the introduction of the Akai S-1100 sampler unit, which together with newly developing sequencers changed the structural sound of recordings across the musical spectrum.

Electro-funk was beloved of the B-boys and hated by those who preferred the organic soul of R&B music. It took off big time in the UK where records like Rocker's Revenge's 'Walking On Sunshine' and Man Parrish's 'Hip Hop Be Bop (Don't Stop)' were club favourites that caught New Order's attention and began the long process of British indie music getting hip to the groove. *Planet Rock* was a big record.

The album did not appear until 1986, bringing together the title track with another early electro classic, 'Looking For The Perfect Beat' and newer songs like 'Renegades Of Funk' and 'Frantic Situation'. It was followed by *Beware (The Funk Is Everywhere),* featuring a roll-call of the coolest producers in the business including Bill Laswell and the old Sugarhill Gang backroom team. Bambaataa also worked with James Brown, Malcolm McLaren and John Lydon in the next few years, and more recently with Adamski and Leftfield. The albums come every few years, but when he isn't making them you can rest assured that the master of records is still buying, and taking it all in.

Place, time, scene: New York 1977. Afrika Bambaataa was one of the original New York DJs and was the first to combine his turntable skills with rapping. It was his open music policy stemming from his hiphop philosophy of cultural inclusion that led to the creation of electro-funk, combining rap and funk with the cold electronic beats and sounds developed by Kraftwerk in Germany during the middle-part of the seventies. Electro found a new audience in the UK in the eighties and took hip-hop, and particularly the concept of 'sampling', international. As hip-hop has grown, Bambaataa has remained its conscience, regularly making his feelings felt when he is concerned that the original philosophies are being surrendered to corporate interest.

What to buy first: *Planet Rock: The Album* 1986

And then: *Beware (The Funk Is Everywhere)* 1986

BAUHAUS

It's difficult to assess Bauhaus as anything other than originators really. Tucked away in Northampton, the four members of the band, Pete Murphy, Daniel Ash and brothers David and Kevin Haskins, were involved in no particular scene to speak of. Pete Murphy has explained in interviews that he is first and foremost, a singer who writes lyrics to enable him to use his voice. In a sense, he was always looking for a band to add the wider musical context.

The other three members had played together in a band called the Craze before meeting Murphy, but immediately they established a musical connection with the vocalist. Daniel Ash, in particular, articulated his guitar style to emphasize the dark textures in Murphy's voice, a relationship not unlike the one between Bowie and Ronson or even Elvis Presley and Scotty Moore on 'Heartbreak Hotel'. Although there's an epic, theatrical feel to a lot of Bauhaus' output which influenced later 'goth' bands, sending them off

in search of ever more over-egged production strategies, Bauhaus themselves were keen to get their songs down on tape spontaneously. The band's debut nine minute-long single 'Bela Lugosi's Dead' was recorded in one take, and remains the benchmark by which dark music has been measured ever since. A prominent bass from which everything is built; insistent, sparse drumming that would later be emulated by drum machines; improvised and intricate guitar-work that is as much about the volume and effects as the notes and chords; and that voice, 'undead, undead, undead'. It was released on the Axis label which changed its name to became 4AD in time for the band's first album *In The Flat Field* in 1980, an album which announced the approach that the label would take over the next decade or so with bands like Dead Can Dance and This Mortal Coil. Not that Bauhaus themselves subscribed to the gloom that would later become a stylistic trademark of the scene that followed. The songs may be sinister sounding, but a glance at the lyric sheet reveals more mundane issues surrounding relationships, sarcasm and a sense of irony which was demonstrated beyond doubt when they released a carbon copy cover of David Bowie's 'Ziggy Stardust', a wilfully perverse riposte to music critics who billed them as mere Bowie copyists and retro glam-rockers. The earlier cover of 'Telegram Sam', the appearance in Bowie's film *The Hunger* and Murphy's androgynous celebrity following a starring role in a TV advert for Maxell tape, might have had something to do with the backlash, but time and Trent Reznor have helped restore Bauhaus' place in history.

First team: Peter Murphy (v), Daniel Ash (g), David J (b), Kevin Haskins (d)

Place, time, scene: Northampton 1979. Along with Siouxsie and the Banshees, Bauhaus pioneered the use of gothic imagery and injected some welcome energy and theatre into a post-punk UK scene which was becoming increasingly heavy. Dark, yes. Gloomy, not necessarily.

What to buy first: *In The Flat Field* 1980

And then: *The Sky's Gone Out* 1982

In retrospect: *1979–1983* 1985

BEASTIE BOYS

The Beastie Boys, and their various collaborators over the years, have kept the spirit of hardcore punk alive by making sure that everything they do has a hard and dynamic musical edge. They also realized before other hardcore bands that there was a connection to be made with New York hip-hop. From the hard rock production of their debut album through to the inspired use of samples for maximum rhythmic and dynamic effect, the central concept of the breakbeat and well-placed shouty rap vocals has remained, and has allowed the band to consistently put out vital, energetic, physical music. In 1987 they captured the hip-hop crossover mood and became international stars, bringing hip-hop to a mainstream rock audience and since then have uncompromisingly done things their own way, eventually being recognized as the alternative band par excellence, the first to incorporate hip-hop and punk/metal styles and culture into a seamless whole. The nu-metal money-spinner that followed a few years later is clumsy and deeply cynical by comparison.

Adam Yauch and Mike Diamond played bass and drums respectively in their own hardcore punk band called the Young and the Useless which played a gig in 1983 on the same bill as Hüsker Dü and the Replacements and was inspired by the punk and reggae onslaught of Bad Brains, a band which they saw live whenever they could. They became the Beastie Boys when Adam Horovitz joined. Those who saw them play live, usually at private house parties in New York, are universal in their criticism and at that point in the early eighties they put the instruments in the attic and adopted a different strategy, inspired by the new trend for block parties in their native and, let's be frank, middle-class neighbourhood in New York. Inspired by the montage science perfected by Grandmaster Flash and his Wheels of Steel, they produced their own hip-hop single 'Cookie Puss' which was built out of a spoof phone conversation, a Steve Martin comedy routine and some beats; the B-side was a throwaway reggae track. Bizarrely, the B-side got picked up by British Airways and a section was used for a TV advert. The Beastie Boys heard it, sued and got themselves enough cash to focus exclusively on their music and their position within the growing New York hip-hop scene. By 1984 they had met with Rick Rubin who, together with Russell Simmons, was in the process of setting up Def Jam Records, a label informed by Simmons' hip-hop knowledge and AC/DC fan Rubin's new found skills as a DJ. It was exactly where the Beastie Boys were at musically. It led to a single 'Rock Hard' that sampled AC/DC's 'Back In Black', and an album *Licensed To Ill* in 1986 that brought together the Beastie Boys' rhyming abilities and Rubin's skills as producer, DJ, and man with contacts book. Run DMC wrote two of the tracks and Kerry King from Def Jam labelmates, Slayer, added the perfect guitar solo to 'Fight For Your Right'. It was the album that made the Beastie Boys internationally-famous rap stars, but partly because of the topics of their rhymes and their middle-class and white background, it didn't get them the respect of their peers. The fact that Rubin had contributed so much to the sound of the album did not help either, but the ability to expertly place rhymes for maximum impact was an early sign of things to come even if *Licensed To Ill* did not, in retrospect, fully demonstrate what the Beastie Boys were capable of.

The follow up, *Paul's Boutique*, released three years later with a different record label, is the point at which the Beastie Boys really start to matter. The rhymes provided a carefully constructed mess of specific and popular cultural referencing. The relentless dropping of lyrics and phrases from the rock'n'roll canon ranging from Public Enemy to the Sweet is genre-busting of another kind, running alongside a montage of music, cut up and pasted back together by the Dust Brothers, that is easily the exemplar of the form. *Paul's Boutique* sold a lot less but meant a lot more.

Having perfected the combination of DJ and MC that is the holy grail of hip-hop, *Check Your Head*, released in 1992, was the point at which the band got out their instruments again, and it was followed just over a year later by their masterpiece *Ill Communication*, an album released shortly after Kurt Cobain's, and consequently, grunge rock's death. Almost overnight, the Beastie Boys were making the kind of music that rock kids wanted to hear, independent in spirit with guitars all over it, but which had a different kind of energy and, importantly, was fun again. *Check Your Head* was an eclectic album made up of live jamming and cool soul and funk samples; *Ill Communication* was more of the same and had some awesome riffing. 'Sabotage' is the defining moment, a rock track built on looped riffs but assembled in sections so that the riffs and the rhythm breaks have more impact; over the top there's some shouty almost-rap, and scratching solos. It's Black Flag's hardcore rock experiments, Fugazi's emo developments, and hip-hop's 'anything goes' philosophy – all brought together for the first, and perhaps only, time. That's why it makes so much sense to so many people. 'Get It Together' and 'Sure Shot' are a similarly constructed mix of loose jam and tight loop but done as jazz and soul. The Beastie Boys were soon the coolest band on the planet, leading the way in sample-heavy rock music, and introducing artists like Money Mark, Buffalo Daughter and Luscious Jackson via their Grand Royal record label. 1998's *Hello Nasty* is the perfection of the Beastie Boys' endlessly-mutating crossover sound. The balls-out rock has gone and has been replaced by a more electro-funk feel on tracks like 'Intergalactic' and 'Body Movin'' but with fellow innovators like keyboardist Money Mark, DJ Mix Master Mike and percussionist Eric Bobo on board, the album flies off in all directions. The collaborators add their own style into the mix but it's all held together by the Beastie Boys' sense of vibe, of what works, where it should go and what words to use to get the message across.

First team: Adam Horowitz (g, v), Adam Yauch (b, v), Mike Diamond (d, v), Money Mark (k), Eric Bobo (p), Mix Master Mike (t-t)

Place, time, scene: New York 1985. From hardcore beginnings, the Beastie Boys soon got turned onto the possibilities of looping and sampling. Rick Rubin helped them achieve the combination of hard rock and hip-hop rhythms on their first album, and from thereon a series of collaborations with the Dust Brothers and then a long-standing team of talented musical innovators ensured that the Beastie Boys had the skills to hand to keep knocking out their unique and subtly mutating mix of styles that is always hard, always fun.

What to buy first: *Ill Communication* 1994

And then: *Licensed To Ill* 1987, *Paul's Boutique* 1989, *Check Your Head* 1992, *Hello Nasty* 1998

In retrospect: *The Sounds Of Science* 1999

BEAT HAPPENING

Beat Happening formed at Evergreen College in Washington, the same one that Matt Groening, creator of *The Simpsons* attended a few years before. They thought of themselves as a punk band despite their gentler, more sensitive approach. Woolly jumpers and floral print dresses were not common on the hardcore scene but that's what the trio of Calvin Johnson, Bret Lunsford and Heather Lewis opted for. Musically, they were haphazard. They shared and swapped guitar and drumming duties, with Johnson and Lewis generally doing the vocals. A Beat Happening gig would usually involve almost as many line-up changes as songs.

Their initial strategy for success centred on moving to Japan to record their first demos and become punk stars in a country where there was no other American or British competition. In effect, the trip consolidated all three members resolve to stick strictly to DIY principles, updated to 'DIN' (Do It Now), and the bare minimum in terms of instrumentation and production. The band's definitive work is to be found on the debut album *Beat Happening* released in 1985. Often just guitar and drums, the songs are thrashy in feel and are about typically pop-oriented subjects – crushes, going out – none of the serious, dark stuff beloved of the hardcore bands of the time. On the long-awaited second album *Jamboree*, the mood is still sassy and thrashy but with added sleaze in the guitar department; 'Bewitched' could easily pass for a Cramps song, only less rockabilly, more hardcore punk. The albums were never long, or wide, or deep for that matter.

They supported the likes of Fugazi and Black Flag, borrowing equipment as a matter of course, while in interviews they talked about their favourite Madonna and Janet Jackson songs. The band found like-minded spirits on a visit to the UK, hooking up with the Pastels and the Vaselines in Scotland and releasing a single on the Pastels' 53rd and 3rd label. Everything else came out on the band's own K label and was distributed through Rough Trade or Sub Pop most of the time. It's a label which has since become key to the development of independent music in the years since, putting out early records by Beck, Jon Spencer Blues Explosion and the Make-Up amongst others. Beat Happening stopped recording in 1992 after five albums which are essential listening for bands wanting to play loud and discordant but can't help writing pop songs. Nirvana, Yo La Tengo, Teenage Fanclub, various Riot Grrrl bands and the White Stripes have all benefited to some extent. And that's why Beat Happening are in the book, duh.

First team: Calvin Johnson (v, g, d), Bret Lunsford (g, d), Heather Lewis (v, g, d)

Place, time, scene: Olympia, Washington 1983. Beat Happening were a lo-fi band that challenged the accepted punk image but still made hard uncompromising music. Calvin Johnson's K Records has been key to the development of independent music through the nineties and like his UK counterpart, Stephen McRobbie of the Pastels, he personally has become a talisman for many projects and events that would not have happened without his involvement.

What to buy first: *Beat Happening* 1985

And then: *Jamboree* 1988

BECK

Beck was the first 'artist' of the sampling generation. Almost a decade after the introduction of the little gizmo which made it possible for musicians to create finished pieces of work at home, in lo-fi, a new set of artists emerged who saw what was once considered the cutting edge of technology, as a key tool in their journey back to where the sound was thin, the playing was loose and the songs were knocked off quickly and ironically. Bands like Sebadoh, Palace Brothers and Pavement spent the early nineties rebelling against the new overground underground that had made stars of Nirvana and Pearl Jam and had compartmentalized independent music old and new into neatly ordered market segments. The idea was a good one and the music was refreshingly original most of the time, but there was a whiff of elitism about it all, and full membership required an up to the minute grasp of the ever-changing rules concerning style and taste. A new game of musical one-upmanship was set in motion where it was essential to build the right record collection and reference the right artists at all times, when discussing influences. Many new musicians and bands talked their eclecticism well but failed to deliver any

evidence of such influences in their work. Not so, Beck. With his trusty sampler, slide guitar and sophisticated understanding of musical and cultural history, he embarked on a career of music-making which has always been clever, and sometimes ironic, but also aware of the fact that useful popular music needs to be artistically inventive and at the same time accessible and non-patronizing.

Beck Hansen grew up in a Salvadoran ghetto listening to ranchero music, playing the blues on slide guitar and perfecting his break-dancing. He was also subject to the influence of avant-garde art and punk too. His grandfather was Al Hansen, the founder of Fluxus, an art collective which had connections with Yoko Ono amongst others in the days before she knew John Lennon. Hansen saw art in the everyday, or at least the potential of everyday situations. What if a piano was placed on a ledge, and it, you know, fell off, now how would that sound? Hansen was also one of Andy Warhol's contemporaries who regularly hung out with the arties at the Factory. Apparently it was his suggestion to name the Velvet Underground 'The Velvet Underground'. His daughter, Beck's mother, Bibbee made her own small contribution to music culture a few years later by letting hardcore punk bands stay at her house. Her own band was called Black Fag, a little joke made at the expense of serious, real popular culture that might just have rubbed off on her boy. Beck got interested enough in the scene that, at the age of 17, he headed off to New York from his LA home to be a punk. He spent time with his grandfather in Berlin too. An excellent apprenticeship that, combined with a little studio time paid for by the independent label Bong Load, produced a bit of tape which became an anthem for an emerging generation, the slacker classic 'Loser'. Its looped hip-hop groove, blues slide, ironic, gospel style chorus and 'don't give a fuck' punk attitude brought together in one perfect pop song.

Labels were queuing round the block but it was David Geffen who offered the best deal, an open marriage that allowed Beck to record for other labels. Beck knew the game right from the start. You gotta have something independent going on if you're gonna mix it with 'the man' on other projects. It's about perception as well as creative freedom. In two years he released four albums on four different independent labels including Calvin Johnson's K Records, and also found time to deliver *Mellow Gold* for Geffen, which demonstrated that Beck's major label work is always just as innovative as his independent releases.

Mellow Gold benefited from the money spent on it. *Odelay* justified a lot more. On it, Beck teamed up with the Dust Brothers, the DJ producers who had been responsible for the Beastie Boys' groundbreaking *Paul's Boutique* album five years earlier. Where the Beastie Boys had settled for rapping over the Dust Brothers' intricate montage of samples, Beck worked with John King and Mike Simpson to ensure that the album retained his voice throughout. For a start he played most of the instruments, and on tracks like 'Jackass' and 'Lord Only Knows', the samples are integral but only ever secondary to the song itself. The key is to know how far to push it. 'Devil's Haircut', 'New Pollution' and 'Where It's At' were all singles with recognizable hooks and choruses, but with weird musical excursions somewhere in the middle, maybe inspired by Japanese noise, free jazz or fierce breakbeats. Critics of Beck are concerned with the free-floating nature of all these styles, and what they perceive as a lack of rooted-ness, but *Odelay*, like all of his albums since, sticks to the central working practice pioneered by Al Hansen back in the (avant-garde) day.

Beck's recording sessions, like the art 'happenings' of the sixties and seventies, are improvised affairs where songs, and parts of songs are created on the spot. The use of musical collage, like Al's refuse-inspired art, is Beck's way of merging sometimes outdated and assumed uncool musical styles, to alter the perception of the underlying song or idea. And if he wanted to, Beck could do it differently every time. Sometimes, Beck's albums sound diverse and fractured, sometimes they appear to be based on a focused conceptual idea. It depends on how you listen. Chuck a CD in the player while you're doing something else and *Midnite Vultures* is a sexy Prince pastiche, *Mutations* which came before it, a sparse singer-songwriter effort held together by Beck's prominent voice and his recourse to traditional instruments, notably the acoustic guitar, harmonica and trademark slide guitar. But listen to both more closely and it becomes clear that a whole stack of musical 'junk' that nobody else had any further use for has been pilfered. Amazingly, *Mutations* was knocked up in two weeks worth of record-ing, many of the songs having been written and performed much earlier. Lyrically they're his most personal songs and benefit from his deftest and most subtle production touch, which draws on mainly acoustic instrumentation, but incorporates electronic textures to fill out the sound without losing the sense of stripped down folk that pervades the album. Ex-Jellyfish man Roger Manning has his synthesizer all over it and 'Tropicalia' even features the much maligned eighties disco-staple, the syn-drum. 'Nobody's Fault But My Own' is Beck's best song yet, melancholic like 'Loser', but with Indian droning and a western string arrangement. The album was promoted as a bit of filler by his record label who clearly didn't listen properly. But that just confirms what Beck, and his dear old grandaddy have always said, doesn't it? Look at the hideous mutilated finger inlay artwork. All those severed nerve endings that are in fact red marker pens: Beck is making his point visually too, we live in a time where perception is all, but where the real skill of perceiving is in decline. The best stuff just gets thrown away. Beck tries his best to retrieve it and make it into something beautiful.

Place, time, scene: Los Angeles 1992. Beck was initially associated with the slacker, lo-fi generation of bands who reacted against the corporate appropriation and institutionalization of independent music. The sampler, linked up to a non-linear software application for mixing and arranging, was key to his initial looped styles and montage work, helped out by the Dust Brothers on his acknowledged masterpiece, *Odelay*. Since then he has demonstrated a deftness of touch when constructing albums that seem stylistically familiar, but are in fact a sophisticated combination of ideas, styles, instrumentation and textures. Badly Drawn Boy operates in similar territory albeit with more jazz and classical references.

What to buy first: *Odelay* 1996

And then: *Mellow Gold* 1994, *Mutations* 1998, *Midnite Vultures* 1999

BELLE AND SEBASTIAN

In the sleeve-notes to their second album, Stuart Murdoch notes that 'Belle and Sebastian were the product of botched capitalism' and goes on to explain how each member was working a dead-end job or 'chain-ganged by employment training' when the band came together in Glasgow sometime in the mid-nineties. The focus was a project for Murdoch's popular music course, and the result was a debut album on the Electric Honey record label operated by ex-Associate Alan Rankine. It's probably fair to assume that the ten-track *Tigermilk* satisfied the learning outcomes and terms of the project brief, especially as several tracks quickly got national radio airplay and launched a series of EPs and albums that eventually led to the band being controversially voted best newcomers at the British music industry Brit Awards three years later. That's not why they're in the book though; they're in the book because they tell uncomfortable stories set to uplifting folk-pop music that recalls the sound and mood of all the best bits of the sixties and seventies so accurately, it's as if they've invented a time machine that can take them back to a specific year and a specific studio at will.

Before embarking on his music course, Stuart Murdoch had relocated from Glasgow to London in a vain attempt to meet his songwriting hero, Lawrence from Felt, and had continued to display something of an obsessional streak in his personality, spending most of the nineties in Glasgow asking anyone who had a bit of free time if they would form a band with him. He eventually succeeded in convincing bassist Stuart David to get involved, and had the core of Belle and Sebastian when Richard Colburn, Stevie Jackson, Chris Geddes and Isobel Campbell joined in too. The very first track on *Tigermilk*, 'The State That I Am In', immediately demonstrates Murdoch's knack for writing vivid lyrics that have a touch of the Ken Loach about them. The song consists of a series of scenes, all apparently symbolic, beginning with a dream in which an older brother announces his homosexuality on his sister's wedding day, and ending with the image of the narrator spending his days turning tables around in Marks & Spencers, 'they don't seem to mind'. From there on in the album is a collection of snapshots detailing poignant moments in tragic lives. *If You're Feeling Sinister* was their first album for the Jeepster label and was followed by a trilogy of EPs that sounded different to anything else released in 1997. Britpop was finished. Blur had just put out their

'whoo-hoo' number and Oasis were eating cakes at Number 10 Downing Street. And in the lull, a whole slew of different sounds and voices finally got heard, including Belle and Sebastian. *Dog On Wheels* was a perfect pastiche of Love's 'Alone Again Or', and it was followed by the epic, swirling *Lazy Line Painter Jane*, a kind of updated 'Like A Rolling Stone' where the Jane in question is told 'being a rebel's fine' but why is she 'sleeping in bus stops' and buying 'lotions and potions' that 'hide your shame from all those prying eyes'. A giant sounding Wurlitzer drives the song home, just like Al Kooper did with his electric organ on the Bob Dylan song. The next album, *The Boy With The Arab Strap*, is probably the best of the bunch, bringing together gentle folk, strings and brass, northern soul and perfect pop. It helped them amass enough public votes to win the best newcomer category at the Brit Awards that year, amid claims that the band and their record company had rigged the vote. Strange that. Just because the industry types and media commentators had not heard the band on the radio, seen a video or read about their night-time exploits in the tabloids, they assumed that the band was not popular amongst the record-buying and file-downloading public. There's something to be learned there, I reckon.

First team: Stuart Murdoch (v, g, k), Stuart David (b), Stevie Jackson (g, v), Chris Geddes (p, k), Richard Colburn (d), Isobel Campbell (cello, v), Sarah Martin (vn, v)

Place, time, scene: Glasgow 1996. Belle and Sebastian are clearly influenced by their own musical expertise and have mastered many styles in their prolific career. Felt are a definite inspiration for Stuart Murdoch's lyrics and there are links to Morrissey's storytelling style, although Murdoch has always managed to avoid specific reference to himself, and although many songs may appear autobiographical, most of the time they seem to be symbolic cameos.

What to buy first: *The Boy With The Arab Strap* 1998

And then: *Tigermilk* 1996, *If You're Feeling Sinister* 1997, *Dog On Wheels* EP 1998, *Lazy Line Painter Jane* EP 1998, *Fold Your Hands Child, You Walk Like A Peasant* 2000

BETA BAND

NME journalist Keith Cameron put it best when he noted that it was refreshing to hear a new band without immediately recognizing their influences, or getting a sense of where they are coming from musically. The Beta Band emerged with a series of guitar and percussion driven shuffles that might be traced back to the laziest, lolloping-est moments of the Happy Mondays, but with stylistic references running from krautrock to acid-house.

Vocalist and guitarist Stephen Mason was a B-boy back in the day, a big electro-funk fan who, like his DJ friend John MacLean, has clearly got the looping bug. For the Beta Band songs develop in a straight line, getting more complex as they go on. The first few EPs are key to understanding what the Edinburgh quartet are all about. The early tracks develop from a strummed acoustic base and maybe a bongo or two, to become multi-instrumented mantras with the key words or phrases repeated to fade. The layered textures of individual instruments are warm and organic, and owe little to studio techniques of multi-tracking, in a period when DJs and producers were increasingly taking over from musicians at the cutting edge of musical creativity. The players come in with their parts when it feels right, building on the underlying looped groove. 'Dry The Rain' is the band at their best. The EPs were so popular that they were eventually collected together on one twelve-track album in 1999, and when listened to in order, suggest a band learning as they go. Radiohead are big fans. They invited them on their 2001 US tour and have plainly admitted to being sufficiently influenced by their Scottish counterparts for the *Kid A* album which changed their sound overnight from intricately constructed and emotive guitar rock into a series of steadily building electronic soundscapes that start in one place and end up somewhere completely different. They called it their Beta Band phase.

Determined to keep to their manual looping techniques, and without any songs prepared before they went into the studio, the debut Beta Band album is a bit messy, form over content, but the follow-up *Hot Shots II* in 2001 put them right back on course. Kicking off with 'Squares' – the one about daydreaming amidst the flowers – an out and out pop song but conforming to no one specific stylistic genre, Stephen Mason's dreamy vocal chants are almost monastic, which when set alongside music that is clearly space age makes for a unique listening experience. The important change on *Hot Shots II* is the shortening of the songs so that there's a higher sound per minute ratio. Textures and styles are constantly changing throughout songs like 'Human Being' and 'Broke' and it is all genuinely exciting to listen to. The Beta Band, when they get it right, are masters of the 'less is more' strategy, and they can do it whether they're making long songs or short songs, and that's about as close to musical pigeon-holing as it gets. A good thing, I think you'll agree.

First team: Stephen Mason (v, g), Robin Jones (d), John MacLean (DJ, samp), Richard Greentree (b)

Place, time, scene: Edinburgh 1997. The lolloping psychedelic hip-hop groove of the Beta Band could be traced back to the Happy Mondays in spirit and bands like Pusherman and Regular Fries in terms of music, but beyond that they are an original piece of work. Their early sound influenced Radiohead's change in direction for the *Kid A* album.

What to buy first: *The Three EP's* 1998

And then: *Hot Shots II* 2001

BIG AUDIO DYNAMITE

To start with, Joe Strummer claimed that Mick Jones was kicked out of the Clash because he had got lazy, not interested in recording, playing or even hanging out with the rest of the band. Later on he retracted that and apologized, placing the blame on his own egotistical shortcomings, perhaps humbled by the poorly received 1985 Clash album *Cut The Crap*, and the rave reviews that Jones' new band was getting for their debut album *This Is Big Audio Dynamite*. Strummer and the Clash still had a voice and motivating lyrics but were sounding a bit too traditional, like the musical stalemate that punk had come to bury ten years earlier. Jones had left at the right time, and knew that whatever he did next had to be different. For a Brixton boy it was obvious: hip-hop had arrived in South London and it was as uncompromising in its sound and philosophy as punk had once been. All he needed was a band who could pull it off.

To start with, Jones was drawn towards Don Letts. He was no musician – he needed stickers on his keyboard to help him remember the order in which he should hit the keys – but he was on his way to becoming a film director of some note, having got a lot of early punk performances and events down on super-8. Scorsese was a fan, Fellini had described him as a cinematic terrorist. He was a punk film-maker with a cultural CV that made impressive reading too. He had managed Acme Attractions, a stall on the King's Road selling punk clothing and records where Lydon, Strummer, and both Jones and Simonon were all regulars, he DJ'd at the Roxy when it opened in '77 playing reggae tunes with just one turntable, and managed the Slits on their first tour with the Clash. Integral as far as the mixing of reggae into punk was concerned – it was Letts who travelled to Jamaica with John Lydon in 1978 after he split from the Pistols, and before the dub-inspired Public Image Ltd took shape – the dreadlocked DJ was, at the very least, a talismanic figure who Jones could rely on as an artistic sparring partner.

In practice, Jones continued to write the songs, his core area of expertise being chords and melodies, while Letts brought a cinematic dimension to proceedings in the form of samples and scripted-lyrics which often drew on film for subject matter. The single 'E = MC2' was inspired by the films of Nicholas Roeg, and many of the samples were cut from film narrative. Musically, the first few albums were a blend of rock, reggae, funk and developing dance styles, drawing on the particular musical skills of the rest of the line-up, keyboard player Dan Donovan, and the solid backline of Leo Williams and Greg Roberts. Sometimes the tracks would be more traditionally Clash sounding, notably 'V-Thirteen', co-written with Joe Strummer, and at other times, out there on the cutting-edge of dance culture, as evidenced on 1989's *Megatop Phoenix* album which was substantially acid-house by design. 1989 was the year that the band split following a life-threatening illness that kept Jones out of action for a period. Lett's continued his film and music video work, and Williams and Roberts formed Dreadzone,

while Donovan became embroiled in a predictably doomed relationship with Patsy Kensit. Jones meanwhile, created Big Audio Dynamite II and continued to explore the evolving musical terrain he could hear about him in Ladbroke Grove after dark. The albums that followed were always interesting, but as he has himself admitted, he did tend to stray too far from his own guitar-based roots on occasion. Having said that, there have been some gems. The single 'Rush' in 1991 is certainly worth downloading and the album *P-Funk* in 1995 is a buyer. He has worked with the Libertines, a band not dissimilar to the Clash at their peak, and the Big Audio Dynamite sound system is often out and about serving the local community with all their beat needs. The ideas may sometimes be difficult to pull off, especially as, rather than simply adding texture to his music to give it a sheen of newness, Jones often throws himself fully into experimentation with new styles, but at least Big Audio Dynamite have always been out there giving it a go, and that's how, well – stuff happens.

First team: Mick Jones (v, g), Don Letts (k, samp), Dan Donovan (k), Leo Williams (b), Greg Roberts (d)

Place, time, scene: London 1985. Big Audio Dynamite were into sampling culture before virtually any other UK band. For them the sampler was not a tool to underpin the rhythm and the sound of their music, it was useful for evoking a more cinematic dimension to their songs. Don Letts was key in this regard, and his DJ knowledge, matched with the funk sensibilities of the rest of the band, made for a refreshing new pop sound that influenced bands like Pop Will Eat Itself, Jesus Jones and EMF. The reformed Big Audio Dynamite II incorporated live scratching into the mix and might be seen as a forerunner of some of the rock/rap sounds of the nineties.

What to buy first: *This Is Big Audio Dynamite* 1985

And then: *No 10 Upping Street* 1986, *P-Funk* 1995

BIG BLACK

Steve Albini has a reputation for being a miserable bastard. It certainly comes across in early interviews with his band Big Black, he has no time for 'laissez-faire

hippie wimps', frat-boys and 'lude-heads doing poppers to his music on the dance-floor', and points out
that his music sounds black 'because everyone else tries
to be so twiddle-dee-dee, lightweight, gee-aren't-we-
having-fun'.[11] It's probably a deserved reputation, but
it's also what makes his creative work so interesting. His
concerns are with truth and honesty – in his life and
especially in his music-making. He avoids pretence
and pretension at all costs. As a result Albini has become an institution in American independent music.
He has produced Nirvana, the Pixies, Slint, Tad, the
Breeders and even Bush. He's also had a hand in the
best work by the Auteurs, PJ Harvey and Robert Plant
and Jimmy Page! He hated the Pixies' *Surfer Rosa* which
he produced in 1987, calling it the work of a bunch
of 'art school students'. Everybody else of course, cites
it as the forerunner of melodic hardcore leading to
Nirvana and all that came after them. It was probably
the 'melodic' bit that annoyed him. His name is
synonymous with a hardcore sound that is dark and
abrasive; just the appearance of his name in the sleeve-
notes, signals an artist's intention to make it honest,
regardless of the consequences. Cynics, as is their
wont, are cynical, and are apt to suggest that the Albini
name on a recording is a shallow attempt to gain
authenticity points. Albini, unsurprisingly sees it differently; bands who come to him are doing it in spite
of their record company's marketing strategies, not
because of them. He is also keen to point out that
his contribution in the role of producer or engineer is
not overly significant, hence his refusal to take more
than a straight one-off payment for his work on Nirvana's *In Utero* (and his criticism of the Pixies!). Since
1989, Albini has pursued his own sonic vision with
Rapeman and Shellac, but which are consistent with
the approach he began, as the sole member of
Chicago-based Big Black back in 1982.

Playing all instruments himself on some tracks,
including a home-made Stratocaster, Steve Albini
issued the *Lungs* EP at the beginning of 1983, but it
was well over a year, two more EPs and various personnel changes before a settled Big Black was finally
in place. In that time Albini made himself a reputation as a mean-spirited music critic who only had time
for bands like Chicago's Naked Raygun and Hüsker
Dü. He hated the hardcore scene. By 1984 he was work-

Steve Albini

ing with his heroes, Santiago Durango and Jeff Pezzati
from Raygun, and a drummer going by the name of
Roland who never said much but belt out a consistent
rhythm for as long as was required. Albini was following the lead of British bands like Sisters Of Mercy and
Echo and the Bunnymen who also used drum machines
to dehumanize their early sound, but with Big Black
the added sheets of guitar noise made for something completely alien, no beauty or melody to rescue
the songs from utter darkness. And then there's the
lyrics – child abuse, messing about in abattoirs and
songs that deal in overt racism and sexism – Albini's
shock tactics designed to get folks thinking.

David Reilly, a bassist who had worked with George
Clinton (and it showed), replaced Pezzati for the debut
Atomizer album in 1984, while Albini plays 'rocket'
guitar and Durango plays 'train' guitar. The album
centres around the twin themes of violence and sex,
and often brings the two together, as on a track like
'Kerosene' which is difficult listening both because of

what it says and the way it says it – it's the musical equivalent of the small-town nihilism and emptiness shown in celluloid on *River's Edge*, where murder, sex and drug abuse are a way of life.[12] Like the accusations thrown at little Eminem a decade or so later, Albini has been accused of revelling in the anti-social. His response: 'As far as I'm concerned, an artist has absolutely no responsibility.' It's a philosophy which extends to the subjects of pornography and drugs, and also informs most of 1987's *Songs About Fucking*, which is certainly the most honest album title of the rock'n'roll era, particularly for a band who 'don't write love songs'. There are songs about South American killing techniques, bread that gets you high, and how 'slowly, without trying, everyone becomes what he despises most'.

When they disbanded in 1987 at their peak, Albini described his band as 'dumb, ugly and persistent'. He switched to production, starting with the Pixies and then fellow noise-mongers, Slint and Jesus Lizard, established himself as house producer and mascot for Touch & Go Records, and then hit the road again with a new band. Hooking up with two thirds of the band Scratch Acid and using the controversial group moniker Rapeman, he immediately upset a lot of people and surely trashed any chances he may have had of major record sales. He had built up a head of steam with the last Big Black album and the production credentials had made him a notable worker on the underground scene. With the album *Two Nuns And A Pack Mule* featuring real drums, Rapeman defined what all rock should sound like, especially when letting rip on the perfect rock song. Rapeman's version of ZZ Top's 'Just Got Paid' is the best cover of them all, no contest. It was five years before he returned with Shellac and the album *At Action Park*. On it, Albini was credited with velocity while his collaborators, Bob Weston and Todd Turner, were responsible for mass and time respectively. With a Steve Albini production it's the only way to describe the sound with any degree of accuracy, and that's why his name alone has become a genre in its own right.

Here's a project: look through the rest of this book and see how many post-Big Black artists have at one time or another 'done a Steve Albini'? You can bet good money that it would be a whole stack more, if he hadn't had such picky taste.

First team: Steve Albini (v, g, d-m), Santiago Durango (g), David Reilly (b)

Place, time, scene: Chicago 1982. Big Black was the most extreme sound in Chicago in the early eighties. Inspired by the sonic thrash of the Swans, Hüsker Dü and Naked Raygun, Albini developed new ways of recording sound in the studio, and made innovative use of the Roland 808 drum machine. His production work for the likes of Jesus Lizard and Slint has been just as influential as his own output. His work with PJ Harvey on *Rid Of Me* and Nirvana on *In Utero* has helped each artist to their rawest and purist sound.

What to buy first: *Atomizer* 1986

And then: *Songs About Fucking* 1987, Rapeman: *Two Nuns And A Pack Mule* 1989, Shellac: *At Action Park* 1994

BIG STAR

When the Beatles made *Revolver* in 1966 it was effectively the end of an era. Never again would they return to the simple folk-pop style that they had developed out of an original rhythm and blues base. The style they had developed gradually from their second *With The Beatles* album onwards, culminating on *Rubber Soul*, had enabled them to write more introspective lyrics and develop their harmonics. The melodies and hooks were straightforward and unforced too – they sounded like a relaxed band. With *Revolver* they began to experiment with studio trickery, mixing styles and surreal lyrics. It was great but meant that the only band of any note left doing the pop stuff was the Hollies. In the last years of the sixties, pop music changed beyond all expectation and in the seventies it just kept going, although by then, there were a few dissenting voices who thought everything had got that little bit pretentious and disconnected. In Memphis, Alex Chilton had just finished making a solo album, having left the successful chart band with which he had sung for several years, the Box Tops. Still barely out of his teens himself, he met a trio of Beatles fans who were just finishing off school and together they picked up where the fab four had left off in 1965, but rather than taking the experimental route that messed about with the musical setting, they opted to keep it simple and make the songs progress instead.

Big Star made three albums, each one different, but somehow all the same. The sound they got down on tape and the mood of the lyrics set the scene for the revitalization of pop music and marked out the territory for alternative, college-radio rock to come. In a period where progressive music was disappearing up its own backside, Big Star brought everything back into perspective as if the weird trip of the previous five years had not happened.

Chris Bell wrote a lot of the songs on *#1 Record* while Alex Chilton took a back-seat. The songs are classically structured and there are some great harmonies to go with the jangly guitars. Reviewers, pleased to be able to assess lyrics and pop sensibilities again, loved it, but tended to focus on Chilton because of his chart-topping pedigree and missed the more extensive contribution Chris Bell had made. It broke the band. Bell did not return when the reformation happened two years later, and it was as a trio, that Big Star made their best album *Radio City* in 1974.

Bassist Andy Hummell has explained how a more direct approach to the sound was achieved, instead of laying down songs and adjusting them in the mix at the point of production, this time the band put instruments through old amps or experimented with microphone placement. The oddness of textures and sounds was created live. An oscillator was used to adapt the sound of the guitar at times. Chilton's songs jarred with the melodic lightness and harmonies, a juxtaposition that made bands like REM, the Replacements and Teenage Fanclub sit up and take note.

On *Third* in 1978 the subject matter gets darker still, although the guitar, bass and drums are still the main weapons of choice. Effectively an Alex Chilton solo album, there was no more from the band and Chilton moved into other areas of music, most notably producing an early session for the Cramps that was startling in its raw directness and simplicity. Like pub-rock veteran Nick Lowe who produced early albums by the Damned and Elvis Costello, and was known as 'Basher' Lowe because he just bashed everything down on tape, Chilton clearly retains the sense of clarity and directness that was always around before punk but took a while to find. New bands found Chilton and Big Star in their droves during the eighties and turned them into a cult band almost as worshipped as the Velvets and the Stooges. In they go.

First team: Alex Chilton (v, g), Chris Bell (v, g), Andy Hummell (b, v), Jody Stephens (d, v)

Place, time, scene: Memphis, Tennessee 1972. Big Star were a band inspired by the British Invasion bands of the mid-sixties who bucked the trend of complex psychedelic and progressive music. They were worshipped by guitar-based, independent bands in the eighties, from REM and Dream Syndicate to the Boo Radleys and most passionately by Teenage Fanclub.

What to buy first: *Radio City* 1974

And then: *#1 Record* 1972, *Third* 1978

BJÖRK

Björk has been making music almost all her life. Establishing herself within the fiercely independent scene with Kukl and the Sugarcubes, Björk found herself in a well-respected position when seeking collaborators for her solo album. Since then, she has experimented with sound and production techniques, and has turned out a series of well-received albums that have won almost universal praise within the popular-music industry and some regard within the contemporary classical field. Unlike musical auteurs before her, she has managed to experiment with her talent without falling prey to criticisms of pretentiousness. She could turn out to be one of the most important musicians and vocalists of the next few decades.

At age 11, Björk Gudmundsdóttir released her debut album. It was an album of cover versions, and went down pretty well in her native Iceland. By the time she was 18 she had progressed through three punk bands, released four albums and was working with Jaz Coleman and Youth from Killing Joke who had relocated to Reykjavik to avoid the apocalypse. It's true, I tell you! The collaboration convinced Björk, together with Einar Orn and Siggi Baldursson, that they were ready to move outside Iceland, forming first Kukl, a band which released two albums on the Crass record label, and then the Sugarcubes who were signed in 1987 to the One Little Indian label securing their own and the label's financial future when the debut album *Life's Too Good* was released in 1988. There were three albums in three years, each experimenting with eclectic musical settings for Björk's unique voice, often set against Einar's mad ramblings. On 'Birthday', inspired by Freudian identification theory – 'today is her birthday, they're smoking cigars' – her timing and phrasing is all over the place and her voice, heard by many for the first time is part howl, part growl and at times is so breathless that it sounds like it has passed through every part of the wind instrument section of an orchestra before finally emerging from her mouth. It was the best the Sugarcubes ever did.

Björk has maintained that the band was always a temporary project, a collection of artists who worked in other fields and just came together to do music. The inevitable split after two more albums saw Björk return to Iceland where she began collaborating with musicians on various projects including an album of fifties doo-wop songs. All through her career, collaboration has been key to her music-making, a process which she describes as 'very intimate, a full-on musical relationship' and each of her solo albums, beginning with *Debut* in 1993, has benefited from such an intimate approach. Nellee Hooper provided the trip-hop and house beats for the debut album although Talvin Singh, Jah Wobble, Tim Simenon of Bomb the Bass and film scorer David Arnold also contributed. The lush orchestration and intriguing textures immediately do more for Björk's voice than the comparatively two-dimensional arrangements she was working with in the Sugarcubes. But then the nineties producers had new technologies to hand and the growth of dance and hip-hop had provided them with a whole set of new rhythms to choose from. 'Human Behaviour' was the first of four singles to be taken from the album, and all crossed over into the clubs with the help of a few well-commissioned remixes. Three tracks, 'The Anchor Song', 'One Day' and 'Aeroplane', are all more obviously Björk's own work, and it's these songs which point the way towards her later albums, and demonstrate a keenness to experiment with sounds and moods that come together at the point of arrangement, when she draws on what she has called her 'more academic, clever side'. 'Hyperballad' and 'Army Of Me' from the follow-up album, *Post*, have very specific textures.

Björk's most extreme album is probably *Homogenic*, released in 1997. Unlike *Post*, which was perhaps Björk's most musically diverse album, *Homogenic* is far more personal and is essentially a return to a simpler and more direct sound. It followed what she called the 'crash' in her personal life, brought about by her high profile romantic relationships and her seemingly desperate need to protect her privacy from media intrusion. Remember the incident at the airport with the photographer? He hasn't forgotten. Picking up where 'Hyperballad' had left off on *Post*, the album is a collaboration between Björk and Mark Bell of techno legends LFO. It's a mix of lush strings and distorted electronics, probably the prettiest hardcore techno that you'll ever hear, with lyrics and vocals that make the whole thing otherworldly. *Vespertine* in 2002 did something similar, just a lot more quietly. The beats are often submerged and it's the strings, classical textures and choirs that give the album its overall sound. The final track, 'Unison', brings beats and strings together in a final crescendo that also manages to incorporate a little jungle. Throughout, her voice is deployed as another instrument, as fragile or as powerful as the music does or does not dictate. After years of getting used to her voice, it is still impossible to predict how she will use it from one second to the next.

It's difficult to say exactly where Björk fits in the great musical scheme of things – it's somewhere between rock and dance, and transcending both. Her experimentation is in emulation of her hero, Karlheinz Stockhausen, who explores the psychological as well as the acoustic effects of music. He's filed under classical and that might just be the way that Björk is headed but for her constant need to surprise and ignore rules. The classical folks don't let people like that into their structured, carefully limited world. That's the beauty of popular music – there's no science, just feel. That's where Björk's at right now, when she's not winning best actress awards at Cannes that is. Clever woman.

Place, time, scene: Reykjavik 1977. Björk came to prominence with her band the Sugarcubes in the early eighties, and was one of the few female voices on the independent scene at that time. The combination of Björk's voice and what the band called their 'clichéd pop' approach was entirely different to anything else at that time, although it had some connections with the melodic noise of Jesus and Mary Chain, with whom they recorded a version of their hit 'Birthday'. When the Sugarcubes split in 1992 she was in a strong position to choose collaborators on her solo projects and has clearly been learning from each project she has been involved with, each new texture, mood and sound gradually percolating into pop consciousness. With her album, *Vespertine*, she has managed to make sense of the links between rock, dance and classical forms of music and is truly operating on the cutting edge of creative music.

What to buy first: Björk: *Debut* 1993

And then: Sugarcubes: *Life's Too Good* 1988, Björk: *Homogenic* 1997, *Vespertine* 2002

BLACK FLAG

Along with Minor Threat and the Dead Kennedys, Black Flag were one of the three great American hardcore bands. Their live shows inspired the formation of a whole new generation of independently-minded bands who witnessed firsthand the way in which a group of noise-mongers could connect directly with their audience. The mosh-pit was established at early Black Flag gigs and with it a new sense of democracy doing away with the aura and cult of personality that had built up around musicians during the seventies. Lyrics still mattered to the hardcore bands but they were always secondary to the primal energy created on stage. The bands hoped that their followers would buy the records and consider the messages of the songs carefully. And even if they didn't, then at least the central message was getting through, namely that this was something different – the sound, the attitude and just as importantly, the infrastructure was new – and anyone could do it. Black Flag played gigs all over the US, and at each place they visited, they sowed the seeds of an independent music scene. Later, when the new scenes bore fruit, they signed up the bands to their own SST record label and made sure that they got exposure and any support they could manage. From 1978 to 1981 they made hardcore punk music and for a large part of the eighties they experimented with their hardcore roots, developing new ways of getting their message across. When Henry Rollins joined, the stories and the language became more elaborate and the music changed to fit the mood. Their later records were

dismissed as unfocused and badly executed at the time, but listened back to now it's apparent that the loose, rock style was a foretaste of the grunge scene to come. Black Flag changed everything.

Greg Ginn and Chuck Dukowski met up when their bands played together at parties in Hermosa Beach, an area which to the outsider epitomized the laid-back Southern Californian utopia of sunshine and hang-tens. Some of it rubbed off on Ginn. He worshipped the Grateful Dead, not because of their hippy ideals, but for their approach to music-making. The Dead, live or studio, were always real, their music was grown organically, and their fan base was built on that principle too. The same could be said of British rock bands like Black Sabbath, who seemed to evoke the sound of the factory floor or leisure time spent fixing up a Triumph or a Norton two-wheeler. He hated prog-rock because it was contrived and pretentious but when he heard Television for the first time he was sold on the new style; Tom Verlaine may have played intricate guitar solos but the overall sound was thin, raw and spontaneous. Seeing the Ramones play live confirmed both Ginn's and Dukowski's belief in the purity of punk because it connected with the audience at a direct and physical level. Calling their first band Panic, they continued to play at private parties around Orange County, playing fast to emulate the Ramones but also to get as many songs in as they could before the cops came. By 1978 they were getting gigs in LA and had changed their name to Black Flag, which worked nicely as the symbolic antithesis of surrender, and was also the name of a popular brand of insecticide.

The band released their first single on Ginn's own SST label – an offshoot of Solid State Tuners, an antique radio refurbishing company which he had set up on his own as a teenager – and with it announced their trademark sound, that of a man (vocalist Keith Morris) and a band at psychological and musical breaking point, and best experienced whilst slamming your body into someone else's at high velocity. It was physical music for those physically able to consume it and the mosh-pit was not advised for those who didn't like the sight or taste of blood. Dukowski and Ginn were keen to point out that Black Flag adhered to the punk ethic of 'live and let live'. If mindless violence was posited as a solution, then maybe it was a solution, at least for those doing the positing.

After Keith Morris left to join the Circle Jerks in 1979 the band hired and fired two vocalists, and occasionally resorted to live shows with an open-mike policy, before taking on Henry Rollins who remained with Black Flag until the band split in 1986. His previous band S.O.A. were one of a number of east-coast hardcore bands that aspired to a scene as legendary as the one that Black Flag had founded in California, and it made perfect sense that a band that effectively opened up the trade routes as far as independent music in America was concerned found the ultimate hardcore vocalist whilst they were out on tour. He was key to the band's development.

The debut album from Black Flag, *Damaged*, is a wake-up call to American youth. 'Gimme Gimme Gimme' mocks consumerism, 'TV Party' bemoans a media-transfixed society and 'Rise Above' calls for the change of attitude that is going to be necessary for the revolution to come. Rollins comes into his own as a songwriter on 'Damaged I' which features one of his soon-to-be legendary tension-filled monologues, in this case forcibly pleading to be left alone in his own private psychological hell. Rollins was able to personify the societal ills that Ginn had always written about, injecting a new personal sensitivity into hardcore that would soon be taken up by bands like Hüsker Dü.

Damaged was finished in January 1981 but unfortunately did not make it to the shops until 1982 due to record company wrangling which ultimately concluded with Ginn and Dukowski serving a five-month jail sentence for attempting to release material during a period of embargo. By the time Black Flag had started work on their follow-up, drummer Robo, guitarist Dez Cadena and most significantly Dukowski had left. Ginn wanted to devlop the musical side of the band and had felt that Cadena and Dukowski in particular were just not competent enough to see it through. Maybe Ginn had glimpsed something more substantial with the addition of Rollins and wanted to frame his words in a more complex musical context.

Extensive touring had allowed Black Flag to work out a lot of new material on the road, resulting in three studio albums being released in 1984. *My War* was nothing like *Damaged* from three years earlier.

As far as Ginn was concerned, hardcore was finished. The new album was purposely slow and heavy and *Slip It In* continued in the same vein. Hardcore fans of old hated the new direction but both albums had a raw metallic power that, in retrospect, connects with Steve Albini's harsh noise work with Big Black and the later grunge sound that perfected the amalgamation of punk and heavy metal at the end of the decade. Throughout, Rollins' existentialist angst is full-on, and by the next album, *Family Man*, his spoken spleen-vents had taken over an entire side of the album leaving Ginn and the band a side of their own with which to wig out dark and heavy.

One album later, Black Flag were done. The Rollins Band gave Henry the opportunity to frame his poetic reportage within a sympathetic musical setting, another outlet that complemented his published writing and spoken-word material. The video age and the development of alternative music television made him a cult celebrity during the eighties and nineties, and a mainstream TV presenter at the turn of the millennium. Ginn and Dukowski carried on at SST doing what they have always done, finding bands, recording them, making records and putting them out. Just a few small bands, you understand: Sonic Youth, Dinosaur Jr, Hüsker Dü, Meat Puppets – that kind of thing. And although the label eventually ran into financial problems, leading to some legal nastiness with bands claiming they had not been paid, for the initial development and construction of an independent music industry infrastructure in America, Black Flag are to be saluted. The sound and availability of alternative music has a lot to do with their trail-blazing.

First team: Greg Ginn (g), Chuck Dukowski (b), Henry Rollins (v), Roberto Valverde (d)

Place, time, scene: Orange County, California 1977. Inspired by the attitude of punk, Black Flag reduced the sound and energy of the movement down to its most basic elements and created hardcore. Bad Brains, Minor Threat and Dead Kennedys did a similar thing at a similar time but none made the same commitment to touring the new sound around the country and inspiring a whole network of scenes. The SST label was crucial to the movement's success and continued to support new independent music as it developed. Black Flag themselves adapted their musical approach to keep the spirit of hardcore from becoming institutionalized and generic. Rollins' personal lyrics and brutally honest stage presence also impacted on a new sensitive strain in independent music that affected bands like Hüsker Dü, the emo movement and ultimately the mix of sensitive songwriting and hard music that broke through with Nirvana.

What to buy first: *Damaged* 1982

And then: *My War* 1984, *Slip It In* 1984

In retrospect: *The First Four Years* 1983, *Wasted . . . Again* 1988

BLACK SABBATH

Black Sabbath may well have killed the sixties. The variety and experimentation of the decade, the relentless incorporation of styles and genres, was not on the agenda once they had discovered that guitar, bass and drums could combine to produce a sound so dark and intense that it actually made listening an uneasy experience. Put that together with satanic and death-obsessed narratives, delivered by a front-man with questionable motives and a mad-eyed stare, and you've got a new development in popular music, a development that the critics and the musicians, cozy in their pseudo-artistic respectable careers, weren't ready to deal with. The fact of the matter was that Black Sabbath had hit a nerve and started a trajectory that would eventually lead directly to the Sex Pistols and beyond. And at the time they were universally panned by a set of cultural intellectuals who, unlike the proverbial 'kids', hadn't yet got a handle on the dark side of rock.

Driven by a love of blues-based rock and Geezer Butler's interest in the occult, they first played together as Polka Turk, then Earth, and finally in 1968 as Black Sabbath. Their trademark fat sound takes its cue from Tony Iommi's guitar technique, brought about by an industrial accident that resulted in him losing the tips of two of his fingers. The metal tips he wears and the loose stringing makes those babies vibrate wider and longer. Place the resulting sound out on right-wing with bass playing outside left, drums at the back, and you have a mess of sludge which is the perfect musical backdrop for Ozzy Osbourne's tales of war, madness and satanic ritual. The first album

was released as Led Zeppelin were putting out their second and the Stones were delivering *Sticky Fingers*, key rock albums that had left flower-power and revolution behind them and put sex at the top of the agenda – the cock-rock manifesto. It's odd that critics were so down on Black Sabbath at that point for a perceived lack of sophistication in their sound and subject matter, in the days before dark was considered cool. Maybe, the working-classes aren't supposed to get existential angst, or at least, should not be able to give voice to such feelings. The reality is that Black Sabbath were better at it than most, and could do it without really trying. The title track 'Paranoid' was written as a filler for their second album (the whole album recorded, incidentally, in five days!). It starts with a classic blues opening 'Finished with my woman' but then proceeds to a tragic personal story full of self-loathing and paranoiac decline.

It's not clear when Ozzy sings the line 'Happiness I cannot feel and love to me is so unreal' if it's him or not. His entire rock persona has always been informed by a nihilism resulting in excess. The decapitated furries, inappropriate defecation and the occasional lapse into arson, notably setting the drummer on fire on tour in the early seventies, are part of rock mythology, and lend weight to the claim that there is something inherently dangerous about certain forms of rock music. Such claims were the basis for later court actions against Ozzy and fellow Brummies Judas Priest following suicides allegedly inspired by specific advice given in lyrics. Of course, in all cases the charges have been dismissed as time-wasting and wholly inappropriate, but what's significant is Black Sabbath's role as the first rock band to address themes of death, murder and suicide, and their psychological causes, at a time when other bands were either escaping into fantasy or obsessing about sex. The songs may not have been based in reality but they hinted at the possibilities for songs about the darker side of everyday life. Add to that the sound that Black Sabbath created on their first four albums, and you have the indirect inspiration for punk and the direct inspiration for the hardcore sound which followed it. Ice-T probably had a couple of Sabbath albums in his collection too.

By 1976 Black Sabbath had succumbed to the temptation to experiment (horn sections?) resulting ultimately in Ozzy's departure in 1977 and that of Butler and Bill Ward by the end of the decade. Ozzy moved to America and married one of the best marketing managers in the history of rock, entrepreneur Don Arden's daughter, Sharon. Together they have created a brand identity for Ozzy that appeals to rebels and the mainstream simultaneously. The Ozzfest concerts keep it real-ish and Ozzy the reality TV star – brought into focus in post-production – has reinvented him as everyone's favourite drug-addled clown. It's all a bit sad really, but it's amazing how one blast of 'Paranoid', 'Iron Man', 'War Pigs' or even the relatively mellow 'Sweet Leaf' from the early days still resonate a spirit that cannot be undermined by any amount of cozy domestic sitcoms or corporate repositioning. Black Sabbath rock!

First team: Tony Iommi (g), Ozzy Osbourne (v), Geezer Butler (b), Bill Ward (d)

Place, time, scene: Birmingham 1968. Initially operating in the same territory as Cream, Black Sabbath soon realized that something much heavier and simpler was the way to go. Their relentless riffing and powerful backline, combined with the dark and sinister vocals of Osbourne, separated them from their more cerebral rock contemporaries and made them a key sonic influence for the punk, hardcore and metal bands to come.

What to buy first: *Paranoid* 1970

And then: *Master Of Reality* 1971, *Black Sabbath Vol 4* 1972

In retrospect: *We Sold Our Souls For Rock'n'Roll* 1976

BLUE CHEER

Keiji Haino from Japanese noise band Fushitsusha, a man who knows about the sonic possibilities of the mighty axe, has referred to Blue Cheer's first album *Vincebus Eruptum* as a paradigm shift in the performance of guitar-playing and rock music in general. Recorded early in 1967 when florists were still experiencing a golden age and before street-fighting revolution had become the new peace, it blew away anything else being done in the name of rock due to its raw power. The MC5, Black Sabbath, the Japanese noise

bands and even Cream learned from it, and the Smashing Pumpkins, the Melvins and Mudhoney all went on to cover the band two decades later.

Leigh Stephens started it. He was a British musician abroad in Boston who used his spare time to develop a new playing technique during which he used his guitar to control the high volumes of sound emanating from his stack of Marshalls – a means to an end rather than an end in itself. When Blue Cheer went into a recording studio to record the debut album it seems that several microphones and at least one studio desk were damaged because the VU meters spent too long in the red. As a result, their second album was mostly recorded outside where microphones could be placed a safe distance away from the amplifiers. The first album contains covers of Eddie Cochran's 'Summertime Blues' and Otis Redding's 'Rock Me Baby' which are templates for the kind of murderous reinterpretation that various punk, hardcore and metal bands have specialized in ever since, a kind of respect for the past that acknowledges the sentiment but destroys the original context for something new. The second album, *Outsideinside*, is better produced and consists of a set of Hendrix-type songs where the lyrics are not as important as the screaming vocal style employed by Dickie Peterson. It was the sound of a rock singer learning from the soul screaming of James Brown and Sly Stone, black singers who were sparking their own revolution against the prevailing smooth-pop style associated with successful black music. Stephens left the band after the second album and the band settled into a seventies rock groove, but for a moment there Blue Cheer were the sound of the cultural zeitgeist, and it was new, heavy and loud.

First team: Leigh Stephens (g, v), Dickie Peterson (v, b), Paul Whaley (d)

Place, time, scene: Boston 1966. Blue Cheer made two albums that redefined guitar music and had a specific influence on bands like Black Sabbath and the MC5, but in terms of the role of amplifiers and effects in recording, has had a much wider and diverse impact.

What to buy first: *Vincebus Eruptum* 1967

And then: *Outsideinside* 1968

BLUR

Dave Balfe, one-time member of the Teardrop Explodes and founder of Food Records, the only label that was interested in signing the nascent Blur, back in 1990, explains his taste in music as 'weird pop', that is, non-mainstream music which makes the charts. It's a pretty good description of what Blur are all about. They have an uncanny knack for achieving major success without compromising their overall aims. Image is particularly important – the need for a strong identity to focus the meaning of the music – but Blur have demonstrated that, once that's taken care of, the message and the music itself can be anything they want it to be. Having said that, it's also true that Blur have suffered due to the power of their image, but such is the quality of their work they have managed to successfully shake off the stereotypes.

In their early days as Seymour, the band specialized in noisy atonal art-rock with elements of jazz thrown in. This side to the band which lends itself to image-shifting was probably why they struggled to get signed early on. Food were apparently the only label interested, and early in their career the band took the label's advice, changing their name and tweaking their sound and image to fit with the prevailing baggy scene. There was a hit single 'There's No Other Way' and a Top 10 album *Leisure*. In Japan they were a cultural phenomenon, a key factor in their retention by Food after baggy's demise, and a bargaining tool to gain record company support for a seemingly unfashionable second album that flew in the face of current music trends. *Modern Life Is Rubbish* was Blur's response to being on the road and discerning a growing demand from audiences for a return to songs that had something to say about everyday experiences, and that doubled as good sing-a-long material too. Baggy was going nowhere, the noise-pop scene led by bands like Ride placed the emphasis on sonics and American grunge and hip-hop tended towards apathy and nihilism. Suede were being hailed as the great British hope with a glam-rock sound and some degree of social commentary but, despite music-industry hype, Suede's ironic and sexually ambivalent art-rock never made it in the big leagues. Blur were more direct with their approach.

The iconic mod image that the band adopted stressed the nature of the issues that Damon Albarn was dealing with in his lyrics, broadly speaking the tedium of social and cultural life in post-Thatcherist Britain, in the ironic tradition of arch-mod Ray Davies of the Kinks. The album was the first in a trilogy that dealt with English life. The image and the subject matter made for easy criticism, but what critics then and now have chosen to ignore is that the vignettes of British life and the characters involved are always ironic, and never celebratory. The theme running through the songs on *Parklife* is escape from the tediousness of British life. The characters, whether it's golfing civil servant Tracy Jacks, America-obsessed Bill Barret ('Magic America') or those 'following the herds down to Greece', are all planning or pursuing their great escape, but as the follow-up 1995 album reiterates, there is no getting away from a universal global culture that is fed in through 'satellites in every home'. There are cynical observations about likely-lad culture, the class system and marriage, as Damon Albarn takes care to distance himself from a celebration of national institutions too. The anagrammatic Dan Abnormal who threatens to shoot up a burger bar for want of a 'McNormal and Chips' is no nationalist, just alienated 'like you, you see'. Just like Bruce Springsteen, who got annoyed when Republican

Damon Albarn, Blur

America didn't listen closely enough to the message in 'Born In The USA', Blur are entitled to feel pissed off. Albarn has recently admitted 'I don't think anybody understood the irony, *Modern Life Is Rubbish* and *Parklife* were angry records. *The Great Escape* was cynical, too cynical … being cynical isn't enough. Music is something that should speak for itself, straight from the heart. It took me a long time to understand that.' Too harsh obviously, but it does help to explain the motives behind Blur's musical transition with their fifth self-titled album in 1997.

The new direction brought together contemporary British and American indie music in the form of the band's fifth eponymous-titled album. Inspired by the likes of Pavement, Guided By Voices and Sebadoh who were putting out records that were self-consciously ironic and avoided slick production and clever musical chops, Blur returned with their fifth album which was not so much a wholesale change of approach as a shift in emphasis. Up to that point their sound had always been uncluttered; Graham Coxon's style of crashing out angry chords or just strumming, leaving room for Alex James' often-complex bass patterns was well-established. The relationship is not unlike that of Buck and Mills in REM where the bassist plays the interesting noodly bits while the guitarist concentrates on making a racket at key moments. (Listen to the opening bars of 'Girls And Boys' from *Parklife* for a masterclass.) It's the mood that changed, the guitar becoming central to proceedings, the electronica and the *Sgt Pepper* isms thrown out in favour of something altogether less upbeat. Coxon lets his guitar come untuned and the chords get wonky, and Albarn's voice is less chirpy. There is no longer the sense of tracks having been constructed, rather they are allowed to flow more naturally, something which comes across even more so on 1999's *13*.

Of course, the key track for Blur Mk II is 'Song 2', a huge American hit with the lo-fi and rock crowds and a song that could be played next to 'Smells Like Teen Spirit' or 'Killing In The Name' at rock and indie nights worldwide. It's a Blur song that has Coxon written all over it, even down to the lyrics that are surely inspired by the energy of the song and not central to it. That said, the lyrics on both albums are as crucial as ever, even if they are no longer printed on the inlay card. The line 'when I feel heavy metal … and I lie and I'm easy' in 'Song 2' is a cutting put-down of the established mainstream underground scene that Lou Barlow or Stephen Malkmus would be proud of, while *13* is a blow by blow account of Albarn's psychological state following his break-up with Elastica vocalist Justine Frischmann. 'No Distance Left To Run' and 'Tender' are uncomfortably personal and are the sound of Blur letting their guard down for a moment. *13* is the album that reveals the band without the frills, musically or personally; it's timeless and culturally unconnected, a fitting one to end on for Coxon who left the band before 2003's *Think Tank*. His departure, taking his guitars with him, has focused the band again. Demonstrating that they still have the ability to make their alternative words and sounds sound like familiar pop music, the singles taken from this album, 'Crazy Beat' and 'Out Of Time', are the weirdest and poppiest weird pop of their career so far, proving once again that Blur, the chameleon band, can do whatever they like as long as they stay connected to the latest developments in modern life.

First team: Damon Albarn (v, g, k), Graham Coxon (g, v), Alex James (b), Dave Rowntree (d)

Place, time, scene: London 1990. From the start, Blur have adapted their image and carefully constructed their music to appeal to an ever-changing non-mainstream audience. *Modern Life Is Rubbish* saw them at the forefront of the scene which was dubbed Britpop, and their shift of emphasis in 1997 reflected the American independent scene's attempts to distance itself from an established corporately-funded alternative, and marked the musical end of Britpop.

What to buy first: *Parklife* 1994

And then: *Modern Life Is Rubbish* 1993, *Blur* 1997, *13* 1999, *Think Tank* 2003

In retrospect: *Blur: The Best Of* 2000

BOREDOMS

Noise music in Japan began with Fushitsusha, a band led by Keiji Haino. In the late sixties and early seventies while most rock bands were concerning themselves with psychedelic complexity and meaningful lyrics, Haino was immersed in the study of sonics. He has made it his life's work to capture the awesome power and explore the endless textures possible while playing and amplifying his guitars. Having been initially inspired by the high volume experimentation of bands like Blue Cheer and Black Sabbath, and the droning techniques employed by Indian sitar-players, a series of albums during the seventies and eighties were classics of the noise genre. Fushitsusha turned on other noise bands, notably High Rise and Mainline, many of whom had direct links with Haino, and the growing music scene was reported on and lauded by amongst others, *The Wire* magazine, resulting in concerts outside of Japan.[13] Sonic Youth, who were pursuing similar concerns, were fans, as were Mudhoney who invited High Rise to tour with them. Not that the respect was mutual, Asahito Nanja of the band has commented that 'I think what they do is trash, I hate it'. Noise and punk, it seemed didn't necessarily go together. Within Japan, a gap opened between the free-jazz-inspired noise originators, keen to pursue their artistic vision, and a new set of bands that retained the noise aesthetic but began incorporating other influences into their sound. Acid Mothers Temple crashed the acid, got communal and incorporated Hendrix and the Dead into their music, Merzbow looked to the industrial experimentation of Neubauten, and Osaka-based band the Boredoms took their cue from hardcore punk and its Butthole aftermath to produce a back-catalogue of work which has been described as the least commercially viable ever released by a major label.

Yamatsuka Eye was a veteran of the Japanese noise scene, only disbanding his previous project, Hanatarash, an experimental Einstürzende Neubauten-inspired 'tool' band, because he came close to losing a leg during a live show. The Boredoms were a continuation of his musical extremism, but without the use of dangerous cutting and drilling equipment. They formed in Osaka in 1986 and released their first EP *Anal By Anal* the same year. Right away it was clear that the Boredoms were intent on pulling popular music apart. Adopting a similar strategy to Frank Zappa, each of their albums is an identifiable project, beginning with a central idea, expertly realized by a set of 'in the zone' musicians, and steeped in lashings of irony, parody and pastiche, the Boredoms are specialists in both. *Anal By Anal*, as the title suggests, is a collection of songs based around the central theme of

arse, following up a Hanatarash album which deconstructed the role of the penis in a set of given situations. *Osozeran No Stooges Kyo ('The Stooges Craze in Osozeran')* in 1988 was filled with straight-ahead noise topped by Yamatsuka's insistent bawling. The fact that the Boredoms refuse to take themselves totally seriously oddly makes the metal freak-outs all the more terrifying, perhaps because there's no sense of control. Producer Mark Kramer, friend to the Butthole Surfers and owner of the Shimmy-Disc label, offered the band a US deal on the strength of the album and when *Soul Discharge* was issued in 1989 the band found themselves being name-dropped extensively by Sonic Youth (for the noise), the Beastie Boys (for the irony) and Nirvana (for the times).

Soul Discharge and the follow-up *Pop Tatari* are the band's most accessible collections wherein they perfect the combination of free-form playing and driving energy. From this point on, the Boredoms used their time in the studio to experiment with new ways of playing hardcore, ska, jazz, lounge and rockabilly surf, effectively introducing a whole new set of noise-inspired mini crossover genres previously explored by avant-garde musicians like John Zorn. But make no mistake, the Boredoms were not merely pursuing art for art's sake; they were invited onto Lollapalooza, signed to Shimmy-Disc and bigged-up by a whole cross-section of the underground because they were breaking rules in pop, not inventing them in art. The quality of musicianship within the context of the Boredoms is judged by the individual players' ability to do the unorthodox to excess, all the while staying true to the noise-central aim, the transference of amplified and textured raw energy to the waiting audience or listener.

By 1998 the Boredoms had left Warners' Reprise label, as the focus shifted from loud rock to hip-hop, Britpop and the development of musical laboratories for the development of new, marketable punk, metal and hip-hop hybrids. Their album *Super Ae* from that year is the band's most traditionally structured, a series of long jams that demonstrate an innate understanding of the post-noise style that they had created, matched with impressive production. The overt confrontational attitude may have been phased out but the Boredoms are essential for anyone interested in being blown away.

First team: Yamatsuka Eye (v), Yamamoto Seiich (g), Yoshimi P-We (d), Hayashi Hira (b), Yoshikawa Toyohito (v)

Place, time, scene: Osaka 1986. The Boredoms are the band that took Japanese-noise music international. Sonic Youth and the Butthole Surfers were already doing similar things when the band broke through but it's worth noting the variety of the Boredoms noise, which included industrial, psychedelia, free-jazz and hardcore influences right from the first album in 1986. Their deals with Shimmy-Disc and then Warner opened up links with Japanese music in general and helped with the subsequent relative success of Shonen Knife, Merzbow and most recently Cornelius.

What to buy first: *Soul Discharge* 1989

And then: *Pop Tatari* 1991

In retrospect: *Onanie Bomb Meets The Sex Pistols* 1989

DAVID BOWIE

With Ziggy Stardust, David Bowie created a stage persona that was simultaneously the ultimate rock-star success story, fronting a loud and very cool band, prone to hedonistic excess, 'bitching about his fans' and revelling in all that the rock star system had to offer, and also the embodiment of failure, a cautionary tale of how that same system can destroy the potential of the rock star, their music and their message, in this instance finally, with a rock'n'roll suicide. It was Bowie's response to the excess that had killed so many of his peers in recent years, as they became unable to detach real-life from rock-life. When a songwriter or an artist made themselves the subject of their music or performance, it was not only egotistical and patronizing for those identified as fans, but it was clearly dangerous too. Bowie, like Marc Bolan who underwent a change of musical direction in his shift from Tyrannosaurus Rex to T.Rex, used the opportunity to dress-up as an opportunity to move away from the more personal and intimate songs featured on previous albums like *The Man Who Sold The World* and *Hunky Dory*, and in so-doing created a new approach to music-making that would be explored further by punks like Johnny Rotten, and

opened up the possibilities for what could or could not be said in popular music.

Of course Ziggy didn't happen overnight. 'Life On Mars' on *Hunky Dory* sets the tone for what was to come. It was the story of a girl who visits the cinema to watch a film which turns out to be about herself. As a character, in drag with make-up, heels and unisex hair-do, Bowie could put into effect his acting skills and could address issues of sexuality and gender, and, as an alien, human identity in a more general sense. He's been doing it ever since.

The Rise And Fall Of Ziggy Stardust And The Spiders From Mars was the album that established Bowie as an alternative to everything else around at that time. Having persuaded the band, consisting of Mick Ronson, Trevor Bolder and Mick Woodmansey, to forgo their denims for Kansai Yamamoto's designer sparkly jumpsuits, the first tour was tough at times. Audiences were not familiar with space-age cross-dressing and guitar blow-jobs but were eventually won over by a realization that Bowie and his band were not just a controversial idea, there was real substance to their sound too. Mick Ronson's guitar style was fundamental – heavy metal like Black Sabbath, and sleazy like Iggy and the Stooges, but designed to fit into arrangements that incorporated strings, keyboards and acoustic instruments. In fact, Ronson was responsible for a large part of the arranging that went into the early Bowie albums, and for the influence of these albums on musicians to come. The singer may have addressed themes of destruction, apocalypse and nihilism in his lyrics and performance, which provided a new angle for rock writing, especially on an album like *Diamond Dogs* which was based on George Orwell's *1984*, but it was Ronson's guitar style that inspired the next generation of bands. Virtually every punk guitarist, from Johnny Thunders to Steve Jones and Mick Jones, owes something to Ronson. Bowie used Ronson's departure as a starting point for his own musical experimentation.

Young Americans was a 'plastic soul' album. Bowie went back to his R&B roots; the saxophone that had so mesmerized him when he saw Sounds Incorporated at the Brixton Odeon back in 1963 is evident on several of the tracks, Luther Vandross supplies silky smooth backing vocals and of course, there's 'Fame', a funk workout featuring vocals and guitar by John Lennon that James Brown would have been proud of. Bowie announced his retirement at this point, claiming that he had 'rocked his last roll' and no longer wanted to be a 'useless fucking rock singer'. It marked a shift from stage performer to studio musician, and coincided with some bad press he received for giving a Nazi salute as he disembarked from a plane in front of the gathered media. A year of partying with Iggy Pop resulted in arrests, drug abuse and a life-long friendship. It also ended with Bowie's move to Berlin where he would stay for the duration of the punk period.

Station To Station in 1976 had brought together R&B with electronic instruments and was inspired by Kraftwerk's *Autobahn* album. The ten-minute long title-track featuring synthesized train sounds, discordant piano and guitar and one of Bowie's best vocal performances for 'the return of the thin white duke' remains a highlight of his career and prompted Brian Eno to get in touch for a collaborative period of creativity that resulted in three albums in just over two years. *Low* is the best. Eno builds ambient sound-scapes for Bowie to construct songs within and around. The first half of the album is made up of new-wave meshings of guitars and keyboards and in the second half there are dense and dark pieces based around synthesizers, and resembling the progressive krautrock of bands like Neu! and Can, mixed with the floaty hymnal constructs of British band Jade Warrior. 'Tone poems' they were called, and 'Warszawa' is probably the most beautiful piece of music in Bowie's back-catalogue, with chord changes determined randomly by a pre-arranged and unrelated system of dots on paper that corresponded to a pre-recorded finger-clicks running throughout the track. *Heroes* and *Lodger* stretched the musical skills of his regular band with relentless experimentation, on one occasion requiring guitarist Carlos Alomar to play drums while the drummer played bass. The result was a hit single, 'Boys Keep Swinging'.

Bowie's last great album is *Scary Monsters* which effectively set the 1980s in motion just like he had done with the previous decade. It was the album that confirmed his status as the musical and iconic figurehead of the new romantics, who revelled in identity-confusion and postmodern irony. Musically he was right there with the new club-based culture too. Fash-ion draws on harsh glam-rock guitar played by Robert Fripp, bubbling synthesizers and low-end bass funk, the culmination of his work up to that point. 'Ashes To Ashes' revisited an old friend, Major Tom, who was now a 'junkie – strung out on heaven's high, living an all-time low', the perfect insight into the decade to come and indicative of Bowie's most socially-aware album, and that, just at the point when everything else was getting so hedonistic and self-obsessed. Bowie, so often referred to as a chameleon, the man with the ever-changing image, summed up his achievements succinctly in a 1993 interview: 'For me a chameleon is something that disguises itself to look as much like its environment as possible. I always thought I did the exact opposite of that.'

Place, time, scene: London 1967. David Bowie came to prominence after almost a decade of making R&B music and, following that, psychedelic folk-pop. It was his Ziggy Stardust persona that launched him into the spotlight and which had a significant influence on the way that rock music was performed and constructed. The punks learned from his experimentation with identity and perception and dug Mick Ronson's guitar sound. His subsequent exploration of soul and electronic forms and work with Brian Eno challenging traditional production methods, before delivering the template for pop music in the eighties, make him one of the most influential individuals in rock history.

What to buy first: *The Rise And Fall Of Ziggy Stardust And The Spiders From Mars* 1972

And then: *Hunky Dory* 1971, *Diamond Dogs* 1974, *Station To Station* 1976, *Low* 1977, *Heroes* 1978, *Scary Monsters* 1980

In retrospect: *Best Of Bowie* 2002

BILLY BRAGG

Billy Bragg writes folk songs and plays them on an electric guitar. The first time Bob Dylan did that, it all kicked off big style at the Newport Blues and Folk Festival. Dylan wanted to use the music of a potentially revolutionary youth culture to give voice to his message. Bragg, writing nearly 20 years later, was aware that the combination of conscious lyrics and rock music had run its course and had become clichéd. He opted therefore for the unthinkable, and for many, the unlistenable: politically conscious lyrics barked out over the sound of a single electric guitar. Neither folk, nor rock, Bragg famously said that he considered himself a 'one-man Clash'.

Having left punk band Riff Raff, and spent time in the services (army and record retail) Bragg's solo 'career' was ultimately inspired by his introduction to the protest songs of Woody Guthrie and Phil Ochs. He used public transport to get himself, his guitar and amp to venues all over the country, and due to the straightforward nature of his act, picked up support slots wherever he went. It's interesting that his break came when music publishers, Chappell, bought him studio time to record his demos, perhaps spotting something in the words that might work long-term. As far as albums go, Bragg has always stuck with independent labels, notably Go! Discs and Cooking Vinyl, and has retained complete control over his songs, even if it has meant putting up a lot of his own money for production and distribution. As he has said 'It's a question of whose pension it ought to be, mine or theirs.'

The debut album *Life's A Riot With Spy Vs Spy*, consisting of just vocals and guitar, was a stark album but was not overtly political. There are a few songs which reflect on the social condition, but in the main the songs deal with smaller concerns of human relationships. The album begins romantically, 'If you're lonely, I will call, if you're poorly I will send poetry. I love you. I am the milkman of human kindness. I will leave an extra pint.' It's what he's done ever since, and yet, perhaps because of his uncompromising 1985 *Top Of The Pops* appearance singing 'Between The Wars', Bragg's image has always been set in stone for those not prepared to listen to the albums. The truth is that Bragg is primarily a songwriter who uses his talent and position as a platform for protest. Crass, for example, adopt the reverse position. The themes of his work have always been socialism and specifically how it could be made relevant to British youth. To this end, his albums have always been just that little bit cheaper than everyone else's – Bragg pushed for the 'pay no more than' sticker. He played free in support of striking coal miners in 1984, toured under the banner 'Jobs For Youth' a year later, and in 1986 became a founder member of the Red Wedge movement which was allied to the British Labour Party and organized gigs and raised funds for the party's election campaigns in 1987 and 1992.

In 1988, Bragg released *Worker's Playtime* – a set of his songs with fuller musical backing than his previous work, giving new life to his basic formula. The album finishes with 'Waiting For The Great Leap Forwards', a song which finds Bragg questioning his own role within a declining protest movement, and the co-option of issues like Third-World poverty and nuclear-weapons testing into something more media-savvy. The song builds to a climax ending with crowd vocals and a full band rockin' out, while Bragg screams out some of his best slogan-lyrics 'If you've got a blacklist I wanna be on it' and 'the revolution is just a T-shirt away'. The crucial part of the song, 'Mixing pop and politics, he asks me what the use is? I offer him embarrassment and the usual excuses' is poignant. Disillusioned with the possibilities of socialist change and possibly having spotted the branded form of New Labour around the corner, it marks Bragg's philosophical shift to a 'socialism of the heart' relating more to the human spirit.

Socialism of the heart entails Bragg's continued support of socialist causes and this he has done by continuing to play live on a regular basis and making it his mission to keep recording and ensure that he's interviewed by both '*Loaded* and *New Statesman*'. His most recent project is the archiving of approximately three thousand Woody Guthrie songs. The folk singer, described by Bragg as the first punk, suffered a debilitating illness in the last years of his life and was unable to record the songs, a task which Bragg has taken on, working with American band Wilco, a project coming the closest yet to a folk-rock album – complete with hammond, violin and a full band – but, due to the quality of the material and the honesty of the vocals (Bragg and Jeff Tweedy from Wilco) the album manages to avoid the pitfalls of the patronizing and self-serving protest-rock of the last two decades. Good bloke, Billy Bragg.

Place, time, scene: London 1983. Billy Bragg's sparse and direct folk-punk was totally original and has not really been followed up as overtly-political protest music has effectively disappeared. There are few protest singers to compare with Bragg, who followed in the footsteps of Woody Guthrie, early Bob Dylan and Phil Ochs.

What to buy first: *Life's A Riot With Spy Vs Spy* 1984

And then: *Brewing Up With Billy Bragg* 1985, *Talking With The Taxman About Poetry* 1986, *Worker's Playtime* 1988, *Mermaid Avenue* (with Wilco) 1998

In retrospect: *Back to Basics* 1983

BUTTHOLE SURFERS

Kurt Cobain once suggested that there are two extremes when it comes to attitudes to making music. On one hand 'you can be either anally serious, sad and depressed like Morrissey, or you can be a big joke like the Butthole Surfers'. It was out of character for Cobain to fall for such obvious stereotypes – Morrissey's lyrics were often funny and life-affirming – but in the case of the Butthole Surfers maybe the stereotype was fairly accurate. There's the name for a start, the unprofessionalism that saw them turn up for TV interviews stoned out of their faces, and the stage shows which often incorporated nudity and pornography – sometimes on tape, sometimes live, featuring vocalist and dancer. Certainly, from the start, the Butthole Surfers seemed intent on shocking their local Texan neighbourhood, but that shouldn't overshadow their musical achievement. Over the course of five EPs and albums released between 1983 and 1987, and with the help of fellow post-punk yippies the Dead Kennedys, the Butthole Surfers hammered a few nails into hardcore punk's coffin, which it might be argued, had always taken itself far too seriously anyway.

Bizarrely, Paul Leary and Gibby Haynes met in business school, training to become a stockbroker and an accountant respectively, but they let a combination of peurile student humour and a creative desire to experiment take them over. Both musicians already, they formed the Butthole Surfers on the understanding that they would attempt to unlearn their craft and start again from scratch. They began with two drummers, a brother and sister no less, while guitarist Leary adapted his guitar so that, for their first EP, he was playing an instrument with six E-strings.

By their 1984 debut album *Psychic Powerless … Another Man's Sac* and the following year's *Rem-*

brandt Pussyhorse, they had begun to experiment with tape-looping and combined it with extreme and dramatic musicianship. The combination of mad violin, found on an old piece of studio tape that the band used to record the track on and left exactly where it was, and creeping piano on 'Creep In The Cellar' is disconcerting to say the least, and with Gibby Haynes' voice fed through a distorted vocoder for many of the tracks, an extra dimension of terror is palpable on songs about progressive Alzheimer's disease, assassins and Chairman Mao's need for potty-training. It's uneasy listening, well for most people anyway, although their spiritual mentor Roky Erickson probably found the whole thing quite cathartic. The disturbed leader of that other great Texan band, the 13th Floor Elevators, once visited the Surfers at their house at 1401 Anderson Lane, Austin, Texas, complete with silver décor and boarded up windows. According to Leary it was to stare at the bathroom wall – but surely it was more than that. Roky knew the importance of the Butthole Surfers and maybe he was glad that they were just about sane enough to carry on where he couldn't.

First team: Gibby Haynes (v), Paul Leary (g), King Coffey (d)

Place, time, scene: Austin, Texas 1983. Butthole Surfers couldn't give a monkeys about anything it seems, but that was the very thing that plugged them directly into the seedy, rotten source of bad rock'n'roll. The insanity inherent in the music and the manic stage performance might have been a put-on or it may have been for real. Marilyn Manson will have taken in a few ideas from the Buttholes.

What to buy first: *Rembrandt Pussyhorse* 1985

And then: *Psychic Powerless … Another Man's Sac* 1984, *Locust Abortion Technician* 1987

BUZZCOCKS

Johnny Rotten and Joe Strummer both sang about the big stuff. Although they did it in different ways and with different takes on solving the problem, they both described how it felt to be part of a disenfranchised culture. The Buzzcocks didn't. They wrote about love and

The Butthole Surfers

sex, the subject matter of pop music since time immemorial. Of course, it was never the pretty bits. In keeping with the ideals of punk, Pete Shelley kept it real, and that meant lust, broken promises, infidelity, confusion and for their major label debut single, masturbation. The thing is, they were so good at making exhilirating, effervescent pop that they got away with it.

The Buzzcocks should have played their first gig on 4th June 1976 supporting the Sex Pistols, but although they were booked as the support they weren't quite ready. Howard Devoto, the Buzzcocks' original lead vocalist, was the promoter who had organized the gig, since to have taken on mythological proportions. In his book of the film *24 Hour Party People*, Tony Wilson points out that Devoto and Shelley were 'miles ahead of everybody in Manchester ... already the Buzzcocks'. As Wilson remembers it, Bernard Sumner and Peter Hook from New Order were there, along with producer Martin Hannett, Morrissey and even Mick Hucknall (of whom, nothing else later in the book). The Buzzcocks' attitude was inspired by the Sex Pistols. A *Sniffin' Glue* review of an early London show explained 'Their sound is very rough, very like the Pistols, but that guitar sound! It was a spitting rasping monster.'

On their debut *Spiral Scratch* EP Devoto's vocals have that certain sneering quality, while the band's version of the Troggs' 'I Can't Control Myself' on *Time's Up*, just like the Pistols' 'I'm Not Your Stepping Stone', underlines the potential for punk to reinterpret and give voice to the previously unspoken and unspeakable. *Spiral Scratch* captures songs first take, apart from 'Breakdown' which the band had a luxurious three gos at, and the fact that the EP was self-financed and released on the band's own New Hormones label represents a key moment too – the beginning of the DIY ethic that spawned the independent production, manufacturing and distribution system of the post-punk years. The EP's release in February 1977 coincided with Devoto's departure from the band to finish his degree, although he remained associated with the band, and particularly Shelley, socially, before forming the more musically expansive Magazine with John McGeogh and Barry Adamson.

It was a reshuffled Buzzcocks that signed with United Artists and made the debut album *Another Music In*

A Different Kitchen in 1978. Shelley took over vocals and played rhythm guitar while Steve Diggle played lead. It was a crucial change that led to the Buzzcocks' trademark wall-of-guitars sound that, along with resignedly realist lyrics, courtesy of Shelley and occasionally Diggle, became the benchmark for the British indie scene to follow, although Shelley has always dismissed any role he may have had as a chronicler of teenage angst, preferring to underplay the meaning of his lyrics. 'I don't take copyright out on ideas. I haven't got a monopoly on them. If a song throws up ideas for people then I'd rather they discussed it amongst themselves. Not discuss each line like I'm a dead poet.'

The songs are generally based around a simple idea and built traditionally with verses and memorable choruses. 'What Do I Get?', 'I Don't Mind', 'Love You More', 'Ever Fallen In Love?', 'Promises' and 'Everybody's Happy Nowadays' all appeared in a thirteen month period between February 1978 and March 1979, and there were three albums in eighteen months. And right from the off, the band began experimenting with styles and recording techniques, notably the leanings towards cyclical drumming and considered chord sequences associated with the likes of Can and Faust, but all within the confines of the three-minute pop song. Having come so far in such a short period of time, Shelley like Devoto before him, was keen to try something different. He began experimenting with tape-looping and cheap new electronic technology. He spent 1980 and 1981 working on solo material, and writing songs for a fourth Buzzcocks album which was eventually released as the solo work *Homosapien* in 1982. On it, Shelley replaced walls of guitar with electronics and disco beats, creating a new texture for his intelligent and ironic lyrics, which dealt quite specifically with his own sexuality. In fact, the stylistic shift that Shelley makes with *Homosapien* helps join the dots between punk and the beat-driven intelligent pop of New Order and the Pet Shop Boys that followed. That's the legacy of punk, right there. But if that's not enough, what about the Buzzcocks' reformation in 1989, which coincided with the new punk-pop of Green Day in the US and Mega City Four in the UK, and which has since become a fully-fledged genre in its own right? Whether you see punk as a musical style, a philosophy or an attitude, the Buzzcocks are the daddies.

First team: Pete Shelley (v, g), Steve Diggle (v, g), Steve Garvey (b), John Maher (d)

Place, time, scene: Manchester 1976. The Buzzcocks were one of the first bands to form having been inspired by the Sex Pistols. Main songwriter Pete Shelley was more concerned with issues of identity and personal relationships than many of his contemporaries. He wrote love songs for goodness sake. The emphasis placed on sex and sexuality, and the solipsistic and awkward character he created through his songs rubbed off on fellow Mancunian Morrissey and inspired an entire generation of more sensitive male post-punkers. The buzzsaw guitar sound became a key signifier of new wave and indie music, although by that time Shelley himself was experimenting with new musical technologies, notably the synthesizer.

What to buy first: *Another Music In A Different Kitchen* 1978

And then: *Love Bites* 1979, Pete Shelley: *Homosapien* 1982

In retrospect: *Singles Going Steady* 1983, *Chronology* 1997

C

CABARET VOLTAIRE

Cabaret Voltaire are the band that started Sheffield's electronic scene back in the mid-seventies and it's been thriving ever since. The cutlery-production capital of the world was provided with an alternative to the straight-forward punk that exploded everywhere else in the UK a couple of years later, and so began a tradition of plinkity-plonk that has included the Human League, Pulp and an entire Warp label.

The trio of Stephen Mallinder, Richard H. Kirk and Chris Watson were, by their own admission, poor musicians in the traditional sense, but, inspired by the methods of editing, looping and sampling perfected by Holger Czukay in Can and the rough-and-ready racket made by sixties garage-bands like the Seeds, they set about creating music using reel-to-reel tape, drum machines and early synths, only picking up guitar or bass when a different texture was required. Vocals often came from obscure films, commentaries, or in the case of a track like 'Sluggin For Jesus', from a TV evangelist. Taking their name from a Dadaist periodical, their philosophical approach to music-making was inspired by modernist experiments with form.

Their early releases through Rough Trade, Factory and the Industrial label (operated by Genesis P-Orridge of like-minded musical terrorists Throbbing Gristle) were never songs in the traditional sense. A common technique developed by the band involved amplifying usually quiet background sounds to take them into the foreground of the mix. By looping such sounds and setting up unusual rhythms, tracks took on a physical dimension, the end result being dance music that it didn't feel quite right to dance to. A press release issued by the record label Mute, collecting together their early work, describes the music as existing within 'the grey area' – neither song or dance – but, instead, a provocation to think.

By the early 1980s Cabaret Voltaire were using bass and drums to create a more traditional rhythmic underpinning, although tracks like 'Breathe Deep', despite having a distinctly funky top-layer, still retained an air of menace mainly due to Mallinder's effects-ridden horror vocal. In 1983, the single 'Yashar' started a fashion for ethno-techno, a mix of contemporary electronica just breaking in Detroit, with traditional middle-eastern vocals, an idea that was pursued by M/A/R/R/S and Coldcut later in the decade. And 'Sensoria', well that was a hands-in-the-air club anthem for a club scene that was still, in reality, a couple of years off at that point. In fact, throughout the late eighties and nineties, Cabaret Voltaire remained at the forefront of the mutating and developing dance styles. Acid house, rave, ambient, and the industrial music of Skinny Puppy and Nine Inch Nails can all be traced back to the Sheffield band's addiction to experimentation.

First team: Stephen Mallinder (b, v) Richard H. Kirk (g), Chris Watson (k, tape)

Place, time, scene: Sheffield 1973. Cabaret Voltaire made their noise with the aid of bits of tape and a variety of electronic gadgetry. Their strategy was to combine found sounds, harsh guitars, distorted voices and drums into a dense percussive whole. Keeping up with technological advances and developing club culture, they have remained omnipresent but hidden away ever since. Along with Throbbing Gristle they are the originators of what has since been dubbed 'industrial music'.

What to buy first: *Voice Of America* 1980

And then: *Red Mecca* 1981

In retrospect: *Golden Moments Of Cabaret Voltaire* 1987

CAN

The legendary rock journalist Lester Bangs once asked the rhetorical question – why are Germans so cool? He was referring to a scene that had been developing since the late sixties that took electric and electronic technology as its main tool and the musical and mathematical experiments of Stockhausen as its guiding philosophy. The idea was to make music that retained the principle of sixties experimentalism but did not allow the sense of limitless possibilities associated with psychedelia to take over the music. Remembering his old teacher's life's work to understand the intricate and microcosmic nature of single musical notes, Holger Czukay, who had studied with Stockhausen, made music with the belief that 'restriction is the mother of invention'. Having said that, one of their earliest tracks, 'Yoo Doo Right', clocked in at just under 20 minutes and they once played a gig that lasted 12½ hours.

Inspired by the Beatles and the Velvets but informed by more contemporary avant-garde classical work, bassist Czukay and fellow-student guitarist Michael

Karoli, shifted their emphasis from the avant-garde to rock and funk. They formed Can in 1968 together with keyboard-player Irmin Schmidt and drummer Jaki Liebezeit and, from the outset, adopted a strategy of recording that was entirely new as far as rock music was concerned. Pieces emerged from jam sessions usually recorded live with no overdubs and all fed through one channel of the mixing desk, with the most satisfying grooves edited together later to create music that was at once loose and tight. The post-recording editing process also allowed for samples to be added to the ostensibly linear mix. Can's original vocalist Malcolm Mooney, was replaced in 1971 by street-singer and busker Damo Suzuki, discovered in Munich by Czukay in the afternoon and on stage performing with the band later that evening. The line-up remained consistent for the next three years and the next three albums, Can's trilogy of masterpieces, *Tago Mago*, *Ege Bamyasi* and *Future Days* all demonstrate that Can, as a set of musicians, were connected in a way that most bands never achieve. Always ensuring that they listen to and work off each other when jamming, they tend to avoid egotistical showboating solos and lazy recourse to standard rhythm'n'blues' structures. The albums have a consistent musical identity that denotes Can but have an individuality which is determined by the surroundings and the situation in which they were recorded. *Tago Mago* was created in a castle by 'instant composition', a term coined by the band to explain their apparent telepathic spontaneity. There are also sections of 'in-between' recording resulting from Czukay's dastardly plan to record his colleagues whilst they were just jamming, blissfully unaware that they were being taped. 'Halleluwah' is the centrepiece, driven on by Leibezeit's machine-like, circular drumming (easy to edit later) and Suzuki's often unstructured, floating vocals (not easy to edit later!). *Ege Bamyasi* was made in an old cinema and is quite a bleak album, due perhaps because of the darkness of the cinema interior, intensified by the 1500 mattresses attached to the walls. Michael Karoli's physical discomfort brought on by a stomach ulcer would not have helped the mood either. *Future Days* was made in the same location but the mood is lighter, perhaps because the band had just scored a number one hit with the track 'Spoon' which was also used as a theme tune to a German TV show. Making it on to the gravy train and the fact that it was a long hot summer in 1973 might well have contributed to the balmy feel of some of the tracks. 'Bel-Air' captures the essence of the recordings, and although it clocks in at well over 20 minutes and is perhaps more complex than their earlier recordings, like all of Can's work in this period it rarely sounds self-indulgent.

There is still a lot of previously lost Can material coming to light from their earlier days, and in 1997 an album of remixed Can material going by the name of *Sacrilege*, which gave those artists most influenced by the band the opportunity to re-envisage their best work, among them Sonic Youth, Pete Shelley and Stereolab. That's a role-call of artists that have consistently demonstrated restraint in their creative endeavours, each in their own way minimalist designers of music and image. Buy some Can.

First team: Holger Czukay (b, tape), Michael Karoli (g), Jaki Liebezeit (d), Irmin Schmidt (k), Damo Suzuki (v)

Place, time, scene: Cologne, Germany 1968. Can approached their work from a classical tradition rather than the traditional R&B root. They played around with repetitive rhythms and devised a new way of working in a recording studio. The endless jams, edited and looped so that the finished result sounds modally structured but loose and organic at the same time was a key influence on many post-punk bands who were wary of the excesses of prog-rock but felt constrained by the strict rules of punk. British bands like the Fall and PiL based entire careers on the 'krautrock' of Can and their more rhythmic musical cousins Neu!.

What to buy first: *Tago Mago* 1971

And then: *Ege Bamyasi* 1972, *Future Days* 1973

In retrospect: *Anthology* 2001

CAPTAIN BEEFHEART AND HIS MAGIC BAND

Don Van Vliet's biographical and musical history will forever be linked with that of his high-school friend Frank Zappa. The two discovered Chicago blues and west-coast R&B together as teenagers at their most idealistic age, and spurred each other to make conscious and subconscious rules about what creativity meant and how it could be judged. Both have left their mark on the development of independently-minded music and were there when pop music met its Other, alternative music, sometime in the mid-sixties. Zappa was the organizer, or to use his description, the composer. His extensive and varied career in music which ended with his death in 1993 has been about a series of projects exploring different techniques and styles, finishing one and moving on to another. Van Vliet, who goes by the name Captain Beefheart, is different. Like Zappa, he has always been concerned with doing things differently in an attempt to nudge those who are listening, and bring them out of their narcoleptic fantasy dream world where reality is not allowed in to disrupt the comfortable rhythm of familiarity, 'I don't want to hypnotize, I'm doing a non-hypnotic music to break up the catatonic state', but unlike Zappa he is less comfortable with delegating aspects of his creativity out. Captain Beefheart the musician, and Captain Beefheart the painter and sculptor, is primarily a solo artist who, at crucial moments, has gone to great lengths to retain complete control over his artistic vision. The resulting sounds and techniques have proven useful for those wanting to disrupt otherwise conventional melodies and rhythms, to the extent that over the years his name has become synonymous with musical weirdness.

Way back before he knew Zappa, Don Van Vliet was a child prodigy who appeared on American television demonstrating his sculpting abilities. He lived with his parents in Lancaster in the Mojave desert, a boomtown that was thriving due to the Cold-War as missile production increased at Edwards air force base. As a teenager he listened to the forbidden fruit – black R&B music – with Zappa and perfected his skills as a saxophone player. Back then it was still the fifties, but pretty soon the sixties came along to replace them and Beefheart, after a break of several years, again hooked-up with Zappa at his Studio Z in Cucamonga, where they recorded a demo as the Soots and sent it off for major label consideration. The combination of Beefheart's Howlin' Wolf vocal style and distorted guitar was not on the agenda in 1963 and the two would not work together again until the groundbreaking *Trout Mask Replica* album in 1969. In the meantime, Beefheart assembled his Magic Band, a group of musicians who shared his love of blues and included 16-year-old slide guitarist Ry Cooder. The band recorded a session with producer David Gates, who would later form Bread, and released their debut album *Safe As Milk* in 1966 on the newly-established Buddah label shortly after Zappa's *Freak Out* was made available through Verve. The album introduced the Magic Band's trademark rhythmic oddness and a form of guitar interplay that was less about lead and rhythm and more duelling banjos. Sure, 'Nuff And Yes I Do' is a hoe-down of an opener, featuring Cooder sliding around a mid-range vocal from Beefheart. The psychedelia creeps in on 'Yellow Brick Road' and 'Electricity', a track which Jerry Moss at the A&M label refused to release for fear of the effect it may have on his daughter, perhaps due to Beefheart's lunatic growl which combines with the ghostly theremin in a most disconcerting way. There's an Engish folk feel to the track, and elsewhere on the album the track 'I'm Glad' is pure Smokey Robinson. It's an amazing debut album. John Peel played it to death on his late-night BBC radio show and there was enough interest in Beefheart for a short tour of the UK in early 1968 when clubs like Middle-Earth and UFO[14] were turning on to the British blues- and jazz-inspired psychedelia of Pink Floyd and Soft Machine.

In the US it was a different matter though, Beefheart and the Magic Band remained a mystery, too far out for the hippies who preferred soothing space guitar sounds and gentle rocking. *Strictly Personal*, which followed later in the year, continued the attempt to capture the sounds in Beefheart's head and contained the epic 'Kandy Korn', a track which showcases Drumbo's polyrhythmic drum patterns, constantly changing direction and leading the nine-minute closing track in all sorts of odd, unexpected directions. Beefheart's voice is at its multi-octave best and the lyrics are vivid and impressionistic. And then came *Trout Mask Replica*.

Matt Groening, the man responsible for creating *The Simpsons*, the most successful satire of contemporary consumer society bar none, calls it the best rock album he has ever heard but concedes that on first listen he felt ripped off only later realizing that 'they meant it to sound exactly this way'.[15] Zappa produced it, or at least set it up as a field recording in the Magic Band house, recording early takes in kitchens, hallways and bathrooms before moving to a proper studio to finish it off. Once there, Beefheart insisted that he record his vocals separate from the music already laid down, preferring to guess where the vocals should come in from just the faintest echo of the backing track being played in the adjoining control room. Even Zappa thought that this was insane. As a result his vocals are not quite in sync with the rest of the band, but then that doesn't really matter much because the band themselves are playing a form of music never before experienced on a rock recording. Beefheart had brought in a few new players for the album including guitarist Zoot Horn Rollo, bassist Rockette Morton and his cousin, clarinettist, The Mascara Snake. Along with existing members Antennae Jimmy Semens and Drumbo, the band had spent six months cramming, learning instrumental parts devised on piano by Beefheart and transcribed by Drumbo. Beefheart was not much of a piano player, which made the whole thing even more interesting still. The resulting album is still the most difficult yet ultimately satisfying listening experience in the whole of popular music. The songs are about human atrocities meted out against other humans, overweight ladies, airships covered in nipples, and of course the neon meate dream of an octafish (sic), a song which contains the charmingly alliterative line 'squirmin' serum 'n semen 'n syrup 'n semen 'n serum, stirruped in syrup'. It's Salvador Dali set to music. *Trout Mask Replica* should be a set text for aspiring musicians.

Beefheart followed it up with the saxophone and percussion-heavy *Lick My Decals Off Baby*, the heavy jazz-funk rock of *The Spotlight Kid*, and his last great album *Clear Spot* in 1972, which nailed the soulful style he had hinted at on several of his earlier albums. 'Her Eyes Are A Blue Million Miles' is a love song par excellence; the Coen brothers used it in their film *The Big Lebowski* to soundtrack one of The Dude's many hallucinations. The critical, and believe it or not, relative commercial success of *Ice Cream For Crow* took everyone by surprise in 1982, but it turned out to be the Captain's swansong and for the last couple of decades he has concentrated his efforts on painting, where his initial figurative approach becoming evermore surreal has placed him at the forefront of weird amongst the canvas-ticklers too. The Captain is dead, long live the Captain.

First team: Captain Beefheart (v, sx, cl), Drumbo (d), Antennae Jimmy Semens (g), Rockette Morton (b), Zoot Horn Rollo (g), The Mascara Snake (cl)

Place, time, scene: Los Angeles 1965. The Magic Band's blues paralleled the return to blues that was happening in the UK around bands like the Yardbirds and the Bluesbreakers, and their psychedelic touches made them a forerunner of bands like Pink Floyd and Soft Machine. They were associated with Frank Zappa in the US and it was this connection that turned many of his fans on to *Trout Mask Replica*, an album which remains a template for non-traditional musical arrangements. Many of the post-punk bands, notably Gang Of Four and the Minutemen have acknowledged their debt to the good Captain and his magic men.

What to buy first: *Trout Mask Replica* 1969

And then: *Safe As Milk* 1966, *Clear Spot* 1972

In retrospect: *Zig Zag Wanderer* 1998

CARDIACS

The Cardiacs may be one of the most influential British bands to have emerged since punk. In fact it was at the height of UK punk that they formed, quickly developing into a 'pronk' band, so named because of their seamless integration of punk and progressive rock musical practices.

Inspired by similarly disposed bands like Television and Pere Ubu, the band's leading light is vocalist and songwriter Tim Smith whose skills at musical arrangement have been likened to those possessed by his hero Frank Zappa at his most epic. His attention to detail in terms of song structures and a knack for effecting affecting key changes are central to the Cardiacs' sound. He writes and arranges, leaving the band to construct, practise and get the best take down on tape. Guitarist John Poole makes the point that 'There's a hell of a lot of bands who build all their stuff out of jams, just do it on the spot from their guts,

but sometimes you need to put your brain to it, to make things more interesting, to find new ways'. Not that the band are boring musos. Their live shows are fast and adrenalin-pumping at times, certainly punk enough to upset a crowd of Marillion fans on their 1984 support tour with Mr Dick and the boys.

The band, which includes Tim's brother Jim and occasionally wife Sara, have a back-catalogue of albums, all released on their own Alphabet Business Concern label, that runs well into double figures although many original cassette-only releases are difficult, if not impossible to find. It is their eighth album, second on vinyl, that is the key one. The release of *A Little Man And A House And A Whole World Window* coincided with the band's only media interest of note, thanks to the good solid journalistic working practice of the *Sunday Sport* who uncovered the shocking revelation that Tim Smith was involved in a relationship with his sister, Sara. An easy mistake to make who'd have thought that two people in the same band sharing the surname Smith might actually be married! (Years ahead of the White Stripes' sibling confusions.) Tim Smith kept the story going as long as he could, not necessarily because of the publicity but because it was in keeping with a notorious twisted sense of humour that comes across in his lyrics. *A Little Man ...* contains the Cardiacs only hit single 'Is This The Life', an epic swirling guitar-scape underpinned by Sara Smith's saxophone and William Drake's 'television organ' – a device made from old television parts that is 'really, really tinny and it's got this sort of washing machine motor in it and you turn it on and it goes "ck-errrrr". If you play a chord on it, it's like "neeyaah, urrrh, urrrh" – it's scary, but it's really gorgeous.'

There were five more albums made with the classic Cardiacs line-up, and then a paired down four-piece band that gave Smith the opportunity to work with tapes when playing live, giving him more control over elements such as sax and keyboards, the sound of which could be perfected in advance. *Sing To God* released in 1996 might be the band's best album yet, a montage of styles and moods which veer between 'lighter-in-the-air' epic balladry and mosh-pit hardcore. They do play the odd gig now and then, easily selling out two thousand-plus venues, record company distribution notwithstanding. With Blur having sung their praises, pilfering a few of the Cardiacs' musical devices on their English trilogy of albums in the mid-nineties, and Super Furry Animals coming out of the closet too, if you want to tick off a few boxes in your I-Spy Book of Inspirational Pop Stars get yourself down to a Cardiacs gig. Those in the know, know.

First team: Tim Smith (v), Jim Smith (b), Sara Smith (sx), William Drake (k), Dominic Luckman (d)

Place, time, scene: Carshalton, Surrey, UK 1977. The Cardiacs were the forerunners of 'pronk', punk combined with prog-rock complexity and theatrical performance. They were resolutely independent, releasing their early albums themselves on the cheaper cassette format. Their sense of dynamics and skills with musical arrangement have been noted by Radiohead and Super Furry Animals of late.

What to buy first: *A Little Man And A House And A Whole World Window* 1988

And then: *Sing To God* 1996

In retrospect: *Cardiacs Sampler* 1995

CARDIGANS

When Abba won the Eurovision Song Contest in 1974 it transformed Swedish popular culture. Initially they were ridiculed by an embarrassed national media and music industry that espoused fiercely socialist ideals, but by the end of the decade a whole new pop-music industry had replaced the classical, jazz and folk scenes that had once been dominant. In recent years Sweden has become a pop superpower. Celine Dion, Britney Spears and N Sync all owe their biggest hits to Swedish writers and producers and there's even been home-grown success for the likes of Ace Of Bass and Roxette. Of course, the growth of mainstream pop invoked its less cynical other too, inspiring the guitar-based rock of the Wannadies, Soundtrack Of Our Lives and Kent amongst others, but it's the Cardigans that are the true inheritors of the Abba crown. They alone have found international success with a sound that seems effortlessly simplistic on the surface but, in keeping with the genius of Ulvaeus and Andersson before them, actually gets a damned sight more complicated the deeper you delve into the production. Vocalist Nina Persson also has that touch of melancholy that cuts through saccharine sweet pop, an art inherited from Agnetha Faltskog

in particular, but made all the more introverted and downright gloomy at times by better lyrics that could pass for the sort of thing that Morrissey might write. For the most part, the sound is more organic – jazz and folk in the early days, leather-pants rock later on – than the techno-pop that Sweden has since become famous for. Throw in the odd Black Sabbath cover and a knack learned from Stereolab for creating futuristic retro pop with a conscience and you have a band that makes Europop the way it should be made.

The band came together in 1992 in Jönköping in the south of Sweden. Two of its members, Peter Svensson and Magnus Sveningsson had played in heavy-metal bands but from the outset the Cardigans were intended as a pop band, albeit with jazz and indie-rock leanings. The debut album *Emmerdale* was a major critical success in Sweden and mixed light jazz-inflected pop with something altogether darker. The single 'Sick And Tired' written by Svensson and Sveningsson is an up-tempo ode to summer, coloured in by pastoral folk flute and crystal-clear guitar textures; 'Rise And Shine' goes faster still, driven on by energetic jazz drumming; 'Celia Inside' goes a stage further bringing in stand-up bass and vibraphone; and 'After

Nina Persson, The Cardigans

All' invokes late-night piano bar with Pernod and Gitanes cigarettes for Nina Persson's microphone-hugging vocal, so upfront and personal it will make you blush and look away. The album finishes with the band's idiosyncratic lounge-funk version of 'Sabbath Bloody Sabbath' which only avoids undermining the whole album as a postmodern exercise in irony because it is so beautifully played. The Cardigans may be taking the piss but when it sounds this good it's difficult to feel cheated.

Five of the songs originally featured on *Emmerdale* were packaged with eight songs from the band's follow-up set *Life* and released as a new album again called *Life* in 1995 on Stockholm Records. The new songs continued in a retro-jazz vein throwing in the odd piece of kitsch like 'Gordon's Gardenparty' – 'we were swinging oh so nice' – among soaring hook-laden sing-a-longs that don't come much better than the lead-off track 'Carnival'. From the moment Nina clears her throat with a clearly audible cough, the stage is set for a swirling string-driven masterpiece that sounds like it originated at some point in the early sixties but actually didn't. Try and tie the sound down to an era or a scene and it soon becomes clear that what you thought was a retro pastiche never actually existed up to that point. Genius.

With the inclusion of 'Lovefool' on the soundtrack to *Romeo And Juliet* the Cardigans broke through internationally and had some success with their album *First Band On The Moon* which dropped some of the jazz chords and padded out the gaps with more traditional rock sounds. The apparent fluff of 'Lovefool' with its chorus 'love me, love me, pretend that you love me' is placed in context as a song detailing a particularly painful break-up. It's followed on the album by 'Loser' during which Persson actually swears, and from there on in *First Band On The Moon* brilliantly combines feel-good tunes with tragic story-lines. By the time the band had recorded *Gran Turismo* the sound was more seductive still but becoming more claustrophobic. 'Erase/Rewind' is particularly moody and trip-hop beats are deployed to evoke a darker feel in general. 'Hanging Around' and radio favourite (and therefore inevitable car advert soundtrack) 'My Favourite Game' still retain big hooks for listeners to latch onto, but overall the sound is experimental. Guitars sound like synthesizers, there's more

texturing and Persson's voice is less naked than on previous albums. It was the last Cardigans album for five years and it's only with the eventual release of *Long Gone Before Daylight* that the band's continued existence has finally been confirmed. Persson's work with Mark Linkous of Sparklehorse in A Camp has obviously had an impact on the songs she is now writing with Svensson, a sad country vibe runs through a lot of the songs which don't half sound good when fed through the pop juicer.

First team: Peter Svensson (g), Nina Persson (v), Magnus Sveningsson (b), Bengt Lagerberg (d), Lasse Johansson (k, g)

Place, time, scene: Malmö, Sweden 1992. The Cardigans were determined to make pop music at a time when rock was in the ascendancy internationally and Swedish music was divided between studio-constructed pop and indie-guitar music. The jazz and folk inflections are traceable back to pre-Abba days, although the attention to detail in the Cardigans' music, the hooks and melodies, and Nina Persson's pop melancholic voice distil the best bits of the ultimate pop supergroup, updated with a form of introspective lyric-writing that has always been apparent in British indie music.

What to buy first: *Life* 1995 (International Release)

And then: *Emmerdale* 1994, *First Band On The Moon* 1997, *Gran Turismo* 1998, *Long Gone Before Daylight* 2003

CAT POWER

Some time around 1992 there was a Nick Drake revival. Island reissued his three seminal albums and a box set including a disc of previously unreleased material called *Fruit Tree*. It coincided with a new era of music-making taking place at home. A movement dubbed lo-fi was given a shot in the arm by the availability of samplers and cheap mini-mixers and artists like Pavement, Silver Jews, Will Oldham's Palace Music and Smog took it upon themselves to undermine the big-rock sound and studio artistry associated with mainstream rock bands and 'indie' bands alike. Several artists connected their sloppy amateurist approach to ironic lyrics and artwork, designed to puncture what they perceived to be a new form of musical pomposity based around production

Cat Power

values and instrumental virtuosity. Sure, it's one thing to have a dig at Butch Vig's production, but quite another to suggest that Kurt Cobain didn't feel the pain he sang about, especially when faced with an act so defiantly 'for real' a couple of years later.

Cat Power, the alter-ego of singer-songwriter Chan Marshall, has never felt the need to pass judgement on things outside her own realm of existence and is certainly not concerned with the business of scoring irony points in a music industry that has become more and more self-referential in its business and marketing practices. Her lo-fi is the real thing. In the tradition of Nick Drake, the key signifiers are introspection and honesty. The times, of course have a-changed and un-like Drake she belongs to a culture where it's possible and perhaps even inevitable that introspection and honesty are occasionally fed through a filter of reflex-ivity. It's not enough to be frank and direct anymore. Thanks to punk and postmodernism, frank and direct artists must now find ways of clothing their naked angst in a further level of self-awareness that requires them to

simultaneously speak from the heart and defend their right to do so. Cat Power knows that the old me gen-eration self-pity and Generation X alienation are just too obvious and, although tangibly real, especially when invoked by a performer of Cat Power's clarity, have somehow become cliché in such untrusting times. Cat Power isn't folk, punk or a member of the singer-songwriter genre. Like Bill Callahan in Smog and the recently deceased Elliott Smith, she is walking a line between personal catharsis and being a role-model for social and political resistance. So far she has succeeded impressively.

Cat Power's formative years having been spent in Georgia, her music is imbued with the blues, especially the sparse structures which give her songs a stillness and an emotional clarity, especially when extremes are called for. Her first album, *Myra Lee* released in 1995 was apparently recorded in one day and features Steve Shelley from Sonic Youth on drums. For the most part, the songs are empty sounding but still manage to pack an emotional punch, building to diffi-cult conclusions. A notable standout track is 'Enough' which traces the growing inevitability of a nervous breakdown. *What Would The Community Think?* was recorded before the end of the same year and brought together Marshall's voice with a musical setting that turned up the power and made a song like 'Nude As The News' vaguely accessible and catchy – a hit in France! Elsewhere the mood is more desolate though. On 'The Coat Is Always On' there are several inter-laced voices giving the effect of multiple personality disorder, and tracks like 'Water And Air' and 'Bathy-sphere' are relentless in their delicate heaviness.

Moon Pix in 1998 is often compared with Van Morri-son's *Astral Weeks*, an idiosyncratic album released almost 30 years before which has never really been fol-lowed up successfully, mainly due to the fact that the musicians who made it were themselves unaware of the precise nature of the magic they were creating at that time. Working with Jim White and Mick Turner from Australian string-driven trio, the Dirty Three, Cat Power is supported by a more free-form musical backing which is light and breezy on 'Cross Bones Style' and is more traditional for the alcoholic's tale, 'Moonshiner'. For 'The Colour And The Kids' she is on her own again though and comes across like

Blue-era Joni Mitchell, except that where music was always a salvation for Mitchell, for Chan Marshall it has become 'boring'. Maybe she was losing faith in her chosen dayjob. The following *Covers Record* seems inevitable in this context although on it she doesn't just opt for quiet originals that reflected her own art and life, there are songs on there by Moby Grape and the Rolling Stones. Her version of 'Satisfaction' makes the point that Liz Phair was aiming for on *Exile In Guyville* but more succinctly and with a degree of understanding of Jagger and Richards' youthful male egotism that Phair was happier to simply lampoon.

For the 2003 *You Are Free* album, the mood is once again deep and heavy. Imagine the first part of Patti Smith's 'Land' from *Horses* where she begins to tell her story in whispered tones, well that's Cat Power throughout the album. Unlike Smith, she rarely raises her voice to press her point home. Be careful when listening, that whispering might just drive you mad. The first track 'I Don't Blame You' tells the story of a performer in a rage because '*they* wanted to hear that sound that *you* didn't wanna play' which might be a piece of self-analysis made from a position of contrived objectivity, via astral projection, or possibly refers to someone else altogether. Maybe Cat Power had been to see Elliot Smith shortly before his apparent suicide, maybe not, but the point she makes relates to the distinction between private and public life that has haunted several key performers during the preceding decades. Cat Power is one of those artists out there on the edge, listen carefully to what she has to say.

Place, time, scene: Georgia 1992. Cat Power is sometimes associated with the anti-folk scene that was prominent around the time of her first album. Along with lo-fi artists like Smog and Elliot Smith she managed to create a powerful music with very little instrumentation and production to back-up her restrained but emotive voice. Where artists such as PJ Harvey and Liz Phair have enhanced their rawer early sound, Cat Power has retained a quietness that resembles the introspective singer-songwriters of the past, fed through a punk filter.

What to buy first: *Moon Pix* 1998

And then: *What Will The Community Think?* 1996, *You Are Free* 2003

NICK CAVE

Nick Cave has been making music for a quarter of a century now, and during that time he's perfected every aspect of his craft – songwriting, arrangement, performance and voice. And it seems that he's always been heading that way, having been introduced to the great works of literature at a formative age by his didactic father who was clearly keen to set high standards for his son to aspire to. The opening paragraph of *Lolita* and the murder scene in *Crime and Punishment* were set texts for the aspiring writer, a basic introduction to the themes of sex and violence, and according to Cave, his pre-occupation with 'death, isolation and prison, basically the same things I've always been harping on about'. Of course, there are the books as well as the music to confirm a level of empathy with words and imagery that follows the poetic tradition of Bob Dylan and Leonard Cohen. Although the thing that makes Nick Cave truly unique is his ability to set such literature to some of the most primal and compelling music committed to tape.

The Boys Next Door began in Melbourne in 1976, a new-wave band formed out of the ashes of Crime And The City Solution, inspired by the attitude of Australian independent pioneers Radio Birdman, musically, the post-punk experiments of bands like the Pop Group from the UK and Australia's Laughing Clowns, and in terms of performance, the Stooges and the Doors. Cave and Roland Howard were the songwriting base of the band, although multi-instrumentalist Mick Harvey, 'in yer face' bassist Tracy Pew and drummer Phil Calvert were fundamental to the band's essence. They relocated to the UK, becoming the Birthday Party on the eve of the trip, and once there, took temporary jobs to pay their way in-between gigs.

The first Birthday Party album was recorded back in Australia in 1980, but the lack of a scene and the band's tendency to get banned from venues due to their unconventional stage antics, led them back to the UK and then on to Berlin. The perpetual travelling mirrored the approach to music-making during the Birthday Party's four year existence, which developed from quite fractured and barely restrained to the relatively coherent which could be even more disconcerting still. The early gigs were, by all accounts, fast

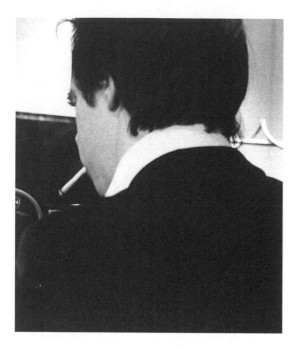

Nick Cave

and direct, brutal and confrontational, some of which seeped through onto the albums *Prayers On Fire* and *Junkyard* which take a basic Stooges template and add more feedback, horns and organ to accompany Cave's wide-eyed screaming.

By 1983, in Berlin, the mood had changed thanks largely to heroin addiction, and Cave's developing friendship and education in the possibilities of musical form from Blixa Bargeld of German band Einstürzende Neubauten. The EPs *The Bad Seed* and *Mutiny* are the best of the best as far as the Birthday Party are concerned. The sound is less claustrophobic and provides a better context for the classical imagery developing in Cave's lyrics. Mind you, although this period represents the beginning of the Bad Seeds, it is still quite clearly the Birthday Party on tracks like 'Sonny's Burning', which is a mix of black humour and relentless punk pounding. Cave's comment that 'I don't know of another group who are playing music that is attempting in some way to be innovative that draws a more moronic audience than the Birthday Party' is probably a fair indication that he was ready to move on.

The Bad Seeds back-catalogue begins with 1984's *From Her To Eternity*, which from the off combines Cave's righteousness and apparent emotional turmoil with experiments in musical form inspired by his colleagues. The title-track is a group effort that is only just kept under control, always seemingly at the point of explosion or collapse, and typical of the dramatic tension that is a recurring motif in every album since. It is the perfect backdrop to a song about intense sexual desire and the need to exorcize the desire before it's too late. The last line 'then ya know that lil girl would just have to go' can be interpreted two ways, one of which is a central theme of Cave's writing and culminated in a whole album of *Murder Ballads* in 1996. The albums in between see many souls dispatched, the towns-children of 'Tupelo' on *The Firstborn Is Dead*, the prisoner on death row in 'The Mercy Seat' on *Tender Prey*, and when it's not murder then it's death by slow decay when a horse keels over and dies during the appalling march of dwarves, mangy cats, dog-boys and rotting carcass, as witnessed by the omniscient Cave in 'The Carny'. He has created some of the most vivid imagery in the whole history of popular music.

Cave plays piano and organ, often the basis of the songs the Bad Seeds play, but he relies on the obvious musical talents of other band members for the realization of his work. Mick Harvey, Blixa Bargeld and Barry Adamson, and later Martyn P. Casey and Thomas Wydler have an understanding of musical and recording possibilities that, combined with Cave's overall vision, has ensured a series of albums that are exemplary in their melding of the avant-garde and cutting-edge technology. His most complete and rounded albums though are his most recent albums, mainly structured around his own playing and containing songs that are personally told rather than through his usual fictional analogy. *The Boatman's Call*, released in 1998, is the closest Cave has come to a solo album, and although the mood is still intense, it is lightened by the pure romance of songs like 'Into My Arms' in which Cave calls on angels and 'Are You The One That I've Been Waiting For?' that tells of a soul comforted. Speculation as to Cave's muse rests on songs entitled 'West Country Girl' and 'Black Hair', and the fact that Cave had recently collaborated with Dorset-born PJ Harvey.

With *The Boatman's Call*, Cave places the focus firmly on his lyrics and opts for a sparse musical arrangement that allows his voice to become the focus of the songs. On 2001's *No More Shall We Part* he variously resembles Bryan Ferry, Bob Dylan and Neil Diamond as well as the several Nick Caves established over the years. The arrangements are more complex, thanks to Mick Turner and Warren Ellis of fellow Aussie band the Dirty Three, but restrained when they need to be. The result is Cave's most perfect, powerful realization of lyrics, musical form and vocal yet. 'God Is In The House' and 'Oh My Lord' played back to back might just represent the high point of his career so far. First, a social plea to Him on behalf of the outside world, followed by a manic, paranoiac song during which he appears to go mad losing 'the plot, the plot'. After 25 years of music-making it seems that Nick Cave is just hitting his stride, and it's going to be a fascinating journey.

First team: The Birthday Party: Nick Cave (v), Roland Howard (g), Mick Harvey (g, k, d), Tracy Pew (b), Phil Calvert (d) Bad Seeds: Nick Cave (v, k), Blixa Bargeld (g), Barry Adamson (b, k, d), Martyn P. Casey (b), Thomas Wydler (d)

Place, time, scene: Melbourne 1979. The Birthday Party combined primal Doors-style blues with punk energy, eventually brought under control by Cave with his next band the Bad Seeds. Cave's vivid imagery and flair for story-telling, combined with powerful, dynamic and expansive musical arrangement, makes for songs of mythic proportions that stay with the listener for a very long time. Tindersticks are about the only band that have got anywhere close to Cave's genius for the melodramatic.

What to buy first: *No More Shall We Part* 2001

And then: The Birthday Party: *Mutiny/The Bad Seed* 1983, Nick Cave And The Bad Seeds: *From Her To Eternity* 1984, *Tender Prey* 1988, *Let Love In* 1994, *Murder Ballads* 1996, *The Boatman's Call* 1997.

In retrospect: The Birthday Party: *Hits* 1999, Nick Cave And The Bad Seeds: *The Best of Nick Cave and the Bad Seeds* 1998

CHARLATANS

'We are fuckin' rock' read the last line of the press release issued by the Charlatans following the death of their keyboard-player Rob Collins in the summer of 1996. It ended a statement that, despite losing the band's founder member, the band were to continue. It also doubled as an acknowledgement that Collins' time spent in the band meant something. To disband would be admitting the end of an era, that what they had been doing all that time was filling space before they got proper jobs. To continue confirmed that they had been an important British band right from the outset, despite the deranged ramblings of critics who had generally dismissed them as industry also-rans who got lucky when they found themselves playing gigs in Manchester when the whole baggy scene kicked-off nationally in 1989. The name probably didn't help.

From the point that vocalist Tim Burgess and guitarist Jon Baker joined forces with Collins, Martin Blunt and Jon Brookes, previously a garage-punk band inspired by the first wave of American psychedelia, the Charlatans became one of the best live bands on the circuit. They specialized in an enveloping sound that positioned each instrument in the live mix for maximum groove appeal. They had learned their art playing venues in Manchester where live music went hand-in-hand with late-licence clubbing. If a band wanted a gig and an audience that didn't peel off to the bar while the DJ took a break, then they had to provide the rhythms to keep them there on the dance-floor. By the late eighties, bands could no longer take it for granted that they would be the main attraction – the democratizing rave culture had seen to that – the groove was the star and the Charlatans sure knew how to groove. Their sound revolved around a big fat Hammond, with crashing guitar parts to add texture and crashing chords, and an unfeasibly high volume bass. Burgess' vocals were usually buried somewhere beneath, and were ambivalent enough not to detract, or steal the limelight from the communal vibe set up between band and audience. The lighting, which was often turned on the dance-floor, made it difficult to stand and simply watch a Charlatans gig. At least, there would be a little shoulder movement.

The early albums never really captured the vibe of the gigs, and the apparent lack or centrality of substantive lyrical content, meant that critics struggled to find clever things to say about *Some Friendly* and *Between 10th And 11th*. That, despite tracks like

The Charlatans

'Sproston Green', a wall-of-sound rocker, and 'Weirdo', featuring the best Hammond and guitar duel ever likely to be committed to tape. And you don't get a much more concise expression of zeitgeist capturing cultural ambivalence than a line like 'Most of the time you're happy, you're a weirdo'. With baggy segueing into shoegazing, and the rise of dark and emotional heavy music from the US in the early nineties, the Charlatans waited until 1994 before returning with their third album *Up To Our Hips*, featuring a more defined Burgess vocal somewhere between Bob Dylan and Liam Gallagher. With production from Steve Hillage, it sounded different too, emphasizing more upfront organic acoustic sounds with the keyboard taking on a more textural role. With the band's obvious understanding of sonic dynamics, they were able to produce themselves on 1995's *The Charlatans* with excellent results, but it's *Tellin' Stories* where they really found their voice, although this sadly coincided with the

tragic death of their keyboardist in a car crash while on his way to the recording sessions.

With most of his keyboard parts in the bag before his death, the band continued with a focus and emotional depth to their songs, perhaps missing from earlier albums. 'North Country Boy', the brooding opener 'One To Another', and the yearning 'How Can You Leave Us', which addresses the subject of the song as 'Darlin'', may be lyrically inspired by their friend's passing; the instrumental piece 'Rob's Theme' definitely is. Elsewhere, the rockers 'How High' and 'Only Teethin' demonstrate where the band's head was at before and after Collins' tragic demise. The Charlatans had always suffered due to the quality of their stylistic contemporaries the Stone Roses and the Happy Mondays, and now with both bands defunct, the time was right for the survivors to move into the limelight. Their amalgamation of classic rock and groove sensibility was better realized than the

Zeppelinism of the Roses' second album, and Burgess' lyrics and delivery more understated and less cartoon than Black Grape's debut. A new dark side and sense of reality had been discovered that gave them an authority that the Britpop bands could not match, and which enabled the band to succeed in post-grunge America where many newer bands failed.

'Forever', the lead-off track on the next album, is perhaps the band's ultimate achievement, the perfect blend of light and shade and as fat and full as a full fat bastard. The 'It's us and us only' line in the song which gives the album its title, is set against the repeated phrase 'I wonder what you people do with your lives?'. Burgess could have someone specific in mind, but it could easily double as an attack on the band's detractors over the years. The album continues with a set of personal songs that are shot through with a sense of resolve in the face of adversity and tragedy, with angels and witches a recurring motif. A song like 'My Beautiful Friend' strikes a blow for the heavenly crowd and 'A House Is Not A Home' finds Burgess somewhere altogether darker. It's what Dylan would sound like if he had the funk.

The band are still knocking out albums. Most recently the lighter, funkier and decidedly soulful *Wonderland*, infused throughout with a positivity that probably has something to do with Tim Burgess' new life and wife out in LA. With the rest of the band still based in the British north-west, attendance at practice night is surely tough to police, and as you would expect, fatally undermines the collective spirit and shared culture of the group members. They're a tough lot to break though, the Charlatans, so don't write them off yet. The 'fuckin rock' thing obviously still applies.

First team: Tim Burgess (v), Martin Blunt (b), Rob Collins (k), Jon Brookes (d), Jon Baker (g)

Place, time, scene: Northwich, Cheshire, UK 1989. They were there when rave infected the indie rock scene and flew in on the baggy breeze, hitting the UK Top 10 with their second single. Their own 'second coming' in 1996 took the initial blend of indie and beats to the next level and transcended the philosophically oppositional American rock and British pop of the mid-nineties.

What to buy first: *Tellin' Stories* 1997

And then: *Some Friendly* 1990, *The Charlatans* 1995, *Us And Us Only* 1999

In retrospect: *Melting Pot* 1999

CHEAP TRICK

In 1977, after four years' solid touring around the US, Cheap Trick released their self-titled debut album. It confounded critics and marketing experts due to its apparent wrongness. Wrong image, wrong songs, wrong production, wrong time. Luckily due to the years the band had spent on the road criss-crossing their native country supporting AC/DC, Kiss and Boston, it sold bucket-loads – in Japan! In fact, for the next two years, Japanese youth culture experienced escalating 'trickmania', culminating in the band selling out the massive Budokan Stadium in just two hours. Back in the US, potential fans didn't catch on until a live album made up of tracks from the Budokan gig was released as Cheap Trick's fourth album in 1979, and then it all started to make sense. The Budokan album revealed an awesome and expert set of musicians who had honed their craft on the road, and in the process joined the dots between pop, heavy metal and punk before anyone else. 1979 was about the time that everyone else caught on. After a good half-decade of trying, Cheap Trick were eventually a right place, right time band. The image was always suspect of course – the poodle perms, outsize specs and inconsistent clothing combinations – but such blatant disregard of fashion suss can only be admired in retrospect.

Songwriter and guitarist Rick Nielson was 32 with 12 years of playing in bands behind him when the debut album was released. Together with Tom Petersson and drummer Bun E. Carlos, he had formed a band called Fuse. Having spent some time playing in Europe and then basing themselves in Philadelphia, they returned to their native Rockford, Illinois in 1970, where they hooked up with folk-pop singer Robin Zander. Four years on the road gave Nielson the opportunity to write enough songs to eventually fill three albums. Always keeping the hook and the melody line central, he set about undermining such blatant pop with fast, crashing metal guitar-riffs and an approach to subject matter and lyrics which was more in keeping with the irony, humour and realism that went together so well in songs by the emerging punk writers. And Zander could be relied upon to get the message across with the minimum of stylistic pretension, having developed a direct and confident vocal delivery style during his formative folk years.

The first Cheap Trick album was recorded in 1976 and opens with 'ELO Kiddies', a vaguely autobiographical song which acknowledges the band's hero-worship of Roy Wood, the founder of ELO, and the reason for Nielson's and Petersson's trip to the UK in 1968. There's also 'Daddy Should Have Stayed In High School', a song about paedophilia, 'The Ballad of TV Violence' which connects mass murder and the media, and 'He's A Whore', the subject-matter of which was confirmed by Big Black, who included the song on their 1987 thematic album *Songs About Fucking*.

Unfortunately, Cheap Trick got sucked into soft-rock mediocrity during the eighties, and in a bid to appease their record company who still expected the sales figures achieved by *Live At Budokan*, agreed to a financially motivated masterplan for the band, which included buying in songs by outside songwriters. Hits followed and album sales increased, but Cheap Trick had lost their direction both lyrically and due to the synthetic production methods imposed on them, musically as well. And that would have been it for Cheap Trick, just another casualty in the ongoing ideological war between artist and corporation, but then at the end of the decade Billy Corgan and even Kurt Cobain started talking about the band's early work in reverential terms. The result: a recording session with Steve Albini (formerly of Big Black), leading to a single for Sub Pop, a slot on Lollapalooza and a nationwide tour with the Smashing Pumpkins.

Rehabilitated and back on track, they played a series of gigs where they exhumed their first four albums, one album each night in their entirety, to hugely appreciative audiences across the US. OK, so on one hand it's an acknowledgement that their best years were behind them, but on the other, it's a celebration of the longevity of inspired creativity in an apparent throwaway commercial medium, even 20 years after the event. The fact that the audiences included a whole new set of admirers, makes Cheap Trick's return far more than simply an exercise in nostalgia.

First team: Rick Nielson (g), Robin Zander (v, g), Tom Petersson (b), Bun E. Carlos (d)

Place, time, scene: Rockford, Illinois 1973. Cheap Trick had a unique sound brought about by unique circumstances. After several years on the road they had mastered a blend of pop and heavy rock but also injected a little punk spirit into their songs, making them the first of the old school bands to wise up to a raw guitar sound and the odd controversial lyric. The combination of melodic pop with a heavy-rock sound retrospectively put them back in vogue with the new American underground bands of the early nineties.

What to buy first: *Cheap Trick* 1977

And then: *Live At Budokan* 1979

CHEMICAL BROTHERS

Tom Rowlands and Ed Simons were a couple of history students studying at Manchester Polytechnic in 1988 when the city exploded to the sound of house and techno music from Chicago and Detroit. The scene, of course, was fuelled by the influx of that 'dance all night' happy substance from Europe – Stella Artois – a pound a pint at the Hacienda Club. New Order were the local heroes, off in Ibiza making their rave-flavoured *Technique* album, the Stone Roses were round town trying out songs for their debut album, and the Happy Mondays were, well, wherever the party was at. Manchester was the place that embraced the rock and dance crossover. With its history of northern-soul clubs, the indie kids had always been happy to dance as well as mope, and the Stone Roses' warehouse gig idea had brought together a rag-tag selection of youth subcultural groups, all with different tastes in music. Someone had to provide the mix.

Inspired by their heroes the Dust Brothers, who were responsible for all that harsh sonic montage work on the Beastie Boys' groundbreaking *Paul's Boutique* album, Tom and Ed, the Chemical Brothers, set about making their university time just that little more vocational. They played various student parties and picked up a residency at a club night called Naked Under Leather run by Justin Robertson of Lionrock. By the time they moved to London, they had enough clout to get themselves a residency on Great Portland Street in central London, Rowlands' CV including a few singles for the Deconstruction dance label, and both with remixes for Leftfield, Lionrock and Republica, a deal with Junior Boys Own Records, and good solid 2:1s in History. The Chemical Brothers know when to party and when to get down to some good old-fashioned work. It's a distinction that's served them well.

The residency at the Sunday Social[16] was their chance to demonstrate that the art of DJ-ing could be more than simply re-enacting beat matches made the night before in your bedroom, or made easier by just using instrumental tracks with the bpm written on the sleeve. Taking their cue from 'Madchester' they mixed everything into everything, but were careful to follow the golden rule that it's not what you play but the order in which you play it. Everyone came to the Social. Bobbie Gillespie of Primal Scream, Noel Gallagher, Paul Weller and Tim Burgess of the Charlatans were all spotted there, and it led to more remix work, although they did turn down Oasis and David Bowie! Their first proper release was a remix of This Mortal Coil's 'Song To The Siren', a previously slow-moving piece of dreamscape etherealness, which took on a new character when subjected to the Brothers' big beat. Kicking off, obviously, with sirens, Liz Fraser's vocals are taken out of context, looped and placed just underneath a pounding real-drum sound with occasional bass rumbles that sound awesome on a 10k sound system. It was an announcement of intent.

During 1994 they turned down big remix money from INXS and Aerosmith who wanted them to add that much sought-after hint of cool to their latest releases, but they chose instead to work with English folk singer Beth Orton who, despite having a totally different musical background and style, obviously had the right attitude. She appears on the debut Chemical Brothers album *Exit: Planet Dust* released in 1995, a whole album of music made with the dance-floor firmly in mind but also perfectly enjoyable when domestically-consumed as well ... providing you turn the whole thing up. 'Leave Home' is their first great construction. Starting ominously with a ship's funnel bass sound, it builds with different textures, a confused-sounding funky guitar sound, rumbling bass, a slowed-down voice intoning 'brother's gonna

work it out', and then the trademark break into an irresistible big beat, that at the very least will have you nodding with purpose, affirming just how downright ace it all is.

'Block Rockin' Beats' which kicks off the second album *Dig Your Own Hole* follows suit and perfects the stop-the-beat, hold it ... start-the-beat again strategy that Fatboy Slim has since made a trademark. They work primarily with computers, samplers and sequencers, often leaving certain tracks 'bubbling away' for months or years until inspiration hits. Ed Simons makes the point that there is not the same division of labour and focus between musicians who compose electronically, and that with two of them working on everything, there is an in-built quality control at all times; musical identity is less likely to be lost than it is in a band where one or two members might emphasize their own role at the expense of others in the sound mix. The Chemical Brothers have strong opinions on what is right musically, and what isn't. Unexplainable to an outsider, it's a form of chemical zen.

Dig Your Own Hole includes songs sung by Noel Gallagher and Beth Orton, hip-hop pioneer Kool Herc can be heard on there too. Rowlands and Simons wrote the track 'Where Do I Begin' performed by Beth Orton, another string to their bow, and perfectly positioned as the calm before the storm of the album's mesmerizing finale 'The Private Psychedelic Reel', an amazing psychedelic trip that makes the link between acid house, folk-rock, Indian droning and Mercury Rev, a link which it didn't seem to need making up to that point, but there you go. *Surrender*, which followed in 2001, picks up where the reel left off and develops sounds and textures as a priority. The single 'Hey Girl Hey Boy' was their biggest dance hit to date and once again there's house, techno and disco beats but they enhance the songs, demonstrating that mastery of beats is crucial in the contemporary business of music production. 'The Sunshine Underground' is the centrepiece of the album, beginning mid-tempo and increasing in pace while more and more sounds are piled on top, finally emerging as pure techno. It gets better with every listen.

With *Come With Us* in 2002, the Chemical Brothers confirmed their ability to mix styles but retain an overall aesthetic that is clearly their own, blending organic and electronic sounds that keeps them in high demand amongst other artists who want their music to affect the head and the body simultaneously, and which – this is the important bit – will never be reduced to cliché. Of course, many ask, and many are turned down. Producers don't tend to do that – for them it's a job. For the Chemical Brothers it's more than that; things like quality, creativity and spirit are what count in the chemical world.

First team: Tom Rowlands (c, k, s), Ed Simons (c, k, s)

Place, time, scene: Manchester 1992. The Chemical Brothers are DJs who have mastered the new software and technology needed to make contemporary music where beats and texture are crucial. Their knowledge of musical genres past and present makes them awesome DJs and informed producers.

What to buy first: *Dig Your Own Hole* 1997

And then: *Exit: Planet Dust* 1995, *Surrender* 1999, *Come With Us* 2002

In retrospect: *Singles 1993–2003* 2003

CLASH

The Clash are the template for all other bands formed after 1976 that want to make music on their own terms without losing sight of the reality in which they are operating. Musically, they reflected the range of popular music tastes developed up to that point, and combined different styles with a revolutionary spirit in keeping with the more progressive political aspects of youth and working-class culture. They balanced utopian idealism with a sense of realism, and in terms of their business and marketing methods, made a clear distinction between expediency and unnecessary frivolity. Signing for a multi-national corporate company like CBS was about getting records made and raising funds for tours; on the other hand, performing to a backing track on *Top Of The Pops* was selling out and allowing the image to become as important as the music. The Clash didn't really do irony either, especially not the playful verisimilitude that was a key part of punk. They once refused to loan the Banshees their equipment because Siouxsie was wearing a swastika. Critics of the band cite such examples as wrong-headed naïvety, while those that revere the Clash as the true punk gods

point to the band's consistent stand against hypocrisy, and lyrical observations about a cultural reality that has nothing to do with the art or artifice peddled by other such punk luminaries.

Mick Jones and Joe Strummer were never like-minded individuals and their backgrounds in music were initially at odds too. Strummer was three years older than Jones when they met up for the first time in 1976, and he had spent a few years playing the pub-rock circuit. His band, the 101ers had made one single, a straightforward driving R&B love song called 'Key To Your Heart'. Jones, by contrast, had very little live-playing experience but had honed his punk taste and philosophy. Together with Tony James, who would later form Generation X and Brian James, later of Chelsea and the Damned, Jones had created the legendary London SS which spent more time auditioning potential members than actually playing. As far as Jones was concerned, musicianship was certainly important but having the right attitude was the crucial thing. Paul Simonon had no discernible musical ability at all but was Jones' one definite in any future projects he might undertake. Both drew inspiration from the Stooges and New York Dolls, but also had a thing for the Rolling Stones so were willing to give it a go with the more traditional Strummer.

With Terry Chimes on drums and scenester Keith Levene on third guitar, the band, operating as the Psychotic Negatives began playing gigs and were signed up by manager Bernie Rhodes, a McLaren acolyte who fancied himself as a rock'n'roll swindler. Rhodes encouraged the band to adopt a direct and overtly political stance in their songs, an approach which Jones and Strummer warmed to, notably on the rewriting of 'I'm So Bored With You', becoming instead 'I'm So Bored Of The USA'. 'White Riot', 'London's Burning' and 'Career Opportunities' followed, and then an eponymous debut album which captured the band, now called the Clash, in all its amateur yet clearly focused glory.

Strummer's experience of pub-rock gigs meant that he couldn't sing without thrashing out chords on his guitar, and vice versa, so his playing is rarely to be heard on the album due to microphone and sound leakage issues. Terry Chimes had been kicked out of the band before the sessions were started but was the only drummer around so he played anyway, and according to producer Mickey Foote, on the few days they had to get the recording done, the band members were unlikely to start work until well after lunch, wasting valuable studio-time paid for by their label. That's punk, you see, right there.

It's a great album though – not as fast and throwaway as the Damned's first one, but equally as anarchic – impassioned vocals, relentless rhythms and concise guitar solos just about squeezed into the sub-three-minuters that make up most of the album. Joe Strummer described it at the time as 'sealions barking over pneumatic drills', but tucked away towards the end of the album there's also a version of Junior Murvin's 'Police And Thieves' which points to the musical route to be travelled in the years to come. The track is reggae done Clash-style, still with the mellow backing-rhythm but somehow more insistent, with Mick Jones adding guitar stabs where there would normally be gaps, the cumulative and simultaneous sound of the Roxy, where DJs mixed reggae, dub and ska with punk in-between live punk sets. Lee 'Scratch' Perry, a reggae producer noted for his broad taste in music, approved of the Clash's new hybrid sound and offered to produce their 1977 single 'Complete Control'. It's one of their best, even if Jones de-dubbed it by cranking the guitars back up after Perry had left.

'(White Man) In Hammersmith Palais' followed, Strummer's cutting observation of voluntary colour apartheid set up by the audience at a Dillinger gig, complete with references to the new punk bands who wear suits bought from Burtons menswear 'ha, you think it's funny, turning rebellion into money'. It was good journalism. However, the reports of punk's philosophical demise came across as just that little bit rich, from a band whose second album was produced by the bloke from soft-rock FM radio heroes Blue Oyster Cult. *Give 'Em Enough Rope* was its unfortunate title. Too clean, too slick. There were still great songs though, notably 'English Civil War' and 'Tommy Gun', which appears to capture the discrepancies in the studio, coming on like a big production number with the full and textured guitar intro before kicking into an altogether more lo-fi and thinner, live-punk sound for the meat of the song.

In contrast, when *London Calling* followed at the end of the year, it was the sound of the Clash getting everything spot-on. It's got rock, reggae, rockabilly, jazz, R&B and melodic pop, and all played with a musical confidence and knowledge of sonic dynamics and structure which could not have been predicted two years before. The tracks are sparse and neat with everything in just the right place in the overall mix, and there are some complex arrangements too. 'Clampdown' is three different songs in the first forty seconds alone, 'Wrong Em Boyo' has a perfectly executed intentional false start and 'The Card Cheat' is Spector's Wall of Sound incarnate. The songs are mostly about London and the real and fictional characters that did or might have inhabited Clashworld. There's Jimmy Jazz, an underworld criminal, Rudie who drinks 'brew for breakfast', and a gun-toting Jimmy Cliff wannabe living in Brixton. On occasion the specific tales are more widely contextualized, so you hear about the 'evil presidentes' working for the clampdown, the lingering effects of the Spanish Civil War, and in 'Lost In The Supermarket', the perpetual consumerism that leads to inevitable political apathy. *Rolling Stone* magazine made it their album of the decade. Nuff said.

Sandanista was a triple-album set to follow-up the double *London Calling*, and gets better with age, especially with hindsight. Made with producer Mikey Dread, it explored dub and rap, and considering the speed with which it was recorded, contains a bewildering array of ideas, both musical and politically. The theme was anti-American. That's the American state, not American culture in general, a simple enough distinction, although many British critics got confused and branded the Clash pretentious hypocrites.

Combat Rock in 1982 was a more focused version of *Sandanista* and had the Clash perfecting their punk-pop. 'Rock The Casbah', written by Topper Headon, and 'Should I Stay Or Should I Go' were both international hits. 'Straight To Hell' was the Clash at their best and had they left it there, the story would be pretty much a flawless one. They didn't. Jones was sacked in a Strummer/Simonon coup, prompting him to form Big Audio Dynamite, Headon left of his own accord to pursue a solo career incorporating one album, a jail sentence and a more rewarding career as a London cabbie, and the fundamentally flawed Clash made the ironically titled *Cut The Crap* before ending it in 1985. Strummer played with Bob

Dylan, the Pogues and his own Mescaleros in the ensuing years, but tragically died of an unexpected heart defect at Christmas in 2002. The tributes, of which there were many, emphasized that he, and his band, were the real thing, the dog's bollocks. Which is about right.

First team: Joe Strummer (v, g), Mick Jones (v, g), Paul Simonon (b, v), Topper Headon (d)

Place, time, scene: London 1976. The Clash were perceived as the Sex Pistols' main rivals. They were more directly oppositional than the Pistols and musically more diverse. Their blending of punk and reggae was a nod to the links between the two cultures in London and pointed the way towards 2-Tone. The anger and passion that Strummer put into his performance inspired Billy Bragg in particular, who carried on the direct political message into the eighties.

What to buy first: *London Calling* 1979

And then: *The Clash* 1977, *Combat Rock* 1982

In retrospect: *The Story Of The Clash* 1988

COCTEAU TWINS

Words don't really express what the Cocteau Twins were about, and that's why for the most part, they didn't use them. In the early days they didn't really use music either. Well, at least not in its traditional sense.

Having met in Grangemouth in Scotland where Robin Guthrie was a DJ at a punk club, they started making music together with bassist Will Heggie, sometime in 1979. Liz Fraser didn't last long initially but returned to the fold when she began seeing Guthrie on a more personal level. As travelling fans of the Birthday Party, they obviously took note of the darkness and intensity of the band's live shows, and having got to know the band, were advised to send a tape of their developing musical style to Ivo Watts-Russell at 4AD Records. Hearing something in the combination of Fraser's soaring vocals and dense, atmospheric backing made-up of layered guitars and hypnotic bass, Watts-Russell invited them to London and gave them nine days in a studio, resulting in an album called *Garlands* which got lots on play on John Peel's national radio show and made it to number two in the UK Indie charts in 1982. The second album, *Head Over Heels*, went one better and for the rest of the decade, the Cocteau Twins' sound became synonymous with the 4AD label, with Fraser's seemingly wordless vocals – often incorporating languages other than English – an inspiration for vocalists, who began using their own voice as an additional instrument to be added to the mix.

Throughout their 14-year career, Robin Guthrie made use of studio technology to create the Cocteau Twins' trademark sound. Specifically, that meant that what the guitar did was not as important as the way it was eventually recorded. A neat musical analogy of Fraser's approach to singing if you think about it? Guthrie makes no excuses about his lack of skills as an actual player, and is keen to point out that his methods are just as creative, and ultimately just as influential. 'I'm playing my guitar and I'm putting it into a Copycat and overloading it. I'm then coming out of that and putting it into a BigMuff and then going into another Copycat. Nowadays, with all the multi-FX and racks, all you've got to do is go to preset number four in order to get the "Robin Guthrie" setting'.[17]

The replacement of Will Heggie, who left to form Lowlife, with Simon Raymonde, who they knew from the shop below the 4AD offices, brought a new structure to the Cocteau Twins' ambient free-floating sonics and the next few releases feature more obviously structured songs. With Raymonde's ear for arrangement – perhaps in the genes, his father having co-written Dusty Springfield's pop gem 'I Only Want To Be With You' – *Treasure* is the most accessible of the Cocteau Twins' albums up to that point. It features extensive use of acoustic guitars and piano, in effect beginning a six year period of development that culminated in the 1990 album *Heaven Or Las Vegas* – the ultimate realization of a new style of music-making that clearly had some influence on bands like Massive Attack and Portishead, even Björk.

Listening to the album, it is apparent that Guthrie has perfected his layering techniques, recording parts separately and mixing them at varying volumes and with varying degrees of delay so that they appear to float unsuspended, while Raymonde establishes the melody with his bass parts and Fraser, sounding at her most relaxed and happy, actually uses proper words in some instances, to convey the emotion of her songs, some of them perhaps inspired by her family life with Guthrie.

Two more albums followed before the couple and the band split. Occasionally, Fraser's voice has cropped up in the public domain, notably on Massive Attack's sparse masterpiece, 'Teardrop', while Guthrie and Raymonde have based their post-Cocteau work around their label Bella Union. Now working with Siobhan de Mare, formerly of Mono, Guthrie's new work as Violet Indiana has been incisively reviewed as 'all trip and no hop' which at least proves that he's consistent.

First team: Robin Guthrie (g, k), Liz Fraser (v), Simon Raymonde (b, k)

Place, time, scene: Grangemouth, Scotland 1980. The Cocteau Twins' experimentation with guitar and vocal textures has inspired many including My Bloody Valentine and is most clearly heard in the work of other 4AD artists including the Throwing Muses.

What to buy first: *Heaven Or Las Vegas* 1990

And then: *Treasure* 1984

In retrospect: *The Singles Collection* 1991

CONTORTIONS

In the first week of May 1978 a series of gigs were held at the Artists' Space in Soho, New York. The bands that played were all part of a scene which had become dubbed 'no wave' – a response to the punk sell-outs who had taken their musical cue from the first wave of American and British punk bands but didn't get that there was an attitude thing that went along with the music that gave it spirit and significance. They did it by taking rock tradition apart and putting it back together again in new and different ways, replacing the accepted rules of pop and rock style with pure energy.

Mars were the first of the no-wave bands to form in 1976, clearly inspired by the Velvet Underground's experimentation with noise, droning and feedback. They narrowly missed being part of punk's first generation but remained on the New York scene while others went international. They were perhaps the

most non-musical of the bands playing at that time and were more concerned with pulling rock music apart so that it became a mess of noise. The discordant and atonal sound that Mars made was rarely resolved; guitar parts in particular went nowhere and there was little attempt at melody. It inspired Brazilian-born non-musician Arto Lindsay to form DNA, a trio which also included a good-looking Japanese girl and a performance artist. DNA made music that was more angular than Mars – 'lots of stop-start' – and which incorporated abstract South American and Asian rhythms and sounds. A non-musical musicologist could probably make a link between Arto Lindsay's guitar style and the stuff that John McGeoch did with Magazine and Siouxsie and the Banshees a couple of years later.

DNA were one of the bands that cropped up on a compilation album called *No New York* which was produced by Brian Eno and is the best document of the scene, which revolved around a relatively small number of bands, all doing something slightly different but connected by a sense of musical adventure. Bands like Material and the Golden Palominos, which featured avant-garde musicians like Bill Laswell, Anton Fier and John Zorn, are sometimes referred to as no-wave but were not at the heart of the original scene, even if they were attempting something similar, but more musically informed at the same time. If it's no-wave originators you want, then you'll be after James Chance and Lydia Lunch.

The two met in 1976 when Lydia Lunch was working as a waitress in a cocktail bar. Five years later on she had the world at her feet with a nicely evolving solo career, but back then she was a 16-year-old punk groupie, desperate to start her own band. James Chance played keyboards and saxophone and had initially come to New York from Milwaukee to take the jazz scene by storm. It didn't work. He claims, because he was too young, had the wrong accent and was the wrong colour, but it might also be down to the fact that he specialized in atonal, screeching sax that undermined all of the traditional rules of playing. When he started hanging out in downtown New York with the punks he realized that his particular brand of jazz music had more in common with the Ramones, and having discovered Lunch, decided to form a band which they called Teenage Jesus and the Jerks.

For six months, Chance meshed his sax with the early hardcore sound of the Jerks, but by the end of 1977 had begun another band, leaving Lunch to make two more singles with the original band before striking out on her own as a solo artist who would later work with the Birthday Party, Einstürzende Neubauten, Sonic Youth and Foetus, eventually setting up her own company called Widowspeak for the purposes of publishing her own books and spoken-word work. Chance's band the Contortions, meanwhile, continued to pursue the atonal and the discordant in music, but underpinned their experimentation with a weird groove that is part rockabilly, part bubblegum pop. 'Flip Your Face', included on the *No New York* compilation, is the ultimate mix of party vibe and brittle punk, overlaid with crazy hardcore free-jazz sax, scratchy guitar and Chance's terrifying screamed vocals. It's psychotic dance music of the highest order.

Buy, released in 1979, is an 'in yer face' collection of songs where the anger, associated with punk, is focused into a no-holds-barred attack on the music. Having said that, there's a good deal of contempt for the world and the human race in general; the tracks 'Roving Eye' and 'Contort Yourself' both have, shall we say, issues. *Off-White*, released the same year by Chance's alter-ego James White and the Blacks, and including many of the original Contortions, is a little calmer, as befits an album which was supposed to be a disco collection, but the grooves are still hard, the structures still unexpected and the subject matter controversial. 'Stained Sheets' features a Lydia Lunch erotic moan, and 'Almost Black' is Chance having yet another dig at racial hypocrisy.

Stories abound of Chance's unreasonable behaviour during the period, his violent tendencies in particular scared off many of his musical collaborators. The final two albums were made with a revolving-door band membership policy, but still featured Chance's insane Beefheart-inspired saxophone playing. The Contortions did a couple of shows in 1991 and that was it.

First team: James Chance (White) (v, sx), Pat Place (g), Jody Harris (g), Georg Scott (b), Don Christensen (d), Adele Bertei (k)

Place, time, scene: New York 1978. The no-wave bands were the rightful heirs to the scene that had been born in 1975 at CBGBs and Max's Kansas City[18], and were themselves inspirational to a whole stack of other bands who formed in the wake of punk and wanted to take their new found life-affirming hobby in interesting new directions. The Contortions had the longest career, driven on by pure spirit. Jon Spencer Blues Explosion must have a couple of James Chance albums surely?

What to buy first: *Buy* 1979

And then: James White And The Blacks: *Off-White* 1979

In retrospect: Various Artists: *No New York* 1979

JULIAN COPE

Julian Cope is a highly principled music fan who happens to have made a living from working creatively within the music industry. Read his book *Head-On* and you'll realize that he has a tendency to get very excited about the music that matters to him, and how it affects him on a personal level. On hearing the Ramones for the first time he explains that 'For about a year after October 1976 the Doors sounded muso, the Velvets sounded reasonable and Can sounded like hippies'[19] but that the Sex Pistols 'Anarchy In The UK' was somehow not as effective as its rawer, thinner sounding B-side 'I Wanna Be Me'. It's a great book, and he's one of the best rock writers around. When he applies such clarity of judgement and enthusiasm to his own music, he's even better.

The Liverpool scene that Cope happened upon in the late seventies and early eighties was a creative hotbed of musicians and writers inspired by the spirit of punk and a lengthy musical tradition in the city. Supported by an established live scene centring on Eric's – a club on Mathews Street just down the road from the original Cavern – and fed by an impressive range of import new-wave and old garage psychedelic records available at Probe Records, bands such as Echo and the Bunnymen, Dead Or Alive, Wah! and Frankie Goes To Hollywood all gestated there and went on to score hits in the British charts in the first few years of the new decade. All but one of the above bands included members who had at one point or another been in a band with Cope, most notably the one-rehearsal session band called the Crucial 3, the first and last retrospective supergroup consisting of Cope, Ian McCulloch and Pete Wylie. Simply put, the object was to become the coolest, sleaziest, most rocking band since the Stooges, or the Pistols . . . or Subway Sect – whoever mattered the most that week.

The melting pot of influences and the production skills of Cope's sparring partner Dave Balfe made Cope's own band the Teardrop Explodes particularly eclectic, demonstrating on a series of singles and three albums – *Kilimanjaro*, *Wilder* and the unreleased *Everyone Wants To Shag The Teardrop Explodes* that they were prepared to incorporate whatever felt right at the time – a mixture of exhuberance and eccentricity that made pop interesting in the first part of the eighties. But by 1983, the unrelenting pop machinery had got the better of him and Cope explained 'I'd stopped caring whether I liked our music really. All I was interested in was getting precisely what I felt down on tape.'

Such honesty and lack of commercial design coincided with a developing drug habit and a period of self-loathing and self-mutilation that culminated in 1984 with Cope slashing open his chest with a broken mike stand on stage at the Hammersmith Palais. By that point the Teardrop Explodes had been obsolete for two years and Cope was rushing headlong into a solo career which was overshadowed by a media image that had him down as a latter-day Syd Barrett. Following the perfunctory debut *World Shut Your Mouth*, rumours and music-industry gossip suggested that the next album would be the final nail in the Cope coffin, and sure enough, when it came out, a few months after the delayed debut, it received short shrift from critics and public alike.

It shouldn't have done. *Fried* is the sound of a troubled man getting a lot of bad stuff out of his system. The opening track 'Reynard The Fox' uses the metaphor of the hunted fox to tell of Cope's own feelings with regard to his media image and state of mind, and is followed on the album by a sarcastic attack on Bill Drummond who, Cope had felt, let him and the Teardrop Explodes down when he was their manager. The music is often sparse, with little or no bass, and there are some odd mixing techniques too. Drums appear on just one channel, and a toy piano graces the album's psychedelic highlight 'Sunspots'.

It failed to sell, but the spirit of *Fried* is evident on everything else he's done since.

After the commercial success of *Saint Julian* and the big budget and associated creative stasis of *My Nation Underground*, the full implications of *Fried* hit home. An album which was essentially a personal document of a particular moment in his own life, made wholly independently and with very little support from his record company, suddenly made sense. 'With expectations from the record company I was shit. Without expectations from a record company I was great.' The slick production and Cope's desire to play the pop star for *Saint Julian* made for a marketable product complete with hit singles, *Top Of The Pops* and magazine covers. The disinclination that Cope felt to do it all again on *My Nation Underground* made for musical dishonesty. Cope learned from his time in the pop machine, many don't.

Skellington came next – recorded in one and a half days – and was totally unacceptable to Island Records. Cope, thankfully, put it out himself. Otherwise the world may never have got to hear the lo-fi gem 'Out Of My Mind On Dope And Speed'. It was a spiritual successor to *Fried*. *Peggy Suicide* took a bit longer to create, a double album of positivity, confidence and purposefulness that was themed around environmental concerns and the family, and contained moments of pure sentimental joy expressed in raw acoustics on 'Beautiful Love'. It also has 'East Easy Rider' and 'Safesurfer', catchy songs which should have had Cope back on *Top Of The Pops* every week, but sadly the world didn't work like that anymore. He followed *Peggy Suicide* with two more environmentally themed albums, one of which, *Autogeddon*, was so-named after his car had spontaneously exploded on his driveway. He walks a lot now, mainly along ley lines and ancient routes. And that's how it has been ever since. Cope the sentimentalist plugged into the essence of the rock'n'roll spirit. Or 'The Andrew Lloyd Webber of garage punk rock' as *Q* magazine billed him at the time.

20 Mothers is a right old mix musically, the Captain Beefheart approach to arrangement is used. Instrumental parts mostly explained to the musicians by Cope from his head, the result of walking the spiritual power-lines centring on the ancient stones at Avebury near Glastonbury. The production is again unbalanced and odd and the subject matter is loosely based on family relationships. 'Wheelbarrow Man' features an elated Cope singing 'I've made up with my brother' and 'Queen/Mother' takes a shot at Courtney Love in the wake of Kurt Cobain's death (she was an old acquaintance of Cope's from the Liverpool days). The highlight of the album though is 'Try Try Try', everything that Cope is good at done to perfection. Perfect hook, perfect powerchords, a perfectly 'nailed-it' vocal and ba-ba-ba-ba-ba-ba-bas to boot. His hero, music fan and writer, the late Lester Bangs, surely would have approved.

Place, time, scene: Liverpool 1978, Tamworth 1983. Julian Cope's first band the Teardrop Explodes pushed the expectations of early-eighties pop but were never really able to get across what Cope really stood for in such a structured pop format. As a solo artist, he has rambled through a career of albums that are at times grand pop statements, and at other times skeletal folk-punk. Both are driven by passion and enthusiasm, and a mysticism that is now rare in British music, even with an annual rock festival at Glastonbury.

What to buy first: *Peggy Suicide* 1991

And then: *Fried* 1984, *Saint Julian* 1987, *Skellington* 1990, *20 Mothers* 1995

In retrospect: *Floored Genius: The Best Of Julian Cope And The Teardrop Explodes 1981–1991* 1992

ELVIS COSTELLO

Along with Nick Lowe and Ian Dury, Elvis Costello and his band the Attractions emerged out of the London pub-rock scene which was a forerunner of the punk scene that followed. Pubs like the Tally Ho and the Kensington in Kentish Town, the Hope and Anchor in Islington and the Nashville in West Kensington were a haven for bands who were keen to get away from the overwhelming arena-accommodating sound systems, and who were happier to plug into the house PA in their local. The music was basically R&B based, just like it was back in the early sixties, but some incorporated country and folk influences into their sets, often notable in the lyrics, phrasing and instrumentation used. Elvis Costello was one of those with some-

thing to say, and boy has the world had to hear it in the 25 years since.

Moving from Liverpool to London in 1974, having been inspired by a conversation with Nick Lowe when they played the city in 1973, Costello spent a year or so on the pub circuit with a band called Flip City, simultaneously holding down a day-job as a computer operator and finding time to be a husband and father for his wife and son. When punk hit in 1976, he was unable to get to the gigs because he just didn't have the time, but a close listen to the first albums by the Damned and the Clash sparked something in him. It coincided with a creeping sense of anger at what he perceived to be a 'moral complacency' within British society that, in his opinion, gave itself away in the notable apathy towards growing xenophobic nationalism and Jubilee celebrations that were at odds with the real working-class experience of living in a less than prosperous society.[20] In the summer of 1977 he wrote some of his angriest and most venomous songs which later appeared on his debut album *My Aim Is True*. 'Less Than Zero' rails against the infamous fascist Oswald Mosley, 'Watching The Detectives' addresses the issue of media-induced de-sensitization and apathy, and for light relief there's 'Alison', a personal, but pointedly non-traditional love song where the relationship in question is anything but straightforward.

This Year's Model continues the trend, and with the addition of a full-time band to set the musical scenery for Costello's songs, is a more complete realization of Costello's abilities. Bruce Thomas and Pete Thomas of the Attractions had their background in pub-rock like Costello, while keyboardist Steve Nieve was a classically trained musician apparently less familiar with traditional rock and pop music. Not that you'd know; 'Pump It Up', 'I Don't Want To Go To Chelsea' and 'Hand In Hand' are all driven by Nieve's pounding organ, right up there with Costello's nasty vocals, and Bruce Thomas' melody-line bass patterns. Nick Lowe's production captures the whole thing pretty much live in the studio, in keeping with his 'bang 'em down' style, and although Costello might claim that his production sweetened some of the tracks, there's still a rough feel to the whole that reflects the band at its best.

Armed Forces drops the full-frontal punk sneer and incorporates a few well-placed pop embellishments. 'Oliver's Army' is one of his most vitriolic political songs but was clearly inspired by Abba's 'Dancing Queen', and 'Accidents Will Happen' is positively light. By the time he made *Imperial Bedroom* in 1982 he was seven albums into his career, and had already messed around with several different styles of writing and performing, but with this album he stripped everything down to basics and let the songs do the work. Probably his most personal album, it contains 'Man Out Of Time' and the Gram Parsons' song 'I'm Your Toy', sung deeply and with a degree of vocal control that had not been apparent on his earlier albums, and which would serve him well in the future. The lyrics are great too, he rhymes 'issues' with 'tissues' and sings of a 'shorthand typist taking seconds over minutes'. Genius.

Punch The Clock contained two of his most affecting political songs, 'Pills And Soap' and 'Shipbuilding', the latter a war-time anti-war song, told sensitively and ironically from the perspective of one of Britain's failing industries. Around this time he produced albums by the Specials, Squeeze and the Pogues and returned himself with two of his best albums in 1986, *King Of America* which had him once more exploring country and rhythm and blues music, linking the indigenous styles with songs that dealt with the British perception of American society, and *Blood And Chocolate* which, for all the talk of his musical genius, is him and the Attractions giving it raw. Back to a live set-up where, according to the sleeve notes, the instruments were allowed to bleed into one another to avoid clear sound separation and make for something muddier, the songs and the band sound more powerful than at any other time in the back-catalogue. 'Uncomplicated' is raw, 'Tokyo Storm Warning' is relentless and 'I Want You', captured in one take, and not altogether dissimilar to the Beatles song of the same name, is just downright ... heavy. For the most part, just a guitar and bass, with occasional kit and keyboards, the song was only performed once, and is probably the most explicit representation of human jealousy ever committed to tape – 'Did you call his name out as he held you down?'

That's jealousy. For anger try 'Tramp The Dirt Down' on the 1989 album *Spike*, wherein Costello looked forward to Margaret Thatcher's death, hoping beyond hope that it would come as soon as possible. This time the bile is not left exposed and raw, it's accompanied by a lilting folk arrangement incorporating bouzouki, Indian harmonium and uillean pipes. Pure unadulterated anger in the form of a personal attack, essentially suggesting that another human being go fuck off and die, and yet played so sweetly that it could almost be an Irish Eurovision entry. That's a new demographic, right there, one for the mums and dads, the nans and grandads, and those who like their pop music just that little bit twisted. Clever bastard.

First team: Elvis Costello (v, g), Steve Nieve (k), Bruce Thomas (b), Pete Thomas (d)

Place, time, scene: London 1977, Elvis Costello would have been a successful singer-songwriter anyway, he didn't need punk to make it. He resonates truth, even in the most obscure of his lyrics. Musically he has tried everything and done it well and his albums with the Attractions are amongst the best of their type, eclectic melodic rock arranged to suit any performance style. Solo artists don't come along very often nowadays, so make the most of the man they call The Imposter while you can.

What to buy first: *Blood And Chocolate* 1986

And then: *My Aim Is True* 1977, *This Year's Model* 1978, *Imperial Bedroom* 1982, *Punch The Clock* 1983, *King Of America* 1986, *Spike* 1989, *When I Was Cruel* 2002

In retrospect: *The Man* 1986, *Extreme Honey: Best Of The Warner Brothers Years* 1997

COUNTRY JOE AND THE FISH

Country Joe and the Fish are the best psychedelic band of them all. No contest.

Jefferson Airplane may have got there first but their debut album was fairly straight folk-rock and the follow-up, *Surrealistic Pillow*, was only better because Grace Slick had joined from the Great Society and brought her two best songs with her, the one about the rabbit, which the Airplane unashamedly set to

Ravel's Bolero, and a fairly straightforward pop song called 'Somebody To Love' which Slick's previous band had done better anyway. And Jefferson Airplane's idea of cultural politics was to shout odd things like 'do away with people laughing at my hair'. Bollocks, frankly.

The Grateful Dead on record was just as disappointing. Clearly they could cut it live as their fourth album in 1969 proved, but the three leading up to that one, whether they took three days or six months to record, ended up as embarrassingly pretentious or psychedelic parody that only really worked as advertisements for their sponsor Owsley Stanley, a leading manufacturer of LSD, the guy who bankrolled their early live tours. As soon as the Haight Ashbury scene ended, the Dead simply ripped off Crosby, Stills and Nash and the Band, and went back to their folk roots, and indulged in a more traditional view of American culture than the one that had been evoked when Kesey's magic bus had arrived, dispensing instant creativity in the form of little pills. And where was the counter-culture in all that? It all seems pretty much in keeping with the corporate American Dream. The Grateful Dead were signed to Warner Brothers, Jefferson Airplane to RCA.

By contrast, Country Joe and the Fish wrote the counter-cultural anthem, a specific attack on specific government policy, recorded three definitive psychedelic albums sticking resolutely to an independent record label throughout, and by the end of the sixties had led the way in terms of progressive music's incorporation of, and into, pop. They spotted, earlier than most, that psychedelia and prog-rock had the potential to get silly and irrelevant if left to their own egotistical devices. And, importantly, although they embraced the creative and cultural potential of LSD, Country Joe and the Fish never staked everything on the drug, musically, and certainly with Joe McDonald's songs they remained rooted in reality. LSD might have allowed its users to widen their consciousness, but it was never long-term. There was going to be a comedown and the Fish knew that.

Having spent a few years playing in folk bands around LA, Joe McDonald started making rock music with guitarist Barry Melton at about the time that Dylan went electric at Newport, but by then had already written his most famous song, the anti-Vietnam war protest of 'I-Feel-Like-I'm-Fixin'-To-Die-Rag' based around the central conceit that 'you could be the first on your block to have your boy come home in a box'. The song was self-produced, not usual practice in 1966, and released as a promotional single to go with folk-zine *Rag Baby*, also edited by McDonald. Signed to the fiercely independent Vanguard Records who had spent many of the preceeding years financing overtly political folk releases, McDonald and Melton, together with Bruce Barthol, David Cohen and Chicken Hirsh, adopted the name Country Joe (after Country Joe Stalin – a joke name for the murderous communist leader coined by McDonald's socialist parents) and the Fish (after a Mao Tse-Tung saying concerning 'the fish that swim in the sea of the people'), and set about making their first album *Electric Music For The Mind And Body* (1967).

Left to their own devices in a studio in Berkeley, they came up with a variety of songs. There's the satirical 'Superbird' written about Lyndon B. Johnson, the dark and maudlin 'Death Sound Blues' and the downright rude 'Happiness Is A Porpoise Mouth', 'I hunger for your porpoise mouth and stand erect for love'. But at the album's core, there are a series of mellow dreamlike songs that are amongst the best examples of psychedelia in that period. 'Section 43' and 'The Masked Marauder' are both instrumentals, spacious, sprawling, eastern-style acid-rock excursion, and weird waltz respectively, and 'Bass Strings' which opens with the line 'Hey mister, won't you pass that reefer around' features the most gloriously stoned vocal of them all. You can virtually smell the incense burning.

Within the year they had added a second album *I-Feel-Like-I'm-Fixin'-To-Die*, which contained McDonald's earlier song of the same name, alongside a love song to Janis Joplin and a jaunty little inter-song commercial for LSD which is satirical or downright blatant depending on your reading. The album sold well, mainly because of all that business with the Fish cheer at a festival in New York, and then at Woodstock where the crowd opted for F-U-C-K at the beginning of the song in place of the original F-I-S-H.

Country Joe and the Fish made one more album with the original line-up and with it, pointed the way towards a useful new direction for psychedelic music. *Together* features a tribute to James Brown, using their newly discovered 'sockin-it-to-ya' riff and 'The Harlem Song', a sarcastic allusion to the social problems of the Harlem neighbourhood, complete with references to Amos'n'Andy and employing racist language for effect. Joe also talked about the media like McLuhan did, bemoaned the arrival of the 'number-people' and criticized his government as a 'death machine'. That was summer 1968. It was kicking off in Paris for real. And of all the 'revolutionary' hippie spokesmen and spokeswomen, only Country Joe and the Fish cared enough to get involved too. They gave hippies a good name.

First team: Country Joe McDonald (v, g, hm), Barry Melton (v, g), David Cohen (g, o), Bruce Barthol (b), Chicken Hirsh (d)

Place, time, scene: Los Angeles 1966. Country Joe and the Fish were an archetypal hippie band, but one of the few to back up their image with songs that expressed specific counter-cultural concerns. The music was grounded in McDonald's earlier folk songs so they were able to adapt their style quite smoothly as R&B and soul became new signifiers of political resistance.

What to buy first: *Electric Music For The Mind And Body* 1967

And then: *I-Feel-Like-I'm-Fixin'-To-Die* 1967, *Together* 1968

In retrospect: *Collected Country Joe And The Fish* (1965–1970) 1998

CRAMPS

Lux Interior and Poison Ivy live in Beverley Hills. Since 1975 they have been prime movers in the gothic psychobilly band which goes by the name of the Cramps. So legend would have it, they used to babysit Bridget Fonda which might explain a few things, especially as a trawl through the back-catalogue reveals a fascination with sleazy sartorial experimentation – g-strings, cha-cha heels, leopardskin and leather thigh-length kinky boots – and a tendency towards writing songs that advocate 'jumping aboard the drug train', pose questions such as 'what's inside a girl' and explain the rules to a dance called 'The Crusher' where one of the moves is 'do the eye-gouge'. But don't get too caught up in the image, the Cramps have the music to back it

up too. Songs about sex, drugs, sex, rock'n'roll and sex are set to a sinister musical backdrop that is drum-driven, feedback splattered and sung in a vocal style best described as voodoo-hillbilly. There's a humour there too but it's shrouded in such darkness that it ends up sounding like the kind of humour indulged in by Freddie Krueger rather than Freddie Schneider. People may do the comparisons but the B-52s could never touch the Cramps.

The band's origins are in the early seventies when ex-carjacker and drug fiend Lux picked Ivy up hitch-hiking in Sacramento, California – 'she was wearing hot pants with a hole in the ass showing her red panties'. After some time spent in Ohio the pair began their music career in earnest when they got to New York just in time for the new-wave explosion in 1977. Together with drummer Nick Knox who had recently left the Electric Eels, and second guitarist, Bryan Gregory, they headed straight for the scene at CBGBs, hanging out with bands like the Ramones, Talking Heads and their heroes, the New York Dolls.

Like other schlock horror bands, notably the Misfits, their chosen musical style was a mix of garage punk and rockabilly but the Cramps also paid significant attention to mood and texture. An early session with Alex Chilton, formerly of Big Star and the Box Tops, was captured on tape at the very same Sun Records studios used by Elvis 20 years before, and resulted in an EP *Gravest Hits* that was described by one unimpressed critic as punk sludge. Listening back now, it can be heard as a pioneering thin, white noise album, required listening for the likes of Pussy Galore and Royal Trux. Made at a time when punk was still fast and was about to get faster still with the advent of hardcore, and new wave was on the trail of new sounds and interesting structures, *Gravest Hits* was sinister and seemed to have taken its creative ideas from the newly rotting corpse of the King himself.

The tracks recorded by Chilton are a mess of noise with all the instruments faded way up in the mix, and Lux Interior's vocal mic up even higher, allowing him to intone dark Jerry Lee Lewis-style whispers and screams over the top. On 'Love Me' you can hear the click of his tongue and the movement of saliva, and the 'buzz, buzz, buzzzz' bit in 'Human Fly' is one of the worst examples of 'mic popping' committed to tape – not that it should ever by tidied up, you understand. Their version of the Trashmen's 'Surfin Bird' is the centrepiece and boasts several minutes of screeching feedback in the middle, so discordant that when Lux returns to the song with his 'Papapapapapa-papapap-oo-mow-mow, papa-oo-mow-mow' and the dustbin-lid clatter of guitars kicks back in, it's actually a form of light relief.

On *Songs The Lord Taught Us* (1978), again made with Chilton at the desk, the band opted for a straighter rockabilly style overlaid with liberal use of fuzzbox and vibrato on the guitar, and lyrics that recalled a version of fifties America that takes in B-movies, disposable technology and rock'n'roll before it got corporate.

With Brian Gregory gone soon after their first recordings, the Cramps moved through a succession of guitarists and eventually bassists, resulting in a fuller, more accessible sound. *Psychedelic Jungle*, featuring Kid Congo Powers of Gun Club is still sludgy but less messy, and *Smell Of Female* is an impressive live document demonstrating the band's grasp of sonics and theatrics. But it's *A Date With Elvis* in 1986 that is the Cramps' most effective distillation of psychedelia, punk and rock'n'roll, where the cheeky humour of songs like 'What's Inside A Girl?' and 'Can Your Pussy Do The Dog?' is set against Nick Knox's ever-straight and minimalist drumming and Ivy's crisp and endlessly satisfying guitar-playing. 'Hot Pearl Snatch' is magnificent, lyrically just plain naughty and musically, a lesson in less is more production, simple drum pattern, buzz-saw guitar stabs, fractured lead breaks and then feedback and distorted Arthur Lee riffing to fade. 'Wop bop a loop a lop a lop boom bam' as the lyric sheet later informs us. Give me 'Hot Pearl Snatch' over Cock-rock anyday!

First team: Lux Interior (v), Poison Ivy Rorscach (g), Nick Knox (d), Brian Gregory (g)

Place, time, scene: New York 1977. The Cramps took their cue from the garage-punk bands of the sixties and with their songs, tapped into sex and madness that was always implicit in rock'n'roll since the days of Jerry Lee Lewis and Little Richard. The primal energy, sex and humour of the band has inspired countless others, notably Pussy Galore and its offshoots.

What to buy first: *Songs The Lord Taught Us* 1978

And then: *A Date With Elvis* 19861

In retrospect: *Off The Bone* 1983

CRASS

Crass emerged out of an Epping commune led by drummer Penny Rimbaud and vocalist Steve Ignorant, sometime in 1977. They picked up vocalists Eve Libertine and Joy De Vivre, guitarists Phil Free and B.A. Nana, and bassist Pete Wright (a made-up name – surely?) along the way but never really considered themselves to be a band. They weren't rock'n'roll and they certainly weren't punk. Rimbaud in particular criticized the Sex Pistols for ripping off their fans, and the Clash for selling out. They had no time for 'blank generations' and ironic appropriation of iconic signifiers. Crass made records to reinforce their political position and not for the music or the art of it. Crass were quite simply 'no fun'.

The early gigs took place at Conway Hall in London and featured some piss-poor playing but some inspirational sloganeering, influencing a new generation of punk bands with something to say. On record, the music was discordant, white noise guitar, relentless one-string bass, bashed drums, and spoken or shouted words over the top of it all. At various times on the first album *Feeding Of The 5000*, there are digs at the prevailing punk industry, notably 'Banned From The Roxy' and on the follow-up *Stations Of The Crass* there's the industry-baiting 'Hurry Up Garry' and 'White Punks On Hope'. Crass liked the idea of punk in essence, but were concerned about its potential for corporate co-option into a new mainstream.

'Penis Envy' is probably their most musical moment where Pete Wright's bass guitar comes into its own and there's added wah-wah guitar and church organ for textural variety. Libertine and De Vivre handle the vocals on the album, with Steve Ignorant nowhere to be seen. Without him they are less committed to their direct and tyrannically rhythmic beat, more able to be musical, an approach which was continued on *Christ – The Album* on his return. But Crass's real place in history hangs on their direct action and use of music as ideological soundtrack.

In 1979, 'Reality Asylum' was judged criminally blasphemous, for which they were arrested, and *Penis Envy* was put before a judicial review and pronounced obscene. In 1982 the Thatcher-baiting 'How does it feel to be the mother of a 1000 dead?' had the xenophobic British tabloid media proclaiming them sick traitors, and was followed in 1983 by the 'Thatchergate tape' which, with clever editing, created a phone conversation between Reagan and Thatcher where she admitted to sinking the General Belgrano while he threatened to nuke Europe.

In all, there were five albums on their own Crass Records label, none of which make particularly enjoyable listening but then that wasn't really the point. And anyway, the joy of consuming Crass was not musical, it was about feeling the injustice and empathizing with it through the passion and spirit coming from the records. *Feeding Of The 5000* is so brutal that, compared with other punk records of the time, it remains fresh and untarnished by the mythology that has grown up around the period.

Along with like-minded signings Flux of Pink Indians, Crass told us about corporate malpractice, governmental hypocrisy, societal sexism and racism, and more specifically documented personal perspectives on sexual abuse and injustice. The *Penis Envy* album in particular stands the test of time, transcending the punk moment and perhaps meaning more in the contemporary reality of a flawed society than it ever did as a piece of punk iconography. Crass could have made films, published articles or robbed banks, but they chose music as their medium of expression, and pointed out some of the inadequacies of its contextual infrastructure in the process. That helped.

First team: Penny Rimbaud (d), Steve Ignorant (v), Pete Wright (b), Phil Free (g), B.A. Nana (g), Eve Libertine (v), Joy De Vivre (v)

Place, time, scene: London 1977. Crass seized on the punk energy of the period and turned in an impressive career as one of the government's most vociferous opponents. Musically they were ahead of the US hardcore bands by about a year.

What to buy first: *Feeding Of The 5000* 1978

And then: *Penis Envy* 1981

In retrospect: *Best Before 1984* 1987

CURE

Chris Parry, manager of the Cure and founder of the independent label, Fiction, which puts out the band's records, has a theory that Robert Smith is a performer 'who lives in his audience's perceptions'. The trademark look, the shy and bumbling interviewee, and most significantly the distinct musical style all contribute to this perception, and have allowed Smith to play by his own rules. His own claim that he only has two songs 'Love Cats' and 'Faith' is surely an attempt to deflect critical attention away from himself and his work with the Cure, and in doing so avoiding fraternization with that part of the music industry that he despises. For the Cure, the competition is not mainstream pop, but the self-important, serious artists who build careers based on critical acclaim and assumed cultural significance. There's never been a Robert Smith solo album, legendary producers have not been wheeled-in to create a new sheen or sound, and at no point have they gone acoustic to expose the truth and honesty of their artistic vision. As a result of not playing the hype or the acclaim game, the Cure have retained the loyalty of an international fan base that is able to judge the band's enormous success in spite of, rather than because of, conventional music industry rules and procedures.

The debut album, *Three Imaginary Boys*, produced by Parry and featuring Smith, Michael Dempsey and Lol Tolhurst but not original member Porl Thompson, reveals an angry band consumed with loathing, of self and others, and in that, it's not dissimilar to other post-punk bands of the period. 'Jumping Someone Else's Train' takes a pop at hypocrites and the fashionably political, and 'Boys Don't Cry' is filled with regret and disappointment at Smith's own failure to act on his emotions. Using the basic set-up of guitar, bass and drums, the overall sound is sparse and the words take centre stage, spat out by Smith, a style which he returned to on later albums, but which was soon replaced by his less punk deadpan delivery.

Seventeen Seconds which followed in 1980 is still minimalist in sound, but less sparse. 'A Forest' is still stark at its core but the song itself is buried beneath washes of keyboard and guitar parts. It is new member Simon Gallup's bass rather than Smith's vocals that provide the central focus. The *Faith* album (1981) continues the shift in style; on the swirling 'Other Voices' the bass maps the way through the sonic mist, and simultaneously sucks the listener into the song. The stillness and claustrophobia that comes through on *Faith* didn't impress Cure audiences who had come to the shows hoping for new-wave energy and catharsis, and it was a new audience that rushed out to buy *Pornography* the following year.

The band's fourth album struck a balance between punk energy and dark psycho-analysis, and is probably the closest they came to making a Joy Division album. It probably explains why they sold so many copies too. Ian Curtis had committed suicide two years before and although a new goth scene was developing around bands like the Cure and Bauhaus, the scene lacked a figurehead that personified the angst that was implicit in the music. With *Pornography* Smith became the figurehead. Songs about the terrors of an abattoir and the claustrophobia of the womb appealed to those who didn't get excited by videos showing Duran Duran on their yacht in the Caribbean or appreciate being told that as young guns, they ought to be 'going for it'. The Cure got their most enthusiastic reviews for *Pornography* and perversely decided it was time to split up.

Over the next two years Smith spent time touring as Siouxie and the Banshees' guitarist, working on a project with Steve Severin as the Glove, and, at Chris Parry's suggestion, knocking out some of the lightest, fluffiest pop music of the decade. Although initially unwilling to identify themselves as the Cure for the singles 'Let's Go To Bed' and 'Love Cats', it ultimately paid off. Smith and Tolhurst accidentally had a hit single, and together with the wacky videos, hair and badly-applied lipstick, suddenly had a new image as ironic, fun-loving weirdoes. And it saw off all those serious rock critics who had fallen for the Cure at the time of *Pornography*. Result!

The band returned as a six-piece later in the year with *The Top*, an album that incorporated light pop and heavy gloom – the two sides of the band's schizophrenia – and followed it with *The Head On The Door* in 1985 which kicks in with the catchy, guitar-toting, synth-fingering 'In Between Days' and ends with the doom-laden angst of 'Sinking'. By the time they had put out the double *Kiss Me Kiss Me Kiss Me*, the band had again climbed to a lofty position, shifting units

hot-cake style in France and South America, and a scene-leader in British alternative music as one of the only post-punk bands still in operation that appealed to a demand for introspective music. Even the Stone Roses were goths at that point, and the only other successful indie bands were the Smiths and New Order.

Kiss Me Kiss Me Kiss Me is a sprawling double album, that commences with the psychotic 'The Kiss' ('get your fucking voice out of my head') and by side three has turned in the brassy 'Why Can't I Be You' and the cool funk of 'Hot Hot Hot'. The horns are joined by strings, eastern instrumentation and wah-wah guitar, and the songs are again a split between light romance and dark thoughts, a perfect mirror to the culture of goth which feigned a sense of tragic and looked sullen, but at heart revelled in the opportunity to play out a role where the mere concept of doomed romance was romantic. The Cure were a band for sensitive and introspective souls, and they had time to get just one more album in before introspection and sensitivity were banished in favour of hedonism and dancing one's ass off.

With *Disintegration*, the sensitive love songs are cloaked in swirling, rich textures that come close to ambient trance at times. 'Love Song' and 'Lullaby' are the two Cures blended at last. In stadiums around the globe at the end of the eighties, the Cure could be heard ushering out the decade of mega-shows and overblown sentiment on a grand scale with their own unique combination of epic intimacy. In the right hands the big music could still be personal, sensitive and captivating.

First team: Robert Smith (v, g, k), Simon Gallup (b), Porl Thomson (g), Boris Williams (d), Roger O'Donnell (k), Lol Tolhurst (d, k)

Place, time, scene: Crawley 1978. The Cure began alongside post-punk bands that were driven by punk spirit, but soon withdrew into themselves and developed a stillness which begat a sense of epic power and served them well for three albums, confirming them as leaders of the goth scene. Unwilling to be typecast, Robert Smith explored the possibilities of pop music and over the course of another four albums reconciled the frivolous and bleak aspects of their music in a way which might have inspired the Pixies amongst others.

What to buy first: *Pornography* 1982

And then: *Three Imaginary Boys* 1979, *Faith* 1981, *The Head On The Door* 1985, *Kiss Me Kiss Me Kiss Me* 1987, *Disintegration* 1989

In retrospect: *Staring At The Sea* 1986, *Greatest Hits* 2002

D

DAMNED

The Damned are probably the most misrepresented of the first wave of British punk bands. It may have been down to the image and the silly names, or even the speed at which they played, but for some reason the Damned never got validated after the first shock of punk hit. Other artists and bands settled into new roles as spokespersons for social injustices or as artists working at the cutting edge of the new musical agenda. They did it with the backing of the corporate big-boys who had eventually seen the light, cut their hair and hit the pub-rock trail looking for new raw talent. The Damned, though, stuck with independent labels until well into the 1980s, and despite releasing the definitive punk album that demonstrated just how punk attitude could be applied to a whole cross-section of musical styles without selling-out to the traditions of any one of them, still remained punk's party boys. That's despite releasing the first punk single and the first punk album, having the first punk chart hit and being the first punk band to play a big London venue before heading off round the country to turn everyone else in the country onto the new attitude. Oh yeah, and they went to the US first too, Britain's first response to the Ramones, and like their speed-driven American cousins, the Damned were a significant influence on the fast and furious hard-core punk that followed. Certainly the Damned were an archetypal punk band, but to ignore their other talents, obvious from the very first releases, is to forever hold them captive in a particular moment in popular music history. And the Damned had a lot more going on than that.

Captain Sensible (Ray Burns) began playing guitar with a band called Johnny Moped in the mid-seventies,

which Roger Armstrong of the independent label Chiswick Records recalls as 'the band further out on the edge than any of the others'. Those who saw the shows, played at various pubs around London, testify that Johnny was a mesmerizing front-man, and that the band, with Slimy Toad on guitar and Dave Berk on drums, was able to play intricate and complex songs at a pace that defied common belief. Folk guitarist Alan Holdsworth was invited down to one gig and was astounded by their abilities. Fans of Soft Machine and the English psychedelic folk scene of the early seventies, it was an influence that carried forward into the Damned when Captain Sensible joined forces with Bryan James and Rat Scabies in 1976, both scenesters who had formed or joined various bands in the previous year or so, some of which, like the legendary London SS, had never made it past the rehearsal stage.

Sensible had played guitar and keyboards with Johnny Moped, but switched to bass for the Damned and the trio got started, backing Nick Kent, the original vocalist with the Swankers, the band that would later become the Sex Pistols. Finding gravedigger Dave Vanian was the key though. With his pseudo-theatrical vocal style that might have been his best attempt at singing big and emotively, or just a piss-take, or maybe a bit of both, he fitted perfectly with a style of writing and playing music that took all the overblown clichés of rock and soul music and, by a combination of playing very fast and trying to get as much as possible into a sub three-minute song as possible, produced songs like 'New Rose', complete with lead-guitar solo and middle-eight vocal section played simultaneously. It was the first punk single available to buy in the shops, thanks to the guerrilla production and distribution techniques employed by

Stiff Records who signed the band in 1976. The album was produced by house producer, Nick Lowe, earning him the name 'Basher' Lowe on account of his style of turning everything up full, ignoring distortion levels and just bashing it down on tape. It's called *Damned, Damned, Damned*, it lasts just under thirty minutes and covers a range of styles, a condensed summary of everything since Elvis. It was the first response to the Ramones' debut no-brainer released the previous year on the other side of the Atlantic, and although it has a similar spirit on the faster tracks that make up the second half of the album, there's always so much more going on musically. It's just easy to miss because there's no egotistical attempts at separation in the mix to draw your attention away from all the other noise – it's all there at the same time and occupying the same sonic space.

The sleevenotes suggest that *Damned, Damned, Damned* is 'made to be played loud at low volume' which about sums it up. Sensible drives the tracks on with his bass, Scabies comes on like Keith Moon behind the kit and the guitar parts are inspired and very cleverly constructed. There are solos all over the album, sometimes hidden, sometimes upfront, always impressive. And on top of it all, Vanian moves from full-on punk on 'Neat Neat Neat', to country on 'Born To Kill' and gothic horror on 'Feel The Pain'.

Just like the Clash on their second album, the Damned opted for an established rock musician to produce *Music For Pleasure* later in the year and suffered because of it. Bringing in Nick Mason of Pink Floyd was on paper a good idea, especially with the band's penchant for the psychedelic, but the album is neither psych or punk, or a mixture of the two, just a step too far, too soon. Another guitarist had been added, James had taken over as creative leader and everybody had got annoyed. They split. . . . And then reformed a year later without Brian James, leaving Sensible free to play guitar with ex-Saints bassist Algy Ward joining in time to make the band's best album, *Machine Gun Etiquette* in 1979. During the split, Sensible had joined a more pop-influenced band called the Softies where he 'learned how to play guitar with a band' and wrote some of his best songs. 'Smash It Up' came in two parts, although Sensible actually wrote four parts which have recently been released, tidied up from the original demo recordings. As a two-part song, it's

impressive enough though, three minutes exploring gradually changing moods, played by Sensible on guitar, lurching into another three with the rest of the band in a chaotic punk workout before emerging drunk on energy to sing 'and everybody's smashing things down' in the style of true self-deprecating comedy amateurism. The rest of the album takes in the pop of 'Love Song', the hard rock of the title track, psychedelia on their cover of 'White Rabbit' and an early hint of goth on Vanian's 'Plan 9'.

The Black Album and *Strawberries* followed in the first years of the new decade, both exploring a variety of styles, resulting in the best mixture of pop and rock music of the period. Just so much music and so many ideas crammed into short bursts of gloriously melodic energy. Nobody's immune to 'History Of The World (Part1)', 'Wait For The Blackout' or 'Drinking About My Baby'. 'Silly Kids Games' is just plain pretty, all harmonies and delicate acoustic guitar, and even when they went long on 'Curtain Call' they did it with a montage of melodic passages and intriguing sound experiments that makes the 17 minutes and 17 seconds fairly fly by, 'a lot of people slagged us off cause it wasn't punk, but they can bog off'. If only more people had got to hear them, they could have been as big as Abba, but just scuzzier. The Damned revival starts here.

First team: Captain Sensible (g, b, k, v), Dave Vanian (v), Brian James (g), Rat Scabies (d)

Place, time, scene: London 1976. The Damned were a first-wave punk band and one of the very first bands in London to play their music purposely fast and with a new attitude. Their musicianship was evident immediately and their folk-rock/psychedelic influences came to the fore later in their career by which time they had been pigeon-holed as a light fun band without the intensity of their contemporaries. The Damned were as important as the Ramones but had the skills and the creativity to develop a long career.

What to buy first: *Machine Gun Etiquette* 1979

And then: *Damned, Damned, Damned* 1977, *The Black Album* 1980, *Strawberries* 1982

In retrospect: *Smash It Up: The Anthology 1976–1987* 2002

DE LA SOUL

The Daisy Age, according to hip-hop chronology, occurred at the end of the 1980s and saw rap into the new decade. It was a period when crews were superseded by tribes, flowers were distributed at gatherings, the rhymes were eco-friendly and colourless, and the vibe was positivity. It was 'DA Inner Sound Y'all' – Daisy – you see. The Jungle Brothers, Prince Paul and A Tribe Called Quest were Daisy Age rappers, but the movement's creative and cultural core was De La Soul, a rap collective formed with the express intention of undermining the growing gangster rap culture led by groups like NWA who traded on descriptions of urban decline and black nihilism. NWA members Ice Cube and Dr Dre claimed that they were simply engaged in reportage, tellin' it like it is, but the way De La Soul saw it, if you weren't part of the solution then you were part of the problem, and tracks like 'Fuck Tha Police' didn't seem to be as dispassionately objective as it was claimed.

De La Soul opted to begin their recording career with a masterpiece. *3 Feet High And Rising* is the first, and maybe only hip-hop concept album, themed around the running motif of a television game-show and containing odd musical interludes. The concept is in the sound rather than the lyrical content and it's backed up by the wildest montage of sampled material gathered together in the name of hip-hop. Hall and Oates, Steely Dan, the Turtles, Willie Nelson and Otis Redding all make a brief and looped appearance.

The rhymes are fully-conscious but never didactic like Chuck D's raps in Public Enemy 'Tread Water' tells the story of ecological pollution from the perspective of a fish, a squirrel and several other of God's disenfranchised little creatures, and 'Ghetto Thang' is brimming with black humour about contemporary neighbourhood life, but stops the comedy long enough to observe 'Negative's the attitude that runs the show when the stage is the G-H-E-T-T-O'. De La Soul were reporting on the causes of social unrest, not the unrest itself.

Podnuos (Sound Op spelt backwards) and Trugoy (Yogurt spelt backwards?) are the main rappers in the trio, and Mase is the DJ, although producer Prince Paul must be given a lot of credit for the mixes and arrangements on the album too. They signed with Tommy Boy Records straight from school, and now have five albums to their name. *3 Feet High And Rising* was a hard act to follow and as yet, they haven't really come close. Concerned that they were being dubbed hippies, they followed up their debut album with *De La Soul Is Dead*, in an attempt to demonstrate their own voluntary distancing from the concept of The Daisy Age.

De La Soul felt that they were not reaching the audience that they needed to reach, and as a result, have opted to continue their progressive and conscious rap message but set to a more traditionally urban hip-hop aesthetic in terms of sound, and a darker, harder and irony-free approach to rapping. Gone are the analogies and metaphors, the message is more direct. *Art Official Intelligence Volume 2: Bionix* is their most commercially focused towards a mainstream hip-hop audience but check the lyric sheet and you'll still find the De La Soul of old, just no cute stories about squirrels.

First team: Podnuos (v), Trugoy (v), Mase (v, sx)

Place, time, scene: New York 1988. De La Soul were a key part of the Native Tongues movement which tried to redress the balance in US hip-hop which they saw becoming more stereotyped as commercial forces emphasized those aspects of the culture that most effectively fitted with an exaggerated emphasis on visual image and the video. Other members of Native Tongues included A Tribe Called Quest and the Jungle Brothers.

What to buy first: *3 Feet High And Rising* 1989

And then: *Best Of De La Soul* 2003

DEAD KENNEDYS

The Dead Kennedys made relentless hardcore punk. Listen to any one of their five albums released between 1980 and 1986 and you'll quickly identify their basic strategy: fast, aggressive, spontaneous and oppositional. You won't catch much of what Jello Biafra is shouting, but the lyrics are always included with the album so, if you can speed-read, you'll be able to pin down the specifics of his, always overtly political, and often satirical, arguments. Even without the lyrics, it's apparent that he's pissed off just from the sheer anger expressed in his voice. The Dead Kennedys are un-compromising, and difficult to consume which makes them essential.

Emerging out of the same hardcore scene as Black Flag in San Francisco, the band initially consisted of Biafra, East Bay Ray on guitar, Klaus Flouride on bass and Ted on drums. Their original deal with Miles Copeland and IRS was enough to persuade Biafra to set-up his own Alternative Tentacles label, but not before re-leasing their debut album *Fresh Fruit For Rotting Vegetables* which, along with Black Flag's *Wasted*, remains a key hardcore album. Commencing with the black humour of 'Kill The Poor', which details the advantages of ridding the world of poor people – 'no more welfare tax to pay unsightly slums gone up in flashing light ...' – the album also deals with war-mongering for a higher economic purpose, greedy landlords and evil media. 'California Uber Alles' is a song about the alleged fascistic tendencies of the sun-shine state's governor, and 'Holiday In Cambodia' attacks apathetic de-politicized students. The cover of 'Viva Las Vegas' is sarcastic genius. *Fresh Fruit For Rotting Vegetables* would make a good set text for schools teaching history as it details all of the key issues facing America between the wars (Vietnam and the Gulf). Uncomfortable listening, even if it's the Dead Kennedys most accessible record!

Once on Alternative Tentacles, the band opted for hardcore hardcore. *In God We Trust* contains eight songs including Biafra's message to certain sectors of his audience, 'Nazi Punks Fuck Off'. New drummer D.H. Peligro was in the seat by this point, allowing the band to up the overall pace from the first album, only slowing down for the parody of an evangelist church service featuring a congregation singing the Mickey Mouse Disney theme, before launching into a song about the Moral Majority's skewed sense of right and wrong. At one point, on 'Dog Bite', which begins with a false start, Biafra chastises the band for not playing fast enough. He was a stickler.

Plastic Surgery Disasters and *Frankenchrist* were similarly pumped up on adrenaline, although Biafra's lyrics are occasionally discernible on both. The drum-ming is impressive throughout, there's the odd guitar solo and even synthesizers can be detected at times. In fact, *Plastic Surgery Disasters* is a particular influ-ence on alternative rock music more generally, with everyone from Big Black to Slayer and loose and lazy old Mudhoney having claimed it as an influence.

The last album, *Bedtime For Democracy*, was a return to fast hardcore, but seemed out of place in a music scene that was busy embracing ironic pop music and doing deals with major labels. The satire was still biting though. The album includes a spoof advert for an MTV sponsored event entitled 'USA for South Africa' which explains that apartheid is big business, and that every American should do their patriotic duty to uphold it. The suits really didn't dig Jello, didn't like his lyrics, didn't appreciate his run-ning for Mayor of San Francisco, and hated the fact that he had his own business financing others in such un-American activities. They nearly got him on a charge of obscenity for the artwork to *Frankenchrist*, H.R. Giger's *Penis Landscape*, which depicted rows of male genitalia apparently entering rows of anuses, a representation of American corporate society. They didn't though. Biafra was cleared and the Dead Kenne-dys' back-catalogue remains intact, and remarkably topical too. Same shit, different generation.

First team: Jello Biafra (v), East Bay Ray (g), Klaus Flouride (b, v), D.H. Peligro (d)

Place, time, scene: San Francisco 1979. An original hardcore band, but one which took an overview of society's ills and made directly oppositional music that encouraged fans to get wise and get involved, America's answer to Crass, complete with their own label and police record.

What to buy first: *Fresh Fruit For Rotting Vegetables* 1980

And then: *Plastic Surgery Disasters* 1982

In retrospect: *Give Me Convenience Or Give Me Death* 1987

DEFTONES

'Sensitive guys' heavy metal' someone once called the Deftones. OK so it doesn't scan that well but it is a fairly accurate description. They were one of the early nu-metal bands that combined metal with funk-inflected beats and elements of hip-hop, but while recognizing the importance of new textures and rhythms in rock music, vocalist Chino Moreno still focuses his attention on the songs themselves. They may have been discovered by Korn when they played Sacramento, and Tool loom large as an influence, but as an admirer of the Cure and PJ Harvey, vocalist Chino Moreno, like Kurt Cobain before him, is far more concerned with the emotional possibilities of lyrics and texture than selling out the music to the groove. And with three albums in the bag so far, each one better than the last, and their music evolving in ever more interesting directions, the Deftones may just yet save metal from disappearing up its big fat, gangster-rap pilfering, commercially viable arse.

The first album, *Adrenaline*, introduces Chino Moreno's impressive vocals that at times, take in elements of rap style but only as one aspect of an approach that sets out to convey a range of emotions. There are lyrical motifs: birth, death, religion and sex – classic goth stuff really. It's also clear from the band's debut album that they are about more than just noise. Citing Bad Brains as an influence confirms their hardcore leanings but also hints at the potential for experimentation with dynamics, something that is instantly apparent on the follow-up album *Around The Fur*. 'My Own Summer', the single that kicks off the album allows Moreno the opportunity to whisper and whine over a solid, reggae-inflected opening section before launching into a full-on metal assault where he screams 'Shove it, shove it, shove it'. 'Mascara' would not be out of place on the Cure's *Faith* or *Pornography* albums, with its dark, gothic guitar sound and a vocal which almost suggests that Moreno is wearing a big black wig and badly-applied lipstick, while 'Be Quiet And Drive (Far Away)' is a wall of sound driven on by pounding drums, infected with screeching guitar and featuring a double-tracked Chino schizophrenically screaming and singing 'FAAAR, awaaaay'. Primal stuff.

The next full set, *White Pony*, took three years to perfect. Again focusing on textures, the album incorporates trip-hop, looped synth beats and sprawling psychedelia – but fused with a guitar sound and pounding drums that isn't that far off being Hüsker Dü. And there in the centre of a canyon of sound there's Moreno's self-trained rock voice, always clear and perfect in terms of pitch and volume, almost as if he has

been studying 'voice as instrument' under the tutelage of Professor Liz Fraser of the Cocteau Twins. There are still tracks that are out and out metal, and there's a turntablist on there too but only to add interesting washes of sound, not to bring the beat back or fill a hole in the mix; but the feeling that you get when you listen to *White Pony* is that this is a band determined to sound like no-one else around. It's not straight metal, not alt-rock and certainly not any form of hip-hop. 'Change (In The House Of Flies)', 'Knife Party' (dealing with the age-old subject of erotic blood-sport!) and 'Passenger' (featuring Maynard James from Tool) are the highlights on the album and point the way towards further progression in the future.

Of late Moreno has been experimenting with a sampler at home and working with Scottish post-rockers Mogwai, so expect more droning and plenty of instrumentals on the next one. Now that would be a radical direction for a vocalist to take!

When metal took over from indie in 1991, it was because the kids wanted physical music, a music that could compete with hip-hop, techno and drum'n'bass, and the independent bands of the eighties didn't have the raw power such a demand required. Metal supplied it but then got suckered into the reiterative mainstream. The Deftones have shown the way out of the mess, and signed to the Maverick label they've done it all with Madonna's money. Nice touch.

First team: Chino Moreno (v), Stephen Carpenter (g), Abe Cunningham (d), Chi Cheng (b)

Place, time, scene: Sacramento, California 1994. The Deftones emerged at the same time as Korn, in a scene inspired by the dark, funk metal of bands like Tool. The band's admiration for earlier goth-rock artists has encouraged them to focus on songs and not the stereotyped gloom that many doom-metal bands picked up on. They have also managed to avoid similar parodies of hip-hop music and marketing strategies, although there are stylistic funk and hip-hop musical elements at play in the Deftones' work too. All in all a subtle blend of diverse influences and expanding all the time.

What to buy first: *Around The Fur* 1997

And then: *White Pony* 2000

DELGADOS

The Delgados claimed that they started the band to get back at former colleagues in previous bands. Both Alun Woodward and Emma Pollock, the band's two vocalists, have independently confessed that the Delgados' primary motivation was revenge, and when it came to the music industry they got their revenge in first. They did not intend to be just another indie band stuck in an alternative system where it has always been considered cool to remain aloof and anonymous from a potential mainstream audience. As Emma Pollock succinctly puts it 'I'm in a band – I want to sell records. Not because I want to live in LA with a swimming pool in the garden, but because I want people to hear what we're doing. I think they should. If I was a member of the public and I didn't get a chance to hear this album, I'd be really f***ed off.' For the Delgados, revenge meant setting up a record label that single-handedly subverted the major labels' successful little sideline, customizing its own 'alternative system'. The Chemikal Underground label reinvigorated an independent scene that virtu-

ally disappeared at the end of the eighties only to be reconstituted as the far more marketable Britpop in the next decade. For most of the nineties the Delgados ensured that independent and independently-minded music had an outlet. Their own work, which revisits the melodic but noisy shambling bands of the eighties but with structures based on Albini dynamics, especially his work with the Pixies, is not a million miles away from what Radiohead were doing at a similar time, although the Delgados' love of pastoral folk and intimate vocals makes them a different proposition altogether.

The Chemikal Underground label was launched in 1994, administered from a kitchen somewhere in Glasgow. The Delgados released their first single through the label and made their first signing in 1995, a lo-fi electro pop band called Bis that, after just two records on the label, got signed to what the Delgados describe as 'a fuck-off record deal'. That meant Chemikal Underground could rent an office, make some longer records and sign the most impressive collection of innovative new artists since the independent

The Delgados

label heyday in the late seventies and early eighties. By 1997 the label was looking after Arab Strap, Mogwai, Magoo, Radar Brothers, Cha Cha Cohen and of course the Delgados themselves.

Just like Postcard and Creation over a decade before, Chemikal Underground was a Scottish solution to developing musical blandness where the so-called cutting edge of British music was at best static and at worst meaninglessly retrospective. For their own part, they took inspiration from the bands that had been swept aside by Britpop. In the UK that was bands like the Pastels and My Bloody Valentine, and in the US, the harsh but organic Steve Albini sound, captured most clearly on the Pixies' *Surfer Rosa* album, especially Joey Santiago's guitar-noise, and the band's overall sense of audio dynamics. *Domestiques*, the debut album, is constructed from layers of guitars and vocal settings that sometimes make it hard to distinguish between Pollock and Woodward. On standout tracks 'Sucrose' and 'Under Canvas, Under Wraps', the songs, although ensconced within or beneath the noise, are still the basis of each track, and on occasion are allowed to speak for themselves, as on 'Smaller Mammals' or 'D'estus Morte'.

Peloton, which arrived just over a year later in 1998, continues in this vein and leaves the songs more exposed. 'Everything Goes Round The Water' is a delicate folk song, augmented by flute and strings that builds to an emotional climax with the dual vocals of Woodward and Pollock, each attempting to outdo the other in terms of sheer plaintiveness. Pollock's talking-singing style is particularly effective on 'Pull The Wires From The Wall', and when the two of them gently sing in fractured harmony, 'I don't know if you're wrong or you're right, oh I don't care. Let's go out for the night, get some chips in the car' in 'Clarinet', you feel like driving up to Glasgow and giving them both a big hug.

The combination of fragility and awe is mastered on *The Great Eastern*, an album which is massive in scope, and marvellously textured. Dave Fridman, who has worked with both Mercury Rev and the Flaming Lips, is the album's producer, and no doubt egged on by the master of all things majestic, the four members of the band are heard tackling an array of instruments themselves. There are also key contributions from arrangers responsible for brass, woodwind and strings. As Woodward expresses so elegantly, 'the decision was made quite early on: if you're going to write with strings and choirs in mind, don't hold back. Don't use eight string parts – go for the full fucking orchestra.'

'The Past That Suits You Best' opens the album and has the feel of northern desolation signified by the maudlin brass band sound, while the album's highlight, 'No Danger', the most beautiful yet discordant piece the band have yet created and which must contain virtually every instrument invented for use in popular and classical music, playing simultaneously by the end of the song, suitably evokes the central conceit of the song that 'now we're singing out of tune'. The lyrics are available for the first time too, on the sleeve-notes, a realization perhaps that for a lot of listeners, the Delgados are saying stuff that really matters and means something. The music draws you in and the lyrics lead you to the song underneath. It's what the Delgados do best, and it makes you want to . . . no, need to listen to them again and again.

First team: Stewart Henderson (b, g, p), Emma Pollock (v, g), Paul Savage (d, k), Alun Woodward (v, g, k)

Place, time, scene: Glasgow 1995. The Delgados picked up where indie music had left off in the late eighties. They combined the sensitivity and noise associated with the C86 bands with a new approach to dynamics taken from the Pixies, and added their own unique brand of plaintive folk – a Scottish tradition in independent music. Their label Chemikal Underground, has introduced the world to Arab Strap and Mogwai amongst others.

What to buy first: *The Great Eastern* 2000

And then: *Domestiques* 1996, *Peloton* 1998

DINOSAUR JR

Dinosaur Jr tend to get lumped in with the grunge set although they were actually plying their hard, loose and melodic songs several years before the Seattle scene kicked in. In fact Dinosaur, as the senior version of the band was known until a run-in with some particularly litigious hippies in 1986, were a major influence on the shoe-gazing scene that preceded grunge in the UK. The Boo Radleys and Ride were both inspired by J. Mascis' effects-laden guitar-work on the band's first album, which at that point also featured Lou Barlow, later of Sebadoh, on the other guitar. Dinosaur Jr managed two more albums with Mascis and Barlow existing in the same band but the situation was always an accident waiting to happen. Two musical geniuses into one band does not go.

Mascis grew up a fan of the Beach Boys but by the time he was at college in his home town of Amherst, Massachusetts he had let his sixties taste slide, primarily because it was associated with drug-addled hippies. Mascis had been turned on to hardcore punk, specifically the kind that espoused the 'straight-edge' philosophy of no drink, no drugs and no meaningless sex. In early eighties America, 'straight-edge' was what rebellion was all about, Mascis didn't even relate to British punk because it had a certain junkie chic attached to it. His first band of note was Deep Wound, which included Bostonian Lou Barlow and a vocalist named Charlie who was key to the hardcore education of both. He was evicted some time in 1984 after his friend Murphy had joined, and Mascis, who had until that point been a drummer, took over vocals and guitar, playing loud and making use of as many effects as possible to make the guitar sound and feel as dynamic as the drums he was used to. According to Mascis, no-one else he knew could get the sound he wanted from the guitar so he did it himself.

For the first three albums the strategy worked. *You're Living All Over Me* is the album that Mascis always wanted to make, and a contender for rock album of the decade. For a man who taught himself guitar, it's an astonishing pastiche of Neil Young at his most, well, Neil. The drumming borders on hardcore and melodies and hooks fly off in all directions, given added cool thanks to Mascis' tuneless and lazy vocal style, entirely new, a watershed moment in the shift from purposeful hardcore to ambivalent grunge. The album is a myriad of dynamic shifts where none of the instruments or vocal tracks seem in balance with one another but that makes for even more exciting guitar experiences. The soaring solos and the crystal-clear jangles are what the album is all about. Apparently Mascis and Barlow had been listening to a lot of

Metallica, Dream Syndicate and Sonic Youth, and with those three reference points you can pretty much build the sound up in your own head.

Bug which followed is more of the same and contains the single 'Freak Scene', which might have picked up more radio play had it not contained one little naughty word. Mind you, it's the best bit of the song, so in retrospect who cares if stupid old radio stations didn't play it, and anyway those that wanted to hear it went out and bought it. Mudhoney were soon doing similar things with their track 'Touch Me I'm Sick', but with just that little bit more passion! Mascis' style was always lethargic, ironic really considering that he fired Barlow from the band for being too lazy and not really into what they were trying to achieve. There's a story told that Barlow let his bass guitar feed back for too long at a gig round about the time of *Bug* and was admonished quite subtly with a guitar smashed over his head, that old straight-edge devotion to excellence rearing itself, maybe. Barlow left to form Sebadoh while Mascis continued with Dinosaur Jr throughout the 1990s, turning in some impressive albums, notably *Green Mind* in 1991 and

J. Mascis

Where You Been in 1993, before disbanding at the end of the decade with Mascis the only remaining original member.

First team: J. Mascis (v, g), Lou Barlow (b, v), Murph (d)

Place, time, scene: Amherst, Massachusetts 1983. Dinosaur Jr took the guitar fetishism of Sonic Youth, the hard rock elements of hardcore and speed metal and the psychedelic pop of the Paisley Underground, and brought them together in a band where the rhythmic and textural assault was mind-blowing. Both Mascis' and Barlow's abilities to write melodic songs with powerful hooks added a dimension that would be picked up by future noise bands in the UK and US, and Mascis' ambivalent vocal style, which got him tagged as a slacker/stoner, became a cornerstone of a whole new set of harsh sounding bands who liked the juxtaposition of energy and couldn't be arsedness.

What to buy first: *You're Living All Over Me* 1987

And then: *Dinosaur* 1985, *Bug* 1988, *Green Mind* 1991, *Where You Been* 1993

In retrospect: *Ear Bleeding Country* 2001

DJ SHADOW

When he was about ten, Josh Davis noticed that there was something peculiarly different about *The Message* by Grandmaster Flash, Melle Mel and the Furious Five. Unlike all the other music he had heard up to that point, it was direct and raw, with barely any music to speak of, at least compared to the new wave and progressive rock that he had been used to hearing. His mind was further blown a few years later when he heard Mantronix's collage hip-hop pieces like 'King Of The Beats', and started to realize that the DJ was central to hip-hop and that rappers were somehow hijacking the form, encouraged to do so, by corporately led financial incentives. He suddenly felt very motivated.

By the time he made it to university, and had been introduced to DJ Zen on the student radio station, and on-campus rapper Lyrics Born, Davis was already making his own hip-hop inspired soundscapes, consisting of samples and breakbeats culled from increasingly obscure sources. It led to the formation of a collective called Solesides that played wherever they could in Davis, California, leading pretty quickly to a deal with Hollywood Basic who gave DJ Shadow, as he was now known, a deal to put out a few singles. 'Entropy', with vocals by Lyrics Born, clocked in at 17 minutes, and was enough to bring Shadow to the attention of James Lavelle at Mo'Wax records, resulting two years later in the culmination of a lengthy period of experimentation with sonic textures and time signatures, when DJ Shadow released his debut album called *Endtroducing*.

Adhering to the hip-hop philosophy of 'unity through music' espoused by Afrika Bambaataa back in the late seventies, *Endtroducing* is a montage of samples and turntable breaks, that goes one stage further than the Dust Brothers, the Bomb Squad or Prince Paul. Where they had cleverly mixed and sampled a cross-section of different styles in their work for Public Enemy, the Beastie Boys and Beck, and De La Soul respectively, DJ Shadow merged different samples in a much more organic way, opting for longer, looped samples that he delicately segued into one another, often foreshadowing certain musical motifs in earlier tracks to build up tension and give the listener a sense of déjà-vu. He also indulged in a little micro-mixing, cutting up beats into minute fragments and using samples as individual notes.

The textures are all important on a DJ Shadow album, especially at the mixdown stage after the sonic jigsaw is complete, so that the overall feel of the tracks he has created are consistent with one another and have a sense of reality even if it is ultimately, hyperreality. *Endtroducing* mucks about with traditional time signatures too. Dance music has always stuck to the rock solid foundation of four to the floor time, but DJ Shadow is perhaps proudest of his deliberate avoidance of the groove. When he does get rhythmic with his music, it's usually just for a few bars before slipping down, or cranking up a gear. Listen to 'Midnight In A Perfect World' for some exemplary slippage between piano and drums.

With his second full-length album, *Psyence Fiction*, billed as UNKLE and working with the label boss of Mo'Wax, James Lavelle, DJ Shadow added electronic sounds and lush arrangements to his hip-hop baseline, and with Lavelle's address book handy, managed to rope in the voices of several contemporary music icons. Continuing with his underlying strategy of 'taking music and articulating it visually' Shadow built custom-made musical environments for his guests to work within. Badly Drawn Boy gets a suitably lo-fi setting, all tinny drums and guitars, Thom Yorke is presented with off-kilter piano for the disconcerting 'Rabbit In Your Headlights', and Richard Ashcroft is set adrift amidst an ocean of strings for the epic and really quite beautiful 'Lonely Soul'.

It took five years to follow up *Endtroducing* and when he did, it took hip-hop somewhere else again. 'If you build something, you should be the first to destroy it before someone else does.' *The Private Press* is more cinematic and is influenced as much by his soundtrack hero David Axelrod as Herc, Flash or Bambaataa, which some hip-hop fans have read as a sell-out, although Shadow himself is adamant that any such pandering to 'the man' has been going on since at least the beginning of the 1990s when rap took over from all other aspects of hip-hop music and culture. He also continues to go out touring with his old Solesides mates, and his Mo'Wax chums who go by the name of Quannum, and which includes Blackalicious, Latyrx, and various members of Jurassic 5, and together with Cut Chemist from the band, he has knocked up a couple of DJ mixes constructed entirely out of 45rpm singles, these were intended as special editions for special fans but have ended up becoming much sought after examples of a dying art, Shadow and his friend digging out old singles and having fun sticking them together over the course of a mad weekend. Such a simple idea, as most things are. And it's the essence of hip-hop.

Place, time, scene: Davis, California 1993. DJ Shadow took up the challenge of resurrecting the importance of the DJ in hip-hop just like Eric B had done before him, but took it a stage further and combined his turntable skills with a sophisticated understanding of sample technology. His music is textured and ambient, apparently a big influence of Radiohead in their *Kid A* period.

What to buy first: *Endtroducing* 1996

And then: UNKLE: *Psyence Fiction* 1999, *The Private Press* 2002

DOORS

'I want it to be dark and moody. Real misterioso. But then I want it to explode into the light. I want the sun to shine in the dark corners,' enthused Ray Manzarek in his book *Light My Fire* describing his musical vision for the Doors in 1965. Psychedelia was not a word being applied to music at that point, and the idea of marrying jazz and rock'n'roll which was the basis of the Doors sound was a completely new one. Of course, it was more than just a cute idea. The Doors, formulated by UCLA cinematography students Manzarek and Jim Morrison and two LA based musicians that Manzarek met at a transcendental meditation meeting, Robbie Krieger and John Densmore, were a force of nature. Intellectual, hip and with wide-ranging music taste, the four Doors nailed their sound the very first time that they played together, and with six albums in just over four years, laid down a blueprint for a style of music-making which is simultaneously structured and improvised, and although often aspired to, rarely emulated by bands that came along later. They didn't conform to the structure in operation at the time, instead they put sounds and words together in new ways that made rock music a cognitive and intellectual experience. Where other pop bands fitted simple stories to the hook or rhythm of the song, the Doors made it their project to build their music around the deep and symbolic stories told by vocalist Morrison. He became the first rock'n'roll shaman, plugged into a spirit that oozed out of him and inspired his fellow musical travellers. Even Robbie Krieger's more traditional pop songs were enhanced with an indefinable energy in their presentation that confirmed the awesome potential of rock'n'roll music as the most important cultural form of the next few decades.

Manzarek grew up on the south side of Chicago, Morrison in Florida. When they graduated from UCLA both had been awakened to the possibilities of art as a communicative form. Using their knowledge of film, particularly concepts such as mise-en-scène and the groundwork of Eisenstein and von Sternberg, they developed their own much copied form of modernist rock'n'roll music. Functional and expositional, there were smooth straight edges to the sound so that each instrument can be identified as a contributing factor to the overall mix, and plenty of wide open musical space for Morrison to inhabit with his symbolist and beat-inspired poetry. His musical relationship with drummer John Densmore was crucial, particularly on epic tracks like 'The End', which the band developed during their period as the house band at the London Fog and later the legendary Whisky-A-Go-Go club on Sunset Strip.[21] Densmore would control the beat in accordance with Morrison's performance while Krieger and Manzarek slid melody lines into the proceedings just at the required moment. There was no bassist in the Doors when they played live, Manzarek took care of that with his boogie-woogie taught left hand and trademark Vox Continental electric organ.

The 11 minutes that make up 'The End', a song based around the myth of Oedipus Rex, demonstrated what the Doors were capable of right from the start. It combined long mesmerizing musical sections that actively encouraged meditative inaction, making the central climatic line 'Father I want to kill you. Mother I want to fuck you' and ensuing musical crashing all the more effective. It tied in neatly with the countercultural agenda of the time too by making the point against war driven by the desire for material possession in a brutal yet artistically sophisticated manner.

The first album for Elektra Records was completed in mid-1966 and released in January 1967. That's way before *Sgt Pepper* and the Velvets, and ahead of the debut album by Frank Zappa too. On it Manzarek inflects his playing with jazz chords, Krieger introduces the world to bottleneck guitar – played with an actual broken bottle – and Densmore contributes jazz rhythms throughout. It's his latin beats that give Krieger's song 'Light My Fire' its exotic edge and helped it become the soundtrack to the summer of love. It stayed at number one on the Billboard charts for most of August before being knocked off the top spot by the Beatles' 'All You Need Is Love'.

The Doors took psychedelia to New York in 1966 on their trip out east to mix their debut album, they played alongside the Jefferson Airplane at the Roundhouse in London in early 1968 and it was at a gig in Cleveland that Iggy Pop caught the rock'n'roll bug from Jim Morrison and immediately set about forming a band called the Iguanas and later the Stooges. Iggy learned stagecraft from Morrison and in many ways kept his spirit alive after the singer's death.

Jac Holzman signed the Doors to his Elektra label as part of the label's continuing move away from folk and towards rock. Love were another band signed to the label, but it was the Doors that made him a rich man. The debut album had been recorded in a matter of days, and the follow-up *Strange Days* followed suit. It was again packed with songs that the band had been road-testing for the previous year. Songs were captured in the minimum of takes, and the extra space left over from their new 8-track mixing desk gave the band the luxury of overdubbing certain parts. Morrison got to bang away on a Moog synthesizer for the title track and Manzarek played his piano part backwards on 'Unhappy Girl' just for the hell of it. 'When The Music's Over', the band's definitive sectionalized masterpiece, was done in just two takes, although it should have been one. The first was without Morrison who was AWOL at the time, forcing the band to improvise around his imagined vocals, and the second take was vocal only where Morrison managed to hit every cue with perfect timing.

Waiting For The Sun was an even more remarkable album, featuring a stoned drunk vocal from the Lizard King on the track 'Five To One'. According to Manzarek, the medics were on standby while Morrison laid down the vocal. Buy the album and have a listen. That guy has a slur! *The Soft Parade* in 1968 had horns and strings and contained the solid gold soul classic 'Touch Me'; *Morrison Hotel* was back to basics heavy blues rock – check 'Roadhouse Blues' for their kiss-off to all things hippy-dippy; and *L.A. Woman*, with its Californian road-trip title track, the primal deep blues spiritual 'The Wasp' and the dark and foreboding 'Riders On The Storm', is the culmination of, let's face it, a near perfect recording career. All that was left was for the singer to top himself, which he did, probably accidentally in a Parisian hotel bathroom on July 3rd 1971. The Doors did not continue. They just shut up shop and left the arena. Their only post-Morrison project was the 1979 *American Prayer* album which gave them an opportunity to once more connect with the spirit of their late friend when some recorded poetry and story-telling was unearthed. They set the words to music and incorporated excerpts of 'Roadhouse Blues', 'The Unknown Soldier', 'Riders On The Storm' and 'The Wasp' along the way. They were never funkier.

Oliver Stone tried to put it all into perspective at the beginning of the nineties in a film that portrayed the Doors as just another counter-culture failure. It was there on the screen in black and white, Jim the innocent and naïve flower-child and the other three, well they were pseudo-hippies, in it for the money, any trio of musicians would have done it seems. Twat. Crass posthumous myth-making just confuses the issue, the Doors were more than just an enigmatic frontman. The Doors were a band until ... the end, beautiful friend.

First team: Ray Manzarek (k, v), Jim Morrison (v), Robbie Krieger (g), John Densmore (d)

Place, time, scene: LA 1966. The Doors made psychedelic head music that changed the way listeners experienced rock music. Their combination of jazz, rhythm and blues, and rock styles together with powerful lyrical imagery made their music vivid and palpable. Many bands that followed failed to realize that the Doors' success was as much about live performance as musical excellence and became detached from the primal source of the music. The Stooges may well be the Doors' closest relatives and it was not until the end of the seventies that bands like the Birthday Party and Echo and the Bunnymen attempted a similar blend of styles and performance albeit without the spiritual LA beach vibe.

What to buy first: *The Doors* 1967

And then: *Strange Days* 1967, *Waiting For The Sun* 1968, *The Soft Parade* 1969, *Morrison Hotel* 1970, *L.A. Woman* 1971, *An American Prayer* 1979

In retrospect: *The Best Of The Doors* 1985

NICK DRAKE

Dead at the age of 26, with three commercially unsuccessful albums to his name, Nick Drake was surely destined for an eternity of non-entity. He certainly didn't make his voice heard while he was alive, stage-fright meant that he rarely ever performed in front of an audience, radio sessions were arranged and missed, interviews almost non-existent, and his own contribution to the promotion of his third album consisted entirely of dropping-off the tapes at his record label's reception desk. The albums were released of course, but the fashion for serious artists not to release singles in the early seventies, and to rely instead on live performance and the serious music press, effectively cut Drake off almost entirely from his potential audience. In the four years that he was recording, Nick Drake was unknown to many and anonymous to the rest, but in the decades since his death his name alone has become a byword, not just for a particular style of music, but for a whole approach to music-making that is best summarized simply as 'real'. Nick Drake wrote lyrics and made music that expressed himself in a way that he struggled to do in his non-musical life. Music, above all else, was Nick Drake's way of communicating with the world, 'If songs were lines in a conversation, the situation would be fine.'

Born in Burma to upper middle-class parents, Drake grew up in Tanworth-in-Arden, near Coventry, in the comfortable and relaxed red brick and green lawns environment of his family home. He attended Marlborough public school and then went up to Cambridge University where he read French symbolist poetry and smoked good quality hashish. He performed at University get-togethers, was spotted by a member of Fairport Convention, and recommended to the American producer Joe Boyd who ran Witchseason Productions from an office on Charlotte Street in London. According to Boyd, the initial tapes were the finished article and Drake was put into a studio immediately. The debut album, *Five Leaves Left*, is the first of three mesmerizing collections, all of which have a purity of mood and spirit that is rarely captured on tape.

Musically, they are a continuation of the development of folk music, from an institutionalized form made for a folk music elite into something more accessible to an audience mostly familiar with popular music. Martin Carthy had begun the popularization with his innovative guitar arrangements, encouraging artists like Bert Jansch, Bob Dylan and Tim Buckley to consider the music as well as the words of folk songs, Jansch and Buckley integrating blues, jazz and styles from centuries past, and Dylan of course blended folk with rock. He also placed greater emphasis on symbolic imagery in his words and with his vocal style brought a personalization to a style of music which had drifted off into self-parody.

Drake, recording at the end of the sixties and the beginning of the seventies, had clearly followed all of these developments, although his own vocal style was what made him so different to what had gone before. The songs may be sad but they're never self-indulgent because Drake's deep, smooth vocal never betrays anger, remorse, irony or anything that stamps his own personality on the recordings. He remains aloof throughout, precisely articulating the words, yet somehow detached from their meaning. It could be down to his middle-class reluctance to bare his soul in public, his crippling shyness, or a determination not to undermine his words and music with a fundamentally dishonest attempt at performance. Drake was never showbiz. It's what makes his work timeless with a style all of its own. It's also pretty punk if you think about it – the erasure of self-important rock star posing, leaving just the music and the message.

On *Five Leaves Left* the mood of the performance is in the music. Drake's guitar-playing is crisp and precise, particularly on the opening track 'Time Has Told Me', and the string arrangements by his university friend Robert Kirby, rising and falling on 'River Man', echo Drake's cyclical guitar picking, becoming more dramatic as the song progresses. On 'Way To Blue' the strings take centre-stage as Drake almost reads his poetry over the top. Elsewhere there's double-bass from Danny Thompson and some congas played by Rocky Dzidzornu, but it's the strings that permeate the album, something that Drake was most firm about when advised to go with a different overall sound.

The songs work as poetry, the imagery that's evoked given time and space to form in the mind of the listener, unhindered by the lush, pastoral soundscapes and Drake's non-committal vocals. It's difficult now, to know how a song like 'Fruit Tree' was initially interpreted without the hindsight of Drake's tragic death, which it seems to prophesy. If Drake himself is connoted in 'Fruit Tree', other characterizations are more vague. Who is Betty, and where was she on her way to in 'River Man'? What are Jeremy and Jacomo fleeing from in 'Three Hours'? And Mary Jane is so mysterious with all that flying, going out in the rain and journeying to the stars, that she may not even be human at all. 'The Thoughts Of Mary Jane' may well refer to something else entirely; let's face it, it was the late sixties when he wrote it.

Bryter Layter invites more reflection and introspection but the mood is lighter, thanks to gentler string arrangements, some jazzy piano, mellow alto-saxophone, some Richard Thompson guitar and a rolling backline of bass and drums courtesy of Dave Pegg and Dave Matacks from Fairport Convention, who provide an uplifting and timeless counterpoint to lyrics soaked in pathos. Revealing lines like 'oh poor boy so sorry for himself', 'what will happen in the morning when the world it gets so crowded that you can't look out the window in the morning?' are sweetened by Joe Boyd's production, but the album's highlights are 'Northern Sky' and 'Fly', both featuring John Cale playing viola, harpsichord and celeste, adding a poignancy that Drake would further explore on his final album *Pink Moon*. Its release in 1972, two years after the abject commercial failure of *Bryter Layter*, came after a long period of depression for Drake, and it feels like it. Apart from a little bit of piano on the title track, the rest is just Drake's voice and guitar. The playing is again crystal clear and expertly picked with Drake letting strings resonate over one another to add texture. He even jangles brightly on 'Place To Be' and 'Road', but for the most part the mood is dark. 'Things Behind The Sun' opens with a fairly concise definition of paranoia, 'Please beware of those that stare, they only smile to make you while your time away', whilst the agonisingly repetitive and almost discordant guitar of 'Know', contains just four lines, ending finally with 'know I'm not there'.

Having recorded the album in just two nights, the now deeply withdrawn Drake, monosyllabic at best, dropped the finished tapes off with the receptionist at Island Records, leaving them to discover what was in the mystery package several days later. There were four more recordings in 1974 including 'Black Eyed Dog' which is about the bleakest thing anyone has ever got down on tape, and is notable for the high-pitched whine of Drake's vocals, no longer able to put the distance between his psyche and his performance. But, no matter how clear-cut it might seem that Drake was on a one-way trip to an inevitable demise, his eventual death of a drugs overdose at his home in Tanworth-in-Arden might not have been his decision.

In the weeks before his death, he was, according to his family, the happiest he had been in a long time. A 'Best Of' album of his songs was selling well and he was talking about writing songs for other people, rather than continuing to perform himself. If he had actually come to terms with his depression then it makes his death even more tragic, and it has needlessly robbed a family of a much-loved son and brother, and everyone else of the continued creative outpourings of a musical and poetic genius. Make Nick Drake's music a priority in your life, for yourself and for the sake of that prophetic line in 'Fruit Tree' 'They'll all know you were here when you're gone.'

Place, time, scene: Cambridge 1969. Nick Drake continued the integration of folk into rock that had begun with Bob Dylan in the earlier part of the decade. His lyrics, and style of delivery mark him out as a sensitive soul, and his ability to contextualize his sensitivity in a variety of musical settings and moods, has become a reference point for introspective rock and pop artists and approaches ever since. It seems that every week at least one album is released that promotes its contents as 'sounding like' or 'inspired by' Nick Drake.

What to buy first: *Five Leaves Left* 1970

And then: *Bryter Layter* 1972, *Pink Moon* 1974

In retrospect: *Way To Blue* 1994, *Fruit Tree* (Boxed Set) 1986

DREAM SYNDICATE

Generally speaking, Steve Wynn has always followed his heart, and with the formation of the Dream Syndicate, that meant looking back before punk hit the US and guitar-based music split into the underground hardcore scene and overground soft-rock, with its fetish for technological gadgetry and high-fidelity sound. Inspired by Big Star, the first self-consciously retro pop band, the Dream Syndicate, along with other bands dubbed the Paisley Underground, notably the Rain Parade, the Long Ryders and the Bangles, made music which recalled the experimental music of the sixties, after the group format had been mastered but before the studio took over and started splitting the group and their sound up. To be precise, the point at which the Beatles unveiled 'Rain', the B-side to 'Paperback Writer' and the band's crowning achievement; a slow fuzz of a

record that brought together the lovable mop-tops' innate sense of pop and group camaraderie and the experimental, darker sounds seeping out of America around the same time. The Dream Syndicate could relate directly to it; they didn't reject all that was good about classic rock but wanted to mess about with it, punk it up. Regardless of the hard punk and experimental post-punk fashions of the time, Dream Syndicate made their 'Rain', not giving a monkey's if it was out of step with everything else.

It took just five hours in the middle of the night to record *The Days Of Wine And Roses*, with each track played as a live jam. Karl Precoda plays circular guitar parts that occasionally veer towards something more free-form and are caked in feedback, while Wynn drones with both his own guitar and voice. It's rocking Velvet Underground but with droning guitars where John Cale's viola would normally have been, and it all culminates in the final seven minute title-track that remains the band's finest moment, loose and assured in equal measure.

On 'Tell Me When It's Over' you can sense the spontaneity and the relaxed effortlessness of a band who are just happy to be playing their instruments at high volume, totally unconcerned about any notion of overdubs or putting it right in the mix. The needle was apparently in the red for a lot of the recording and Kendra Smith's bass is really only felt, not heard for large parts of the album. *The Days Of Wine And Roses* captures a mood on tape in one take (ish), the very antithesis of the slick and carefully produced music being played on Californian radio at that time, yet still sunbaked and dreamy in its own way. Having said that, the lyrics are certainly not cheerful and a couple of them hint at suicide, but it gets darker still on the later albums 'arson, necrophilia, incest, and all of those things … look, I was wallowing in complete self-degradation'. Kurt Cobain was a big fan.

The Medicine Show was cleaner sounding but still soaked in guitar noise; *Out Of The Grey* is wilfully discordant and *Ghost Stories* is the sound of the Dream Syndicate getting their wayward electrical excursions under control, having finally worked out what those things in the studio with knobs and faders on were all about. But then the Dream Syndicate were best when they didn't really give a damn about all that stuff.

First team: Steve Wynn (v, g), Karl Precoda (g), Kendra Smith (b, v), Dennis Duck (d)

Place, time, scene: Los Angeles 1982. The Dream Syndicate brought about the Paisley Underground scene which returned garage psychedelia and free-form jamming to eighties studios. Their recording methods were straightforward, and the resulting loose psychedelic-punk set off a new trajectory in American underground music, inspiring Dinosaur Jr's more 'wimpy, jangly' aspects.

What to buy first: *The Days Of Wine And Roses* 1982

And then: *The Medicine Show* 1984

In retrospect: *It's Too Late To Stop Now* 1989

IAN DURY

When Ian Dury and the Blockheads released *New Boots And Panties* in late 1977, Dury was at last in sync with the times. The anti-rock stance that he had always taken, from his early days playing the pub circuit in London with his first band Kilburn and the High Roads, won him the label 'godfather of punk' and boosted his record sales accordingly. The follow-up album, *Do It Yourself*, sold even more and in between, the band effortlessly dropped three singles into the UK Top 10 with 'Hit Me With Your Rhythm Stick' going all the way to number one, pop pickers. Like Elvis Costello, Dury was not directly connected with the punk scene; unlike Costello, who altered his approach to writing when he realized that a new attitude was emerging, Dury didn't need to revise his attitude, it was spot-on already. The irony, the humour, the stark realism, and the straight non-patronizing relationship with his audience was and always had been his stock in trade right from the beginning.

Having received his first dose of reality at the age of seven when he contracted polio from a public swimming pool visit, leaving him with a stricken hand and leg, Dury's early songs with Kilburn and the High Roads were shot through with anger and cynicism, and in his own words he got 'bored with the screaming and the ugliness of it all' after a first album recorded for a subsidiary of Warner Brothers. The album, called *Wotabunch!*, wasn't released until Dury had become a household name at the end of the decade, due to the fact that the band had been dropped after the label's managing director saw them play live. It's probably safe to say that he was unable to spot star potential in the badly dressed bloke in his thirties, admonishing the audience and singing songs about rough kids from the council estates.

By the time of their demise in 1976 and following a second album, *Handsome*, which focused more on Dury's vocals, he was on the lookout for a different musical context in which to work, and discovered what he was after in Chas Jankel, a keyboard-player who helped Dury arrange his songs so that he could more or less talk through his lyrics. On *New Boots And Panties*, Jankel comes up with some amazing funk backing for the track 'Wake Up And Make Love To Me', 'Sweet Gene Vincent' is given a ghostly rockabilly feel, and the final 'Blackmail Man' is pure punk-parody with controversial lyrics and bad attitude.

There was no record deal at the time but Stiff Records finally put the album out and were rewarded for doing so with its biggest-selling album up to that point. With a new band, the Blockheads, Dury quickly came up with a new batch of songs, including the single 'Hit Me With Your Rhythm Stick' – a nonsensical travelogue that has perhaps the greatest musical climax of them all. Over a minute of wild call-and-response, as Dury screams 'Hit may-ee' at the top of his voice, the instruments reply ever more manically the sax complains, the guitar twangs, what sounds like a harmony group from the 1950s croons (or maybe that's a keyboard trick), while the bass and drums somehow hold the whole discordant mess together. Fantastic. The best number one single the UK has had since the Beatles.

There were a couple more albums with the Blockheads, both placing perhaps an overemphasis on the music at the expense of Dury's vocals and by extension his lyrical message too. Jankel left after *Do It Yourself* and the band were no more by 1982. Since then there have been a few solo albums, a musical, and two decades of positive role-modelling.

Ian Dury died in 2000.

First team: Ian Dury (v), Chaz Jankel (k), Norman Watt-Roy (d), Charlie Charles (b), John Turnbull (g), Mickey Gallagher (k), Davey Payne (sx)

Place, time, scene: London 1971. Ian Dury was a pre-punk punk. He had played the pub-rock scene for several years with earlier bands and had developed an uncompromising performance-style to go with an energetic band set-up and gritty social realism lyrics.

What to buy first: *New Boots And Panties* 1977

And then: *Do It Yourself* 1979

In retrospect: *Reasons To Be Cheerful* 1996

BOB DYLAN

Within the context of popular music Bob Dylan is the original alternative artist. All others with a claim to having consciously set out to work outside the prevailing institutional framework, be it commercially, artistically or culturally defined, should be judged against him. In terms of working practice, creativity and communication with a like-minded audience, Dylan is the genuine article. The Beatles and the Stones, the Beach Boys, James Brown and Bob Marley may have all bucked trends later in their careers, but it was fashionable to do so then; record companies even encouraged it, because innovation and having something to say sold records. OK, the Beatles took a chance with *Revolver* and *Pet Sounds* didn't shift units at the time, and there's an argument to be made that the Rolling Stones' first Decca recordings captured a rawness previously unheard in the pop world, but like Elvis Presley, the Stones quickly settled into a career trajectory that, to be frank, matched mainstream cultural and commercial expectations (even if the mainstream culture of the time was a progressively liberal one).

As for the Beatles, the Beach Boys, Brown, Marley and other great innovators of popular music not included in this collection, well they all warmed to their role, but only after a period of acquiescence with prevailing music-industry practice. The Beatles wrote their own songs but they were quite clearly aimed at a notional target-audience of teenage girls; the Beach Boys sang about surfing and Californian hedonism but, with the exception of Dennis, didn't partake themselves; James Brown had a stunning live show, but it only served to bolster his own ego, songs like 'Please, Please, Please' and the theatrics that surrounded his performance did

Bob Dylan

not challenge the industry set-up, and the succession of singles that he put out during the late fifties and sixties were R&B standards that demonstrated Brown's commercial aims; and Marley, well he spent the sixties pleasing the mainstream Jamaican market with gospel inflected, Americanized rocksteady that got played on Jamaican radio but was out of touch with sound system culture. But enough already. It feels wrong to be criticizing such giants of popular music who have all been revolutionary in their way. The point is that although each of them, at some point, stepped up to the challenge of making crucially important music that held little regard for commercial imperatives and careerism, it was Bob Dylan (you know, the bloke I started talking about back at the beginning), who showed the way.

It was Dylan who demonstrated that you could start outside the mainstream and never have to move into it. Eventually, of course, the mainstream came to him, like it has to many other artists in this book. But where some of those artists may have displayed a tendency to become self-absorbed in their own perceived importance, or have somehow justified a less musically-honest practice with regard to their music, Dylan has remained immune to such industry bullshit and supremely confident in his own honest creativity. Dylan has done it all on his own terms and retained his voice throughout – that's his message-voice, you understand, not his actual voice, that's shot to ribbons.

Back home in Hibbing, Minnesota, in the fifties, Dylan grew up listening to Muddy Waters and John Lee Hooker on a radio show 'blastin' in from Shreveport' and learning guitar from Hank Williams records. He saw Buddy Holly and Richie Valens on their fatal tour and formed a few high school bands playing R&B and rock'n'roll, a musical approach which he stuck with for a few years, even getting a gig playing piano for Bobby Vee's backing band at one point, but which he dropped in 1960 when in his own words 'rock 'n'roll was pretty much finished'. He heard Woody Guthrie and 'that was it, it was all over'. He headed for Highway 61 in New York to visit the ailing folk singer, played him some songs, got dubbed 'the kid' by his hero and quickly set about changing the rules and bucking the traditions of folk music in the United States.

In 1961 he was singing his own talkin' blues songs to folk traditionalists in New York clubs, audiences and performers alike who were used to hearing the accepted canon of folk songs played out. Of course, four years later, he twisted the knife with his performance at the Newport Folk and Blues Festival when he plugged in his guitar and sold out the institutionalized traditions of folk to the all-consuming power of rock. In the years in between, Dylan had found a wider audience with his first five albums, each one demonstrating an increasing blending of folk and rock styles. The debut *Bob Dylan* is largely made up of folk traditionals, but the next three contain the definitive protest songs of the decade in 'Blowin In the Wind', 'A Hard Rain's Gonna Fall' and 'The Times They Are A Changin'', banded alongside more pop-oriented subject matter dealing with love and relationships, but always with an acknowledgement that such subjects are not necessarily without their complications. 'It Ain't Me Babe' is an honest admission that the singer is not ready for a full relationship, not prepared to protect and defend his lover, and that she should 'go at her own chosen speed'. Not a love song, not a kiss-off, more a frank assessment of a doomed relationship.

Not even Lennon was that mean yet, and it was a good two years before the Stones fully realized their astounding potential for misogyny.

By the time he made *Bringing It All Back Home* in 1965, he was being name-checked by the Beatles and just about every other beat-pop band then in existence. His albums were topping the charts in the UK and the Byrds had taken his acoustic reading of 'Mr Tambourine Man' and made it a full blown popsong. Not that Dylan was waiting to hear such a marriage of folk and pop before he chanced it himself. A whole side of *Bring It All Back Home* is electric, featuring members of the Paul Butterfield Blues Band who would later back him at Newport, and lyrics like 'Take me on a trip aboard your magic swirling ship' were just begging to be set to electric music (for the mind and body) that was as detached from straightforward acoustic performance as the symbolic wordplay was detached from straight denotative speech. Taking on board the literary influence of the French poet Rimbaud and the American beats, particularly novelist William S. Burroughs, Dylan's lyrics on *Bringing It All Back Home* and the follow-up *Highway 61 Revisited* became less direct, providing an opportunity for record-buyers to draw their own conclusions as to the meaning of the apparent stinging criticism of a line like 'You never turned around to see the faces on the jugglers and the clowns when they all did tricks for you'.

Musically, *Highway 61 Revisited* captures the revolutionary mood that the band must have been in, coming straight from Newport to the Columbia Studios in New York to bang out the songs in seven days at the beginning of August 1965. It's rough and ready with most of the songs captured in the bare minimum of takes. 'Like A Rolling Stone' was done in one (!) and legend has it that it was the first time that Al Kooper had ever played the organ (!!). 'Tombstone Blues' features superb lead guitar by Mike Bloomfield, but then there's 'Queen Jane Approximately', where the guitar is completely out of tune, and 'Ballad Of A Thin Man', where replayed piano parts are spliced back into the final mix to cover up earlier mistakes.[22] Sounds great, though.

Blonde On Blonde was started six months later, at the beginning of 1966, a double album recorded in a couple of sessions with Al Kooper again, Robbie

Robertson of the Band and the best musicians in Nashville at that time. It kicks off with 'Rainy Day Women # 12 and 35', all dumb-ass brass and speeded-up tape 'everybody must get stoned', and finishes with an entire side of 'Sad Eyed Lady Of The Lowlands', inspired by his wife Sara Lowndes. In-between, there's a stack of Dylan originals, not necessarily preaching protest or acknowledging the growing counter-cultural forces that he was acutely aware of, but instead, demonstrating what could actually be achieved with the newly matured rock-music form when there's someone up front who has something to say and knows how to say it with the maximum emotional impact. The whining, nasal drawl has become a signifier of irony and authenticity, affected by everyone from Lennon to Lydon. The hooks are numerous, especially on lighter songs 'Just Like A Woman' and 'I Want You', and the mood shifts subtly and continually across the album. It came out the same month as the Beatles' *Revolver* album, but pointed further ahead to what was to happen after psychedelia, the flower children and Woodstock or, as Dylan put it, 'the sum total of all the bullshit'.

Blonde On Blonde is the precursor of rock, as opposed to pop music. An influence on anyone who came afterwards who tries to say something with their lyrics, but who knows that the music and the performance are integral parts of that process. In other words, pretty much everyone else in this book. By October of 1966 even Levi

Stubbs of the Four Tops was doing 'a Dylan' on their international Motown hit 'Reach Out (I'll Be There)', taking his voice up at the end of each line to make it feel more heartfelt. What about that? Even soul music had come round to Dylan's way of doing things. Keep it real and the mainstream will pick up on it sooner or later. That's the moral of this particular tale.

Place, time, scene: New York 1961. Bob Dylan, the folk artist was always a rock'n'roller at heart; he had turned to folk because rock'n'roll got predictable in the early sixties. It was no surprise then that he connected his new-found genius for making folk music with a heavier blues-based sound as soon as he and pop music were ready. His lyrics and vocal style changed the face of pop music, and his politics, direct or obliquely surreal, fed into the counter-culture that he soon came to despise. His refusal to be treated like a pop star, with all of the inanity that went with it, made him a role model for a new maturity in pop, and was the key factor in the shift to a new rock paradigm that focused on albums and took popular music seriously.

What to buy first: *Blonde On Blonde* 1966

And then: *Bringing It All Back Home* 1965, *Highway 61 Revisited* 1965, *Blood On The Tracks* 1974, *Basement Tapes* 1975, *Desire* 1976

In retrospect: *The Essential Bob Dylan* 2001, *Biograph* 1986

E

808 STATE

The problem with Detroit techno was that it was too damned cheesy. The Belleville Three, Juan Atkins, Derrick May and Kevin Saunderson, the man behind Inner City ('We're having big fun'): talked-up the intellectual and culturally significant aspects of their electronic music. They were, in their own words, 'technicians with human feelings' who were concerned with making records that focused on the sound and texture rather than tunes, and were informed by a new approach to

music production that mirrored the shift from the human-built Ford cars and Motown music in the sixties to a process in the late 1980s where it was all done by machine. Derrick May's 'Nude Photo' and 'Strings Of Life' were exceptional pieces of work and set the international club scene reeling, particularly in Manchester where DJs at Factory Records' Hacienda club made Detroit techno the main attraction of their house-driven sets. Sure, techno was listening music, especially for those who understood that the criteria by which they should be judged was in the sounds and the production, but it was first and foremost party music played by DJs in clubs. Its British offshoot changed all that, and Manchester's 808 State were, let's be frank, the band that rescued techno from disappearing up its own rectum.

The original techno coming out of Detroit quickly mutated into acid house, a catch-all term for unfeasibly fast beats and high-pitched bleeps that reached its nadir with D-Mob's appalling trebly piece of shit, 'We Call It Acieed', a hit single and moral panic all rolled into one. Danny Rampling's Shoom[23] club night in London was acid central throughout 1987 and 1988, but the really interesting stuff was going on in the north of the country. In Sheffield, the Warp record store run by Rob Mitchell became Warp Records and signed LFO and Nightmares On Wax, purveyors of a new, darker from of techno that emphasized the bass again (hooray!). Richard Kirk of Cabaret Voltaire put out a single as 'Sweet Exorcist' which joined the dots between techno and industrial, and in Manchester it was another record store that inspired the formation of 808 State. Owner of Eastern Bloc Records, Martin Price, his friend from the café over the road, Graham Massey, regular DJ punters Darren Partington and Andy Barker, and a guy called Gerald Simpson, began the band in 1988 and within two years had spewed out four albums – two on their own Creed label – and had tapped into the developing Manchester dance scene to the point that they could fill the city's G-Mex stadium. That's right, 808 State played techno live

The first album *Newbuild* makes a feature of outdated technology deemed too crass and unmusical for 1988. Like Afrika Bambaataa seven years earlier, they used their Roland 808 drum machines as the basis for their sound, and layered samples, synths and turntables on top, making particular use of the Roland TB303, which spiked and snarled but was in no way pleasant. From the first track 'Sync/Swim' it's clear that 808 State had stumbled across a new energy that didn't necessarily inspire hands in the air abandon, or for that matter, chin-stroking reflection. The sounds and textures that Gerald Simpson would later build his magnificent 'Voodoo Ray' from are here, and it's clear that the likes of Stakker-Humanoid, Altern-8 and later bands like Autechre, Squarepusher and Boards Of Canada all managed to find a copy.

Of itself, not an easy task. *Newbuild* is acid house before it got crap, techno that ain't pretty, and attitude that made those more used to wielding guitars stop and reconsider the merits of dance music. It spawned baggy Madchester.

By 1989, 808 State had a hit single with the decidedly prettier 'Pacific State', and were beginning to work with song-writing vocalists who, as Graham Massey has noted, helped 808 State take the techno aesthetic across accepted musical boundaries: 'After "Pacific State" we went off at so many tangents that it's amazing people stuck with us. We've never followed a single with another one that sounded anything similar. That's our mistake and I'm proud of it.'[24] Björk, Bernard Sumner, James Dean Bradfield and Ian McCulloch have all worked with the remaining trio of Massey, Partington and Barker over the years, and Björk in particular was inspired in new rhythmic and textural directions by the collaboration which took place a year before she began working on her debut solo album.

808:90 and *Ex:El* released at the beginning of the decade both demonstrate the band's intent and ability to build sophisticated technologically-informed music, which marked the beginning of the great dance/rock collapse. 808 State albums come round again from time to time and A Guy Called Gerald still noodles, but the technology is so much more difficult to undermine nowadays. More's the pity.

First team: Graham Massey (808, 303), Martin Price (808, 303), Gerald Simpson (k, 808, 303), Darren Partington (t-t), Andy Barker (t-t)

Place, time, scene: Manchester 1987. 808 State stepped back from the head-on rush into acid house and took techno in a different direction. Working with relatively cheap keyboards and drum machines they came up with an album that had more of a nihilistic punk feel than the happy-clappy techno on offer elsewhere. Their live shows complemented the Stone Roses' warehouse shows and were attended by indie kids and Goths as well as clubbers. A big influence on the Chemical Brothers, Underworld and the Prodigy.

What to buy first: *Newbuild* 1988

And then: *808:90* 1990

In retrospect: *808:88:98* 1998

ECHO AND THE BUNNYMEN

Echo and the Bunnymen are the lasting survivors of the early 1980s' post-punk scene based in Liverpool. In the late seventies the city had resembled itself in the late fifties, except that rock'n'roll and R&B imports had been superseded by Television, Suicide and Pere Ubu. New punks like Ian McCulloch and Julian Cope collected as much as they could afford and shared their purchases around the newly-developing scene. Of course, punk was only the catalyst for the music that was soon to emerge from Liverpool; most of the sound and musical inspiration came from much further back. Scenesters needed to know about the Doors, the Velvets, the 13th Floor Elevators, and anything else of interest that cropped up on the reissued Nuggets albums compiled by Lenny Kaye. Echo and the Bunnymen were the sum of all these influences, but the focused sound that eventually emerged on their first four albums was something different entirely. The starkness and power of the Doors was evident, confirmed in McCulloch's vocal sound and delivery, but with a new realism that relates to a time no longer lost in the possibilities of the hippie dream. Where Jim Morrison seemed unstoppable, a shaman plugged into an ancient spirit, McCulloch is more cynical, his power comes from knowing that life sucks and there's not a lot that can be done about it.

Along with Julian Cope, his fellow arbiter of taste and band-mate from the Crucial 3 and A Shallow Madness, McCulloch ensured that he kept up with all the latest hip developments on the American music scene, and together they traced the origins of the music they were hearing. Will Sergeant was another scenester who bought import vinyl at Probe Records, and who frequented Eric's on Mathews Street, gaining inspiration from the first wave of British punk bands and then the more cerebral post-punkers, notably Warsaw, who would later become Joy Division. Sergeant invited McCulloch to add vocals to his developing minimalist sound sometime in 1979.

Based around one or two-note guitar parts, Les Pattinson's rumbling bass and a drum machine (Echo), it was the perfect backdrop for McCulloch's Jim-isms. Mind you, the ubiquitous long overcoat and refusal to get caught freaky-dancing on stage placed McCulloch firmly in 1980s' Liverpool, and not the far less self-conscious LA of the late 1960s. The Bunnymen may have pursued a similar sound to the Doors as their career progressed, but post-punk commitment to distance and irony dictated that the band should always remain wary of cliché. McCulloch's comment that 'the 80s made stars out of people who dressed like plumbers' was a thinly veiled attack on the likes of U2 and Simple Minds, who had got their priorities wrong as far as McCulloch was concerned. In the tradition of Mark E. Smith of the Fall, another music press 'motor-mouth' who expressed similar dissatisfaction with the growing trend for authentic and credible artists, McCulloch used cynicism and sarcasm to deflect attention away from any scholarly critique of his own band's music. It's indicative of a confidence born of the knowledge that they were way better than any of their contemporaries.

The debut album, *Crocodiles*, in 1980 is an awesome debut. The three albums in the three years that followed are the sound of the band perfecting their craft, particularly in terms of lyrics and arrangement, but in terms of raw talent and focus, *Crocodiles* is it. Having signed with Korova Records, a sub-division of WEA, managed by the corporation's chairman-in-waiting, Mr Enya, Rob Dickens, they were immediately told to get a real drummer to replace the drum machine. Typical music-industry stuff really, informed by 'the rules' and insensitive to claims that 'Suicide use a drum machine', especially as Suicide didn't have a drop dead gorgeous lead singer and the potential to shift serious rock/pop units.

And the bastards were right; when Echo and the Bunnymen got their drummer, Pete De Freitas, he was fundamental to their creative success. His John Densmore rhythms are immediately evident on the album's opener 'Going Up', propelling the track while Will Sergeant weaves and floats guitar over the tight but simultaneously lazy rhythm, and there's an expanse of space on the track for McCulloch to deliver his vocals and neo-psychedelic Morrison ad-libs. The single, 'Rescue', appears to have at least four Will Sergeants playing guitar on it, each one keeping their part minimal. There's the introductory simple lead-pattern, some lazy background strumming, overlaid effects stabs, and a relentless solo that eventually breaks down into a sparse funky opportunity for McCulloch to repeatedly intone the line 'Is this the blues I'm singing, is this the blues I'm singing?' The whole album is a triumph of arrangement, and a demonstration of how guitars can be used to texture songs instead of competing with the vocalist for equal billing. Johnny Marr of the Smiths, William Reid of Jesus and Mary Chain, and John Squire of the Stone Roses all owe Will Sergeant a huge debt.

The next three albums, *Heaven Up Here*, *Porcupine* and *Ocean Rain*, represent the best run of albums released by a British band in the first half of the decade, and show the band developing their abilities to create a specific mood that is dark and sinister but poppy and melodic at the same time. *Ocean Rain*, released in 1985 is, for many fans, their finest moment. Awash with strings, providing a suitably melodramatic setting for McCulloch's evocative imagery, often based around the twin concepts of love (maybe lust) and death, the album contains several epics – the watery title track, the quasi-religious 'Thorn Of Crowns' and the night-time drama of 'The Killing Moon' – allowing McCulloch to use the full extent of his vocal range and theatrical style. Very gothic.

Two years later, Echo and the Bunnymen were big news in America with their fifth album *The Game*, but that was more through luck than judgement, due to the inclusion of 'People Are Strange' on the soundtrack to that year's big teen movie *The Lost Boys*, demonstrating that even Hollywood had discovered irony. But thankfully no amount of success could convince first De Freitas, then McCulloch that they were creatively flogging a dead horse. Things were moving on in the UK, De Freitas in particular had succumbed to the lure of the ecstasy pill and McCulloch was sensing a change of mood both within and outside the band; a cynical media-friendly reinvention wasn't really on the cards as far as he was concerned. He left, and by 1989 had released his debut solo single and album *Candleland*. The band's demise had been confirmed a few months before that though when Pete De Freitas, who had initially left and then returned to the band, was killed in a tragic motor cycle accident on the A51 near Rugeley in Staffordshire.

But then it got weird. Rob Dickens at WEA convinced Sergeant and Pattinson that they could still make it in the States with a new lead singer (Ha!). Without thinking any of it through the band set about what their biographer Tony Fletcher refers to as 'fucking

with their legacy'.[25] The album that came out in 1990 was embarrassing in its inappropriateness, and would have been a disappointing swansong to an important musical career. Fortunately the band reformed in 1997 for the album *Evergreen*, and there have been a couple more since. *Flowers* in 2002 is a particular favourite amongst the band's die-hard fans. As of this moment, it's good to have them around. A revered back-catalogue is always just that little bit more alive when the original perpetrators decide to get the songs out and give them a good kicking every once in a while. It just reminds everyone what alternative music sounds like when you get it right.

First team: Ian McCulloch (v, g), Will Sergeant (g), Les Pattinson (b), Pete De Freitas (d)

Place, time, scene: Liverpool 1979. Echo and the Bunnyman were in the vanguard of a new set of bands that formed after the post-punk bands, that were driven by artistic and political aims. The Bunnyman were more concerned with making music that didn't try and change anything in particular, but sounded cool, looked cool and made people who listened to it feel cool. Using the powerful and expansive backdrop created by Sergeant's guitar and De Freitas' drumming, McCulloch was able to cast himself as a latter-day Jim Morrison, a shamanic figure in an overcoat for a more cynical generation.

What to buy first: *Crocodiles* 1980

And then: *Heaven Up Here* 1981, *Porcupine* 1983, *Ocean Rain* 1985

In retrospect: *Ballyhoo: The Best Of Echo And The Bunymen* 1997

EELS

Mark Everett has been making records since 1992. Whether working under the name of E or as the main creative force in the band Eels, the defining characteristic of his work is his continued efforts to control the musical elements that convey meaning in his songs. Like Brian Wilson, he creates music in the studio drawing on the specific skills of a core of musicians and engineers, and then, when he goes out on the road with a band he uses his songs as a basis for performance.

E does not create songs with live performance in mind. It's his way of dealing with a dilemma that has faced musicians for the best part of forty years, an acknowledgment that he has two quite different creative roles to play, and for Everett the aim of creating just the right sound and mood for his music is a process that cannot be repeated again in a live setting. Some critics don't like the idea, and have dismissed his odd blend of folk styles and techno beats as Beck plagiarism, ultimately shallow and lacking in any real content, because all of the usual instrumentation, passionate vocals and meaty rock bits are apparently missing. The reality is that the sounds and styles that E uses are carefully chosen so that the words 'become something of themselves' – different to simple prose or poetry. Black humour and unconventional styles combine to create a twisted back-catalogue made all the more poignant when the subject matter is a firsthand account of personal tragedy.

After two albums, credited simply to E, featuring Everett, a sampler and a selection of self-played instruments including a euphonium, he got a deal with the Dreamworks label in 1995. Opting to work as a band, which he called Eels so that the records would be filed next to his solo work in record stores (momentarily forgetting about the Eagles and Earth Wind And Fire – 'I didn't quite think that one through'), *Beautiful Freak* was an impressive start, shedding several hit singles internationally. 'Novocaine For The Soul' carried on where the world-weary Kurt Cobain had left off, and 'Susan's House' made the shift from existential angst to a form of social reportage that demonstrated E's knack for combining lyrics and music for the desired emotional effect. The sad little piano part that accompanies the repeated line 'going over to Susan's House, can't be alone tonight' (recalling Gary Portnoy's theme to the pathos-ridden TV comedy show *Cheers*), suggests a sort of sanctuary from the depressing, harsh reality of a world on the streets where drug abuse and teenage pregnancy are commonplace, an aspect of the song that is musically represented by a persistant trip-hop rhythm and disturbing voice effect.

By the time of the second Eels album, E had had to face the end stages of his mother's cancer and his sister's suicide, leaving him with no immediate family. It gave *Electro-Shock Blues* a darker feel as he worked out his loss through the creation of appropriate songs. The album begins with the direct and specifically detailed 'Elizabeth On The Bathroom Floor', 'my name is Elizabeth, my life is shit and piss', and soon moves to 'Cancer For The Cure', preceded by an ominous soundscape of percussion and ghostly electronics which run as a motif through a relentless keyboard-driven rocker that hinges on the chorus, 'cancer for the cure, buckle up and endure now baby'. A gravestone pictured inside the CD libretto bears the legend 'sing along at home' but the cathartic nature of the album is confirmed by a later gravestone that announces 'everything is changing'. *Electro-Shock Blues* is not a depressing album.

On *Daisies Of The Galaxy*, which followed in 2000, the lyrics are even quite cheering. The album opens with 'Grace Kelly Blues', which sees E run through a series of scenarios, ending with the observation that in comparison 'me, I'm feeling pretty good as of now'. The black humour and juxtaposition of meaning is there in 'Its a Motherfucker', a pretty song with an ugly title, and there's the irony-laden 'Mr E's Beautiful Blues', in demand by a slew of advertising agencies, keen to appropriate the song's feel-good factor. Mr E, of course, will have none of it. Oddly, the track, easily Eels' biggest single, is not even credited on the album cover and is added as a hidden track, which any major record-label employee will tell you is no way to market a product. Mind you, George W. Bush ensured that the collection got its fair share of promotion when he objected strongly to the title of the track 'It's A Motherfucker' on the back cover, arguing that the album's artwork, in the style of a child's storybook was an attempt to somehow indoctrinate America's youth. It makes you shudder, doesn't it?

What Bush 'thought' of an album released on the 24 September 2001 called *Souljacker* featuring E on the front dressed like the Unabomber, well that's not a matter of public record. *Shootenanny* pursues the theme of societal decline too, with its central theme of state-encouraged violence. According to E, 'it's only a matter of time before we need some MTV-style street catch phrase for "shooting spree". I thought I should be the one to coin the term. It's a hip, "edgy" catch phrase for something so serious and so ugly and so likely to happen at any moment, to me, it kind of sums up the times that we live in.' Eels' irony is not for the easily offended.

First team: E (v, g, k, b, d, samp), Butch (d, v), Ryan Bosech (prog)

Place, time, scene: LA 1992. Eels have their roots in the sampler-led lo-fi 'scene' of the early nineties. By the time of *Beautiful Freak* E had a more cohesive sound to go with his dark lyrics, and he has continued to write about difficult subjects, often ironically. As a result he seems to have been more successful in the UK than the US.

What to buy first: *Electro-Shock Blues* 1998

And then: *Beautiful Freak* 1996, *Daisies Of The Galaxy* 1999

EINSTÜRZENDE NEUBAUTEN

'I was making my way down the stairs when an eerie hypnotic sound came floating from the TV room, insidiously seductive, irresistibly sad ... as I stepped into the room all the notions of music that I held so dear were obliterated – in toto – by what I saw upon the screen'[26]

So writes the ever poetic Nick Cave describing his first encounter with Einstürzende Neubauten on Dutch TV. It was, it seems, enough to make him reconsider his position in the Birthday Party and set in train the formation of the Bad Seeds, in which guitarist Blixa Bargeld would be his chief-lieutenant, the man who he describes later in the same piece of prose as 'the most beautiful man in the world'.

'Einstürzende Neubauten' is German for 'Collapsing New Buildings', an apt name for a band that specializes in using the arts of noise to give voice to their musical soul. Half a decade after Italian futurist Luigi Russolo had first confused and angered audiences with his noise montages created out of motorized sound and 'noise intoners', inspiring avant-garde classical musicians like John Cage and Lamont Young, Einstürzende Neubauten applied the same practice to rock music. And yes, they did start as a rock band, not as pretentious artists looking for a gimmick.

Having grown up skint and squatting in West Berlin, 'a utopia for unusual young people', Einstürzende Neubauten were never far above the breadline, and it was poverty that inspired a change of fortune. Drummer Endruh Unruh was forced to sell his kit for food, but invention being the child of necessity, he collected together metal tools to hit instead: mallets, saws, screws, corrugated sheet-metal, anything that could keep a rhythm. Alexander von Borsig followed suit with a selection of drainpipes, 'The Thirsty Animal' became his favourite, and Blixa Bargeld played guitar. Well after a fashion – he preferred to coax noises out of it with very little concern for traditional musical practice.

Over the years, the sound that Einstürzende Neubauten make has become more sophisticated, not because they have shifted emphasis towards traditional instrumentation, but because they have developed a unique knowledge and understanding of how the performance and recording of noise, whether emanating from a carefully tuned and played guitar or a 'dog rooting around in a steaming pile of pig guts', can mess with the listener's normal perception of sound. Or as Bargeld explains it 'how it is within us to hear music in things that have no musical intentions whatsoever.'[27]

Their early concerts received media attention due to the band's tendency to destroy instruments and, going a stage further than Hendrix and the Who, that too. The band's first full-length album was called *Kollaps* released in 1981 and there has been an album approximately every two years since. The band has played site-specific events all over the world, from the ICA in London to the Mojave desert, and have contributed sounds to various visual mediums including several films. The focus of the early albums is on percussion and the undermining of accepted rhythmic practice, although Bargeld's voice is a thing to behold as well, a series of screams and whispers that defy traditional understanding of scales and harmony, often used as another form of percussion, as on the track 'Negativ Nein'. *Zeichnungen des Patienten O.T.* (*Drawings Of Patient O.T.*) is inspired by an artist committed to a Swiss psychiatric hospital, the perfect muse for an album which is an assault on the senses, quickly changing mood and pace without warning; it is the band's most hardcore punk record, although there are no buzzsaw guitars, just buzz-saws.

By 1989's *Haus Der Lüge* the band, perhaps influenced by Bargeld's work with Nick Cave, Mick Harvey and Barry Adamson, had begun to use the technological subtleties available in the recording studio to strike a balance between noise and melody, and the placement of sounds in the overall mix. 'Fiat Lux' is split into several sections, but starts with the sound of insects buzzing while a cacophony of destruction is played out at a lower volume underneath. In 1991 Einstürzende Neubauten experimented with motorized playing of guitars and gongs, and incorporated electronic frequency interference as a new texture, most recently using the interference caused by mobile phones on *Silence Is Sexy* in 2000.

Einstürzende Neubauten, along with Throbbing Gristle, remain an inspiration to industrial noise bands, and the two blokes discussed below – Alec Empire and Brian Eno – probably own a few albums too. U2 even cited the band as an influence on their *Achtung Baby!* album. In recent years their experimentation has supported more song-based work, notably tracks like 'Blume' on *Tabula Rasa*, their 1992 'blank sheet' album, and 'Redukt' on *Silence Is Sexy*. But it's a testament to the band's deftness of experimental touch that the really odd stuff is not always obviously apparent. The important thing is that it's there and that you sense it's there. Alternative working practice, alternative sounds and squarely aimed at a set of fans defined neither commercially nor as self-consciously arty. Einstürzende Neubauten meet all the criteria set out in the introduction to this book.

First team: Blixa Bargeld (g, v), Endruh Unruh (perc), Alexander von Borsig (pipes)

Place, time, scene: Berlin 1980. Einstürzende Neubauten are originators of industrial music, becoming interested in the sounds that could be made after starting as a rock band. Bargeld's guitar ensures that the band retain a connection with rock music, and as a result they have influenced other like-minded artists including Trent Reznor of Nine Inch Nails.

What to buy first: *Kollaps* 1981

And then: *Zeichungen Des Patienten O.T.* 1983, *Haus Der Lüge* 1989, *Tabula Rasa* 1992

In retrospect: *Strategies Against Architecture I* 1984, *Strategies Against Architecture II* 1991, *Strategies Against Architecture III* 2001

ALEC EMPIRE

Alec Empire's theory for why Berlin was the key German city as far as youth culture and music was concerned throughout the sixties, seventies and eighties is that it was a truly international city, home to British, American and French soldiers who were there to keep order, and a mecca for artists and musicians, notably David Bowie, who wanted that war-torn and post-apocalyptic feel in their work. When Empire was in his teens, he fell for hardcore punk and by the mid-eighties was a convert to the techno music coming out of Detroit, quickly setting himself up as a DJ, dominating the crossfader at the numerous disused warehouse parties that kicked off in West Berlin, a city of numerous disused warehouses. But then in 1989 it all went wrong. Some clever dick went and tore down the Berlin Wall. Raves lost their edge, no longer a sign of resistance, just happy hedonism, and as far as Empire was concerned a sinister new German culture emerged out of the reunification. It inspired him to act.

Together with Hanin Elias and Carl Crack, he formed Atari Teenage Riot in 1992 and set about a sound clash of hardcore and techno which he dubbed digital hardcore. The idea was simple and it could be argued that Empire just got there first. Certainly the Prodigy, who did the same thing five years later, have had more commercial and critical success, but to write off Atari Teenage Riot as one-trick ponies is to ignore the sound they make, which is not allowed – in this book at any rate. Atari Teenage Riot aren't just about the beats and the attitude, it's far more subtle than that. On *Burn Berlin Burn* here is a commitment to the possibilities of noise that has led the band and Empire in particular, to 'subvert' existing digital technology by running everything created on computer through analogue recorders to ensure that the bass retains its low end frequencies and the guitars don't get compressed and sweetened in the mixdown. Empire's latest collaborator is Japanese musician and IT expert Nic Endo, who has further strategies for keeping the noise and textures at optimum shock levels. In fact Empire, who disbanded Atari Teenage Riot in 2000 due to the continuing illness and eventual death of Carl Crack, has moved away from techno entirely of late, preferring to explore the potential of noise when crossed with metal. Members of Nine Inch Nails and the Japanese avant-garde noise artist Merzbow have both assisted him on his latest work.

Atari Teenage Riot and Empire have also focused on alerting those in the nascent German democracy to the issues arising from their new situation. The band's second album *The Future Of War* contains a set of songs that 'warn of a Germany that strategically ignores its own hostility towards foreigners (as well as the inherent anti-Semitism and racism) because of its over-ambitious national pride, and therefore tolerates the crimes and violence committed by the extreme right and neo-nazis'.[28] 'Deutschland (Has Got To Die)' sums up the central message and is probably the reason why the album was blacklisted in Germany. But Alec Empire is interested in defeating apathy the world over, and he's still out there doing it, providing a service.

'We see our music as functional music, not as pop music; it's music that's there to make you feel aggressive, to push the adrenaline in your body, and get this vibe across. Most of the music on MTV or the radio stations or whatever is just there to calm people down. And with the way we program the beats and use certain frequencies, it has this effect on your adrenaline. That's very important.'[29]

First team: Alec Empire (prog, v), Carl Crack (v), Hanin Elias (v)

Place, time, scene: Berlin 1992. Alec Empire is the inventor of digital hardcore techno music, drawing on his background as a DJ and before that a politically-motivated punk. He is the man responsible for techno beats crossing over into rock. The Prodigy have incorporated his sound and reinvented a whole new career for themselves. It has seeped into metal too, but without the crucial political dimension that gives the thrash sound its full meaning

What to buy first: *Burn Berlin Burn* 1997

And then: *The Future Of War* 1997

BRIAN ENO

'The manipulative thing I think is the American ideal that here's nature, and you somehow subdue and control it and turn it to your own ends. I get steadily more interested in the idea that here's nature, the fabric of things or the ongoing current or whatever, and what you can do is just ride on that system, and the amount of interference you need to make can sometimes be very small.'[30]

Brian Eno does not write music, he just sets up the possibilities for music to be made, and it's why he's such a good producer. Whether it's working with U2, Talking Heads, John Cale, David Bowie, Television or a whole string of independently 'no wave' bands he's effectively done the same thing, and that's to help them understand the noise they make relative to other possibilities. It helps to know an instrument intimately, to be aware of what sound can be made, but there are so many other options as well. And Eno's trump card is always that he has the uber-instrument at his disposal, the instrument that determines all others: the recording studio. To that end, on his own records, Eno is as happy to use players who, like him, have no dextrous ability with an instrument, and place them in the same mix as those, like his regular collaborator Robert Fripp, who are acknowledged to be at the top of their profession. Not that Eno has any specific musical agenda when he is working. He doesn't have a list of computerized settings that he can refer to that he knows will elicit a certain sound, and he has always maintained that he keeps no notes based on what he has done before. Sounds are manipulated, processed and messed about with until something interesting emerges. That's what he claims anyway.

There are three distinct phases to Brian Eno's own musical career. He began in Roxy Music, joining accidentally having come along to a band practice session with his friend Andy Mackay and impressing all present with his apparent mastery of Mackay's synthesizer. His skill was in coaxing interesting noises from the machine and especially, as evidenced on their second album, *For Your Pleasure*, encouraging the rest of the band to play and create more spontaneously. During this period he began referring to himself as a non-musician, a claim he continues to make today. Unfortunately, as Bryan Ferry succinctly put it, 'there's not enough room for two non-musicians in one group'. Eno left, taking most of the band's spirit of adventure with him.

The second phase of Eno was a continuation of what he achieved on *For Your Pleasure*, and is spread across four albums that effectively demonstrate the new creative potential of studio technology. Of course, such potential was wasted on musicians who lacked interesting creative ideas, and not forthcoming for artists who may have wanted to work innovatively but were let down by formally-trained studio engineers and producers who viewed technology as primarily a labour-saving device. But hey, it wasn't the 1980s yet! Eno's first solo album, *Here Come The Warm Jets*, was released in 1973 and featured contributions from Mackay, Paul Thompson and Phil Manzanera, his chums from Roxy Music, alongside arch-modernist Robert Fripp from King Crimson and proto-punk motorbikin' man Chris Spedding.

'Cindy Tells Me' is an homage to the man who first showed the way to studio nirvana, Phil Spector; 'Needles In The Camel's Eyes' is glam-punk, which is ... let me check ... a-ha yes, before the New York Dolls; and 'Baby's On Fire', well that's just the weirdest of the weird. Eno has explained that he writes his lyrics after the basic track, with all of its textures and rhythms, has been completed, giving him an opportunity to come up with words that fit the mood. Hence, the 'eye' sound in 'fire' is suggested because it is a thin, sharp sound in keeping with the guitar-onics of the overall track. There's no point analysing the lyrics directly therefore, although any psychologist worth their salt must surely be keen to discuss a lyric like 'Father we make claims on our knees, leave us alone we've nothin to pee'. Mind you that may not be the actual lyric from *Here Come The Warm Jets*, as it seems that Eno might have recorded several sets of different lyrics and superimposed them, the trickster.

Taking Tiger Mountain (By Strategy) is Eno's best album. Again, featuring the same list of players, but with Phil Collins also in on the act, it's a perfect marriage of previously unheard sounds and arrangements with, on the surface, traditional pop/rock motifs. It's very easy to sing-a-long to 'Mother Whale Eyeless', or play air-guitar to 'Third Uncle', although the real joy of listening to the album is in the details. There's the synthesized vocals on 'The Great Pretender' and the odd-sounding piano in 'Fat Lady Of Limbourg'. He also manages to coax a consistent and enjoyable sound out of the Portsmouth Sinfonia, a group like himself (allegedly) devoid of any traditional musical ability, on 'Put A Straw Under Baby'.

Another Green World marks the beginning of his more avant-garde ambient work. Nine out of the 14 tracks are instrumentals conceived as soundtracks to imaginary films, and in his own words, 'less personality-based, more evocative of times or places'. The contributions of John Cale, Phil Collins and of course, Robert Fripp, who were all instructed to play, for want of a better word, unusually, makes for the definitive collaboration of musical expertise and technology. As a collection of ambient pieces, it points the way towards his later albums like *Music For Airports* which was designed specifically to be played in an airport. Music for living, functional and designed to fit into a specific space or time. It was consistent with Eno's evolving interest in a natural and minimal approach to music-making, but his musical voice only really remains in the form of the idea. Although his ambient work may still be concerned with music that addresses the listener directly without being filtered through the institutional expectations of the self-consciously creative art world or its apparent antithesis, the niche targeted market, from this point on Eno became musically anonymous, effectively severing the link that connected him to his audience. He became an artist-auteur working independently of popular music.

Brian Eno is a clever man. His early albums proved that he was an independently-minded clever man, and that's a fiendish combination.

Place, time, scene: London 1973. With Roxy Music he was able to encourage spontaneous playing styles that inspired many post-punk bands, and indeed Eno's claim to be a non-musician was an early defence of punk and hip-hop forms before they even existed. If he is not considered a musician and yet is responsible for some of the most fascinating music of the last century, then being a musician isn't really relevant when it comes to making fascinating music. His expertise with a recording studio is legendary although it's his production ideas that have influenced so many artists since, notably David Bowie, Talking Heads and U2.

What to buy first: *Here Come The Warm Jets* 1973

And then: Roxy Music: *For Your Pleasure* 1973, *Taking Tiger Mountain (By Strategy)* 1974, *Another Green World* 1975

F

THE FALL

Mark F. Smith was always concerned with self-sufficiency in the early days of the Fall. He wanted his band to exist outside the traditional bounds of the music industry, 'we don't dig promoters, backhanders, publicity (bought that is), backers, agents etc'[31], and that included what he perceived to be a quickly evolving official alternative music industry that thrived on middle-class notions of liberalism and political correctness. This was confirmed by the Fall's time on the Rough Trade label where they were thankful for the independent practice of getting maximum royalties to the artist, but resented input into the creative process. 'They had a whole meeting over the fact that we mentioned guns in one song. Y'know ... it is not the policy of Rough Trade to be supporting fuckin' ... And I'd go, What the fuck has it got to do with you? Just fuckin' sell the record you fuckin' hippy.'[32] That was how Smith saw it anyway. If there's one thing that has become apparent over the years, it's that no-one messes with the music. Not even the audience. The Fall make music for themselves, or more accurately, of themselves. If anything, the audience is encouraged to interpret or come up with their own understanding of what the band is about. The Fall have never been about making things easy. There have been moments when the band has ventured towards commerciality or art, but never to the detriment of their central sound and identity, which is as clear and focused as it ever has been, and that's after 26 years and 32 albums. The glue that holds it all together is Mark E. Smith himself, the only remaining original member, who over the course of 21 different band line-ups has managed, as a non-musician, to convey his musical requirements without ever losing control of the band.

The Fall were formed in 1977 in Manchester as part of a scene that included the Buzzcocks, the Prefects and the Worst. Consisting of Smith, guitarist Martin Bramah, keyboardist Una Baines, bassist Tony Friel and drummer Karl Burns, the Fall's sporadic early gigs introduced audiences to a new form of 'ordinary' performance. The look was the same onstage as it was off-stage, and the songs were straightforward narratives that told it like it was, or at least how Smith saw it, without any attempt to offer a solution or suggestion for change. More Pistols than Clash, but without the showbiz. Critics called it empty and negative, Smith considered it pure and free from pretension and posturing. Musically, it recalled the Velvet Underground and the Doors, mainly due to Baines' electric piano sound, but a track on the first EP called 'Repetition' also emphasized the band's regard for German group Can, due to its sheer, well, repetition. 'The Three R's ... Repetition ... Repetition . Repetition. All has been forgotten as repetition is forbidden.' Of all these early styles, it is the influence of Can in particular that resounds throughout the Fall's extensive back-catalogue.

When the first line-up fell apart later that year, Smith and Bramah were able to develop their sound with the addition of new members who could be trained in the Fall style. Mark Reilly and Yvonne Pawlett were both barely out of school when they joined, and Reilly in particular found himself re-learning bass before progressing to guitar, schooled by Smith as if he were a member of Captain Beefheart's Magic Band. Smith has said on more than one occasion that he doesn't encourage his band to practice, adding 'It's not good for them'. The first album *Live At The Witch Trials* is not a particularly inspiring musical collection, with only Bramah's guitar-work really standing out alongside Smith's striking monotone, barking vocals, but the lyrics and the attitude make up for any musical shortcomings. As expected, there are songs that attack the music industry and the fashion scene, but there's also tracks like 'Frightened' which give Ian Curtis a run for his money in the angst stakes 'I don't wanna dance I wanna go home. I'm frightened.' Of course, the difference between the Fall and Joy Division came down to spontaneity. The debut album was recorded in a day, and the sense of immediacy has always been a trademark of the band's albums since.

With the addition of Craig Scanlon and Stephen Hanley for the second album *Dragnet* in 1979, the Fall became a much tighter musical unit, and for a while played with two drummers, following in the footsteps of their krautrock heroes with odd rhythms and unexpected tunings. Smith's lyrics became more obscure too, in keeping with his developing vocal style that, like the guitars, could be de-tuned for effect.

The next album, *Hex Enduction Hour* is a weird one. The first album released after the band left Rough Trade, it is a real band effort; Smith's words (of which there are many) are buried in the cacophony. 'And This Day', the ten-minuter that ends the album is a randomly edited jam, the ultimate punk take on Czukay's work in Can. Some loved it, some hated it and some thought that they'd better get over to the UK, marry the miserable bastard and make a few changes.

As Brix, the former Mrs Mark Smith, has explained 'The words really infuriated me because I didn't understand them at all. In fact, the first thing I ever said to Mark was, "That gig was the best I've ever seen, but those words . . . they infuriate me so much!!" '

The influence of Brix Smith on the five albums recorded between 1985 and 1988 is in the shading, bringing in an indefinable lightness of mood on *The Wonderful And Frightening World Of . . .*, *This Nation's Saving Grace*, *Bend Sinister*, *The Frenz Experiment* and *I Am Kurious Oranj*. Die-hard fans were concerned that she was taking over. And maybe she was, but with Smith's full consent. *The Wonderful And Frightening World Of . . .* is a much more diverse set of songs than anything else they had done previously, different moods and textures and ending with 'Disney's Dream Debased', a harrowing true story of the Smiths' visit to Disneyland during which they witnessed a tragic accident on a ride that ended in a woman's decapitation.

This Nation's Saving Grace might be the band's best album, certainly their most accessible due to the debut of melody into proceedings. The production is better too, giving tracks like 'Bombast' and 'Spoilt Victorian Child' an extra punch. *Bend Sinister*, like its predecessor, is varied but spontaneous, and *The Frenz Experiment* puts together good production and minimalist textures to produce the perfect setting for Smith's

incanted lines and phrases repeated over and over, but each time voiced differently so that the experience of listening remains compulsive. On it, the Fall update the Kinks' 'Victoria' and R. Dean Taylor's 'There's A Ghost In My House', extracting any organic warmth that the originals might have had, and making them 'shrill and fuzzy'. The centrepiece of the album is 'Bremen Nacht', a ten minute terror-blues workout that was also used in the staged ballet entitled *I Am Kurious Oranj* the following year. The central themes of social mediocrity, brought on by the McDonaldization of contemporary life, are played out in music and dance, while the Fall performed stage-left on a large Big Mac. The accompanying album has Smith at his sneering best on the band's take on Blake's 'Jerusalem', while the title track is a trance-inducing hypnotic swirl that Spacemen 3 would be proud of.

Brix' departure and liaison with Nigel Kennedy (!) resulted in Fall mark four, and coincided with the rise of Madchester to national prominence; 'Idiot groups with no shape or form' he scolded.

It's the same age-old problem that he's been banging on about for years and as far as Smith sees it, it's not getting any better. Music, fashion and cool. The Clash, the Pistols, Joy Division, the Bunnymen, the Mary Chain, the Smiths, the Roses, Mark E. Smith has slagged them all off. In fact, he has on more than one occasion slagged off his own band. He's not that keen on *Bend Sinister* for example, which a lot of Fall fans rate as one of their best albums. He's a card, that Mark E. Smith.

The thing is, he's bloody clever with it. Ignore the words for a moment and listen to the music. Throughout the band's entire career it has been the crucial thing. Smith was the guitarist in his first band, the Outsiders, and although he never got beyond the basic understanding that it made a noise, it didn't matter because that was all he needed to know. Since then he has used his voice, and chosen his band-mates to create the ultimate rock'n'roll sound. It's a mix of fifties rock'n'roll, especially the guitar sounds (rockabilly and surf guitar), with the studio-based work of his heroes Can and Neu!. It's raw and it's intellectual, and it gets better with every release. The turn of the millennium albums, *The Light User Syndrome*, *Levitate* and *The Marshall Suite* explain it better than anyone could in words. Get them and listen!

First team: Mark E. Smith (v, g, k), Craig Scanlon (g), Stephen Hanley (b), Brix Smith (g, v), Paul Hanley (d). Honourable mentions: Una Baines (k), Tony Friel (b), Martin Bramah (g), Karl Burns (d), Mark Reilly (g, b), Marcia Schofield (k), Julia Nagle (g, k, prog)

Place, time, scene: Salford 1977. The Fall based their own part in the post-punk revolution in music on the most dynamic musical styles of the previous decades, blues, rockabilly, garage rock, psychedelia and the progressive techniques of the German bands Can and Neu!. Mark E. Smith has retained ultimate control for the most part and it is his vision that has driven the sound of the band throughout.

What to buy first: *This Nation's Saving Grace* 1985

And then: *Dragnet* 1979, *Hex Enduction Hour* 1982, *The Frenz Experiment* 1988, *I Am Kurious Oranj* 1988, *Shift-Work* 1991, *Levitate* 1997

In retrospect: *In Palace Of Swords Reversed* 1987, *458489 A Sides* 1990

FLAMING LIPS

'I can see where people get those Brian Wilson comparisons, you know, the nuts loose in the studio doing crazy things. But then the rational side of us kicks in, because we don't actually want to be like Brian Wilson. I don't mean that in a bad way. I want to get this perspective of, is this music actually entertaining people? I don't make music because I have some message to tell the world. I am making music for the reason I listen to music: I want something pleasant to listen to while I'm driving to work. I don't need my fuckin' life changed by some retard. In the end, that's what I want our records to represent. I'm all for weirdness and eccentricity, but I also want people to listen to it with some urgency.'[33]

That's right, there's no escaping the fact that the Flaming Lips consciously set out to make 'pleasant' music that helps people get through their busy and sometimes difficult lives. It's a strategy that fits nicely with the aims of their multi-national corporate label too. In fact, Warner Brothers seem to have chucked money at the Flaming Lips since the 1993 success of the single 'She Don't Use Jelly'. So what the hell are they doing in this book? Their working practice is time-consuming and fractured – an original idea mutates into something quite different after days, maybe weeks of working in the studio. They ditch songs that may cause offence. And worst of all, when Nirvana and their Seattle cousins were keeping it real, dark and well, grungy, the Flaming Lips were making a guest appearance on that paean to shallow capitalist ideology, *Beverley Hills 90210*. Your honour, the Flaming Lips are quite clearly the mainstream. I move that we waste no more of the court's valuable time. But whoa, whoa, whoa, listen to the music. The Flaming Lips are out there.

OK so they've had all the breaks, but let's examine what they've achieved. The money's been well spent on a series of albums that defy generic categorization where even the individual songs stand apart from each other. Wayne Coyne, the group's leader since their inception in 1983, has explained that since multi-instrumentalist and drummer extraordinaire Steven Drozd joined the band in 1992 the process of recording has focused on building songs in the studio, importantly completing one song before moving onto the next one. The Flaming Lips don't go in and lay down drum parts, bass parts etc for lots of songs at once, they approach each song differently. And then, when they go back to a song recorded earlier, they can listen to it objectively 'like it's by another band' and then make any alterations. It's an expensive craft industry, and it's an approach that has influenced the likes of Mercury Rev and Grandaddy to name but two. Wayne Coyne's fragile, high pitched Youngian voice has carried over to both Jonathan Donahue and Jason Lytle too, and adds a dreamy, childlike quality to Flaming Lips' songs that are already fantasy constructions.

Jonathan Donahue was once a member, having joined the Oklahoma based band for their 1990 album *In A Priest Driven Ambulance*. It was the band's fifth, and best attempt at nouveau-psychedelia. Swirling layers of guitar wrapped around songs with daft titles and humorous lyrics, that sneak up on you when you're not expecting it, and get you thinking, or perhaps even smiling at the wonder of it all. There are songs about babies raining down from heaven, and on the next album a similar idea but this time with frogs. It's most likely a biblical reference; there are a lot of Jesus mentions scattered throughout the Flaming Lips' back-catalogue, and occasionally Coyne gets direct: 'Do you realize that everyone, some day, will die?' The odd thing is that it never feels dark or foreboding, Coyne's voice is just too sweet. On *In A Priest Driven Ambulance* there's a cover of Louis Armstrong's 'What A Wonderful World', supposedly laden with irony, but as Coyne himself has admitted, it just sounds too damned positive. The 1993 album *Transmissions From The Satellite Heart* is the first to feature guitarist Ronald Jones and drummer Steven Drozd. It's got the jolly jelly single on it and is crammed full of melody and hooks from start to finish with feedback and distortion deployed carefully throughout.

The follow-up *Clouds Taste Metallic* has Drozd sharing most of the music composition with Coyne, and thanks to production from Dave Fridmann, occasional member of Mercury Rev, it is the first album to really explore the sectionalising and dynamic possibilities of the band's songs. 'The Abandoned Hospital Ship' which opens the album features a lonely Eddie Hazel-inspired guitar interlude by Jones that explodes into a musical sequence that calls to mind the passing of a bizarre magical carnival parade containing fractured guitar and bells, driven on by Drozd's big-beat drumming. 'This Here Giraffe' seems to be the sound of guitarists, bassist and drummer playing with no real knowledge of what the other is doing, only meeting up at pre-established points when Coyne sings 'And you hear yourself swimming'. And as for 'Bad Days', well that's just the most life-affirming song yet written that advocates shooting people to get that warm fuzzy feeling. Schizophrenia can be fun.

Zaireeka, a four CD set released in 1998, exemplifies the band's desire to get the full extent of their sound out to the audience. The same tracks are on each CD, but mixed differently so that when played together,

The Flaming Lips

the music overcomes the limitations of a single CD. It's the same kind of thinking that has led to the band giving out headphones to audience members at gigs, patched directly into the mixing desk, an attempt to overcome the limitations of the venue and its acoustics. Coyne has also attempted a 'car stereo symphony' where 20 or so cars are parked up in such a way that cassettes of different sounds can be played out simultaneously. Loopy.

The albums *The Soft Bulletin* and *Yoshimi Battles The Pink Robots* have brought the Flaming Lips to an international audience, and are so chock-full of good songs that the wibbly production techniques and odd song structures are easily assimilated by a more mainstream audience. Even British radio stations, notorious for their cautious approach to programming, have begun playing the band's singles, 'Do You Realize??' in particular, with its overt reference to the inevitability of death for everyone, has picked up extensive daytime play on the country's easiest-listening station Radio 2. The Flaming Lips are subverting the accepted rules of subject matter and musical accessibility now, as you read this, and they're doing it with a smile and a stack of corporate dosh. If this is what the fall of independent rock sounds like then it's just possible that everything's going to be alright.

First team: Wayne Coyne (v, g), Michael Ivins (b), Steven Drozd (d), Ronald Jones (g)

Place, time, scene: Oklahoma 1984. The Flaming Lips picked up a major label deal with Warner in 1992 after the breakthrough of Nirvana the year before. A new opportunity beckoned for underground music to get promoted to a larger audience and Flaming Lips were at the forefront. They soon had a hit with 'She Don't Use Jelly' and for the next few years were ever present on college radio with a quirky sense of fun that was not as bitingly satirical as Pavement. Their focus on studio technique distinguishes them from lo-fi bands to some extent, but they do retain a wobbly, loose sound that seems to appeal to an ever widening audience.

What to buy first: *The Soft Bulletin* 1999

And then: *Transmissions From The Satellite Heart* 1993, *Clouds Taste Metallic* 1995, *Yoshimi Battles The Pink Robots* 2002

FUGAZI

The way that Ian MacKaye of Fugazi tells it, his aim has always been to document music, his own and that of others. The only criterion of value as far as he is concerned is that it is music that communicates contemporary experience without getting caught up in ambitions of commercial or artistic success. I'd like to think that he'd approve of the artists included in this book. He has been independent since the start, setting up his own Dischord label to put out records by his band Minor Threat, a band that came complete with their own philosophy – 'straight edge'. His most recent band, Fugazi, retains the independent ethic, and the blasts of emotion that made up the short hardcore songs of Minor Threat are still there in Fugazi, except there tends to be several different types of blast in one song. Now that he has his audience's attention, MacKaye, along with his co-writer Guy Picciotto, can explore the combination of sound and message in more complex ways.

MacKaye formed his first band in the summer of 1979 following an inspirational show by the Cramps. Called the Teen Idles, they were playing Madam's Organ in Washington DC with Bad Brains within the year. By December 1980, almost a year to the day after the Teen Idles played their first show, MacKaye formed Minor Threat and in order to distribute their own records, the Dischord label. A series of 7" singles capturing the cream of the DC hardcore scene on record followed and Minor Threat, MacKaye in particular, along with Black Flag and the Dead Kennedys, became a key musical and cultural part of a new musical American independence, the significance of which is still evident today.

Where Black Flag toured relentlessly across the US, inspiring scenes wherever they went, and the Dead Kennedys took on the establishment and state government, Minor Threat kept their hardcore message more parochial and specific. Minor Threat were 'straight-edge'. They didn't do drugs, drink alcohol, eat meat or engage in meaningless sex. The song 'Straight Edge' was 45 seconds long, a blast of pure energy best experienced while jumping up and down erratically in a sweat-drenched mosh-pit. The first few singles were typically speedy, driven on by Jeff Nelson's drumming (try tapping a pencil faster), but the band's only album proper, *Out Of Step*, which contained just eight songs, took hardcore in a different direction, two guitars, a few more chords and even a string section at the end of the album. When Minor Threat split, MacKaye's next band Embrace experimented further with the possibilities of the hardcore sound, but it's Fugazi that nailed it.

A few gigs with Rites Of Spring in 1985 led to a deal with Dischord to put out their album *End On End*, and convinced MacKaye that their 'emo-core' style was what he was striving to achieve in Embrace. A new approach where guitars got more angular and choppy and the drums adopted different patterns, stopping and starting to create different sections and moods within individual songs. Over the top, vocals were raw and emotional, and rather than dealing with societal and political issues directly, songwriter Guy Picciotto's lyrics were more personal, sometimes so inward-looking and buried in the mix that only the voice offered any clue as to what he was feeling. Together with Picciotto and drummer Brendan Canty from Rites Of Spring, MacKaye formed Fugazi in 1988 and, in keeping with Dischord philosophy of old, ensured that the emphasis was placed on playing live, charging just enough on the door to match overheads and take a wage. The first two EPs were put together on an album called simply *13 Songs*, followed in 1990 by the band's definitive collection, *Repeater*, the ultimate mix of ethics and honesty set to a lean, well-practised and organized backing track.

Fugazi are one of the tightest bands in rock history. It goes with the territory. There's no room for self-indulgence on a tight budget, and that goes for the music too. The title track on *Repeater* is definitive. Complex and constantly changing bass and drum parts, innovatively-played guitar, sometimes angry, sometimes pretty, and dual shouted vocals, demanding '1,2,3. Repeater', all combine to produce a track which hits the ear like a gust of fresh air, clean and crisp. It's all the best bits of punk but controlled and focused – the opposite of Black Flag's loose rocking during the mid-eighties.

Lyrically it remains timeless. MacKaye and Picciotto deal with the big issues in local contexts, a style of writing that is perfected on the follow-up album *Steady Diet Of Nothing* the following year. The first

song is a haiku, opening with the word 'Exeunt', and there are songs addressing issues of broken family relationships, body fascism and ideologically unsound media. 'Polish' is typical of the approach, setting the tale of television escapism in the reflective thoughts of a person polishing their television screen. 'Language keeps me locked and repeating' goes the line in 'Stacks', and it might as well be a statement of intent; to escape from such confines. Musically, *Steady Diet* is a leap into the realms of Sonic Youth-style experimentation. The consistency and repetitiveness of hardcore is still there as a base but the songs are anything but linear; sounds fly off in all directions and, like Sonic Youth at their best, the music is never really resolved. Dissonance is the key word, notes left hanging, musical passages not completed and the whole lot often disappearing into loud musical soups of noise. An unenlightened musicologist would probably call the whole thing 'wrong'.

Albums like *Red Medicine* and *End Hits* are the sound of Fugazi perfecting their sectionalized hardcore blasts, mixed with everything from reggae to rockabilly, often on the same track. They are albums that, together with cheap all-age shows, have influenced a new generation of emo bands, notably At The Drive-In and their various spin-off projects. Fugazi are still an important band. They are still the same band, same four members, and their aims are still the same too. They still call the shots, musically and in terms of working practice, and that means they are free to create whatever they want regardless of fashion and commercial imperative. They are required listening for any new band interested in being a . . . band.

First team: Ian MacKaye (v, g), Guy Picciotto (v, g), Joe Lally (b), Brendan Canty (d)

Place, time, scene: Washington DC 1988. Having been a key player in the hardcore scene with the Dischord label and the band Minor Threat, MacKaye has worked with Picciotto and Fugazi to retain the energy and sound of hardcore within a new setting. Dubbed emo, their music is characterized by fits and starts, passionately delivered vocals and sonic elements of hardcore and noise. At The Drive-In and Drive Like Jehu are two of the bands inspired by the approach.

What to buy first: *Repeater* 1990

And then: Rites Of Spring: *End On End* 1985, Fugazi: *Steady Diet Of Nothing* 1991, *End Hits* 1998

In retrospect: Minor Threat: *Complete Discography* 1988

FUGS

Some say that the Fugs were the first punk band. Formed in 1964 by a bunch of proto-hippies who could not play a note, they decided that they were not going to bother practising to get good. It wasn't necessary. As far as they were concerned, the message was the medium, and it had to be told straight up.

Ed Sanders had done time in prison in 1961 for boarding a Polaris missile submarine, and had used his time to focus his poetry writing. When he got out he moved to New York and set up a publication called *Fuck You – A Magazine Of The Arts*, and through it met fellow poet and publisher Tuli Kupferberg. With Sanders on toy piano, Ken Weaver on cardboard boxes and Tuli singing, they formed the Fugs in 1964. Inspired in equal parts by the new folk of Bob Dylan and Phil Ochs, and the 'Happening' culture which made art out of the mundane, they used the band as a setting for their poetry.

Bolstered by the members of folk band, the Holy Modal Rounders, the Fugs played around the lower east side of New York and secured a residency at The Dom, a dive-bar underneath the famed Electric Circus club which was a meeting place for boho artists and socialites alike.[34] Andy Warhol took it over in 1965 as the setting for his Exploding Plastic Inevitable nights that would later feature the Velvet Underground. At the Dom the Fugs played their satirical, anti-war songs, mixed in with sarcastic digs at current pop music, commercial culture and artists who took themselves too seriously. The lyrical content bordered on the obscene at times, and their tendency to play songs called 'River Of Shit', 'Bull Tongue Clit' and 'Coca-Cola Douche', before physically performing 'The Turkey Gobble', made sure that they remained a cult attraction.

The band recorded two albums for the specialist jazz label ESP but had one set rejected due to apparent obscenity concerns. Atlantic Records offered them a deal in 1967 but cancelled it when they heard the material. Those first albums were made up of initial sessions, recorded by legendary folk-music archivist Harry Smith, with Peter Stampfel and Steve Weber providing most of the musical input. The problematic second album was eventually released as *Virgin Fugs* in 1968. Alongside Saunders and Tuli originals like 'New Amphetamine Sheik' and 'CIA Man', there's a version of Alan Ginsberg's poem called *I Saw The Best Minds Of My Generation Rot*. The band were threatened with legal action over the track 'Coca-Cola Douche' but, despite Saunders' pleas to the contrary, they were never sued. The band later discovered that they were routinely investigated by the FBI during this period but their songs were deemed not to be obscene, 'If we'd only known about this, we could have put a disclaimer on the record, "Ruled NOT obscene by the FBI!"' Instead the Fugs had to settle for the advisory sticker that read 'For Adult Minds Only'.

The Fugs' third album was in fact *The Fugs Second Album* (concentrate now) and is a far more accomplished set of songs. It even made the Billboard Top 100, sparking several television appearances and a run of shows attended by the leading lights of the counter-culture, and anyone else who wanted to partake a little of that old revolutionary spirit. With a band consisting of keyboardist Lee Crabtree, Vinny Leary and Pete Kearney on guitars, and Jon Anderson on bass, the album is the band's best, complete with harmonies and musical expertise to bring the best out of sloganeering lines like 'Near or middle or very far east, far or near or very middle east, kill, kill, kill for peace'. A deal with Reprise provided four more albums before the decade's end, during which time, the Fugs exorcized the Pentagon, stuffed flowers into the gun barrels of young nervous soldiers, got bomb threats and then actual bombs in the post, attended every demo going and were at the forefront of the change from beatnik to hippy to yippy.

By the end of the sixties, Sanders and Tuli were fully-fledged counter-cultural icons and they had a pretty good band together too. At which point we leave the story of the Fugs and their various reincarnations across the last three decades; it all gets a touch too Grateful Dead for my liking.

First team: Ed Sanders (v, perc), Tuli Kupferberg (v, perc), Ken Weaver (d), Lee Crabtree (k), Vinny Leary (g), Pete Kearney (g), Jon Anderson (b)

Place, time, scene: New York 1964. They couldn't play, they used makeshift instruments and their records were obscene. Yeah, they were the first punks.

What to buy first: *The Fugs Second Album* 1966

And then: *The Fugs First Album* 1965

FUNKADELIC

George Clinton grew up in New Jersey. During the late fifties he ran a barber shop specializing in hair-straightening and was able to fund his own doo-wop group called the Parliaments. By the mid-sixties, Clinton was a jobbing songwriter and the Parliaments were having hit singles in the US with Motown-inspired pop soul records, but that all changed in 1967 when Clinton heard the free-form experiments of Cream and started noticing that other psychedelic bands like the Doors and Country Joe and the Fish were adding horns to their music. Within a year he had recruited Billy Bass Nelson, Eddie Hazel, Tawl Ross and Tiki Fulwood and had changed the name of his band from the Parliaments to Funkadelic. The next three albums were the original genre-busters and stereotype-killers. And it was all done in the name of pure funk. P-funk to be concise.

The debut album *Funkadelic* begins with the track 'Mommy What's A Funkadelic?', which is answered musically with a loose mix of rock and soul styles, and lyrically with phrases like 'a funkadelic will pee on your afro'. As it goes, not that helpful, but that's the deal – funkadelic is about freedom from the institutionalized way of doing things. The second album *Free Your Mind ... And Your Ass Will Follow* contains a set of songs that point to the definition of funk as an inner understanding of self, while *Maggot Brain*, released in 1971, opens with a short speech that concludes 'I knew that I had to rise above it all or drown in my own shit' which roughly translated, is a call-to-arms for individuals to get involved and sort out society's ills. The idea culminates in the album *One Nation Under A Groove* where a whole new society, Funkadelia, is envisioned. It's hippy shit, basically, but not far off what Afrika Bambaataa was talking about with his

Zulu Nation and the original philosophy of hip-hop.

The first two albums are the sound of Funkadelic tightening everything up ready for a killer album to come. You'd have thought that it would be a heavy soul masterpiece and in a way it is, but *Maggot Brain* is so much more than that too. High on confidence, the band jumps from one style to another, making it sound totally normal for a black soul band to get down to switch from folk to gospel and then create a little heavy metal thunder.

'Can You Get To That' is the aforementioned folk gospel, with an invigorating combination of strummed acoustic guitar and sublime chorus singing. 'Wars Of Armageddon' is a relentless metal-funk monster that pushes the studio to its limits in terms of the amount of sheer noise thrown in there, although it's not quite clear why all those farts are there at the end. 'Super Stupid' is pure Black Sabbath with Clinton singing like Hendrix and some tripped-out organ from new boy Bernie Worrell. By the end of the track, guitarist Eddie Hazel plays dumb and heavy, riding his guitar like a rodeo horse. But then that's Eddie Hazel for you.

You can forget about everything else on the album if you like and just play the title track. Those who have heard 'Maggot Brain' testify that it is the best individual guitar solo they have ever heard – sad and mournful to begin with, becoming more optimistic as Hazel plays on. The solo itself is about nine minutes long with barely any other accompaniment. Apparently Clinton told Hazel to play as if his mother had died, but then is told that she is alive after all. It clearly worked.

Within a year, the line-up that had made *Maggot Brain* had disintegrated with just Clinton and Worrell remaining as the core of the band. The emphasis shifted to a new band, Parliament, that was possibly the best funk band of them all – it included Bootsy Collins on bass, Maceo Parker on brass and Fred Wesley on saxophone. Ultimately the line between Funkadelic and Parliament became so blurred as to make no sense, and no-one really cared, the vibe was the thing and the shows took care of that. The Mothership Connection tour was a series of huge productions that effectively updated the big-band swing shows of the 1940s but with weird specs, nylon tights and mind-boggling indoor spaceships. Clinton wrapped the whole thing up in a fantasy extra-terrestrial piece of theatre, and the music was tight as. But you know, I can't help feeling that it was all a trip too far. Too many people, too many voices. Give me one Funkadelic creating a groove over a whole nation succombing to one any day. Buy *Maggot Brain*. Defo.

First team: George Clinton (v), Eddie Hazel (g), Tawl Ross (g, v), Bernie Worrell (k, v), Billy Bass Nelson (b), Tiki Fulwood (d)

Place, time, scene: Detroit 1968. Before Funkadelic, George Clinton was in a soul band that played Motown-type numbers. Not surprising, he was from

Detroit after all, but with Funkadelic, Clinton started looking around to see what was going on outside black music, and together with Eddie Hazel surely stumbled across other Detroit bands like the MC5 and the Stooges. Funkadelic's cosmic rock/funk hybrid, and later on their electro-funk, made an impression on the little purple feller, that's for sure.

What to buy first: *Maggot Brain* 1971

And then: *Free Your Mind ... And Your Ass Will Follow* 1970

In retrospect: *Ultimate Funkadelic* 1997

G

GANG OF FOUR

Gang Of Four were already in existence when punk really hit in the summer of 1977. The attitude of those early London punk bands was clearly an influence on the Leeds-based quartet and, if nothing else, confirmed that they were heading in the right direction with their 'tell it like it is' take on society and culture, and het-up and angry delivery, but it didn't do a lot for them musically. As far as guitarist Andy Gill is concerned, the early British punk bands were 'not a whole lot different from a lot of your heavy metal acts' – rhythmically unsophisticated, guitars played with full distortion and shouty-screamy vocals.[35]

Gang Of Four were more influenced by the more interesting pub rock bands that came before punk, particularly Dr Feelgood with their more constructed and considered style of playing, specifically original guitarist Wilko Johnson's approach, which was to drop chords and solos in at key moments as dressing, rather than strumming or riffing all the way through a song. And then there was Television's 1977 album *Marquee Moon* and early Talking Heads singles which were equally vital in defining new ways of using guitar, bass and drums, which avoided the rock clichés that had

become established in the previous two decades. All grist to the mill for Gang Of Four.

The band formed at Leeds University and, with their debut 'Damaged Goods', immediately set out their stall as a new band with a new approach. With their first album *Entertainment*, they nailed it. The album is funky with a capital F, but jerks around and is played at such a speed that there's no time to properly get down and dirty in one groove before the next one kicks in. It's funk put to a different, more immediate use; it gets people fired up and ready for action. Punk-funk with a message inbetween the shifting grooves.

Throughout the album, Dave Allen and Hugo Burnham set up bouncing, jerking rhythms and Andy Gill fires off rounds of guitar over the undulating soundscape when the coast is clear, usually at the moments when the song is at its most sparse. It's as effective as hell. The single 'At Home He's A Tourist' might as well be Chic, with its galloping bass, but it's soon apparent that it's not with all that clanging guitar falling about all over it, and as for 'Not Great Men', well the groove setup on that one is serious, as in grave. Try smiling when that one's twitching about. Gang Of Four will have you dancing, but they'll make it feel like an act of social resistance every time.

Throughout the album, Jon King's vocals jump in and out, his voice clips words to give them more impact, and each sneered line is enunciated clearly, because the words are important, and shouldn't drift off lazily out of sync with the mathematically precise music. If it's sweet melodies and harmonies you're after, well you're in the wrong album, as Andy Gill points out, 'We saw all the elements, the four voices of the band as working together to create this rhythmic groove.' The lyrics are just as organized with both King and Gill working together to come up with well-scanned old-school Marxist analysis. A central theme of the album is representation, of ideas and events, particularly through the media, and the effects of such bad ideology on people's personal lives, especially in the bedroom, 'repackaged sex keeps your interest'. On the inner sleeve there are a series of pictures of television representations anchored by lines that explain that 'However unsavoury, events are shown in a palatable way' and 'Dramatic events on the other side of the world made simple at home'. The Gang Of Four were didactic; what of it?

Live, they were inspirational, insisting through the construction of their songs that the audience continually shift their attention from King to Gill to Burnham to Davies. The tension between King's vocal rants and Gill's knowing guitar retorts were described by writer Greil Marcus as representative of the singer's 'bad conscience'. The guitar undermines the angry young man, dropping in clanging chords to mark the discrepancy between what the 'character' sings and the way he lives his life.[36] Not that Gang Of Four could ever themselves be accused of not walking the walk. They avoided hypocrisy at all turns, refusing to play the same bill as a stripper at an early gig in Scotland, and in 1979 walked out of *Top Of The Pops* after opting not to replace the word 'rubber' in the song 'At Home He's A Tourist' with the alternative suggestion of 'rubbish.'

The band toured the US at the turn of the decade and turned on a whole generation of American independent bands, notably REM who played some shows with them on their 1981 tour, apparently joining the Gang Of Four on-stage for a version of Funkadelic's 'One Nation Under A Groove' at one point. Peter Buck rates their Washington DC show as one of the best he has ever seen, and Michael Stipe has admitted on more than one occasion that he 'stole a lot from them'.[37]

Solid Gold followed in 1981 and is equally as stirring, although any band would have difficulty following *Entertainment* as it is pretty much a complete album. It begins with 'Paralysed', another bass driven, guitar textured funk-punker, with spoken lyrics from King, and moves on to other songs dealing with fast-food, militarism and general social malaise. The grinding 'What We All Want' is a highlight, along with the enigmatically titled 'Cheeseburger'.

Bassist Dave Allen left before the third album to form his own band Shriekback, and without his pummelling bass the band had no option but to change tack, and eventually split in 1984 after another two albums and having made little impression on the mainstream charts. Still, there was enough interest to lead to a brief two album reformation in 1990, and Andy Gill has certainly been kept busy since producing albums by Killing Joke, Boss Hogg, Bis, the Red Hot Chili Peppers and notably Jesus Lizard who wanted Gill, because Steve Albini was not available. Okay.

First team: Andy Gill (g, v), Jon King (v), Hugo Burnham (d, v), Dave Allen (b)

Place, time, scene: Leeds 1977. Gang Of Four were one of the original post-punk bands responsible for invigorating the fairly standard punk approach. On their first album they demonstrated that angry music could get down too, and along with the Pop Group, made an impression on politically-motivated bands, particularly in America, who didn't want to express themselves through the more basic hardcore set-up.

What to buy first: *Entertainment* 1979

And then: *Solid Gold* 1981

In retrospect: *A Brief History Of The Twentieth Century* 1990

GIANT SAND

Howe Gelb was born and raised in Pennsylvania and spent some time in New York in his early band days, but his spiritual home is Tucson, especially the desert that surrounds the Arizona stronghold. He first moved there when he was 15 years old to be with his father, and has been heading back whenever he can, ever since. The heat, the space and the overwhelming sense of being free from structure and rules has clearly affected his music. Often dubbed desert-rock, the running theme is relaxed spontaneity and it has rubbed off on all who have assisted him in his work over the years. Many, like Evan Dando of the Lemonheads, Joey Burns and John Convertino of Calexico, Juliana Hatfield and Victoria Williams, and the band Grandaddy, continue to display Gelb's influence in their own music, while Gelb himself remains a cult obscurity who, after two decades and nearly 30 albums (including side-projects) still struggles to get record deals and has long since given up on media support.

Gelb got turned onto country music when he met guitarist Rainer Ptacek on his first visit to Tucson. The two remained very close friends until Ptacek's death from cancer in 1997, and formed their first band together, the Giant Sandworms, in 1980. Another Arizona-based band the Serfers, who would later become Green On Red, started at the same time, and over in LA the Paisley Underground bands, Dream Syndicate, Rain Parade and the Long Ryders, who were re-establishing a more organic sixties rock sound, were coming round to the idea that roots music was where it was at, especially in terms of mood, subject matter and a darn good strummed acoustic gee-tar. The Giant Sandworms headed for New York (just to be different) and managed a couple of EPs that blended country-rock with soul music, an influence that seeped in from their living quarters in the bad end of a Puerto Rican neighbourhood. Gelb has continued to make music organically, inspired by his surroundings and collaborators. As Jason Cohen of *Stereophile* magazine has noted when compiling the band's discography, each of the 15 Giant Sand albums released since 1985 has essentially reversed the process of playing live to support the album, and perhaps more sensibly (in terms of music, not sales), uses the live set-up to perfect the mood and the craft of the eventual album which then stands as a document of a certain musical moment.

The early albums feature bassist Scott Gerber who remained from the Giant Sandworms days, and Gelb's first wife, ex-Go-Go Paula Jean Brown. 'Ballad Of A Thin Line Man' is typical of the band's early stark sound, but by 1988, with the release of *The Love Songs*, the addition of drummer John Convertino and the assistance of original Green On Red member Chris Cacavas, the band had begun to rock, leaving the more overtly country references to Gelb's other band the Band Of Blacky Ranchette, who were doing the kind of twisted new country that must have inspired accepted alt-country pioneers Uncle Tupelo who were still seven years away from releasing their debut album when the first eponymous Blacky album was recorded.

The Love Songs is one of the four essential Giant Sand albums, along with *Ramp* in 1992, *Glum* in 1994 and *Chore Of Enchantment* in 2000. These are the albums where the band perfected their spontaneous approach to making music in the studio, feeling their way to a particular sound, inspired by invited guests, including vocalists Victoria Williams and country original Pappy Allen, Peter Holsapple on slide, Rainer Ptacek on dobro and slide, Mark Walton of Dream Syndicate on bass, Lisa Germano on fiddle and the ever-reliable Chris Cacavas on keys. Pappy Allen and Victoria Williams, in particular, have become the central voice of songs on which they have sung. Pappy's version of Hank Williams' 'I'm So Lonesome I Could Cry' from *Glum* is the rare sound of the old world fused with the new and brings together the alternative country styles associated with the Depression eras at both ends of the twentieth century. He died before the album came out.

The core of the band throughout the late 1980s and 1990s has been Gelb, Convertino and Joey Burns and it's that line-up which is responsible for *Ramp*, a perfect blend of city and desert that should have made them all stars. There are big pop epics, fragile and lonely piano pieces and good old-fashioned hoedowns involving as many people as would fit into the studio at the time. It's a good mix. Skilful musicianship meets lazy, wonky writing and playing, where the hook is always the real throwaway bit. 'Yer Ropes' off *Glum* is a good example. The strumming is laid-back and loose, and Gelb's vocals give the impression that he's busy doing something else more important while he's singing. The giveaway is when he sings what sounds like 'I dunno ... ropes' just before launching into one of the best guitar solos heard that decade. You can blame a certain Canadian for such behaviour. 'His guitar playing was my inspiration – his electric playing, like the way he made the wrong notes work. I don't like everything he does, and I love it even more that he can do that. He's my ideal... like if there was a neighbourhood to live in, it's Neil's neighbourhood.'[38]

Of course, like Neil Young, Howie Gelb is serious about his music, it's just that he doesn't hammer home his talent by adopting the now trade-marked persona of the perfectionist genius – the 'Brian Wilson syndrome'. He rarely does any promotional work, and is unwilling to take the major credit for Giant Sand. For him the band is a family thing. Some have referred to Giant Sand as the natural successors to the Grateful Dead but that's just missing the point.

First team: Howe Gelb (v, g, p), John Convertino (d), Joey Burns (b), Paula Jean Brown (b), Rainer Ptacek (g), Victoria Wiliams (v), Pappy Allen (v)

Place, time, scene: Tucson, Arizona 1980. Giant Sand are the original desert-rockers, a band that brought together punk and hippie, or maybe even beatnik attitude in a way that very few other bands could possibly pull off. Gelb's family approach to recording and little concern for record sales has ensured that every new album combines a spirit of adventure and a sense of comfort. Alt-country bands and lo-fi slackers all have a little bit of Giant Sand in their soul.

What to buy first: *Ramp* 1988

And then: *The Love Songs LP* 1988, *Centre Of the Universe* 1992, *Glum* 1994, *Chore of Enchantment* 2000

In retrospect: *Giant Songs* 1989, *Giant Songs 2* 1995

GO-BETWEENS

Growing up in Brisbane, Queensland in Australia during the 1970s taught Robert Forster and Grant McLennan one great lesson – get out and get started somewhere else. According to the two founding members of the Go-Betweens, Brisbane had no youth subculture. It was not civically encouraged by the prevailing administration of the day. In terms of music, the Saints had started in the city, but had been whisked away to Britain by EMI before they had chance to influence a new

organic scene in their hometown. In 1977 when the Go-Betweens formed there wasn't an Australian music scene beyond the mainstream rock of bands like Skyhooks and Cold Chisel. By the time they made it to Melbourne in 1979 that had changed. The Birthday Party represented Melbourne's seedy musical underbelly and Radio Birdman had made a similar breakthrough in Sydney, which was developing a musical avant-garde led by ex-Saints' guitarist Ed Kuepper and his band Laughing Clowns.

The Go-Betweens were inspired by the new musical opportunities but the nearest like-minded writers and musicians were in Scotland. The Go-Betweens, along with Orange Juice, Aztec Camera and later on, the Smiths, were onto something a lot gentler and more considered than their punk-inspired contemporaries. Not for them, the anger of punk or the brooding dark experimentalism of post-punk. The Go-Betweens were concerned with telling stories, evoking images and encouraging reflection. They combined lyrics and melodies to create songs that operate on a smaller scale, personal songs that draw you in and make you think.

Robert Forster taught Grant McLennan the bass guitar while they were at university together in Brisbane, and together with drummer Dennis Cantwell they recorded some of Forster's songs, inspired by themes of declining society and collective guilt. Typical art student material really. Forster was a fan of Salinger's *Catcher In The Rye* and, like Holden in the book, he adopts the character of a sensitive soul adrift in an ugly world. McLennan's songs, when they finally emerged, were more personal. 'Cattle And Cane', a song on the band's second album *Before Hollywood*, is an autobiographical reflection on his youth growing up in the rural north of Queensland. He followed it up with 'Unkind and Unwise' on the next album, giving further details of his fatherless upbringing and relating his experience to the cultural norm of male identity machismo that he recognizes as his other on a daily basis, all very sensitive. Forster is less poetic in his writing, more conversational, and prone to the odd barbed comment. 'Part Company', a song from the 1984 album *Spring Hill Fair* is a story of lost love, sung-spoken like many of his songs, over a series of interlocking melodies. 'That's her handwriting, that's the way she writes, from the first love letter to this bill of rights'.

The Go-Betweens' focus on songs and melody was what prompted Glasgow-based Postcard Records' boss Alan Horne to sign the band in 1980, however they only released one single with Postcard and headed back to Australia. Just like the Birthday Party at that time, the Go-Betweens became a nomadic band constantly on the move between Melbourne, London, Eastbourne, Paris and Sydney, recording in new locations with new producers for virtually every album. Amazingly they retained a consistency to their work that is down to their absolute focus on songs rather than stylistic changes. There were three label changes and five critically acclaimed albums, but no hits.

It's interesting that the Smiths had more success with a similar approach but, crucially, had an image to attach their music too. The Go-Betweens, with a female drummer, a seven-foot lead singer and songs about film stars, apparently didn't. But then, maybe the Go-Betweens pushed it just that little bit too far. Forster and McLennan may have had more traditionally tuneful voices than Morrissey, but although their songs were always melodious, well written and carefully produced, they often contained little quirks that endeared them to many but distanced them from others – usually those running the radio stations. In the sleeve notes to the 1999 *Best Of* album, Forster explains that in the case of 'Cattle And Cane', perhaps their best shot at early success, 'the song itself is damn weird, it has no noticeable chorus and the outro is too long'. It was also the most evocative and beautiful three minutes of music released that year, but then radio programmers aren't after beauty, they're interested in familiarity and consistency.

The first two albums, made by Forster, McLennan and drummer Lindy Morrison, featured the three members playing guitar, bass and drums respectively. By the third, Robert Vickers had joined as the band's new bassist, allowing the two songwriters more freedom to develop melodies, while the rhythm section kept their parts as simple as the sparseness of the songs required. The four albums, running from 1984's *Spring Hill Fair* up to 1988's *16 Lovers Lane* are all excellent, and with the addition of strings played by Amanda Brown on the last two albums, the Go-Betweens' sound became even more expansive and

swirling. On *16 Lovers Lane* the ten songs that comprise the album are easily the most consistent the two writers had come up with up to that point. The single 'Streets Of Your Town' nearly charted too!

The band split later that year, leaving behind one of the great undiscovered back-catalogues.

First team: Robert Forster (v, g), Grant McLennan (v, g), Lindy Morrison (d), Robert Vickers (b)

Place, time, scene: Brisbane 1978. The Go-Betweens moved between Melbourne and London in their early days, settling in the UK for most of their career. They were initially associated with the new pop scene based around the Postcard label in Glasgow which also gave starts to Orange Juice and Aztec Camera, and in terms of lyrical importance, were a forerunner of the Smiths. The *C86*/shambling scene[39] that brought bands like the Pastels and Talulah Gosh to public awareness, and later Belle and Sebastian, owe a little something to the Go-Betweens

What to buy first: *16 Lovers Lane* 1988

And then: *Before Hollywood* 1983, *Spring Hill Fair* 1984, *Liberty Belle & The Black Diamond Express* 1986

In retrospect: *Bellavista Terrace* 1999

GOLDIE

Bill Brewster and Frank Broughton in their book *Last Night A DJ Saved My Life* explain the sudden acceleration in techno beats as a reaction to cheaper Ecstasy tablets that contained more amphetamine than previous batches. It sounds feasible, especially as new scenes formed in geographically specific locations. Clubs in the Midlands were the centre of the new hardcore techno culture, notably The Eclipse in Coventry, formerly a bingo hall that began attracting psychedelic speed freaks and those who fancied a dance from all over the surrounding area, and did it under the noses of the city's moral elders, and without the knowledge of most of the city's student and townie populations. Hardcore techno DJs Fabio and Grooverider were the stars of the scene. They started their own night at Heaven in London which they dubbed Rage, and it was there that Goldie, who had been working away on his own thing, got his first jungle track played.

Goldie was a B-boy back in the day. He upheld three of the five hip-hop elements laid down by Afrika Bambaataa. He span on his head, he sprayed walls and he was dedicated to the knowledge. It was an impressive enough CV to get him a small part in a 'graffer' documentary film called *Bombing* alongside Afrika Bambaataa himself, and enabled the Walsall-born orphan to hang out at the heart of hip-hop culture in New York.

When he returned to the UK at the end of the 1980s it all seemed a bit tame, especially as acid house had caught hold and the bass had given way to a series of bleeps. Mind you he still got into the scene, carried along by the euphoria. He dropped E, danced himself stupid and became best buddies with Bristol scenesters 3D and Nellee Hooper. Their future was in trip-hop, dance music that you didn't dance to. Goldie went to the other extreme and was ready for the challenge when acid and techno went up a notch.

Picking up tips from Fabio and Grooverider he made his first jungle track in 1992. Early singles, notably 'Terminator', which starred a sampled Arnie Schwarzenegger, were built using the skills and knowledge he had picked up at Reinforced Records, a dance label operated by the production team known as 4 Hero. Following the example of hardcore, Goldie's beats per minute often reached as high as 170, and the ultra-fast breakbeats were combined with a much slower bass-line that gave the tracks a dark, brooding sound. Using a studio tool called a hoover, which sounded like . . . a hoover, and making use of an amazing bit of kit made by Akai called the S-1000 Sampler which enabled him to slow down samples without altering the pitch, he created his masterpiece album *Timeless* in 1995 which, in comparison to his heavier jungle singles, is much lighter and soulful.

The title track clocks in at 22 minutes and comes in three parts, each one marking a shift in mood that evokes iconic urban images, especially during the section entitled 'Inner City Life'. Tracks like 'Angel' and 'State Of Mind' are just as smooth, with speed beats occasionally discernible in the background, and there's the full-on headrush of 'Kemistry', named after his girlfriend of the time. He later hooked up with Björk and followed with a second album that was universally derided for being self-indulgent. In retrospect, with an opening track that was 60 minutes long, and another with 'mad for it' guitar by pseudo-rebel flavour of the decade Noel Gallagher, *Celebrity Big Brother* with a former topless model, two retro TV presenters and a former member of Take That, was always on the cards. But for a moment there, Goldie was the sound of cool and innovative British culture at its last great peak.

Place, time, scene: London 1993. Goldie was not the first jungle artist but he was the first to really get to grips with the new technology available to him and spotted the potential of the new beats when combined with other music genres. He made jungle records that could be listened to at home, still beat-driven but beautifully textured as well.

What to buy first: *Timeless* 1995

GRANDADDY

Alt-country is a term which has been bandied about for a number of years now, and tends to crop up in press releases and artist biographies, and by extension, reviews, of artists who are a) from any American small-town not close enough to a major conurbation to be fitted into a scene, and b) dressed like drug-store truck-driving men in jeans who are somehow wise beyond their youthful years. Grandaddy fit both criteria in terms of their base in the desert town of Modesto, California, and dishevelled sartorial-ism and weird beards. They do not, however, play country music.

Experts in the field have traced alt-country back to Uncle Tupelo and their 1990 album *No Depression* which, from the first few bars, puts together the old style with punk guitars, and tells stories about guilt, remorse and despair in a contemporary setting. Grandaddy's lyricist and singer Jason Lytle is similarly pessimistic but pays specific attention to the despair associated with the inroads into contemporary life made by science and technology, and the damaging effects of this on nature and culture. Musically though, short of a strummed acoustic guitar, there are no country licks to speak of anywhere in their back-catalogue. Lytle's weapon of choice is the analogue synthesizer while the rest of the band specialize in fuzzy guitar, relentless rolling bass and loud Flaming Lips-style drum parts. Their favourite band is Talk Talk, who, to the best of this writer's knowledge, never played The Grand Ole Opry, and to top it all, Lytle and guitarist Jim Fairchild are ex-pro-skateboarders.

Lytle has explained that the country in Grandaddy's music is more to do with 'honesty and purity. It's more the sentiment that we try and pick up on, rather than the twanging guitar, or the lap-steel, or whatever.' On the debut album proper, *Under The Western Freeway*, released in 1998, the sentiment seems to revolve around the idea that change is bad and that stability and familiarity are good – 'Go progress chrome, I won't be at your unveiling, I like it how it's always been'. 'Summer Here Kids' advises against summer madness and 'AM 180' pleads with a friend 'Don't change your name, keep it the same, for fear I may lose you again'. Musically, Grandaddy get every-

thing right and achieve a blend of guitar sounds (with their three guitarists) and electronic noises that only Radiohead were to better on their *Kid A* album.

'Laughing Stock' is the standout track, a tribute to the Talk Talk album of the same name, featuring guitars fed back on themselves, kept low in the mix but gradually allowed to come to the fore as the mood builds. There are odd static and bubbling noises expertly deployed at key moments throughout, and in the middle of it all, Lytle's fragile Neil Young voice – a signifier of a delicate soul, cast adrift in an unkind world. The song opens with the line 'We do believe it ends right here' and to be honest, it could have done, and Grandaddy would still be in this book. However by 2000, they'd gone up another notch with *The Sophtware Slump*. The sound had become clean, lush and less understated, and like their fellow sonic travellers, the Flaming Lips and Mercury Rev, they

Grandaddy

demonstrated that they knew how to get the most out of a studio without recourse to cliché.

The opener 'He's Simple, He's Dumb, He's The Pilot' is a ten minute epic that is both haunting and spine-tingling. 'The Crystal Lake' is a perfectly executed pop song that is bursting at the seams with sheer weight of music. And 'Jed the Humanoid', a tale of a highly evolved computerized robot that didn't get enough attention, turned to drink and 'fizzled and popped ... until finally he stopped' – a cautionary tale told over sparse but melodramatic piano and spurious robotic noises that is just plain daft on paper but 'staring into space' tragic when set to music. It's the millennium equivalent of hillbilly songs where dogs die and friends and lovers let you down. Alt-country, anyone?

First team: Jason Lytle (v, g, k), Kevin Garcia (b), Aaron Burtch (d), Jim Fairchild (g), Tim Dryden (k)

Place, time, scene: Modesto, California 1994. Grandaddy have blended a Luddite anti-technology philosophy with an electronic-based sound that ex-udes a yearning country heart. Radiohead's American cousins?

What to buy first: *Under The Western Freeway* 1998

And then: *The Sophtware Slump* 2000, *Sumday* 2003

GRANDMASTER FLASH & THE FURIOUS FIVE

Grandmaster Flash is acknowledged as one of the founders of hip-hop music. Along with Jamaican raised block DJ Kool Herc, he put into place the key elements of the DJ's art. Often, his innovations were the result of neccessity – to move the crowd – but he has not gained entry into this book just because he was a clever technician. Flash is the turntablist extraordinaire, the original and best who could cut it live and in the studio. He invented the tools and with them perfected his craft.

Kool Herc was the first person to spot the problem with disco. There was too much going on, all those instruments, the melody lines and worst of all, singing. The 120 bpm kept people dancing but it didn't encourage them to go wild. There was potential there though. Most disco tracks released during 1975 and 1976 had

sections where the beat was most prominent and didn't have to compete with all the embellishments. If this came in the middle of the track, Herc noticed that dancers got that little bit more excited and could focus all their energy into nailing the beat with their moves, having had their attention diverted away from singing or mouthing lyrics. Herc called it the breakbeat and set about building his DJ sets around these moments of physical ecstasy. It meant spending more money. He had to buy two copies of each record so that a breakbeat could be extended by switching from one copy to another to keep the beat going. It also meant buying records that he wouldn't normally bother with, just for a few seconds of sound. Mind you it paid off big time. With his huge sound system, for years louder than anyone else's, he became the main attrac-tion in the Bronx area of New York. He developed his crude mixing techniques and kept the party going by shouting over the top of the beats like the toasters he'd witnessed back in Jamaica in his youth. He was good. Flash was better.

In his book *DJ Culture*, Ulf Poschardt explains that with Herc as his role model, Flash the trained electrical engineer, built his own system but with several tech-nical innovations. He made great use of turntables that could spin backwards as well as forwards and perfected his beat-matching with a pre-fade facility that enabled him to audition records on one turntable while playing out the other turntable live to the crowd. By adding a third turntable he was able to keep the beat with the first two, and embellish the often sparse rhythms with washes of music, musical riffs and even spoken-word or comedy. He developed 'clock theory' so that he could find breakbeats quickly using the record label as a compass, and arranged his library of records into categories determined by tempo and type. He mixed, back-span and scratched, and when he heard about this thing called a metronome that drum-mer's used, he hooked one up to his system, christened it the beatbox and launched the DJ on a career that would soon extend beyond the turntables.

His definitive sonic moment is a 12" single release called 'The Adventures Of Grandmaster Flash On The Wheels Of Steel', an eight minute montage of music taken from such diverse sources as Chic, Blon-die, Queen and the Sugarhill Gang, which stands as a testament both to Flash's technical ability in the days when sampling and looping were done without the aid of an electronic gizmo, and the progressive positivity associated with the DJ's art. Each track is chosen for its potential to create a vibe. Musical and cultural boundaries don't come into it, and although an academic textual analysis of the various elements might draw conclusions about the ironic use of rock songs that have themselves appropriated an arguably cynical rap or disco aesthetic, we can be pretty certain that Grandmaster Flash was solely interested in laying down a groove. It's the ultimate postmodern text. It celebrates difference and artistic possibilities, and by taking no critical position, at the same time somehow suggests one.

Flash's best work is most likely scattered around homes across New York. There were no record deals for mix DJs in 1977 because there was no media outlet for them. Radio really didn't catch on for a long time, so the culture revolved around cassettes and taxi cabs. A new mix was circulated among the cabbies in the neighbourhood who played them to customers on long, often unnecessary fares, unless, of course, the punter bought a copy. When Flash did get a deal with Sugarhill Records it was because he had teamed up with the Furious Five, a crew of MCs that rapped over his breakbeats.

Led by Melle Mel and Cowboy, they rapped about the reality of street life in long narratives that became 'The Message' and 'White Lines (Don't Don't Do It)'. Like everything else that Grandmaster Flash did, he got the rappers right too. And they were good enough to draw the audience's attention away from his technical work. A party just isn't the same if everyone is gathered around the DJ watching instead of dancing. On record, Flash took responsibility for arranging the backing track to the Furious Five's tales, and it's a further sign of his immaculate ego-less hip-hop philosophy that he kept the arrangement relatively simple for the most part.

In the studio his focus shifted from content to form, and he began taking time to create mood pieces that worked because the often-sparse backing track was set at the right tone and tempo, with breakdowns and drum fills carefully scheduled into the arrangement. The empty, dark sense of foreboding that is built up at the beginning of 'White Lines' was perhaps only bettered by Massive Attack nearly ten years later when there were a lot more electronic toys to play with.

For a period of about five years, Grandmaster Flash was the master of his art and was responsible for the shaping an entire style of music-making. When rap took over and the DJs were replaced by technology that could do the work more cheaply, he was out of a job. Life sucks sometimes.

First team: Grandmaster Flash (t-t), Melle Mel (v), Cowboy (v), Kid Creole (v), Duke Bootee (v), Raheim (v)

Place, time, scene: New York 1977. Grandmaster Flash was the DJ that turned DJ-ing into an artform. His then unique skills, combined with a sense of technological adventure and innate feel for the groove, launched a new cultural and aesthetic form. His collaboration with the Furious Five brought him together with the best rappers around, and their street-suss social realism rhymes have become the template for all rappers since.

What to buy first: *The Message* 1982

In retrospect: *Greatest Messages* 1984

HAPPY MONDAYS

The Happy Mondays had no agenda. They weren't here to rescue the kids from a cruel and heartless world, or provide a social commentary on contemporary life, they never claimed to be changing music or updating culture, they couldn't give two f**ks about the notion of independence and the Marxist ethics that underpinned it, and they weren't even that interested in being pop stars. That was the image anyway, and it was backed up by virtually everything they did. Of course, individual members were driven by the same sense of moral philosophy and life expectations that everyone has but when they got together as a group, on stage or in the studio, all of that got sacrificed to the vibe. The Happy Mondays were a party band. They existed in leisure time, not real time. This was the key to their success and the reason that they connected so completely with their audience. There were Bez's onstage dancing lessons, Shaun Ryder's up to the minute lyrical anecdotes and barfly philosophy, and the band's awesome groove. Musically, lyrically and most of all in their performance style, they were the archetypal 'weekender' band. Oh, and all that stuff I listed in the second sentence, they did all that too.

Named after the day when unemployment benefit is doled out, the Happy Mondays announced their working-class credentials from the outset. The basis of the band was the Ryder family: Shaun who sang and wrote the songs, Paul, the northern-soul fan who played bass, and Derek their dad who did the sound at their early gigs. They were a breath of fresh air when they broke through at the forefront of the post-techno rave scene in 1990 but that was five years after they formed, a period during which they struggled to gain any recognition for their blend of seventies-style funk and sixties psychedelia. Guitarist Moose played wah-wah guitar and keyboardist Paul Davis (PD) added James Taylor style funk while Shaun Ryder intoned his street-poetry over the top using his football terrace chant vocal style. They were fairly ropey at that point but what stood out were Ryder's lyrics.

Tony Wilson has compared Ryder to T.S. Eliot, W.B. Yeats and Bob Dylan, his argument resting on an apparent effortless ability that he has to evoke powerful imagery and engage in clever wordplay. He invents characters to tell his stories and sets them up in tragic situations. The couple in 'Tart Tart' might be in a relationship together, or they might be punter and client, what's certain is that the woman has had 'tests on the blood' and received conflicting results, while the man in the story gets bothered about the 'spots on his chest, chest, chest'. It's not a pretty story, drugs, STDs, who knows, but it's a subject that few other songwriters would tackle.

The band played at a Hacienda Battle of the Bands night in 1985, an event organized by DJ Mike Pickering who would later form M People, and caused such a stir with their on-stage fighting that the next thing they knew they had a record deal with the Factory label. By that point Bez had become a permanent member of the band, the Happy Mondays' very own Chas Smash. He played maracas and danced, shoulders out, arms flailing like a novice swimmer who has not learned how to do the front crawl properly yet, and piercing eyes staring out into space, straight-ahead, transfixed. There were those who didn't see the point of Bez, but for anyone who attended a Mondays gig it was clear how crucial he was. He showed the crowd how they should interpret the music, how to freaky-dance.

The band's music improved steadily from 1985 to 1987 when they recorded their first album with Velvet Underground legend John Cale. It contained some good early songs, notably '24 Hour Party People' which replaced a track called 'Desmond' due to an uncleared Beatles' sample. The album managed to gather some good reviews, although those who knew the band considered it a flat production compared to their astonishing performances at the Hacienda. With their next sessions for 'Freaky Dancing', 'Lazyitis' and 'Wrote For Luck' they turned a corner, and it helped that Ryder was writing his best songs. Martin Hannett, the Factory producer who had recorded Joy Division, produced their second album, *Bummed*, and got the result required. It's a mark of his skill that he could move so easily from dark, brooding productions to something far groovier and trippy, but then maybe those tabs of E that the band encouraged him to take did their bit.

'Wrote For Luck' was remixed by Paul Oakenfold in 1989 and reissued as the 'Think About The Future' mix, and with another remix by Vince Clarke of Erasure hot on its heels, 'WFL' as it became known became the club anthem of the summer of '89, a whole year ahead of Primal Scream's 'Loaded'. A filmed performance of the band playing at Manchester's G-Mex in March of 1990 caught the spirit of the period perfectly as the stage gets invaded for the 12 minute long bass-heavy 'WFL' finale. Whistles blowing, freaky dancing and general good vibes take over the huge venue, capturing Madchester in all its glory.

As 1990 progressed, the Happy Mondays, along with the Stone Roses, went from leading a new Manchester culture to a new national culture. As ecstasy poured into British clubs, it was noted that football hooliganism was on the decrease as clubbing took over as the favoured pastime amongst male youth in Britain. The Roses played a major gig at Spike Island which attracted just about every subculture going, and when the Mondays released their 'Hallelujah' 12″ single, both bands were on *Top Of The Pops* in the same week. If Nirvana's *Nevermind* was the point that American underground music broke through to the mainstream, that edition of *Top Of The Pops* was the British equivalent. 'Step On' followed and then the band's crowning moment, the *Pills, Thrills, n'Bellyaches* album.

Recorded in Los Angeles with Oakenfold and Steve Osbourne at the helm, it was an organized period that had members of the band turning up individually to lay down their parts and Ryder sauntering in at night to do the vocals. 'Kinky Afro' has some of the best guitar sounds ever committed to tape, the jangled opening and the slithering lead part, and on top, Ryder's complex tale of complicated parenthood. 'God's Cop' has him skinning up with notorious moral guardian James Anderton, 'Donovan' pays tribute to the Scottish mystic, and 'Loose Fit' is a paean to the baggy trouser. It was the last great thing the Happy Mondays did.

The recording of the last album was a disaster, and is now well-documented as such. The band went to Barbados, discovered crack and ignored the album totally. Producers Tina Weymouth and Chris Frantz, formerly of Talking Heads, struggled to get anything down on tape and at one point Ryder was seen loading Eddy Grant's studio furniture into a van to take downtown to sell for crack. *Yes Please!* had a few worthwhile tracks on it but is otherwise a symbolic album that coincided with some well-publicized ecstasy-related deaths in the UK, a clampdown on clubs and imposed restrictions on their operation, and the switching of allegiance from Madchester to Seattle. The Happy Mondays and the so-called second summer of love were over.

First team: Shaun Ryder (v), Paul Ryder (b), Moose (g), PD (k), Gary Whelan (d), Bez (mar)

Place, time, scene: Manchester 1984. The Happy Mondays took several years to get their blend of northern soul, acid house and folk-pop right. Ryder's lyrics were always the band's trump card, but as with Jarvis Cocker and Pulp, the words take on an added power when the music falls into place. Martin Hannett, Paul Oakenfold, Steve Osbourne and even Vince Clarke all lent a hand when it came to perfecting the band's sound, but the hijack of British youth culture was another thing entirely. The band that allegedly handed out ecstasy pills at their early gigs were on top of that one.

What to buy first: *Pills, Thrills n'Bellyaches* 1990

And then: *Bummed* 1988

In retrospect: *Loads: The Best Of* 1995

RICHARD HELL

When interviewed in 2002, on the occasions that Richard Hell was asked about his early punk days and his involvement with three of the key bands of the period, he continually avoided details and instead, said enigmatically that he finished with each of them because he knew how it was going to turn out. It didn't make sense to me at the time, but thinking back now, it's exactly the sort of statement that a writer would make. What's the point of commencing work on a novel if you don't know what the story is going to be? And that's Hell's real passion, writing. He was doing it before he discovered rock'n'roll and he's been doing it ever since. Poetry, novels, collected short stories, essays and autobiographical reflections. Buy his book *Hot And Cold*, it's a nice little greatest hits package.

As far as music is concerned though, Hell's legacy as a punk pioneer rests on his belief in the positive power of the music. He may have snarled and got angry like other punks but he also knew how to inject humour onto the proceedings. He abhorred pretentiousness, and saw hard, fast, physical music as something that should be celebrated and which could in turn be celebratory. His song 'Blank Generation' was widely misinterpreted when it was first issued in 1977. 'Blank' didn't signify nihilism, it suggested possibilities for a generation that was at last starting to get real. Hell's punk was utopian.

The bohemian literary world which Richard Myers was trying to break into really started to piss him off after a while. Together with his friend Tom Miller he had left Lexington, Kentucky and gone to New York in the late sixties. Once there, they worked in bookstores and set up their own publishing press to print their poetry and short stories. Miller took the surname Verlaine after his wordy hero and Myers became Hell because that was the frame of mind that the relentless onslaught of pretentious literary society had imposed on him. In 1971, the two gave it up for music and a free electric band and formed the Neon Boys with drummer Billy Ficca.

At that point, Verlaine was already showing signs of becoming the best guitarist of his generation and, although Hell was no slouch with a four-stringer, the musicians won out. When the Neon Boys became Television in 1974, Hell didn't stick around too long, and took his trademark anti-glam slashed clothing and customized slogan T-shirts – an idea which McLaren pilfered – with him to hook up with Johnny Thunders and Jerry Nolan from the New York Dolls and formed the Heartbreakers.

The Neon Boys had only recorded two songs, one of which was the overt 'Love Comes In Spurts' which had something to do with the transitory nature of romantic love, although it might also have alluded to fucking. It was a song that had all the characteristics of the punk boom to come – directness, humour, coarseness – and certainly when Hell played it with his own band, the Voidoids, it featured stripped down Mick Ronson riffs and a half-shouted, half-whined vocal that was the antithesis of the confident, controlled rock vocalists of the time.

The Voidoids were a much more viable option for Hell than the Heartbreakers. They were busy pursuing the perfect rock'n'roll riff and getting out of their heads on whatever was available to people who really liked getting out of their heads – a lot! With guitarists Bob Quine and Ivan Julian and drummer Marc Bell, Hell could keep it real. The Voidoids were signed to Sire Records and together they made the excellent *Blank Generation* album, complete with intelligent, literate lyrics that usually worked on more than one level and were shot through with themes of identity, relationships and death. They were funny too. The title track is of course, the Void-oid's crowning achievement and

demonstrates that Quine was a guitar-player like Wayne Kramer and Fred Smith before him who had more than a passing interest in the improvisational possibilities of free-jazz. The guitar break is awesome.

Hell stopped at that point, and uncharacteristically pushed the self-destruct button for a few years but thankfully returned to writing, sporadic recording, notably with Thurston Moore and Steve Shelley of Sonic Youth in a project called Dim Stars, and on occasion, some film acting too. You can't help but feel that he knew that it would all be okay in the end.

First team: The Voidoids: Richard Hell (v, b), Bob Quine (g), Ivan Julian (g), Marc Bell (d)

Place, time, scene: New York 1971. Hell's band the Neon Boys picked up where the Stooges left off and concocted a combination of musical virtuosity and amateurish presentation. Television would go onto perfect this approach while the Voidoids kept it simpler. Hell's lyrics and look, and the Voidoids' sound were a major influence on UK punk.

What to buy first: *Blank Generation* 1977

HÜSKER DÜ

Hüsker Dü made hardcore punk music respectable. By their 1983 album, *Zen Arcade*, they had demonstrated that musically and philosophically, the 'pull no punches' and 'take no prisoners' approach could transcend the two-minute noise assault format, and could in fact be developed across a conceptual double album. In a relatively short period, hardcore had become a parody of itself and was being adopted by the American jock culture who saw it as a good opportunity to have a ruck. As a result, many of Hüsker Dü's contemporaries covered up their hardcore past and opted for the relatively safe classic rock/pop styles of the sixties and early seventies. Hüsker Dü didn't, they kept the faith, reinvigorated the sound and widened its scope. Songwriters Bob Mould and Grant Hart wrote personal songs about personal issues and paved the way for the loud, independent guitar music to come. Even the mainstream record industry spotted their trailblazing potential. Hüsker Dü were the first 'scene' band to get a major label deal and that changed everything. Within a few years independent music had gone overground which was the point all along, wasn't it?

Student Bob Mould, record shop employee Grant Hart and bassist most likely to grow a very camp handlebar moustache Greg Norton formed the band in 1979. The Ramones provided the formal inspiration, and in terms of content, guidance ranged from the Beatles to the dub-inflected post-punk of Public Image Ltd. Early gigs got them noticed by Jello Biafra who invited them on tour with the Dead Kennedys, and there was also a support slot with Black Flag as they dropped by on one of their transnational mega-tours. They were so impressed that a number was passed to Mike Watt of the Minutemen leading to a deal with the band's New Alliance label.

The first few releases are honest to goodness enervated hardcore punk rock, the debut album *Land Speed Record* is basically a series of explosions clocking in at just under half an hour in total, but by the time they released their 1983 *Metal Circus* EP, Hüsker Dü had begun taking pot shots at the increasingly clichéd hardcore scene, and were incorporating more melodic elements into songs that were less generalized in terms of subject matter, and instead dealt with specific issues or events. They were beginning to tell stories about the world and on occasion, their own response to it. You know, all that self-reflexive 'me' stuff that the more pious pioneers of punk had fought so hard to eradicate. Hüsker Dü didn't deal in the set rules pertaining to smashing the system. They weren't about answers, they were about provoking questions.

Zen Arcade is definitive. The central concept is the tale of a mixed-up kid on the run from his parents and their parent-class culture. It might as well be *Quadrophenia*, but updated and moved to Reagan-era America where attempts to re-embed conservative values into a liberal economic structure were not only at odds, but were also in the process of dismantling the progressive integration of class, race and creed that had been ongoing since at least the 1960s. Mould and Hart both wrote songs for the album, and both were writing from the perspective of the alternative culture of their creative lives and perhaps in some way, the culture emanating from their personal lives as gay men. This was something that both men were totally open about should the topic come up, but did not see as integral to appreciating their work with Hüsker Dü. Nevertheless, the theme that runs through *Zen Arcade*, of a teenager exploring the world alone

for the first time and finding it a harsh and uncompromising place, is better told with some empathy, and both songwriters are able to do that.

The music is hard throughout, and consistent, probably due to the fact that it was recorded in its entirety in one 45 hour session. That's 25 songs in two days! It ends with a first-take swirling maelstrom of noise going by the title 'Reoccurring Dreams', which is a fitting instrumental summation of the unresolved tragedy and alienation that has just preceded it. Released on SST, *Zen Arcade*, along with Minutemen's *Double Nickels On The Dime* made the label an overnight independent success after four years of trying. Unfortunately, the label was unable to meet initial demand and sales probably suffered in the short-term. As Hüsker Dü received more and more play on the newly evolving college-radio network, particularly with tracks from their next two albums, *New Day Rising* (Dave Grohl lyric check!) and *Flip Your Wig*, both knocked out within a year of *Zen Arcade*, the band caught the attention of major labels who were keen to point out that their big thing was, er, distribution.

A deal was done with Warner Brothers, who got a hard-working band at their prime, having perfected the ultimate blend (and brand) of intensity and melody. *Flip Your Wig* is an album of scorching guitar sounds, big choruses and stylistic shifts between psychedelia, folk and soul. Critics and fans loved it alike. If the band hadn't split two albums into their major label career, Warner would have had the new alternative mainstream sewn up. REM at the point of crossover and Hüsker Dü just that little bit further in before the really hard stuff on the other side. The problem, it seems was that the acrimony always rife in the band seemed to flare up more dangerously when even the lightest pressure gets applied by those intent on unit-shifting. Hüsker Dü may have broken through on college radio, but even if the music industry was willing to take a chance on tougher sounds, you can guarantee that, even now, mainstream radioheads won't be interested if the loud, fuzzy guitars don't 'test' that well. *Candy Apple Grey* and *Warehouse: Songs And Stories* certainly have their moments and are worthy additions to the Hüsker Dü back-catalogue which remains one of the most impressive canons of work in American music. Musically and philosophically, Hüsker

Dü were uncompromising. And this time the word is being used advisedly and correctly, not as hyperbole or generic shorthand by lazy-ass music journalists. Hüsker Dü. Uncompromising. Yeah!

First team: Bob Mould (v, g), Grant Hart (d, v), Greg Norton (b)

Place, time, scene: St Paul, Minnesota 1978. The band picked up on the hardcore craze that followed on from US and UK punk. They steered clear of classic retro sounds which evolved in many US cities as a response to the hardcore backlash, and continued to develop the thrash/speed form into something more longform and suited to a non-live environment. Their combination of energy, noise and tunes became the blueprint for independent music at least up to Nirvana, taking in the Pixies along the way.

What to buy first: *Zen Arcade* 1984

And then: *New Day Rising* 1984, *Flip Your Wig* 1985, *Candy Apple Grey* 1986, *Warehouse: Songs And Stories* 1987

I

ICE-T

Ice-T, or Tracy to give him his real name, has taken a strange route through rap. As the first major rapper to emerge from the west coast in 1983, he is credited/discredited with the invention of gangster rap. His early albums walked a fine line between glorifying black nihilism and attempting to do something about it. This can be read either as a mixed message or a specific strategy to conform to a generic type in order that he may sell more records and get a progressive message out on the streets. As his career has progressed it's become clear that Ice-T wants to be progressive, in which case his albums are an interesting insight into the marketing practices of major labels dealing in hip-hop.

Tracy Morrow has been shot twice, once while carrying out an armed robbery. He was a member of a troublesome LA gang and keeps a well-stocked armoury of guns in his home. Apparently, his life changed when he met black author and former pimp Iceberg Slim, and his influence is detectable across most of Ice-T's albums since *Rhyme Pays* in 1987. Iceberg Slim's books are graphic in dealing with the seedier side of life on the street, although they were written as a form of catharsis and often included moralistic messages (and sometimes didn't). Ice-T's albums can be taken the same way.

On *Rhyme Pays* the beats are tinny and his voice has not yet developed the deep, sinister growl that he would later perfect. 'Squeeze The Trigger' and '6 'N the Mornin'' are stories of gang life where the message is left ambiguous. 'Squeeze The Trigger' addresses the stand-off between the police and the youths on the street, but hints that that whole situation may be blown out of proportion. The second album leaves stories of the street aside for the most part but replaces them with bragging songs that thrive on misogyny, but then on album number three, *The Iceberg*, who else but angry old Jello Biafra turns up to add vocals to two of the songs. Does that mean Ice-T has got the politically correct thumbs-up from the most principled man in America? The rhymes deal with censorship, sex and there are a few more street tales.

The next album is acknowledged by Ice-T fans as the best he ever did. *Original Gangster*. It sounds awesome, as if the samples have been done by the Bomb Squad boys who work with Public Enemy, and the raps are about child abuse, black pride, saying no to guns (!) and features a sampled montage of real-life prisoners explaining why prison is not such a cool place to be. There are no bragging sex songs either, in fact one song actually goes so far as to parody exactly the sort of song he was making two albums previously.

Ice-T was getting preachy. Who could have guessed what would come next.

Bodycount, a full-on, balls-out, Lollapalooza-playing metal album, that just happened to include a track called 'Cop Killer' which told the story of a law-man's murder from the perspective of the killer. It was an anti-violence song, but so complicated in terms of its characters and identifications that the message was not one hundred per cent clear. It was banned, which of course raised its significance and became a firm favourite at rock clubs throughout America and the UK. White rock fans dug the controversial sentiment and tried to get hold of a copy by whatever means necessary. They were in it for the irony of course, and the fact that it kicked ass.

In the end, the power of the track to encourage violence, no matter how misguided, was neutered by the fact that Ice-T's audience had switched. He lost his black hip-hop audience because he gained a white rock audience, although as a black icon who had crossed over into white culture, the long-term effect of 'Cop Killer' has been a gradual shift of taste amongst new hip-hop fans to a position in-between rock and beats, and vice versa. Ice-T can take some credit for tearing down the boundaries between black and white musical cultures, leading to new forms which borrow from both camps. The result, nu-metal. Hmmm, now why have I included him again?

Place, time, scene: Los Angeles 1983. Ice-T may have been the originator of gangster rap, but for the most part, he has attempted to retain a progressive message, a difficult balance when popularity hinges on meeting certain generic characteristics like homophobia and violent imagery. Of course, if like Ice-T you have a belief in human goodness and are aware that nobody really takes anything seriously anymore anyway then the odd reference to bootie or a drive-by doesn't really matter. Eminem is currently exploring a similar hypothesis, motherfucker!

What to buy first: *(OG) Original Gangster* 1991

And then: *Rhyme Pays* 1988, *Bodycount* 1992

In retrospect: *Ice-T Greatest Hits: The Evidence* 2000

J

JANE'S ADDICTION

Jane's Addiction were peddling a mix of prog-rock, punk attitude and metal on their home turf in LA when everyone else in town was more concerned with the poodleness of their perms and the sumptuousness of their chest-hair. The band's iconic lead vocalist had neither, his hair was a jet-black scraggle and his front-age, skinny and smooth as a baby's bot. The other three members may have flirted with rock hair before they joined Jane's Addiction but Perry Farrell (peripheral – get it?) was a fully-fledged goth, straight out of the Cure influenced Psi-Com before he started the band with Eric Avery in 1987. As such, their artistic aims were at odds with the glam and thrash metal circulating at the time. It was more cerebral than the punk attitude just discernible in Guns n' Roses and less obvious than the muso pretensions hiding just beneath the surface of bands like Faith No More and Primus who may have appeared dumb and comical, but every now and then, let their mask slip. By contrast, Jane's Addiction were not always the tightest of bands but they knew their musical dynamics, had a good grasp on the art of melody-writing and had listened to enough folk, jazz and funk-inspired rock music from the previous two decades to establish an authentic after-punk, neo-hippy image that might just have been the birth of heavy metal's alternative other, and the saviour of a genre of music that was becoming increasingly irrelevant.

Having moved from Miami to LA and sang in a band called Psi-Com which disbanded in 1986 so that the two of its members could join the Hare Krishna movement, Perry Farrell, together with bassist Eric

Avery who had played the same scene as Psi-Com in his bands Flower Quartet and the excellently named Scrunge, began playing gigs as a duo. Jane's Addiction followed on from this with a series of drummers and guitarists, before settling on Stephen Perkins and later Dave Navarro from the glam-metal band Dizastre. They played the Roxy with Gene Loves Jezebel, various gigs with thrash and hardcore bands, and by 1987 had enough songs to record a demo which secured them a deal with the Warner label. Songs that would eventually appear on their debut studio album *Nothing's Shocking*, notably 'Mountain Song' and 'Jane Says' were already perfected at this stage, but despite this the band opted to release a live album for their official full-length release as an act of defiance against the carefully produced rock of the period, slaved over in studios at the expense of spontaneity.

Jane's Addiction set in place the mix of styles and control over dynamic range that was to become their trademark. It also introduced Farrell's high-pitched vocal style that resembled a more excitable Neil Young, and porn-ridden lyrics that took on a darker edge when filtered through his pre-pubescent child-like squeal. *Nothing's Shocking* arrived in 1988 with a cover picture of two burning naked Siamese twins and another set of songs dealing with the kind of thing that just wasn't talked about in rock music. The thrashers like Slayer and Metallica may have addressed historical themes of war, violence and all manner of ugly social practices but Jane's Addiction made it more personal. Farrell tried to get inside the mind of Ted Bundy and told stories about junkies and prostitutes. The album title relates to the desensitization of society by media, a subject explored by the likes of Gang Of Four, Dead Kennedys and the Minutemen, but never by those from the rock fraternity. In fact Jane's Addiction seemed to bring together the glamour of metal and the sincerity of independent guitar music in their utopian blend of styles. 'Ocean Size' is loud and metallic, 'Had A Dad' has the funk, 'Ted, Just Admit It' incorporates reggae, 'Summertime Rolls' is an exotic, erotic epic, 'Mountain Song' is heavy spiritual and 'Jane Says' has a mantra feel that the Beta Band might well have internalized at a formative stage – there are steel drums in there too!

In 1990 the band released *Ritual De Lo Habitual*. The stylistic experimentation continued apace but it's the constant switching between harsh manic noise and gentle, rolling extended instrumental jams that steals the show. On the lead-off track, 'Stop', the band rocks up a storm with Perkins' drumming particularly noteworthy, but then takes it all down in the middle-section segueing into a scorching Navarro guitar break and a brief multi-tracked a capella respite before the final crash. 'Been Caught Stealing' has the dancefloor in mind and stars Avery's growling bass, and then just when the listener has got the gist of the album, the band lurches into four tracks that have a combined playout time of 32 minutes. Scheduling suicide maybe, but once you're in the zone, it becomes apparent that 'Three Days', 'Then She Did', 'Of Course' and 'Classic Girl' are pointing the way towards a new form of heavy psychedelia that is refreshingly spontaneous, if a little loose and unfocused for the technique-obsessed times. It works for me at any rate. Much of the album was apparently recorded in chunks and pieced together, but certainly on 'Three Days' the band is all there and going at it at once.

Navarro's inability to kick his drug habit, Farrell's arrogance and Avery's deep-seated need to kick Farrell because he was severely pissing him off spelt the end of the band. There was a headline appearance at the inaugural Lollapalooza – it was after all, Farrell's idea – and then nothing from the band whose ability to get dark and ugly while continuing to party hard was lost on the grungers, industrialists and punkas that followed. Had they stayed together they might have led the international field after the coroner's report had come in on grunge, but as it was, the Beastie Boys walked off with the title and Jane's Addiction could only muster a brief reconciliation in 1997 before disintegrating again for the best part of another half-decade.

First team: Perry Farrell (v), Eric Avery (b), Stephen Perkins (d), Dave Navarro (g, k)

Place, time, scene: Los Angeles 1987. Jane's Addiction were a rock band with a very broad brief. They threw several styles into the mix and altered the texture and sound of rock music as it existed at the end of the eighties. They dealt in dark and violent subject matter and imagery but managed to retain a spiritual dimension that was often uplifting. They put the glamour into indie music and the seediness into metal, lit the touch paper and stood back waiting for the ensuing explosion that never really came.

What to buy first: *Ritual De Lo Habitual* 1990

And then: *Nothing's Shocking* 1988

Retrospective: *Kettle Whistle* 1997

JESUS AND MARY CHAIN

There was nothing going on in the British music scene in 1984. Even the new romantic scene was dying a slow and painful death. Howard Jones, Eurythmics and Nik Kershaw were the bright new pop things and as far as the indie scene was concerned, it started and ended with the Smiths. American bands led by REM and the Paisley Underground scene were clearing up on the gig circuit and in the music press. In short, there was a gap, and as it turned out, one good idea would be all that it required to plug it. British alternative music needed some excitement and Scottish band Jesus And Mary Chain got in there and provided it. Their idea was noise, or to be specific, feedback. Almost by accident they stumbled across the sound that would revitalize the British independent scene, and then when everyone least expected it, the chancers with the back-combed hair got really good.

East Kilbride, circa 1983; two brothers make a demo tape with only the most basic musical skills at their disposal. The songs are melodic and there's the hint of feedback coming from a broken effects pedal. The tape finds its way into Bobby Gillespie's hands and he sends it to his friend Alan McGee who runs a struggling record label called Creation in Clerken-well Road, London. McGee the idealistic punk with delusions of entrepreneurialism covets the tape and sets about telling everyone he knows that he has the future sound of rock music in his grasp. A gig is organized at the Roebuck on Tottenham Court Road, the Jesus And Mary Chain play a short set completely shrouded in white noise and feedback, attack their drummer and promptly pick up a deal with Creation Records. It's that easy.

For the next year, the band were effectively hyped as the saviours of British music as they played a series of gigs around the country, and managed to incor-

porate violence or controversy into just about every show. Through it all, the guitars fed back and a rich feller wearing no clothes was spotted lurking around the stage convinced that his new outfit was the smartest in all the land. The Jesus And Mary Chain's first single, 'Upside-Down' was indicative of the live performance, a painful listening experience due to the incessant layered white noise consisting of effects and feedback that ran across the entire song. The B-side, a version of a Syd Barrett rarity called 'Vegetable Man' confirmed their record collection credentials and constant referencing of the Velvet Underground in interviews helped to perpetuate the myth that the Mary Chain were here to reclaim the primal spirit of rock'n'roll.

'Upside-Down' became the biggest selling record in Creation's short history and was followed by three more singles and a deal with Warner's new pseudo-indie Blanco Y Negro. 'You Trip Me Up' was a magnificent single, at heart, a plaintive ballad played on acoustic guitar, but drenched in feedback, and the fourth, 'Just Like Honey' demonstrated that they had got the feedback under control as the simple drum part played by Bobbie Gillespie, and loudly recorded but almost-spoken vocals started to come into clearer focus amid the swirling noise. When *Psychocandy* was released in 1985, the melodies were even more apparent and it was becoming possible to ignore or embrace the sound of feedback depending on taste. The Jesus And Mary Chain had changed their audience's perception of music.

And with that done they stopped and started again, this time with the definitive blend of light and shade, *Darklands*. The Reids recorded it without Gillespie who had left to pursue the holy grail of noise pop in Primal Scream, and in fact played all of the instruments on the album themselves. The chugging 'April Skies' with its ghostly Beach Boys vibe where everything seemed to have been fed through an echo machine was a hit single, and once again confirmed that the duo were effective songwriters, and 'Happy When It Rains', another great single, pegged them as goths, or, following the banning of the single 'Some Candy Talking' because of its alleged drugs reference, goths who took lots of drugs.

The first two albums by the Jesus And Mary Chain covered a lot of ground and established them as an evolving band that might continue to surprise with future releases, but instead the band have opted to stick with a dark and decadent formula. And there's nothing wrong with that. Of the five studio albums that have followed, *Honey's Dead* is the best. Kicking in with 'Reverence', and its repeated mantra 'I wanna die like Jesus Christ', the album demonstrates that the Mary Chain can do screech and jangle equally well, and even finishes with a return visit to 'Reverance', this time done like Jonathan Richman's 'Roadrunner'. That's the boys having a laugh, who'd have thought it?

First team: William Reid (g), Jim Reid (v), Bobby Gillespie (d)

Place, time, scene: Glasgow 1984. The Jesus And Mary Chain jumped in to save indie music in the mid-eighties, and did it by injecting a little old-fashioned rock'n'roll debauchery. Nobody really expected them to make *Psychocandy* or *Darklands* because they seemed to be so lacking in musical ability when they played their first gigs. Just like Dinosaur in the US, they seemed to have stumbled across a sound and were quickly able to bend it to their will; small venue acoustics surely played a part in both bands' sophisticated understanding of feedback control. The Mary Chain were a key influence on My Bloody Valentine in particular.

What to buy first: *Psychocandy* 1985

And then: *Darklands* 1987, *Honey's Dead* 1992

In retrospect: *Barbed Wire Kisses* 1988

JOY DIVISION

In his autobiographical 'book of the film' *24 Hour Party People*, co-founder of the Factory label, Tony Wilson muses that the common factor in all the music that has meant something to him during his life is that in each case the musicians involved didn't have a choice in the matter; they had to get their words or ideas out to a wider public. In other words, they meant it. That's why it means something. Ian Curtis clearly meant it and he wasn't going to be put off by an unspoken rule of punk rock which seemed to dictate that real emotions and

real physical suffering weren't allowed on stage. Punk had arrived with a powerful and simplistic new agenda but it took another set of bands to interpret the new independent attitude and figure out how to express something more complex and long-lasting. Joy Division's sound was unique. With the exception of Wire, not many punk bands had consciously built their music, preferring instead, something more visceral and spontaneous. Joy Division were more intense.

From their early days as Warsaw, a name tellingly inspired by a track on David Bowie's *Low* album (produced by Brian Eno), the individual musicians had apparently realized that less is more, and left space in the mix for Curtis to inhabit with his brutal and frank poetry. In a sense, they were creating a quiet space, a void into which the watching audience could peer. Bernard Sumner, Peter Hook and Stephen Morris were happy to stay in the shadows coaxing strange sounds, extreme textures and unusual rhythms out of their instruments, leaving the focus on Curtis. Producer Martin Hannett was a key factor in getting the Joy Division experience onto record. He separated the instruments even further apart and created a new listening experience where a sonic structure is created out of instrumentation that sounds mechanical and inhuman, a frightening place for such an honest and troubled voice to be wandering around. It was all gloomy enough before Ian Curtis hanged himself; afterwards, listened to in retrospect, everything somehow sounds like the approaching inevitability of death. It's no wonder that the surviving members opted for something a lot lighter with their next project. Heavy stuff, Joy Division; the heaviest, in fact.

Bernard Sumner and Peter Hook met Ian Curtis with his wife, Debbie, at the second Sex Pistols show at the Lesser Free Trade Hall in Manchester. By then Curtis had been married for just under two years and was not yet 21. There were no children at that point, but a family was certainly on the cards as the birth of daughter Natalie in April 1980 attests. Not the traditional route into rock'n'roll but then Ian Curtis clearly had no intention of being a traditional rock'n' roll star. Warsaw played their first gig in Manchester in May 1977, took a trip out to Eric's[40] in Liverpool the following month, and with a line-up consisting of Sumner, Hook, Curtis and third drummer Steve

Brotherdale, recorded a session at Pennine Studios. By the time they had recorded a second session at the end of the year, they had replaced Brotherdale with Curtis' friend Stephen Morris and were starting to attract the attention of major record labels intent on keeping in touch with new musical developments at all costs, many of their older roster of artists having been dealt a body blow by punk and its philosophy of new beginnings.

A session paid for by RCA eventually cost the band over a thousand pounds to retain the rights to, and that was enough to convince them that the mainstream music industry may not always work entirely in their favour. In the end they signed with Factory Records in a deal in which they kept all copyright control of their material, received a fair royalty rate and were not expected to pay for additional expenses like artwork. Joy Division, along with Durutti Column and A Certain Ratio became the first creative musical aspect of a new brand that brought together studio production, live gigs and visual arts to support cutting-edge popular cultural products at its own expense. Local TV celebrity Tony Wilson used inheritance money to fund the recording of Joy Division's *Unknown Pleasures* album and was lucky that it was a relative success. There were distribution problems – how do you pay for a new pressing run if you haven't yet received the money for the last one? – but the band never considered jumping ship despite the effect that such problems were having on their potential success.

Thanks to some extensive touring and John Peel support, *Unknown Pleasures* soon became an essential purchase for those punks who had not got the retro ska or soul bug, and were keen to discover an entirely new approach to music. Curtis's songs dealing with dark shadowy forces and the loss of individual control – 'the bodies are tamed' – were matched with heavy bass, guitar-work that Tony Iommi of Black Sabbath would be proud of (check 'Day Of The Lords'), and a drum sound never heard before on record. Martin Hannett's digital delay echo system working in tandem with Morris's powerful drumming brought the drums to the centre of the overall sound and had the effect of isolating the voice, bass and guitar from each other instead of holding them together. And what the hell did he do to Curtis's voice on the first verse of 'She's

Lost Control'? Working with Hannett again, Joy Division made 'Transmission' and 'Love Will Tear Us Apart', neither of which appeared on albums – a policy which continued long into New Order's career – and in the first few months of 1980 recorded nine songs for the *Closer* album.

By now the band had toned down some of its rockier elements and was constructing a sound that restrained the raw power, and when it wasn't being all hushed and haunting, was actually quite poppy. 'Love Will Tear Us Apart' is the band at their most melodic, although Curtis' voice of course stops us getting caught up in the unfettered beauty of the melody and reiterates that the song is actually meant to be tragic. (Paul Young's version was tragic for an entirely different set of reasons.) 'Heart And Soul' and 'Isolation' get into a groove that marks them out as prototype New Order, but for balance 'Twenty Four Hours' is the darkest they ever got and allows Morris to demonstrate his remarkable skills as a drummer. 'Atrocity Exhibition' reflects on Curtis' epileptic illness as performance – 'for entertainment they watch his body twist' – and provides some insight into a possible reason for his suicide a few weeks after the track was recorded.

One notable epileptic attack had happened at a London gig lit by strobe lighting that forced him into such a fit that he fell into the drumkit, the audience applauding wildly thinking it to be a particularly extreme version of his jerky 'dying fly' dance. Such incidents may have led him to believe that the band would be better off without him and, because he had recently indulged in an extra-marital affair, he may have considered it best for everyone if he was no longer around. He hanged himself on May 15th 1980 having written a suicide note addressed to his wife. Iggy Pop's album *The Idiot* was on the turntable.

First team: Ian Curtis (v), Bernard Sumner (g), Peter Hook (b), Stephen Morris (d)

Place, time, scene: Manchester 1977. Joy Division were one of the first bands to reinterpret punk and channel its energy in a different musical direction. The sound and the subject matter clearly influenced the goth scene that followed, based around bands like Bauhaus, Sisters of Mercy and the Cure, and the involvement with Factory Records set up the label for a long period of creative work at the cutting edge of Manchester culture. New Order became the label's flagship band and were a vital link in the crossover culture that produced the Happy Mondays.

What to buy first: *Unknown Pleasures* 1979

And then: *Closer* 1980

Retrospective: *Permanent* 1995

K

KENICKIE

At about the same time that the Spice Girls were being put through their paces, learning to dance, strike a pose, and er, sing, all under the auspices of Simon Fuller – the man who often gets accused of cheap cynicism, but was actually only ever concerned with reinvigorating the feminist movement! – another group of young women were attending a party somewhere in Sunderland. They were very drunk, singing songs and when asked by a local record company executive if they were in a band, Lauren Laverne, Marie du Santiago and Emmy-Kate Montrose lied that they were. Out of nowhere they had a record deal, and with Laverne's older brother Johnny X on drums, they had a band too, Kenickie.

The first few singles, along with releases by Bis and Dweeb, signalled that something was missing in Britpop that wasn't being catered for. Following the high profile death of Kurt Cobain and the subsequent Blur vs Oasis media hype, guitar music was back on the teenage agenda. With the demise of Take That at the same time, it looked like manufactured pop – the worst kind, the false and misleading stuff that demands emotional and pubescent sacrifice to the cause – was dead. Hooray! But then Fuller marched into town with his ginger headed general at his side and kicked rock's big hairy ass. He had won the kids. And it was nearly all so different.

When Bob Stanley from Saint Etienne, who was now running Emidisc for EMI, announced that Kenickie, who he had just signed from Fierce Panda, would be millionaires by the end of the year, he was probably basing his comments on seeing Bis on *Top Of The Pops* and Kenickie singles like 'Punka', 'In Your Car' and 'Come Out 2Nite'. This was real girl power stuff, but not like Shampoo who simply went to different nightclubs from the ones you'd expect to see the Spice Girls at and just sang about 'having fun' from a slightly different perspective; Kenickie had fun but also appreciated that teenagers had brains, and a sense of responsibility too. This was after all, the band that turned down Alan McGee at Creation Records because they had to concentrate on their A'levels. Seen live, Kenickie were all sass and intelligence, brimming over with a confidence based on the knowledge that they were doing it all just the way they wanted to do it.

The album, *At The Club*, is all Buzzcocks energy, sarcasm and camp, right down to the Shangri-Las reference, 'tell us exactly', at the beginning of the first track. Musically, it's new wave, electro-punk with brass, strings and Indian bells thrown in, all played by the multi-instrumentalist band members. Not one single cracked the Top 20 in the UK, and that includes 'I Would Fix You' from the second album, which was easily the best single of summer 1998, crisp acoustic guitar, hook, singalong chorus, vibraphone, ba-ba ba's to fade. Not a radio record it seems! Kenickie split in 1999.

Du Santiago and Montrose have filled their time with another band, Rosita, and DJing club nights; Johnny X has become J. Xaverre and has concentrated on exploration and experimentation; while Lauren Laverne has decided to have her revenge on cloth-eared radio programmers by presenting regular shows on Xfm where the likes of Kenickie don't fall through the net.

First team: Lauren Laverne (v, g, k, cello), Marie Du Santiago (g, v, k), Emmy-Kate Montrose (b, v, k), Johnny X (d, k)

Place, time, scene: Sunderland 1995. Kenickie, together with Bis were tipped as the next big thing. The new-wave influence on their sound carried on a theme running through bands like Elastica and Sleeper, although they had a pop sheen to their punk and an exuberance that was quite different. It should never have gone away, and you can rest assured that every time I see Lauren Laverne at the Xfm studios I will be nagging her to get more stuff out!

What to buy first: *At The Club* 1996

And then: *Get In* 1998

KILLING JOKE

Killing Joke were surprisingly one of the very few post-punk bands to give their sound a heavy-metal edge. The fallout from punk obviously retained a deep-rooted distrust of longhairs with guitars. In America, hardcore bands like Black Flag were happy to admit their liking for Black Sabbath, but it was up to Killing Joke to muscle up the sound in the UK, producing a set of dark and gothic, industrial metal albums that seem to have inspired Steve Albini's production sound and the industrial/techno combination perfected by Trent Reznor of Nine Inch Nails, in other words, all dark music since 1981.

The band came into existence in 1979 when Jaz Coleman, from Cheltenham but of Egyptian descent, and drummer Paul Ferguson left the Matt Stagger Band, and together with bassist Martin Glover aka Youth from punk-band Rage, and guitarist Geordie, began to experiment with a new sound that put them up there with PiL, Wire, Joy Division, the Pop Group and Gang Of Four as crucial post-punk pioneers. Keeping the drumming low and rumbling – no hi-hats or cymbals – and layering synths and distorted punk guitar on top for Jaz Coleman to get all angry over, the first album is a foreboding and sinister affair, perfectly contextualizing the subject matter of the songs which are anti-capitalist and pro-environment. The single 'Wardance' and tracks like 'The Wait' and 'Tomorrow's World' pound along, sometimes fast and punk, sometimes slow and funky, but always brutal and brooding.

For the second album, *What's THIS For . . . !* in 1981, Killing Joke opted to stick with the rhythmic base of

their sound and Geordie's soon-to-become trademark high-end guitar. The tribal drum sound and restrained minimalist and repetitive musicianship complemented Coleman's increasingly paranoiac visions of a future world, where apocalypse was just around the corner and the only safe hiding place would be Iceland. After one more album – the harsh and occasionally atonal *Revelations* – in the spring of 1982, during the promotion for the album, Coleman, followed by Geordie, fled to Iceland where they remained for about a year. Youth joined them some time later, but returned to England to form Brilliant with Paul Ferguson and bassist Paul Raven, only to have his plans put on hold when Raven and Ferguson too fled to Iceland. Coleman had somehow managed to convince them all that his psychic and occult research was for real. And that's the sign of a great storyteller.

Youth did not rejoin the band when they returned to the UK in 1983 to make their most effective album up to that point, *Fire Dances*, which centred on Coleman's spiritually informed narratives. Ian Astbury of the Cult was influenced by Coleman's strong beliefs and split Southern Death Cult to reform as Death Cult to explore further his own connection with native American culture. 'Rejuvenation' and 'Frenzy' are fairly self-explanatory as titles, and are solid musical workouts bristling with confidence and energy, as well as being tuneful and to the point. It took them two years to follow it up with the commercially successful but unrepresentative *Night Time*, which contained hit singles 'Eighties' and 'Love Like Blood'. It's Killing Joke at their most accessible and enjoyable, and for a while their attempts to replicate it led them way off course, and resulted in at least two more break-ups and well over a decade of unfocused mediocrity.

Coleman, Geordie and Youth got back together for *Pandemonium* in 1994, which slotted nicely into a release schedule that included Nine Inch Nail's *The Downward Spiral* and Marilyn Manson's *Portrait Of An American Family*. Critics and fans of the breakthrough industrial bands bought it in their droves and re-launched the band, who put out the equally well-received *Democracy* two years later. Their legacy had caught up with them at last.

First team: Jaz Coleman (v), Youth (b, k), Geordie (g), Paul Ferguson (d)

Place, time, scene: London 1979. Killing Joke blended punk, metal and synthesizers to create a sonic environment in which Jaz Coleman's apocalyptic imagery could thrive. It inspired other mystically motivated types like Ian Astbury of the Cult and also the more darkly inclined industrial bands like Ministry and later Nine Inch Nails.

What to buy first: *Killing Joke* 1980

And then: *What's THIS for ... !* 1981, *Fire Dances* 1983, *Night Time* 1985, *Pandemonium* 1994

In retrospect: *Laugh? I Nearly Bought One* 1992

KRAFTWERK

Ralf Hütter and Florian Schneider, the core of Kraftwerk, began making electronic music after training as classical musicians. They claim they were first drawn to it because machines are more efficient. There was no need to practice endlessly to develop supple joints to play the piano or the violin more easily, and with electronic music the notes are the same every time, they can be relied on to do the job in hand, which in Kraftwerk's case was the creation of tone-films where the sounds evoke the mental images. Their breakthrough album, *Autobahn*, inspired Bowie and Eno in the mid-seventies, and two tracks from the following album *Trans-Europe Express* were used as the basis of 'Planet Rock', the Afrika Bambaataa track that launched electro-funk and then techno. As a result, the band is cited as a key influence on virtually all electronically-based music, whether it happens to be rock, pop, dance or hip-hop.

The duo's introduction to electronic music came via a late-night radio show on Cologne-based station Rundfunk. Listening to the sounds, it occurred to them that they would be able to construct music that did not require lots of other musicians who would need time to learn parts and then would only be able to play the more relentless repetition of sounds that they wanted them to for relatively short periods between breaks. The band still retained their learned classical music philosophy though, for them structure remains all important – no room for emotive interpretation and soloing – just play what has been composed.

For the first album, *Kraftwerk* – German for 'power-plant' – the duo signed up two drummers, one of whom was Klaus Dinger who left after the album to set-up Neu! with Michael Rother, a far more relaxed and more spontaneous project which led to three albums over five years. The *Kraftwerk* album featured Schneider's flute and Hütter's piano, along with the latest Vox and Farfisa organs, minimoog and Arp Odyssey synth. It also had a series of electronic oscillations that might have been inspired by New York band the Silver Apples. On their second album, recorded at their developing Kling Klang studio in Dusseldorf, they used a drum machine for the first time on record. It was 1971. It followed in 1972, introducing drummers Karl Bartos and Wolfgang Flur, and then the big one in 1974, *Autobahn*.

Hütter and Schneider recorded various examples of automobile noise and then attempted to recreate the noise using synthesized sounds. Together with a catchy motorik rhythm, a speciality of their old friends Neu!, a few travelogue lyrics and some timeless melodies, they created their longest and most evocative tone-film up to that point. David Bowie apparently spent most of 1975 and 1976 driving around with the album playing repeatedly on his car stereo, transforming him from an ex-glam rocking soul boy into a Teutonic modernist, with the haircut, the salute (oh dear that caused trouble) and the trilogy of electronic-music based albums. Although he was ahead of them with his *Station To Station* epic which had the synthesized sound of a train at the beginning of the track, Kraftwerk eventually went much further.

Unique rhythms and textures were recreated painstakingly and evocatively by the band on the 1977 album *Trans-Europe Express* from sounds gathered at Dusseldorf station just over the road from Kling Klang studios. Again, the travelogue feel is there in the occasional words of the title track, and the floating melodies are once again so beautiful that they put the traditional composing and instrumental dexterity of non-electronic artists and bands to shame. The image may have been cold and harsh but the sound was another thing altogether. 'Showroom Dummies' played on their evolving image and, what with the uniform suits and haircuts, they weren't exactly punk. But do you really think they cared? Remember, these guys were classical, although they were about to be given honorary degrees in the funk.

In 1977 they became the toast of black music. Afrika Bambaataa, working with Arthur Baker, used the Metal On Metal section of the title track to create 'Planet Rock' and with Baker's help, tried to create the rhythmic finesse that Kraftwerk had managed on that album, and Grandmaster Flash used their electronics as a template for his singles at the beginning of the eighties. The band played a sell-out show at the Ritz in New York in 1977, performing to a mainly black audience, and when they released the follow-up *The Man-Machine* album it became their biggest international hit. In the UK, the single 'The Model' went to number one at the end of a year which had also seen Ultravox, OMD, Human League and Depeche Mode break through. In 1981, with a decade of experience behind them, Kraftwerk were most definitely the original article though. Their electronics had a warmth and a fluidity that the young pretenders would never be able to match. The tracks on *The Man-Machine* were born out of improvised jam sessions and individual sounds created and treated so that they ultimately existed in a neverland between technological fact and musical fantasy. And they could do it time and again. That Kraftwerk, they were plugged-in guys.

First team: Ralf Hütter (k, p, v), Florian Schneider (k, fl, v), Wolfgang Flur (d, k), Karl Bartos (d, k)

Place, time, scene: Dusseldorf 1970. Kraftwerk used electronic instrumentation to bridge the gap between classical music and popular music. Dubbed kraut rock along with Can, Neu! and Faust who all had different sounds and musical agendas, Kraftwerk began to experiment with recreating everyday sounds and using them to surround or constitute melodies. David Bowie and Brian Eno were influenced by their sound, New York rhythm scientists working in hip-hop were turned on, and ultimately the electronic branch of new romantic pop was too. Dance music of every description owes something to the groundbreaking work of the power-plant boys.

°**What to buy first:** *Trans-Europe Express* 1977

And then: *Autobahn* 1974, *The Man-Machine* 1978

ED KUEPPER

At the same time that AC/DC were getting their act together in Sydney, led by Malcolm Young's search for the perfect amalgamation of Black Sabbath and the Rolling Stones, the Saints, along with Sydney's Radio Birdman, were inventing the Australian punk scene. Both bands took their inspiration from the Stooges, the MC5 and the New York Dolls, although there was a subtle difference. The Saints had a thing for classic R&B, while Birdman were always more Blue Oyster Cult than James Brown. By the time the Saints moved from Brisbane to London in 1977, they were already trying to shake off the punk tag that had been attached to them. They were a garage band with no specific philosophy or strategy. For them, the buzz was playing dynamic rock music in a locale where there had never been dynamic rock music before. After three albums and a couple of years operating from London, guitarist Ed Kuepper quit the Saints and returned to Australia to form the Laughing Clowns, once again pushing new forms of music, this time in a developing artistic musical community in Sydney. Both bands should be given credit for accelerating the potential of non-mainstream music in Australia, but also for working independently of and staying ahead of the game being played out in the US and the UK too.

Kuepper, like Deniz Tek in Radio Birdman, the Youngs and Bon Scott in AC/DC and Irish band-mate Chris Bailey, was not born in Australia. He was moved there from Germany as a child and within a few years had become a budding rock'n'roll star in a city with no rock scene. The first Saints album was called *The Most Primitive Band In The World* and it was recorded in Kuepper's garage onto a mono-cassette deck. The band could not get any gigs in the staunchly conservative Queensland capital. The Joh Bjelke Peterson administration came down strongly on anything deemed socially undesirable and that included nasty, rowdy rock'n'roll. It meant most of the gigs happened in the band's own front rooms, and that would have put paid to any further career development had it not been for a perfectly timed mailout.

The Saints recorded the single 'I'm Stranded' in June 1976, paid for 500 copies to be pressed and sent a couple to the UK music press. With punk just getting into gear, and with first singles by the Damned and the Sex Pistols still a few months away, the Saints' single was just what the British music press needed. By September it was *Sounds*' single of the week. EMI issued instructions to EMI Australia to sign the band – and quick, and by the end of the year the Saints were label-mates with the Sex Pistols. The debut album proper was recorded in two days with EMI's money, and turned out to be straight garage punk-rock, which according to Kuepper, they could have knocked out any time in the last couple of years. It's fast, full of attitude and is chock-full of ringing power chords and concise little lead-guitar fills. And as far as the Saints were concerned, had absolutely nothing to do with punk – they hadn't even heard of the stuff!

Still, a few gigs in London and selected enlightened venues around the country, and vocalist Chris Bailey was well on his way to becoming an icon of sorts. He had the classic 'couldn't give a toss' attitude, set off with long greasy hair, barely concealed fat gut and could take a drink or two. Well, that was how he was portrayed in the music press at any rate – a blend of punk, anti-punk and Irish/Aussie stereotyping. Of course, the band were more interested in being judged on their musical output, especially as they were clearly amongst the best in the country at that time. They specialized in a muddy, growling hybrid of rock and soul and often included strictly non-ironic versions of 'River Deep Mountain High' and 'Lipstick On Your Collar' in their set.

When the follow-up album, *Eternally Yours*, released in 1977, introduced horns into the band's sound, the Saints lost more supporters than they gained, such was the growing entrenchment amongst the new puritans. In fact, *Eternally Yours* is the band's best album. 'Know Your Product' reflects the band's own experiences with the music industry up to that point, and is a lesson in controlled anger; 'This Perfect Day' is the band's masterpiece – a short statement of resistance, delivered over a chugging beat and inventively deployed guitar. Kuepper's growing interest in jazz certainly helped with some of the arrangements on *Eternally Yours*, which can be seen as a launchpad towards the rest of his career. There was one more album with the Saints, the far more experimental *Prehistoric Sounds*, which toned down the guitars and brought the horns to the forefront of the Saints'

sound. Bailey didn't get most of it and new bassist Algy Ward, a heavy-metal freak, had difficulty feeling the R&B. Kuepper left the Saints and London and headed for Sydney where he formed the Laughing Clowns. Bailey stayed in London and the Saints marched on into obscurity.

Drawing on the individual musical talents of a group of musicians, most of which had a background in the Australian jazz scene, the first fruits of Kuepper's ambitious project to bring together R&B, jazz and Saints-styled rock were impressive. Eddy played guitar while a rotating line-up blew horns, huddled up to stand-up basses, and all the while Jefferey Wegener kept time. The early EPs and tracks, later collected together on *History Of Rock And Roll Volume 1*, combined complex arrangements with an energized improvisational feel that certainly inspired Nick Cave's later work with the Birthday Party and the Bad Seeds, and may have made its way back to the UK to influence post-punk funkers the Pop Group. The band's output does not follow any obvious developmental trajectory. Its success was determined by the musicians involved at the time and the mutual connectivity between them.

Looking back, Kuepper maintains that 'the Clowns would have been able to blast off into the stratosphere had there been someone that knew where we should draw the line on certain things. It was such an insular society ... trying to do so much – in some ways too much in that framework.' Many of those involved with the Clowns became key to the Sydney scene that followed, including the Apartments, the Moodists and the rejuvenated Crime And The City Solution. There is even a direct link to the formation of the Big Day Out festival, Australia's very own touring Lollapalooza that began with a stationary event in Sydney in 1992 but became an important step in the development of scenes in other Australian cities.

The Laughing Clowns' 1984 album *Law Of Nature* is probably their definitive work, even if definitive in this sense actually emerges from a sound that is actually indefinable. The Laughing Clowns disbanded in 1986 and Kuepper moved on to a similarly eclectic solo career, during which time he has run up over 20 albums, often eschewing focus in favour of experimentalism. And that's his prerogative. More than any other Australian musician, he can claim to have been integral in the formation of a totally different approach to making music.

First team: The Saints: Ed Keupper (g), Chris Bailey (v), Ivor Hay (d), Kym Bradshaw (b)

Place, time, scene: Brisbane, Australia 1975. The Saints took their inspiration from UK and US bands of the sixties, and particularly the Stooges' first two albums. They were adopted as punks by the developing UK scene but were always more interested in classic R&B. When Kuepper moved on to the Laughing Clowns he pursued this, and brought in elements of jazz which in turn gave the Birthday Party, the Bad Seeds and the Triffids some ideas. Post-punk bands such as the Pop Group in Bristol were doing something similar at the same time.

What to buy first: The Saints: *Eternally Yours* 1977

And then: The Saints: *I'm Stranded* 1977, Laughing Clowns: *Law Of Nature* 1984, Ed Keupper: *Electrical Storm* 1986

In retrospect: Laughing Clowns: *History Of Rock And Roll Volume 1* 1984

FELA KUTI

The history of popular music in the developed world is a history of incorporation. The music we have to listen to now has grown out of numerous and varied influences, some of which are technological, others cultural. When an existing style brings something new to the mix, it progresses into a new style, and artists and musicians who come along next internalize the new style and take it somewhere else again. The hub of pop is Anglo-American, and anyone who wants to connect with an Anglo-American industry and set of listeners must adapt their own creativity and spirit to fit into one of the many models available to them. If a new artist doesn't do this then they remain at the edge, not really part of popular music at all, not mainstream and not an alternative to the mainstream. Only Fela Kuti has managed to alter this situation. Trained as a classical musician in London, turned on to jazz in his spare time, and funkin' politicized when he got to LA, Kuti took these influences back to his native Nigeria and incorporated them into his own raw, powerful and political music. He called it Afrobeat, and since the early seven-

ties when he was lauded by rock, soul, funk and reggae fans and practitioners alike, no-one has been able to get close to his idiosyncratic sound and energy. Afrobeat died with Fela, his own genre done his way.

Born to a relatively affluent family in Abeokuta in Nigeria, Fela learned social resistance from his parents, who had been revolutionaries in the fight for independence from the British. His first recordings leading a band in London called Koola Lobitos were a direct result of his refusal to focus on classical music when jazz was the new rebel music in town.

By 1969 the Highlife Jazz Band was well established, playing a mixture of highlife, a form popular in Lagos, Nigeria during the fifties and sixties, and Fela's own style of jazz developed after several years of travel. After his visit to LA in 1969 though, he focused his music to reflect his new political awareness, which had been awakened by the Black Panther movement led by Malcolm X. He took the 'on the one' funk of James Brown's band and overnight transformed highlife jazz into 'Afrobeat' jazz. This was a big deal, not necessarily because Fela was an African, but because he was the first jazz artist to embrace funk, full stop. From now on, his band was called Africa 70 and it played regular shows at Fela's own Lagos venue dubbed The Shrine. Bootsy Collins, a member of James Brown's band, has told how he saw Africa 70 play there in this period and how the rhythms alone put the JBs in the shade. The *'69 Los Angeles Sessions* and *Fela's London Scene* are the two key albums from this period.

Fela's politics ran through everything he did from that point on. He twice ran for the presidency of his beloved Nigeria. He was arrested and attacked on numerous occasions including an incident in 1977, when he and some of his followers who lived together in his Kalakuta Republic were attacked and raped, an attack in which Fela's mother died, and in 1985 he was jailed by the state on a trumped-up charge, inspiring artists such as David Byrne from Talking Heads to add their voice to the protest for his release.

Byrne's favourite Fela album is apparently *Zombie* from 1970, which deals with the issue of military fascism in two long pieces. Like most of his Afrobeat recordings, the pieces build from piano or sax, bringing in horn sections and complex rhythms before breaking into call and response singing. Brian Eno is a fan of all of Fela's output, and has explained that he's particularly fascinated by the bass, which plays melody and is a percussion instrument simultaneously. Drummer Tony Allen was essential to the sound of Africa 70 and its later transformation into Egypt 80 when Fela slowed down the Afrobeat to a more meditative pace. *Beasts Of No Nation* is the standout from that period. Fela played sax, trumpet and piano, and sang. He also took the opportunity at his concerts to spend anything up to an hour talking to his audience about crucial political issues that affected Africa in its entirety, and black culture globally. James Brown never wanted to meet him. I wonder why?

During the eighties he made albums with producer Dennis Bovell who had worked with the Slits, the Pop Group and Linton Kwesi Johnson – all Fela fans – and Bill Laswell, at the hub of the New York avant-garde punk/funk scene. According to Bovell, Motown once offered Fela a million dollars for the rights of his back-catalogue which runs to approximately 75 albums. He refused, and consequently there's not a lot available unless you're really tenacious. He died in 1997, aged 58, of an AIDS related illness, even in death drawing attention to a major issue not yet acknowledged and addressed in his homeland.

First team: Fela Anikulapo Kuti (v, p, sx), Tony Allen (d), Ojo Okeji (b), Yinka Roberts (g), Isaac Olasugba (sx), Tunde Williams (tr), Eddie Aroyewu (tr), Tex Becks and Uwaifo (t-sx), Fred Lawal (g)

Place, time, scene: Lagos, Nigeria 1962. When Fela returned to Nigeria he combined the local highlife jazz with some Miles Davis and John Coltrane moves, but then in 1966 began incorporating funk into his performances. By 1969 he had created a highlife/funk/rock hybrid which he dubbed Afrobeat. Politics were a constitutive part of the style, which remained beyond the capability of other jazz or funk artists because, African or non-African, they did not have the background and melting pot of influences that Fela had. Talking Heads have incorporated Afrobeat rhythms into their music.

What to buy first: *Fela's London Scene* 1970

And then: *Zombie* 1977, *Black President* 1981, *Beasts Of No Nation* 1989, *ODOO* 1990

In retrospect: *The Best Best Of Fela Kuti* 2000

L

LAMBCHOP

There's something about Tennessee. Alabamians Hank Williams and Sam Phillips moved to Nashville and Memphis respectively just after the second world war setting up Tennessee to become the focal state for the sophistication of country music and the development of rhythm and blues, and ultimately the birthplace of rockabilly and rock'n'roll. Of course it was rock'n' roll that grew into the dominant musical force of the next half-century while country and R&B became slick, urbane money-spinning forms with their institutionalized corporate rules and hefty niche audiences. A few dissidents thrived, notably George Clinton and Sly Stone on one side of the colour bar and Johnny Cash and Willie Nelson on the other, but the crucial line of development was the country-soul hybrid that provided an alternative to rock music's obsession with art and technology in the late sixties and seventies. The Memphis based Stax label with its liberal multi-racial polcies, bringing together musicians and songwriters like Booker T, Steve Cropper, Don Nix, Isaac Hayes and Joe South with vocalists raised on gospel and country – Otis Redding, Rufus and Carla Thomas, Solomon Burke, Wilson Pickett – was an inspired alternative to the Grand Ole Opry and Motown. Tough rhythms, riffing horns, clean country guitar licks and most importantly an honest, direct approach to vocals and lyrics that ranged from personal and fragile to hard-hitting and political. Everyone from the Stones to the Allman Brothers and Creedence Clearwater Revival picked up on some aspect of the Stax style and did their bit turning on the next generation of post-punk influenced artists including Giant Sand and the Minutemen, even Mudhoney. Mind you, somewhere along the line the sophistication associated with country-soul got lost in favour of a focus on loose roots, art and politics. Eventually, it was a band from Tennessee, Lambchop, who realized the full potential of the old styles, authentic enough to sound timeless and with just enough punk irony to let people know that they have a point to make too. The fact that they couldn't get arrested in their home town is just plain old irony at work again.

Kurt Wagner started the band in 1986 as an excuse to hang out and have fun with some friends. Most of the early practice sessions and actual gigs occurred on various porches out of town, although they did eventually get a few gigs at Lucy's record store in Nashville, opening up for the likes of Guided By Voices, Vic Chesnutt and Superchunk. Spontaneity is key to the band's success with core players Deanna Varagona who plays saxophone, steel guitarist Paul Niehaus and organist John Delworth creating unusual sounds and moods simply by the combination of their individual instrumental skills. Wagner plays a vintage Gibson guitar from the 1920s, quietly and deliberately picking out notes to make simple melodies which add a Hank Williams dimension to his plaintive singing and storytelling in songs about automobile maintenance, garden irrigation techniques and throwing up. From this simple basis, an array of instrumentation from what is essentially a small ten-piece orchestra develops the songs into dense, lush and sweeping soundscapes that are accessible and experimental at the same time. From the outset on the debut album *I Hope You're Sitting Down* the instruments are massed, with more sophisticated arrangements emerging on the follow-up, *How I Quit Smoking*. There's also a swipe at bland country music entitled 'Garf' – I'll let you work that one out.

The 1997 album *Thriller* kicks off with two surefire hit singles although the titles suggest that chart success isn't high on the band's agenda. 'My Face Your Ass' is a gentle ballad that Smokey Robinson would have been proud to call one of his own, complete with euphonious backing vocals, traces of 'tracks of my tears' guitar and Wagner's delicate threat 'I'll show your punk rock ass'. It's followed by 'Your Fucking Sunny Day' wherein glorious horn riffs get the funk and this time the more energetic vocalist delivers the most venomously delivered 'fucking' this side of Lennon's 'Working Class Hero'. Yeah! The title-track is six minutes of experimental drone-work and there are three songs by Wagner's songwriting hero F.M. Cornog, demonstrating a degree of copyright altruism rarely found in the dog-eat-dog day-to-day machinations of the music industry.

What Another Man Spills, released in 1998, contains a relaxing stroll through the band's stylistic influences, including some nice Spanish guitar work and blue-note jazz on the lead-off track 'Interrupted'. There's another Cornog song and a version of Curtis Mayfield's 'Give Me Your Love' with hot-buttered blaxploitaion groove strings and a note-perfect pastiche of the great man's voice by Wagner. It took them two years to follow it up but with an expanded line-up of 13 members for their fifth album in 2000 they let rip with the amazing *Nixon* album. Wagner's alternating croak and falsetto vocals once again combine with epic arrangements. 'The Sound of Philadelphia' is lovingly recreated on a lot of the songs, many of which deal with the effect that Nixon-era politics had on Wagner and his generation when they were children. 'Up With People' is the standout track, a sanctified gospel dressing down for 'those clean-cut Pat Boone looking motherfuckers, young republicans telling us how to live our lives, imposing their values on the captive audiences that were their prey'. The repeated phrase 'C'mon progeny' is a little more chilling when understood in this context, and then for the final two tracks the band eschews all irony and musical beautification altogether for the sinister and brooding 'The Petrified Forest' and the blind noise terror of 'The Butcher Boy', a track which makes the links between a traditional murder ballad and a murderous society. It seems that there are times when a little dissonance is called for; Hank, Sam and Otis would have been impressed, even if they never quite mastered the feedback squall themselves.

Is A Woman? (2003) is a much less opulent affair, the orchestration replaced by a quieter, smaller sound that gives more room to Wagner's voice and lyrics. The songs are piano-based and the country-soul stylings have been muted in favour of ambient jazz and barely audible guitar dissonance. Just when everyone thought that they had a handle on what the man who lays floorboards for a living was up to, he goes and changes it all around. This entry might need some serious updating in a few years time.

First team: Kurt Wagner (v, g. k, p), John Delworth (k, p), Deanna Varagona (sx), Paul Niehaus (pedal steel, g), Allan Lowery (d), Jonathan Marx (tr), Marc Trovillion (b), Paul Burch Jr (vib), Mark Nevers (g), Dennis Cronin (tr, cor), Alex McManus (g), Matt Swanson (b)

Place, time, scene: Nashville, Tennessee 1986. Lambchop brought together country and soul music in the tradition of the Memphis-based Stax label of the sixties. Kurt Wagner's songs and vocals provide the country while the awesome collective talents of the band bring on the soul and funk. The attitude though is strictly nineties, inspired by punk and informed by art and experimentalism. In short, Lambchop are the definitive nineties band – contemporary retro. It will be fascinating to see where those influenced by the band take it next.

What to buy first: *Nixon* 2000

And then: *Thriller* 1997, *What Another Man Spills* 1998, *Is A Woman?* 2003

In retrospect: *Tools In The Dryer – A Rarities Compilation* 2001

MARK LANEGAN

The Screaming Trees were never part of the urban Seattle grunge scene. They existed on the periphery and took a more central role as grunge began to look to its more rural folk-blues roots. Had Kurt Cobain not died in 1994, it's probable that he would have worked more closely with Mark Lanegan, who has set up an excellent solo career as one of a dwindling number of contemporary singers able to interpret songs deeply and affectingly. He has most recently joined forces with ex-stoner rockers, Queens Of The Stone Age, as vocalist and spiritual guide.

The Screaming Trees were formed in 1984 in a relatively small rural community on the outskirts of Seattle. Vocalist Mark Lanegan had been a slacker youth who spent some time in jail for drug-related crime and was taken in by the Conner family who gave him a job debt-collecting for the family firm, of itself not a great career move, although the band he put together with the Conners' boys panned out pretty well, all things considered. After a year or so of gigging around the Washington area, with occasional forays into Seattle, they got a call from Greg Ginn, guitarist with Black Flag and manager of the SST label who offered them a deal.

The three albums for SST issued between 1986 and 1989 brought together hardcore punk with elements of psychedelia, both sonically and in Lanegan's occasionally mystical lyrics. The Meat Puppets, on SST at the same time, were clearly an influence, but the Screaming Trees, particularly Lanegan, remain an important link to the more melodic, lyrics-based, folk-blues styled songs that Kurt Cobain was writing by 1991. In fact, Lanegan's 1990 solo album *The Winding Sheet* released on the Sub-Pop label featured contributions from Cobain and Krist Novoselic from Nirvana, notably on a version of Leadbelly's 'Where Did You Sleep Last Night?', which the band resurrected on their *MTV Unplugged* special in 1994. Lanegan and Cobain became firm friends, a fact borne out by entries in Cobain's diaries that detail the music-swapping that went on between the two. Everything from Leadbelly, mentioned above, to the raw Seattle punk of the Fartz.

The early albums are hard rocking affairs but have their reflective acoustic moments too, and there's a glorious organic psychedelic streak running through it all. Lanegan's particular love for traditional folk-blues was explored further on *The Winding Sheet* though, produced by grunge figurehead Jack Endino. The Screaming Trees put out their major label debut *Uncle Anaesthesia* in 1991 – the same year as *Nevermind* was released – and neatly set itself apart from other grunge albums released in the following year, mainly because the Screaming Trees were never really committed to the same musical territory and urban subject matter that other grunge bands were then mining. *Sweet Oblivion* released in 1992 was the band's best album up to that point, but only until they issued their most complete and fully realized final collection *Dust*, in 1996.

Obviously, the album draws tragic inspiration in the first-person from the events and emotions surrounding Cobain's apparent suicide two years earlier, and musically it has a classic rock sound, perhaps benefiting from keyboard-player Benmont Tench's significant input. Lanegan's voice is at its blues and whiskey-soaked best, and tracks like 'Halo Of Ashes' with its coral sitar and 'All I Know' featuring Tench's refreshing electric piano are the best American rock has sounded in the last 20 years. It's just a shame that the band couldn't hold it together for another album. Socially, the Screaming Trees were at breaking point, and had been for several years mainly due to the titan-clashing relationship of the two brothers, Lee and Van Conner, a situation described by Lanegan as being in a band with two huge egos emanating from two men who take up the same space as three. Big blokes you see – the Conners. The all-in wrestling fight that the two had during the recording of *Dust* was the end really, even if it was par for the course as far as brothers in bands is concerned. Still, having made their point with their best album, the Screaming Trees disbanded in 1997.

Lanegan meantime, has released solo albums, each one focused on his remarkable voice, maturing into a blend of Tom Waits and Leonard Cohen singing delta blues songs. His regular side-kick Mike Johnson, formerly of Dinosaur Jr, helps with the mainly sparse arrangements for the albums, providing settings for songs about love, loss and despair, given a deep spiritual dimension by Lanegan's genius for interpretation. He lives every song that he sings whether it is one he has written himself or a cover. *Scraps At Midnight* released in 1998 and *Field Songs* in 2001 are the best examples of his art, although he can now also be heard fronting up Queens Of The Stone Age, having recently signed on full-time. Keep an ear out for Lanegan – after two and a half decades in the business he's only just getting started.

First team: The Screaming Trees: Mark Lanegan (v, g), Gary Lee Conner (g), Van Conner (b), Barret Martin (d)

Place, time, scene: Seattle 1984. The Screaming Trees were always just outside the Seattle scene, and brought a different, less dark and urban perspective, to the grunge that developed in the late eighties and early nineties. Kurt Cobain was a fan, particularly of Mark Lanegan's connectivity to the blues. It was becoming a more obvious influence by the *MTV Unplugged* session and might have continued further had events not dictated otherwise. Lanegan himself has continued to sing the blues like no-one else of his or the generation following.

What to buy first: The Screaming Trees: *Dust* 1996

And then: The Screaming Trees: *Sweet Oblivion* 1992, Mark Lanegan: *The Winding Sheet* 1990, *Scraps At Midnight* 1998, *Field Songs* 2001

M

MANIC STREET PREACHERS

The Manic Street Preachers were dead set on becoming pop stars. They used pop music for their own political ends, realizing that dissenting voices are a lot more powerful when shouted from the centre of the mainstream than the official sidelines. In short, they wanted to subvert from within. Songwriter Nicky Wire has always believed that lyrics, especially the wilfully controversial type, 'Repeat after me, fuck Queen and country', could have a significant effect on an impressionable young audience and ultimately they did, although it took the psychological breakdown and eventual disappearance of a founding member to make it happen. The band had a tough start, choosing to do things the hard way by avoiding identification with what they considered to be a stale indie scene. They dressed flamboyantly, wore make-up and criticized the accepted canon of serious pop music from Lennon to Cobain. In return, their own output was derided as shallow and meaningless by reviewers who claimed to hear nothing new in the band's basic pop-punk approach and uncomplicated reading of social history and politics. Pretty quickly the Manics reached a stage where just their very existence pissed people off because they didn't play by the rules. Looking back now, it's clear that when the Manics rolled into town it changed the existing preconceived notions of what constituted alternative, independent music, and importantly, begged questions about a set of institutionalized rules that governed the apparently progressive and free indie scene.

By the time the Manic Street Preachers had a record deal they were a tight-focused unit, musically and socially. Drummer Sean Moore had lived with his older cousin James Dean Bradfield and his family in Blackwood, Wales for several years, and bassist Nicky Wire was a close friend of Bradfield from their university days together. The other bloke Flicker was only ever temporary, his second guitarist role handed to the slightly older Richey Edwards shortly after the original Betty Blue became the Manic Street Preachers and recorded their first single 'Suicide Alley'.

From the outset, the roles in the band were a clearly defined division of labour with Wire and Edwards contributing lyrics and philosophy and Bradfield and Moore handling the musical arrangement including vocals. They gigged extensively during 1990 and 1991 and practised their own form of musical socialism. One notable instance being a double-booking at a musicians' co-operative in a wintry Coventry where the band selflessly encouraged the local band booked with them to take the slot while they headed on their way – time and money apparently not an issue.

Early reviews suggested that they were hopelessly out of step with both prevailing trends in independent music. They weren't introspective and moody and they weren't groovy party heads. Actually, in a way they were both, but the band never went so far as to say that, preferring instead to just slag everyone else off. The combination of glam fashion and glib comment that seemed to confirm their status as indie chan-

cers was only dispelled when Richey Edwards carved '4 Real' into his forearm with a razor blade during an interview. Julian Cope did something similar eight years earlier with a jagged microphone stand when faced with similarly negative media coverage. Sometimes popular music's status as a hollow and insignificant creative form is too much to take for artists wanting to demonstrate that they are in fact '4 real', and the only way past the branding and irony is to invoke the real physical existence of the human behind the image. It worked. The cartoon brand was suddenly cast aside and in a moment the band had a new image and a new audience without playing a single note.

The debut album *Generation Terrorists* released in 1992, brought together uncomplicated punk-pop songs with extravagant string-driven epics. Songs like 'Stay Beautiful', 'Slash And Burn' and 'You Love Us' related directly to their own early need for directness. According to Wire, not only was punk a tried and tested style for socially and politically charged lyrics, stretching back to the Clash, but it also provided the necessary clout for a band fighting its way out of a small working-class Welsh town, 'If you're from Manchester or London you already have the confidence, it's built-in, we needed something to give us our own confidence'.[41] But then there's 'Motorcycle Emptiness', which is still the band's finest achievement. It's a road movie of a song, right down to its wide-open driving production (the guitar even sounds like a motorbike) and lyrical insight into the nature of society and a person's place within it. The line 'All we want from you are the kicks you've given us' still stands as the band's most cutting indictment of contemporary culture.

Gold Against The Soul, which followed a year later, again divided the politics up into the social, by Wire, and the personal, by Edwards and set the wordy lyrics amidst some pretty Bradfield melodies, even if it did lack the bite of the one before it. Fortunately they spent less time on the next one and as a result captured the band's essence just in time, before it was lost. *The Holy Bible* was recorded in south Wales, the band having turned down the opportunity to work in Barbados, and it opens with a shot at themselves. 'Yes' was surely inspired by their close shave with rock cliché on the previous album, and was followed by a series of songs written by Richie Edwards which continue the loathing motif, of corporate America, of the holocaust and of his own physicality.

The songs are given the patented Gang Of Four treatment, all angular with odd drum patterns and carefully deployed guitar, and there's extensive use of sampled narration, often at the beginning of songs, dropped in like quotations to add weight to the arguments the band are making. All that's missing is the Harvard referencing system. 'Faster' and 'PCP' are tough songs, 'The Intense Humming Of Evil' is disconcerting and 'Yes' and 'Die In The Summertime' are actually quite pretty in spite of their subject matter. Although Bradfield must have felt the pain of his close friend in a lot of the lyrics, and sings the words in a detached way, fast and quite shouty, to do them quietly and straight would have been too overwhelming. The lyrics in the inlay card printed next to a picture of Edwards aged about two on the beach read 'I have crawled so far sideways. I recognise dim traces of creation. I wanna die, die in the summertime.' Six months after the album's release the toddler at the seaside disappeared and the band were never the same again.

The albums that have followed *The Holy Bible* still benefit from Nicky Wire's political nous and sense of classic Bevan-era Labour party principles. He talks good history too 'Libraries gave us power, then work came and made us free'. *Everything Must Go* in particular is a flawlessly-produced album that does credit to Bradfield and Moore's musical capabilities. They have recovered well. The music was never really going to be a problem, but as Wire recently explained, losing Edwards was as much about losing a right-winger as a guitarist, the two having grown up playing football together. It broke the band's heart.

After a while it becomes a career thing, and the bands that make it to the top of the pile have the choice of surrendering to commercial expediency and taking the easy route or continuing to push themselves, often answerable only to their own rules and ethics. Alongside bands like REM, Pulp, Primal Scream, Blur, Radiohead and the Beastie Boys, the Manic Street Preachers continue to be admired for their continued independence in the face of huge earnings, corporate deals and concerns and responsibilities outside of music. It's a situation which the Manics helped to bring about by openly questioning the structures that once kept all the interesting music locked away in the indie cupboard away from mass exposure. Their deal was with CBS right at the beginning and that took a long time and a lot of pain to live down. Some may say that Richey Edwards would be appalled at the new Manics who appear to be the very thing that he always railed against. Who can know? But surely it's better that people hear songs that warn of cultural mediocrity than having to just settle for those that are riddled with it.

First team: James Dean Bradfield (v, g), Nicky Wire (b), Richey Edwards (g), Sean Moore (d)

Place, time, scene: Blackwood, Wales 1990. The Manics didn't emerge from the Welsh-language scene prevalent at the time of their formation. From the outset they were determined not to be ghettoized or attached to a scene of any sort. Their breakthrough, just as baggy was being superseded by grunge as the official alternative, inspired the New Wave of New Wave which also included S.M.A.S.H and These Animal Men, a scene which paved the way for Britpop.

What to buy first: *The Holy Bible* 1994

And then: *Generation Terrorists* 1992, *Everything Must Go* 1996

In retrospect: *Forever Delayed* 2002

MARILYN MANSON

Brian Warner's agenda was mapped out right from the beginning. He wanted to fuck shit up. He knew he'd have the kids with him when he did it because he knew how to get them on board. All he had to do was get them on his side by tapping into their generationally-defined post-structuralist culture. He could put on all the clobber, the make-up, the eye thing, sing songs about death, torture and suicide and they would identify with him, become his followers. That would do it, put the cat among the pigeons, get him even more publicity. And then he would have achieved his aim, namely, the emancipation of American youth, freedom from a 'religion and media-induced coma' with freedom to think for themselves. They're parents and unreceptive friends wouldn't get it at all of course, and would join in the inevitable chorus of disapproval. Even better.

He put together his band in 1989 in Florida, insisting that each member took a name which brought together the greatest female sex symbols and the most infamous murderers of the present century. Daisy Berkowitz played guitar, Twiggy Ramirez bass, Madonna Wayne Gacey looked after the all-important organ and Sara Lee Lucas pounded drums leaving him, Marilyn Manson to concentrate on the audio/visual message, starting with statements like 'I don't think people understand how deep Marilyn Manson goes into my existence.'

By the early nineties, the band, also called Marilyn Manson, had caught the attention of Trent Reznor of Nine Inch Nails who signed them to his Nothing label, helping out on the debut album *Portrait Of An American Family*. They recorded it at Reznor's Nothing studios, Sharon Tate's former house in Hollywood and the scene of her brutal murder at the behest of Charles Manson two decades before. The promotion that went along with the album made much of the connection. To fans it was way cool, to concerned parents it was sick. On the album, Manson performs grotesquely over-the-top songs dealing with drugs, sexual deviancy and the perennial issue of lunchbox violence. Throughout, he keeps his mask well and truly up, a different approach to that adopted by Alice Cooper, who the audience was sure they knew really. Of course, kids listening to the album are sure they know Manson anyway, and are totally aware that he is playing a part; it's the adults who don't watch horror movies or play violent beat 'em ups that fall for the act, and they're the ones doing the reviewing too. OK, so musically, it's a fairly standard re-run of the stuff that Ministry and Nine Inch Nails used to do, but as an alternative to the sterile, standardized pap that is routinely forced down their throats, it has the potential to get a generation of kids kicking some big fat rock ass.

On the grab-bag *Smells Like Children* (1995), the band covered Screamin' Jay Hawkins and Patti Smith's 'Rock'n'Roll Nigger' which is never a bad thing, before releasing the second album proper, *Anti-Christ Superstar* later in the year. More industrial rhythms and gothic, doom rock combined with suitably mocking voice to express the dark matters afoot in the songs, which this time dwell on the subject of suicide, making Manson the latest in a long line of heavy metal artists to do so. High-profile cases centring on songs by Judas Priest and Ozzy Osbourne have made it a controversial topic, despite both previous claims having been dismissed and roundly criticized by the justice system looking into them. It's Manson's intention to show that those caught up in the censorship debate are not loony right-wingers getting their morality kicks, but when faced with a character as apparently grotesque as himself, it draws in whole sections of the American public. Of course, he hadn't expected to be implicated in the Columbine School killings, and really shouldn't have been, the kids doing the shooting were not particularly interested in Manson's music or message, they were just kids doing the shooting, which was Manson's whole point.

The continued focus on artists like himself ignored the underlying problems that were actually provoking such behaviour. He didn't need to explain that to the kids listening to his records because, if anything, they were the more sensitive, thoughtful and well-adjusted group. For them, the age old rule of rock'n'roll rebellion applied, they found in Manson a channel for their rebellion, just like their grandparents had, the rock'n'rollers or the hippies, and their parents had in Alice or punk. With *Anti-Christ Superstar* Manson was doing nothing more than following in the traditions of several generations past, what had changed was the organization of the opposition. No longer were they sighing parents shaking their heads and admitting that they don't understand the youth of today. At the turn of the millennium, right-wing America had organized middle-of-the-road America into a fearful, misinformed and easily-led mass sector of society, primed and ready for the next stage. Now that's scary.

First team: Marilyn Manson (v), Daisy Berkowitz (g), Twiggy Ramirez (b), Madonna Wayne Gacey (k), Sara Lee Lucas (d)

Place, time, scene: Florida 1989. Marilyn Manson are a politically motivated band. Originally calling themselves Marilyn Manson and the Spooky Kids, they eventually emerged onto the hard rock scene with their mix of gothic rock and industrial rhythms and slotted into an alternative music culture still reeling from the death of Kurt Cobain and finding catharsis in Nine Inch Nails' album *The Downward Spiral*. With the higher profile of underground music,

Manson has become a celebrity figure who, in interviews and with his other artistic projects, is successfully meeting his political aims within the context of a postmodern society.

What to buy first: *Anti-Christ Superstar* 1996

And then: *Mechanical Animals* 1998

MASSIVE ATTACK

Massive Attack have been known to win dance music awards although they are self-confessed two left-footers. Perhaps dub, reggae, soul or hip-hop describes what they do, or that genre invented just for them: trip-hop. It's irrelevant really. There's no slavery to generic convention in Massive Attack and no kowtowing to any of that individual ego bullshit either. A quick bit of content analysis confirms that the three core members have used their own voices on just a third of the group's recorded output. They opt instead for outside voices that bring their own history and personality to bear on the eclectic montage of musical styles. Shara Nelson enhances the soul, Horace Andy teases out the reggae, Tricky disconcerts, Sinead O'Connor makes it political and Elizabeth Fraser contributes the indefinable ethereal. The core of the band, until 2002 was Robert Del Naja, nicknamed 3D, a former graffiti artist with a sophisticated understanding of texture and colour that has clearly dominated the sonic arrangements of the band's four albums, and fellow rapper and musician Daddy G (Grant Marshall) and DJ/musician Mushroom (Andrew Vowles) who both have an extensive knowledge of songs and sounds that can be selected and incorporated at crucial moments. Ultimately, it is these three individuals who have been responsible for creating an entirely new listening experience based entirely in sound. Musical style is still relevant but secondary to the needs of the mood being developed. Massive Attack do sonic architecture.

Leaving aside Beki Bondage and Julie Burchill's questionable contribution to Bristol punk, the really class act were the Pop Group, a band regularly cited by Nick Cave as a major influence. They spent the late seventies perfecting a punk funk hybrid that took on an even greater significance after they split. Two bands: Pigbag, and Rip, Rig and Panic emerged from the fall-out and Mark Stewart, the band's vocalist, became a permanent fixture on the Bristol scene, pursuing new funk and hip-hop rhythms with Keith LeBlanc and Doug Wimbish of the American Sugarhill label. It was Stewart who got the Wild Bunch collective their gigs at the Language Lab in London, alongside their local residencies at Bristol clubs like Thekla and The Dug Out.

The Wild Bunch were a set of like-minded artists, DJs, rappers and musicians which included Nellee Hooper, Smith and Mighty, Trickykid, a young Geoff Barrow, who later came up with the idea of Portis-head, and the three members of Massive Attack, who distilled the variety of styles found in the Wild Bunch, losing the party vibe but retaining the punk philosophy, the soul vibe and the dub foundational structure. Soul II Soul may have caught the moment back in 1987 but the mood had changed by 1991. Jazzy B's inspirational appeals for a universal groove had given way to a pragmatic realism; it was still 'them and us' and Massive Attack knew that. Tracks like 'One Love' at the individual level or 'Hymn Of The Big Wheel' at the global level, which both appear on *Blue Lines*, preach utopia but with an added reality check – not everyone out there conforms to the same ideals. It's there in the lyrics and confirmed in the sonics.

The mood of *Blue Lines* is most definitely heavy, it's all bottom end. 'Daydreaming' may have Shara Nelson 'floating on air' but it's only a brief release from the dark urban monotony, signified by the reiterative and very phat bass line holding it all in place. 'Five Man Army' demonstrates the trio's innate understanding of dub, with rocksteady guitar stabs, sonic repeats and what sounds like a little wah-wah towards the end. Even the love songs are tough. On 'Safe From Harm' Shara sings 'And if you hurt what's mine I'll sure as hell retaliate' and then there's 'Unfinished Sympathy', the song of the album and let's face it, the decade. The lyrics contain some of the best love poetry written in the name of popular music set to an epic blend of yearning soul, hip-hop beats and dub reggae technique that is then taken to a different place completely when those major chords, swirling strings and pseudo-choral 'hey, hey, hey-e-heys' are added.

Blue Lines is an album of depth, a series of sound-scapes where the song is actually born of rhythm, non-existent without it, that's why the only person to cover, or rather exhume Massive Attack so far, is dub producer Mad Professor. Sure, you can take the tracks apart, but only Massive Attack know how to put them back together. *Protection* released in 1995 is a very good album. *Mezzanine*, three years later, is a better one. Both reinforce the continued relevance of Massive Attack's aesthetic, which like all good trip-hop is about creating an atmosphere and then selecting the right vocalists to draw the listener into the depths.

'Protection' is a romantic song but with just that suggestion of entrapment and suffocation depending on how you interpret the blend of lyric and music. It features vocals by Tracey Thorn and was so convincing that it set Everything But The Girl off on a totally different career trajectory, mixing their gentle folk with sophisticated beats. Similarly, 'Teardrop' is probably the best thing that Elizabeth Fraser has put her voice to and let's face it, she was hardly working with chancers in the Cocteau Twins. The music is kept to a minimum but it actually sounds like it took three years to get just the right texture and resonance in those piano chords and spurious other effects that contribute to the song's three-dimensional vibe. On other tracks the music is full to overflowing. There are scorching guitar solos in 'Angel' and 'Rising Son' and the oxymoronic 'Inertia Creeps' is terrifying in its otherworldliness.

By the time *100ᵗʰ Window* was released in 2003, only 3D remained of the original trio, and with such a long period of gestation it could be concluded that the concept of Massive Attack had become harder to define, especially with the likes of DJ Shadow taking giant leaps into the realms of the unknown. Like *Mezzanine*, there is a theme of sorts running through the album that is not unlike Roger Waters' doomed-culture lyrical observations on the later Pink Floyd albums. Sinead O'Connor sings three of the songs including 'A Prayer For England', and right through the album there's a sense of restrained anger. 3D's vociferous campaigning against the war waged on Iraq around the time of the album's release may well have removed some of the old anonymity associated with Massive Attack, their philosophy and working practices, especially now the original collective of mysterious figures has gone.

3D is at the beginning of a new phase and it will be interesting to see what comes next. Mind you, if he sticks to his usual timetable the next album won't come around until 2010. In the meantime it's enough to say that Massive Attack have readdressed the integration of music and culture that fell out of favour after the demise of the Clash and the Specials, and then moved it on a bit. Reason enough for them to be in a book like this.

First team: 3D (v, k, samp), Daddy G (v, k, samp), Mushroom (v, t-t, samp), Guests: Horace Andy (v), Shara Nelson (v), Tricky (v), Tracey Thorn (v), Elizabeth Fraser (v), Sinead O'Connor (v)

Place, time, scene: Bristol 1989. The philosophy of the collective was central to Massive Attack, just as it was for the group's previous incarnation as three key elements of the Wild Bunch. The Wild Bunch was the first artistic expression of a specifically Bristol-based subculture that can be traced back to the national outbreak of punk in the late seventies and perhaps in part a local reaction to the St Paul's area riots in 1980. Musically its basis was in US breakbeat but its devotees eschewed B-boy posturing for the more progressive form of cultural resistance associated with the non-segregated punk and two-tone philosophies circulating on their own block. Massive Attack took the punk, soul and dub aspects of the Wild Bunch music and culture and came up with a darker sound to set against Nellee Hooper's work in Soul II Soul.

What to buy first: *Blue Lines* 1991

And then: *Protection* 1995, *Mezzanine* 1998

MC5

'Hearing that you made a person decide to start a band – that's the ultimate compliment. Of course, I care what the MC5's work means to "civilians" too but the musicians are my own tribe.'[42]

Guitarist Wayne Kramer has always maintained that the MC5 were about action and not just entertainment, and over the years their influence has inspired whole scenes to develop. Together with Iggy's Stooges, they are probably the key performance band of the pre-punk era, regardless of the music they made. Their first album was a live one because they had decided that that was what they did best, and would be the most honest account of the band as it sounded in 1968, or to be precise, how the band sounded on the nights of October 30th and 31st at Russ Gibb's Grand Ballroom in their hometown of Detroit. All that stuff about being ready to testify dates from that album, which is launched with the question 'Are you part of the solution or part of the problem?'

The MC5 saw themselves as the solution, taking their music to the American people and offering an alternative to the hippies, who were becoming an official counter-culture complete with reality-dulling drugs and vague philosophizing. When they played outside of Detroit, they were met with disbelief and incomprehension by crowds that weren't ready for such directness. In fact, the hatred that the band provoked went some way to confirming the class divide that existed between the flower children with white-collar potential and the blue-collar fans that still wanted to experience the physical spirit of rock'n'roll like Elvis had done it. The MC5 made body music, not head music.

The band formed in 1966 with the intention of playing a freer form of R&B than that practised by most other garage bands of the time. More importantly they were determined not to lose the spirit of the music by mastering it and creating something that sounded good in someone's front room. The two guitarists, Kramer and Fred 'Sonic' Smith concentrated their efforts on a twin attack that was improvised in keeping with the free-jazz style of their heroes Sun Ra, Ornette Coleman and John Coltrane. With everything turned way up high in the mix, the sound of their early singles 'I Can Only Give You Everything' and 'Looking At You' resembles nothing else of the time. When chords are not banged out on the beat, there's fuzz and feedback strewn across the songs, leaving vocalist Rob Tyner no choice but to scream vocals over the top. Such an oppressive musical approach and a tendency to incite violence and vomit on stage (on at least one occasion, onto a Beatles album) lost them a lot of work in Detroit and when they did get a gig at a battle of the bands competition, ensured that they lost.

Fortunately, John Sinclair, co-ordinator of the revolutionary political group the White Panthers, liked them and took over management that very night. His input moved the band onto an even more confrontational political agenda. Stars and Stripes were ripped and burned, groupies defiled for promotional purposes and lyrics written that documented the growing social discontent in Detroit specifically, and more widely the spirit of revolution growing across America and the world as the sixties drew to a messy end.

The live album *Kick Out The Jams* contains a set of songs that espouse White Panther rhetoric and throughout, the 'fuck-off' knob is turned up to just over maximum. You can almost see Smith and Kramer administering blows to their guitars and Tyner on his knees gripping the microphone. The energy is palpable. The title track is of course, the highlight but there's also 'Rocket Reducer No. 62' which demonstrates beyond doubt what a great set of musicians the MC5 actually were. It's pure heavy metal. 'Rama lama fa fa fa' indeed. Rock writer Lester Bangs hated it, which was odd as he's normally on the money with this kind of thing. Mind you he did take it back eventually and anyway, that other great writer of the period, Jon Landau was impressed enough to volunteer his services as producer for the band's first studio album. It was his first too, and somehow he managed to get the band into tip-top shape for the job in hand.

Back In The USA is classic AM-radio pop music, complete with harmonies, fast and tight rhythms and a patented buzzsaw guitar sound that was eventually used by the Ramones to great effect on their songs about sniffing glue and teenage lobotomies. *Back In The USA* was packed with songs about high school and teenage lust where the irony is only apparent when you hear tracks like the anti-draft song 'The American Ruse' and 'chop, chop, chop, chop, chop, chop, chop, chop, chop, chop, chop chop' 'The Human Being Lawnmower', which confirm that the MC5 still had an axe to grind even if their mentor Sinclair had inevitably ended up doing time for crimes he did commit by then. It's a totally different sound to that of their first album, which, with a couple of well-placed gigs, got them noticed in the UK by a stack of musicians who were about to take over the pubs and initiate the ultimate attack on bloat rock which the Motor City 5 had warned everyone about a decade before.

There was one more album in 1971 before the band split. Fred 'Sonic' Smith married Patti in 1980, Wayne Kramer formed Gang War with Johnny Thunders, Michael Davis put together Destroy All Monsters, and Dennis Thompson did New Race. Rob Tyner tried a new MC5 but died in 1991. Xfm came on air in September 1997 – the first record played was 'Kick Out The Jams'.

First team: Wayne Kramer (g), Fred 'Sonic' Smith (g), Rob Tyner (v), Michael Davis (b), Dennis Thompson (d)

Place, time, scene: Detroit 1966. The band was certainly inspired by the garage psychedelic bands of the period, but was actually alone in initiating an original punk sound. When Iggy arrived in Detroit in 1967 and began the Psychedelic Stooges, the MC5 had already done the groundwork.

What to buy first: *Kick Out The Jams* 1969

And then: *Back In The USA* 1970

In retrospect: *The Big Bang: Best Of The MC5* 2000

MEAT PUPPETS

Kurt Cobain loved 'em. That's why he invited the two brothers that set up the Meat Puppets in 1981, onto Nirvana's *MTV Unplugged* special in 1993. There were three Meat Puppets' songs performed that night, each one fitting perfectly with the stripped down semi-acoustic Nirvana material that Seattle's most famous sons were experimenting with. Cobain was reportedly worried about doing his songs quietly and no longer being able to retreat into the metallic shadows in-between verses when the band usually hit the loud bits. The thing was, people wanted to hear his words, unlike the other grunge bands he seemed to have something personal and significant to say. And where had he found his inspiration for such an approach? Why, the Meat Puppets of course. They may have started out as a hardcore punk band but there was always this connection to roots music and ability to write poetry that suggested that hardcore was only ever going to be a temporary thing. By their second album they had mastered what Barney Hoskyns at the *NME* called 'hillbilly metal hardcore' which gets it about right. Others started calling it cowpunk but having never heard any specifically bovine music, I'm loathe to consider its cross-generic potential.

Curt and Cris Kirkwood didn't have the most idyllic of childhoods. They grew up in Mexico, Arizona and Texas during the 1960s. Their parents split when they were small and Ma Kirkwood married a succession of unsuitable suiters, exposing her boys to random acts of violence which culminated on one occasion in having to flee a burning house set alight by their stepfather du jour. Life was pretty shit, until that is they inherited a large amount of money from their millionaire inventor grandfather. It's true! Realizing that they probably wouldn't have to work like normal people for a while, they decided to start a band instead.

The Bastions Of Immaturity became the Meat Puppets with the addition of jazz and punk fan Derrick Bostrum, and after a series of gigs around Phoenix they were signed up by Greg Ginn's SST label and found themselves playing with Black Flag in support of their debut eponymous album released in 1981. On it the trio demonstrate that they are excellent musicians even when playing at high speeds, and lyrically the tone is pure roots, evocative, self-deprecating and tinged with tragedy, but with the usual old-timer regret replaced by a more youthful and positive sense of hardcore purpose, 'The rain falls softly on the barren trees, across the ocean blows a little breeze. Soon my factory's gonna shut down, I'll go back to the accepting ground. But until that day this walking mire to greater heights will aspire.'

The follow-up, *Meat Puppets II* contains the three songs performed with Nirvana 11 years later. 'Lake Of Fire' is driven by some immaculate strumming and sparkling vibrato acoustic fills but descends into a blaze of searing electric guitar – the quiet-loud dynamic that Nirvana perfected with such skill. 'Split Myself In Two' is the blueprint for the amalgamation of country and punk that the No Depression alt-country bands ran with at the end of the decade, and 'Plateau' is the definitive slacker-stoner track 'who needs action when you've got words'. *Meat Puppets II* is the desert and small town America, home-spun philosophy and a few smiles along the way. To give it a commercial strap-line, let's say 'Roots music for the post-punk generation.'

The next one, *Up On The Sun*, pursues the desert vibe and is even looser and more stoned than its predecessor. Recorded in just three days, it incorporates psychedelia and jazz, but once again the blend of styles, notably on a track like 'Enchanted Pork Fist', is subtle and never . . . ahem, hamfisted. If you buy the recent version of the album which contains extra demos you'll hear a lengthy jam version of 'Hot Pink' which is the trio at their improvised best. 'Maiden's Milk' has some excellent porch whistling and lyrically the album overall is another collection of songs mulling over both the big ideas and the everyday chores of mid-west American life. The Meat Puppets continued with a string of impressive albums right through until 1998, rocking or rootsy-ing at will. Some say that they were as good as Cream. Bastards. They were much better than that.

First team: Curt Kirkwood (v, g), Cris Kirkwood (b, v), Derrick Bostrum (d)

Place, time, scene: Phoenix 1980. Originally attached to the west-coast hardcore scene, they were one of the first bands to incorporate roots music into their punk rock. Along with X and Wall of Voodoo, they spearheaded the roots revival that begat Dream Syndicate, Long Ryders, Giant Sand, Green On Red, Flaming Lips and arguably REM too.

What to buy first: *Meat Puppets II* 1983

And then: *Up On The Sun* 1985, *Mirage* 1987, *Huevos* 1987

In retrospect: *No Strings Attached* 1990

MERCURY REV

Mercury Rev have always aspired to make dream music and have spent the best part of a decade developing their craft and waiting for technology to catch up sufficiently so that they could finally realize their aim. Their fourth album *Deserter's Songs* is not just the culmination of Mercury Rev's work, it is perhaps the ultimate studio album, traceable back to the noise experimentations begun by Cocteau Twins and My Bloody Valentine in the early and mid-1980s and stretching much further back to the first studio-art of Phil Spector and Brian Wilson. Then, the goal was to make real instruments sound other than of themselves, to create fantasy noise, a task which required an intuitive sense of sonic manipulation and a desire to bypass the cosy settings and functions of the studio desk. Dream music can only really be created when individual sounds do not sound

quite right. Put a whole stack of those sounds together in a heady mix of noise and you've got brain-meltdown. Of course, if you can hang it all on melodic hooks and use the right words to map a course through the melange of sound then a whole new world of possibilities opens up for future listening pleasure. Mercury Rev may not have been the pioneers of so-called noise-rock but they've taken all the work on board, attached it to the roots of popular music learned in their impressionable years and have created something darn pretty in the process. They're as far as we've got, where we're at right now.

Jonathan Donahue helped out his friend Dave Fridmann with the sound for the Flaming Lips before he joined them as a full-time member in 1990. By then he and Fridmann already had their own band which eventually became known as Mercury Rev. There was little in the way of financial backing for the band and sessions for their first album *Yerself Is Steam* became protracted and stretched out over several years. Fridmann's sound engineering course stood the band in good stead right from the outset and he became a key part of the band's success with his ever-expanding knowledge of studio technique. Guitarist Grasshopper provided 35mm magnetic film stock for their first recordings because he felt that it provided a warmer overall texture, and when the band played live, guitars were hung from concert hall ceilings so that the inevitable feedback added another dimension to the sound.

When *Yerself Is Steam* was eventually released, it was too late for the heyday of the noise scene on both sides of the Atlantic but it connected with British critics who appreciated the psychedelic feel and loose jamming. The band worked to a tighter schedule on the follow-up *Boces* but with less impressive results. Mercury Rev were clearly a band who needed to take their time. Heated band arguments led to vocalist David Baker's departure from the band. It was the best thing that ever happened to them.

With Donahue and Grasshopper in charge of the songwriting on *See You On The Other Side*, a new structure was imposed on the sonic soup, and Donahue's stoned immaculate voice was the perfect narrator for their warped and wobbly audio-scapes. Again, the album received enthusiastic reviews but nothing in the way of commercial success. For three years the band hid away in their country home in Catskills, north of New York, only returning with the mighty *Deserter's Songs* when the time was right.

The way Donahue saw it, the music scene was moving away from its roots in the mid-nineties, 'I didn't think that people were looking back and remembering some of the great music that had been made. A lot of groups seemed to be trying to escape history, rather than learn from it.'[43] The emphasis was on the constant reinvention of genres with songs themselves, secondary to the search for new combinations of styles. Not that Mercury Rev wanted to return to and regurgitate old styles; the key was to create something that sounded new but which was informed by a knowledge of all that had gone before, retaining the complete spirit of the original and not just a reconfigured and recontextualized sample of the original. How strange then that they happened upon Levon Helm and Garth Hudson from similarly-minded sixties archivists the Band when they were in the Catskills. One of those things that was meant to be.

Mercury Rev

Helm played drums on 'Opus 40' and Hudson contributed saxophone to 'Hudson Line', but the spirit of the Band is there all the way through the album. Donahue calls it 'the search for the timeless song', the spirit of the past. Various songs on the album evoke iconic, often filmic images that are part of a shared history, 'the way I lit your cigarette', 'well I got us on a highway, I got us in a car'. Musically, there are a few references to what has gone before, 'Goddess On A Hiway' has a nod to the Beatles' 'Golden Slumbers', 'Opus 40' recalls 'The Night They Drove Old Dixie Down', 'Hudson Line' runs through soul music from Booker T to the Crusaders, and 'Delta Sun' combines a techno beat with some natty little Chicago house piano.

Jack Nitzsche who arranged Phil Spector's Goldstar Studio sessions, and later, the man behind Neil Young's symphonic country with Buffalo Springfield and on his own *Harvest* album, reckoned that *Deserter's Songs* was the best album released in years and offered to produce their next one. Unfortunately he died before work started on *All Is Dream* but his excitement and enthusiasm confirmed that Mercury Rev had successfully re-awoken the ghost of music's past. Nitzche and Spector were the first people to recognize and realize the potential of multi-track recording for the popular song. After years of experimentation creating new textures and combinations of sounds by producers and musicians alike, it was about time that somebody came along with a new take on the old songs to put all of that technological development to good use. Mercury Rev bided their time but got there in the end.

First team: Jonathan Donahue (v, g), Grasshopper (g), Dave Fridmann (b), Jimmy Chambers (d), Suzanne Thorpe (fl), Adam Snyder (k)

Place, time, scene: Buffalo 1988. The band's noise-rock beginnings tie in with the coming to prominence of bands like My Bloody Valentine and Dinosaur Jr. Their focus on the spirit contained within songs and a desire to replicate the spirit in a new setting led them to *Deserter's Songs*, a studio-built album that sounds completely organic. Flaming Lips and Grandaddy have both released similarly inspired albums since.

What to buy first: *Deserter's Songs* 1998

And then: *See You On The Other Side* 1995, *All Is Dream* 2001

METALLICA

Let's see, how exactly did we get from the poodle rockers of the early 1980s to the grunge rockers at the end of the decade? What changed rock from being a joke genre that appealed to young nerdy boys and denim-clad Quo-heads played by perm-haired, bare-chested lotharios singing songs about girls, girls, girls and cowboys on steel horses, to something altogether more real and less patronizing? Well, for a start, the knob rockers were an American invention, or more specifically an LA thing. It's funny how LA sucks the goodness out of music; the same happened with hip-hop and rap when it went west. But then the city of angels did provide the Doors and Black Flag so it's obviously not all bad. In the UK, rock had learned a thing or two from punk and in the late 1970s there was talk of a movement dubbed The New Wave Of British Heavy Metal which took its cue from the likes of Iron Maiden (Dianno era) and the granddaddies of speed metal, Motorhead. In fact, Lemmy didn't even consider his band to be metal, he thought of them as punk.

At the heart of the NWOBHM scene was a young Danish drummer named Lars Ulrich who had recently returned from LA. It was a move that must have annoyed his parents because they had moved to the US with young Lars' professional tennis career in mind. Just take a moment to picture that. OK. Good.

In London, Lars got some work with *Kerrang* magazine and was responsible for compiling an album which collected together the cream of the NWOBHM scene. The dark, dank clubs, warm beer, smell of patchouli oil and 'Ace Of Spades' must have lodged themselves deep inside his system because when he returned to LA he was ready to start a metal band that would piss all over the Hollywood glam scene. Not that Metallica ever really got properly down to business in LA. Importantly, Ulrich met up with guitarists James Hetfield and Dave Mustaine while he was living there in 1981, picked up bassist Cliff Burton in San Francisco in 1982, and completed the band with the addition of Kirk Hammett in New York in 1983, losing Mustaine in the process. He formed Megadeth, who along with Metallica, Slayer and Anthrax were the fourth riders of the metal apocalypse who, by 1987 had changed the rules of rock music forever.

In New York, Metallica shared a house with Anthrax, whose comics and skateboards mentality must have made for some interesting 'odd couple' moments when set against Metallica's more cerebral and politically-motivated interests. The two bands released their debut albums within a few months of each other. Both were fast and intense and with more and more practice and plenty of gigging both bands got faster still. By 1984 the key difference between the two bands was that Anthrax's new vocalist Joey Belladonna was beginning to contribute to a slightly more melodic sound. Metallica kept it straight.

Kill 'em All announced the Metallica sound and immediately put heavy metal back in its rightful place. Once again, a metal record had power. The guitars blaze and the backline pulverizes. Motorhead had applied punk energy to their metal, but Metallica made it hardcore. Just as Black Flag were winding up after a period of experimentation with heavier sounds, Metallica fused their own metal with original Black Flag power and for the next two albums pummelled it out of their collective systems.

Ride The Lightning got more primal again as Hetfield had his way and injected his guitar-playing with elements of garage rock. His vocals are at ripping point for most of the album too, but fortunately remained in good nick for the follow-up *Master Of Puppets* in 1986. Once again, the rhythm is tight as, the guitars are recorded a la Glenn Branca, multi-tracked for extra velocity, and because of a straightforward approach to song structure, jump out of the mix like fireworks exploding from an arsonist's bonfire. This was not just an important metal album, it also inspired new guitarists like J. Mascis of Dinosaur Jr, who learned his craft listening to Metallica and then went and made the definitive noise-guitar album for the indie world, *You're Living All Over Me*. The subject matter of the songs takes in drug addiction, war and insanity, nothing particularly new but given a new intensity that had been lacking from heavy metal since the first two Black Sabbath albums. But then it all stopped.

Cliff Burton's death in a traffic accident may not have been the cause but when they reconvened for their next album in 1988, the energy and the spirit had gone from the band. ... *And Justice For All* gave them a hit single in 'One', but the atmosphere of gloom and the tendency for the individual band members to indulge themselves with their playing, rather than working for the greater good of the group, killed Metallica the thrash-metal band off overnight, and they have not really attempted to get the power of oneness back since. The black *Metallica* album contained the chugging 'Enter Sandman' which did alright in the rock clubs and got MTV rotation, but since then its been symphonic collaborations and corporate whinging about how the sharing of music files is taking the food from their very mouths. Hmmm.

First team: James Hetfield (v, g), Lars Ulrich (d), Kirk Hammett (g), Cliff Burton (b)

Place, time, scene: New York 1983. Metallica brought together NWOBHM and American hardcore style and attitude to produce a fast, no-nonsense form of thrash metal. Together with Anthrax, Slayer and Megadeth they made heavy metal relevant again, and by their third album *Master Of Puppets* had widened their audience to include those on the indie scene who wanted something that bit harder.

What to buy first: *Master Of Puppets* 1986

And then: *Kill 'Em All* 1984, *Ride The Lightning* 1985

MINUTEMEN

San Pedro's Minutemen did everything 'econo'. It was a working philosophy which ensured that they never spent unnecessary time or money on their music or its promotion, and importantly allowed them time to focus on their real objective – teaching. From an early age, D. Boon and Mike Watt had been turned on politically and had made the most of their learning opportunities, particularly when it came to history. By the time they formed a band they had a stack of stuff to say and when punk hit they were able to say it. After 1976 it was suddenly okay for a bunch of out-of-town kids with no specific star appeal, or readily apparent musical ability, to play the rock'n'roll game. The old rules had gone, you could do-it-yourself and do it any way you wanted. The Minutemen grabbed the opportunity, set up their own rules, and stuck to them. It makes for an impressive history.

In his book *Our Band Could Be Your Life*, which incidentally, is just about the best set of band histories

dealing with the key American independent bands of the early 1980s, Michael Azerrad includes a detailed chapter on The Minutemen, whose lyric provides the title for the overall book. He explains that the relationship between Watt and Boon was based on mutual admiration, and willingness to debate crucial social and political ideas. Both wrote their songs individually but then had to defend them in the inevitable discussions, and occasional wrestling contests, that followed. From the outset the plan was to relate big issues to personal situations, and each had their own way of doing this. Boon was direct, Watt more nuanced. There are no choruses though, that was deemed wasteful. A typical Minutemen song takes the form of a short story or scenario which serves as anecdotal evidence to support a position taken in relation to a particular underpinning theory or issue. The words may be spoken or sung but are always clear and concise. They have to be. Nearly all Minutemen songs are less than three minutes in length, many less than two.

Musically, like so many other American bands of the period, the Minutemen were inspired by the angular and unexpected structures of British bands like the Gang Of Four and the Pop Group, where the guitar is used for effect rather than structure and the bass and drums are given freedom to dictate the groove. It was the next stage on from the hardcore punk played by Black Flag, who had given the band their first break, choosing the Minutemen as support on their first tour and giving them a deal to release records on the SST label. As far as Boon, Watt and drummer George Hurley were concerned, punk was an attitude, not a style, and as long as you played 'fast and loud ... beyond that, you could do almost anything you wanted'.[44]

The band's working-class roots clearly informed their lyrics, but unlike so many other 'political' bands and writers, the Minutemen walked it like they talked it. The econo philosophy extended to every aspect of their set-up. In the early days they all had jobs at Greg Ginn's SST label headquarters, throughout their career they were their own roadies, they booked studios for short periods and used cheap tape, and made sure that they kept a tight rein on their expenses. Records were a necessary promotional tool for the gigs, and the gigs were all-important, because that was where the band could demonstrate to their audience that the stuff they were saying was important and needed to be thought upon some more. In addition, Boon ran his own *Prole* magazine featuring pro-socialist essays, tracts and cartoons.

In 1981 they formed their New Alliance label and signed up Hüsker Dü for their debut album, launching a healthy sparring contest that continued for the next few years. Both bands were trios intent on developing punk ideals through the incorporation of apparently non-punk musical styles, and both had a democratic policy with regard to songwriting. By the time the Minutemen released their key album *Double Nickels On The Dime* in 1984, all three members were writing songs, and like Hüsker Dü the objective was to get the material out there into the public sphere. In three years the Minutemen released six albums, and Hüsker Dü put out four including their conceptual and multi-faceted double-album *Zen Arcade*, which was recorded in just three days.

Double Nickels On The Dime was a gut reaction to such a work of scope and concision, and resulted in 44 songs being recorded in two two-day sessions. On it, the band covered ecology, the media, the tyranny of language, American foreign policy, Van Halen and Steely Dan. The majority of the songs though dealt with the music industry and the Minutemen's relationship to it. There's 'Political Song For Michael Jackson To Sing', 'Do You Want New Wave Or Do You Want Truth' and 'History Lesson, Part 2' wherein D. Boon explains how punk music saved his life. In 'There Ain't Shit On TV Tonight' Boon delivers a sermon on the state of contemporary culture and ends with the line 'We are responsible'. What he would have made of the album's sudden sales leap in 2002 after the use of the song 'Corona' as the *Jackass* TV show theme, we will sadly never know.

After another EP of ironic cover versions and one more album which took the Minutemen a step closer to mainstream success, Boon died in a tragic road accident, breaking his neck after being thrown out of the back of a van. A cruel irony for a man who had relied on that particular mode of transport as a key tool in his attempts to spread his message for so many years. The Minutemen ended right there in December 1985. Watt and Hurley later formed fIREHOSE a band which continued the fight against 'mersh' imperatives but lacked the directness, focus and concision of their previous band. The Minutemen deserve to be heard. Do some listening.

First team: D. Boon (v, g), Mike Watt (b, v), George Hurley (d)

Place, time, scene: San Pedro, California 1980. The Minutemen were there at the beginning of the Californian hardcore scene, but were among the first punk bands to incorporate different styles into their sound inspiring other hardcore bands like X, Meat Puppets and most notably Hüsker Dü to do something similar. REM were also big fans.

What to buy first: *Double Nickels On The Dime* 1984

And then: *Buzz Or Howl Under The Influence Of Heat* 1983, *3-Way Tie (For Last)* 1985

In retrospect: *Post-Mersh Volume 1* 1987, *Post-Mersh Volume 2* 1987, *Post-Mersh Volume 3* 1989

MISSION OF BURMA

Hardcore punk demonstrated that raw noise could make a real impact on people who witnessed it live. Mission Of Burma reckoned they could make an even greater impact by harnessing that power and letting rip at crucial moments. The three-piece band evolved an innovative sound working together with their live engineer, and should be credited with a whole new approach to music making that shifted the emphasis from the traditional rock method of experimentation with style to experimentation with texture and the dynamic potential of amplified sound. Hüsker Dü, Sonic Youth, Dinosaur Jr, My Bloody Valentine, Fugazi and Yo La Tengo were surely all taking notes.

Clint Conley and Roger Miller had both moved to Boston in 1977 and had joined an art-rock band called Moving Parts. It dawned on them pretty quickly though, that this new punk thing was a lot more exciting. Miller suffered from a developing tinnitus problem and had vowed not to play loud music again but could not resist thrashing about one more time. Once formed, Mission Of Burma lasted four years during which time they failed to break out of the toilet circuit scene and only managed one full-length album and an EP, but both are crucial.

The band made their name playing live. Miller would crank his guitar amp up real high and create sounds that relied as much on the shape of the room as anything else. Instead of playing fast thrashy chords like the hardcore bands of the period, he held back; just at the point when it seemed a solid rhythm was called for, Miller would take his sonic assault off in another direction entirely. With Conley and drummer Peter Prescott filling in the structure while Miller bounced his guitar off the walls, the Mission Of Burma live experience was different every time. To add to the melee, sound engineer Martin Swope took it upon himself to record sections of the live shows and play them back at random moments – his front-of-house area must have been a mess of discarded tape and razor blades.

The band's first single was 'Academy Fight Song', which became an integral part of REM's live set for the ensuing years, and their first EP contained the mighty 'That's When I Reach For My Revolver' covered by Graham Coxon and Moby in his heavy-metal phase. It's the first song of a type that became familiar in the ensuing years, racked with tension in the verses as the guitar threatens to get away from Miller, and then finally exploding into the chorus apparently sung by a man on the edge. In sound and content it's spookily prophetic. The album was called *Vs*, recorded in a large cavernous studio to get those textures and harmonics down on tape, and is a template for the possibilities of noise. The band thinks nothing of firing out discordant random thrashes, picking up an off-kilter groove and then segueing into a gloriously hooky chorus. It's the kind of exciting musical structure that can be so effectively created by hip-hop producers working with loops and stylistic juxtapositioning and is clearly indebted to the groundbreaking work of Can in particular, where the excitement is in the combination of raw noise and rhythm. The maturity of the lyrics and subject matter, literate, philosophical and emotional, and the manic shouted delivery are yet another example of the band's crucial contribution towards post-punk's development as a uniquely physical and cerebral artistic form. It's just a crying shame that they bloody well split up just before everything kicked off.

First team: Roger Miller (v, g), Clint Conley (b, v), Peter Prescott (d, v)

Place, time, scene: Boston 1978. Mission Of Burma put the art into hardcore punk. The three members of the band shared a desire to experiment with free-jazz, krautrock and the kind of art-punk being made by Pere Ubu. They harnessed the power and textures of punk noise and structured it in terms of tension and release so that the overall effect was even more overwhelming. Their sense of dynamics and power had a profound influence on all independent rock-guitar music to follow.

What to buy first: *Vs* 1982

And then: *Signals, Calls And Marches* EP 1981, *The Horrible Truth About Burma* 1985 (Live)

In retrospect: *Mission Of Burma* 1988

MOGWAI

As far as Mogwai are concerned, post-rock is just another music industry cliché, 'Isn't that having a beer after the gig's finished?' Unfortunately, it's a label they've been saddled with which alludes to a way of making music which has somehow gone beyond traditional rock music practice. Bands like Squirrel Bait, Slint and Tortoise were the first post-rockers, picking up on the experimentation of Sonic Youth. These were bands that made considered decisions about how sounds should interact with one another to create mood pieces with unexpected rhythms and strange combinations of noise. My Bloody Valentine were developing the art of noise-rock around the same time at no small cost to Alan McGee's Creation label, focusing on guitars, harmonics and the mathematics of interaction between sounds. When Mogwai came into existence in 1995, post-rock had become a catch-all term for cleverly constructed instrumental music mostly consumed by those wanting an alternative to the backward-facing rock and pop music exemplified by the also-rans of grunge and Britpop. When the Glaswegian teenagers marketed their own T-shirts bearing the legend 'Blur Are Shite' they were not just confirming their musical position, but also making the point that they were in the game to have some fun. Mogwai made clever music cool.

The core of the band since their inception has been guitarists Stuart Braithwaite and John Cummings, bassist Dominic Aitchison and drummer Martin Bulloch, although Brendan O'Hare from Teenage Fanclub was an honorary member for one album. Their early gigs were played out at The 13th Note in Glasgow, a place where they probably offloaded a few copies of their early EPs on their own Rock Action record label. Seen live, it's obvious that Mogwai are very much a rock band. They have the volume and they have the musical chops, even if the presentation is marked by a stillness and refusal to be captured 'getting into the music'. They even sit down for large chunks of the shows.

Of course, Mogwai *are* into the music. They're right there at the centre of the sound, just not jumping around on top of it. Their songs are slow-release epics, beginning and concluding with the sound of single gently operated instruments, but at their most ferocious moments are a perfectly executed cacophony of noise. The key is in the harmonization of the instruments and the inter-modulation between them. Knowing what the pedals do and how feedback works helps too, I suppose.

The debut album was released in 1997 on the Chemikal Underground label, and was immediately hailed as a classic by British reviewers. 'Mogwai Fear Satan' is the album highlight; a lone flute floats above distant, approaching guitars that eventually become terrifying in their confusion, sounding for all the world like distressed birds of prey. It's definitive Mogwai. At the heart of the noise there is always a fragile beauty that separates them from other more cerebral bands of their ilk. There is obviously some planning but *Young Team* is not an experimental album based on maths and science, it is felt, spontaneous and organic.

The second one, *Come On Die Young*, features vocals from Braithwaite and Iggy Pop and draws on the multi-instrumentalist talents of new member Barry Burns who contributes various woodwind and brass sounds. Importantly, it introduces producer Dave Fridmann of Mercury Rev who has worked on all Mogwai albums since and whose knowledge of the studio allowed the band to realize some of the sounds

Mogwai

that they were not able to fully develop on *Young Team*. Check out the drum sound on 'Kappa' and the astonishing grasp of channel mixing and volume levels as more and more sounds are thrown in during the ten-minute track 'Chocky', and yet the pretty little sad piano at the song's heart stays audible and clear throughout. 'Come On Die Young' takes a lot longer to get loud too, and listened to as a whole is like experiencing a full album version of one of the individual songs on their debut.

In 2001, the third album *Rock Action* which is the band at their most textured and nuanced. The 20-minute single, 'My Father, My King' followed, a 'two-parts beautiful serenity, one part death metal' take on a traditional Jewish hymn produced by that other master of noise, Steve Albini. 'There is noise, it's just subtle. It's like someone mowing the grass a couple of doors away, rather than someone doing the hovering in the same room while you watch TV.'[45] Contrary to what you might have heard, Mogwai are not an acquired taste, just a taste that most people haven't bothered to acquire yet.

First team: Stuart Braithwaite (g, v), Dominic Aitchison (b), John Cummings (g), Martin Bulloch (d), Barry Burns (w-w, br, g)

Place, time, scene: Glasgow 1995. Mogwai are spiritually connected to the other Chemikal Underground bands, particularly Arab Strap and the Delgados, but musically take their cue from the post-rock bands predominant in the US during the late 1980s and 1990s. These include Squirrel Bait, Slint, Labradford and more recently Sea and Cake, Tortoise, Aerial M and Trans Am.

What to buy first: *Young Team* 1997

And then: *Come On Die Young* 1999, *Rock Action* 2001

MOTORHEAD

Lemmy really deserves a lot more credit than he gets. For five years and as many albums he was the driving force behind space-rock band Hawkwind. No, he didn't write the songs and he didn't have the hippy kudos of chief muso Dave Brock or fantasy poets Robert Calvert or Michael Moorcock who were perceived to be key to the band's success without even being official members, but his bass-playing was the crucial thing

that kept Hawkwind grounded. It was solid and hard, and gave them a groove that other bands like Gong always strived for but never really got to grips with. They'd always go and blow it with too much fairy-dust. 'Silver Machine' made it to number three in the UK chart on the strength of that bassline, and albums like *Space Ritual Alive* and *Warrior On The Edge Of Time* which, as you'd expect, swoosh and swirl very nicely indeed, ultimately appealed to the nascent taste of John Lydon and Jello Biafra because of Ian's menacing bottom-end. When he formed Motorhead, it was a totally new idea. Fast, heavy metal with distortion and gruff shouted vocals. Just like the Sex Pistols, but less produced and more raw and direct, musically and yes, even lyrically. Motorhead, who played their first shows in 1975, took their cue from the MC5, and were setting the benchmarks for hardcore punk and speed metal before the 1976 version of London punk had even caught on. Mind you, don't go accusing Ian Kilmister and his band of being punks or metallers. He'll just get annoyed and tell you that all he's ever done is play rock'n'roll.

Let's get the facts out of the way. Lemmy is the son of a vicar, he used to score acid for Hendrix, his band the Rocking Vicars wore Finnish national costume and dog-collars and were the first western rock band to play behind the Iron Curtain at the request of President Tito of Yugoslavia, and for a while he lived at Ron Wood's mother's house. He was evicted from Hawkwind after being busted for possession of drugs in Canada, and although the charges were dropped, the eviction stood probably because of his increasing links with a chapter of Hell's Angels. His replacement in the band pointed Hawkwind in a firmly progressive jazz-rock direction and led to a good two decades of tedious noodling, the very antithesis of what Lemmy would set about doing with his band Bastard, renamed Motorhead in 1975.

Having settled on a core line-up of Lemmy, guitarist Fast Eddie Clarke and drummer Philthy Phil Taylor, Motorhead's first album proper was *Motorhead* on punk label Chiswick Records. It contained a version of their title song, originally written for and recorded by Hawkwind two years earlier. Released in 1977, it blew the tinny punk records out of the water and was followed by a series of albums, all recorded quickly and demonstrating that Motorhead were a band firmly connected to the blues and rock'n'roll of yore, but keen to play it louder and often faster than it had gone before. *Overkill* kicks in with the relentless drum-driven title track, and switches gear to the blues of 'Metropolis' and the get-down rock boogie of 'No Class', none of it that far away from what ZZ Top were up to at the same time down in Texas, just more energized. *Bomber*, *Ace Of Spades* and *Iron Fist* all contain well-executed heavy rock'n'roll and songs about gambling, women and drinking with the road crew, but it all really makes sense on the 1981 album *No Sleep 'Til Hammersmith*, a warts and all document of the band as they should always be heard, live with no overdubs and studio cleanliness, just no-nonsense, low-down, dirty rock'n'roll.

There have been twelve more albums since. *1916* got a Grammy nomination, *Orgasmatron* received subsonic production from bass scientist Bill Laswell, and *We Are Motorhead* sounded bloody good last thing on a Saturday night on Xfm when Xfm's Ian Camfield discussed it track by track with Lemmy two days before its release. After 27 years of Motorhead there was still a tangible sense of anticipation for their latest collection. It's the same when the live show rolls into town, except then the anticipation is mixed with trepidation. Motorhead are still scary. How many other rock bands can you say that about?

First team: Lemmy (v, b), Eddie Clarke (g), Phil Taylor (d)

Place, time, scene: London 1975. Motorhead preceded the New Wave Of British Heavy Metal by at least three years. They were accepted as spiritual brethren by the punk bands that set up at the same time and were given record deals by both Stiff and Chiswick labels who primarily focused on the pub rock scene and punk.

What to buy first: *No Sleep 'Til Hammersmith* 1981

And then: *Ace Of Spades* 1980, *Overkill* 1979

In retrospect: *The Best Of Motorhead: Metal Is* 2000

MUDHONEY

By the end of 1991 the term grunge had become a marketing term used by the music and fashion industries alike. It was a handy way to define, and therefore,

understand and make safe, a nihilistic youth culture that had got so used to being fucked over that they no longer gave a fuck. The 'whatever' kids became a marketable type that couldn't necessarily be sold to but could be sold on. Supermodels sported grunge frocks and bands that played grunge rock were invented for advertising purposes. The bands that had initiated the style either, self-consciously embraced the new opportunities, or began plotting ways to escape the descriptive tag. I'll let you fill in the gaps there! Steve Turner of Mudhoney, who probably first-used the term in a Seattle music paper to describe the music his new band was making, created out of sustained chords and fuzz-box effects, didn't seem to care either way, 'I'm not just into grungy, two-chord rock, I'm into, uh, less grungy two-chord rock too.'[46] For guitarist Turner, grunge had nothing to do with image or generic categorization, it was simply the sound his band made.

Mark Arm appears to have been there right from the start of the Seattle scene. His first band was formed at school and had a name inspired by a maths class, Mr Epp and the Calculations. By 1981, the band was recording and within the year was getting played on DJ Rodney Bingenheimer's KROQ new music show. Arm did vocals and played guitar, occasionally drums. The band's legacy is one compilation album and an acknowledgement that they were 'the worst band in the world'. Not mere bragging though, it was just that kind of review that attracted Steve Turner and soon he had joined both Mr Epp and Arm's other band the Limp Richerds. In addition, he set up another called the Thrown-Ups for whom Arm played drums, Turner looked after the guitar and a local nutter called Ed sang and took to the stage dressed as the baby Jesus. For Arm and Turner, the important thing was to keep it fun.

In 1984 they launched Green River, naming themselves after the Green River killings and, together with bassist Jeff Ament, drummer Alex Shumway and second guitarist Stone Gossard, set about making a riotous din that took its cue from the Meat Puppets' second album, hard, loose and laid-back with lashings of fuzz and feedback. It got them a deal with the Sub Pop label and a few gigs at CBGB's in New York. An EP entitled *Come On Down* was released in 1985 before Turner quit, and an album was finished for

Mudhoney

release in 1987 but by then Arm had gone too. The basic problem was that Ament and Gossard wanted to make it big with the band, and such naked careerism reared its ugly head for the last time when Arm was told that he couldn't get guest-list places for a couple of mates because Ament had already set them aside for some A&R men. The band split. Ament and Gossard formed Mother Love Bone with Andrew Wood of slightly funkier Seattle band Malfunkshun and then, when he OD'd on heroin, they invented Pearl Jam instead.

Turner, who had expressed his distaste for his former colleague's tendency to 'play like Iron Maiden or Venom or something' reunited with Arm forming Mudhoney to continue to explore the possibilities of feedback-laced lazy hardcore, or for brevity's sake, grunge. They did it together with Matt Lukin from the Melvins and Dan Peters from Bundles of Hiss. The debut EP *Superfuzz Bigmuff* on Sub-Pop is their defining moment and includes 'Touch Me I'm Sick', which together with Dinosaur Jr's 'Freak Scene' released the same year, represents the perfect melding together of the influences that had preoccupied American bands for the previous decade. The key difference is in the vocal. J. Mascis is laconic and ambivalent compared to Arm's more animated screaming on 'Touch Me'. Put the two together with slow-fast, soft-hard, stop-start songs and that's your basic Nirvana right there.

Every Good Boy Deserves Fudge was released in 1991 on Sub Pop using cheap tape and a small eight-track studio desk. Suitably unsophisticated, it's the very antithesis of the big production, major label debuts of their contemporaries. 'Fuzz Gun '91' is a heavy jam, built on the always-present muddy bass and features a soaring fuzztone lead guitar part, 'Don't Fade IV' is pure psychedelia complete with a twang that Country Joe would have been happy with, 'Thorn' is fast and loud hardcore, and 'Let It Slide' has a surf-rock feel. The lyrics are resentful and complaining, and although the sixties are invoked in some of the garage-rock psychedelic riffing, the attitude is pure 1991 in all its non-deluding honesty, 'Dream, don't fade away into another shitty day'. Mudhoney never wanted to be spokesmen for a generation, and they never were.

First team: Mark Arm (v, g), Steve Turner (g), Matt Lukin (b), Dan Peters (d)

Place, time, scene: Seattle 1987. All four members of the band had contributed to the early-eighties Seattle music scene before forming Mudhoney. Green River in particular were a founding moment of the grunge aesthetic, having taken their own cue from the mix of hardcore punk and roots music developed by the Meat Puppets and X.

What to buy first: *Superfuzz Bigmuff* EP 1988

And then: *Every Good Boy Deserves Fudge* 1991, *Green River: Come On Down* EP 1985

MY BLOODY VALENTINE

One thing that's abundantly clear about Kevin Shields is that he is a perfectionist. His band, My Bloody Valentine, have released two of the most innovative and influential collections of recorded music since 'pop' records began, and yet he's not happy with either of them. It's something to do with not being able to let go. Unfortunately, perfectionism has tragically stalled his output to the extent that there has been nothing released by My Bloody Valentine since 1991. In fact, with the exception of a few remix projects there has been very little from Shields in any capacity. Thankfully, he re-emerged in 2001 to work on Primal Scream's *Xtrmntr* album, which gave him an opportunity to get his teeth into a proper musical project again – a chance to work with songs and live performance which may just spark him back into life. We could do with him back. Hell, even Brian Eno referred to My Bloody Valentine's work as 'setting a new standard in pop'.

To start with, My Bloody Valentine, led by Shields and Colm O'Ciosoig, were a fairly straightforward post-punk band playing gigs in their native Dublin. Over time they developed a more gothic sound, always a risk when a band spends too much time in Berlin, and with the addition of bassist Debbie Googe when the band moved to London, put together an intense live show not unlike the Birthday Party. But then Shields discovered noise. It was the Jesus And Mary Chain who were to blame, with their feedback-laden white noise. By 1987 My Bloody Valentine had changed their sound entirely and emerged out of the intense darkness to create songs which brought together light bubblegum pop and guitars that sounded like a disturbed hornet's nest, all buzzing and angry. When Alan McGee of Creation Records signed the band in 1987 they had a new vocalist, Bilinda Butcher, and were ready to experiment further, removing the last vestiges of traditional rock practice.

The album *Isn't Anything* is astonishing. Quite clearly it prioritizes sound over song, but the whole album is still darn catchy. 'Feed Me With Your Kiss' is driven on by a hard bass riff, features Shield's trademark 'glide' guitar — all done with delay and sticky-taped tremolo arms apparently — and a fairly energetic piece of drumming which bizarrely fades out and in on the drum roll at the end of each chorus. The vocals, shared between Shields and Butcher, are buried in noise or hidden behind sustained power chords, and on the occasions that you can pick them out, sound like Sandie Shaw and Shane McGowan, real vocals, not the affected singing of the multifarious shoegazing bands that followed in My Bloody Valentine's wake.

And 'Feed Me With Your Kiss' is one of the more traditional songs on the album.

Many tracks don't even feature guitars, just the effects unit that produces the final sound. According to engineer Dave Anderson, interviewed in David Cavanagh's book chronicling the history of Creation Records, the original guitars were erased after the effect had been achieved, just leaving the effect.[47] The *Glider* EP contains the band's crowning glory 'Soon',

complete with shuffling hip-hop rhythm and a jolly little sea-shanty motif afloat amidst the white noise. The production is full and mighty, and it got Creation into the groove a full year before *Screamadelica* danced its way out of the studio. Even Andrew Weatherall felt the urge to get involved and remix the track.

Loveless came out in 1991 and it's said that Shields' quest for perfection nearly broke Creation Records — maybe that deal with Sony came just in time. It took two years, £300,000 and 17 engineers to make, but is a fine example of what could be achieved when the guy in charge has an innate understanding of the potential of sound, depending on its spatial and temporal placement in the mix. Live, the *Loveless* shows were an experiment in sonic possibilities, and contrary to popular belief there was nothing on tape. So here's a band that could cut it live too. And how? The sheer volume and the intensity of a My Bloody Valentine show have since passed into legend. 'I learned that audiences are like one organism, with a head, a body and legs, with the legs at the back while the head's at the front shaking itself. When we did "You Made Me Realise", it transformed the audience into a different thing altogether. All the people at the front could behave no differently from the people at the back. It put everyone into their own head, because they couldn't talk to each other either.'[48]

And that was pretty much it, a blueprint for future generations, followed by nothing. Sure, Primal Scream's album was great but some more My Bloody Valentine, now that's what the world of music needs. Soon.

First team: Kevin Shields (g, v), Bilinda Butcher (g, v), Colm O'Ciosoig (d), Debbie Googe (b)

Place, time, scene: Dublin 1984. Initially My Bloody Valentine were followers of existing scenes, before getting turned on by Jesus And Mary Chain. By 1987 they were at the forefront of the emerging retro noise-rock scene which centred on Creation Records, and were soon perceived to be the godfathers of the shoegazing scene that included Ride and Slowdive. Their musical aesthetic and discoveries have influenced many bands since.

What to buy first: *Isn't Anything* 1988

And then: *Loveless* 1991

N

NEU!

Neu!'s great contribution to alternative music was the invention of a rhythmic pattern, something called 'motorik'. Picking up on the looping techniques of Holger Czukay in Can and the sequencing nous of their old band Kraftwerk, they developed a style of music that pulsed along as if it was motorized, hence the name. Some have pointed out that the rhythm combines the syncopation of rock'n'roll and the four to the floor beat of dance music – sounds about right. Kraftwerk and Can both used the motorik style as did later electronic oriented bands like Ultravox – in the early days when they were good – and Stereolab, who have made the pulse beat the basis of their Europop hybrid work.

The two members of the band were drummer Klaus Dinger and guitarist Michael Rother, who came up with the idea for Neu! whilst still working with Ralf Hütter and Florian Schneider. They made one album together but realized that they were less concerned with what Schneider referred to as 'tone-films' that used sound to recreate a romantic realism, and more interested in getting into the groove. The duo released three albums between 1971 and 1975, *Neu!*, *Neu! 2* and *Neu! 75*. They're all chock-full with drawn-out minimalist instrumental mantras that are guaranteed to make you feel spiritually uplifted, a bit like chanting 'Hare Krishna' or doing the Rosary, although all the work is done for you and you can just drift off on a hypnotic motorik excursion. 'Hallogallo' is track one, side one of *Neu!* and is definitive. It fades straight into a bass and drums rhythm that it is impossible to avoid getting physically involved with and then for ten minutes or so overlays immaculate guitar sustains and drum fills to fade. Oh Yeah!

After the split, Dinger began working with his brother Thomas in the more punk-influenced La Dusseldorf – one of David Bowie's favourite bands, and a key influence on his Berlin trilogy of albums, while Rother put together the funkier Harmonia, a band which Brian Eno at one point referred to as the best band in the world. Not that Dinger necessarily agrees – I think his response to Eno's comment was something along the lines of 'cheap La D copyists, bullshit' – the two have apparently not spoken since those days in the seventies when they made some of the most glorious synchronized and harmonious music of the rock era.

First team: Klaus Dinger (d, k), Michael Rother (g, k)

Place, time, scene: Dusseldorf, Germany. 1971. Neu!, along with Kraftwerk and Can developed new ways of structuring and arranging music which tends to be generalized as 'krautrock'. Neu! perfected the motorik rhythm that echoed Can's jammed and edited linear-looping techniques, but with more hypnotic and expansive results. Bowie's *Low* album in 1977 followed a period of concerted Neu! listening (mainly in his car, of course), Ultravox were the key British electronic band to pick up on the band's style and more recently, Stereolab have used the Neu! vibe as a basis of their own sound.

What to buy first: *Neu!* 1971

And then: *Neu! 2* 1972, *Neu! 75* 1975

NEW ORDER

Having opted to continue after their friend's suicide, the three remaining members of Joy Division recruited Stephen Morris's girlfriend, Gillian Gilbert, and with a different name started to tease the lighter, more pop-inflected aspects out of their previous sound. Several tracks on the second Joy Division album, *Closer*, had been danceable, and there was brightness to melodic songs like 'Love Will Tear Us Apart' that suggested that the musicians in the band had not always shared their lead singer's gloomy approach to writing. After an initial album, produced by Martin Hannett who had always emphasized the cold, dark aspects of Joy

New Order

Division songs, New Order came into their own when they discovered the possibilities of electronic music and its link with the growing hip-hop scene in America. As major shareholders in Factory Records they were free to choose their own musical direction without the usual creative pressures being applied from forces outside of the band.

There were four albums released between 1983 and 1989 and a slew of 12″ singles, all aimed squarely at the dancefloor and drawing on rhythms, textures, melodies and arrangements that made clubs an interesting listening experience before the tyranny of the anonymous, production-line beat took over. Their 1989 album *Technique* remains the ultimate realization of blended pop and dance styles by a band totally immersed in both worlds. New Order had fun in the eighties, indie figureheads and forerunners of a new type of independent music.

It's important to realize that New Order, as their name attests, were intended as a completely different project from Joy Division. The band had always promised each other that if one member left they would end, and start again as something different. That wasn't quite what happened. An initial tour as a trio, performing some new songs and a selection of Joy Division tracks, was followed by the release of 'Ceremony' and 'In A Lonely Place', both of which had been written with Ian Curtis, but they had brought in Gillian Gilbert

as keyboardist by then and although much of the first album, *Movement*, had definite echoes of their previous band, it was obvious that the band was moving in a specific, more electronic direction. Their first London gig was at the gay club Heaven and by the time they had released their follow-up album, *Power, Corruption And Lies*, they were riding high on the success of what would eventually become the biggest-selling 12″ single of all time, the minimalist epic, 'Blue Monday'.

Based around the experimental non-linear computer composition techniques that Morris and Gilbert had figured out, the song was driven by digitized drums and fleshed out with keyboard washes, bass growls, immaculate guitar cameos, synthesized vocals and vocalized synthesizers. But despite all that, it's the breaks that make it, the moments when nothing else is there except the electronic percussion. Rumour has it that even Kraftwerk wanted to know how the band had achieved such timbre and texture when dealing with a set of zeroes and ones. The rest of *Power, Corruption And Lies* sets the agenda for the next few years, combining warm lush string-scapes and melodies with cold electronic beats and the occasional passing guitar. Their experience of New York club culture while working with producer Arthur Baker on the 'Confusion' single ensured that singles like 'Shellshock', 'The Perfect Kiss' and 'Bizarre Love Triangle' were as danceable as they were melodic and exhilarating in both respects, although occasionally, as on *Low-Life*, New Order momentarily left the dance-floor to work out more traditional songs like 'Love Vigilantes'. Their 1987 single 'True Faith' was another milestone, a straightforward pop song with short intro, verses and a chorus which made it perfect for radio. It was also Bernard Sumner's best lyric up to that point, kicking in with the exuberant 'I feel so extra-ordinary, something's got a hold on me'. Released just before club culture exploded, it captured a new mood of optimism that was taking hold in the band's home town of Manchester, most of which would have been witnessed firsthand by the band in their many trips to the Hacienda nightclub, open seven days a week and at the cutting-edge of the new house and techno sounds coming out of Chicago and Detroit.

As Manchester became Madchester at the end of the decade, New Order became a series of spin-off projects. Sumner joined forces with Johnny Marr and Neil Tennant to form Electronic, Peter Hook formed Revenge and then Monaco, and the other two set up shop as The Other Two. The *Brotherhood* album in 1986 had been a relative disappointment and the release of the double *Substance* career retrospective even suggested that the band had effectively called it a day. But then at the beginning of 1989, the year that would end with the Roses and the Mondays on *Top Of The Pops* and a geo-musical power shift from London to Manchester, New Order released the album that effectively started the ball rolling.

Worked out in Ibiza and finally realized in Peter Gabriel's Real World studios in Wiltshire, *Technique* was a 'hands in the air' club meets rock album where two very different types of song rubbed shoulders. 'Fine Time' was out and out acid house, and was followed by the Cure-like jingle-jangle of 'All The Way', while 'Round And Round' is both musical approaches in one song. New Order's *Technique* has a much safer claim to being indie-dance than anything else that came out of Manchester in that whole period. It was happy and smiley, light and bouncy and featured a whole stack of songs cataloguing Bernard Sumner's self-loathing brought on by his own relationship problems. *Technique* is a key album. If only dance music, hell, even rock music had carried on in that direction instead of blowing apart after just over a year of wedded bliss. The Roses and the Mondays couldn't keep it together beyond 1990 and when Claire Leighton col-lapsed and died after taking an ecstasy tablet before going down the Hacienda, things turned sour all round. There was no New Order album until 1993 and by then the band had perfected their craft but were no longer leading musical innovation; they had settled into a role and that's not what this book is about. Still, they had made a major impact on the direction music was to take in the next decade and beyond, even if few have managed to emulate their massive contribution. When the coolest DJs on the planet, the Chemical Brothers were asked what record they would be playing as 1999 shifted into 2000 they replied instantly that it would be 'True Faith' by New Order. Enough, as they say, said.

First team: Bernard Sumner (v, g, k), Peter Hook (b, k), Stephen Morris (d, k), Gillian Gilbert (k, g)

Place, time, scene: Manchester 1980. By the time that New Order got into their stride, they had embraced electronic sounds and, with 'Blue Monday', set a standard that few could follow. Too pop for the goths and too gloomy for the mainstream, they pursued their own course, waiting for the rest to catch up. 'True Faith' captured the mood just before rave culture took off and *Technique* came along two years later to announce the new mood to the rest of the country. It's not to say that there wouldn't have been a Madchester if not for New Order but they certainly contributed to the cultural context due to their involvement with the Hacienda and Factory Records, which signed the Happy Mondays.

What to buy first: *Technique* 1989

And then: *Power, Corruption And Lies* 1983

Retrospective: *Substance* 1987

NEW YORK DOLLS

That term 'art-rock' gets bandied around quite a lot. And do you know, I haven't got the foggiest idea what it means. It might be a description of the way the music is put together – less spontaneous, more contrived. It might also have something to do with the packaging – where the look of the artist serves to emphasize the underlying conceit or concept. Or maybe, it's more pejorative than that, and the prefix is only given to those who seem to be just that little bit cleverer than the rest.

In Britain, David Bowie and Roxy Music were apparently art-rock, as were King Crimson, although Robert Fripp and his men did thankfully decide against flamboyant stage-wear and settled for creating a difficult modernist (or should that be postmodernist? – Discuss.) blend of classical, jazz and rock music. Genesis, another art-rock band, were unable to rein in frontman Peter Gabriel however. He thought nothing of rifling through the dressing-up box so that he could look like a pansy or what appeared to be an unsettling attempt at a 'Dr Who' baddie which he called the Slipperman. On the other hand, those that just stomped their feet in stacked heels and wore make-up that was inevitably, clumsily applied and really not suited to their own colouring, were called 'glam'. They, it seems weren't so clever. 'Are you ready Steve? Andy?' In America, art-rock was thin on the ground. When the Velvet Underground ceased to exist, it seems that the art aspects of their work were ignored in favour of the sleazy bits. The cultural high of the sixties was replaced with a period of debauchery and decay. The new trannies in town were certainly glam – progressive musical experimentation was not their idea of fun – but where UK glam-rockers like the Sweet and Mud were dressing up to cash-in, and the middle-class musos fresh from university and the teaching profession were dressing up to support their art, for a band like the New York Dolls, dressing up *was* their art and it was going to make them a stack of cash.

Guitarist John Anthony Genzale hit the New York rock scene in the early seventies with friend Arthur Kane. At that time, Genzale was calling himself Johnny Volume but became Johnny Thunders when he and Kane formed the New York Dolls with Billy Murcia and Sylvain Sylvain from another band called Actress. The plan was to play low-down dirty and trashy rock'n'roll – the sort of thing the Stones had recently perfected on their four decade-turning albums culminating in *Sticky Fingers* and *Exile On Main Street*, but without the country bits – and they found the perfect frontman in David Johansen, a Jagger clone and former porn star who had recently finished dancing with a theatre troupe going by the name of Fast Eddie and the Electric Japs. Bowie's cross-dressing on *The Man Who Sold The World* and Russ Meyer's sexploitation films provided the look, and the attitude

was inspired by the underlying camp which was evident in those early sixties girl-group records which themselves exploited teenage angst. The trashy teenage trio the Shangri-Las were the undisputed leaders of that particular pack and just like the girls, the New York Dolls would eventually allow themselves to be used in the pursuit of other people's aims.

But let's not get morbid just yet. This was still 1972. They were gigging all over New York. There were a few nights at Max's Kansas City where the Velvet Underground played regular shows in their early days, and a residency at the Mercer Arts Center in Greenwich Village.[49] They were so hot that they got invited to the UK to tour with the Faces. They did some recording, and picked up a few fans who needed some gender-bending live action now that Ziggy had gone to America. It was all going really well, until Billy Murcia died in an alcohol-related incident after a night of heavy partying. It took them another six months to get over his death and find a replacement, the suitably glam Jerry Nolan, whose drumming really brought the band's music into focus. The self-titled first album, produced by a less than enthusiastic Todd Rundgren (art-rocker you see?) is the important one. Fitting perfectly with the image, you get 'Trash' and 'Personality Crisis' plus songs about everybody's new favourite city circa 1972, New York. There's even a touch of politics. The central idea of 'Vietnamese Baby' deals with the impact of the ongoing war on everyday activities that should be fun but are somehow undermined by thoughts of collective guilt. You see, there was substance there too. It's just that the New York Dolls weren't in the business of emphasizing self-congratulatory liberalism like their contemporaries.

Unfortunately the second album was a letdown. On paper it should have been a scorcher because it was produced by the enigmatic Shadow Morton who had recorded the Shangri-Las. The problem was that he saw the album as his project. He hadn't read the new rock'n'roll script which, had he bothered, would have told him that the singers and musicians now had something to say about what should be on their album. They may have been Dolls' songs but the production certainly was not. The Ramones would have a similar experience when they worked with Phil Spector a few years later. *Too Much Too Soon* was exactly that and effectively killed off the New York Dolls as the harbingers of a new cultural mood. By the time Malcolm McLaren stepped in as their new manager, they were up for anything – a combination of desperation and intravenous Class A drug-induced ambivalence. He immediately changed their image, decking them out in red leather and hammer and sickle commie chic, which went down really well when they toured the south of America. The idea was simple: cause controversy by appearing to advocate support of America's sworn enemy. It worked better two years later back in London, where anarchy was deemed the UK's nemesis rather than hardcore socialism. The Dolls' attempts at shock were met with disinterest and in 1975 Thunders and Nolan left the others to it and put together a new band, the Heartbreakers, with ex-Television guitarist, Richard Hell.

Hell's early exit from the band confirmed that the Heartbreakers were in disarray from the start. The album *L.A.M.F. (Like A Muthafucker)* was sponsored by the makers of heroin and included the tie-in promotional theme song 'Chinese Rocks'. 'Born To Lose' was also on the album, a sentiment that captured the spirit of Thunders in particular for the next few years. The band toured the UK in the punk summer of '77, including the Pistols' ill-fated Anarchy tour. Still, it led to Thunders getting a gig in Sid Vicious's band the Living End which was not the best of career moves. There was some solo material in the 1980s but no more after 1991 due to his death in mysterious circumstances. Nolan followed a year later. David Johansen however, has faired better. He's now a part-time film star and goes out touring as Buster Poindexter, doing a kind of Blues Brothers-inspired R&B and lounge show. It's good wholesome entertainment by all accounts.

For a moment there the New York Dolls parodied the narcissistic world of rock'n'roll while others parodied themselves. It was a key distinction, which influenced the attitude of the next lot who were better organized and, thanks to the lessons of the Dolls, ready to take on the ugly, bloated rock beast, and win.

First team: Johnny Thunders (g), Arthur Kane (b), Sylvain Sylvain (g), David Johansen (v), Jerry Nolan (d)

Place, time, scene: New York 1972. The Dolls took their cue from the MC5 and the Stooges but their atti-tude was the important thing. They identified image as an important aspect of their work and, along with Alice Cooper and the Tubes, were forerunners of particularly the UK punk scene. Malcolm McLaren claims to have based his model for promoting the Sex Pistols on the New York Dolls.

What to buy first: *New York Dolls* 1973

And then: The Heartbreakers: *L.A.M.F.* 1977

In retrospect: *Best Of The New York Dolls* 1985

NINE INCH NAILS

Nine Inch Nails is the name Trent Reznor uses to make sensitive, melodic industrial music. He has taken the experimentation of Throbbing Gristle and the Young Gods, the beats of Cabaret Voltaire, the song structures of Ministry and Skinny Puppy, and the dark mutterings of Killing Joke, the Cure and Joy Division, and in blending them all together has forced popular music to catch up with the technology available to it. He doesn't work quickly mind, there have been five albums in fourteen years, demonstrating a dedication to sound that separates him from other branches of music production that have become increasingly production-line based. Reznor wants to ensure that his work transcends the period in which it was made, and never becomes dated because he settled for a familiar sound or setting. With Nine Inch Nails, every constituent part of every track is chosen with care. Reznor is pushing cyber music to its limit, and with every new project gets closer to a sonic reality that traditional methods can never achieve.

Reznor is a trained classical pianist who chose to compose as well as perform, but the medium he had chosen to work in meant a course in computer engineering and music at Allesley College in his hometown of Cleveland. For some extra cash he worked as a security guard at the recording studio down the road, and with plenty of dead time in the middle of the night, he had the perfect opportunity to mess around with mixing desks, microphones and whatever else was lying around. He formed a band to record three of his songs, sent a demo tape to ten different record companies, got accepted by all of them but chose independent TVT to sign with. The deal done, he reverted to working on his own and by 1989 had the ten songs that would become his debut album, real drums and guitars recorded, looped, manipulated and edited together on his Apple Mac at home. The only point at which he collaborated was after the hard work was done, and some of the finest producers in the business helped him with the finishing textures and arrangements. Flood, Adrian Sherwood, Keith LeBlanc and John Fryer all chipped in and the completed *Pretty Hate Machine* transformed the sound of song-based music overnight.

For Reznor, the lyrics are most important, an emphasis which separates him from all other previous industrial artists. Skinny Puppy and Ministry may have had an axe to grind when it came to society and its ills, but Reznor writes from a more personal perspective, and in his own words from a very black place, his appeals to God and Jesus throughout the album make for heavy listening, but bloody good for dancing to.

The live shows to support *Pretty Hate Machine* gave Reznor the opportunity to get out of the house and away from the computer, and by all accounts, he really cut loose. With Chris Vrenna and Richard Patrick assisting, Nine Inch Nails blew away headline acts Jesus And Mary Chain and goth-in-chief Pete Murphy with their sonic rush, and everyone agreed that they won Lollapalooza in 1991 probably due to the wall-of-guitar sound that he had perfected with Patrick. A year later he got the guitars down on tape (sorry, hard-disk) on the mini-album *Broken*, which inadvertently won him a Grammy for the track 'Wish'.

By the time of the second album proper *The Downward Spiral*, Reznor had his own label, Nothing, and studio premises at 10050 Cielo Drive, the scene of the Manson family murders a quarter of a decade earlier. Not that he knew that at the time he bought the place, and by the time he had finished promoting *The Downward Spiral*, he was pretty sick of questions summizing that there was some kind of gory link. In fact, the album is themed around the vices that people indulge in to forget how they're throwing their life away. There's a song which delves into the mind of a serial killer and the title track refers to the ultimate dulling sensation, suicide by shotgun. It was 1994, Kurt was dead and the mood was heavy. As for the sound on *The Downward Spiral*, Reznor was 'more concerned

with mood, texture, restraint and subtlety, rather than getting punched in the face 400 times'. The highlight of the album is definitely 'Closer', based around a harsh slow-march electronic drum pattern and an x-rated bass-line that is just perfect for the dirtiest disco track of them all, 'I want to fuck you like an animal'. Indeed.

Reznor's working practice focuses around Pro-tools software. He, or one of his many supremely talented guest musicians, spends half an hour or so getting down with their instrument and the result is chopped up and stored away on the hard-drive until it's needed. If a musician plays a really good or interesting bit, that can be saved and the stuff around it dumped. With a process of looping and sequencing Reznor can then create perfectly synchronized patterns out of organically created parts. It's just what Can used to do back in the early seventies, but without all the tape.

The Downward Spiral had a substance that the debut album didn't, but then came *The Fragile*. Several years in the making, it's a double album packed with awesome sonics, big music for loud times. The industrial dance stuff is still there but the rhythms are slightly odder, there are quiet moments, pant-pooing loud moments, discordant moments, and sublime moments. Reznor's voice has taken on a slight rock-god tinge and his classical training serves him well on tracks like 'La Mer' which could almost be one of Claude Debussy's. Other tracks are symphonic as befits a big album, and tracks like 'The Day The World Went Away' and 'We're In This Together' are rock monsters like they used to make in the seventies. The album title is apparently a reference to the Yes album *Fragile*. Trent goes prog, but with a battery of electronics that would scare the willies out of Rick Wakeman, with or without his magic staff.

First team: Trent Reznor (v, g, k, prog). With help from: Chris Vrenna (d), Richard Patrick (g), Adrian Belew (p), Stephen Perkins (d), Charlie Clouser (k), Robin Finck (g), Danny Lohner (b, k), Jerome Dillon (d)

Place, time, scene: Cleveland, Ohio 1988. Nine Inch Nails was inspired by the heavy-metal techno of bands like Ministry and the darker industrial noises created by bands like Throbbing Gristle and Skinny Puppy, although Trent Reznor is determined that his work is judged in its totality, not just the sonic textures. His lyrics add depth to the surface noise, and on albums like *The Downward Spiral* and *The Fragile*, Nine Inch Nails put two-dimensional metal bands to shame. This is the big music.

What to buy first: *The Downward Spiral* 1994

And then: *Pretty Hate Machine* 1989, *Broken* (mini-album) 1992, *The Fragile* 1999

In retrospect: *And All That Could Have Been* (live album) 2002

NIRVANA

Unlike many of the entries in this book, Nirvana are not so much originators and innovators as completers. The band, who hail from Aberdeen in Washington, are the culmination of over a decade of independent music-making, a period during which the structure of the music industry and the sound of independently-produced music changed and developed, eventually reaching a point where it was able to invade the main-stream and introduce a whole new audience to a range of styles and a succession of voices that had previously existed beyond the scope of everyday lives. People who only listened to chart or Top 40 radio, who had hobbies or interests that didn't necessarily include keeping up with the latest new musical and associated cultural developments now had an in. The good stuff was nationwide and because they were 'right place, right time', knew their music and scene, and were led by an individual who was just too darn interesting to ignore, Nirvana were the band that crossed the line and took the plaudits. Each of their three studio albums was an improvement on the last and everything was set for an even better fourth, but we never got that.

In 1989, when they released their debut album *Bleach*, Nirvana were just another grunge band. The album was a good solid piece of work, and those who had seen Nirvana play live around Seattle must have had an inkling that the band that had made it might just be onto something. The best that the band, their fans and their record company Sub Pop could have hoped for, and probably even wanted, was for healthy sales and the opportunity to play more gigs.

The independent scene, and certainly individual independent scenes, are generally self-sufficient and

sealed off from wider economic or social concerns. Back then, the possibility, especially in America, of a band breaking out of the scene and getting a major deal was just not considered. At that time, independent music had its roots in the hardcore punk scenes with labels like SST, Dischord and Alternative Tentacles, and it was an unspoken rule that abandonment of the little label that signed and nurtured you was unethical and immoral. It was a rule that was fairly easy to stick to because major labels clearly can't sell independent music to a big enough market, and so it's just not likely to happen. But look at it long-term and it becomes apparent that Sun Records passed Elvis, Johnny, Jerry and Carl on to the masses, Motown ruled the sixties, and most of the CBGB's crowd picked up a major deal before the first wave of punk had had its day. Up to that point the majors lagged behind, it's a historical fact. And they knew it too, that's why a whole series of deals had been done in the early 1980s. Major labels buying up independents, or setting up sneaky licensing arrangements where it

Nirvana

seemed that the label was independent but actually they were being bankrolled in return for their connection to the street. The game was set.

In 1986, Hüsker Dü made a deal with Warner. In Seattle it began with Soundgarden, who moved to A&M, and after that Mother Love Bone signed with Polydor. In 1989 the coolest band on the planet, Sonic Youth, went with Geffen and Nirvana were signed within the year. Geffen provided the security and the marketing clout. It was up to Nirvana to provide the product.

Of course, the difference between Sonic Youth and Hüsker Dü, perhaps even Soundgarden, and Nirvana, was that Nirvana had an appeal that went beyond just the music. Let's be frank, Kurt Cobain was pretty. He also had a personality and stage presence that was not the recognisable cliché of the independent artist. He was not a muso like Thurston Moore, he wasn't weird like Black Francis or serious and intense like Bob Mould. He didn't preach and get worked up like Rollins and he wasn't out of it like J. Mascis. In fact, Kurt Cobain and Nirvana as a whole avoided all clichés and they did it by retaining a real link with their audience. In the songs, Kurt Cobain appeared to be himself. He had a sensitive side that he didn't disguise.

The sudden appearance of slow, personal songs like 'Polly' and 'Something In The Way' on a grunge album was an indication that Cobain was not afraid to lay himself bare, but it's the likes of 'Smells Like Teen Spirit' and 'Lithium' which are most effective. The soft, slow parts introduce a controlled Cobain telling his stories, but then when he launches himself whining, screaming and incomprehensible into a roar of power chords and energized drumming, he almost seems psychotic. Black Francis had adopted a similar approach in the Pixies, although he never seemed quite as fragile; it's Ian Curtis of Joy Division that makes the better comparison.

Like Curtis, Cobain's writing is also imbued with a sense of self-loathing, although it's difficult to really get to the bottom of his songs as they are written often in a fractured style and perhaps with the conscious aim of throwing listeners off the scent. By his own admission he could not write personal songs and so any attempt to decipher Nirvana lyrics in the hope of discovering more about the songwriter would take a good deal of time and a lot of background information. Cobain loved his serious American independent music, but he was quite the aficionado when it came to UK-based indie too; as well as Joy Division and the Raincoats, he also collected bands like the Pastels and the Vaselines, who were not noted for their searching and introspective angst-ridden songs. In fact, listen to the Vaselines' original version of 'Molly's Lips' complete with bicycle horn accompaniment or their 'Jesus Doesn't Want Me For A Sunbeam' and then compare them with the versions by Nirvana, and it's immediately apparent that the songs take on a deeper significance when sung by Cobain. His voice exudes pain and suffering and the tension and manic release in the songs suggests that he is having a hard time dealing with life and gaining fame and success, but as for real personal catharsis, the next album was the one that got closest to that.

Cobain in particular could not connect with *Nevermind* as an album because of the extraneous production that Butch Vig had added to it. Nirvana's ability to control the tension in the dynamic structure of their songs is one of the things that make them a great band. Knowing the exact moment to open it up and when to shut it down, and how best to do it – it's not always a nod and a snare shot from Dave Grohl – is classic Nirvana, but also owes a lot to Vig. As he later demonstrated with his own band Garbage, he's the master of sonic impact, but for Cobain it was all too clean. It's not a grunge album. Each sound is crystal clear, from the string fingering on 'Lithium' to the dead breaks on 'Teenage Pissings', and then there's the stuff Vig has added to texture the album, the whole thing is very definitely hi-fi. Still, those extra touches might well have helped the band breakthrough where others had not. It also gave them a platform from which they could fire off a new round of songs that were far more representative of the US underground scene in terms of psyche and sound.

For *In Utero*, Nirvana worked with producer Steve Albini, an interesting choice for a grunge band as Albini tended to work with more experimental bands like Slint and Jesus Lizard, and he hated the Pixies who Cobain had a deep respect for. The plan was to get back to Nirvana's real sound. From the off, 'Serve The Servants' launches the band into a raw and heavy album that sounds like they've got something to prove.

In typical Albini style, the guitars are corrosive and the drums are upfront, demonstrating what a crucial role Dave Grohl played in Nirvana. In keeping with the overall sound, Cobain's songs are generally hateful, and on *In Utero* it seems that he hates himself more than anything else. Selling out is a recurring theme, as it was on *Nevermind*, but the language is uglier – 'smells like semen', 'I'll kiss your open sores', 'my milk is her shit' – and every now and then, a peek at Cobain's own sadistic demons, as opposed to the ones that are supposed to resonate more generally with those doing the listening. He mentions the term 'bi-polar' in 'Radio Friendly Unit Shifter', a condition that requires lithium to treat it and which many suspect was a problem he faced along with his relentless stomach cramps; 'Heart-Shaped Box' has marriage problems stamped all over it; and the final 'All Apologies' has him questioning his moral right to even be Kurt Cobain, the voice of a generation. Ian Curtis killed himself because of exactly these sorts of personal problems. Kurt it seems, did not subscribe to the view held by some, that Curtis was a twat for doing such a thing, and within a year of recording *In Utero*, he too had killed himself. His mother released a statement the morning after his death was announced, explaining how she had begged him not to join *that* club, and having heard what he was capable of as a songwriter and vocalist, demonstrated further on the acoustic selection of covers and originals that were performed for the *Unplugged* album released just before he died, an entire generation of music fans felt let down by his actions too.

Nirvana launched the nineties with a breakthrough album that made the underground overground. The music industry learned their final big lesson. They knew that new music came from where they least expected it and Geffen had covered that one by investing in Nirvana before they broke big. They also knew that once the breakthrough happens, they must move quickly to cash-in with clones and sound-alikes, but they didn't count on the new generation of alternative kids using *Nevermind* as a starting point to dis-

cover and support they're own discoveries, whether in back-catalogue or via new signings to independent labels like Roadrunner, Grand Royal, K, Matador, Domino and Chemikal Underground. Nirvana exploded the alternative decade, which because of their own eclectic influences and roots, meant interest bloomed in all sorts of areas, punk, metal, indie, goth, noise, lo-fi, alt-country and stoner rock. OK so the industry has benefited too, there are now mini-mainstreams and dedicated TV channels and sponsorship deals in each of the areas listed, but that also means there are more specific routes to all of those styles. Remember, wherever 'the man' has set-up a mainstream, there's an alternative lurking just the other side.

First team: Kurt Cobain (v, g), Krist Novoselic (b), Dave Grohl (d, v)

Place, time, scene: Seattle, Washington 1988. Nirvana emerged out of the grunge scene. More Mudhoney than Soundgarden or Pearl Jam, they made the breakthrough into wider consciousness on behalf of the entire American underground. Once there, they spent the rest of their career documenting how much they didn't want to be there in the first place, although Cobain's own songs were taken as criticisms of 'selling out' more generally. As a spokesman for a generation, his apparent suicide deified him and the band further. Their immediate contribution was to inspire a wider definition of alternative music. Their long-term contribution is probably more profoundly related to a final acceptance by fans, that pop stars don't have all the answers and that their work shouldn't be treated as a straightforward reflection of their life. Or something like that – I'm still working on that one ok! Let's just say we're all more realistic.

What to buy first: *Nevermind* 1991

And then: *Bleach* 1989, *In Utero* 1993, *MTV Unplugged in New York* 1994

In retrospect: *Incesticide* 1992, *Nirvana* 2002

O

OASIS

There was a time in the eighties when independent music was a very cerebral thing to get involved with. It was the same in the UK and the US. Bands may have been loud and even aggressive sometimes but they were always fired by intellectualism; existential angst and disappointment were characteristics of being independent, and the music and words reflected that.

Punk's to blame of course. When 1977 struck in the UK, a couple of years later in the US, a new oppositional and uncompromising youth culture was born, at least that's how the media portrayed it. The look, the swearing, the lack of respect for what had gone before and general unruliness reported on TV and in the papers was linked indisputably with the music. Music was held responsible for a perceived decline in standards that, if it existed at all, had been happening at least since the fifties. Of course, by stirring up a moral panic about youth gone bad, the media just made the whole thing more appealing to those on the lookout for something which would immediately confirm their own identity as a bad person doing bad things. Punk music and fashion became a rallying point for anything that considered itself oppositional or dangerous, which meant everything from naughty schoolkids to sickeningly racist fuckwits. The National Front and BNP began recruiting at punk gigs, eventually setting up on their own with bands like Skrewdriver who changed almost overnight from a right-minded punk band to an extreme right-minded bunch of racist thugs. The hardcore scene in the US was perhaps less overtly racist after its initially progressive beginnings, but hardcore gigs did become an excuse for mindless violence and bullying.

The result was a split. Those disgusted with the hijacking of their music and culture began to distance themselves from the badness; they restrained overtly physical displays of enjoyment, and emphasizing their intellectualism and sensitivity, retreated inside themselves. At least, that's what they did in public to confirm their identification with the more progressive message of punk. Post-punk independent music was still powerful stuff – it could be dark and disconcerting, loud and disturbing. The Velvet Undergound were the scene's founding fathers (and mothers) for bands and fans alike. Vocalists and songwriters became inscrutable; musicians were experimental and well-versed in 'alternative' music history. They discussed music, art, literature and philosophy in interviews, and their beliefs and tastes became more nuanced. As cultural leaders, they could change opinion and resurrect careers; Big Star, Can and even the Carpenters started getting referenced as key influences on important music, and the Beatles were once again revered as gods.

Martin Carr of the Boo Radleys was one of those who knew his music, and became adept at synthesizing his influences into something new. He remembers having a conversation with new labelmates, Oasis, about the progressive influence of the Beatles in particular, although as he tells it, it was not a deep discussion of the music, lyrics or production, more an acknowledgement from the Gallaghers that, when it came down to it, the Beatles were, when all things are taken into consideration … 'mad for it'. In reality, and despite the fact that *NME* had just put Suede on the front cover of their magazine, indie was dead. In 1993, after nearly half a decade of a continually expanding club culture in the UK, *physical* appreciation of music was back on the agenda, and there was a whole new audience for music of all types, that was less concerned with how clever the music was, just whether it was, well, mad for it.

Alan McGee was on to the change. He'd been struggling to sell guitar bands for a few years, and had had extensive firsthand experience of the pleasures of body music too, when he saw Oasis at King Tut's Wah Wah Hut in Glasgow in May 1993. He may not have known it at that point, but Oasis were what the world was waiting for. The Stone Roses had been there much earlier, but then they had messed up by taking so long over the second album, and although Brown, Mani and Reni were northern soul and rock boys, Squire still clung to the old ways. Oasis were a united front. The story goes that the band had arrived mob-handed for the Glasgow gig, and had bullied their way onto the stage because they had a bus full of mates who were expecting a party that night. Oasis didn't leave Manchester much at that time, and so, double-booking or not, they were going to play. McGee's girlfriend, Debbie Turner and her band, Sister Lovers (a Big Star reference!) pulled out and by the end of the night, Oasis were a Creation band.

The debut album was awesome. The songs all had memorable hooks and melodies, some robbed from the best in the business (and the New Seekers), and the sound was big and swirling, visceral and dumb. Noel Gallagher made sure of that. There's no separation between the instruments because the whole thing was recorded live and simultaneously with the needle in the red, so that in his words it sounded like an aeroplane taking off. 'Rock'n'Roll Star' is exactly that, the definitive introduction to an album that is all about playing loud and heavy, and feeling like you're the most important person in the world. If, in the process, you catch yourself sounding like the Beatles or T.Rex that's even better. I'm not sure that I'd take that stuff out either when the band sounds so fucking 'on it', and let's face it, like they own the riff, the hook or the attitude anyway. 'Live Forever' has a drum sound that must have had Bonzo smiling in his grave. 'Up In The Sky', 'Columbia' and well everything else on the album are master-classes in the possibilities of the rhythm-guitar when cranked up really high. 'Bring It On Down' has a raucous guitar solo that can induce head-banging, 'Cigarettes And Alcohol' confirms that the levels are generally far too high in that studio with its introductory mains rattle and hum, and 'Shakermaker' and 'Supersonic' were just catchy enough to get the whole noisy roar into the pop charts. And that hadn't happened since the piled-on guitars and up-front sneering of the Sex Pistols. In fact, that's the best reference point of all, Oasis were the Sex Pistols without the irony or the anger, but with the arrogance and belief in the spirit of rock'n'roll intact and in spades.

By the time they released the era-defining *(What's The Story) Morning Glory*, the focus had gone, and the band subsequently lost its awesome power. There are still moments of course, like the title track, 'Cast No Shadow', and 'Some Might Say', which could all have been on the first album, and 'Don't Look Back In Anger', a song sung by Noel which suggests that at some point he might make a great solo album. The sentiment of the song is amplified because of the band's reputation for straight-talking and a perceived absence of any considered political or philosophical subtext. Noel's plea for inner peace, for people to stop the world and get off, is his 'Imagine', 'Let It Be' and 'Revolution' all rolled into one, the piano and slightly fuzzy guitar intro sees to it that we know that. The lyrics are personal and reflect on his new-found spokesperson role 'please don't put your life in the hands of a rock and roll band' and there's even the pay-off line at the end 'least not today', as Gallagher stops himself before the idealism and naïvety of his appeal gets the better of him. It's exactly what Lennon used to do years before to stop the inner hippy from taking over completely – in his case there's 'I wonder if you can' and the more extreme 'you can count me out (in)'.

'Don't Look Back In Anger' was chosen to close Peter Flannery's epic TV serialization, *Our Friends In The North*, a dramatization of post-colonial British society and politics, set over ten hours, from the Beatle-mania era onwards. It's played as one of the main characters looks on at his friends enjoying a moment of unbridled happiness as children play and loving looks are exchanged, a stolen moment before he and they return to their difficult and occasionally tragic lives in mid-nineties Britain. For that moment, critical thought and socially defined reality are suspended as love, joy and positivity takeover. Pure words and music for a pure moment. At their best, whether it's 'Don't Look Back In Anger' or 'Rock And Roll Star', Oasis can effortlessly reproduce such moments.

First team: Noel Gallagher (g, v), Liam Gallagher (v), Paul Arthurs (g), Paul McGuigan (b), Tony McCarroll (d)

Place, time, scene: Manchester 1993. Oasis are led by a former guitar tech for the Inspiral Carpets, an indie band that flourished as part of the new groove-inspired scene in Manchester at the beginning of the nineties. Noel Gallagher, ably assisted by his brother Liam, connected a spirit of anti-intellectualism with classic guitar rock/pop and tapped into the prevailing cultural vibe, a post-rave demand for melodic and familiar sounding pop, but played by a proper band in the tradition of the great British bands of the past. It got dubbed Brit pop.

What to buy first: *Definitely Maybe* 1994

And then: *(What's The Story) Morning Glory* 1995

In retrospect: *The Masterplan* 1998

ORANGE JUICE

The problem with alternative music, before punk and now still, is that it tends towards the dark, the didactic and the tragic. Very few of the entries in this book are for artists who, having adopted an independent approach to their creative work, have subsequently opted to make self-consciously happy or humorous music, and those who have, have often been struck off completely later on, or at the least have divided opinion as to their worth. Of course, the main problem is that high spirits and lightness of being are classic signifiers of pop music, and it's assumed that those who make pop music are avoiding the real issues, and are driven by a desire to cash-in at the expense of truth and an uninformed and depoliticized public.

Orange Juice made pop music, they must have done because every review that was ever written about them described them as fey, a word of Scottish origin that means 'in high spirits'. Those reviews usually placed the word within the sentence 'could sometimes be annoyingly fey' which speaks volumes about the sad lives of those doing the reviewing and nothing about the music or the band. So let's put that right, right now. Orange Juice were probably the first band to fit the description 'indie', although many of the indie bands that came after them didn't share the same aims at all.

For Orange Juice and their manager Alan Horne, there were two models of independent music, the Velvet Underground and Motown Records. Horne's label Postcard Records was set-up specifically to sign Orange Juice and make them stars, but he also fancied himself as a new Berry Gordy, almost going as far as

signing a house band to the label to back any future signings. His record collection had a major impact on the band's chief songwriter, Edwyn Collins, who had fronted a punk band called the Nu-Sonics before forming Orange Juice as a response to the hard-headed Glasgow punk scene led by bands like the Exploited. Collins was familiar with certain obscurities – the first time Horne saw them, they played a track off one of the later Velvets' albums – but he could get down to some significant listening in Horne's flat.

The first few Orange Juice singles released by Postcard were enthusiastically received by music journalists hungry for a new scene, and Orange Juice along with labelmates Josef K and Aztec Camera, and colourful popsters Altered Images, were dubbed the 'sound of young Scotland'. 'Falling And Laughing', 'Blue Boy' and 'Simply Thrilled Honey' were notable for their slapdash playing, Collins' proto-Morrissey anti-vocal and knowing lyrics that were self deprecating, romantically-themed and got in the odd pop reference. The band at that point consisted of Collins, James Kirk, Steven Daly and David McClymont and while they remained on Postcard they could do no wrong as far as the indie scene was concerned. But when they opted to record their debut album with Polydor, they lost their protective indie shield.

The songs on *You Can't Hide Your Love Forever* released in 1982 were as good as the first singles, but playing by the new rules the operative phrase now became 'annoyingly fey'. The version of Al Green's 'L.O.V.E. Love' on the album was picked on as a sign of Orange Juice's wrongness, but the other songs that blended punk spirit and guitars with northern soul were ignored. Collins plays some neat jazz chord progressions while Kirk, who wrote several of the songs on the album, weighs in with slightly refined but still quite abrasive guitar parts.

Kirk and drummer Daly left before the next one *Rip It Up*, and were replaced by Malcolm Ross and Zimbabwean drummer Zeke Manyika who had to keep a low profile on account of him being an illegal immigrant. Not that it stopped him writing and singing two tracks on *Rip It Up* though, and adding some fiery beats to an album that was out and out funk-pop. The title track features a magnificently minimalist guitar solo, saxophone played by professional scary person Jim 'Foetus' Thirwell and lyrics that reference that key punk song, 'Boredom' by the Buzz-cocks. The lyrical referencing, romanticism and lo-fi musical approach became indie trademarks that were picked up by the shambling bands of 1986 and even made their way over to bands like Pavement by the end of the decade, but this is where it started.

Before McClymont and Ross left to branch out on their own, the line-up that made *Rip It Up* produced a mini-album with producer Dennis Bovell who had worked with the Slits and Fela Kuti. Called *Texas Fever*, it is probably the band's best work, where all of the elements, almost-soul, almost-funk, almost-punk and immaculate songwriting come together like they never had before. The soul is never entirely sweet and the punk never entirely discordant. With Bovell's dub-infused production, the plastic sheen that was always there on the earlier two albums is peeled away and confirmed on its release that it was just a damned shame that the band couldn't stay together in this form. Whatever happened to Ape The Scientific anyway?

Collins and Manyika chose to work with Bovell again on the final album *The Orange Juice* which was effectively Collins' first solo album. 'Salmon Fishing In New York' may be a funk pastiche, it may be for real, certainly the band nails the music in a way that they had never managed before; 'Guess I'm Just A Little Too Sensitive' is a coy reflection on the established indie scene that he helped to establish; 'The Artisans' is the tale of Orange Juice in all but name; and 'Lean Period' might be commenting on his creative flow, or on the reality of his situation, left without a band and a record deal with a future far from mapped out.

It was five years before a solo album appeared, and another six years after that before he had a hit single with the fuzzy pastiche of sixties pop entitled 'A Girl Like You'. How did it go now, 'too many protest singers, not enough protest songs'. Right on, Eddie.

First team: Edwyn Collins (v,g), Malcolm Ross (g), David McClymont (b), Zeke Manyika (d)

Place, time, scene: Glasgow 1979. Orange Juice took the irony and commitment to DIY working practices from punk and musically fused the Velvet Underground with northern soul and funk. Their apparent sell-out signing to Polydor Records left them in a no-man's land between the pop charts and the underground, a position which the Smiths later made their own. The Smiths themselves learned a lot from Orange Juice as did most other 'indie' bands of the decade even if they lacked the groovier elements. An early incarnation of the Stone Roses was heavily based on Orange Juice.

What to buy first: *Rip It Up* 1983

And then: *You Can't Hide Your Love Forever* 1982, *The Orange Juice* 1984

In retrospect: *The Very Best of Orange Juice* 1992, *The Heather's On Fire* 1993

P

GRAM PARSONS

Gram Parsons is credited with the invention of country-rock. Picking up where the original rock'n'roll stars left off, and keen to bring psychedelic rock back down to earth, he made what he called 'white soul' music. Just as Iggy and the Stooges were making their stand against 'head music' and were returning to the primal source of rock'n'roll, Parsons with his International Submarine Band were bringing back the soul and the emotion that had transformed country music when it first met the rhythm and the blues back in the mid-fifties. Despite selling relatively few of his own records while he was alive, Parsons was able to dedicate his short life to music because of his financial inheritance and, like a travelling gospel preacher, influenced the Byrds, the Rolling Stones and one of the first punks, Jonathan Richman, with his musical vision. His struggle to get clean of the addiction to drugs and drink which eventually killed him in 1973 is inscribed in his music. Relentless temptation, regret and elusive redemption have always been the themes of country music, from Hank Williams to Johnny Cash, and Gram Parsons neatly and tragically fits the tradition. His specific drug, heroin, was the ultimate negation. He attempted to live the rock'n'roll life, but it didn't give him enough. Unlike his trad contemporaries the Band who could fantasize about an America that was almost gone, Parsons at least tried to connect with the new culture even if he didn't care much for its escapist music, and that's the distinction. The Band were totally independent and existed outside of pop culture but Parsons was in it, always trying to talk to his peers and turn them onto his music. He offered an alternative.

Cecil Connor got the itchin' to play music when Elvis Presley turned up at his school one day and did a gig! He was nine at the time and although he made it through high school and got to Harvard University, rock'n' roll won through in the end. At Harvard he studied theology but lived music. Confident of his financial future due to a trust fund set up by his land-owning Georgian family, he formed the International Submarine Band, and so began a well-funded hedonistic lifestyle and whirlwind period of musical innovation and inspiration that only ended with his own death.

Guitarist John Nuese of the International Submarine Band was a kindred spirit who turned the then Beatles-obsessed Parsons onto a range of traditional music. Immediately and effortlessly the International Submarine Band produced a perfectly blended country-psychedelia album that brought together the otherworldliness and unstructured experience of LSD with the grounded reality and tradition of roots music. *Safe At Home* was released on Lee Hazelwood's LHI record label in 1968, but because both the band and Hazelwood were so appalled by Parsons' drug-induced approach to music-making, there was never a follow-up. Gram Parsons joined the Byrds as a replacement for David Crosby. In the short time that Parsons was with the Byrds he had a major effect on their music. Together with Chris Hillman, he actively pushed band-leader Roger McGuinn towards country music. 'Sweethearts Of The Rodeo' had steel guitars, mandolins, Merle Haggard and gospel.

It was a critical success, but by the time it had been released Parsons had moved on again, having left the band because he refused to play to segregated audiences during a South African tour – Parsons was no redneck country honk! Next, he formed the Flying Burrito Brothers, taking Byrds bassist Chris Hillman with him, and put out two albums in under a year combining country, rock and soul music into what Parsons called 'cosmic American music'. On *The Gilded Palace Of Sin*, Parsons and Hillman shared the song writing, coming up with songs that dealt with Vietnam, groupies and drugs, although 'Hot Burrito #1' takes the winner's trophy as one of the most beautiful love songs ever written.

Before the second Burritos album was even released, Parsons had moved on again, spending more time with his new best friend Keith Richard. Together they played country music and mainlined heroin. He was a major influence on the Rolling Stones' albums of the period, namely *Beggars Banquet*, *Let It Bleed* and *Exile On Main Street*. He played and sang backing vocals on several tracks for *Exile On Main Street* recorded round at Keith's house, and received a special thank you in the sleeve-notes. His two solo albums, recorded with the help of Elvis Presley's Las Vegas TCB (Taking Care Of Business) backing band, were out and out country, and *Grievous Angel* in particular was informed by the old themes. His relationship with Emmylou Harris and consequent split with his wife, combined with continued drug and alcohol abuse made for a passionate and honest album, made all the more resonant due to the fact that he was dead by the time it came out.

The band that he was considering with Jonathan Richman in 1973 never happened, which is a shame because Parsons would have made a good punk and would have been an interesting bloke to have around when all that back to roots post-punk started happening. He certainly would have approved of the alt. country pioneered by Uncle Tupelo and Lambchop in the late eighties too. But, hey, he's dead. It was apparently the result of an overdose – tequila and morphine – although many claim to this day that the lack of those specific narcotics in his blood during the autopsy might just point to other factors. And then there was all that stuff about his body being kidnapped by friends who took it back to the desert town of Joshua Tree and set fire to it to stop him being buried in New Orleans. A cremation pact apparently. That was 19 September 1973. He was 27.

First team: Flying Burrito Brothers: Gram Parsons (v, g), Chris Hillman (v, g, mand), Chris Ethridge (b, p), Sneaky Pete Kleinow (steel g), Jon Corneal (d)

Place, time, scene: LA 1966. Gram Parsons was combining country and psychedelia at a time when traditional roots music was a no-go area for electric rockers. Dylan and the Band were doing something similar at the same time, although the Band in particular were always consciously opposed to psychedelia and eventually opted for something much more organic, while Parsons was happy to incorporate the latest studio technology and synthesized sounds into his music with the Flying Burrito Brothers. His 'cosmic American music' inspired the Stones and country-rock more generally, but in terms of attitude, his most important influence is on the likes of Steve Earle, Will Oldham, Giant Sand, Uncle Tupelo, Wilco and Lambchop.

What to buy first: Flying Burrito Brothers: *The Gilded Palace Of Sin* 1969

And then: International Submarine Band: *Safe At Home* 1968, Gram Parsons: *GP* 1973, *Grievous Angel* 1974

In retrospect: *Anthology: Sacred Hearts And Fallen Angels* 2001

PASTELS

Alan McGee reckons they should try a bit harder. Stephen McRobbie contends that the Pastels are not that kind of band. When the alternative became the mainstream in the 1990s and got divided into easy-to-manage genres with specific niche audiences, the Pastels were not part of the deal. During their 22 year existence, the group has managed to release four full albums. If the members of the band did nothing else with their lives then that would have to be regarded as a pretty dismal strike rate, but the thing is, Stephen works in a bookshop, Aggi Wright is an illustrator and Katrina Mitchell, in lieu of any other administrative personnel, manages the band. They have set up two labels and maintain international links with Calvin Johnson's

K Records in Washington, as well as a working musical relationship with underground American bands like Half-Japanese. The Pastels were the template for the shambling 'anorak' scene which was given impetus by the *NME*'s *C86* compilation and remain an inspiration for anyone aiming to avoid rock cliché ever since. They have total control over their work and output, and are rightly proud of that fact. They are an independent band.

The band formed in 1981 when the Glasgow underground was buzzing with the success of Orange Juice and Alan Horne's independent Postcard label. With the addition of Aztec Camera and the Go-Betweens, it soon became clear that DIY-punk attitude could be filtered through musical styles other than straight-ahead rock. Lyrics didn't have to be harsh and didactic either; Edwyn Collins, Roddy Frame and Grant McLennan all specialized in innocent romanticism and clever and poetic turns of phrase. Brian (Superstar) Taylor, who shared a flat with Horne at that time, was suitably inspired and instigated the Pastels with Stephen McRobbie, Martin Hayward and Bernice Simpson. Initially the band took their cue from American band Beat Happening and seemed to have an almost wilful amateurism, which has been retained in their releases throughout the 1980s and 1990s. They continue to work to the principle that, in McRobbie's words, 'a good idea badly expressed is always better than a bad idea very well expressed'.[50]

Unconcerned with musical skills in a traditional sense, the Pastels have focused on texture and emotion in their music. There is also a strong folk-song element underpinning what they do that continues a Scottish tradition from the original Postcard releases, and which has worked its way into more recent work by the Delgados and Belle and Sebastian. The Pastels may have remained in the background all this time but their ubiquity on the Glasgow scene has been crucial in the maintenance of an avant-garde in rock music outside of London.

The first few singles were released on several different labels, starting with 'Songs for Children' on the Whaam! label operated by anti-punk ironists the TV Personalities, that led to deals with Rough Trade and Creation and eventually two albums released on Glass and Chapter 22. *Up for A Bit With The Pastels* was released shortly after the band's inclusion on the *C86* tape compiled by *NME*, which placed the Pastels at the forefront of a new musical approach based around a certain sense of amateurism, innocence and fun, notably absent from the over-produced slickster pop stars of the period. They were an indie band. Of late, McRobbie rightly makes the point that indie should not refer to a style of music and is rightly annoyed when the term gets used in that way. Initially the word carried with it a sense of empowerment and resistance, but is now more often used as a term of abuse by some and as a generic descriptor by many. They may have appeared cute and naïve on the surface, but listen to the albums and you'll realize that they are stylistically challenging and always clued-up.

Norman Blake and Gerry Love of Teenage Fanclub, Eugene Kelly of the Vaselines and David Keegan of the Shop Assistants contributed to the first albums, and the family feel was continued when McRobbie and Keegan set up the 53rd and 3rd label, named after the sick (sic) Ramones song, which has put out albums by the Vaselines and Beat Happening.

The Pastels

In the nineties, with *Mobile Safari* and *Illumination*, the trio of McRobbie, bassist Aggi and drummer Katrina have achieved a textured sound where a mood is created through the placement in the overall mix of various sonic elements. On *Illumination* those tuneless voices are right there next to your ear, while the musical backdrop whirs away somewhere in the background. The lead-off track 'The Hits Hurt' makes the most of Dean Wareham's guitar and jazzer Bill Wells' Gershwin piano; 'Cycle' is beautifully pastoral; and 'Unfair Kind Of Fame' will have you running for the window, the claustrophobia is so tangible. Hard and sensitive music, it's an increasing rarity.

Recently, the band have concentrated their efforts on the new Geographic label, which has provided an outlet for musician Bill Wells, Nagisa Ni Te and a project going by the name Sister Vanilla that includes Jim and William Reid from Jesus And Mary Chain, their sister Linda and My Bloody Valentine recluse Kevin Shields. There's a school of thought that Stephen McRobbie would have made a better critic than artist because he knows his music and has an innate sense of quality. That's all true, but surely it's better to have someone like that on the inside where he can marshal sounds and players into cohesive and worthwhile projects. The *Illuminati – Pastels Music Remixed* album is a case in point. It brings together Stereolab, My Bloody Valentine, Cornelius, John McEntire, Third Eye Foundation, Jim O'Rourke, Kid Loco, To Rococo Rot, Future Pilot AKA, the Make-Up and Mouse On Mars on one album, all creating their own art from the same raw material. It's hard to think of any other person currently operating anywhere in the music industry who could bring together such an impressive array of cutting-edge musicians. McRobbie and the Pastels are crucial.

First team: Stephen McRobbie (v, g), Aggi Wright (v, k, b), Katrina Mitchell (d)

Place, time, scene: Glasgow 1982. The Pastels emerged out of the same Scottish scene that produced Orange Juice and Aztec Camera, and were part of a second wave which included the BMX Bandits, Soup Dragons, Primal Scream and the Boy Hairdressers, who would later become Teenage Fanclub. Dubbed a 'shambling' band, they have stayed true to a form of harsh and simultaneously sensitive music, and with their impressive independent label and contacts, have remained key to the continued availability and promotion of non-mainstream artists.

What to buy first: *Ilumination* 1997

And then: *Up For A bit With The Pastels* 1987, *Mobile Safari* 1995

In retrospect: *Truckload Of Trouble 1986–1993* 1993

PAVEMENT

Stephen Malkmus has been called the songwriter of his generation, which probably means the nineties; before that, in the late eighties, it was Mark Eitzel of American Music Club. What's the difference? Well, Eitzel was a hard drinking, sensitive soul fired by the righteous energy of hardcore, who got angry at himself and the world and expressed his anger eloquently and concisely backed by a top-notch set of musicians. Malkmus must get angry at himself and the world sometimes too, but it's difficult to know because he wouldn't feel comfortable talking about it in a song. It might be something to do with his background, the upper middle-classes are notorious for keeping emotions under wraps, but it's more likely that he, like Lou Barlow in Sebadoh, Will Oldham of the Palace Brothers and the king of lo-fi Daniel Johnston, was fed up with the growing emphasis on the high fidelity in independent music. The brutal honesty of his lyrics, matched with flawless, or at the least, sympathetic musicianship, was somehow reminiscent of the dinosaurs that roamed the charts before punk. Chief punk John Lydon pointed out what he perceived to be a return to the bad old days in Nirvana's output, so, like it or not, there was a groundswell of opinion working against the new commercially-successful underground.

At its core, Pavement's anti-rock was the same as Cobain's of course, they just had a different way of expressing it, and because they never really broke through and could talk clever, the critics and budding little critics loved 'em. I reckon that probably annoyed Stephen Malkmus almost as much as Pearl Jam did.

The origins of Pavement are in Stockton, California where Malkmus and Scott Kannberg attended high school together, although they didn't get it together musically until they had left school, forming a band called Straw Dogs that played hardcore and dug industrial experimentalists, Chrome. At 18 Malkmus left for the University of Virginia where he met Bob Nastanovich and songwriter David Berman, who DJ'd together on the university radio station, and formed a band called Lakespeed, and then the Silver Jews, as an outlet for Berman's exceptional songs. On returning to Stockton, he once again hooked up with Kannberg, who was by now calling himself Spiral Stairs, and together they recorded two songs for a single EP which they called 'Slay Tracks', and then Malkmus left again, this time to tour the Middle-East. Kannberg got the single pressed up and credited to a new band called Pavement and when Malkmus returned from his wanderings they had a hit on their hands.

Roping in Nastanovich, bassist Mark Ibold and middle-aged drummer Gary Young, who was on hand to engineer the 10″ single 'Perfect Sound Forever', Pavement suddenly became a going concern. At which point Malkmus left again for another stint in Virginia with Berman, working as a museum guard. Getting Pavement started, it turns out, was as difficult as breaking them up almost a decade later – a period of immense procrastination too. In fact, with members of the band consistently living on opposite sides of the country from each other for the duration of the band's career, Pavement seemed to walk it like they talked it, they were a band who to quote one of Malkmus' lyrics 'could really give a fuck' (for an English translation, replace 'could' with 'couldn't'). They regularly claimed that being famous was not part of their agenda, perfectly happy to not move to the next level.

Eventually the debut album *Slanted And Enchanted* was released in 1992 and was an immediate critical success. The music had a lackadaisical spirit, all loose guitars, detuned, possibly on purpose, possibly because they couldn't be bothered to tune them, and plenty of off-kilter la-la-las and laid-back drumming that sets the pace of the songs at slow-ahead. The obvious comparisons were with REM because of the country/folk vibe and the obscure lyrics, although Malkmus' hidden meanings were actually decipherable provided you had a keen ear for irony.

Crooked Rain, Crooked Rain followed in 1993 and was easier to follow because it was so obviously targeted at the music industry and music culture in general. 'Cut Your Hair' is about being in a band, from the early days when gigs are hard to get to the end days when nobody's interested anymore, and in-between when 'songs mean a lot when songs are bought, and so are you' – that's satire on at least two levels, and counting. 'Range Life' adopts an outsider's view of the independent scene, 'someone', according to Malkmus, from 'Lone Justice or Dream Syndicate not being able to keep up with what's going on today'; there are digs at the Smashing Pumpkins and Stone Temple Pilots but only in the name of good storytelling, of course, and the whole thing is given the patented Pavement loose vibe. The breaks at the end of each verse and chorus segment hang in the air until somebody brings the beat back, and each time it's different – guitar, piano, drums – almost as if the band can't really be bothered with continuing the song, but then one of them feels guilty and we're back with another verse.

At that point, Malkmus reckons they should have stopped, before *Wowee Zowee* showed them up as experimental, serious artists after all. The charade was up, Pavement did care, it wasn't all a 4-track attempt at democratizing the recording industry, showing how great albums could be made on the cheap and with the minimum of fuss. But then again, maybe they had been misjudged all along. In interviews the band had always maintained that they were in it for real as far as the music was concerned, they just weren't interested in being stars. The reviews for the album veered from masterpiece to 'crock', although when listened to it's clear that the songs that make up the first half of the album seem more complete than the shorter ones in the second half, maybe they just couldn't be arsed after all? Boy, this is a complex band to decipher.

Brighten The Corners is a more concise offering and includes their best rocker in 'Stereo', which pulls the old Nirvana trick of controlled verse and manic all-out screaming chorus but with a few tantalizing sonic twists; and their most melancholic and downright disconcerting song 'Shady Lane', which appears to be a warped story of domestic violence. On *Terror Twilight* the songs are just as good, the lyrics just as well-constructed, but with lines like 'The damage has been done, I'm not having fun anymore' in retrospect it seems the end was nigh. It took over a year of saying

they were splitting for them to actually do the terrible deed, probably because they couldn't find everybody to let them know. In the end, Malkmus emailed Spiral Stairs to ask him to post the break-up of the band on the website. It was the first his old school chum knew of it.

First team: Stephen Malkmus (v, g), Spiral Stairs (v, g), Bob Nastanovich (k), Mark Ibold (b), Steve West (d)

Place, time, scene: Stockton, California 1989. Pavement's lo-fi approach was a reaction to the seriousness that had developed in American underground music. A mass ego, they reckoned, needed to be burst. Along with Sebadoh who regularly satirized indie rock in this period, Pavement kept to guitars and basic recording methods for the first few albums and when they did begin to broaden their musical palette they strove to keep the basic melodies and rawness intact. Their final two albums came at a time when bands like U2 were taking giant lemons on tour and phoning world leaders mid-show, and Radiohead were being touted as the new Pink Floyd. Even though Nigel Godrich who produced *OK Computer* worked on the last Pavement album, the band retained their sense of proportion.

What to buy first: *Crooked Rain, Crooked Rain* 1994

And then: *Slanted And Enchanted* 1992, *Brighten The Corners* 1997, *Terror Twilight* 1999

In retrospect: *Westing (By Musket And Sextant)* 1993

PERE UBU

Pere Ubu, more than any other, deserve to be called an art-rock band. From their very first single '30 Seconds Over Tokyo', released in 1977, it was clear that they were in the business of constructing meaningful and evocative music that had required some advance planning. But unlike the progressive rockers of the seventies, they were also a band that retained a fundamental connection to balls-out rock'n'roll. From their inception in 1975 David Thomas has led Pere Ubu with a series of different line-ups and musical focuses, and like his British counterpart, Mark E. Smith of the Fall, has managed to collaborate with and communicate his musical intentions to a range of differently motivated musicians with a large amount of success. It says a lot about the quality of his own songwriting and his assertiveness and negotiating skills, that he has managed to get the best work out of some of the most strong-minded and innovative musicians around. Or maybe it's all about having focus, knowing how to develop it without resorting to the latest trend. It's a difficult balancing act, staying in touch and relevant without sacrificing independence. Goddammit, it's what this book is all about.

Pere Ubu began life as a pioneering garage-punk band called Rocket From The Tombs, key players in a Cleveland scene that also included the Electric Eels and the Mirrors. Thomas, the music journalist, who wrote under a number of aliases including Crocus Behemoth, was the band's instigator. He formed Rocket From The Tombs in 1974 to play MC5 covers at the Viking Saloon in Cleveland. By the time the band recorded its first session in 1975, live in their rehearsal space, the line-up included Peter Laughner on guitar, Cheetah Chrome on another guitar, drummer Johnny Blitz and bassist Craig Bell. The version of '30 Seconds Over Tokyo' recorded in that first session is amazing to listen to. Already an epic eight-minuter, the guitar interplay between Laughner and Chrome, starting restrained and eventually cranked up well into the red for maximum screech, is addictive. Like Tom Verlaine's playing with Television around the same time, it is all about feel and effect and has no real connection to rhythm and blues at all. It's not what the guitarist is playing, it's what it sounds like. There's a touch of Pink Floyd's 'Interstellar Overdrive' about it which is never a bad thing. Thomas's lyrics tell the story of the WW2 Doolittle raid on Tokyo and showcase his strong but disconcerting voice, later to turn into a falsetto-yowl with Pere Ubu.

RFTT lasted one more recording session and a handful of live shows, including a Cleveland date supporting Television which effectively finished the band off. Chrome, Blitz and their new friend Stiv Bators formed the Dead Boys and Laughner and Thomas put together Pere Ubu. Of the existing RFTT song catalogue, the Dead Boys took 'Sonic Reducer' written by Thomas, and Pere Ubu had '30 Seconds Over Tokyo' and the equally compulsive 'Final Solution', which

Thomas refers to as his follow-up to Blue Cheer's 'Summertime Blues': 'I wanted "Summertime Blues" reduced to the minimal – a throb and then a big burst of noise and then back to a throb.[51]

The debut album *The Modern Dance* does not feature Laughner, who died in June 1977 before recording commenced, but it does harbour his art meets rock'n'roll spirit with guitarist Tom Herman doing a fine job alongside drummer Scott Krauss, bassist Tony Maimone and keyboardist Alan Ravenstine. The first track 'Non-Alignment Pact' sets the scene, with Ravenstine's high-pitched EML synthesizer squealing throughout a basic rocker that has an ascending rather than a descending bass-line. The live feel of the album and Thomas's non-melodic vocals qualify it for punk status, although the odd arrangement and rhythms suggest that Pere Ubu had already jumped forward to post-punk. And there's a humour and almost party feel to certain tracks that was missing in many of the CBGB's generation punk bands.

Dub Housing followed within six months and may even be better than *The Modern Dance*. Ravenstine's keyboards are more prominent but are used in such a way that the overall sound is still raw and immediate, still organic. The songs are chock-full of sound, to the point that on first listen it all sounds a bit of a mess, but then that's punk musique-concrete for you. Tape loops and found sounds are scattered around liberally, the drum parts are constantly changing and Tom Herman's guitar thrashes around over the top of it all. The album was a big influence on the no-wave scene that followed in New York, led by bands like DNA and the Contortions, who learned from Pere Ubu that all that stuff they go on about in Rock School is only the first stage. Once you've learned the rules then you can go off and break them. Somebody in Hüsker Dü and in Sonic Youth quite obviously bought a copy too.

The fourth album, *The Art Of Walking*, featured new guitarist Mayo Thompson, the man behind Red Krayola, an inspirational band that operated in the late sixties specializing in musical freak-outs when all other garage bands were mimicking the British invasion groups. He fitted in perfectly. As did drummer Anton Fier who led the no-wave jazz-punk band the Golden Palominos and who joined for the 1982 release *Song Of The Bailing Man*. Both albums moved Pere Ubu away from the art/rock synthesis and, led by

Thompson, who has made a life's project out of this sort of thing, edged their way towards pop music, stopping short of actually getting there of course. Melodies start sensibly but then veer off just before they reach a satisfying destination, tempos constantly change and Thomas's lyrics are based around the central theme of animals and science. He provides some impressive farmyard noises on 'Big Ed's Used Farms'.

Following a split and reformation, Pere Ubu have recorded sporadically since 1988 and David Thomas has additionally worked on several musical projects featuring an impressive list of musician muses including Richard Thompson, Andy Diagram and Jackie Leven. In 1996 he was asked to produce a paper reflecting on his experience of making music. It was entitled 'The Geography Of Sound In The Magnetic Age', a keenly observed and concise summary of the forces at play in the production and consumption of popular music, which calls for critical listening by those doing the consuming. It's not just down to the musicians to do all the work.

First team: David Thomas (v, sx, k), Tom Herman (g), Alan Ravenstine (syn), Tony Maimone (b), Scott Krauss (d)

Place, time, scene: Cleveland, Ohio 1975. Pere Ubu emerged from the Cleveland proto-punk scene that fed into the New York punk scene centred around CBGBs. The band themselves, like Television and Talking Heads, incorporated elements of the progressive rock sound into their music but without falling into pretentious art parody. Most post-punk bands were inspired by Pere Ubu.

What to buy first: *The Modern Dance* 1978

And then: *Dub Housing* 1978, *Song Of The Bailing Man* 1982, *The Tenement Year* 1988, *Pennsylvania* 1998

In retrospect: Rocket From The Tombs: *The Day The Earth Met...* 2002, Pere Ubu: *Terminal Tower: An Archival Collection* 1989

LEE 'SCRATCH' PERRY

Lee Perry is in this book because he changed the way music was made. Of course, he was a pioneer of reggae, bringing rocksteady back to its Jamaican roots, but it was his competition with his friend King Tubby that really motivated him to use the recording studio as a primary instrument. He and Tubby might have been commissioned to re-mix Jamaican rocksteady hits, but they were effectively re-constructing them. Version and dub are the studio bases of contemporary dance music, where the beat and the texture are prioritized above the song and melody. The way Perry saw it, he was creating a spiritual sound that did away with unnecessary egotistical embellishment, which struck a chord with punks too who were fighting their own battle against increasingly irrelevant pomp-rock.

The long hot Jamaican summer of 1966 was an important time for Caribbean music. Duke Reid took the beat down a few notches transforming ska into rocksteady, U-Roy began toasting, and the Upsetter, aka Lee 'Scratch' Perry finally decided to leave Joe Gibbs' studio in Kingston to set up on his own. He'd been with Gibbs since the late fifties, progressing from runner to unofficial A&R man, during which time he had discovered the Maytals and Delroy Wilson. He was one of the first people to produce Bob Marley and the Wailers and in 1968 had an international hit with 'Return Of Django' released through his own Upsetter Records. All good, but his real achievement was not the internationalization of Jamaican music, more the fact that he was taking it back to its 'roots'.

Perry began to incorporate the traditional 'mento' style into his productions and slowed down the rhythms again, creating a style which was ready for the consciousness words of singers like Marley. As reggae replaced rocksteady, Perry and King Tubby also created 'version', removing the Americanized soulful vocal track from existing rocksteady hits, leaving just the instrumental backing track. 'Dub' was next. By performing autopsies on the tracks, splitting the music into its constituent parts, cranking up the bass part and treating the whole thing with varying degrees of echo, an entirely new sound, based on texture and rhythm was invented.

For Tubby the electrician, it was vocational. Stories abound of his eagerness to fix toasters (that's the things you put bread in rather than the proto-rappers) in-between recording sessions. For Perry, it was political and cultural. For him, dub provided an opportunity to be rid of standardized musical structures and learned techniques, taking it free-form instead. He included sound effects and general noises of everyday life into his dub pieces and messed around with volume levels, echo and unexpected sonic interruptions. The subsonic bass made the whole thing sound dark and sinister, and was particularly effective when played through a powerful sound system. Perry's keenness to connect with an audience on a direct level led him to explore the possibilities of beats and textures, and in 1971 he was playing two or more records simultaneously to create new rhythms. Turntablism was rife in Jamaica before it caught on in New York it seems.

In 1974 he opened up his own Black Ark studios where he worked with U-Roy, I-Roy, Dillinger, Augustus Pablo, Jah Lion, and the Mighty Diamonds, and put out a succession of key reggae albums under his own name. The one to get is *Super Ape* from 1976. Perry wrote and produced all the tracks, which were played by a crack team of musicians, including Boris Gardiner on bass, Earl Smith on guitar and Perry organizing percussion himself. At Black Ark he recorded Max Romeo's *War In a Babylon* and Junior Murvin's *Police And Thieves*, and worked with Sly and Robbie, Ernest Ranglin and Augustus Pablo. The Clash covered 'Police And Theives' on their first album as an acknowledgement of the influence Perry's brand of reggae had had on the punk culture in London at that time. Like just about every other reggae star following the success of Bob Marley in the mid seventies, he was signed to Island Records internationally, but when Marley died in 1981, reggae took a body blow and Perry found himself less in demand outside of Jamaica. He hit the rum and the ganja hard and spent the eighties in a stupor, having burned down his Black Ark studio, possibly by accident, possibly to get out of paying the weekly protection money. Visitors tell stories of him worshipping bananas and eating money and he lost his deal with Chris Blackwell at Island Records after calling him a vampire and accusing him of murdering Bob Marley.

Fortunately, he made it through the bad times and by 1989 he had a new studio in Switzerland and an address book that included Adrian Sherwood and Mad Professor. His workrate has slowed during the last decade but with a set of musical disciples that includes Massive Attack, Leftfield and the Dub Pistols – the new generation of dub scientists – let's face it, his work is done.

Place, time, scene: Kingston, Jamaica 1966. Lee 'Scratch' Perry was there for ska, rocksteady, reggae and dub. His technical innovations are widely-used throughout popular music, and his 'less is more' philosophy of production coupled with a desire to make direct music gave him respectability amongst punks in particular. His musical style – part dub, part everything else – has been emulated by Massive Attack, Leftfield and anyone else making darker forms of dance music.

What to buy first: *Super Ape* 1976

And then: *From The Secret Laboratory* 1990

In retrospect: *Arkology* 1997

PINK FLOYD

Thanks to the Beatles and Bob Dylan, pop music had undergone an image change between 1963 and 1965. They had taken control of their own music and were no longer perceived as performers but were beginning to be thought of as artists, and were judged as such. With evolving recording techniques and the availability of new equipment like the Vox keyboard, Farfisa synthesizer and even something dubbed the Super Beatles amplifier, new sounds were emerging too. The feedback that George Harrison gets at the beginning of 'I Feel Fine' turned on a lot more bands than the first Velvet Underground album did, and probably had a hand in the formation of Pink Floyd, a band whose early performances were mixed media extravaganzas that pegged them as experimental artists right from the start. At a time when being 'underground' meant bands could do anything they liked, Pink Floyd led a schizophrenic existence. They constructed lengthy free-form freak-outs and, courtesy of their hugely gifted lead singer and main songwriter, Syd Barrett, knocked out perfect pieces of nursery-rhyme pop on the side.

By early 1968, with Barrett gone from the band and the birth of a new industry structure where pop and rock, singles and albums, underground and chart became opposing forces, Pink Floyd 'the underground band' became Pink Floyd 'the official underground band',

and struggled to produce a fully cohesive piece of work until 1973 with the release of *Dark Side Of The Moon*, which was held together thanks to Roger Waters' themed exploration of insanity and its social causes. 'Wish You Were Here', 'Animals', 'The Wall' and 'The Final Cut' were similarly themed and constructed from often quite diverse musical ideas contributed by individual members of the band. There's no argument that the band that continued without Barrett wasn't in many ways much more experimental and simultaneously able to tap into the tastes of a very large audience once they had identified what worked, but that's not what this book is about. Pink Floyd Mk II sound great, and something must be said for Roger Waters' continued politicization of his lyrics and themes when other successful progressive-rock bands were happy to remain neutral and bland but were never alternative. As part of the London underground of the mid-late 1960s Pink Floyd were. And here's why.

In 1965, whilst a student at the Camberwell School of Art, Roger 'Syd' Barrett found himself living in a Highgate flat with his old friend from Cambridge, Roger Waters, an architecture student at Regent Street Poly, on the same course as fellow musician/architects Rick Wright and Nick Mason. Together with Bob Klose, and following some guitar lessons from his other Cambridge pal David Gilmour, Syd joined their band, the Architectural Abdabs. Within a few weeks they were called Pink Floyd, Pink after Pink Anderson and Floyd after Floyd Council, both Georgia bluesmen who had pride of place in Barrett's record collection. They played early gigs at the All-Saints Church in Notting Hill billed as 'sound and light workshops', mixed media events often incorporating jelly and from there they progressed to local entrepreneur, Joe Boyd's UFO club on Tottenham Court Road where they played alongside the likes of Soft Machine and Arthur Brown. They performed at the launch party of the underground magazine *International Times* in October 1966, an event which Paul McCartney attended dressed as an Arab sheikh, and ultimately headlined the opening night of the Roundhouse in Chalk Farm in 1967. For two years Pink Floyd were the band to see in London and word got round.

From the start the gigs were themed pieces thought out and structured in advance, with each member contributing their own often individually prepared audio/visual installations based around key themes of life and death, and the phases of the day. Barrett's lyrics provided the focus of the proceedings but the concept was imbued within the sound of Pink Floyd as a whole. The instrumental piece 'Interstellar Overdrive' was the band at their peak, drawing together structured themes with free-form playing, a template for their own music and British progressive music in general for the next decade. For their first recording session though, they were able to distil their extensive jams into a sub three-minute pop format. 'Arnold Layne' told the story of a transvestite thief set to a chugging backing track that let's go with a Rick Wright farfisa solo in the middle. 'See Emily Play' recorded a little later was the sound of the band at their most adventurous but concise. Taking five days to record, it featured feedback guitar, various swooshing noises and recurring classical piano motifs. By the time they went in to record the album *Piper at the Gates of Dawn*, recorded in 16 sessions at Abbey Road, the band were on a roll.

The album is one part space-rock jam session and two parts psychologically-disturbed nursery rhymes during which we learn that Barrett is friends with a homeless mouse called Gerald and knows a scarecrow who is 'sadder than me'. 'Astonomy Domine' kicks off the album, showcasing Barrett's innovative fractured guitar style and is driven by Mason's manic drumming and Waters' ascending/descending bass patterns. It sounded like nothing before it. The album was recorded at the same time that the Beatles were finishing off *Sgt Pepper*, so who knows what kind of cross-pollination was going on there? Picture the scene, Paul McCartney sneaking back into the studios when everyone has gone home to have a quick flick through producer Norman 'Hurricane' Smith's tape collection (that's all fantasy speculation you understand!).

Syd Barrett's mental state became cause for concern during the band's first tour of the US. He wouldn't mime on live television and began a policy of silently staring at interviewers rather than responding to their questions (but then would you have anything useful to say to Pat Boone?). Back in the UK, he often went AWOL during tours and when he actually made it onto the stage he might as well have not bothered. He detuned his guitar to the point that the strings would flap about making any sound impossible and spent more time staring blankly at the audience. Psychiatrists have suggested that this is classic psychotic behaviour brought on by the excessive use of LSD, readily available through his coterie of hip-cat friends. Maybe Syd perceived too much through those open doors, or maybe like his replacement Dave Gilmour suggested, it was something more than just a drug-induced decline. He left Pink Floyd in April 1968 after recording two more songs for the follow-up *A Saucerful Of Secrets* album wherein Pink Floyd mark two began to take shape as a specifically musical project where tracks like 'Set The Controls For The Heart Of The Sun' and 'A Saucerful Of Secrets' allowed individual members to retreat inside themselves, and self-consciously maintain an intellectual distance from their art as they played extended solos and developed themes.

The soundtrack to *More* could be passed off as the band composing to a visual brief, but there was no excuse for *Ummagumma* which consisted of several suites of music composed by each member individually. With the 17 minute group-effort 'Echoes' on the 1971 album *Meddle* they eventually found their focus and this was sharpened on the immaculate *Dark Side Of The Moon*, developed during live shows before being recorded in a relatively short period during 1973, but by then the band and their themed art and extravagant sight and sound had become the mainstream. Album artists were big money-spinners for the record companies, and the increasing distance between the bands and the people who bought their records was soon questioned by a pub-rock scene which returned the music to its basics and spoke directly, if a little ironically to its audience. *Animals, The Wall* and *The Final Cut* were all extremely political albums that were far more articulate, satirical and downright nastier than most things done in the name of punk, but ultimately took themselves too seriously musically and lyrically, to appeal to the new punk fans en masse (although it's clear that many older punks and a lot of those at the tail-end of the revolution bought the albums and listen to them now a lot more often than they stick on, let's say, Stiff little Fingers' *Inflammable Material*).

By then Syd Barrett was living in Cambridge, one report claiming 'disguised as a glow-worm'. His legend led to offers of work from both the Sex Pistols and the Damned to produce them, but when it became apparent that such a task would be beyond him, the plans were dropped. Nick Mason produced the Damned on their second album with disastrously overcooked results. Art music had not gone, it had just been redirected. Pink Floyd's early modernism had successfully deconstructed the pop music form back in 1967 without getting all po-faced about the way they did it. When a new set of rules for 'serious' pop music became obvious shortly afterwards it was only a matter of time before they got deconstructed too, especially as progressive music had focused on complexity and individual skill at the expense of 'having something to say'. Pink Floyd, like Henry Cow and perhaps even King Crimson, had something to say but the way they said it just didn't connect in the same way after 1977. Still sounds great though, especially in high-resolution stereo surround sound direct stream digital audio (through headphones).

First team: Syd Barrett (v, g), Roger Waters (v, b), Richard Wright (v, k), Nick Mason (d), David Gilmour (v, g)

Place, time, scene: London 1966. Pink Floyd pioneered the underground scene in London alongside such luminaries as Soft Machine and Tomorrow. Their experimentation was inspired by and perhaps re-inspired the beat groups who spent the late sixties making more constructed and surreal pop music. Space rockers like Hawkwind and art-rock bands like Genesis appear to have taken something from the first Barrett-led album, and progressive music in general moves forward from that point. The evolution of the album format in the UK owes a lot to Pink Floyd too.

What to buy first: *Piper At The Gates Of Dawn* 1967

And then: *A Saucerful Of Secrets* 1968, *Dark Side Of The Moon* 1973, *Animals* 1977, *The Wall* 1979

In retrospect: *Relics* 1971, *Echoes: The Best Of Pink Floyd* 2001

PIXIES

The Pixies arrived on the scene just as underground American music was crossing over into the mainstream. Several key independent bands were in the process of

The Pixies

signing major label deals, others had self-imploded and to cap it all, pop music was being re-evaluated and found, in some cases, to be less predictable and pretentious than a significant proportion of that credited to the indies. The Pixies were brash, sassy, dynamic and determinedly different. They incurred the disdain of Steve Albini because they were not sufficiently dark and heavy, but then their ironic and wilfully amateur approach to music wasn't enough to excite major labels looking for long-term albums bands either. Like their Boston neighbours, Throwing Muses, they signed to the British 4AD label, perhaps because Ivo Watts-Russell heard something that continued in the tradition of his earliest signing, Bauhaus. The Pixies had that same knack for the theatrical and gothic in their music and lyrics, and with Mrs John Murphy, aka Kim Deal, in the band there was always the possibility of the band exploring the more culturally specific issues that Throwing Muses were opening up. For two and a half albums the Pixies were on track to do exactly that, but then they got out of sync, and instead of making great albums, settled into a rut of making albums which were just very good. Still, by then they had wielded enough influence on a generation of bands interested in exploring the possibilities of slightly skewed pop. Their approach can be detected in everything that came next, from Ride, Blur and Radiohead on one side of the Atlantic to Nirvana, Kyuss and Black Rebel Motorcycle Club on the other.

It's an astounding achievement that the Pixies stayed together for six years considering the apparent desperate urge that Charles Thompson and Kim Deal had to create music on their own terms. Both were self-taught musicians driven by a powerful combination of scientific, and in Thompson's case, religious zeal. His parents had belted the bible Pentecostal style back in California, before moving east to Boston where Thompson renamed himself Black Francis and set about a course of anthropology. It was at the University of Massachusetts that he met Filipino Joey Santiago before spending six months in Puerto Rico studying Spanish, a period of cultural immersion that would significantly influence his upcoming musical project. That was sometime in the summer of '85. Kim Deal, meanwhile, was planning her wedding and was about to move from her home town of Dayton, Ohio to live as Mrs John Murphy in Boston. She had her degree in cell biology, eight years experience of playing garage folk-rock with her twin sister Kelley and in her own words knew how to 'weld her own patch cords' (that's studio-tech talk). In Boston, Deal read an advert for 'a bassist into Hüsker Dü and Peter, Paul and Mary', and by summer '86 was a member of the Pixies together with Francis, Santiago and a drummer friend of hers called David Lovering.

The Pixies supported Throwing Muses at a Boston club called the Rathakellar and were invited to record a session at Fort Apache studios by engineer, Gary Smith. The session got handed round and found its way over to Ivo Watts-Russell at 4AD Records in the UK, who immediately signed the band and released eight of the fifteen songs as a mini-album entitled *Come on Pilgrim*. The tracks are in the vein of Calvin Johnson's Beat Happening, driven by Black's acoustic guitar, enhanced by Santiago's effects and given a twee-pop finish thanks to the combination of boy/girl vocals, mainly sung but sometimes spoken across one another. There's a touch of fellow Bostonian Jonathan Richman about the songs, especially his nursery rhyme period, but the lyrics are a lot more disconcerting, 'I've got no lips, I've got no tongue, I got a broken face'.

Surfer Rosa, produced by Steve Albini, followed in 1988. It was the moment when the Pixies' heraldic synthesis of hard rock and hardcore punk, shot through with moments of surf rock and psychedelia a la the Cramps, really got explained properly for the first time. Albini has since commented that his time producing the Pixies was time wasted with college-radio wannabes, but then he's rarely had a good word to say about anyone. The fact is *Surfer Rosa* is band and producer at their zenith. Just like Martin Hannett in Manchester eight years earlier, Albini used his built environment in and around the studio to get new sounds. Lovering's drums are right up front throughout and Santiago's guitar is fierce and abrasive. As far as the songs go, Francis might be speaking personally but the attempt to get his thoughts out are intentionally hampered by his surrealist approach to lyric writing and the fact that he is often forced to shout to be heard. His vocals seem to come from behind the guitar, bass and kit so that the lyrics that might make sense are often inaudible, and the stuff you can hear about somebody's 'bone having a little machine' might as well be.

Kim Deal's song 'Gigantic' was the single and when it was released the three extra CD tracks were sung by her too. She'd have written more if it hadn't been Francis's band to start with, a fact which explains her decision to set up the Breeders in 1990 with Tanya Donnelly from Throwing Muses, Josephine Wiggs from Perfect Disaster and Britt Walford of Slint. The first album consisted mainly of Deal's songs but they are not of the same quality as her Pixies work. Having drafted in Wiggs to play bass she demonstrates that she's no slouch on the guitar though. By the Breeders' second album, *Last Splash*, and working alongside her sister Kelley, Deal finally made the album that she was always capable of, an album that pisses all over anything done in the name of Riot Grrrl. It's the one with 'Cannonball' on it, and also takes in a little country, some Beatle-esque pop and on 'Le Roi' shows what a Deal-fronted Pixies would have sounded like.

Meanwhile, back in 1989 the Pixies were busy breaking through into the 'almost-mainstream' with their album *Doolittle*. Produced by Gil Norton, the album is less raw than *Surfer Rosa* and reins in Francis's screaming and Santiago's slashing guitar to create a fuller sounding collection where the bass and drums actually make most of it danceable, an important factor in the album's success in baggy Britain where 'Here Comes Your Man' could be played at the same indie club nights as 'Made Of Stone' by the Stone Roses. The album launches with 'Debaser', a paean to the eyeball-slashing modernist cinema classic *Un Chien Andalou* by Salvador Dali and Louis Bunuel, and concludes with 'Gouge Away', a suggestion as to how that eyeball might be acquired. Somewhere in the middle there's 'Monkey Gone To Heaven', the definitive lesson in how to build and release tension where Francis starts by telling a story, restrained and spoken, and ends by screaming out numerological references to God and the devil.

There were two further albums: a heavy one, *Bossanova*, in 1990 and the surf guitar-inflected *Trompe Le Monde* a year later, then a lull before Black Francis announced the dissolution of the Pixies on Mark Radcliffe's Radio 1 radio show in 1993, explaining that 'some people can pull that off, but a lot of times people just end up boring fans, and stick around a little too

long'. So that was that. Kim Deal carried on with the Breeders and then formed the Amps, while Black Francis became Frank Black, more California than Boston, but still a mean strummer-screamer. The Pixies' brew of indie attitude, punk-rock screaming and loud guitars was apparently what Nirvana had in mind when they recorded 'Smells Like Teen Spirit', so enough legacy points there I reckon.

First team: Black Francis (v, g), Kim Deal (v, b), Joey Santiago (g), David Lovering (d)

Place, time, scene: Boston 1987. The Pixies followed Throwing Muses out of Boston onto the UK owned 4AD label. Their independent spirit encompassing the twee pop-punk of Beat Happening and the raw metal sound elicited by Steve Albini's production was simultaneously a reaction to the gradual acceptance of key underground artists into the mainstream and the declining scope of what was left.

What to buy first: *Surfer Rosa* 1988

And then: *C'mon Pilgrim* 1987, *Doolittle* 1989, *Bossanova* 1990

In retrospect: *Death To The Pixies* 1997

PJ HARVEY

This book is about alternative music, and as explained in the introduction, alternative refers to a different way of doing something, but importantly it is also about undermining the mainstream so that the next performer or writer along does not have to take up an oppositional position. Good alternative work makes it easier for similarly-minded artists to come along in the future without having the same struggle. The Riot Grrrl bands of the early nineties set themselves up in opposition to what was perceived to be a male-dominated industry and set of practices, and on occasion they made some changes. For a start, women in rock suddenly became more visible and had a platform to speak from on issues that were maybe seen as feminist, maybe not. The long-term effects are not that obvious though, unless you count Courtney Love's higher celebrity profile which may work for her, but is pretty damn tedious for the rest of us. Polly Jean Harvey on the other hand, who released her debut album, *Dry*, just after Riot Grrrl hit, has effected a change. Along with the

PJ Harvey

likes of Patti Smith, Kat Bjelland and Kristen Hersh, she wrote and recorded several albums' worth of honestly articulated and innovatively sounding female-oriented music that are still listened to today and have taken up a rightful position amongst the best work of the last decade. PJ wasn't oppositional, she was alternative. She refused to comply with the mainstream role accorded to female pop stars, but also avoided its easily stereo-typed opposite, and all of that talk of feminism just really got up her nose. She made the music she wanted to make. End of story.

Polly Jean Harvey was born in Dorset in a small village where she was the only girl around and Charlie Watts of the Rolling Stones used to drop by to play jazz gigs in the village hall, organized by her mother. Polly played saxophone with a jazz group called Boulogne and wrote and performed folk songs with a trio called the Polekats. At college she hooked up with a band called Automatic Dlamini and toured Europe with them. When she left the band to pursue a career of her own, bassist Ian Olliver and drummer Rob Ellis left with her and together they called themselves PJ Harvey.

The first single 'Dress' was released in 1991 and immediately gained notoriety as a song that had Riot Grrrl feminism stamped all over it; a simple reading of the song's message pegged it as a challenge to male hegemony through the symbolic refusal to wear tradi-tional female clothing. As Harvey saw it, there was an element of resistance within the song but it also had funny lines about how wearing a dress makes walking more difficult (something to do with heavy-loaded fruit on the top half of the body). Talking of which, she posed for a topless photo that graced the cover of the *NME* at the time of the debut album, *Dry*, in a pose that Siouxsie Sioux had done years before and which had a passing resemblance to the sorts of shots Patti Smith was most fond of. She became the agitprop fem-inist icon, or the confused novice who had undermined the cause by allowing herself to be photographed in line with the prevailing power of the male gaze, depending on the politics of the person doing the gazing. For her part, she was only really annoyed that it set her apart from the rest of the band. They were after all her fellow travellers in stripped down, raw blues-based music attempting to redefine the sound normally associated with a rock power trio. By

the time *Dry* was released Olliver had been replaced by Stephen Vaughan on fretless bass and it was clear to anyone listening properly that her words were only part of the PJ Harvey experience.

The stark sound of *Dry*, released as Nirvana fever hit the UK, made it unappealing to many, while others possibly over-analysed some of the lyrics look-ing for a consistent thread running through the songs where there probably wasn't any connection at all. 'Sheela-Na-Gig' was the album's centrepiece, a refer-ence to an ancient fertility goddess statue that appears to be laughing as she gestures towards her available vagina, which taken in tandem with the opening track 'Oh My Lover' where the narrator of the song begs to share her lover with another woman, might add up to a weak woman driven to give herself to be loved, or, as the laughing 'Sheela' represents, just a couple of smutty moments. The album has a magical and timeless quality that makes it the best folk album of the last decade.

For the follow-up the band enlisted the produc-tion skills of Mr Black himself, Steve Albini, who set up the studio in his own inimitable way and got all the screams, manic whispers, disconcerting moans, harsh guitars and animal rhythms down on tape. The rural, mystical feel of *Dry* is sacrificed for something more intense and maybe just a little bit contrived at times, but with tracks like 'Rid Of Me' and '50 Ft Queenie' it's churlish to get too critical. When the gui-tars fire up, you get a sense of what Led Zeppelin might have sounded like with an Albini production number done on them. You can almost feel the air pump-ing from the speakers as Harvey loses herself in the power of the sound, sometimes off-mic, sometimes dead on it. Her cello playing rocks too. Like *Dry* at times, Harvey's songs are occasionally ambiguous when it comes to the matter of who is doing the narrat-ing and the genders of the characters involved, a little trick borrowed from Kate Bush, who often portrayed herself as an ambiguous, possibly male character in her songs. Once again, the imagery in the language is vivid and harangues the mind for some time after lis-tening, although the killer line has to be 'you leave me dry'. Right on sister!

The third album came with a change of image for the singer. She scrubbed up, applied a bit of lippie and became a solo goth sophisticate. With guitarist John

Parrish and a pool of excellent musicians to draw from she made *To Bring You My Love* in 1995, a collection that is out and out sex and blues, given a crisp sound and a haunting atmosphere by co-producer Flood. She pleads with the father of her son to return home and tells another that she may be pregnant, reflects on her loss of sexual innocence 'down by the water', turns in a vocal performance that begs and longs for love on 'Send His Love To Me', and forsakes heaven and lies with the devil so that she may get her man. It's the sort of stuff that Robert Johnson used to write and perform, and in this setting the messages are just as stark but the spirit pours out of Harvey and her band, making it compulsive and uplifting listening.

In 1996 she recorded with Nick Cave, a kindred spirit when it came to developing tales and imagery around themes of love, desire, loss and regret. Together they recorded the murder ballad 'Henry Lee' and Cave wrote two songs for his most personal album *The Boatman's Call* in 1997, 'Black Hair' and 'West Country Girl' that point to Harvey as his artistic muse during that period. Her own career has moved up a notch commercially in recent years. There have been two more albums and a Mercury Music Award for the last one in 2001.

First team: PJ Harvey (v, g, strings), Robert Ellis (d), Steven Vaughan (b), John Parrish (g)

Place, time, scene: Yeovil, Somerset 1992. PJ Harvey made a powerful sparse folk-blues that bore no relation to the Britpop and grunge scenes of the period. Attempts were made to link her work with the Riot Grrrl scene although she and her band refuted any form of feminist agenda and preferred to let the music speak for itself.

What to buy first: *To Bring You My Love* 1995

And then: *Dry* 1992, *Rid Of Me* 1993, *Stories From The City, Stories From The Sea* 2001

POP GROUP

The Pop Group is a cheeky name for a band that steadfastly claimed to have very little time for popular music of any sort, including their own. It was the time for action, not music. Punk had highlighted social ills and many of its leading lights had made records that called for a new era of youthful revolution. When they formed their first band Mark Stewart, Gareth Sager and Bruce Smith were still at school and the punk mantra hit them squarely between the eyes. Together with Simon Underwood and John Waddington, and with very little initial musical skill between them they seized on the opportunity to get polemical. Like Crass, they opted to focus their attention on the things they stood for and that included uncompromising free-form music, the likes of which had never been heard before.

Before the Pop Group there was no Bristol scene to speak of, and leaving aside Beki Bondage and Julie Burchill's questionable contribution, not a lot of punk either. Their early gigs were at nightclubs rather than venues specifically set up to encourage any kind of scene. Yet, the Pop Group did not head for London and defiantly refused to sign a record deal for a long period of time. The proceeds of their first tour were given to Amnesty International, benefits were played in support of changes in legislation to free up civil rights, and woe-betide any music journalist who dared to ask them about . . . their music.

The reality was that, with the exception of drummer Smith and guitarist Waddington, the rest of the band taught themselves. Due to the nature of their collective record collections, jazz, funk and reggae were added to the basic rock underpinning to create totally new approaches to arrangement, and as the soloists progressed and practised, some innovative playing too.

The single 'She Is Beyond Good And Evil' is equal parts funk, dub and rock, and it sounds magnificent. The effects-laden guitar crashes in over the funk stabs, echoed drums and busy bass while Stewart puts in an intense falsetto off-key vocal performance that clearly inspired Billy Mackenzie of the Associates. The first album, *Y*, addressed issues of general exploitation and veered between the plaintively pretty and the intensely ugly in terms of the music. Mark Stewart screams throughout most of it, only calming down for the closing track. The music sometimes seems all over the place but then the album's standout track 'We Are Time' is the tightest seven minutes of punk-funk ever laid down. *How Much Longer Do We Have To Tolerate Mass Murder* was even more political but tracks like 'Feed The Hungry' and 'Rob A Bank' were now fully-fledged groovers and at the album's end there's a funked-up mess of a track which features the overlayed vocal by revolutionary proto hip-hop collective the Last Poets – just because they could. D. Boon of the Minutemen held the album in high regard, especially the direct political messages contained within the lyrics, and Nick Cave reckons they're single 'We're All Prostitutes' is the best thing they or anyone else has ever done.

When the band split in 1981, two bands, Pigbag and Rip, Rig and Panic, emerged from the fallout and Mark Stewart became a permanent fixture on the Bristol scene. He was instrumental in organizing London gigs for the Wild Bunch, the collective that begat Soul II Soul and Massive Attack. He worked with Adrian Sherwood and the band which would later become Tackhead, and his 1987 self-titled album was the first recorded use of those lazy beats that eventually got dubbed trip-hop. There'd be a few gaping holes in alternative music history if the Pop Group were left out.

First team: Mark Stewart (v), Gareth Sager (g, sx), Simon Underwood (b), John Waddington (g), Bruce Smith (d)

Place, time, scene: Bristol 1979. The Pop Group were the Bristol scene when they started. They self-consciously distanced themselves from the punk venues and played in nightclubs. Their sound incorporated black music influences, and like the Gang Of Four and PiL, they were a key influence on several American bands and the new romantic scene in the UK, although the latter tended to leave aside the Pop Group's political message.

What to buy first: *Y* 1979

And then: *How Much Longer Must We Tolerate Mass Murder* 1980

In retrospect: *We Are Time* 1981

PORTISHEAD

Portishead are important for two main reasons. Firstly, they developed an entirely new way of capturing and using instrumental sounds, and secondly, those sounds provide the backing and surrounding for a singer, the like of which, rarely turns up in popular music. Together Geoff Barrow and Beth Gibbons – the two official members of Portishead – created something that took everyone by surprise when they first heard it. They made music that you could see and feel.

In the Arnolfini Gallery in Bristol there apparently exists a videotape of a 1985 exhibition of graffiti art that included the work of Robert Del Naja, soon to be a member of trip-hop collective Massive Attack. In a bid to contextualize the graffiti and bring it to life, a DJ crew played at the Gallery and, according to Phil Johnson writing for *The Independent* in 1995, it's all there captured for posterity.

> Looking at the tape is like scanning through the quaint historical newsreel. There, gathered around the turntables, is the Wild Bunch: Miles Johnson and Nellee Hooper, cutting up tracks. Grant Marshall (Daddy G) picking out the next record as the very young Andrew Vowles (Mushroom) stands by his shoulder looking on. In the audience are the Pop Group's Mark Stewart, the producers Smith and Mighty, Tricky and, on his first trip to Bristol without his mum, the barely adolescent Geoff Barrow, late of Portishead.

I'm not sure how he knew that Geoff Barrow was on his first trip to Bristol without his mum but I'll take his word for it. The Wild Bunch certainly inspired him to make music. He joined a local band in Portishead, his home town and then moved on from drums to turntables. He got his first real job at eighteen as a tape operator at Coach House Studios and was soon being asked to lay down some demos for Neneh Cherry's *Homebrew* album. At around the same time, he remixed singles by Depeche Mode, Primal Scream, Paul Weller and Gabrielle, and when Massive Attack booked themselves in to make *Blue Lines* in 1990, Barrow was on hand to share his technical know-how – although that depends on who you ask – he may have just made the tea and sandwiches.

In 1991, to avoid having his dole stopped, he went to a business/enterprise initiative training-type event and met Beth Gibbons – a shy singer from Bath who had grown up on a farm in the middle of the Dorset countryside. She didn't fancy the idea of becoming a farmer's wife, and although she knew her way around a cow's udders and could fix tractors, it soon turned out that she had another talent. She asked Barrow to work on one of her own songs with her, 'It Could Be Sweet', and within three years they had an album, a record deal, a couple of musical accomplices and the Mercury Music Prize for best album of the year. Gibbons' compelling voice, shot through with rural blues, honest and true like a Dorset-born Billie Holiday, was matched with an equally attention-grabbing musical backdrop constructed out of full-bodied, vivid and palpable samples, perfectly positioned, edited and looped by Barrow.

The track appears on the debut Portishead album *Dummy*, and although the least complex of the tracks, is a perfect example of Barrow's art – he plays a short passage on a Rhodes keyboard and then loops it throughout the track. The only other instrumental sound is a programmed drum part, yet there's natural warmth that comes through, backing Gibbons' impassioned but controlled vocals and which belies the cold technology that has been used to create the song.

Other musicians play on the album, notably drummer Clive Deamer and guitarist/bassist Adrian Utley, acknowledged as one of the best jazz guitarists currently working in the UK. Dave McDonald is the other key player in the team, a studio engineer who works textural magic on the sounds, both sampled and live. One of his neat tricks is to dub the manipulated sounds to vinyl for Barrow to mix and scratch on his turntables. For the most part, the actual instrument playing is kept to a minimum, with short sections treated and looped, and in the case of the singles 'Sour Times' and 'Glory Box' funky film scorers, Lalo Schifrin and Isaac Hayes provide the central hooks. It's this combination of repetition, enhanced sound and texture, and iconic cinematic signifiers that make Portishead so tactile and graphic, and with Beth Gibbons' voice on top, so real too.

There have been few interviews over the years, Beth Gibbons likes to keep her lyrics to herself and Geoff Barrow isn't keen on having his picture taken. The albums have been thin on the ground too. The follow-up album was in 1997, a relatively long gap due to Barrow's and Utley's decision not to use the same technology and instrumentation as on the first album. Both had become fed up with hearing cheap parodies of their original sound used to sell what became known

as coffee-table or dinner party music, and used to soundtrack car adverts on the telly. The eponymous follow-up centred on live performance and that couldn't start until they had built a library of new samples from scratch. Strings and horns crop up this time, again sampled and manipulated, and Utley finally gets to show off his guitar playing on a couple of solos. Gibbon's voice is treated on various tracks, making it sound alien and robotic thereby reversing the usual set-up. 'Half Day Closing', which is apparently inspired by weird psychedelic band, the United States Of America, really needs to be explored further on a third album, but apart from the live tracks recorded with full orchestra at the Roseland Ballroom in New York released in 1998, which demonstrates that Portishead are not just a bunch of studio-based tricksters, it's been six years at the time of writing since anything new appeared. Let's hope it's not terminal.

First team: Geoff Barrow (k, d, t-t, prog), Beth Gibbons (v), Adrian Utley (g, b, k), Clive Deamer (d), Dave McDonald (eng)

Place, time, scene: Bristol 1992. Portishead were formed at the height of Bristol's trip-hop ascendancy and so were initially considered as part of the same scene. Barrow's background is in hip-hop but Portishead's real pioneering work was in the studio, and the combination of sound textures with Gibbons' transcendent folk/blues voice. There were many imitators, some good, some mediocre, but we await Portishead's return to take their cinematic, soulful sound forward.

What to buy first: *Dummy* 1993

And then: *Portishead* 1997, *Live At Roseland Ballroom* 1998

PRIMAL SCREAM

Primal Scream is a band of alternative music journeymen. Led by music fan Bobby Gillespie they have developed through a series of musical scenes and styles and, in spite of critics who have moaned that the band is only ever as good as its collaborators, have earned their position as a crucially important band precisely because of the way such projects have worked out. Primal Scream have always chosen the right people and have adapted their working practices to suit each project. This has never been a cynical decision though. Gillespie and the Scream have always believed in everything they have done and have enthusiastically thrown themselves into each new sound and culture they have been introduced to. Primal Scream may have begun as a fairly traditional indie guitar band at a time when indie guitar bands were drawing their last breath, but since then they have embraced acid house, discovered their American gospel and rock roots, got dubbed up and psychedelic and ultimately put it all together effortlessly on one album where each track is imbued with the internalized knowledge that comes from privileged time spent amongst a set of musical innovators and practitioners with access to experience that spans the history of popular music.

In his book charting the career of Alan McGee and Creation Records[52], David Cavanagh refers to Bobby Gillespie as Glasgow's leading scene-maker and in the early 1980s, its greatest undiscovered star. Back in 1977 as teenagers, he and McGee had been gig buddies together, and it was after seeing the Clash at the Apollo that Gillespie decided, like McGee, that he wanted to be in a punk band. He joined one called Captain Scarlet and the Mysterons and worked on his role as a rock'n'roll front man while McGee headed for London with his new band the Laughing Apple, which at that point included future Primal Scream member Andrew Innes.

As the first and second waves of punk fizzled out, Gillespie stayed on the Glasgow scene and got involved with twee indiepop band Altered Images. He was their roadie, happy to wear the anorak and everything. After that he joined post-punk goths the Wake as a bassist, but got a lot more out of his experimental work with Jim Beattie, a guitarist who sang and played guitar over pre-recorded backing tracks. The two of them spent 1983 experimenting with the possibilities of feedback, screaming and the much underexplored genre of cacophony. They called it Primal Scream. With the addition of bassist Robert Young and with Gillespie playing drums they started getting talked up by Alan McGee who put the band on at his London venue The Living Room.[53] That was 1983, but it would take another four years before a debut album came out, as Gillespie headed out on tour for two years with McGee's other great discovery,

Jesus And Mary Chain – his job spec, to hit a snare drum and wear shades.

In 1985 Gillespie, Beattie, Young and guitarist Andrew Innes reconvened and recorded a track for the *NME* compilation tape *C86* which gathered together the cream of the indie scene at that time in an attempt to inject some life into a dying music scene which was still a few months away from the hip-hop and house revolution. A few bands like REM and Hüsker Dü had signed major deals and the Smiths were right on top of their game, but other than that it was left to Prince to really get the weekend crowd excited. *C86* did not save the indie scene, it may well have killed it, but at least it gave people a taste of Primal Scream at their melodic noise best. 'Velocity Girl' was 80 seconds of abrasive guitars and buried tune. It still sounds immaculate, and mostly down to Jim Beattie's patient experimentation in the years leading up to its creation. The album, *Sonic Flower Groove*, was heavily influenced by late sixties psychedelia and Jim Beattie's 12 string guitar, and although it got pretty good press, the band themselves didn't really feel that it represented them as a band. In fact, Gillespie and Young were keener to move towards a rockier sound and when they and Innes moved to Brighton, Beattie decided it was time to leave, taking his 12 string with him.

The follow-up album was simply called *Primal Scream* and despite featuring no bass player and having little groove to speak of it became a firm favourite of Shoom club DJ Andrew Weatherall, who Gillespie had met at a Shoom summer rave in Brighton. Keen to capture the mood of the times, the band asked him if he would remix one of the tracks, 'I'm Losing More Than I'll Ever Have', and Weatherall created 'Loaded'. It was late 1989 and Madchester had just gone national with the Roses and the Mondays on the same edition of *Top Of The Pops*. Primal Scream caught the groove at just the right time. The track sounded nothing like the original – it had bass, piano and horns, Nellee Hooper break-beats, a little Peter Fonda and a few effects. It didn't have any Bobby Gillespie. *Screamadelica* followed, an album which threw together five more Weatherall productions, a symphonic dub piece by the Orb and two southern fired productions by Rolling Stones collaborator Jimmy Miller. All the songs were written by Primal Scream and they played on most of the album but in reality the album is a collective effort and a leap forward in terms of the band's potential. Rather than recording as a band, each member added their skills when they were needed, a working practice that reflected the culture of democracy, collectiveness and lack of ego associated with the acid house scene at that time.

Screamadelica went deeper than the Stone Roses or the Happy Mondays in terms of musical innovation because it actually linked rock and dance music in the songs themselves, not just in the way they were presented. 'Slip Inside This House' was originally recorded by the 13th Floor Elevators and makes the link between acid-rock and acid-house. 'I'm Coming Down' has a Beach Boys feel flowing through it and 'Movin' On Up' is straight rhythm and blues with a celebratory hands in the air message. Even tracks like 'Higher Than The Sun' and 'Don't Fight It Feel It' that had no apparent common ground with the band's previous work were played live on subsequent tours. In fact, the shift in emphasis on the next album *Give Out But Don't Give Up*, recorded in the American south with legends like Miller, Tom Dowd and George Drakoulias only really removes the acid house extremities, the strong rhythms and gospel vibe are still there. It may not be as inventive as *Screamadelica* but *Give Out But Don't Give Up* is a positive album with some fine playing and good songs.

By the time 1997's *Vanishing Point* was ready, Mani from the defunct Stone Roses had joined the band and had brought his love of dub and psychedelia with him. The band had their own studio in London and were able to persuade Jamaican dub legend Augustus Pablo, the Memphis Horns and various krautrockers to join in on some of the tracks. Brendan Lynch was the chief advisor in terms of production, although Andrew Innes who had learned so much from working with Paul Weatherall on *Screamadelica* was crucial too. 'Burning Wheel', 'Star', 'Kowalski' and 'If They Move, Kill 'Em' are four of the bands best and most definitive tracks, and each one sounds totally different due to the subtle differences between each mix of hip-hop, dub, acid house, soul and psychedelia. They are the sound of the band's entire history run together. Adrian Sherwood was contacted to oversee the accompanying *Echo Dek* dub album, which was easily the biggest-selling straight dub album of 1998.

Mind you, the Scream's best album may well be 2000's *Xtrmntr* which is easily their most terrifying sounding album, and the one which sounds best live especially with the added bonus of Kevin Shields' guitar playing. The Chemical Brothers pull out their hardest techno production for 'Swastika Eyes', Jagz Kooner of the Aloof also chips in with his trademark dirty production, and there are times when it sounds like it might just be the album that My Bloody Valentine never managed to make, an updated version of Jesus And Mary Chain's *Psychocandy*, an album which Gillespie contributed to right back at the start of his musical career. Noisy guitars and full-on beats, it's the holy grail of physical music past, present and future. With a little help from their friends, Primal Scream have nailed it.

First team: Bobby Gillespie (v), Robert Young (g), Andrew Innes (g), Martin Duffy (k), Mani (b), Paul Mulreany (d)

Place, time, scene: Glasgow 1983. Primal Scream began experimenting with experimental noise styles at roughly the same time that Jesus And Mary Chain were starting out. They were associated with the *C86* 'shambling' movement that only really existed as an exercise in media hype. Their subsequent mixture of guitar-based psychedelia and acid house was a blueprint for all rock/dance crossover music since, and they have been experimenting with the combination of styles featured on *Screamadelica* ever since, getting progressively darker and harder as the post-rave ideal of cultural democracy continues to fade away in the face of more successful corporate pigeon-holing and niche marketing.

What to buy first: *Screamadelica* 1991

And then: *Primal Scream* 1989, *Vanishing Point* 1997, *Xtrmntr* 2001

PRINCE

Picking up where Sly Stone and George Clinton had left off, Prince consciously made music that did not fit the accepted rules of mainstream black music. Just as those trail-blazing revolutionaries had refused to sing the sweet soul expected of them and had opted to make albums that showed off instrumental virtuosity normally associated with white rock bands, Prince made it his business to do the same and more. From his first album in 1978, which was heavy on cold-hearted synthesizer through to the punk funk of '1999' and the detached, sparse bass-less beats of 'When Doves Cry', he demonstrated a healthy disdain for musical or cultural rules. By the time he released *Parade* and *Sign O' the Times* in the middle of the decade, he had not only dismantled the colour bar which had been re-established at the beginning of the 1970s, but he was also making inroads into the hearts and minds of punks, goths, metallers, indie kids and art-rockers who were getting a little bored of the same old same olds that passed for dangerous, cutting-edge music, and that which was being flogged to death by a set of independent record labels that had stopped searching for anything wilfully different the minute they got their licensing deal with the 'big' boys who promised to take care of the money and the marketing (just so long as the their little friend kept coming up with the readily marketable product). Prince may have pissed a lot of people off with his precious artist act, but then a lot of people forgave him because, to be completely frank, he was saving rock'n'roll.

Prince Rogers Nelson was already a multi-instrumentalist by the age of 12. He had his own band at 14 and had created his own Minneapolis-based scene by the time he left school. All the kids knew about 'Uptown', the little guy's very own musical genre played by his band Flyte Tyme, a band which included soon to be legendary producers Jam and Lewis, vocalist Alexander O'Neal and Morris Day, later of the Time, on drums. It was only a matter of time before he got a record deal, and it was a good one too. Warner gave him a huge amount of money and access to the best studio equipment to make his debut album, and he grasped the opportunity to experiment. Prince played every instrument on *For You* and followed it up with an album each year until 1992 such was his working ethic.

The second album, *Prince*, contained the single 'I Wanna Be Your Lover' and followed an earlier release called 'Soft And Wet' setting the general theme of most of his songs, although, like Madonna, he has an ongoing fascination with religion. Not that he allows his vocals to give too much away. He may

credit singers like James Brown and Joni Mitchell as major influences, but his own style of delivery has always been purposely distant and impersonal. He is neither the heartfelt soul singer nor the self-absorbed singer-songwriter. In fact, his entire public persona gives away nothing.

The 1983 double-album *1999* was his breakthrough, mainly due to the success of the title-track single, a solid, punchy piece of funk that was as direct as any new-wave track of the period. The gist of the song is one that Johnny Rotten would have been proud of. Namely, the end of the world is nigh. Live with it. The party he sings about is just his own preference to political anarchy. On *Purple Rain* the following year, Prince left the funk out completely, on occasions settling for straightforward metal instead. The fast electric guitar introduction to 'When Doves Cry' demonstrates his first musical love, and when the song gets going it's soon apparent that there's no bass there. The off-kilter rhythm and strange harmonies just add to the bizarre sound and the whole thing is easily as groundbreaking within the traditions of rhythm and blues-based music as Sonic Youth's experimentation with texture and noise happening around the same time.

Sign O' The Times is the last great Prince album, another double set, this time inspired by the work of Miles Davis. It's a sprawling epic that jazzes around 'Play In The Sunshine' and 'I Could Never Take The Place Of Your Man', does straight up stairway to heaven old time religion on 'The Cross', gets all reverse-gender on 'If I Were Your Girlfriend' and tumbles out four minutes of free-form storytelling and non-repetitive melody for the dream-inspired 'Ballad Of Dorothy Parker'. Apparently Prince recorded that particular track on a new studio desk that was not fully installed, such was his desire to get what he had just dreamt down on tape. The Bangles and Sheena Easton both dropped by during the sessions and ended up on the album. Little Sheena, the former housewife from Scotland who used to sing songs about waving her husband off to work became a funk rocker in the company of Prince, and yes she did sing the line 'let's get to rammin!' Of course, the title track warned of the dangers of loose living, although 'the big disease with the little name' is associated with intravenous drug use and not sex in the context of 'Sign Of

The Times', but even so, the dichotomy is there for all to hear. Prince's document of contemporary life is pretty much a series of sexual encounters or sexy situations played so hot that it's difficult to take a moral stand, but then the purposely sparse title track and the funk-less 'The Cross' are there to remind you of the consequences, and how 'man ain't truly happy 'til man truly dies'. With all the irony floating around in rock-based music since punk, it took someone like Prince to bring back straight talking, be it x-rated gutter speak or pulpit-preaching. Rappers as diverse as Chuck D and Ice-T and Manchester's finest street-beat poet, Shaun Ryder, all benefited from that.

Calling *Sign O' The Times* the last great Prince album is perhaps a little unfair. *Lovesexy* and *Diamonds And Pearls* had their moments, but a lot of his adverse media has probably stemmed from his rampant egotism. Maybe all that stuff about being a slave didn't endear him to people with real problems that didn't involve working creatively on something they loved while a multinational record company paid them copious amounts of money for the privilege of doing it. There's no doubt that he has the talent and the wherewithal to make another great album, it's just a case of when.

Place, time, scene: Minneapolis 1978. Prince picked up where Sly Stone left off. As the eighties music industry once again segregated music along race lines, drawing distinctions between soul and rock, Prince was there to blow the cozy little scheme wide open. His guitar-playing, his enhanced voice and his writing style all went against established stereotypes. Not only that but he almost single-handedly kept interesting music alive in the middle of the decade. Rock, indie, goth and hip-hop fans all dug what Prince was doing.

What to buy first: *Sign Of The Times* 1987

And then: *1999* 1982, *Purple Rain* 1984, *Parade* 1986

In retrospect: *The Hits* 1993

PUBLIC ENEMY

The story of hip-hop in the US begins with the playground parties and youth club appearances by DJs like Grandmaster Flash and Kool Herc and has its initial focus on turntablism and 'the breaks'. Rap grew from that, with many crediting Herc as the first rapper because he started 'toasting' over his mixes. Others like DJ Hollywood did the same, but most of the time the raps related directly to the music and the dancefloor, the words meant nothing on their own. The first rappers credited with saying something original were Flash's MC crew the Furious Five, led by Melle Mel, Cowboy and Kid Creole (different one!), but Russell Simmons who later formed Def Jam Records with Rick Rubin reckons he saw his first solo rapper, Eddie Cheba, in 1977, and his friend Kurtis Blow had been around before that. There's also the small matter of Gil Scott-Heron's 1971 diatribe against media-induced apathy, *The Revolution Will Not Be Televised*. OK, so it's not spoken over a breakbeat backing, but it is brimming over with attitude, politics and humour, and the words are rhythmic and direct.

It took nearly a decade for Melle Mel and his cohorts to follow it up with the release of 'The Message' and 'White Lines', but it was Public Enemy who ultimately became the critical voice of hip-hop and icons of black culture during the eighties. Mainman Chuck D referred to his crew as 'the black CNN' and for three albums at least they were essential listening for anyone wanting to know, in Flavor Flav's words, what time it is. They also attacked the corporately-owned media and its skewed representations of black culture and identity. Sometimes they were direct – 'read a book' – and sometimes they did it subtly with humour as in their track 'Night Of the Living Bassheads', which parodies the generic and racist nature of mainstream horror movies. Their philosophical underpinning was part Black Panther, part Nation Of Islam. They may not have fully subscribed to Afrika Bambaataa's inclusive Zulu Nation as far as complete colour blindness was concerned, but their music was rock enough to get white kids interested too, and their oppositional yet considered stance on many issues was taken on board by many, black or not. The gangster rap that followed was quickly ingested by the corporations and pretty much destroyed the good honest work that Public Enemy had done by stereotyping black identity in line with saleable media representations. That pissed Chuck off, and he's been trying ever since to find a way of negotiating a way back.

In 1982 Rick Rubin got hold of a tape by a Long Island-based rapper going by the name of Chuckie D, a graphic design student enrolled as Carlton Ridenhour at Adelphi University. He was the house rapper on a hip-hop radio show hosted by Hank Shocklee which went out on WBAU, Adelphi's student station. Chuckie D and Shocklee were partners in a rap collective called Spectrum City which was the focal point of the hip-hop scene in Long Island, responsible for organizing many of the local jams, and encouraging up and coming DJs and MCs.

It soon became clear that it wasn't enough for Rubin to offer D a solo deal, Rubin had to expand the offer to a whole musical and socio-political collective. He at least got to choose the name, Public Enemy, a recurring phrase in Chuck D's rhymes. The first album released on Def Jam was *Yo Bum Rush The Show* which blew away the hip-hop audience with its combination of consciousness lyrics and full-on sonic assault. That came out in '87 and was followed a year later by *It Takes A Nation Of Millions To Hold Us Back* which crossed over to the mainstream rock audience thanks to the breakthrough made by the likes of Run DMC and the Beastie Boys, and of course due to the quality of the material.

Public Enemy were produced by the Bomb Squad, a crew of producers assembled by Hank Shocklee who seemed able to locate samples that nobody else could find. Once they had been processed, looped and mixed with sirens, urban wildtrack and innovative beats, the experience of consuming a Public Enemy track became more like watching a film with no pictures than just a one-dimensional exercise in storytelling. On 'Fight The Power' Chuck D narrates the urban experience with his all-powerful booming voice while short snippets of other tracks and sound effects seem to spill out onto the street as he speaks. Then on 'Rebel Without A Pause', the Bomb Squad indulge in a little audio cross-cutting: Chuck D can be pictured outside in what sounds like a howling urban nightmare while his little jester friend (and multi-instrumentalist) Flavor Flav, the light relief, responds and backs him up from a club in full swing somewhere in a different part of the city. The other two core members of Public Enemy were essential to the live aspect of the message: Terminator X the DJ and Professor Griff the choreographer, responsible for the militaris-

tic moves of the 'Security Of The First World' dancers. It was Griff, the most overtly political member of the band, a devotee of Louis Farrakhan and the Nation of Islam, who perhaps provided Chuck D with a sounding board and sparring partner for the articulation of Public Enemy's important and sometimes controversial rhetoric which was becoming difficult to ignore as rap took over.

Rolling Stone put the band on the cover of their magazine and it became clear that rock was being challenged by a new musical form that didn't rely on the traditional guitar, bass and drums set-up. To top it all there was that rhyme about Elvis Presley hijacking black music. There had to be a payback – that's how democracy functions – give a bit, if it gets out of hand snatch the power back and restore the hegemony. Professor Griff made some anti-Semitic comments in an interview and Chuck D was forced to eject him from the band.

There was also the growth of gangsta rap to contend with, which, depending on your perspective, was either corporate profiteering or an honest expression of an increasingly nihilist black identity. Let's blame the cowboy president on both counts shall we? The title of the next Public Enemy album *Fear Of A Black Planet* summed up the band's position, a straightforward statement, a headline that seemed to suggest that Public Enemy were no longer the cultural vanguard. On it, Chuck D's rhymes were objective, reporting on the culture, consciously distancing themselves from the fray. With his writing, journalism and television work, alongside sporadic releases with Public Enemy, he has continued to do the same ever since. For the moment it seems that Public Enemy have been written out of mainstream rap history, which rarely gets back beyond the coastal gangster rap wars of the mid-nineties. Public Enemy, De La Soul, Boogie Down Productions – a heritage lost?

First team: Chuck D (v), Flavor Flav (v), Professor Griff (choreography), Terminator X (t-t)

Place, time, scene: New York 1986. Public Enemy were part of the first generation of hip-hop collectives inspired by the block parties, break-dancing and graffiti art that was a major part of black cultural life in New York. Once they signed with Def Jam they shared a label with Run DMC, LL Cool J and the Beastie Boys, which helped them get noticed very quickly. Chuck D's rapping was socially aware and political unlike many of his contemporaries who quickly learned that they had a platform to work from. D's style of rhyming was an influence on the gangster rappers that followed, notably NWA, but where he wanted to change things NWA were content to leave things as they were and therein lay the problem.

What to buy first: *It Takes A Nation Of Millions To Hold Us Back* 1988

And then: *Yo Bum Rush The Show* 1987, *Fear Of A Black Planet* 1990

In retrospect: *20th Century Masters: The Best Of Public Enemy* 2001

PUBLIC IMAGE LIMITED

In his autobiography, *No Blacks, No Irish, No Dogs*[54], John Lydon is apologetic about the music the Sex Pistols played. He acknowledges that it was good listening and had a spirit that connected with its generation, but as far as he was concerned, it just wasn't interesting enough. Now Public Image Limited on the other hand, that was a different matter.

On Christmas Day 1977 Lydon had played a gig for some children at a youth centre in Huddersfield. Sid Vicious had been off his head as usual, and to shelter the kids from his foul-mouthed foulness, Lydon had played about with them with a Christmas cake. He's a nice bloke Johnny Rotten, it seems, too nice for the nastiest band on the planet, and fast becoming a one-dimensional media cliché which appalled him. Within the month he had left the band, bowing out with the line 'Ever feel you've been cheated?' at a gig in San Francisco. He headed for New York, and then at Richard Branson's behest, for Jamaica with DJ/film-maker Don Letts to check out new talent for the Virgin label. When he returned, he was rejuvenated, immediately got in touch with his old friends Keith Levene and John Wardle (Jah Wobble), and together with Canadian drummer, Jim Walker formed Public Image Ltd. They played their first show together on Christmas Day 1978.

By then the debut single, 'Public Image', was riding high in the national charts and had introduced punks

to a different sound entirely, a relentless wall-of-sound driven by dub-deep bass, upfront drums and squealing guitar splaying out all over the top. Lydon still sounded like himself, at least. The album that came along with it contained straight rock tracks and indulgent art-punk, mostly inspired by the repetitive jams of German band Can. Lydon, it seemed, was covering his tracks back to the Sex Pistols, and doing it well. With the second album, the band moved further into krautrock and dub exploration, and due to the nature of the sonics involved, chose to release the tracks on 12" singles inside a round metal tin. The album, called *Metal Box* at that stage, is now available as *Second Edition* on CD, and remains one of the deepest albums released by a rock band. Wobble's bass all but speaks on every track of the album, keeping everything earthed while Levene fires off guitar stabs and the odd jerky piano or synthesizer line. Lydon's vocals are sometimes impressionistic, sometimes more coherent, as in those sections of 'Memories' where a slow ska rhythm kicks in for him to whine and scowl over. 'Careering' features some sci-fi effects and swooshes that Lydon's other musical heroes Hawkwind would be proud of, and 'Swan Lake', released as the single 'Death Disco', is a dark dub take on one of Peter Ilyich's most popular tunes with Lydon wailing into the microphone about the death of his mother.

Wobble had had enough by the time the band went to work on *Flowers Of Romance*. He went off to drive tube trains while Lydon and Levene set about making the bass-less third PiL album that featured songs constructed around relentless drum patterns and overlayed with violently-played violins, accordions and anything else left lying around the studio. The single 'This Is Not A Love Song' was not a love song, and no amount of re-recording will ever change that.

With Levene also gone by the end of 1983, Lydon made the most of his position and for the next few albums gathered together musicians that he had always admired to back him. On *Album* from 1986 Ginger Baker plays drums on 'Rise', Steve Vai adds guitar to 'Home', Ryuichi Sakamoto provides enigmatic genius, and Bill Laswell plays bass and produces. On *Happy?* former Banshee and Magazine member John McGeoch is the new guitarist and Bruce Smith of the Pop Group plays drums, and Stephen Hague is the man brought in to produce *9*. Not quite the Pet Shop Boys but certainly not the Lydon of old either. All three albums are effectively punk accounts of the new studio fetishism that was churning out dull and lifeless albums by has-been pop stars of decades gone by. Lydon would never let that happen to him.

Working with the best musicians and producers in the business, Lydon was responsible for some of the best heavy dance-rock music of the decade. It's not surprising that Leftfield picked up on the possibilities and cast him in the role of evil MC Rotten for their groundbreaking 'Open Up' in 1993. It doesn't take a rocket scientist to get from there to 'Firestarter' now does it?

First team: John Lydon (v), Keith Levene (g, k, p), Jah Wobble (b), Richard Dudanski (d)

Place, time, scene: London 1978. With PiL, John Lydon was determined to distance himself from the straight rock of his former band and set about bringing punk attitude to the music too. Inspired by the dub and reggae scene in Jamaica and with a collection of musicians who could combine dub, rock and the progressive music of Can, he made three albums of raw experimentation around a groove, before settling into a dance-rock niche and impending inclusion on the nationally polled 'Greatest Britons' coming in at 87. Result.

What to buy first: *Metal Box* (*Second Edition*) 1979

And then: *Flowers Of Romance* 1981, *Album* 1986

In retrospect: *PiL: Greatest Hits So Far* 1990

PULP

Jarvis Cocker is a great storyteller. He knows what we want to hear about and how to tell us the best bits. He chooses his words well for maximum effect, sometimes he's sarcastic, sometimes he's poignant, and he let's us know where he stands on any issues that arise from his tales too. He has a well-developed sense of irony and knows that his core audience of fans would hate to be lied to or patronized in any way. He therefore writes about what he knows about, namely everyday British life from the perspective of a member of the mediocre classes, situated somewhere between the workers and the bosses. It took him and his band, Pulp, a good few

years to perfect their craft, to learn how the words and music should fit together, and just when they got it right, along came this thing called Britpop which revelled in songs about everyday, parochial British life. After 12 years of development Pulp were suddenly in the right place at the right time, and it was a perfect opportunity to get satirical.

Arabicus Pulp is something to do with coffee beans. Jarvis Cocker discovered that in a boring economics lesson at Sheffield City Secondary School sometime in 1978. It seemed like a good name for a band, or if not a band, then maybe a creative arts troupe. It's possible that Cocker didn't really mind as long as, one way or another, he could attract people's attention. Tell them stories about stuff.

Cocker, Mark Swift, Peter Dalton and David Lockwood began making home movies on Super 8 film and showing them in the school hall at lunchtimes charging 10p a time. They also practised as a band, and played their first proper gig at the Rotherham Arts Centre in the summer of 1980. A demo tape was despatched to John Peel and by 1982 they had completed an album. *It*, it was called, recorded at Southern Studios in London and heavy on acoustic-based material and badly deployed keyboards. It consisted of songs that owed a lot to Edwyn Collins' coy style that annoyed a lot of people who found his words too self-consciously clever, or if they missed the irony, too sentimental. It's a difficult thing to get right, a matter of balance, and it also needed to be backed up by a shit-hot sound that made any perceived arrogance, cleverness or moralizing difficult to criticize because the music was so confident and assured. Orange Juice could do that, the Smiths were good at it too a couple of years later; Pulp still needed time.

By 1984, the line-up had been through several changes and now included guitarist/violinist Russell Senior, basically a Pulp fan who had been writing about the band in his fanzine since the first few gigs, and Candida Doyle on keyboards. Doyle's heavy new-wave sound eventually became the band's trademark and when Steve Mackey joined in 1988, the classic Pulp line-up was in place and ready to take on the world, well at least get some radio play. Unfortunately, their record company was not fully committed to the band but was unwilling to let them leave, and for the next five years a state of stalemate existed during which time just one album, *Freaks*, was released and everything else that the band recorded stayed locked away. The band were experimenting with disco and sparse arrangements that enabled Cocker to elaborate on his stories and emphasize his words and phrasing, and the results were finally heard in 1992 when the *Separations* album and a five-track EP called *Intro* were released within months of each other. Island Records were impressed enough by *Intro* in particular and from that point Pulp were reborn.

His N' Hers contained three hit singles, 'Lipgloss', 'Do You Remember The First Time' and 'Babies', and was nominated for the Mercury Music Prize. The Pulp sound was now more focused, driven by keyboards and big on production, but importantly it supported a set of songs that had content as well as style. 'Babies' is typical. Cocker sets the scene, the place and time of his teenage voyeurism, taking care to name the street for added authenticity. He then proceeds to tell his friend what drove him to hide inside her sister's wardrobe to get a peep at her sister with her boyfriend, and how when he had the opportunity to sleep with the sister he only 'went with her 'cos she looked like you'. Comedy, sex and betrayal and all set on a street somewhere in Britain in the seventies.

The *Different Class* album came out a year later and it was basically more of the same, except that by then Jarvis Cocker had become a Britpop icon. Many had him down as a future film star or chat show host, and it was all down to his ability to hold a conversation and say interesting and witty things when interviewed. He was the first British pop star since Boy George to become a media personality, and just like George who famously claimed that he preferred a cup of tea to sex, Cocker held the nation enthralled with his down to earth observations about Britain in the nineties. 'Common People' remains the band's finest moment. From Cocker's sniff before he starts singing, getting into character, to the observation that the spoiled rich girl studying sculpture will never 'fail like common people', and finally the explosive finish complete with those keyboard stabs that recall the final throes of Television's epic 'Marquee Moon'. The album also featured 'Sorted For E's And Whizz' which questions the continuing relevance of the rave scene, 'Mis-shapes' which might be a celebration of the sensi-

tive indie geek and Cocker's own sense of belonging, or a callous put-down, and amidst all the cynicism, the poignant 'Disco 2000' which, like all good love stories, ends with the realization that the clock can never be turned back.

Different Class went into the charts at number one and won the Mercury Music Prize in 1995, and following a gap of three years the band returned with a darker perspective on contemporary life where optimism had been replaced by terror and fear. The title track, 'This Is Hardcore', is shot through with emptiness and despair and the prettiest song on the album, 'Help The Aged' notes that ultimately we are all 'running out of time'. It's their best album, but sold poorly relative to their previous effort, and 2001's *We Love Life*, produced by Scott Walker, fared even worse. Until then though Cocker's popularity had remained high, especially during that spat with Michael Jackson, when he mooned the moonwalker during Jackson's crucifix scene at the Brit Awards, in a characteristic attempt to undermine pompousness.

The British public and tabloids alike were fully behind him, probably because he was making a stand for everyone fed up with being sold crap. There may not be revolution in the air in the comfortably developed world anymore but that doesn't mean that everyone is happy with being patronized and lied to on a daily basis. We all watch bad telly, listen to mediocre music and read poorly researched and non-contextualized news reports. We don't believe in it, we just accept it. When it matters, people make stands against unjust wars and unfair social policies, and those smaller things that make life that little bit cheaper. On this occasion the little feller who's really not sure if he's black or white discovered that the game was up, and that he'd been rumbled. His song was alright, the pop was fine, and everybody knew he was self-obsessed, it was the fact that he thought everyone should take it seriously that pissed people off. Manufactured, branded pop has been a laughing stock ever since and a whole genre of television programmes has been developed, dedicated to destroying the myth and showing the cynicism at work in the production of cheap, pop junk. I'd like to think that Jarvis Cocker had a large part to play in that. Dressing up as Rolf Harris for a celebratory edition of *Stars In Their Eyes* was just the ironic postscript.

First team: Jarvis Cocker (v, g), Russell Senior (g, v), Candida Doyle (k), Steve Mackey (b), Mark Webber (g), Nick Banks (d)

Place, time, scene: Sheffield 1982. Pulp had a long gestation period during which time they evolved a unique sound, bringing together new wave and electronic music with Cocker's knack for storytelling. Their retro sound and parochial subject matter tied them to the Britpop scene although they have since transcended that period with a much darker set of songs that are currently gloriously out of step with either the mainstream or its alternatives.

What to buy first: *Different Class* 1995

And then: *His N' Hers* 1994, *This Is Hardcore* 1998

In retrospect: *Pulp Hits* 2002

Q

QUEENS OF THE STONE AGE

Queens Of The Stone Age are the first overground success for a dirty, bottom heavy, form of rock dubbed 'stoner rock'. Think grunge, but then take out the bleak urban atmosphere and send the music into the desert or into outer-space, basically anywhere that allows it to breathe, relax and meditate. Blue Cheer may be the godfathers of the scene in terms of sheer dirty guitar volume, but Black Sabbath are surely the spiritual guides. Some say that *Master Of Reality* was the first stoner rock album. Of course, it wasn't. Back in 1971 it was just a heavy metal album and Black Sabbath were *the* heavy metal band so there was no need for other categories. But after *Paranoid*, *Master Of Reality* was a completely different trip altogether. The album kicks off with 'Sweet Leaf' (you're thinking what I'm thinking right?) and runs through a series of tracks which are just about the heaviest rock ever got. There's a spiritual vibe running through the album too, a vibe which made sense in Birmingham at the beginning of the seventies, and re-emerged in the Californian desert 20 years later where Kyuss picked it up and took forward what the Sabs had begun all those years before.

Along with Monster Magnet, Fu Manchu and Masters Of Reality, Kyuss carved out a sound that was distinct from the grunge emanating from America's east coast. Monster Magnet were a New York band and developed a space-rock take on stoner that owed something to Hawkwind and Kyuss drew inspiration from the desert on their doorstep. The second album is their best. Produced by Chris Goss of Masters Of Reality, *Blues For A Red Sun* is all overdriven guitars fed through mighty amps, big fat-ass bass and driving drums. The music is so big that lyrics can't really compete, so they tend towards stoned immaculate phrases like 'I am drinking, I am rolling' and 'my hair is real long'. It was the last Kyuss album that bassist Nick Oliveri played on, and he didn't work with guitarist Josh Homme again until the formation of Queens Of The Stone Age in 1997.

After some initial desert sessions, the new band emerged with their debut album *Queens Of The Stone Age* in 1998. They still retain the Kyuss sound as is to be expected when all three members were once in the band, but Homme and Oliveri create more concise songs with the fat-bottomed bass and down-tuned guitar sound, and throw in a few electronic noises too. Rather than mellow jamming, the songs are more structured and cyclical, pretty similar to the way that Holger Czukay worked in Can. *Rated R* followed in 2000 and made a breakthrough into mainstream rock radio with the instantly catchy but, no matter how many times it's played, never tedious, 'Lost Art Of Keeping A Secret'. Homme's voice is coolly laid-back over the top of a hypnotic, chugging guitar and bass link-up. Oliveri sings two tracks, recalling his days in nasty hardcore band the Dwarves, and Mark Lanegan formerly of the Screaming Trees lends his whiskey-soaked voice to 'In The Fade'. The whole album is a paean to drugs, although the album's opener sets the boundaries. 'Feel Good Hit Of The Summer' lists 'Nicotine, Valium, Vicodin, marijuana, Ecstasy and alcohol, c-c-c-c-cocaine' but doesn't go any further. Rock stars have to be responsible sometimes you know.

Songs For The Deaf added Dave Grohl to the expanding supergroup line-up, and Lanegan was back for more too. He sings on the album's highlight 'Song For The Dead', which is uncharacteristically dark and heavy, and obviously so, having followed the single 'No-One Knows' featuring Homme's lethargic vocals and sprightly guitar. Grohl plays a blinder too. With the pressure of being a frontman off and that relaxed desert vibe all around, he puts in his best performance since *In Utero* on 'Songs For The Deaf', and for a while rumours abounded that he was joining on a full-time basis. He hasn't, but don't rule it out. Mary Jane can be a very persuasive mistress.

First team: Josh Homme (v, g), Nick Oliveri (b, v), Mark Lanegan (v), Dave Grohl (d)

Place, time, scene: Palm Springs, California 1997. Queens Of The Stone Age completed the project started by Kyuss nearly a decade before. Stoner rock didn't make the breakthrough like grunge, and bands like Kyuss, Monster Magnet, Fu Manchu and Masters Of Reality were sidelined as cult artists, rarely heard at all outside of the US. The emphasis on softer drugs is still there in Queens Of The Stone Age but there's a stricter code of practice that has tightened up the jamming style and focused the band so that they are poised to become a major international success. Wait and see.

What to buy first: *Rated R* 2000

And then: *Queens Of The Stone Age* 1998, *Songs For The Deaf* 2003

R

RADIO BIRDMAN

And with the formation of Radio Birdman, an alternative Australian culture was begun. Before that there was no real music scene to speak of in any of the country's major cities. Leaving aside Rolf Harris, the Easybeats, led by Harry Vanda and George Young in the late sixties were the only significant pop music success, and they were a bunch of European immigrants formed in a Sydney Migrant Hostel. Their success was never really followed up, and it took another migrant, Deniz Tek to move things on again when he arrived in Australia from Michigan in 1972. Around the same time that George Young was producing his younger brothers Malcolm and Angus in their band AC/DC, across town, Tek was turning his new friends onto the delights of the MC5 and Iggy and the Stooges, two bands which he had seen play live back home shortly before he ventured across and down a bit, to his new home in Sydney. Naming his band after an Iggy lyric, Tek became a garage-rock missionary and filled Radio Birdman's early live sets with the Detroit classics. Radio Birdman became the first Australian punks, complete with their own pseudo-Nazi imagery and must-have logo. Their performances broke down the traditional barriers between band and audience and the gigs that they played at the Oxford Funhouse in Sydney between 1974 and their fateful trip to the UK in 1978 are the stuff of legend, which together with their two legacy enhancing albums, have inspired most of the Australian bands that came after them.

Sometime in the middle of 1974, Sydney's two leading garage bands, the Rats and TV Jones, reassessed their strategies. The Rats opted to break up, while TV Jones decided that they wanted fame and money and figured they were more likely to get it if they sacked their oddball guitarist, Deniz Tek. Of course TV Jones never did get what they wanted, but it did enable Tek to get together with Rob Younger from the Rats and, together with fellow American medical student and keyboardist Pip Hoyle, drummer Ron

Keely and bassist Carl Rourke, they were able to form Radio Birdman. For gigs they stuck mainly to the Oxford Funhouse because they were effectively banned from most other venues in town. The imploding TVs, non-specific experimentalism and Hell's Angels following didn't really help their case, but there's nothing like having your own den when it comes to trying out new stuff and fixing your own rules. It also meant that the band could arrange their gigs around Tek's and Hoyle's medical studies. The scene that developed around the Funhouse was Australia's answer to CBGBs. It happened at the same time and for years afterwards the venue was the Holy Grail of the Sydney alternative scene.

The band's first recordings were made at Trafalgar Studios in Sydney, at night when they didn't have to pay as much. The band and the studio joined forces to form the Trafalgar label and printed up records to sell direct to fans at a seriously reduced price. The first single 'Burned My Eye' is classic garage rock, and features a suitably Iggy-esque vocal by Rob Younger. Tek's concise little guitar solo is just about fitted in at the end of the song, and the perfect tease for a repeat-playing. From that point on, the best comparison is with the Damned. Radio Birdman developed out of an Australian scene that was steeped in progressive rock music, and Tek and Younger were both huge fans of Blue Oyster Cult. Mix this with late sixties garage-punk and you're onto a winner. Their two-album back-catalogue is full of songs dripping with energy. The rhythm section is speedy, the vocals, theatrical and the guitar-work, surgically precise. Let's face it, the fact that Tek is now an ER surgeon having spent just under a decade flying planes for the US marines (nickname: Iceman – yes he was apparently the inspiration for Mr Kilmer's character in the propagandist mid-eighties epic!) goes some way towards confirming the link between his intellectual and dexterous skills.

Radios Appear was recorded at Trafalgar and then re-recorded for worldwide release when Seymour Stein of Sire Records signed them up, having stopped off at the Funhouse after signing the Saints. *Rolling Stone* magazine gave it a full five stars when they finally got hold of a copy, and it was followed by the single 'Aloha Steve And Danno' which pilfered the Hawaii 5-O theme music as Tek's tribute to the surf-

guitar sound. The single was a cult hit in Australia but the band never managed to capitalize on its success. They toured the UK in 1978, but with punk on the wane, it was without the financial assistance of their record company. Like the Birthday Party and the Go-Betweens a few years later, the band found themselves living on the bread-line while they paid their own way around the country and put up the money themselves to record their second album, *Living Eyes*, in Wales. The album is fiery, reflecting the mood of the increasingly frustrated and hungry band. Tracks like 'Alone In The End Zone' and 'Time To Fall' are amongst their best, with the band playing like their lives depended on the outcome. Ultimately, it was all too much and despite potential success awaiting the band on return to their native country, they split up in June 1978 after a gig at Oxford University amid much recrimination and rancour. It was 1996 before they could work together as a complete band again, but that was only for a few shows. Tek, Younger and Warwick Gilbert managed some live shows and an album with Ron Asheton of the Stooges and Dennis Thompson of the MC5 in 1981 going under the name New Race, and Younger has led his own band New Christs since 1983.

Radio Birdman, along with the Saints in Brisbane got things started in Australia by demonstrating to a new generation of Australian bands that there was another way to do things. Rock band Silverchair, whose members weren't even born when the band split up in 1978 recently acknowledged their influence by adding a Birdman track to their live set. In 1996 the reformed band played at the Big Day Out festival (Australia's very own Lollapalooza) and received universal praise from audience and reviewers alike and, outside of sport, that kind of thing doesn't happen very often in Australia.

First team: Deniz Tek (g), Rob Younger (v), Pip Hoyle (k), Chris Masuak (g), Warwick Gilbert (b), Ron Keely (d)

Place, time, scene: Sydney 1974. Radio Birdman combined the rush of garage-punk with the musicality of progressive rock and, independently of UK and US bands doing something similar at the same time, set up a musical and infrastructural template for future Australian independent music. The

Celibate Rifles are often seen as their natural heirs, although bands like the Birthday Party, the Go-Betweens, the Church and even INXS owe something to their trailblazing.

What to buy first: *Radios Appear* 1977

And then: *Living Eyes* 1978

In retrospect: *The Essential Radio Birdman (1974–1978)* 2001

RADIOHEAD

Radiohead got their license to issue music through EMI two months after the release of Nirvana's *Nevermind*. There was clearly a connection there in the band's approach to sonic dynamics and the way in which they combined with vocalist Thom Yorke's heartfelt and sensitive wordplay, but there was also a crucial difference. Nirvana stood at the end of a tradition that had gradually been feeding personal thoughts and emotions into what was effectively post-hardcore punk music. Hüsker Dü and various emo bands had helped with that. Radiohead, by contrast, had used their guitar fireworks, melody-tracing bass and upfront drums, to beef up the traditionally thin and trebly sound of British indie music. That meant the dynamics were more defined, the sound more textured and the vocals more introverted and for the most part, restrained. They were also at the end of a trajectory. One that began with Joy Division and Orange Juice, moved through Jesus And Mary Chain and the Smiths, and landed at the end of the decade with the patented Creation sound of Primal Scream, the House Of Love and that other Oxford band, Ride. Radiohead, as you'd expect, took elements of all of the above – it's what they grew up listening to. The odd thing, though, was that they were the only band around that did.

In 1993 the *C86* generation of indie bands had either disappeared, or had mutated in unexpected ways following their flirtation with the rave scene and hip-hop. New guitar bands like Suede were tracing their roots further back to the less relevant sound of seventies' glam-rock, Blur were embarking on a postmodern project that attempted to satirize contemporary British culture by using the signifiers of a swinging pop scene now long gone (for which they would later be unfairly pilloried by critics who just didn't get it – such is the problem with postmodern satire), and the Manic Street Preachers were trying to bring socialist politics to the masses by steadfastly refusing to acknowledge independent music in any form after the dissolution of the Clash. The British indie scene was effectively being taken over by what American critics disparagingly call 'haircut bands'. Radiohead, on the other hand, had something more substantial and the Americans seemed to like that more than the band's home crowd did. That substance is based on an unquestionable ability to write great pop melodies which are carefully enhanced and brought into focus by the sounds and textures that surround them. By their second album they had won over the UK audience and had set the standard for all rock music ever since. Their continued experimentation with form has led them in interesting new directions as the band attempts to keep up with Thom Yorke's ever deeper explorations inside his own head.

By the time Thom Yorke started at Abingdon School just outside Oxford, he had lived in Scotland, undergone five separate eye surgeries and taught himself to play guitar. He met bassist Colin Greenwood when he joined the school punk band TNT in his first year, and guitarist Ed O'Brien when they started their own band called On A Friday. Phil Selway played drums and Colin Greenwood's younger brother Johnny played guitar. The name referred to the band's practice night at the Clifton Hampden Village Hall. The old lady who lived next door kept the key. By 1987 though Colin, Ed and Phil had all moved away from Oxford to attend various universities around the country, leaving Thom and Johnny on their own for a year during which time Thom improved his lyric-writing skills and the two of them experimented more closely with the interaction of voice and guitar in a more focused environment. When Thom did eventually go off to university in Exeter he spent most of his time creating techno music with a friend.

1991 was the key year. With all members of On A Friday back in Oxford, they picked up more gigs and recorded several demos, one of which Colin gave to an EMI sales rep whilst working behind the counter at Our Price Music in the Oxford Westgate Centre.

Keith, the rep in question, did his bit and in November 1991, On A Friday found themselves playing to 25 different flavoured A&R people at the Jerico Tavern in Oxford. They signed to Parlophone a few days later, calling themselves Radiohead.

While *NME* were printing reviews describing the band as 'a pitiful, lily-livered excuse for a rock and roll group', EMI were working on the American market, and sure enough the debut album *Pablo Honey* was selling well due to the success of the single 'Creep', which had been picked up by San Francisco's Live 105 radio station, got high MTV exposure and was a particular favourite of Beavis and Butthead. The album sold two million copies. The band that had hardly played outside of Oxford a year before were suddenly weighed down with a potentially crippling sense of expectation for their second album. Working with John Leckie who had worked with the Beatles, and Pink Floyd and produced the Stone Roses' debut album, they were initially unable to get

down to work, lacking a sense of focus brought about by a perceived need to cater for what was a vague American market (*Pablo Honey* had really sold on the strength of the unrepresentative 'Creep') and a grudging British one. There was also the problem of the studio, which Yorke later told *Mojo* magazine was never 'an extension of what we were doing, more an obstacle to get round'. John Leckie showed them how to use the studio as 'an instrument' and they haven't looked back since.

The Bends is a masterpiece of textured rock music. The sounds are crisp and expertly positioned in the mix for maximum aural impact, and perfectly complement Thom Yorke's voice which is usually dropped in the gaps between the electric lash of the guitars. On 'Fake Plastic Trees', his voice is stripped naked towards the end of the song for the delivery of the line 'if I could be who you wanted all the time'. The intensity of the moment and the vulnerability with which Yorke sings is light years away from anything

Radiohead

that appears on the first album, and is surely a real personal reflection on the elevated social and moral role he had recently been thrust into. The title of the album confirms the band's accelerated elevation sickness, and the rest of the songs suggest that Yorke, at least, is not having the time of his life. Everywhere he looks things are broken or falling apart – relationships, bodies, society and dear old mother nature.

For *OK Computer* Yorke was still disgusted at the tragedy of it all, but his way of expressing it had become more manic, in keeping with the theme of madness that runs through the album. The fractured phrases and sentences and adoption of different vocal styles, especially on 'Paranoid Android' indicate that we are dealing with somebody who should be kept away from the scissors at all costs, but they also fit more easily around the sectionalized songs which change mood, tempo, volume and density at the drop of a hat. There are of course less dynamic songs like 'No Surprises' and 'Karma Police', which progress linearly and relentlessly to their end, a fact emphasized in the videos that accompanied the tracks as singles. On 'No Surprises' Yorke's head is gradually immersed in a jar of water, and for 'Karma Police' a frightened man is chased methodically along a dark road by a car. You can see where Coldplay may have got their ideas from now can't you?

The songs on *Kid A* continue where 'Karma Police' left off. The wailing guitar and Yorke's choking voice are calmed down, and poor old Phil Selway's drums are all but completely removed. The new medium for their intensity and shattered worldview was electronic and organized by computer. This time the musical undercarriage is opaque and unrelenting. The pulsing electric piano on 'Everything In Its Right Place', the thick bass of 'The National Anthem', and the church organ and operatics on 'Motion Picture Soundtrack' are all up close to Yorke's voice where previously he would have been given room in-between the heavier sounds. Most of the time his voice is just another instrument and it's treated with the same effects as other instruments, dehumanized completely on the title track. Where the band's angular dynamics once reigned, there is now a series of blocks of sound which looked at as waveforms on a computer would make very dull viewing. But dynamics or not, the whole album is orchestrated perfectly, it just requires a closer, more critical listen. Everything is there and in its right place. Dissonance and structure rub shoulders on every track, so the sublime quiet and circular motion of 'How To Disappear Completely' is interrupted by an off-key high note, and the solid groove of 'The National Anthem' gives way to mad brass squall. On its release, reviewers struggled to assess the album using the usual criteria: meaningful lyrics, musicianship, context, authenticity? The album was considered so alien when it was received that it was difficult to even use Radiohead's previous work as a benchmark. In fact, it seemed that new Radiohead had ruthlessly killed old Radiohead in order that they might start again.

Amnesiac was drawn from the same sessions as *Kid A* and was issued very soon after the parent album. In fact, there were plans for a double album in the first instance. The tracks are more song oriented and the electronica is in a supporting role this time. 'Pyramid Song' is a return to the Thom Yorke vocal style of old albeit with a woozy piano melody, and 'Knives Out' and 'I Might Be Wrong' are near as damn it, classic Radiohead, although place them next to anything on *The Bends* and *OK Computer* and you'll quickly realize that what you thought was 'normal' Radiohead is in fact a state of mind. A couple of guitar solos might act as signifiers of glories past, but as should by now be apparent, the sound of Radiohead is a much bigger construct.

The 2003 album *Hail To The Thief* proves the point, the sound of Radiohead returning to pop world and demonstrating that they have such a sophisticated understanding of the textural possibilities of music that quite bizarre sounds and techniques can be twisted, shaped and combined to constitute songs that, if you're not paying proper attention, seem almost normal. On first glance it seems that Radiohead are following in the footsteps of other bands who have taken an excursion into the experimental and having adopted a position of artistic independence within the music industry, simultaneously leaving some of their original guitar-fetishising fans behind, have returned to something more real. Certainly Yorke's lyrics on *Hail To The Thief* bring the band back to their old society-weary ways, and the singer has described the album as *OK Computer 2* in interviews, but listen carefully and he's not fooling anyone. For Radiohead it's gone way beyond mixing genres, revisiting styles and experimenting with the textural fabric of the music. This is a band not just driven by a desire to continue offering an alternative to, or remain independent from, contemporary music. They're leading from the front, taking music into the unknown, and, if we're prepared to go, taking us with them too. The pied pipers of Oxford are here to show the way. What was the word I used at the beginning? That was it, substantial.

First team: Thom Yorke (v, g, k), Johnny Greenwood (g, k), Ed O'Brien (g), Colin Greenwood (b), Phil Selway (d)

Place, time, scene: Oxford 1992. Radiohead were virtually alone amongst British bands drawing on the indie guitar tradition in the early nineties. The close geographic proximity to Ride clearly encouraged a deeper understanding of the sonic possibilities of guitars, and Joy Divison's intensity was also an influence. Their muscular sound and noteworthy first single got them rolling in the US before they broke through in the UK, although that situation was rectified with the next two albums which confirmed the band as an album band par excellence, and allowed them to release the groundbreaking *Kid A* without any accompanying singles. The band's mastery of electronic technology and software has set new standards for hitherto unmoving and sterile electronic music and unadventurous sampler and sequencer based rock bands alike.

What to buy first: *The Bends* 1994

And then: *Pablo Honey* 1993, *OK Computer* 1997, *Kid A* 2000, *Amnesiac* 2001, *Hail To The Thief* 2003

RAGE AGAINST THE MACHINE

Like British punk band Crass, Rage Against The Machine were a political band that happened to use popular music as their medium. Or so they claim. The fact is that the relentless rebellion and lessons in social and political historical injustice are actually matched and given power because of a combination of skilled musicianship and carefully considered structural arrangement. Tom Morello's funk-rock background combined with the hardcore punk history of

the other members is crucial to the band's sound, which gives vocalist Zack de la Rocha room to spit out his uncompromising, rabble-rousing lyrics. Both de la Rocha and Morello come from revolutionary stock. Morello's mother is a noted activist who set-up the anti-censorial Parents For Rock And Rap organization and his father fought with the Mau-Mau guerrillas in Kenya, while de la Rocha's father is an artist who led the Chicano mural movement in Los Angeles, designed to promote positive cultural identity. Their lives have been political since the start, and in order to fully appreciate Rage Against The Machine's three album back-catalogue, it's also important to understand the need for continued questioning of the concept and reality of American cultural assimilation policies, and the problems of carrying out such policies and maintaining democracy in a fundamentally capitalist society. There are those who refuse to contextualize something as transient and unsophisticated as pop music in this way, and end up accusing bands like Rage Against The Machine of peddling white racism and encouraging violence. In vain, various critics and representatives have called the band communists hoping that American youth will think twice before attending a gig or buying an album. Right on – music that caused trouble again.

The band formed when guitarist Tom Morello left Illinois-based Lock-Up, a band signed to Geffen with one album under their belt, and joined with Zack de la Rocha and Tim Commerford late of popular local hardcore band Inside-Out. With drummer Brad Wilk on board they recorded a 12 track demo before they had even played live. They sold the tape at their shows, shifting around 5000 in a few months. Friend and fan Perry Farrell booked them to play his new invention, Lollapalooza and by the time they had finished their set on the second stage, they had a deal with Epic Records. An odd move for a steadfastly independent band, but as de la Rocha tells it, Epic were the only label prepared to leave them alone and who didn't accuse them of being a gimmick political band. Besides 'when you live in a capitalistic society, the currency of the dissemination of information goes through capitalistic channels' – and getting the information out there is what Rage Against The Machine were all about.

The debut album, released in 1992, took the basic template provided by Faith No More in the late eighties of funk and rock licks combined, but did something useful with it instead. The result was a collection of tension-release songs built around hard guitar, funky bass and hardcore energy that appealed directly to the new dancefloor rockers, recently introduced to the heads down, eyes-closed, arms loose delights of Nirvana, Tool and the Smashing Pumpkins. Of course, Rage were offering something more directly political with their songs but it's difficult to know whether or not a lot of their listeners got past the more individualistic statements of resistance, notably the 'Fuck you, I won't do what you tell me' cry in 'Killing In The Name'. Maybe if they bought the album they would get a clearer idea.

The band did their bit while they had a platform to shout from. They played gigs in support of the Anti-Nazi League and Rock For Choice and took on the Parent's Music Resource Centre, responsible for censoring democratic musical activity, by stripping naked on stage with the letters PMRC taped to their mouths. The audience got an eyeful for about 15 minutes. In 1996 they had a number one album entitled *Evil Empire*, a none-too-subtle reference to the mother country, and when *The Battle Of Los Angeles* set was released they caused all sorts of corporate ructions when they performed 'Guerilla Radio' on TV shows that had links to the institutions being criticized in the song. The final album was a covers project called *Renegades* which paid tribute to various revolutionary artists and bands who had inspired the band.

Morello, Cummerford and Wilk recently teamed up with Chris Cornell, late of Soundgarden, on a project which they called Audioslave and, according to his website Zack de la Rocha is working out some solo material and is 'working on his Judy Garland angle, he's experimenting with his Judy side that wasn't always immediately apparent in Rage Against The Machine'. Sarcasm, I think.

First team: Zack de la Rocha (v), Tom Morello (g), Tim Commerford (b), Brad Wilk (d)

Place, time, scene: Los Angeles 1991. Rage Against The Machine melded hardcore punk with the funk-rock played by Faith No More and Red Hot Chili Peppers and immediately made it sound vital and con-temporary alongside the breaking grunge scene. Their music was infused with politics and anger, and they managed to upset some key people during their nine-year existence. Their directness and sense of purpose is already missed.

What to buy first: *Rage Against The Machine* 1992

And then: *Evil Empire* 1996, *Battle of Los Angeles* 1999

RAMONES

When the Ramones were formed in 1974 there was very little straightforward rock'n'roll music around. The MC5 and Iggy and the Stooges had folded, and the New York Dolls had just released a turkey called *Too Much Too Soon* produced by legendary pop producer Shadow Morton, which had robbed the band of their own raw power and substituted it for smooth gloss. In New York, even Richard Hell and Tom Verlaine were making their move away from early songs like 'Love Comes In Spurts' and towards something more complex with their band Television. Way before the punk disease hit in the UK, the American strain seemed to have mutated into something more considered and artistic, and by the time punk was ready to leave New York and spread the word around the union and across the ocean, it was the Ramones that were left holding the torch. Their high energy and simple riffing was inspirational and their ironic attitude, learned from comic books and B-movies, became a central tenet of UK punk and hardcore bands like the Dead Kennedys. They also had a strong connection with their audience. When they played, the audience went wild. It was probably at a Ramones gig that the first mosh-pit originated, and the audience often turned up with placards baring slogans such as 'Gabba Gabba Hey!', which had become the band's rallying call. The Ramones have often been referred to as a cartoon band, the implication being that they were not directly relevant to the real world. As far as alternative music is concerned nothing could be more wrong.

John Cummings was a big fan of the Rolling Stones. It stood to reason therefore that when he got dragged along to see the Beatles at Shea Stadium on their last US tour, he took a bag of rocks with him (for the throwing thereof). Of course, anyone who has seen the pictures of the Beatles playing at Shea will know that even launching from the front row, a fairly sophisticated catapault would have been required. Maybe that was what bothered Johnny, the lack of real contact between band and audience, the breakdown in communication which would only get worse as musicians retired to the studio for the next ten years. He obviously didn't hold it against the Beatles for too long, the name of his next band the Ramones was a reference to Paul McCartney's early career alter-ego Paul Ramon.

The Ramones were a high school band. Johnny played guitar, Douglas Colvin played bass and sang, and Jeffrey Hyman played drums. To give them their proper punk epiphets: Johnny, Dee Dee and Joey Ramone. By 1974 they were good enough to play in New York, which they did, at CBGB's and Max's Kansas City on many occasions. The band had made a crucial change. Tommy Erdelyi had taken over on drums to let Joey Ramone concentrate on the vocals. A big fan of the Who, when Joey spoke to his generation he didn't overstress his concerns like a chest-beating Roger Daltrey. His voice simply reported that Judy was a punk and Suzie a headbanger, or made blank statements such as 'I want to be sedated', or 'now I'm gonna sniff some glue'. He may have been speaking the truth, but let's hope not. The song '53rd and 3rd' is the story of a male prostitute who waits for business on a street corner but waits so long that when a punter does eventually show, he murders him in cold blood. Don't worry though, it's just cartoon violence. 'Beat on the brat with a baseball bat' is just a set of words that sound good when sung over the top of a suitably no-brainer riff. Joey's 'whatever' vocals confirm that. Americans, immune to irony. As far as punk goes, The Ramones bloody well invented it.

The band put out four albums in two years. The first one was recorded in three days and is a fairly straight recording of the band playing live in the studio. And what's clear is that the Ramones could play after all. Throughout, the band is tight as, it's just the attitude which is loose. For the next three albums, it was a case of keeping the energy levels high, and providing anthems for a generation. 'Gimme Gimme Shock Treatment', 'Carbona Not Glue' and 'Teenage Lobotomy' are all, in their way, constructive solutions for the blank generation. 'Rockaway Beach' is just an out and out paean to beach culture as American utopia. The Ramones made people feel good.

By the end of the decade their iconic status led to an appearance in *Rock And Roll High School* playing themselves, and in 1980 there was an album with legendary reclusive producer, Phil Spector. To some it was the end of the Ramones, to others it was an intriguing experiment. The Ramones' rough-and-ready approach to music-making and Spector's mind-boggling quest for perfection seemed contradictory, but Spector had perhaps heard something in Joey's voice and Johnny's guitar-playing that he could elaborate upon.

It apparently took ten hours to get the first chord of 'Rock And Roll High School' just the way Mr Spector wanted it, but as Joey later reflected, it *is* a great sounding chord. Spector of course applied his 'wall-of-sound' techniques, notably on the track 'Danny Says' which features an unfeasibly fat acoustic guitar strum. Maybe it was an attempt to take the dynamic punch of the band and turn it into a full-on body check. The resulting album *End Of The Century* was however, disappointing. The Ramones were always best when they didn't try – just operated on instinct – and, like the New York Dolls before them, they had discovered that more always meant less in the end. Still, the single 'Baby I Love You', basically Joey with strings, got them on *Top Of The Pops* in the UK and network television coast-to-coast, and got a whole new set of people talking about the hairy, skinny blokes in leather jackets and shades who did an old sixties song but seemed so bored all the way through it. A whole new approach to performance was created, and a brand was born that ensured the Ramones a lengthy career as postmodern rock'n'roll icons. There was a new album every two years on average and hundreds of shows, but in 1996 the band which had already lost Tommy and Dee Dee decided to call it a day. Joey succumbed to cancer in 1998 and Dee Dee died in 2002. The Ramones. R.I.P.

First team: Johnny Ramone (g), Joey Ramone (v), Dee Dee Ramone (b), Tommy Ramone (d)

Place, time, scene: New York 1974. The Ramones played gigs at CBGB's alongside other more artistically motivated bands, but really got down to work when they toured, inspiring most of the first generation UK punk bands and the hardcore scenes in New York, Los Angeles and San Francisco.

What to buy first: *Rocket To Russia* 1977

And then: *The Ramones* 1976, *Leave Home* 1977

In retrospect: *Loud, Fast Ramones: Their Toughest Hits* 2002

RANCID

Rancid are so 1979. Over the course of five albums since 1992 they have concocted a mind-blowing mix of the Clash's *London Calling* album, The Ruts' *The Crack* and the debut one from the Specials. Musically it's all punk, ska and rockabilly, and lyrically they piss all over their So-Cal punk colleagues. Tim Armstrong and Fredericksen's songs are always about something other than boredom, getting wasted and self-loathing. They are unswervingly positive about working shit out. Sorry about all the gutter-speak but it's what happens when you enter Rancid world. They swear so well. Every time vocalist Tim Armstrong uses the fuck word he emphasises it with passion and vigour. Since rappers started dropping mutha-fuckers like they were handing out sweets, it's difficult to get shocked anymore. Armstrong, who can do a perfect Joe Strummer vocal impersonation, uses the received English pronunciation too. Excellent. In terms of American chronology, they are indebted to Bad Religion, who signed them to their Epitaph label and have demonstrated in their own lengthy career that enervating and uplifting melodic punk music can get serious too.

Blue-collar town residents Armstrong and Matt Freeman attended pre-school together at the age of five. They're still best mates a quarter of a century later. Their first band was created in their friend Dave Mello's garage in 1987 and was called Operation Ivy. Together with Mello and vocalist Jesse Michaels, they began playing gigs around their home town of Berkeley in California, notably the Gilman Street club where Green Day would soon make their name. Ska-punk, a jollier form of hardcore, was a big hit locally and internationally. Operation Ivy's album, *Energy*, released on the Lookout label in 1989 got rave reviews in the UK and sold well back at home. Unfortunately the band could not stay together, mainly due to vocalist Michaels' personal decision to become a Buddhist monk. Armstrong and Freeman spent the next

two years trying to get various other ska bands off the ground before trying out drummer Brett Reed who had been sharing a room with Matt Freeman, and Rancid was born.

The first album picked up where Operation Ivy had left off with a set of songs about survival in a messed-up world. The variety of styles and Armstrong's need to be freed-up to play his guitar more insistently almost meant Billie Joe Armstrong of Green Day joining, but in the end they opted for Lars Fredericksen who immediately contributed to the songwriting and on-stage dual vocals. *Let's Go* contained the single 'Salvation' which got high MTV rotation and led to a deal being offered by Madonna herself who sent a nude photo along to help sweeten the deal. They turned her, and Sony, down, preferring to stay with Epitaph. In any case Brett Gurewitz's label was fast becoming the most successful independent label in the country thanks to the breakthrough of the Offspring in 1994. Both the Offspring and Green Day signed major label deals that year and went on to mainstream sales success.

By the time *And Out Come The Wolves* was released, the band were being dismissed as sell-outs by other US punks who hadn't been paying attention at all. Their gigs may have become huge events attended by teenage punks, skaters, zoots and metalheads, but the music and the message was more focused and fiercely working-class than ever – 'get organized and get somewhere, oh and while you're at it fuck "the man"'. 'Roots Radicals' is an unofficial Rancid theme tune, 'Time Bomb' got the radio play and 'Ruby Soho' was a ballad! The next album enlisted help from some former Specials and dancehall bad boy Buju Banton and was followed by a straight punk album called *Rancid 2000* that shot through 22 songs in under 40 minutes. *Indestructible* in 2003, produced by Brett Gurewitz and a joint release through Epitaph and the band's own Hellcat label, may be their best. The title track is a heartfelt and passionate tribute to recently-deceased punk legends Joe Strummer and Joey and Dee Dee Ramone, and the rest of the album deals with issues of homelessness, unemployment, rampant consumerism, urban surveillance and the political situation in the Ivory Coast. The London gigs were awesome. Rancid. Proper punk, and don't let anyone else tell you otherwise.

First team: Tim Armstrong (v, g), Matt Freeman (b, v), Lars Frederiksen (g, v), Brett Reed (d)

Place, time, scene: San Francisco 1992. Formed out of the ashes of Operation Ivy, Rancid continued with the ska-punk hybrid that Ivy had pioneered, essentially a Clash sound with the reggae replaced by ska, and became part of the third generation of So-Cal punk bands. They tend to be thought of as contemporaries of Green Day and the Offspring although they are closer in style to Less Than Jake, No Doubt and the Mighty Mighty Bosstones. The thing that sets Rancid apart (and gets them in this book) is their independent attitude and refusal to compromise anything in their live performance.

What to buy first: *And Out Come The Wolves* 1995

And then: *Indestructible* 2003

RED KRAYOLA

'We were not hippies, we weren't involved in the worldview which informed the counterculture. We wanted to be the dissidents of the people to whom we should most propitiously belong.'[56]

When Mayo Thompson formed the Red Krayola in 1966 it was not to emulate the 'British Invasion' bands. With a few notable exceptions that was what American garage bands did. And some of them were very good. The 13th Floor Elevators and the Electric Prunes deserve all the credit they get for their psychedelic experimentation, but it was still built from a rhythm and blues base. Zappa was R&B too, even if he did combine elements of jazz, doowop and blues, and by the time the Captain had finished his first album, well the Red Krayola were already on their second full-length experiment with musical form. The Red Krayola were the first non-classical, non-jazz band to approach their music as an artform. As the quote above confirms, Red Krayola ignored musical and cultural fashion and did it their way. Thompson himself has continued to operate at the cutting edge of alternative music ever since.

The band got their break when Kenny Rogers' older brother Lelan spotted them playing in a shopping mall. He claims that they were so 'out there', particularly the fact that they seemed unable to actually play their instruments, that the mere fact that people were stopping to watch them meant there had to be a market in what they were doing. *Parable Of Arable Land* was released in 1967 on Lelan Rogers' International Artists label, the same label which had recently put out the first 13th Floor Elevators album. It consisted of songs interspersed with free-form freak-outs, a highly experimental concept whereby a group of their Texan friends dropped by the studio and made as much free-form noise as possible and used whatever happened to be lying around. The band played over the top of the cacophony and eventually songs emerged. Thompson's guitar-work on the album turned out to be a forerunner of the less rhythmic, more textural style later adopted by many of the post-punk bands, notably the likes of Andy Gill of the Gang Of Four.

The second album, *God Bless The Red Krayola And All Who Sail With Her* is completely different. The psychedelia is pushed aside in favour of short, fragmented musical sketches played simply with guitar, bass and drums, which become so damned catchy after a couple of listens, you'll wonder why other bands bother with all that arrangement and production stuff. On it, only Mayo Thompson remains from the early line-up, but it's to his own credit that the record still feels like a group effort, such is the nature of improvisation.

The next official Red Krayola album did not come out until 1979, although that one featured playing from most of Pere Ubu and there had been a couple of albums before it which had Thompson playing with Art and Language. In fact, Thompson's musical career is made up of a series of collaborations. He joined Pere Ubu for a couple of albums and was producer and mentor at Rough Trade Records in the late seventies, offering musical and artistic advice, as well as tips on inspirational political texts. His direct and indirect influence can be heard on music made by Scritti Politti, Stiff Little Fingers and the Monochrome Set in that period. He has explained how he was able to discuss a specific musical passage within a Monochrome Set song that he considered to be a retreat into style, and therefore untruthful. The tendency for musicians to fall back on accepted styles and generic techniques, even their own, has always been his biggest bugbear and it has informed his own work since the beginning.

'Soldier-Talk' and 'Kangaroo' by the Red Krayola deal respectively with military issues and the history of Soviet communism, demonstrating perhaps that Thompson had ultimately opted to use his music to raise specific issues in the full knowledge that musical experimentation had moved beyond organic sound and was becoming the preserve of those who were more technologically motivated. Of late however, he has teamed up with the new American avant-garde who have spent the nineties making music which has at last managed to catch up with technological advancement, post-rockers like Jim O'Rourke, David G. Stubbs, David Pajo and John McEntire who can provide a contemporary setting for Thompson's musical imagination. There's plenty of collecting to be done, so I'd start asap if I were you.

First team: Mayo Thompson (v, g), Steve Cunningham (b), Frederick Barthelme (d)

Place, time, scene: Texas 1966. The Red Krayola are at the beginning of the great tradition of slightly warped Texan bands that also includes the 13th Floor Elevators and the Butthole Surfers. They moved from psychedelia to a sparse experimentalism on their second album, which in attitude and aesthetic, had a significant influence on several post-punk bands. Mayo Thompson's later career as an alternative music journeyman helped focus the British indie scene through his involvement with Rough Trade, and he also revitalized Pere Ubu in the later part of the seventies.

What to buy first: *God Bless The Red Krayola And All Who Sail With Her* 1968

And Then: *Parable Of Arable Land* 1967

REM

REM were one of the first American bands to de-punk their initial sound and return the music to its roots. Using songs as their medium of expression and unencumbered by the stylistic restrictions that hardcore punk set for itself, they have used a more traditional approach that has allowed songwriter and vocalist Michael Stipe the opportunity to structure his stories and choose his words to convey a range of ideas. He can do politics, history, philosophy and odd little events or situations, all served with lashings of symbolism and surrealism. Blame Patti Smith and her fantasy stories about horses and such like.

From their first recording sessions with Mitch Easter, right up to the present day, they have had the songs – subject, melody and chorus – and have managed to record them in a way which makes them sound timeless, using little more than the basic band set-up that they started with back in 1978. The committed hardcore fans may have found REM's fragile folk-punk a little too comfortable for their tastes, but with the mainstream becoming more and more obsessed with image, and fantasy, multi-dimensional sound production, for other music fans, REM's real and direct musical approach was a refreshing alternative. It wasn't long before hardcore bands like Hüsker Dü and the Meat Puppets followed REM's lead and adapted their approach to remove themselves from the increasingly clichéd punk scene. REM's success went hand-in-hand with the sudden emergence of college radio in the US, itself an alternative to the stagnant sounding corporate stations driven more than ever by the perceived need to maximise audience figures. This meant taking no chances, because as radio industry logic dictated, it only took a second for the listener to switch channels. It had to be safe, conventional and familiar. As a result, that part of the audience that had aligned their music taste with the punk and new-wave movement were not catered for and within a few years, thanks to bands like REM, college radio had become a crucial platform for new music. Maybe the bands that took independent music into the mainstream were not listening to REM, but the wider public were, for most of the eighties, and that made it easier for all those who came after them.

By most accounts, REM began as a fairly ropey covers band playing old Troggs and Them tunes. Peter Buck was, by his own admission, a novice guitarist who relied on big chords and Mike Mills' driving bass patterns to disguise his inadequacies. And according to biographer Marcus Gray[55], Michael Stipe the accomplished, innovative and idiosyncratic lyricist was at this point barely recognizable judging by the ill-considered and sometimes misogynist rants that he came up with to fill time in the middle section of 'Gloria' or

'Louie Louie'. Stipe had grown up listening to classical and country music and only really got into the good stuff when punk hit in 1976. He became obsessed by Patti Smith's album *Horses* and before long was fronting a punk band called Bad Habits. When he met Peter Buck who worked behind the counter at Wuxtry Records, he took advice on filling the gaps in his music knowledge, and crammed for the day that he would be a rock'n'roll star. Buck's musical career up to that point had centred on collecting obscure garage psychedelia and punk records, and then thrashing away to them with his guitar. Between them they had the spirit of REM sorted. Mike Mills and Bill Berry, veterans of the same school orchestra and various semi-professional bands, brought the expertise.

REM got the practice they needed through constant gigging all over the American south. Playing two or three shows a day on some occasions, they developed their own unique sound. A Peter Buck guitar-smashing incident, designed to impress a female audience member, forced him to resort to acoustic guitar for several shows, which instantly changed the group dynamic and enabled Stipe to calm his vocals and use the space in the songs to expand his stories and develop a more colourful and symbolic form of prose. It's easier to tell the history of British pirate radio or an allegorical tale about a bloke who gardens at night when you haven't got a guitarist going at it full-tilt in your right ear. An early session with producer Mitch Easter provided the final touch to the REM sound. He encouraged the band to add organic audio or 'found sounds' to enrich the texture of their songs, and Stipe's vocal.

Chronic Town (1982) was followed by a session with pop producer Stephen Hague who attempted to bolster the band's thin sound with synthesizers, but the band were having none of it and to this day have not used a single electronic keyboard note on one of their records. REM realized early on that their sound grew organically, often from Stipe's narrative lead, and synthesizers just undermined this. There's a depth to their songs that comes from the real interaction of acoustic instrumentation in the studio. Rather than separate the sounds, they let the instruments blend together, and the perfectly named album *Murmur* has a live, outdoors feel where sounds appear muffled by ambient noise and atmospherics, the very opposite of where new technologies were leading mainstream pop and rock. The album demonstrated where independent American music should go next, out of the metropolis and into the small towns, the punk philosophy filtered through the great traditions of country, folk and blues music. Punk could be done more quietly, it could be murmured.

On *Fables Of The Reconstruction* Stipe began to write songs that looked back to the history and traditions of the American south, specifically drawing on characters associated with their own hometown of Athens in Georgia. It's a social history album and there aren't that many of those around. Joe Boyd, who produced Nick Drake and the first Pink Floyd sessions, got it all down on tape in a studio in wintry London. 'Wendell Gee' is folk-rock complete with banjo, 'Driver 8' has a country twang, and 'Feeling Gravity's Pull' is the band's brief nod to technology – it has feedback guitar. It coincided with the new folk of the Pogues and Billy Bragg in the UK and the expanding demand for traditional, less obviously produced music, inspired by Peter Gabriel's Real World label and WOMAD festivals. *Fables* brought REM to the attention of a British audience, but with the rockier *Document* in 1985 they made the transition from music critics' favourite to cult indie band.

With the mainstream music industry at its nadir as the major record labels focused their efforts on marketing a few major international artists and creaming off the immense profits to be made on compact disc back-catalogue sales, REM suddenly found themselves on a sharp upward turn. Each of their next four albums outsold the one before it, and by the release of *Automatic For The People* their fan base was fully inclusive and fully international. *Document* and *Green* were packed with hook-laden, uncluttered and thought-provoking songs with the best sounding guitars this side of Salford. Stipe's vocals were more prominent too, but unlike Morrissey in the Smiths or Bono in U2, he steadfastly tried to avoid becoming the focus of the band. Until this point the whole band had managed to remain relatively anonymous. There were no group photos on the album covers, very few interviews and even the celebrated lyrics were only available to those prepared to listen – never written down. The problem was that with songs like 'It's The End Of The World As We Know It (And I Feel Fine)', inspired by a dream Stipe had where everyone at his party had

REM

the initials L.B., and 'The One I Love' with its murderous overtones, Stipe was being referred back to as the author for fans desperate to decipher his lyrics. His reputation as an intellectual symbolist poet grew and with singles like 'Stand', 'Losing My Religion' and 'Everybody Hurts' he was promoted to philosopher/guru, a role he had never sought.

REM has never made decisions about their music based on commercial imperatives. For each of their albums following the hugely successful *Automatic For The People*, they have opted to release 'difficult' first singles, there have been no cash-in remix projects and, most tellingly, no abrupt changes in musical style or image designed to woo a new audience. Similarly, they have not pursued a self-consciously artistic direction or divided themselves up to work on projects that represent their 'real musical passions and creative ambitions'. REM has always been and will always be a band first and foremost. When drummer Bill Berry opted out following a life-threatening (and changing) illness, the band made some comment about a dog with three legs and knuckled down to business, effortlessly producing the acclaimed *Up* album.

Good timeless pop music made with the right attitude, deconstructing as it goes, innit.

First team: Peter Buck (g), Michael Stipe (v), Mike Mills (b, k), Bill Berry (d)

Place, time, scene: Athens, Georgia 1978. REM, like the 'Paisley Underground' bands operating in and around San Francisco, were inspired by the New York punk bands but were influenced musically by sixties garage bands and local folk tradition. Their audience did not desert them when they moved to a major label (in a sense, they had always been a major label band at IRS) and, unlike most independent American bands formed in the wake of punk, they had no hardcore history and philosophy to uphold. The combination of Stipe's oblique socially aware songs and the band's refusal to enhance their music by resorting to studio trickery or incorporating fashionable stylistic devices has kept their sound and their central message consistent and focused. Similarly, they have not adopted a self-consciously artistic approach to their music-making or attempted to constantly update their image, and after over 25 years, still appeal to a wide-ranging international audience,

happy to accept them as an independently-minded band that shifts vast quantities of each new record they release.

What to buy first: *Document* 1987

And then: *Murmur* 1980, *Fables Of The Reconstruction* 1985, *Green* 1987, *Out of Time* 1990, *Automatic For The People* 1992, *New Adventures In Hi-Fi* 1996, *Up* 1999

In retrospect: *Eponymous* 1987, *In Time: The Best of REM 1988–2003* 2003

RESIDENTS

The Residents may be the ultimate alternative band. They not only exist outside of the mainstream industry but also shun the accepted notion that musical performers should at least be engaged in a communicative relationship with their audience. The Residents subscribe to the theory of obscurity. If they remain obscured from their fans then they can't be influenced by their expectations and so can get on with the creative process of making music that is in no way commercially motivated. It's a shame really because the Residents have an impressive back-catalogue that many potential listeners remain acutely unaware of. For a period in the mid–late seventies, when those interested in new music, particularly in the UK, were buying import copies of anything that got a decent write-up in the *NME*, either through mail order or from clued-up record stores, the Residents were just another mythical American band. The difference is that while others have passed into rock'n'roll history, the Residents still remain an enigmatic rumour that becomes more difficult to comprehend as time goes on. How do you judge a band that will not reveal itself? Just on the music, of course. It's what they want and it's what they've got. Just as they have continually been ignored by the media-based promotional infrastructure, the Residents will never be allowed into the official histories because they are not complete. Let's change that right now.

It's thought that there are four Residents and that they are based in San Francisco. As far as personal background goes, that's it. Since 1974 the group has released music, videos and interactive multimedia products through their own Ralph label, each release seemingly intended to expose the anomie of contemporary existence and the unethical role played by the music industry. The early albums, notably *Meet The Residents* in 1974 and *Third Reich And Roll* in 1976, used original material and covers of counter-culture anthems to demonstrate the potential hollowness of supposedly oppositional music which means nothing when stripped of its context. In the end, all that's left are nostalgic money-spinning opportunities for the corporate record companies who own the rights. Of course, 'the man' made money off the Residents too. They had to pay for the right to cover, but listen in and you'll see that it was well worth it. 'Satisfaction' is stripped of its youthful revolutionary fervour and mocked as a naïve and irrelevant song where the singer's concerns about smoking the right brand of cigarette is embarrassing in its immaturity.

In keeping with the band's theory of obscurity, the 1975 album *Not Available* was purposely left unreleased because if nobody hears it then nobody can influence its reception and consequently impact on the artist who made it. The *Eskimo* album followed in 1978 and on it the Residents used the cheapest instrumentation available but made sure that it was recorded on the most expensive studio technology. The ambient sound of the album evokes the polar wastelands and the sleeve-notes include well-written short stories that can be read alongside the music, encouraging a narrative engagement with the music, and therefore getting a feel for Eskimo culture. Again, those playing the music are given a back seat. In 1980 the *Commercial Album* collected together 40 songs, all about a minute long, perhaps intended to demonstrate the paucity of expression in popular music, but in fact demonstrating, how bloody clever the Residents were at making concise yet complex pop music. They have continued to experiment with the concept of authorship and context since their key albums in the late seventies, notably with projects focusing on great American composers that matched up James Brown and Hank Williams songs on the same album, and later a Residents-style interpretation of the songs of Elvis Presley. If nothing else they make you think for a moment, and on more recent CD-Rom releases, physically interact with the band too.

The argument runs that the Residents have managed to avoid personal fame and that their work can be judged on its own terms with the identity of the artists remaining consistent and therefore irrelevant. Occasionally a live Residents event will bring them out to play, but the band are only ever seen in tuxedos and top hats, their faces at all times obscured by eyeball masks. A bit like the Wombles or Slipknot I guess, except with an ethically sound moral message. Although that's a little unfair on the Wombles, they at least wanted us to stop dropping litter.

First team: ?

Place, time, scene: San Francisco 1974. The Residents may have taken some inspiration from Frank Zappa, particularly his lifetime crusade against pretentiousness and commercial imperative. They ultimately remain outsiders attached to no particular scene but continue to lead by example.

What to buy first: *Third Reich And Roll* 1976

And then: *Eskimo* 1978, *Commercial Album* 1980

JONATHAN RICHMAN

Jonathan Richman and the Modern Lovers were the first band to put what they had learned from the Stooges to good use. It's been commented on that Richman was one of the first guitarists to use his right strumming hand more than his left fret-board hand. That was something he picked up from Lou Reed on songs like 'Waiting For The Man', a song which had the dirty, sleazy energy that would later inform the sound of punk-rock. Richman was a Velvet music groupie, an entirely new profession in the late 1960s, and an original archetype of the purposely oppositional outsider that would come to support and make alternative music in the next decade or so. After making the perfect punk album in 1973, he quickly shifted his position to that of the anti-punk who didn't do music that 'hurt the ears of little children'. His wilful difference and lo-fi approach to music-making is discernible in later bands like Beat Happening and fellow Bostonians the Pixies in their early days.

On the sleevenotes to the first Modern Lovers album, Jonathan Richman courteously makes the point that the album would not exist had it not been for the Velvet Underground and the Stooges. For him, the Velvets in particular had provided him with a focus that he had been searching for throughout his teenage years growing up in Cambridge, Massachusetts. Since the age of 15 he had played music and written songs which he performed in public at outdoor events and on campus at the University but was the archetypal outsider in a youth culture full of hippies. He hated overblown, pretentious music-making, mistrusted the ultimately conservative ideals of the counter-culture and didn't do drugs. Stories are told of his tendency to walk around town shouting 'I don't do drugs, I'm not a hippy' at the top of his voice.

The Velvet Underground live at the Tea Party in Boston in 1968 was a necessary confirmation of his own ideas and identity up to that point. He followed them to New York, got to know Lou Reed well enough to stop overnights at his home and even got a gig supporting them at a 1969 show. It must have been like a masterclass in cool for Richman. In keeping with the Factory ethic, Richman was getting workshops in guitar style, performance and composition. He returned to Cambridge in 1970 after a brief trip to Israel and convinced his younger friend John Felice to join his new band. Within a few months the Modern Lovers was a going concern with drummer Dave Robinson and film students Jerry Harrison and Ernie Brooks also signed up. Astonishingly, the first record company interest came from the infamous corporate hippy David Geffen, who whisked them out to California to make their debut album with John Cale, now an ex-Velvet, who had produced the first Stooges album.

John Felice never made the trip, which happened in the summer of 1972, and the band themselves could never quite get it together to finish a whole album, or even complete songs to Cale's satisfaction. After an initial session the band nearly folded but thankfully kept it together for a second session in late 1973, which provided enough material for an album. (Richman befriended Gram Parsons who was almost inspired to get straight and join the Modern Lovers at one point during the California trip but couldn't and died instead.) The band returned to Boston after the album's completion and promptly split.

Harrison later joined Talking Heads and Dave Robinson formed the Cars with Rik Ocasek. The album went into limbo, Warner didn't want to release it giving an excuse that they didn't have enough money! It wasn't until 1976 that it finally made it on to record shelves.

'Roadrunner', 'Pablo Picasso', 'Astral Plane' and 'I'm Straight' are all on that album – direct lyrically and musically. There are no unnecessary guitar solos or enhancing musical textures, Richman and Cale had seen eye-to-eye on that issue, and there was no psychedelia – not even the Velvet Underground variety. The vocals were a different matter though. On 'Pablo Picasso' Richman sounds very Lou Reed, but then at other times he adopts a kind of nonchalant and ambivalent 'whatever' style, anti-singing which is particularly clear on 'Roadrunner', and which became the template for vocalists like Joey Ramone and John Lydon to work from.

The *Modern Lovers* album came out on Bezerkley Records at the same time as Richman's next project with a completely different set of musicians and a totally different musical agenda. The 1977 *Jonathan Richman & The Modern Lovers* album was perhaps a statement against the genre of music which he had inadvertently invented in 1972, nursery rhymes, calypso rhythms – a guiding philosophy that 'people who make loud music that harms babies' ears are not cool'. It was generally disliked because it was being experienced alongside the first Modern Lovers album, and those who didn't dislike the second project found it, at the least, confusing. Richman of course didn't care and has pursued his own idiosyncratic vision ever since, and that in itself is inspirational.

First team: Modern Lovers: Jonathan Richman (v, g), Jerry Harrison (g), Ernie Brooks (b), Dave Robinson (d)

Place, time, scene: Boston 1971. With the Modern Lovers, Richman became the first person to strip down the rock musical form into its essential parts. There were no solos and the vocal style was throwaway. Many punks cited the Modern Lovers as the first truly punk band because of this approach. The Ramones were similarly inclined musically, and the bang-it-out lo-fi style in which Richman has continued to work also inspired the consciously anti-rock and anti-everything archetype of the next few decades.

What to buy first: *The Modern Lovers* 1976 (recorded in 1973)

And then: *Jonathan Richman & The Modern Lovers* 1977

In retrospect: *Home Of The Hits* 2002

REZILLOS

Back in 1977 when punk was at its most menacing, causing outbreaks of moral panic and concerns about a new set of teenagers who might just grow up believing all this anarchy, no past, no future, destroy the monarchy stuff, a band like the Rezillos didn't quite fit in. They played music like it was punk and you could certainly pogo along to it, but the problem was they seemed to be having too much fun. Their tendency to cover songs by Screaming Lord Sutch and instrumental rockabilly hits by the Piltdown Men, combined with their own songs about flying saucers and girls who were really into sculpture didn't seem to fit. The go-go dancer, the saxophonist and the fact that they had two vocalists, a girl/boy call-and-response thing, that was surely kitsch, not punk.

It didn't help that they were from north of the border. It's not that the punk officianados of the period didn't rate the Rezillos, but they couldn't see how they could possibly be originators. After all punk was invented in London! This despite the fact that they had formed in 1976 before anyone in Scotland had been made aware of UK punk. That made it more difficult still. There was no industry ready for them, so Sensible Records was set-up – the same year as Stiff Records in London – to release their punk-pop.

The first single was 'I Can't Stand My Baby' in August 1977, followed by a major label battle frenzy to sign what appeared to be a punk band with an ear for bloody good pop music. Sire got them, and the Rezillos were flown to New York to make the debut album *Can't Stand The Rezillos*, produced by the same guy who made the Ramones' *Rocket To Russia*. The album is superb, it has 'Top Of The Pops' and 'Flying Saucer Attack' on it and is exactly the kind of thing that the B-52s and possibly even the Cramps might have listened to and been inspired by. There was one American show at CBGB's in New York, then a huge tour of the UK before the band split citing musical differences as the reason. Fay Fife and Eugene Reynolds

continued, after much legal wrangling, as the Revillos, and Luke Warm aka Jo Callis moved on to his next project, Shake, before joining the Human League in 1981 – where he wrote amongst other things their number one hit and licence to print money for the rest of his life, 'Don't you Want Me'. Pop fact.

First team: Jo Callis (g), Eugene Reynolds (v), Fay Fife (v), Hi-Fi Harris (g), Dr D.K. Smythe (b), Angel Patterson (d), William Mysterious (sx), Gayle Warning (v)

Place, time, scene: Edinburgh 1976. The Rezillos were the first Scottish alternative band. They had an ironic approach to pop music, which they played in a dumb-ass, direct and very punk style. They were recording before both the B-52s and X-Ray Spex who seemed to be cut from the same cloth. The formation of Sensible Records kick-started the independent scene in Scotland and paved the way for other iconoclastic labels from Postcard to Chemikal Underground.

What to buy first: *Can't Stand The Rezillos* 1978

In Retrospect: *The (Almost) Complete Rezillos* 1995

RIDE

Ride were one of the last indie bands. They worshipped 4AD and Creation and took the time to try and understand what the beejeezis Kevin Shields and his band My Bloody Valentine were actually up to secluded away in expensive studios reinventing the sound of the guitar. Their own contribution was to connect such harshness to something more accessible. They were less song-orientated than the House Of Love but had a sense of rhythm that connected with the indie-dance scene. For all of two years, Ride were very relevant.

They acted quickly. Formed in the summer of 1988, they had knocked up their first demo and played their first live gig by the end of the year, and had got a record deal and main stage performance at the Reading Festival under their belt by the following summer. That's quick, but what makes the whole thing so astonishing is that until Ride formed there wasn't even a scene in their native Oxford (unless you count Talulah Gosh). Bass player Steve Queralt has to take a lot of the credit for getting things moving. As singles buyer in a branch of Our Price Music in Oxford, he, together with store manager Dave Newton, made sure that the store was always well-stocked with the House of Love, Jesus And Mary Chain and My Bloody Valentine. The two of them set up a fanzine and a live music night in Oxford called *Local Support* and, it seems, struggled to fill the weekly schedule. Lucky really because it was due to a cancellation and a lack of options that Ride got their debut gig.

Queralt had played bass for a few years and had spent some time messing about with synth-based bands, even trying his hand at reggae. He got Andy Bell involved, a connection which quickly led to the formation of a band with two of Andy's fellow students from Banbury College of Art, Mark Gardener and Loz Colbert. With the exception of Queralt, all the others were only just adult size. Ride recorded demos in the cramped studio environment that was Steve's bedroom and hallway, and created an expansive electric sound that became the benchmark for their subsequent career. Three of the demo songs made in that period later made it on to the band's first EP, and one of the tracks passed to DJ Gary Crowley in London was heard by Jim Reid of Jesus And Mary Chain, leading inexorably to the deal they always wanted with Alan McGee's Creation Records. The fact that the band routinely covered the Beatles' 'Tomorrow Never Knows' and more importantly, the Creation's 'How Does it Feel To Feel?' confirmed that Ride were at the right label, and McGee's input into their career was by most accounts a good balance of support and creative freedom.

By 1990, Ride had put out several EPs that confirmed sonically that they were separate from what was going on in Manchester – 'House of Love with chain-saws' – but still very much aware that guitar music had to groove too. Loz and Steve could easily have filled in for Reni and Mani in the Stone Roses if it had been necessary. It's an important aspect of Ride's sound that gets forgotten amid the lazy summaries of Ride as a 'shoegazing' band. On more than one occasion Mark Gardener has explained that the reason he and Andy Bell spent so much time staring at the floor during gigs was due to the array of effects pedals needed to achieve their sound. Give me wah-wah over freaky dancing anyday.

The *Smile* and *Nowhere* albums were compilations of the songs on their first four EPs. Tracks like 'Drive Blind' and 'Chelsea Girl' were amongst the earliest the band had written. Cymbals crash around on both albums and the guitars are faster and crisper than My Bloody Valentine, a pop approach to feedback and white noise. 'Taste' on *Nowhere* has a decidedly baggy vibe while 'Vapour Trail' is a gentler acoustic-based song which made them stars in Japan. *Going Blank Again* which followed in 1992 includes the epic 'Leave Them All Behind', which, released as a single, took the Creation label into the Top 10 for the first time, somehow fitting that it was an eight-minute chunk of psychedelia. 'OX4' from the album was notable for the variety of guitar styles and sounds it melds together, a five-minute lesson in the 25-year history of the use and abuse of the electric guitar.

The band split in 1996 after the album *Tarantula*, which was deleted after just a week. Andy Bell had taken on most of the songwriting at that point as Gardener fell into a period of creative inertia. It's one of those situations where an extended break might have done the trick instead of a fatal one. Oasis fever had just taken hold and the raw white-noise sound which Ride had made accessible to an indie and mainstream audience was suddenly too extreme and contemporary for a listening public that was returning to a fantasy version of the sixties. Of course, there was Radiohead who had just issued *The Bends* when Ride split, so it seems that they had done their bit; they had reminded people just how great guitars can sound, and got a record label and a whole scene going in the city of the dreaming spires.

First team: Mark Gardener (v, g), Andy Bell (v, g), Steve Queralt (b), Loz Colbert (d)

Place, time, scene: Oxford 1988. Ride took the effects-laden guitar science of My Bloody Valentine, Sonic Youth, Jesus And Mary Chain, Dinosaur and the Boo Radleys, and made it palatable for a wider audience. Making it groovy was the key thing. Radiohead took note.

What to buy first: *Nowhere* 1990

And then: *Smile* 1990, *Going Blank Again* 1992

In retrospect: *OX4: The Best Of Ride* 2003

ROCKET FROM THE CRYPT

John 'Speedo' Reis lives for the moment. If he decides that he's going to form a band then he forms a band, it really doesn't matter to him that he's got several other bands on the go at the time. Right now he is in Rocket From the Crypt, Hot Snakes and the Sultans. There's always the possibility that he might reform Drive Like Jehu and he has his own record label called Swami to run too. His home town is San Diego, and during his formative years there the local heroes were the Battalion of Saints, a band every bit as uncompromising as Black Flag in their early days. Full-on in your face punk with slam dancing and good old-fashioned mindless violence on offer for those wanting to show allegiance. Suitably inspired, Reis formed Pitchfork with vocalist Eric Froberg but after one album released in 1990, found himself in two other bands. Together with Froberg he formed Drive Like Jehu, an emo band – earnest vocals, poetic lyrics, angular guitars and stop-start drum parts – and at virtually the same time, his own Rocket From The Crypt.

Rocket From The Crypt are a no-nonsense rock'n' roll band with a garage-punk ethos. Reis is the vocalist, right up there above the horns, the feedback guitar and relentless drum pounding, testifying primal urges like Wayne Kramer of the MC5 – 'I want it, I need it, I'll steal it'. Where Drive Like Jehu spend time creating moods and agonising over lyrics, Rocket From The Crypt just bang them out. That's not to say that the band are ever slack. Experienced live, the band is as tight as the JBs, and in the studio there are nods to Phil Spector's legendary 'wall-of-sound' strategy. The band even went to the trouble of using his Gold Star studio and original equipment for *Scream Dracula Scream*.

Recorded on a four-track desk, the brass parts were added afterwards. The sound is immense and has a rawness that Spector never had on his work with the Ramones. It broke them internationally with hit singles 'Born In 69', 'Young Livers' and 'On A Rope', and the follow-up *R.F.T.C.* shed a couple of hits too. Rocket From The Crypt then retreated while the party-punk that they had inadvertently inspired took over the charts worldwide. Of course, bands like Blink 182 and most recently Sum 41 may have the looks and the

lifestyle but they aren't connected to the R&B core like Rocket From The Crypt. Those other zig-zag wanderers and purveyors of primal r'n'r, the Jon Spencer Blues Explosion, popped up with their bid for mainstream acceptance in 1998, perhaps inspired by the possibilities opened up by Speedo and the fellers. The first Jon Spencer Blues Explosion album was released in 1992, just as Rocket From The Crypt were putting out their second. The Blues Explosion called theirs *Crypt Style*. Go, as they say, figure.

First Team: John 'Speedo' Reis (v, g), ND (g), Apollo 9 (sx), JC2000 (tr), Petey X (b), Atom (d)

Place, time, scene: San Diego 1990. Rocket From The Crypt was Speedo Reis's other band, but the one which gave him the chance to party while independent American music was embarking on a particularly tortured and heavy period of creativity. Along with the Jon Spencer Blues Explosion, Rocket From The Crypt kept the R&B and funk heart beating, ready for release when everybody needed cheering up again half way through the decade. They looked like they might blow Britpop away too, for a while.

What to buy first: *Scream Dracula Scream* 1995

And then: *Circa Now* 1994

ROYAL TRUX

The Neil Hagerty and Jennifer Herrema story really is a romantic one. She was in her senior high school year in Washington DC when she saw him playing guitar with his band and developed a crush on him immediately. Within a few months, after she had plucked up the courage to speak to him, she found herself spending three days at his flat with him, her girlfriend and an old man who, to paraphrase Herrema 'drank Colt 45, was tripping off his head and was surrounded in his warehouse room with bottles of piss'.

The acid-dropping continued for a year, during which time Neil and Jennifer began making recordings together. In 1986 they moved to New York with Jon Spencer and Julie Cafritz. Neil played guitar with their band Pussy Galore, encouraging them to re-record the Rolling Stones' *Exile On Main Street* in its entirety, and Jennifer took up a place at The New York School For Social Research. Hagerty managed one more album with Pussy Galore, the thin white trebly noise classic *Right Now,* and then set about organizing a record deal for himself and Jennifer using the name Royal Trux.

The first album was untitled, and domestically recorded in mono, the idea being to take the music of the current New York noise scene back to its garage roots. It was followed by a double album of material recorded in San Francisco at the end of the decade called *Twin Infinitives,* based on AC/DC, Stones and Zeppelin riffs but in their rawest form with no bottom end, the audio equivalent of an x-ray. Their first few albums came out on the Drag City label and always got such good reviews from the indie critics that a deal was offered by Virgin Records in 1994 which resulted in the *Thank You* album recorded live on stage and overdubbed by producer David Briggs. It became the first in a trilogy of albums, continuing with *Sweet 16* in 1997 and *Accelerator* in 1998 that progressed through the studio techniques, instrumentation and overall musical philosophies of the sixties, seventies and eighties respectively. No song on *Sweet 16* could be less than four minutes long and *Accelerator* was full of soft-rock solos and desk-affected echo to represent the overproduced, over-budgeted excess of the greedy decade. It still sounds like classic garage-punk though.

The band's most recent albums for the indie label Domino have continued to look back to an earlier sound, which is then fed through a lo-fi punk filter. They come on like 'Exile' period Stones on *Veterans Of Disorder* and *Pound For Pound,* and as the Stones aren't up for that stuff anymore, I'll take a Royal Trux homage anytime.

First team: Neil Hagerty (g, b, v, k), Jennifer Herrema (v), Ken Nasta (d)

Place, time, scene: Washington 1985. Pursuing a deliberately amateur approach to production, Royal Trux were one of the rawest sounding bands to commit to tape since the garage bands of the mid-sixties. Their art is based in a form of pastiche that attempts to remove the technological trappings of studio-based recording, and that seems to include bass guitars.

What to buy first: *Thank You* 1995

And then: *Sweet 16* 1997, *Accelerator* 1998, *Veterans Of Disorder* 2000

In retrospect: *Singles, Live, Unreleased* 1997

RUTS

The Ruts could have been the great British punk band if their lead vocalist and songwriter hadn't gone and died on them. They were a west London based band with a unity of purpose that really only comes from going to the same school and attending the same life-affirming gigs together. The band idea happened sometime in 1977, inspired by the whole of London going punk. They played a series of gigs at the White Hart in Acton and were regulars on the Rock Against Racism gigs together with reggae band Misty In Roots. Just like Clash gigs in Brixton and Bad Brains riots in Washington DC, the events were a satisfying mix of pogo and skank, shout and groove, and tension and release, which rubbed off on the Ruts' musical style.

The deal with Virgin was done in 1978 and the debut album was a bona fide groundbreaker. It followed up on the Clash's reggae and dub experiments, but whereas Joe Strummer in particular was losing faith in the possibilities of progressive race relations, evidenced in the lyrics to 'White Man In Hammersmith Palais', Malcolm Owen's words seemed to place the blame for social unrest with external forces. 'Babylon's Burning', the opening track on *The Crack,* begins with a police siren which signifies the source of racial tension. 'Dope for Guns' continues the theme of institutional anomaly, and the closing 'Jah Wars' is a song entirely inspired by the UK riots that kicked off in April 1979. Throughout the album, the throbbing basslines supportively echo what Owen is singing, and there are harsh guitar sounds that at times evoke the experience of bodies clashing in the midst of riot. All of it topical, all of it angry, and done before the real villains got into office.

Owen's fatal heroin overdose put paid to a 1980s Ruts which was a crying shame. The rest of the band continued without him, but lacking a strong punk voice, decided instead, and with some success, to focus on reggae and dub with a less direct lyrical approach. Still, the territory had been mapped out for a bunch of pissed off Midlanders with time on their hands.

First team: Malcolm Owen (v), Paul Fox (g), John Jennings (b), Dave Ruffy (d)

Place, time, scene: London 1978. The Ruts were a punk band that consciously addressed a multi-racial audience and attempted with a good deal of success to incorporate reggae and dub into their music. They were active in Rock Against Racism and would have fitted neatly into the 2-Tone scene to come.

What to buy first: *The Crack* 1978

In retrospect: *Something He Said: The Best Of The Ruts* 1995

S

SAINT ETIENNE

Bob Stanley was a writer for the *NME* in the late eighties just after the illustrious weekly had tried, and failed, to reawaken the traditionally student passion for indie guitar music with their *C86* compilation. The Stone Roses were left off that particular collection but they had their own strategy for success and it involved warehouse parties and a little northern soul, where Primal Scream who were on *C86*, gave up indie three years later and enlisted the help of DJ Andrew Weatherall to create 'Loaded'. That was December 1989, the point at which the final nail got hammered into the indie coffin. Stanley had heard M/A/R/R/S, checked out the Chicago scene and finally witnessed Bobbie Gillespie and Alan McGee rave on about ecstasy and acid-house. Together with his childhood friend Pete Wiggs with whom he use to make party tapes as a teenager, he succumbed to the groove, invested in a sampler and made a dance record.

Stanley and Wiggs were both fans of sixties pop music, especially when it was fronted by female singers who sang soul but retained their own personality and didn't fall into cliché. Dusty Springfield, Sandie Shaw and Françoise Hardy were big favourites, and the style of future pop that Hardy's husband Jacques Dutronc arranged for her to sing was a big influence too. Saint Etienne were into French pop in particular, way before it became cool ten years later and, just for the record, their *Foxbase Alpha* album released on Creation in 1991 preceded Stereolab's debut by a year. The comparison is irrelevant though. Stereolab combine France's legacy of electronic music with a traditional rock set-up, ready for Laetitia Sadier's vocals to float in over the top; Saint Etienne mess with dub, hip-hop and disco beats and are as happy to use sampled instruments as those played in real time. There are flutes, harpsichords and crucially those female voices. Moira Lambert sings on the cover of Neil Young's 'Only Love Can Break Your Heart' deadpan and monotone like Ronnie Ronette, but it's Sarah Cracknell who steals the show with her blended innocence and sex appeal, sometimes Dusty, sometimes Sandie, always Sarah.

Cracknell has pointed out that thankfully she is 'no Whitney Houston' – all overblown sentiment and production sheen, and hence the perfect vocalist for Saint Etienne, a band which has always been keen to avoid rock and soul posturing. 'Girl VII', 'London Belongs To Me' and especially 'Nothing Can Stop Us' are celebrations of bohemian London life set to a retro musical backing that pre-dates Britpop, and although pastiche in terms of sound, are underpinned by a contemporary cut'n'paste, mix and match approach to rhythms and samples.

Critics tend to dwell on the band's sense of irony, mixing them up with the Pet Shop Boys, probably because they make electronic-based pop and one of them used to be a music journalist, but then that's fairly standard response to artists who make pop music that is not necessarily aimed at the traditional pop market. In fact, it's not easy to pin down Saint

Etienne to any particular style or set of aims when surveying their back-catalogue of albums since *Foxbase Alpha* in 1991. *So Tough* once again brought together a range of sixties influences from Brian Wilson's *Pet Sounds* to classic girl-group, but threw in a little latin jazz too, and had dub and reggae moments that were more akin to the punk take on bass science learned from PiL and the Slits. By 1994's *Tiger Bay* they were less pop and more ambient in sound. Ahead of bands like Air in the 'dance music it's impossible to dance to' stakes, they took a four-year break to let everyone else catch up during which time Stanley and Wiggs ran a cutting-edge record label for EMI called Emidisc, and Sarah Cracknell put out a solo album. They returned with *Good Humor* which swung back from dance to classic pop. And it was released on Sub Pop! – the home of grunge rock. Go figure.

First team: Bob Stanley (samp, k), Pete Wiggs (samp, k), Sarah Cracknell (v)

Place, time, scene: London 1990. Saint Etienne led the indie crossover into dance music, and having little or no experience of being in a band, were able to embrace the new technology available at cheaper prices and use their record collections and immense pop knowledge to construct a sound that was simultaneously dated and right up to date. It was dubbed indie-dance and coincided with the release of Primal Scream's *Screamadelica* album. Since then they have continued to lead the field in electronic, sample-based dance music, becoming ever more sophisticated with their production and arrangements. Britpop and the French Touch scenes owe a little something to Saint Etienne.

What to buy first: *Foxbase Alpha* 1991

And then: *So Tough* 1993, *Tiger Bay* 1994, *The Good Humour* 1998

In retrospect: *Smash The System: Singles And More* 2001

SCRITTI POLITTI

Green Gartside, the auteur who operates under the name Scritti Politti, occupied an interesting strategic position within independent music at the beginning of the eighties. Having started by releasing a record on his own label in 1980, the explicitly political *Skank Bloc Bologna*, he suffered a long illness, and emerged from the experience having done a lot of reading and a lot of thinking. He was deeply cynical about the intentions of many of the bands that had formed in the aftermath of punk, who seemed collectively to have created a set of puritanical rules that kept the music purposely guitar-based and essentially based in white musical culture. A dichotomy had been established between the mainstream and the marginal where the former was, by definition, safe and uninspiring and fatally connected to market forces, and it was understood that the mainstream could never achieve the musical and cultural goals that existed at the margins. Green disagreed. He thought that the days of prog-rock were about to return, just a bit darker and more discordant. He made it his job to do something about it.

Having signed to Rough Trade Records, Green sold his ideas to Geoff Travis, the label's founder, and began work on a debut album, *Songs To Remember,* which drew heavily on disco, reggae and soul, but was focused in its main aim to be an out-and-out pop album, even if it did include songs about cultural theorists and had some neat beat-poetry influenced lyrics. Rough Trade spent £60,000 alone on the recording of the first single 'The Sweetest Girl' – a mix of industrial funk and dub with subtle attacks on Thatcherism discernible in the lyrics – which compared to much smaller amounts for entire albums. Philosophically it pushed Rough Trade and the independent sector to something of an impasse, where potentially enlightened independent workers saw the political importance of what became dubbed 'the new pop' and others saw the whole thing as nothing short of a sell-out. Finally it seemed that it was the latter when Scritti Politti upped sticks and signed with a major label after *Songs To Remember* sold poorly.

Green was a fake then? Or was following the money to Virgin Records just the next stage of his attempts to subvert the mainstream from within? Certainly, the follow-up *Cupid And Psyche 85* was a subtly crafted soul-pop album and there was a small collection of hit singles too, 'Wood Beez (Pray Like Aretha Franklin)', 'Absolute' and 'The Word Girl', which boasted cleverly constructed satirical lyrics and some interesting experiments in rhythm courtesy of John Maher, who joined the band as a drummer having cut his teeth playing with no-wave pioneers like Bill Laswell in New York. Some have claimed Scritti Politti to be the undervalued link between the independent music industry and the increasing importance and development of more populist dance-music styles later in the decade. Green Gartside, the man who made disco cool – hero or villain? Tough one that.

First team: Green Gartside (v, g), David Gamson (k, prog), Fred Mahlar (d)

Place, time, scene: Leeds 1978. Originally an experimental post-punk band, Scritti Politti as a solo project led by Green Gartside questioned the monotony of punk-musical lore and dared to go pop. By the mid-eighties, many others associated with the independent scene had acknowledged a passing respect for mainstream artists like Prince and Madonna, and eventually the whole house of cards tumbled when club culture became the new cool. Scritti Politti were there at the start of it all.

What to buy first: *Songs To Remember* 1982

And then: *Cupid And Psyche 85* 1985

SEBADOH

Sebadoh were out to deconstruct indie music. Although Dinosaur Jr were hardly the epitome of muso noodling and production fetishism, Lou Barlow's time in the band, playing loud and cool had convinced him that indie-rock was in danger of becoming clichéd. With a whole decade of development behind it, underground music was on its way to becoming an eminently marketable genre by the time Sebadoh made their first lo-fi incursions. Subversive but also intentionally song-driven, along with Pavement and Guided By Voices, Sebadoh were trying to distil the best bits of alt-music by removing the more overblown aspects that could pass for old-fashioned rockism. The new lo-fi bands were not going to get caught taking themselves too seriously or getting too 'into' the music, and if that meant writing the odd parody or taking the piss, then that's what had to be done. Hey, it even became a genre in its own right and that confused everything.

By the time Dinosaur Jr recorded the *Bug* album they had created a unique sound based on a strategy of writing classic pop songs and then burying them beneath layers of guitar. Any pretentions of pop were further undermined by J. Mascis's slack and lazy vocal with expletives deployed prominently in the hook of the song to ensure it didn't crossover into the mainstream. But just as Dinosaur Jr were being lauded as the vanguard of what was about to become the most important development in American rock since punk, Lou Barlow upped and left.

His new project was inspired by the minimal recording techniques that stretched way back to Robert Johnson and are perhaps best exemplified by Nick Drake's last work. Working with friend and fanzine writer Eric Gaffney who shared his honest and direct vision, but focused his efforts on raw sound rather than songs, Barlow had been home-taping sessions on a 4-track cassette recorder since the mid-eighties in an attempt to get back to the basics of the recording process, the song before the technology takes over. The first two albums rely on quantity rather than quality, a single pure and unfettered idea for a song put down on tape, followed by another single pure and unfettered idea for a song after that. These early, very rare albums are not the easiest listen but do form the basis for Sebadoh's finest moment – *Sebadoh III* released in 1991. With teenage multi-instrumentalist Jason Lowenstein on board, Sebadoh switched to studio recording but kept their guiding lo-fi principles intact, and that meant getting hold of a sampler so that certain sounds and instrumental sections could be laid down on tape before going in and playing them through the big desk to accompany the vocals. The key thing according to Barlow was that it remained 'something that you were doing yourself. You were in control of the recording. No-one else was fucking around with it and making it sterile.'[57]

Sebadoh III is a 20-track album with songs written individually by all three members that comes on like the Beatles' *White Album* – reflective and sometimes sensitive songs by Barlow opposed to the direct and firmly-opined lyrics attributed to Gaffney. Throughout, delicate and simple song structures are fouled by dirty instrument abuse. Sebadoh's early lo-fi version of 'Brand New Love' was taken up to mid-fi on the following year's *Sebadoh vs Helmet* mini-album in

1992, an album which also contained a cover of Nick Drake's sparse 'Pink Moon', mullered with abrasive guitars, feedback and hardcore shouting.

It's an interesting cover, one of many in fact that make you wonder whether or not Sebadoh are, in fact, taking the piss. You see, another key tenet of lo-fi is the stripping down of overblown sentiment, the big ideas and the didactic polemics that are often hopelessly misplaced within the context of a primarily entertainment-based form. That's not to say that politics is out, or emotion should not be expressed, but the setting and delivery should be right. Dylan managed it, Lydon did too but less directly. I'm pretty sure that they wouldn't be dissing Nick Drake, but there are other moments such as 1991's 'Gimme Indie Rock' that, depending on your perspective, sneers at or affirms the then overground success of grunge in particular: 'renew Stooges, undeniably cool, took a lesson from that drone rock school, getting loose with the Pussy Galore, cracking jokes like a Thurston Moore'. It's good old-fashioned sarcasm and antagoism in the tradition of that other Boston stirrer, Jonathan Richman.

Gaffney left Sebadoh in 1994 and since then Sebadoh has been a band of two halves, Barlow's reflective and often tragic love songs on one hand and Jason Loewenstein's more aggressive sonic attacks on the other. *Bakesale* and *Harmacy* are albums where, regardless of the style of the songs, the overall impression given is that Sebadoh have just knocked the stuff off in one or two takes. The love songs are achingly beautiful and the rockers are motivational kick-assers. *The Sebadoh*, released in 1997, is the album where the two sides come together, and there was even a UK hit with, 'Flame', a relentless drum driven reflection on getting on a bit in life. *The Sebadoh* is definitely the band's most accomplished album, which is just the sort of comment that probably sets the alarm bells ringing for Barlow. Check his solo albums, out-take compilations and work with John Davis in Folk Implosion for evidence of his, perhaps pathological need to work the avant-garde quickly without too much planning and little or no tidying up afterwards.

First team: Lou Barlow (v, g), Eric Gaffney (v, d), Jason Loewenstein (v, g, b, k)

Place, time, scene: Boston 1987. Returning to basics after the effects and noise of Dinosaur Jr, Lou Barlow

set up Sebadoh as a self-sufficient concern that made music quickly and simply. His ironic view of the music industry and what he perceived to be its cynicism and tendency to take itself a little seriously at times led to a series of apparently sarcastic digs and for many, linked Sebadoh with Pavement as the instigators of a new anti-rock scene which was briefly successful in the late nineties.

What to buy first: *The Sebadoh* 1998

And then: *Sebadoh III* 1991, *Smash Your Head On The Punk Rock* 1992, *Bakesale* 1994, *Harmacy* 1996

SEPULTURA

The story of Sepultura is a story of musical and cultural roots, or to put it into Max Cavalera speak 'roots, bloody roots'. Most of the artists and bands in this book emerged out of local music scenes, inspired by local heroes who had gone before, and supported by an infrastructure of venues, fanzines and labels that helped them on their way. Nothing like that for Sepultura. There was no local metal scene in Belo Horizonte in Brazil in the early 1980s, in fact there weren't even that many places where you could get a guitar, let alone the latest Exodus or Venom album. Brothers Max and Igor Cavalera managed to find some though, and by 1985 they were in a band with friends Andreas Kisser and Paolo Jr which was part of a much larger scene, a global scene, where even demo recordings and bootlegged rehearsal sessions were much sought-after by extreme metallers the world over.

The first two albums *Schizophrenia* and *Beneath The Remains*, both recorded in Brazil at the end of the eighties, are definitive death metal: Igor's fast in-yer-face drumming, sheets of indistinct guitar riffing and broken English screaming. It didn't matter that the band's first language was Portuguese, death metal was global and the language of the global music scene is English. Sepultura didn't sing about Brazilian issues or lifestyle either. Brazilian audiences didn't need local cultural references to identify with the songs. To them Sepultura came from the same place as Slayer or Metallica – metal-land.

It's a strange irony then, that when *Arise* was released on premier metal label Roadrunner Records in 1991, the band who had by then moved to Phoenix, Arizona, suddenly started dropping Brazilian flavours into their lyrics and music, and then continued, adding a healthy dose of politics on their next two best-selling albums, *Chaos AD* and *Roots*. 'Refuse/Resist' on *Chaos AD* is a dig at state-sponsored violence and when asked, Max Cavalera explained that 'the President has been impeached and they're creating a whole bunch of industries and companies that are really stealing and weaseling the money from the people. So it's pretty chaotic there right now. It's pretty fucked-up and it isn't getting any better.' Perhaps inspired by Metallica's social conscience albums of the nineties, *Chaos AD* was an entirely new type of Sepultura album. The follow-up, *Roots* in 1996 was an entirely new type of metal album.

On it, Sepultura slow the whole thing down and go for a darker, more moody sound that incorporates an array of different percussive rhythms drawn from their samba school roots. Brazilian percussion and strings are incorporated alongside the basic set-up of guitars, bass and drums, but are played hard and fast. In addition, there are several collaborative moments with the Xavante tribe, and the central theme of the album is confirmed by the line 'these roots will always remain' from 'Born Stubborn'. But with guest appearances from Jonathan Davis of Korn and DJ Lethal of Limp Bizkit, that's roots in the very widest sense. Sepultura took a free-floating global scene and tied it down to their original home in Brazil (their personal roots) and their new home in America (their metal roots). Moreover they've used their new elevated position to make a point, regardless of the risks. Acutely aware of the cultural blacklisting and violence that had gone on in Brazil during their teens, and with the added disincentive of Cavalera having been shot at in 1994, possibly for the views he was espousing, Sepultura and Cavalera's new band Soulfly have continued to make oppositional metal. Proud to have them in.

First team: Max Cavalera (v, g), Igor Cavalera (d), Paolo Jr (b), Andreas Kisser (g)

Place, time, scene: Belo Horizonte, Brazil 1986. Sepultura were part of a global metal scene and were inspired, in particular, by Slayer and Venom. Their incorporation of social and political themes into their

music is rare in a hard-rock band and has been carried on by vocalist Max Cavalera in his new band Soulfly and several other bands on the Roadrunner label roster, notably Fear Factory, Machinehead and Type O Negative.

What to buy first: *Roots* 1996

And then: *Arise* 1991, *Chaos AD* 1994

SEX PISTOLS

Spirit and intensity were the making of the Sex Pistols. When they played live, they meant it, and the sound, the performance and the message were all there, upfront and in the face. And that was with or without a proper bassist. Glen Matlock, often described as the most musically accomplished of the band, brought structure and width to the band at the early gigs but, if legendary reviewer Greil Marcus is to be believed, the band's last shows in America featured 'the only great two-man band in the history of rock and roll'. It was all down to the primal connection that Steve Jones and Paul Cook had to each other and the violent possibilities of amplified noise. And it takes a certain kind of bravery to make an album and then go out on tour knowing all the time that the bloke on bass guitar is only there for the image.

But then the Sex Pistols didn't have a history of giving a damn about most things. Jones, the ex-soccer hooligan, was originally the singer with the Swankers, only taking up the Les Paul when Malcolm McLaren, their stylist-manager, sacked guitarist Wally Nightingale and suggested that John Lydon might be a more viable front-man. Dubbed Johnny Rotten, on account of his bad teeth, finding Lydon was like the Spiders From Mars finally discovering their Ziggy Stardust. Well, sort of.

Jones taught himself guitar by listening to Mick Ronson on Bowie's early records, and Matlock and Cook were both fans of glam's chugging rock sound, particularly Chris Thomas' work with Roxy Music, who went on to produce the first couple of Sex Pistols singles. But although Rotten, a fan of Alice Cooper as well as Bowie, seemed to be adopting a character just like his heroes, it was never clear whether this was actually the case. Ziggy was essentially an opportunity for Bowie to play out his destructive and narcissistic theoretical other self and doubled as a cautionary tale for anyone who might see parallels in their own life, although the process was primarily a cathartic one for Bowie personally. Rotten was operating in a different time and knew that his audience craved something different. Existentialist catharsis of a type associated with the singer-songwriters of the 'me-generation', even delivered once removed, like Bowie, was not what those who attended Sex Pistols gigs or bought Sex Pistols records, wanted to hear.

So instead Johnny Rotten sneered. That laugh at the beginning of 'Anarchy In The UK' makes the point clear from the start. Anarchy is suggested throughout the lyrics, but not for the masses. Just for a self-proclaimed 'anti-christ' that hates the world so much and preaches such utter destruction and loathing he surely cannot be taken seriously. It's a complex and convoluted guise that actually ends up being the most revolutionary statement of cultural alienation ever delivered in a pop song. And it's all down to Lydon's clear understanding of his peers, his culture and the centrality of irony as the only weapon of resistance at that point in British history. The singles that followed – 'God Save The Queen', 'Pretty Vacant' and 'Holidays In The Sun' – continue with Lydon's central theme of disgust at the state his world is in, and his desire to escape and shut it out. 'I don't want a holiday in the sun, I want to go to the new Belsen' neatly encapsulates his preference for a society where the living is hard but relatively guilt-free, or as *Rolling Stone* journalist Dave Marsh interprets it 'the culture on the other side (of the wall) seems better able to keep its citizens numb'.[58]

The combination of the right intellectually-considered message and the right physically-felt and hook-laden music made the Sex Pistols *the* definitive influence on everything else that has followed, and pretty much blows away everything else that came before too. It's a shame that the album *Never Mind The Bollocks – Here's The Sex Pistols* does not do the band's legacy justice. It contains all the singles, and there's 'Bodies', 'Submission', 'Liar' and the more specifically pointed 'EMI'. All the tracks spit bile and are suitably discordant, but they seem to lack Glen

Matlock's pop sensibility (and bass-playing taken on by Steve Jones at the last minute) which had made previous singles all the more powerful because they could be sung in the pubs, on the terraces and in the playground.

What's more, Lydon has since complained that some of the first-take spirit was sacrificed due to too much time getting multiple guitar parts down on tape, and studio-built intensity is no substitute for the real thing. Not that the album had prog-rock intent. Shit no. It was still fast and loose, filthy and furious, just not as focused as *Rocket To Russia*, *Blank Generation* or *L.A.M.F.*, all released the same year, and that's a shame because the Sex Pistols *were* the greatest punk band. Perhaps they are to be remembered as a singles band. Clearly, the band that should have made the debut album no longer existed by mid-1977, and maybe that's the way it should be. Do you really want to know what a fifth Sex Pistols album would have sounded like?

Lydon left the band at the end of a tour of the US, Jones and Cook went to Brazil to work with Ronnie Biggs – a fairly pointless and irrelevant idea that only seemed to afford McLaren the opportunity for a little egowank – and Vicious made no discernible contribution to anything in the months leading up to his inevitable and tragic death. Lydon had got out at the right time it seems. He took a trip to Jamaica with Don Letts and then, as the only Pistol who remained rooted in reality, set about reflecting the sounds coming out of multi-cultural urban Britain with Jah Wobble, Keith Levene and Jim Walker in Public Image Ltd.

First team: Johnny Rotten (v), Steve Jones (g), Glen Matlock (b), Paul Cook (d)

Place, time, scene: London 1976. The Sex Pistols were not the first punk band – there was a whole American scene based in New York operating before they formed – but they were the first to politicize the new direct style that refused to acknowledge rock's past and demanded that everyone start again. The Sex Pistols took punk music to the masses and inspired generations of musicians to come. John Lydon's particular legacy is in the way he addressed his audience. He was non-patronizing and impersonal. He told it like it was, but retained the right to offer no solutions. His main weapon was irony.

What to buy first: *Never Mind The Bollocks – Here's The Sex Pistols* 1977

In retrospect: *The Great Rock And Roll Swindle* 1979, *Kiss This* 1992

SHONEN KNIFE

Tapping into that aspect of Japanese youth culture that collects training shoes and revels in shallow, image-driven pop, Shonen Knife, a trio from Osaka – also home of similarly amateur punks the Boredoms – wrote their first songs about ice-cream, jelly, chocolate and Barbie dolls, and translated them into English for their debut internationally released album in 1990 called simply *Shonen Knife*. It hooked them up with a lot of fans in both the UK and the US, arriving just as the independent scenes in both countries were lightening up and ready for some quirky and crucially, ironic, Japanese pop.

To start with, Shonen Knife – Naoko Yamano, her sister Atsuko Yamano and friend Michie Nakatani – were a determinedly amateur group who used pop music as an excuse to celebrate consumer culture. After several years of just Japanese record sales, they suddenly exploded overnight as an international alternative phenomenon. Pretty soon there was a double tribute album entitled *Every Band Has A Shonen Knife Who Loves Them* and an opening slot for Nirvana on their 1991 tour, in support of *Nevermind*. This was a band which appealed directly to the independent sensibility and somehow managed to get a tick in all the boxes relating to credibility, innovation and working practice. Like the Boredoms, they were apparently free from westernized rock and pop cliché, and by the end of the eighties when everything had been done in both of those areas, and only hip-hop and dance music seemed to have any future, they were a breath of fresh air.

Craig Leon, who had produced the first Ramones album, was brought in to mix their major label debut *Let's Knife* in 1993. Their seriously improved musicianship, combined with re-recordings of their Japanese greatest hits marks the album out as easily their best effort. Effectively, the band had the opportunity of returning to the beginning of their career to start again

with years of touring and studio time behind them. Perfect pop to give it a name, complete with giggling.

Of the albums that followed, *Brand New Knife* and *Happy Hour* have their moments but unfortunately the band has got better at playing and has taken to writing more meaningful songs. The last album *Heavy Songs* is so-called because, as Naoko explains it, 'heavy means not only heavy but strong, deep, aggressive, thick, boring, strict, sad, important, wonderful, fabulous, a great quantity, and so on'. That's far too deep. What was wrong with 'I like chocobars, any kind of chocobars. I eat chocobars, every day two bars per day'? For a moment there, they were the future of pop, now they're just a fairly good rock band.

First team: Naoko Yamano (v, g), Atsuko Yamano (v, b), Michie Nakatani (d)

Place, time, scene: Osaka, Japan 1985. Operating outside the Japanese noise scene which placed a premium on musical precision and expertise, Shonen Knife were steadfastly amateur in their approach. Their international success occurred because they seemed to be without pretension and because they resonated fun, two things which distinguished them from the twee pop and serious rock of the period.

What to buy first: *Shonen Knife* 1990

And then: *Let's Knife* 1993

SILVER APPLES

By their own admission the Silver Apples were one of the weirdest bands in New York – and that was in the late sixties when New York was particularly weird. Their thing was oscillators, and it was just enough of a gimmick to get them onto the bill of every 'happening' happening. Their first single went into the national charts and created a buzz around the space-age sounding band who were in the right place at the right time, but as band member Simeon so concisely puts it, 'Our revolutionary nature always got the better of us'.

To summarize, the Silver Apples were a duo, Simeon and Danny. Simeon was a child prodigy, painting at the age of three and experimenting with free-jazz trumpet at eight. As soon as he was old enough he made for Mexico and then New York where he somehow got in with the avant-garde hipsters and started visiting composer Hal Rogers to play with his rescued World War One oscillator, which they discovered sounded great when fed through an amp and played along to records. When Simeon joined his first band in Conneticut, he introduced his oscillator into the sound and immediately pissed-off several members of the band until just drummer Danny remained, and the Silver Apples were born.

They headed for New York in 1965 and took a room at the Albert Hotel on 10th street just down the corridor from the Lovin' Spoonful, the Mothers of Invention and Mike Bloomfield, and pretty soon became the toast of the avant-garde. They were the first band to play at Max's Kansas City. Danny played drums, often two sets at the same time, and sang, and Simeon; who was by now building his own oscillators, devised a system where different machines oscillating at different frequencies could produce a much fuller sound. Simeon explains, 'the grandfather oscillator remained the big sound-sweeper and the rest were wired into telegraph keys mounted in front of me on a table. Never having played a piano keyboard, this arrangement made much more sense. So that I could differentiate all the different telegraph keys, I put different colours on different ones so I could make out the relationships visually as we were playing. That meant that "Oscillations", our first hit was not played in the key of C for instance, but in the key of BLUE.' There were on stage electrocutions, gigs alongside the Norman Mailer, Allen Ginsberg and the 1910 Fruitgum Company, and even a show in Central Park organized to coincide with the moon landing. The mayor of New York declared the Silver Apples the official New York sound for the landing on the moon.

By the time of the first album the 'Simeon' had been invented, a collection of nine oscillators, lead and rhythm played with hands, elbows and knees and bass played with the feet. With Danny Taylor's unique percussion style, creating mathematical pulsating systems, they both effectively made melody and rhythm, creating hypnotic sounds that were not heard before or been heard since. Their songs are about whirly-birds, hair, colours and oscillators, and Simeon sings them in a high-pitched voice that cuts through the wobbliness all around him. There are

banjos, recorders, eastern sounds and some fancy tape-looping in there too. Go on, I challenge you to listen to a whole album.

First team: Simeon (v, os), Danny Taylor (d, p)

Place, time, scene: New York 1966. A psychedelic band that looked outside of the traditional pop set-up to create music to freak out to. Theirs was a home-made response to the corporately produced Moog, Vox and Farfisa of the day, which added a completely new and workable sound to rock's armoury of instrumentation. Kraftwerk have been known to get down and oscillate.

What to buy first: *Silver Apples* 1968

And then: *Contact* 1969

In retrospect: *Silver Apples* 1997

SLAYER

Slayer brought together hardcore punk and metal at a time when the two just didn't mix. We're talking 1983, when heavy metal, as it was referred to back then, was in a pretty sorry state. Bon Jovi and Def Leppard were the cutting edge! They were good musicians of course, and it was rumoured that Black Flag copped a few tips off Def Leppard when they made their *Slip It In* album. Up to that point the hardcore guys had been more concerned with undoing traditional musical rules in line with the central hardcore rule to play hard and honest regardless of talent or skill. Slayer had the skills, it was the playing hard that rocked their world.

Slayer and the other extreme metal pioneers, Metallica and Anthrax, combined the speed and thrash of hardcore, but they practiced too, a lot. They needed to so that they could get faster and faster and keep it all together, guitar, bass and drums. Two albums in and AC/DC fan Rick Rubin decided that Slayer had something that rock music was lacking at that time, namely a directness of approach that mirrored that going on in the evolving rap industry. In fact, extreme metal was the only viable response to bands like Public Enemy and Run DMC, and the various collaborations that went on in the mid-eighties confirmed that the two forms went well together. Slayer's guitarist and main songwriter, Kerry King, had already got in on the act.

It's his guitar you can hear on the Beastie Boys' 'Fight For Your Right'. He apparently got paid a couple of hundred dollars for that! Mind you, it did lead to a Rubin/Slayer partnership that has lasted the best part of 20 years, starting with the 1986 album *Reign In Blood*.

Kicking off with 'Angel of Death', a song about notorious Nazi murderer Josef Mengele, the band move through a selection of songs dealing with satanism, necrophilia and any other number of bad crimes, all touchingly played from the heart. To quote King, 'I just wrote how I speak. And I speak in a very hateful manner usually.' The album is definitive of its genre, and although there's not a suggestion of hip-hop anywhere on the album, there was something in the perfectly spaced and crisp riffs and rhythms that recalled the breakbeat work of the best hip-hop DJs, and had an impact on Ice-T for one who was soon putting together his own metal band, Bodycount. Plus, you could hear the words, and rappers live for words, especially when they're delivered with confidence and attitude, and stark imagery. The album lasts 28 minutes in total with almost every song segueing into the next to create a listening experience like no other before it. Somebody once said that the guitars sounded like human screams. Yeah! Metal was back and it wouldn't go away again.

First team: Kerry King (g), Tom Araya (v, b), Jeff Hanneman (g), Dave Lombardo (d)

Place, time, scene: Los Angeles 1983. Slayer were the west-coast branch of the new thrash-metal scene that also included Metallica, Megadeath and Anthrax. The need for speed and attitude had been inspired primarily by the new wave of British heavy metal led by Iron Maiden, who cranked the volume and the screaming up in the face of punk. Pretty soon there were death, doom, and speed metal bands, as a scene which had stayed underground in the US, but vibrant and independent, internationally exploded into the void that had been created by the decline of hardcore punk.

What to buy first: *Reign In Blood* 1987

And then: *South Of Heaven* 1988

In retrospect: *Decade Of Aggression* (live) 1998

SLINT

Musically speaking, it's not really clear where Slint came from. Their big idea was that the guitar didn't have to be the main star of rock music, it could take a more democratic role and allow other instruments to have the opportunity to take the music off in other directions. Similarly, the vocalist didn't need to be so obvious either, and traditional song structures, well, they could go out the window. Slint made two albums which launched what has since been dubbed 'post-rock', which claims to deconstruct traditional rock practice through careful and mathematical precision. It's all about which chords go where and at what point the tempo changes to create the most unexpected and disturbing effect. Steve Albini, who knows a thing or two about disturbing people, loves Slint.

Led by guitarist Brain McMahan and drummer Britt Walford formerly of Kentucky-based band Squirrel Bait, Slint were formed in 1988. The other two members were guitarist David Pajo and bassist Ethan Buckler. For the first album *Tweez*, they enlisted the Touch & Go label's house producer Steve Albini to work with them, and immediately nailed their combination of loud abrasive guitar, almost inaudible vocals and upfront drums – an Albini speciality. Each of the songs is named after band members' pets, perhaps an acknowledgement that the songs themselves are irrelevant, it's the sound that counts. Some sections are packed with the stuff, others are more sparse, the volume sometimes matches the density of sound, sometimes doesn't and the speed at which everything happens veers from ultra-fast to tortoise-slow.

Having learned some useful lessons from their time with Albini, Slint's second album, featuring new bassist Todd Brashear, was an innovative masterpiece. This time there were songs propelled by bass and with guitars and voice synchronized. They constructed songs that made the most of the dynamics of hard and soft passages in their music. Where grunge and emo bands had distinct breaks where the guitars crashed in and the vocals went from almost spoken to screamed, the drums acting as a kind of starting pistol for the melee to begin (think 'Teen Spirit' and you've got the idea), Slint did the same but made the transition when it was least expected. For 'Good Morning

Captain' the bass and drums are right up front while McMahan speaks over a fairly sparse introductory section, off-kilter guitar separates the verses and then with one minute of a seven minute song to go, all hell breaks loose with McMahan screaming so hard it reputedly made him sick. 'Nosferatu Man' appears to have a repeated bass note played and sustained throughout as guitars scrawl and crawl over the hard-working drums, spider-like and creepy, hence the album title, *Spiderland*.

The band, who played less than 30 live shows, never recorded together again such was the intensity of the experience of making their second album. Rumour has it that one member took psychiatric advice soon after its completion. David Pajo joined forces with John McEntire in Tortoise who became leaders of the Chicago-based post-rock movement, while Britt Walford joined the Breeders and later the Palace Brothers with a revitalized McMahan who now operates as The For Carnation.

First team: Brian McMahan (g, v), Britt Walford (d), David Pajo (g), Todd Brashear (b)

Place, time, scene: Kentucky 1989. Slint were formed out of the ashes of the experimental Squirrel Bait, which also included David G. Stubbs, and Archer Prewitt, later to form Gastr Del Sol and the Sea And Cake. Their musical approach may have some antecedents in the no-wave scene in New York in the early 1980s and in the experimentation of Sonic Youth and the production techniques favoured by Steve Albini. They instigated the 'post-rock' genre which now includes Tortoise, the Sea And Cake, Mogwai, Sigur Ros and Godspeed You Black Emperor amongst others. It's a state of mind more than a set of musical rules.

What to buy first: *Spiderland* 1991

And then: *Tweez* 1989

SLY AND THE FAMILY STONE

Rhythm and blues-based music got split in two at some point in 1963, and to the collective shame of all involved, the boundary was drawn with colour in mind. Somehow this got mapped onto an accepted idea that if you were white you could do your own R&B. Form the band, play the music, write new R&B-based songs and if you had the wherewithal to do it, get experi-mental on R&B's ass. If you were black, you could sing and ... well, dance. The possibilities of developing popular music from an R&B base were so great, both in terms of musical innovation and commercial reward, that major record labels were bending over backwards to accommodate artists who wanted to try something different. White R&B got a new name, rock. So did black R&B; it took on the generic descriptor, soul, a term which emphasized the emotional aspect of the music which was evident in the directness of the singing, and the subject matter which dealt almost exclusively with matters of the heart.

Unfortunately, this drew attention away from the musicianship, and lessened the chances of songs that spoke about society, politics, philosophical ideas and pretty much anything that took popular music in new and interesting directions. It wasn't just a corporate thing. Motown, the most successful black music label of the period, was an independent, and yet it kept black music simple and formulaic. The musicians that played on the production line of hits were black but they were generally heard and not seen, instead the stage was filled with dancers and spare singers. When the definitive soul label, Atlantic Records, decided to add a little rock to their artist roster, they went for Vanilla Fudge and Led Zeppelin. By 1968, with one or two notable exceptions, the potential that had existed back in the late 1950s when both black and white rock'n'rollers were knocking out epoch-defining songs sowing the seeds for a more tolerant culture and society in general, had been squandered. The world of music needed Sly And The Family Stone.

By 1964, Sylvester Stewart was a songwriter and producer at Autumn Studios in San Francisco. He was 20 years old and had already been making records for 16 years, having played drums and guitar on a song recorded by his family when he was four! He spent his high school years in various bands and while working at Autumn DJ'd on hit music stations, KSOL and after that KDIA. He produced hits for the Mojo Men and the Beau Brummels, both bands at the forefront of the San Franciscan folk-rock scene, and by 1966 having taken on board everything he had learned up to that point, he put together his own band, the Stoners. A good name, I think you'll agree, for a psychedelic soul band.

Following an expedient change of name, the Epic label signed Sly And The Family Stone later that year and the band, which consisted of trumpeter Cynthia Robinson, sax-player Jerry Martini, pianist Rosie Stone, guitarist Freddie Stone, drummer Greg Errico and most importantly, bassist Larry Graham, put out their debut album *A Whole New Thing* in 1967, a collection which combined the energy of the best Motown pop with the latest psychedelic licks and socially-aware lyrics. It was quickly followed by a single, 'Dance To The Music', which successfully deconstructed the technical skills that went into the making of a contemporary R&B record by introducing each element from drums through to voices. It emphasized that the Family Stone were most definitely a band, and a damned funky one at that.

Three more albums followed in under two years, each one further perfecting the blend of rock and soul styles by creating a groove out of fuzz guitar, bottom-end bass and horns. *Stand*, released in 1969 was one long positivity trip. 'Everyday People' and 'I Want To Take You Higher', which both celebrated the potential of contemporary life, were matched up with a warning song, 'Don't Call Me Nigger Whitey' which in the lyric pulls the old vice versa trick, making it an anthem for progressive cultural unity.

There's A Riot Goin' On, which followed *Stand* in 1971, is the last great Family Stone album, which is a testament to the band's innate understanding of their craft. To be frank, Sly Stone was out of control. The drugs had kicked in big time by the time they hit the studio which, considering the fact that they rarely got it together enough to play live, was an achievement in itself. Stories abound of stoned Stone sessions, incorporating a succession of lady friends who were invited back for a little night jamming and were recorded getting down if you catch my drift. Still, it contains the band's most sinister and simultaneously soulful moment, the incest-inspired 'Family Affair' and a whole stack of musically out-there rock/funk joints that must have inspired George Clinton to take it to the next level with his band Funkadelic. Sly And The Family Stone lasted another few albums but were torpedoed below sea level and they went down slowly and painfully before calling it a day at the end of the 1970s.

First team: Sylvester Stewart (v, k), Larry Graham (b), Cynthia Robinson (tr), Jerry Martini (sx), Rosie Stone (p), Freddie Stone (g), Greg Errico (d)

Place, time, scene: San Francisco 1966. Sly And The Family Stone were a kickin' rhythm and blues band which incorporated psychedelic folk-rock into their music. Sly Stewart's background producing rock and folk artists was a key factor. Their multi-race, male/female line-up was also a first. The music and the philosophy were carried over into George Clinton's Funkadelic and later on, Prince and Afrika Bambaataa and the Zulu Nation.

What to buy first: *Stand* 1969

And then: *There's A Riot Goin' On* 1971

In retrospect: *The Best Of Sly And The Family Stone* 1992

SMITHS

The Smiths were frank. Even the name was chosen to avoid unnecessary confusion and was an attempt to discourage critics and fans from tracing the historical circumstances and cultural references associated with its use. The music was always straightforward and effortlessly simplistic, beautiful and rhythmic. The lyrics were direct and concise. Yet for a period of four years, during which the Smiths notched up enough hit singles to comfortably fill two greatest hits albums and four albums which proved to be critical and commercial successes, the attempts to understand the band and in particular unmask the charlatan posing as Morrissey, were relentless. The Smiths did it all so easily that somewhere surely somebody was getting conned? Critics were voracious in their negativity. The music ripped off the Bunnymen and REM, the singer couldn't carry a tune, and the subject matter was self-pitying and on occasion downright distasteful. But then similar things were said about the Sex Pistols who were equally as direct. It was the bands in between that were surely more worthy of suspicion, the post-punks who hid behind complex musical techniques and oblique lyrics, or the rabble-rousers who preached lifestyles and quoted punk lore about the necessities of creative innovation and DIY ethics. Morrissey was there that night in Manchester at the Lesser Free Trade Hall when the Sex Pistols took the north all guns blazing. Just like his heroes Oscar Wilde, James Dean and Johnny Thunders, Johnny Rotten must have struck Morrissey, firstly as a star complete with his own unique, perhaps affected, personality, and secondly as someone with a message. Unlike other punk visionaries, Rotten did not profess to have any answers, he simply said what he thought. The words delivered with wit and irony, the underlying themes: loathing and despair. Sound familiar?

The first track on the eponymous debut album by the Smiths begins with the line 'It's time the tale were told ...' and it's a fitting introduction to a back-catalogue of songs that, put bluntly, tell stories. Morrissey's youthful preoccupations were literature, cinema and pop music. He ran the New York Dolls UK fan club and wrote a book about James Dean. He also expended a good deal of energy writing letters and reviews to the music press. By the time he was composing lyrics for songs with Johnny Marr, he had mastered a variety of writing styles, and was particularly adept at the pithy Wilde-styled ironic one-liners that fitted perfectly within the pop song medium. These were dropped into stories for maximum impact. He was able to write about issues that related directly to himself, songs that addressed a wider topic but which were told through his own experience, and songs that dealt with specific events and issues in which he did not feature at all. Criticisms that he was narcissistic and self-pitying are just plain wrong. 'Suffer Little Children' may be based on events (the Moors Murders) that impacted on his childhood, but the song is specifically about the murders and the way in which they reflected on Manchester as a whole. It has nothing to do with Morrissey himself. He's telling a tale. More recently, Eminem has suffered the same ignominious criticisms from those keen to ensure that pop music never succeeds in becoming a valid form of expression in line with other more traditional artistic pursuits.

The Smiths made pop music literate. Dylan, Drake and Cohen had brought in poetry, both symbolic and surreal, but Morrissey, alongside bands like the Go-Betweens and Nick Cave, described situations and invoked a narrative voice that had not been fully explored before. 'This Night Has Opened My Eyes',

The Smiths

a previously unreleased track which appears on *Hatful Of Hollow*, is the tragic story of a woman who has to give away her unwanted baby and is inspired by the film *A Taste Of Honey*, 'The Headmaster Ritual' looks back to a pre liberal violent school system, and 'Rusholme Ruffians' is a seedy night out at the fair. Elsewhere the imagery is evocative too, especially the scene-setting first lines: 'Punctured bicycle on a hillside desolate', 'Park the car at the side of the road', 'A dreaded sunny day, so I'll meet you at the cemetery gates' and so on. His lyrics are nostalgic, although criticisms are still made claiming that they paid little attention to contemporary, multi-cultural Britain. But that's just missing the point.

Julia Stringer has pointed out that Smiths lyrics relate to a social type that was not often represented in pop music, namely the sensitive young adult.[59] The band had formed against a backdrop of war in the Falklands and all of the xenophobia that went with it. Lads were lads and the British were bulldogs. Goths of course, had a sensitive side but over-romanticized life and revelled in self-pitying angst. Morrissey never did either of these things. He wrote from a realist standpoint and when he was properly romantic, it could kill you. 'There Is A Light That Never Goes

Out' is the best example of that, the imagery of a road accident accompanied by the line 'to die by your side, well the pleasure and the privilege is mine'.

The key pre-occupation for Morrissey was of course sex and sexuality, mostly his lack of it, and an inability to decide what sort of sex he wanted if indeed he wanted any at all. Pete Shelley seemed to have the same issues during his time with the Buzzcocks. On record, both deal with the subject humorously and aren't afraid to get a little crude at times too. Morrissey is at his best when he's being cheeky – 'it was dark as I drove the point home' – and he's no slouch when it comes to being funny, romantic or angry either. *Meat Is Murder*, the second album, released in 1985, captures Morrissey developing his writing and Marr and the band experimenting with different arrangements and styles, which gel impressively on tracks like 'The Headmaster Ritual' and 'That Joke Isn't Funny Anymore', and most obviously, the B-side which became the band's most requested song, 'How Soon Is Now', which combined an awesome slow groove with a mournful guitar that mirrors the despairing lyrics perfectly. Across the album, Marr's guitar-playing is immaculate – the sparse, electrified jangle and chime has never been bettered.

But if *Meat Is Murder* is a great album, then *The Queen Is Dead* is a magnificient one. Kicking off with the wilfully confrontational title track, the heaviest thing the band ever did – huge drums, wah wah guitar and Andy Rourke's trademark busy Motown-inflected bass – the album moves through a variety of styles and textures and features Morrissey at his lyrical zenith. 'Cemetery Gates' is a cautionary tale aimed at those who might pretend to be something they're not, cleverly setting up Morrissey as the master of the one-upmanship that he warns against – always there with an answer and a witty riposte because he's read well and Wilde is on his side. 'Vicar In A Tutu' commences with the deliciously sketch-show image 'I was minding my business lifting some lead off the roof of the holy new church', and proceeds to a scenario that is provincial yet surreal, with Rose collecting money in a canister while the vicar in a tutu comes sliding down the banister. It's a piece of well-observed social commentary concerning the current state of church-based religion, and is Freud-rude at the same time.

In the ten months that followed *The Queen Is Dead*, the band knocked out four singles that rank amongst the best British pop released up to that point, namely 'Panic', 'Ask', 'Shoplifters Of The World Unite' and 'Sheila Take A Bow', and with barely a year gone since their last album, issued their fourth and final collection, *Strangeways Here We Come*. The album was morbid in places, with several tracks dwelling on death and depression. 'Last Night I Dreamt That Somebody Loved Me' commences with over a minute and a half of foreboding major chords and disconcerting background chatter, before launching into Morrissey's most sustained self-pity yet, 'Unhappy Birthday' is just plain mean, and 'Girlfriend In A Coma' is a particularly negative context for a love song. There are still a few cheeky smiles to be had of course – 'I grabbed you by gilded beams, that's what tradition means' – but overall the fractured sound of the album signified the end of the band who had effectively split before the album was released. They left the indie world in 1988 and although Morrissey in particular had a few more moments of genius left in him (*Viva Hate* in 1988, *Your Arsenal* in 1992, *Vauxhall And I* in 1994), song-based music missed the Smiths. They had shown that loud guitar music and sensitivity actually did go together after all. If there had been a gender bias in alternative music, they put paid to it, and demonstrated to blokes who might be considering a few years in a hard rock band, perhaps around the Seattle area, that it was okay to be sensitive.

First team: Morrissey (v), Johnny Marr (g, p), Andy Rourke (b), Mike Joyce (d)

Place, time, scene: Manchester 1982. The Smiths succeeded where Orange Juice had failed in bringing a new sensitivity to alternative music. Johnny Marr's immaculate guitar-playing certainly helped, making for a memorable overall sound when supporting such an unusual voice with perfectly executed bright and catchy guitar riffs and jangles. The northern-soul feel of Rourke's bass made the band danceable too. The *NME* recently conducted a poll amongst musicians and critics who picked the band as the most influential artists of the rock era, suggesting that the combination of personal lyrics and classic pop structures are still held in high regard among musicians and are ultimately more important than experimental and stylistic concerns. The Smiths split in 1988 as dance music and heavy rock styles took over. Indie music has never quite recovered or again come close to their archetypal sound.

What to buy first: *The Queen Is Dead* 1986

And then: *The Smiths* 1984, *Meat Is Murder* 1985, *Strangeways Here We Come* 1987

In retrospect: *Hatful of Hollow* 1984, *Louder Than Bombs* 1987, *Singles* 1995

PATTI SMITH

Just to take a rock chick at random on the subject of Patti Smith, I'll use Carla Bozulich of country hardcore fem-rockers the Geraldine Fibbers, who explains most eloquently her first exposure to the punk poetess: 'When I was 12 I saw her do "Gloria" on television. She disturbed me. She was the most defiant woman I had ever seen. No make-up, no bra. Unshaved. Singing about another chick. This one had circumvented everything by which other women had secretly agreed to abide. She didn't care about seeming sweet, or pretty or nice, or fuckable. It was dirty, like the insides of a real person.'[60]

And it's safe to say that other female rock icons such as PJ Harvey, Kat Bjelland, Courtney Love and Björk would say something very similar. She made it so gender just didn't matter anymore when you were making meaningful rock music. There are those that will argue that she adopted a self-consciously non-feminine pose, but what the hell does that mean? She's a woman, isn't she? How much more feminine do you want to get? A better argument might be that she sneaked into rock music through the backdoor, being a published writer and poet for several years before she chose music as her medium of expression, but she still did her time out on the road before starting work on her first album, and was a key draw at CBGB's right from the start. And it was her spoken-word background which she incorporated into the rock format that is her lasting legacy. John Cooper Clarke and Henry Rollins have literally followed her style, while the likes of Michael Stipe in his early days tried to emulate her apparent stream of con-

ciousness-tumbling word formations. Nobody could do it like Patti though.

She was born in Chicago and left school to work in a factory. Pregnant at an early age, she gave up the baby for adoption and buried herself in symbolist poetry and painting during which time she met Bobby Neuwirth, a friend of Bob Dylan, who took her to New York where a conversation with rock critic and guitarist Lenny Kaye led to the formation of a band which would help her become 'a leather Liza Minelli'. The poetry publications and the single 'Piss Factory', inspired by her earlier 9–5 life, got her some influential friends including Lou Reed, who told Clive Davis of Arista Records that he should sign her immediately, and within the year Reed's old sparring partner John Cale was recording her rock-poetry in Electric Lady studios, New York.

Right from the off, the *Horses* album demonstrated her innate understanding of the rhythmic power of words. 'Land', the epic centrepiece of the album, tells the story of male rape in an American college set to the groove of Wilson Pickett's 'Land Of A 1000 Dances'. The beginning of the song is spoken evocatively, as you would expect from a poet, and the music builds as the horrific story is told until the boy floats off into a dream of fiery horses. As Smith sings 'And then he saw, horses, horses, horses, horses . . .' Lenny Kaye brings the band in and Smith hits the vocal as the band crunches into the Pickett number, without missing a beat. Her version of Them's 'Gloria' follows a similar pattern, 'Jesus died for somebody's sins but not mine' goes the lyric before the rock'n'roll rhythm strikes in to offer salvation.

The whole album is about the power of rock'n' roll redemption, using the key motifs of sex and death. 'Redondo Beach' deals with a lesbian's suicide, 'Birdland' is about a boy's dreamtime visit to his dead father, and 'Elegie' is a paean to Jimi Hendrix. Throughout, Patti Smith plays the rock'n'roll shaman, but minus the bulge down the front of her trousers that Jim Morrison was so keen to display.

Patti made three more albums in the following years of which *Easter* was the most successful critically and commercially. The cover photo featured her bra-less, and she went to the trouble of masturbating over the picture to check that teenage boys would be able to get off on the image. The album itself were a collection of concise rock songs, tightly played by the band and sung emotionally by Smith. The epic and yearning 'Because The Night', which she co-wrote with Bruce Springsteen, was a major hit on FM radio and would have launched her as a major star had she not started taking it all a bit too seriously. On *Waves* she lost touch with the primal energy and shamanic spirit that had made her so listenable and with the album's consequent failure she gave the whole thing up, instead choosing to live with her husband Fred Smith, formerly of the MC5 and another ex-rock visionary.

Dream Of Life was released in 1988 but was again lacking in focus and power. It was tragically with the death of her husband that she found her voice again, notably on the 1996 album *Gone Again*, a touching tribute to her soul-mate, that captures Smith again at her most intense with heart aching. When she joined REM for their magnificant 1996 single 'E-Bow The Letter', her significant contribution to rock music was once again confirmed.

First team: Patti Smith (v, g), Lenny Kaye (g), Ivan Kral (b), Richard Sohl (p), Jay Dee Daugherty (d)

Place, time, scene: New York 1972. Patti Smith came into rock'n'roll from the New York boho art set and immediately set the music alight with her track 'Piss Factory'. Her no-nonsense approach made her an awesome female role-model for those that saw her perform, and inspired a deepness and sensitivity in other performers keen to emulate her powerful writing and delivery. Michael Stipe began his time with REM attempting to incorporate the stream of consciousness poetry and symbolism that was her trademark.

What to buy first: *Horses* 1975

And then: *Easter* 1978

SMOG

As far as misnomers go, the term hi-fi has got to qualify as one of the worst. The thinking was that improved recording technology, and the ability to add volume and beef up voices and instruments in the mixing process meant higher fidelity, or, to put it another way,

more truth. In the seventies it tended to be used to describe domestic sound systems that were growing ever more equal to the task of reproducing the subtle nuances of sound being created in the studio, and it all came together in the magnificent and sonically multi-faceted work of . . . Dire Straits. Compact discs were the obvious next stage – they were mostly digital sound which made everything even more hi-fi. It was all done with the listener in mind of course, and was nothing to do with the discovery of a completely new format opportunity that enabled major entertainment corporations to flog everything again, those old vinyl LPs having given up the ghost by then. But I digress. The real truth about hi-fi was that, to put it bluntly, it destroyed truth.

Bands could no longer reproduce live what they had attained on disc. There's a limit to how many guitars can be played at once, and the extent to which a human voice can operate in several different temporal and spatial realities at once. Bands could use snazzy tapes and stuff but that ain't really that truthful now is it? By the late eighties the situation was getting out of control. Bands were playing gigs where they played the album and that was it. It took so long to set up the fantasy sonic surroundings that to break away from that particular aesthetic and do an older track or, heaven forbid, something that they might want to try out on the road before they recorded it, was impossible. And that's where lo-fi came in. Of course, lo-fi wasn't lo-fi at all, it was fuckin' hi-fi. Those bedroom musicians who laid down their own songs on 4-track mixers had no gimmicks to hide behind, their music was truth! The first songwriter to get landed with the term was Daniel Johnston, although all he was doing really was taking up where first Robert Johnson and later Nick Drake had left off. Basic music and straight vocals. The difference was that Johnston's music was quirky and clever compared to his forerunners stark brutal honesty. It was a few years after Johnston started that a more obvious successor, particularly to Drake, came along. His name was Bill Callahan and he operated under the nom de musique, Smog.

Bill Callahan may have started by recording his music at home on a 4-track mixer and then progressed to a 24-track studio to work with some of the great studio techno-musos currently available, but despite the transition he has kept to his original plan, and continues to create minimalist music that is sometimes so soft and fragile that it hardly seems to be there at all. But then again, he also makes very loud music too. The key thing is that at all times the music is kept separate from his deep, resonant vocals. Callahan's strength is in his words, and unlike fellow lo-fiers like Slint, who hid the voice deep within the mix, sound is only a part of what Callahan focuses on.

First and foremost, he is a lyricist, specializing in mature, reflective and significance-packed storytelling. And he knows it too, that's why he speak-sings his words slowly and deliberately and leaves space after each line for you to take in what he has just said. A line like 'our sentences will not be served, we are constantly on trial' may crop up in a story about Callahan the prison guard taking the prisoners swimming, but his delivery gives it a resonance far beyond that particular scenario. And 'Father left at eight, nearly splintering the gate' is a lesson in concise writing where an entire story is told in just a few words.

Both come from songs on the 1999 album *Knock Knock*, which is perhaps his most accessible and positive sounding collection! Under normal circumstances, bleak and black are the order of the day, yet like other so-called miserablists, there's something about the combination of confident, open vocals and minimalist arrangements that just reeks of positivity. Callahan, like Drake and Cohen before him, is not afraid to speak difficult truths. 'And when I think about my brother dying and my parents trying to slowly do themselves in inch by inch, day by day' it's because he's up there saying it and not avoiding the issue that makes it seem possible to say anything, no matter how painful, to experience a form of catharsis.

If anything, his albums have got better and better with every release. The last few, *Knock Knock*, *Red Apple Falls* and *Rain On Lens* have also benefited from production input or creative advice from some of the best in the business. Jim O'Rourke and John McEntire have helped Callahan develop his musical textures without compromising his basic approach and I'll tell you what, take a listen on a really good hi-fi through ridiculously expensive headphones and you'll be in for a real aural treat.

First team: Bill Callahan (v, g, k, p)

Place, time, scene: Silver Springs, Maryland 1988. Bill Callahan's gloomy and pessimistic songs arrived at a time when American independent music was embracing stoner, Generation X culture and building a set of local scenes to help deal with the dissaffection. Before long, grunge had become a fashion statement and new artists and groups found themselves making a choice between assimilation into a commercial underground or ironic piss-taking. Throughout it all Smog kept it introspective and brutally honest, and with a sparse skeletal sound dubbed 'lo fi' provided a new aesthetic for music-making, specifically taken up and identified as 'sad-core' by the likes of Will Oldham (Palace) and David Berman (Silver Jews) but which also provided a source of inspiration for the more mocking songs of Pavement and Sebadoh.

What to buy first: *Julius Caesar* 1993

And then: *The Doctor Came At Dawn* 1996, *Red Apple Falls* 1997, *Knock Knock* 1999, *Rain On Lens* 2001

SOFT MACHINE

In 1964 if you wanted an alternative to the Beatles you had to look outside pop music. They were better at it than anybody else, and had made teen music cool again after the era of teen idols and bad Elvis impersonators. If like Londoner Robert Wyatt you wanted an alternative, then it had to be jazz – Ornette Coleman and John Coltrane, free jazz, the type that Beefheart, Reed and Zappa were also listening to on the other side of the Atlantic. Wyatt, like his American counterparts, was not a jazz musician, he wanted to make pop music, only he thought it could be done differently.

In 1962 Wyatt met Australian Daevid Allen who wrote poetry and had spent the last year living in Paris at the Beat Hotel with William S. Burroughs and Allen Ginsberg. Together with Wyatt's friend Hugh Hopper who would contribute looped sounds to Wyatt's drumming and Allen's poetry, an art project was considered, but when Allen left again on his travels, the two remaining found keyboardist Mike Ratledge and instead formed the Wilde Flowers which played around the Canterbury area giving rise to the scene of the same name. The Wilde Flowers invented prog-rock. It was 1965.

A year later the band had changed its name to Soft Machine and had expanded with the addition of guitarist Kevin Ayers. They played at the Roundhouse and the UFO clubs in London alongside Pink Floyd, and gradually extended their songs as the audience made the crucial shift from dancing to gyrating to sitting down on the floor listening. Allen was drafted back into the band when they visited Paris and recorded a session, but he had gone again before a second session in America which produced the first Soft Machine album in 1968. It was free-form rock'n'roll. Wyatt kept slightly squiffy beats while Ayers' guitar solos floated over the top and off into the distance, rejoining the rest of the band at a later point many musical bars further into the song. With Ratledge's keyboard set to distort, the sound was pure psychedelia.

The songs that Soft Machine had were far from drippy though. 'Joy Of A Toy' is a thinly-veiled attack on manufactured band the Monkees, delivered in a proto-Richman style that is best described as ambivalent and disinterested. Syd Barrett adopted a similar style in Pink Floyd, and both bands were effectively undermining false singing styles that were supposed to pass for sincerity in other parts of the pop world.

Ayers left after the first album and headed for Ibiza, and soon formed his own band the Whole World, who continued to make odd but appealing psychedelia for the next two decades. In 1970 Soft Machine made *Third*, an album that didn't include a guitarist at all. The noodling psychedelia had been replaced by a stricter modal approach to structuring songs, and allowed each member of the band one side of a double-album to go to work on. New boy Hugh Hopper had horns emerging out of a electronic wash, and then proceeding to what is effectively noise and all kinds of looped sounds on tape, oh and flutes, lots of flutes. The Wyatt piece, 'Moon In June' is similar to earlier 'poppy' Soft Machine to begin with, but then moves into jazz-rock territory with a superb bass solo and keyboards played off against one another while Wyatt sings wordlessly.

He left after one more album and Soft Machine, having invented prog-rock, then proceeded to give it a bad name with a succession of unfocused but cleverly played albums. Wyatt embarked on a sporadic solo career which peaked with the album *Rock Bottom*, written and recorded after a tragic accident which has kept him in a wheelchair ever since. In 1982 he recorded a version of Elvis Costello's 'Shipbuilding' which many believe to be one of the best interpreted covers of a song ever made.

First team: Robert Wyatt (d, v), Mike Ratledge (k), Hugh Hopper (k, b, tape), Kevin Ayers (g, v)1

Place, time, scene: Canterbury 1966. Soft Machine made a jazzy form of psychedelia, featuring satirical and surreal lyrics and experimental playing. They played the same underground clubs as Pink Floyd but by their third album had moved away from rock as the basis of their sound and instead focused on modal forms of jazz that could sound harsh and unrelenting at times.

What to buy first: *Soft Machine* 1968

And then: *Third* 1970, Kevin Ayers: *Joy Of A Toy* 1969, Robert Wyatt: *Rock Bottom* 1974

SONIC YOUTH

Sonic Youth have always been just that little bit out of step with prevailing music trends. They were just too late for the first wave of New York punk, had too many old sixties records to really fall for the anti-history of hardcore, and had too much long-term ambition for the here and now of no-wave. Their music and approach though, is in essence a mixture of all three, an achievement which demonstrates their acute awareness of styles and how they can be used for optimum effect. Their experimental blend of hard music has survived where the original sounds and ideas have fallen by the wayside, and because they have resisted the Talking Heads route of progression, preferring to combine textures and sounds rather than styles and content, Sonic Youth remain a touchstone of alternative music, an invaluable source of learning material for the bands that have followed them. For over 20 years the band has been at the heart of an expanding and mutating music scene. It means that when Sonic Youth make recommendations, people listen. They were key to the increased cultural awareness of contemporary Japanese music and were integral in the major label signing of both Hüsker Dü and Nirvana. They are as much part of the art world as

Sonic Youth

the independent music world and have a cultured and mature approach to music which transcends any specific time or place. Sonic Youth have the potential to be cool forever.

Thurston Moore arrived in New York when the CBGBs scene was in full swing. He loved the Ramones and Television, Johnny Thunders and Patti Smith, the dumb-ass thrash and the clever conceits. He hung around to watch the next lot to come along too, namely the Contortions and Teenage Jesus And The Jerks who briefly perfected the blend of energy and art dubbed no-wave, but what really knocked Thurston Moore sideways was Glenn Branca's guitar sextet. The idea was to experiment with the textural and harmonic possibilities of electrified strings. Play it loud and it's like being in a sonic wind tunnel. Moore booked Branca to play at a noise festival he was organizing and sounded-out guitarist Lee Ranaldo on the idea of

forming a band to harness guitar noise within a rock band structure. With Moore's new girlfriend, the artist Kim Gordon, playing rudimentary straight-forward bass and Richard Edson playing jazz drums, Sonic Youth set their guitars to stun and began the process of reinventing the sound of rock music.

Moore and Ranaldo did not tune their guitars in the traditional way, making for unexpected harmonics and expected dissonance between the two players. By placing pieces of metal, paper or rubber under the strings at certain points on the fret-board and striking the strings in a certain way, the sound could be further distorted. With practice and a process of trial and error whole sections could be developed. Throw in a hardcore drummer to replace Edson, a guy named Bob Bert, and a bass-player who could be taught to play specific bass patterns and the effect was every-thing modern art should be, difficult and ground-breaking. Sonic Youth live meant lots of guitars, all tuned differently, and lots of hanging around between songs while the correct sound was achieved. Once the two guitarists had internalized the tangible possibilities of their sound though, there was no stopping them.

The early thrashy hardcore-inspired sound gradually gave way to something more controlled. Short musical interludes were developed in between the more epic pieces and by the time they recorded the 1984 album *Bad Moon Rising* the band had even got itself a neat groove going too. There was something compulsive about 'I'm Insane' and 'Death Valley 69', featuring no-wave icon Lydia Lunch, which dealt with that perennial American enigma, the Family Murders, and was actually built around a chunky riff. The album was well-received in the UK and was surely an inspiration for Jesus And Mary Chain, My Bloody Valentine, Spacemen 3 and the new psychedelia which led ultimately to the rock/dance crossover at the end of the decade.

Sonic Youth followed it up with *EVOL* featuring new drummer Steve Shelley. It was released on the SST label but was still very much a New York album. There's still the familiar Velvet Underground drone sound and in the lyrics, a dark fascination with celebrity and popular culture. 'Madonna, Sean And Me (Expressway To Yr Skull)' is the beginning of their apparent obsession with the ambitious blonde, which even ran to a side project dubbed Ciccone Youth and a cover of her 'Into The Groove'. In the mid-eighties, the puritanical nature of the independent music scene was starting to feel a little silly and immature when set against the new cool of mainstream artists like Madonna and Prince who were clearly sussed up when it came to making music on their own terms, tearing down the accepted social structure as they went. Sonic Youth had enough confidence in the challenging nature of their own music that they didn't shy away from mainstream mingling. Kim Gordon certainly scrubbed up well when she opted for a different look, and the band even found the time to organize a tribute album to the Carpenters, explaining that uber-geek and pin-up boy for the sixties squares, Richard Carpenter, had been an inspiration to them all along. The best track on *EVOL* is the last one 'Expressway To Your Skull'. It's the definitive Sonic Youth track, and the one which *The Wire* magazine tellingly chose to include on their retrospective

triple-album set charting the development of avant-garde music across the century, released in 2002. The dynamics are perfectly realized, gale-force guitars giving way to the reflective quiet after the storm. Hell, Neil Young loves it too.

Sister followed in 1987, largely inspired by Philip K. Dick's dystopian writing and aspects of his personal life. Frank Zappa would have called it a project. Take an idea, develop it, perfect it and move on. *Sister* is a Sonic Youth rock-chugger of an album which attempts to make their harsh, dissonant and sometimes cold electric lash sound just a bit more human. Of course, they can't ultimately succeed because their sound is too alien to be considered traditional, just like the futuristic robots in Dick's 'Do Androids Dream Of Electric Sheep'. But then, on the follow-up *Daydream Nation*, they actually transcend the dissonance of their sound. More than just a project, *Daydream Nation* was the culmination of everything they had learned, played with feeling, from the soul. *Daydream Nation* feels real. Listening to the album is an emotional experience, and the fact that so many sections are off-kilter and out of tune just adds to the pathos exuding from the album. Its pervading themes are still alienation and isolation in a world fast losing its grasp on, or concern for, truth. The opener 'Teenage Riot' sets the scene, bemoaning the lack of real direction in supposedly oppositional youth culture, a realization that anarchy and liberation is not just around the corner. It's delivered in the first person too, less angry and disappointed than Johnny Rotten, and not so heartfelt and whiny as Kurt Cobain, it's just delivered. The album veers between low-down dirty rock and scrawl and the ornate orchestration of carefully arranged guitar noise, finishing with the suitably epic album-in-microcosm of 'Trilogy'.

Sonic Youth signed with Geffen for their next album, *Goo*, and have remained with them ever since. Three albums standout: *Dirty*, *Washing Machine* and *A Thousand Leaves*, but really, taken at random, anything by Sonic Youth has the potential to make the listener stop and consider for a moment. The sound they make is always just that little bit wrong, and that's the thing that makes Sonic Youth oh so right.

First team: Thurston Moore (v, g), Lee Ranaldo (g, v), Kim Gordon (v, b), Steve Shelley (d)

Place, time, scene: New York 1980. Sonic Youth were most closely linked with the no-wave noise-inspired scene that brought together the art community with the independent music scene of the time. They were the only band to make anything of their early noise beginnings and inspired bands on both sides of the Atlantic, notably Dinosaur Jr, Big Black, Jesus And Mary Chain and My Bloody Valentine.

What to buy first: *Daydream Nation* 1988

And then: *Bad Moon Rising* 1985, *EVOL* 1986, *Sister* 1987, *Washing Machine* 1994, *A Thousand Leaves* 1997

SPACEMEN 3

There used to be a little family-run record store in Rugby town centre that for years put up an impressive period of resistance against the high street record retailers who would normally swallow whole such small-town demand for recorded music. The thing that kept them going, and the reason that other independent retailers lasted to the end of the eighties, and depending on their white-label policies, into the nineties, was a reputation amongst music fanatics for having a caring ordering policy. The corporate boys didn't bother with import distributors like Pinnacle and Greyhound, they didn't take the time to go out back to the bloke in the SPS van who had all those discontinued releases, and rarely had enough to reach the minimum order requirement for all those cool independent distributors like Southern, APT, Ninemile, Rough Trade and Jetstar. Of course, the little independent stores struggled to get the minimum order too but then a few exceptions were made in the name of the ongoing battle against 'the man'.

Anyway, if Jason Pierce or the enigmatically named Sonic Boom (real name Pete Kember), pioneers of 'record-collection' rock, wanted to get an obscure release by the 13th Floor Elevators, Glenn Branca or Can, then a small 'mom and pop' shop was the place to go – they'd order it, it might take a few months to come through, but eventually they'd get it. I once served Sonic Boom in the Rugby Our Price store, but we never got enough together for a minimum order of the album he wanted. Mind you, by then Spacemen 3 were no more, Sonic Boom was pursuing his fascina-

tion with contemporary psychedelia in Spectrum, and Jason Pierce was on the verge of mainstream success with Spiritualized. It was payback time for their innovative years fusing repetitive waves of white guitar noise with a laid-back spiritualist vibe that some have gone as far as to call gospel music.

The obvious comparison is with Sonic Youth who had just released their opus *Daydream Nation* when Spacemen 3 formed, but where Sonic Youth were interested in noise as a textural project that impacted directly on the body and the ear at a physical level, Spacemen 3 wanted to get at your soul. Their initial recordings were made in Northampton in 1986 and are available on the reissued *Taking Drugs To Make Music To Take Drugs To.* By their second album *The Perfect Prescription* (spot the connection), they had filled out their thin white sound with a greater understanding of the sonic possibilities of playing the same few chords over and over again at full volume and with full effects. Throw some occasional lyrics on top that, mainly about the transcendental possibilities of getting monged, and you have the perfect music to take drugs to, or just pretend you are taking drugs to, if you like. The album contained covers of songs by Red Krayola and Roky Erickson's pre-13th Floor Elevators band the Spades, plus Spacemen originals that sound as fresh and alien today as they did then. 'Walking With Jesus', 'Come Down Easy' and 'Call The Doctor' are worth downloading if you can't find the album. Sonic Boom fondly remembers the sessions in the VHF studios in Rugby, explaining that

> 'mattresses were installed into the studio's lounging space and our kaleidoscopic light show stayed on throughout the session, permanently focused on the studio's revolving mirror-ball, myriad rays of micro-psychedelic worlds (and whirls) mixing with our minds and music. Actually the projector's fan noise permeated most of the recording and was considered an unfortunate but necessary evil.'[61]

Hardly anyone bought the album of course, but they had more success with the follow-up *Playing With Fire* which arrived just as 'chill-out' and 'ambient' became overused words to describe anything chucked together on Pro-Tools software or its progeny, and invariably included hamfisted attempts at dream-sequence sampling where Glen Campbell is just detectable in the background behind a gentle keyboard wash – oh and there are sheep too. They know who they are. Spacemen 3 did their stuff live in the studio where possible, and by their third album, had perfected a quieter approach that still involved the marshalling of noise but much more subtly and ultimately even more powerful when the inevitable release of noise came. With new members Will Carruthers and Jon Mattock, *Playing With Fire* was Spacemen 3 at their most incandescent. Various live albums are available that demonstrate how plugged in electrically and spiritually the band were when they made their psychedelia on the spot, and the final *Recurring* album in 1990 is a suitably impressive swansong, even if it is effectively Kember and Pierce in two separate studios at separate times, such was the irrevocable breakdown in communication at that point. Next time you're in your local record store looking for Spiritualized records just take the time to look a little to the left where the Spacemen 3 section is. If it's there at all it will probably be empty of course, but if you get lucky maybe they'll order you something. Or alternatively check their website at www. sonicboommusic.info. It's a music retail revolution in cyberspace, don't you know?

First team: Sonic Boom (g, v), Jason Pierce (g, v), Willie Carruthers (b), Jon Mattock (d)

Place, time, scene: Rugby, Warwickshire 1986. Coming into existence after Sonic Youth and Jesus And Mary Chain and eschewing their respective textural and melodic experiments with noise guitar, Spacemen 3 combined the repetition of krautrock, the minimalist full-tiltistness of Glenn Branca, the experimentalism of Red Krayola and the righteous psychedelia of the 13th Floor Elevators – 'record collection rock'. Spiritualized and Spectrum carried the flame into the nineties with a series of impressive albums.

What to buy first: *The Perfect Prescription* 1987

And then: *Playing With Fire* 1988, *Recurring* 1990

In retrospect: *Taking Drugs To Make Music To Take Drugs To* 1994, *Translucent Flashbacks* 1995

SPECIALS

2-Tone was the culmination of the punk experiment with Jamaican music. The dub and reggae connection had been made right at the start of the movement; in clubs, before and after the main punk band had played, the DJ inevitably spun something moodier and slower as a tension builder or comedown depending on the circumstances. The Clash had paid their tribute to Lee 'Scratch' Perry on their first album by including a version of 'Police And Thieves', and bands like the Ruts in west London were singing about Babylon and Jah and trying to blend reggae with their venomous guitar sounds. Both were good attempts but somehow the slower pace subsumed the spirit and energy of punk and those tracks ended up sounding like something completely different. The Coventry Automatics, later to become the Special AKA, tried punk and reggae too, but by the end of 1977 they had hit on a better brew. Going back just that bit further in Jamaican music history and maybe remembering how the skinheads made ska their own in the late sixties, the Automatics had a sound that could contain the anger and oppositional energy of punk and the tuneful and rhythmically addictive patterns of ska. When vocalist Terry Hall was added to the mix, his deadpan, sardonic delivery made the whole thing complete. Refusing to be angry, oppositional, tuneful or dancing, he brought the distance and irony that Johnny Rotten inspired, and in his own way influenced a whole generation of post-punk vocalists who would forever feel far more comfortable not getting down with the groove and keeping their dignity intact instead. The Specials, as they were by now, kicked ass and were cool with it.

Keyboardist Jerry Dammers formed the band in the summer of 1977 after a series of recording sessions at his flat in Coventry. Armed with a Revox tape-to-tape recorder and a good set of contacts he eventually settled on a traditional rock set-up and two vocalists, Hall to sing and Neville Staples to reggae toast. The rhythm section was of the solid swinging variety, but just darkened enough by some punk guitar courtesy of Roddy 'Radiation' Byers and fierce wood-on-metal from drummer John Bradbury aka Prince Rimshot. The band could punk it up or party out depending on the situation, although once the 'upside-down R&B'

ska sound was settled on, Dammers' stabbing piano and Lynval Golding's circular up-strumming of his rhythm guitar were ever-present on the offbeat. Immediately, fast songs like 'Too Much Too Young' and 'Little Bitch' (which bore more than a passing resemblance to the Stones' 'Brown Sugar') were transformed, and the urge to pogo was replaced by the need to skank.

Following an early recording session with Pete Waterman in Coventry, the Specials played an early set of dates with the Clash in 1978 but quickly discovered that the punks attending the gigs were not ready for anything new just yet. Racist comments were rife and only served to embolden the band, who returned to Coventry and set-up their own label, 2-Tone, a name chosen to emphasize their commitment to racial equality. The single 'Gangsters', recorded independently and manufactured and distributed by Rough Trade, sold enough to enter the lower reaches of the charts and launched an inevitable 'A&R frenzy' which even extended to Mick Jagger turning up at one of their gigs as a representative of Rolling Stones Records. Ultimately though, the band signed with Chrysalis who were the only company prepared to let them operate 2-Tone as an independent company. Of course, in reality, the 'tight-loose' deal which was soon to become commonplace in the 1980s music industry – where the label has control of signing bands and developing them and the record company balances the books and holds the purse-strings – never really made 2-Tone any money, but it did allow them the opportunity to sign the likes of the Selecter, Madness (for one single) and the Bodysnatchers. It also meant that for just over a year, Britain went 2-Tone crazy. From schoolkids wearing Harrington jackets with slogans on the back to open-air gigs that doubled as political rallies and ultimately the high profile of Rock Against Racism, the ska revival was responsible for politicizing the mainstream with pop music in a way that was unprecedented in the UK.

The debut *The Specials* album included tracks like 'Concrete Jungle' which addressed the problems of violence and racism in declining city centres at night, and more specific tirades against youth throwing their lives away, as in 'Too Much Too Young', a disappointed lament on teenage pregnancy that ends with the line 'trying wearing a cap' – not an obvious sub-

ject for a number one single, but hey! The second album *More Specials*, had Dammers experimenting with light jazz muzak and latin styles, a decision perhaps brought on by his and the band's declining enthusiasm for an upbeat celebratory music which was constantly being undermined at gigs by violence and misunderstanding as the National Front and BNP used Specials gigs as an opportunity for recruitment to their fundamentally racist causes. On *More Specials* the band made the music less obviously antagonistic and as a result more powerfully brooding. 'Stereotype', 'Do Nothing', 'International Jet-Set' and 'Man At C&A' are the standout tracks, and were a kind of lull before the storm. In the summer of 1981 the band issued the 'Ghost Town' single which reached number one in the UK charts in Royal Wedding week. While Charles and Di were getting hitched there were riots breaking out in Brixton and Toxteth in Liverpool, and hearing 'Ghost Town' on the radio brought into sharp focus the dichotomy of economic living conditions in the country at that time. The track has a suitably eerie and sinister musical backdrop and the scariest sneering backing vocals ever committed to tape. The B-side 'Why?' was written by Lynval Golding, a heartfelt plea to NF sympathizers who had recently brutally attacked him, to help him understand why they had done it. And that shortly after Dammers and Hall had been arrested for attempting to intervene to stop a riot at one of their gigs. It's no wonder the band split up.

Dammers and Bradbury regrouped a few months later and together with Rhoda Dakar from the Bodysnatchers relaunched the band as the Special AKA. The first single was Dakar's 'The Boiler', a disturbing and personal song dealing with the issue of rape, that was followed by 'Racist Friend', and as Dammers got more involved with Artists Against Apartheid, the anthemic 'Nelson Mandela'. By 1988 the band were playing the song to a packed Wembley Stadium and an international audience at Mandela's 70th Birthday Concert. Hall, Staples and Golding formed the Fun Boy Three and managed to inject a little irony and oblique political references into a mainstream chart made up of poseur new-romantic bands. Hall then moved on to the Colourfield and ultimately a sporadic solo career. He was not with the band when they recently reformed and recorded an album's worth of material, with Ali

Campbell of UB40 producing. It was not particularly well received but it's interesting that there were very few dissenting voices when it came to the issue of their actual reformation. Most other legendary bands are routinely criticized when they decide to reform, but in the Specials' case, it was always the message and the way they operated that counted. A truly inspirational band.

First team: Jerry Dammers (k), Terry Hall (v), Lynval Golding (g), Neville Staples (v), Roddy Radiation (g), Sir Horace Gentleman (b), John Bradbury (d)

Place, time, scene: Coventry 1977. The Specials began as a punk band but incorporated first reggae, then ska into their sound and created a new post-punk vibe that was as suited to partying as getting angry. The 2-Tone label ensured that a whole movement came into being simultaneously, and for about a year soundtracked a difficult period in British social history. By 1982 the punk energy had gone underground again, to be replaced by a new club-based 'new-romantic' pop scene, and the only noticeable directly influenced bands were Operation Ivy and Rancid in the US. The Specials' importance was always cultural first and foremost.

What to buy first: *The Specials* 1979

And then: *More Specials* 1980

In retrospect: *Singles* 1991

JON SPENCER BLUES EXPLOSION

Pussy Galore called it a day after half a decade of making 'hatefuck' music, which loosely translated meant thin trebly white noise devoid of bass guitar, and carnally-obsessed lyrics. During that time Jon Spencer had met his future wife, Christina Martinez, a New Yorker who had once worked in the same Haagen Dazs ice-cream parlour as Henry Rollins (it's true ok!), and shortly before the band collapsed, had played a gig at CBGB's with Martinez as Boss Hogg when the headline act didn't show. Martinez did the gig entirely naked (also true). The set was so successful that Boss Hogg became a full-time concern with guitarist Spencer happy to take a back seat while his wife led the band. By 1992 Spencer was keen to get back up front again

and so formed the Jon Spencer Blues Explosion with Judah Bauer and Russell Simins, a band which continued Spencer's postmodern deconstruction of rock music through the medium of electrified folk-blues. Again with no bassist in the band, the Blues Explosion opted against any attempt at songwriting in the traditional sense, i.e. verses, choruses, melody, and just got down to plain old-fashioned goofing around and making a racket. For some, it's the essence of rock'n' roll, for others they're clearly taking the piss. It could be both, of course.

Following two independent album releases which set the scene for the band's merciless parody of the blues, the band landed a deal with Matador Records in 1993 and put out *Extra Width*, which once again had Spencer howling like a blues screamer of yore while the music around him funks up a storm. On the standout track 'Afro', he veers between sounding like Prince and Captain Beefheart, and is punctuated by a theremin break cranked-up beyond acknowledged levels of ear-safety. The next album *Orange* is filled with more scratchy, spidery guitar, introduced right from the start over a beatific arrangement of lush Sound Of Philadelphia strings, but then segues into the band's most demented primal recorded moment, a paean to the much maligned fashion statement that is 'Bellbottoms'. On that one, Spencer at times sounds more like Jerry Lee than Lux Interior of the Cramps has ever managed, and the foul rhythms and textures are plugged directly into the same source that got rock' n'roll up and running in the first place. On 'Flavor' we are informed that the Blues Explosion is number one all over the world, keeping with the theme that pervades the whole band's output – the Blues Explosion love themselves.

Now I Got Worry, released in 1996, featured vocals from old Mississippi bluesman R.L. Burnside whose career was effectively resurrected by his association with Spencer, and *Acme*, the album that followed in 1998, starts with a tribute to Calvin Johnson, the founder of K Records and lo-fi pioneers Beat Happening who were operating the same time as Spencer's first band Pussy Galore. It's an interesting point to bring up the connection, just as the band were finally embracing studio technology to smooth out their sound. And the man who brought in the balance and sheen? Steve

Pussy Galore

Albini! The band that had never quite given away their game-plan – were they for real or just messing about? – finally went commercial by bringing in the producer famous for dirtying up the slick stuff to make them sound more radio-friendly. Genius. Notwithstanding the postmodern fucking around, *Acme* is a great album and the star is the bass guitar, so long absent from the Blues Explosion's anti-funk, it makes you wonder what might happen to all the old songs if it was retrospectively added to the earlier albums. Now there's a project.

First team: Jon Spencer (v, g, theremin), Judah Bauer (g, v), Russell Simins (d, v)

Place, time, scene: New York 1992. Jon Spencer Blues Explosion continued where Pussy Galore left off, except with added funk, perhaps inspired by James Chance and the Contortions who had made a career out of primal performances in New York in the early–mid eighties. The return of the New York garage-punk scene in 2001, especially with the White Stripes, themselves heavily influenced by Spencer's various bands, has completed the cycle.

What to buy first: *Orange* 1994

And then: *Extra Width* 1993, *Now I Got Worry* 1996, *Acme* 1998

STEREOLAB

Tim Gane attended the same school in Barking that Billy Bragg had left a few years before. It was there that Gane met the other three members of McCarthy, a guitar-based indie quartet that featured on the *NME's*

C86 cassette and which spent the remainder of the eighties writing and recording fiercely socialist songs that drew on ever more extreme Thatcherist policy as their creative muse. There must have been something about Barking Abbey Comprehensive. By 1990, McCarthy and an entire genre of indie bands, had become obsolete. John Major and the new groove had taken over from Mrs Thatcher, and for Tim Gane the choice was stark. If he was to remain in important, cutting-edge music he had to try something different.

The last McCarthy album, *Banking, Violence And The Inner Life Today* saw Gane experimenting with a layered production style that was subtly different from the straighter guitar-pop of the previous albums. It also featured his French girlfriend Laetitia Sadier on backing vocals, and it was through her that he was introduced to a whole new world of sound. Always a fan of pop music, especially the jangly Beatles variety, he now took on board the more keyboard-based futuristic retro of sixties producers, Jean-Jacques Perrey and Jacques Dutronc. Gane began playing analogue Moog and Farfisa keyboards and with the addition of ex-Chills' bass player, Martin Kean and Joe Dilworth, drummer with th'Faith Healers, created a whole new pop sound that brought together Europop with the motorik drone and pulse music of German bands Neu! and Kraftwerk. Laetitia became the vocalist, often singing in French.

Signed to Too Pure in 1991, but allowed to release their work under the logo Duophonic, Stereolab's first album was a compilation of their first three EPs. *Switched On* introduces the Stereolab sound, linear and layered and always underpinned with a motorized pulse that drives the guitar, bass and drums along. Sadier's voice, combined with guest vocalist Gina Morris on several tracks has a woozy, dreamy texture and has a jazzy sophistication that recalls Astrud Gilberto. 'High Expectations' with Sadier's repeated 'I don't, I don't, I don't, I'm sorry' is aural bliss. *Peng!* followed in 1992 with Sadier joining Gane on analogue keyboards for twice the effect, and then in 1993 a shift in personnel made room for Sean O'Hagan to join.

O'Hagan had been one half of Microdisney with Cathal Coughlan, who had since gone on to form Fatima Mansions, while O'Hagan spent a longer period developing his own project which he called the

High Llamas. At the point of joining Stereolab he was perfecting his own retro sound based on the harmonies and string and brass arrangements that Brian Wilson had so cleverly devised for the *Pet Sounds* and *Smile* albums in the sixties. *Gideon Gaye* and *Hawaii* are essential albums for anyone who has the time to meditate on a fairly regular basis. Watch out though, if you have a busy lifestyle it's just possible that your life could fall apart as the High Llamas addiction kicks in and stops you from getting stuff done. O'Hagan first appeared on Stereolab's 1993 mini-album *The Groop Played Space Age Bachelor Pad Music*, the band's first real foray into ambient music. O'Hagan also cropped up on *Transient Random Noise-Bursts With Announcements* which includes the 18 minute long 'Jenny Ondioline', a mess of noise and hidden melodies incorporating a socialist rant that ends with Laetitia chanting 'give me the strength to live for the struggle'.

The driving moog-rock of singles 'French Disko' and 'Lo Boob Oscillator' helped establish Stereolab's reputation with indie and dance crowds simultaneously, largely thanks to the groundwork laid by the declining baggy scene. A wider breakthrough might have been on the cards too had the indie-dance momentum continued, but as it was Britpop came along and scuppered everything. Both the Charlatans and Primal Scream went rock, Saint Etienne went on holiday, and it was not until the emergence of Bis and Super Furry Animals in 1996 that the experimental electronic vibe was back in vogue.

Emperor Tomato Ketchup is the band's best album so far. More varied than previous collections, virtually every track is different from the one before it and recalls a different period in the band's development. 'Percolator' is an analogue fantasy, 'Cybele's Reverie' has the patented O'Hagan strings, 'Emperor Tomato Ketchup' itself is the ultimate motorik throwdown and 'Les Yper-Sound' has all those wonderful countermelodies and layered vocals; it's also a directly political song. Amongst those who seek out challenging and innovative music, Stereolab are well established as the most accessible 'difficult' band operat°ing today. Take any one track by the band in isolation and play it to any one person in isolation, and the response will invariably be positive. Their music is weird but never unpleasant, and always underpinned by a pop sensibility and an insistent groove.

First team: Tim Gane (g, k), Laetitia Sadier (v, k, g), Mary Hansen (g, v), Sean O'Hagan (v, k), Duncan Brown (g, b), Andy Ramsay (d, p)

Place, time, scene: London 1991. Stereolab were formed out of the ashes of McCarthy, one of a multitude of guitar-based indie bands that changed their musical approach in the wake of dance and hip-hop music's sudden ascendancy. Their sound is a mix of Europop and krautrock, particularly the motorik pulsing rhythms of German band Neu!. Their futuristic retro sound has fed into work by Air and the High Llamas and can be discerned in recent electronic artists like Röyksopp.

What to buy first: *Emperor Tomato Ketchup* 1996

And then: *Switched On* 1992, *Transient Random Noise-Bursts With Announcements* 1993

In retrospect: *Refried Electroplasm (Switched On Vol Two)* 1995, *Aluminium Tunes (Switched On Vol Three)* 2002

STONE ROSES

The Stone Roses saved rock music and did it by giving the impression that they were playing dance music. Everyone goes on about their blend of two opposing musical styles and the reality is that the sound made by the kings of baggy was pretty close to the sound that countless guitar bands had made for a good two decades before they came on the scene. No, what happened was that the Stone Roses blended cultures. They removed the cultural distinction that had made independent guitar music the preserve of the critical, listening set and opened it up for the dancing hedonists. It's been possible to dance to pop and rock music for years. Dancefloors have filled to the opening bars of everything from the Stones to the Smiths, and there was that whole new-romantic movement which gave itself up to a new groove in the eighties, but body movin' was not a crucial part of a guitar band's job description until Manchester '88 when a handful of bands changed the rules.

Hip-hop and house music were given a warm welcome in the north where northern-soul all-nighters had long been part of the cultural heritage, and any band wanting to draw a crowd in Manchester had to tap into that vibe. By the mid-eighties the post-punk heaviness of Joy Division had given way to the more rhythmically inclined New Order, the seven-night a week Hacienda nightclub was starting to come alive, and there was even a drug available that took users up instead of down, and out instead of in. The context was communal and so the music had to be too. For one album and a few singles the Stone Roses led the way, followed closely by their looser fitting contemporaries, the Happy Mondays. Both bands connected with their audiences more closely than any other rock-based band before them, and possibly since, and in the case of the Stone Roses, this connection was made not just in performance but within the music as well. The relative failure of the second album (despite sounding great at high volume) happened because in the five years it took to get the damn thing made the band lost its cultural moorings. *The Second Coming*, like the first 'lemon' album, features some great guitar, an awesome backline and some pithy one-liners that sound great chanted communally; it's just not as perfectly blended as its predecessor, an era-defining rock album that, after nine years of trying, made the Stone Roses an overnight success and for just over a year, had everybody raving.

The first gig that Ian Brown and John Squire played together was in 1980 with guitarist/vocalist Andy Couzens and drummer Si. At that point the band was called the Patrol and Brown played bass, providing an early indication that his front-man role to come would not be based on a driven desire to speak his soul to an ever-attentive audience. He, like Squire, had been fired by the punk fury that he saw on television and heard on records by the Sex Pistols and local revolutionaries, Slaughter And The Dogs. As senior school acquaintances, they moved in the same circles and both attended an early Joy Division gig, although apart from music, their personalities were at odds, like all great creative duos. Brown did karate and might on occasion get physical at a football match; Squire preferred painting and during the eighties carved himself out a useful career in animation, working on cartoon projects for Cosgrove Hall which included the Terry Wogan voiced surrealist classic, *Chorlton And The Wheelies*. In fact, for the first part of the decade, after the Patrol split, Brown and Squire went in different directions, and Brown was not initially involved in Squire's band the Waterfront, which included new bassist and scally archetype Gary 'Mani' Mounfield.

The Waterfront were inspired by the jagged jingle-jangle of Scottish band Orange Juice, a band which had taken the attitude of punk but retained earlier sixties influences to their sound, particularly the bits that dealt with melody and romanticism. The Waterfront had the wedge haircuts, the sports-casual clobber and a vocalist named Kaiser who was replaced by Ian Brown, the scooter boy and northern soul fan, in 1983 just before the band became the Stone Roses. In 1984 the band consisted of Brown, Squire, Andy Couzens, former roadie Pete Garner on bass and new drummer Alan Wren or 'Reni', a heavy rock fan who might just have been the drummer of his generation. Pete Townshend certainly thought so. When the band was invited to play at an anti-heroin benefit gig he organized in London, he chose Reni to play in his backing band for part of his set. The event should have got things moving for the band but at that point, as a recording session with Manchester legend Martin Hannett revealed, they were still a band in progress, not quite ready.

They already had songs like 'I Wanna Be Adored' and 'This Is The One' when they made their debut album and were pulling good size crowds to their gigs, one of which was organized in a warehouse behind Piccadilly railway station in the centre of Manchester. But although they were establishing a communal vibe it wasn't until John Squire started acting on what he was hearing in new bands like Jesus And Mary Chain and Sonic Youth, and specifically in the guitar-work of Johnny Marr and Will Sergeant, that a distinctive sound began to emerge that was subtler than the more straightforward style of playing that can be heard on the first Stone Roses' album entitled *Garage Flower* recorded in 1985, but only issued after the band became successful. By the end of 1986, with Mani and his northern soul bass-shapes back on board, the Stone Roses had finally put together all of the influences – melodic pop, punk, post-punk and soul – that had been shaping them for the last six years. They were ready.

The album *The Stone Roses* was recorded in 1988 and early 1989 in London with producer John Leckie who had a CV which at that point included George Martin, Phil Spector, Pink Floyd and XTC's perfectly executed pastiche of sixties psychedelia, the spin-off band Dukes Of Stratosphear. 'I Wanna Be Adored' opens the album, emerging slowly and broodingly out of white guitar noise before being picked up and given direction by Mani's bass; there's the ghostly echo of pop's past 'She Bangs The Drum'; the gentle pastoral feel of 'Waterfall'; which changes tempo and texture repeatedly before being repeated backwards in its entirety as 'Don't Stop'; and that's just the first four tracks. The album also contains 'Made Of Stone', a complex and beguiling montage of all the best bits of pop music since the whole thing got underway a good 30 years before, a track which brings together life-affirming melody and stark, dark urban imagery. There's 'Shoot You Down' showcasing Reni's shuffling rhythms and expert harmonizing, and the two crowd-pleasing anthems that conclude the album, 'This Is The One' and the mighty 'I Am The Resurrection', both inviting the listener to testify along with vocalist Brown as the band pulls out all the stops and chops around him.

The thing about the Roses was that Ian Brown was always equal to his colleagues. In performance he was an anti-front-man. Of course he had the swagger and stage presence, but that was just his role in the band; his vocals never allowed his ego to take over and control the band. On record his singing voice is just another texture, restrained rather than weak, with an echo-like quality that suggests he is one of the crowd. His voice is communal, it encourages chanting. The Stone Roses' audience was the same audience that went to raves and that was all about democracy. Not necessarily the hippy ethic of giving everyone the freedom to do what they want to do, but more the sense that everybody is in this together. The Stone Roses dressed like their fans, and as their notoriously difficult interviews prove, they were not in the business of telling anybody what to do. They were egoless, classless and saw no need to attach themselves to any one scene or style. When they played their legendary gig at Spike Island it was attended by a cross-section of sub-cultural groups, the like of which has not been seen since, unless you count Glastonbury festival, although that is carefully divided along tribal lines. The 'Fool's Gold' single which got them into the Top

10 and onto *Top Of The Pops*, appearing the same week as the Happy Mondays, was a suitable mixture of hip-hop sampling, krautrock looped structure, rock-funk wah-wah guitar and bass, and restrained dreamy vocals. Together with 'One Love', which followed 'Fool's Gold' into the charts, the band looked good for a cracker of a second album but it was a long wait.

The Second Coming was finally released at the end of 1994 and although tracks like 'Love Spreads' and 'Breaking Into Heaven' were monolithic groovers, the emphasis was firmly on John Squire's guitar which he wanted to sound fuller and fatter than the thin jangly feel of the first album. There were apparently some Mani-Reni jam sessions during recording that never made it onto the album (check Ian Brown's 'Can't See Me' on his first album for one rescued session), and Brown never got round to writing anything in the five-year lay-off which meant that all the songs were Squire's too. Listening to tracks like 'Ten Storey Love Song' and 'How Do You Sleep', which are more in keeping with tracks from over a decade earlier, there's a sense of missed opportunities, and the heavier Zeppelin-esque songs, many of them jammed rather than worked out carefully, seem like the work of an entirely different band. It's still an ace album, and rock fans in particular probably see it as an improvement on the debut. But too much time had passed by.

The Stone Roses were never prolific. It took them nearly a decade to get the first album together, and even then they had their detractors who couldn't see how delicately the band's sound hung together. With Oasis about to release their second album made up of familiar hooks and big bully-boy sounds, and a vaguely class-inflected battle with Blur brewing, the Stone Roses' egalitarianism probably wouldn't have made any sense anyway. *The Second Coming* never really got promoted properly. The band had to pull out of a Glastonbury headline slot because Squire broke his arm, and it wasn't long before first Reni, then Squire left the band. An ignominious Reading appearance sealed the band's fate.

First team: Ian Brown (v), John Squire (g), Mani (b), Reni (d, v)

Place, time, scene: Manchester 1984. The Stone Roses went through a long period of gestation before finally establishing their own sound, fashioned from many sources including the proto-indie guitar sound of Orange Juice, the guitar experimentation of noise bands like Jesus And Mary Chain and a crucial dollop of R&B soul rhythm. Their ability to connect with their audience mirrored the cultural mood instigated by ravers and clubbers and, together with the Happy Mondays, the Charlatans and Inspiral Carpets they were key to a new scene dubbed 'Madchester' and 'baggy' which grew up around this cultural mood. Ian Brown has continued to pursue the vibe he helped create, although that textured guitar sound and infectious rhythm has rarely been attempted since.

What to buy first. *The Stone Roses* 1989

And then: *The Second Coming* 1994

In retrospect: *The Complete Stone Roses* 1995

STOOGES

When they made their Halloween live debut in 1967, the Psychedelic Stooges changed the rules of garage music. Shortly before their first gig, lead vocalist Iggy Pop had seen the Doors and the Velvet Underground, heading in opposite directions on their way through America's heartland. In April, Iggy had witnessed the dark, seedy, droning of the Velvets and in October, the erotic, uninhibited, psychedelic R&B of the Doors. He took what he learned from those two crucial master-classes and with a blistering set of musicians in place to back him to the hilt, he launched himself into a three-year period of rock'n'roll abuse, of himself and anyone who took their chances by coming to one of the band's gigs. The Stooges made their reputation on stage, and that reputation for primal release spread down the years, reaching the next generation of nihilist rebels who made Iggy their god and the Stooges their musical template. There are several contenders for the title but in terms of sheer indifference and lack of respect for what had gone before, the Stooges were the first punks.

James Newell Osterberg was born in Ann Arbour, Michigan in 1947, the son of an Englishman living abroad. He joined his first band, the Iguanas at age 17. He drummed his heart out for two years in between a series of bad car crashes from which he always emerged unscathed and feeling ever more fearless and immortal. By 1965 he was a member of the Prime Movers, and calling himself Iggy Pop – Iggy because he used to be in the Iguanas and Pop after local junkie Jim Popp. He spent a few months in Chicago hanging out and talking blues with Sam Lay, drummer with the Paul Butterfield Blues Band, and returned to Detroit in 1967 ready and able to take on the hippies and beat them. Playing around Detroit at the same time as the MC5 and against a backdrop of civil unrest in the motor city, the Stooges had plenty to draw inspiration from in terms of bad stuff going down, and their gigs reflected the sense of emptiness that the working-classes were feeling.

His band consisted of Asheton brothers Ron on guitar and Scott on drums and bassist Dave Alexander, who between them conspired to conjure up a hazy, filthy sound that sounded so much more blended than other similarly tooled-up bands of the period. Ron Asheton's ability to harness feedback and make the most of simple effects technology was only really matched at the time by Leigh Stephens in Blue Cheer, and the debut album *The Stooges* in 1969 blew away their punk rivals the MC5, who could only muster a thin white noise sound. The introduction to 'I Wanna Be Your Dog', with the archetypal descending bass line cutting through a wall of feedback, is the best guitar music ever got – no contest. The album also contains '1969', 'another year with nothing to do', and to emphasize the point further, 'No Fun'. John Cale of the Velvet Underground produced the album and is probably to blame for the extended 'We Will Fall' which includes chanting and droning. The Stooges however, nailed the extended jam format on their next and best album, *Fun House*.

This time produced by Don Gallucci of the Kingsmen, the band that gave 'Louie Louie' to the world, the Stooges actually calm things down but end up with an album that buzzes and pulses with electricity. 'Down On The Street' starts at medium pace with a solid backline, expertly deployed guitar screech and an Iggy vocal that growls the words. By the end of the album the pace and the manic depravity has increased, making the white noise 'LA Blues' a disconcerting listening experience. It would be the last time that the band recorded together in that formation.

They split after the album's release in 1970 with all four members exhausted after three years of relentless rock'n'roll abuse.

It was only in 1973 when Iggy Pop and guitarist James Williamson were holed-up in London as part of David Bowie's Ziggy entourage that the bug bit again, and with the Ashetons' arrival at Iggy's behest, the band went back into a studio to record what was to become the *Raw Power* album. On it, Ron Asheton played bass as many of the songs had been written by Pop and Williamson. Some have said that Asheton's playing is infused with anger throughout due to his effective demotion, but if true, this only served to make the album sound even rawer.

The best tracks are 'Search And Destroy', 'Gimme Danger' and the title track, which does exactly what it says on the tin. It was dropped off at Columbia, who hated it and asked David Bowie to remix the album and give it a glam-rock sheen to improve its chances of radio play. The mix has since gone down in rock history as one of the worst crimes against the artist ever perpetrated, which is a little unfair on Bowie considering he was only given one day in the studio with the tapes and was acting under instruction from the label and the band, who were keen to resurrect their career. The album, with its raw power amputated, did not sell well and after one more tour of the US, during which Iggy may have gone too far with the body-slashing, the oral sex and the first recorded instances of stagediving and crowd-surfing – once a drummer, always a drummer – the band split for the final time.

Iggy Pop worked with Bowie again in 1977, the year punk broke, and at the height of his notoriety as the Godfather Of Punk, he opted to make two albums which explored the possibilities of electronic music on several of the tracks, the sinister 'Nightclubbing' reflecting Bowie's own current fascination with cold, pulse-driven music. Of course there was also 'The Passenger' and 'Lust For Life' which revealed some of the Iguana of old, and he managed to get Tony Wilson's television show *So It Goes* taken off air for good with one of his performances. In fact, tales of gore, of ripped flesh, crushed bones, shattered teeth, of hot wax poured over naked bodies and peanut butter abuse still circulated, and as the millennium approached the cleaned-up Iggy Pop still couldn't resist the opportunity of wearing see-through plastic trousers for ajust about post-watershed television performance. The music's important of course, but it's even more important with added shock factor.

First team: Iggy Pop (v), Ron Asheton (g), Dave Alexander (b), Scott Asheton (d)

Place, time, scene: Detroit 1967. Iggy Pop combined the outrageous performance antics of the Doors with the sleaze of the Velvet Underground and together with his band the Stooges transformed the look and sound of garage-rock music. Their legend and their attitude inspired punks en masse and their primal, instinctive, yet skilful mastery of sonic dynamics was picked up by a more tuned in set of pre-punk, punk and post-punk musicians and producers, including Tony Visconti, Mick Ronson, Tom Verlaine, Chris Thomas, Martin Hannett and Steve Albini.

What to buy first: *The Stooges* 1969

And then: *Fun House* 1970, *Raw Power* 1973

In retrospect: *Nude And Rude: The Best Of Iggy Pop* 1996

THE STROKES

When the Strokes stumbled onto the international scene in 2001 they focused everyone's attention back on New York again after two decades of relative obscurity. The last rock based scene had been no wave in the late seventies, which celebrated raw art-punk-funk. Key scenesters like Bill Laswell, Anton Fier and Arto Lindsay got deeper into beat science and embraced sampling culture, former hardcore punks the Beastie Boys adopted a hip-hop stance, and only a few guitar bands like Sonic Youth and Hoboken neighbours Yo La Tengo carried on with experiments in good old electric lash. As far as the rest of the world was concerned, New York's music scene consisted of rappers, graffers and B-boys. It was an image that Mayor Giuliani tried hard to temper, with his war on night-clubs an integral aspect of his no-tolerance policy on crime during the nineties. During that period the formerly vibrant bohemian areas of the city became stale as their reputation for artistic creativity and the cultural capital that went with it attracted a new set of residents who priced the real artists out of the neigh-

bourhood. Aspiring musicians, in particular, were unable to afford the price of rehearsal rooms, studios or most crucially, digs. Gone were the days when out-of-towners like Patti Smith, Tom Verlaine and Richard Hell could breeze in and breathe life into the scene. It helped then that the Strokes were loaded rich kids, and that their privileged upbringing had affected them in such a way that by the end of the century they were ready to get primal on New York's ass. They resurrected the spirit of the Big Apple's rotten core with their blend of all the best bits of rock'n'roll music since the seventies (and voice effects).

Three of the band's five members attended what vocalist and main songwriter Julian Casablancas has called 'a school for rich fuck-ups'. Casablancas started writing songs as he became more disillusioned with his surroundings, and by the time the band formed in 1998 with the addition of bassist Nikolai Fraiture and guitarist Albert Hammond Jr, son of the 'Free Electric Band' man, whom Casablancas met during his corrective time at a Swiss boarding school, he had an impressive set of songs destined for the band's debut album. The debut single 'The Modern Age' found its way to Geoff Travis at Rough Trade Records in London, and after one listen he was hooked, proclaiming it the best record out of New York since the city's late-seventies heyday. Driven on by a syncopated drum which turns into something more relentless when an up-strummed guitar breaks in to emphasize the off-beat, the song was a refreshingly sparse alternative to the fatter sounds beloved of just about every other musical genre at the time. It was weedy indie with a groove and an understanding of the music's angular and textural potential, learned from the likes of Gang Of Four, Joy Division and of course the masters of thin syncopated punk, Television.

'The Modern Age' was issued in January 2001 and the album *Is This It* followed in the summer, confirming the band's grasp of minimalist-maximumist production techniques. Guitar parts are played against each other (a Television trait) but never sound cluttered or confused, and Casablancas' voice, fed through various effects, is an odd mix of disinterested ambivalence and impassioned screaming. There are some blinding solos, memorable melodies and the whole thing is tight as, hell even drummer Fabrizio Moretti

The Strokes

comes on like a drum machine. Why it all feels so slack and fucked up then, lord only knows. Some kind of genius I guess. 'Someday' and 'Last Nite' made great radio songs (unashamedly pilfered as they are from soft rock hits of the past – check 'Last Nite' against Tom Petty's 'American Girl'), 'Hard To Explain' was effortlessly mixed into Christine Aguilera's 'Genie In A Bottle' by Freelance Hellraiser, 'New York City Cops' and 'Barely Legal' dealt with, you know, issues and 'Alone, Together' remains the perfect summation of everything yet done in the name of punk, from the Rancid ska-shaped opening and the Hooky/Wobble bass bits, to the firebrand Tom Verlaine guitar break to finish. British critics loved the album, probably influenced by the band's undeniably cool haircuts, while American critics were less impressed, probably because of the band's undeniably cool haircuts.

The follow-up *Room On Fire* was started with Radiohead producer Nigel Godrich but halfway through recording they opted to reunite with Gordon Raphael who produced the first album. The taut guitar sound remains intact, although some of the space is filled in with a few soul moves and some Cars-style new-wave keyboard, and Casablancas' voice is kept on a tighter leash, less manic, more controlled. There's a whole stack of New York-based bands like Interpol, The Rapture and Radio 4 following in the wake of the Strokes. It could well be that other bands emerge as far more influential over time, but for the moment the Strokes have managed to create their own distinct sound from a variety of historical sources and have made thin weedy music cool again, just as if thumping bass-lines and fat beats had never happened.

First team: Julian Casablancas (v), Albert Hammond Jr (g), Nick Valensi (g), Nikolai Fraiture (b), Fabrizio Moretti (d)

Place, time, scene: New York 1998. The Strokes revived the New York scene with their self-conscious pastiche of the original New York art and punk scenes of the previous decades. Taking the dual guitar sound of Television and staying true to the thin sound of the Velvet Undergound's *White Light/White Heat* period and Television's 'Little Johnny Jewel', they have managed to get people interested in a more primitive sound that is emphasized in the vocal effects used by singer Casablancas. For listeners who don't know a

world without hip-hop, the new sound is a revelation and is even being used by DJs in clubs as a different texture to set alongside the more bass-heavy beats that make up a typical dancefloor experience. The Strokes are possibly at the forefront of the American equivalent of Britpop, and as the experience of bands like Suede and Blur attests, that's both an exhilarating and an exasperating place to be.

What to buy first: *Is This It* 2001

And then: *Room On Fire* 2003

SUEDE

Suede made introspective glam rock. It's not something that many other bands have tried. Even Bowie, who glammed up his early folk leanings for Ziggy Stardust, was playing around with a theatrical creation. Brett Anderson, who began his musical life as a punk, understood that the kids don't dig heart on the sleeve honesty and knew that a dose of rock'n'roll ironic role-playing is always necessary, but drew the line at competing with an ever-expanding party culture by setting himself up as a fun-loving beered-up grebo (see Ned's Atomic Dustbin or Pop Will Eat Itself). If indie music was to be saved and restored to its rightful position as the soundtrack of bedsit/room society when the Smiths ruled all things sensitive and solipsistic, something a little darker and personal was required. Anderson took London life at night as his muse, and his troubled characters and seedy scenarios were given a veneer of glamour by musical collaborator Bernard Butler, the greatest simultaneous lead and rhythm guitar player of his generation, who managed to create his very own wall-of-sound built out of T.Rex bricks and Ride mortar. For at least the time it took to make two albums, Suede reinvigorated the indie scene and focused attention on the minutia of contemporary cultural life at the same time as those other glam-rockers the Manic Street Preachers were dealing with the bigger issues. Britpop followed as a matter of course, but by then one of the best teams in nineties alternative music had destroyed itself.

Brett Anderson and bassist Matt Osman played in a band together in Hayward's Heath in the late eighties and formed Suede when they made the 40 mile trip into

London where they met drummer Simon Gilbert, a fellow immigrant from Leamington Spa, and discovered guitarist Bernard Butler via an advert in *Melody Maker*. Gilbert was working at the University of London Union (ULU) selling tickets and led the band to their early manager, comedian and later Xfm Head Of Speech Ricky Gervais, who also worked at the venue booking acts. Anderson's girlfriend Justine Frischmann was also drafted in for early gigs and demos as a second guitarist but it soon became apparent that Butler could effortlessly handle being Mick Ronson and Johnny Marr simultaneously so she left to form Elastica. Suede hammered away at promoters, venues and audiences with their unique blend of balls-out rock and effeminate posturing, and eventually started winning hearts and minds around 1992. They were on the front-page of *Melody Maker* without a record deal, and when they signed with

Nude Records, managed to place two singles in the Top 20 within weeks of each other. Suede-mania took hold and at last Britain had a dynamic response to the grunge hegemony that had held sway for the previous few years.

The debut single 'The Drowners' introduced the band's playful approach to sexual ambiguity which, coupled with Anderson's early television appearances, made for a return to Bowie era gender-bending techniques. 'Metal Mickey' and 'Animal Nitrate' followed, rockers that made big melodic anthems of songs about a stripper and a drug-addicted victim of sexual violence. By the time they got to the album the band had perfected their art and could switch between dark ballads like 'Sleeping Pills' and seedy romps about sex in cars in the cheekily titled 'Breakdown'. The single that followed, 'Stay Together', clocked in at eight minutes and pointed the way towards the

Suede

more elaborate album to come. It remains one of the most impressive single releases by a British band.

By the time of *Dog Man Star* in 1994, Britpop was well underway and Suede's seventies retro didn't fit with the official sixties signifiers that provided the new London pop with its postmodern 'roots'. Suede were more 'Lola' than 'Waterloo Sunset' – a key distinction. As a result, the album that is regarded by many as one of the best released during the nineties was relegated to the position of new album released by yesterday's could've-beens. Maybe it was a contributing factor to the creeping mutual hatred developing between Anderson and Butler, but from amongst the personal wreckage emerged a collection of songs that were soaring, dramatic and at times satisfyingly dense. Strings and horns are deployed effectively on orchestrated epics like 'Daddy's Speeding', and 'We Are The Pigs' thunders along with an awesome power that Oasis bottled and rolled out on their debut album a year later. The standout track though is 'The Asphalt World', an epic musical experience which succeeds in interpreting Anderson's tale of a love triangle where he might be the cuckolded lover or the interloping novelty and his rival, perhaps a man, but probably a woman – 'When you're there in her arms and there in her legs, well I'll be in her head'.

Just before the release of the album, Butler announced his departure from the band and was soon working with David McAlmont, a better vocalist technically than Anderson and equally suited to Butler's big production sound, but without the knack for cultural reportage and the skinny white boy's affecting ability to combine disgust and fascination in equal measure when singing about the world he sees after dark. The next three Suede albums still have their moments although feedback on the freaks is at times exchanged for identification with them. The subjective recognition that 'we're trash, you and me' and the more removed observation that 'here they come, the beautiful ones' kept Suede dear to the self-consciously sensitive outsiders but also saw them sailing dangerously close to self-parody. Of course, both tracks were trebly-thin pop classics that showed off new boy Richard Jake's leaner and more concise guitar style, and the album *Coming Up* and its long awaited follow-up, 2000's more muscular *Head Music*, were the very epitome of indie-pop, but with that kind

of throwaway approach to song production, Suede had become a pale imitation of their darker, denser earlier incarnation. In 2003, after their fifth album *A New Morning*, they announced their plans to call it a day, but don't rule out a Suede revival and reformation at some point in the future cycle of pop, especially with Mr Butler back on the loose.

First team: Brett Anderson (v), Bernard Butler (g), Matt Osman (b), Simon Gilbert (d)

Place, time, scene: London 1991. Suede reinvigorated an indie scene that had lain dormant since the Smiths disbanded in 1988. Where the Manic Street Preachers brought back glamour, Suede returned to a darker form of glam and an altogether seedier and closer look at society's ills than the sweeping grand statements of their Welsh counterparts. Britpop took the basic idea and ran with it.

What to buy first: *Dog Man Star* 1994

And then: *Suede* 1993, *Coming Up* 1996

In retrospect: *Sci-Fi Lullabies (B-Sides Collection)* 1997

SUICIDE

Alan Vega and Martin Rev were funded by New York State when they started making their otherworldly form of music. Not that New York State knew that was the case. As far as the state department were concerned they were paying for a performance and gallery space called the Project for Living Artists. During the day there were exhibitions and creative workshops, but at night when it closed it became a project for homeless artists to live in. As one of the curators, Alan Vega had the keys and regularly let his friend Martin Rev sleep there, or more to the point crank out his bizarre electronic sounds.

The two had worked together in 1971 on an event entitled A Punk Music Mass, apparently the first historical reference to punk as a musical concept. Having bonded through their mutual admiration for electronic pioneers the Silver Apples, who made music with amplified oscillators, the duo began to work together on their own darker version of what was effectively hippy music when the Apples did it back in the sixties. Vega's voice was, as near as damn it, Elvis Presley, and when put to use intoning urban tales and poetry concerning disreputable characters and seedy situations, sounded fucking ace. Martin Rev, a classically-trained pianist, composed melodies on primitive electronic equipment and underpinned them with stark pulsing rhythm. They even managed to get hold of an early drum machine, and eventually had a new sound that was totally alien to New York audiences. When punk broke at CBGB's in 1974 they soon became a much talked-about act but were less fortunate in securing a record deal with record companies, who seemed to equate punk with guitars not electronic music.

When they finally got a deal with independent label Red Star in 1977, the resultant eponymous debut album resolutely failed to sell outside of New York, although a series of selected performances in Europe went down well, and as Alan Vega remembers it, Soft Cell came along to a gig in Leeds. It makes sense as Soft Cell are the most obviously indebted to Suicide of the eighties bands that followed, although the Human League's 'Being Boiled' single, the first all-electronic track to be released as a single in the UK, has a similar darkness to it. The album's centrepiece is the ten minute 'Frankie Teardrop' and the 'should've been a hit single' is 'Rocket USA' which still sounds as fresh and contemporary as any other electronic music currently being released in the name of electro-clash or techno. It's driven by a huge bass rhythm and sounds like it was recorded in the Royal Albert Hall, the sound is so expansive.

A second album followed in 1980, produced by Rik Ocasek of the Cars and given a smoother sheen which must have seemed like a good idea back then, but makes no sense when listened back to now. After years of deletion, the debut *Suicide* album was finally reissued on Mute in 1998 and coincided with Alan Vega's collaboration with producer Stephen Lironi, working as the Revolutionary Corps Of Teenage Jesus, which *NME* described as 'the best use of violent demented narrative on a dance record to date – convulsive and terrifying'. Good to know that he hasn't lightened up over the years.

First team: Alan Vega (v), Martin Rev (k)

Place, time, scene: New York 1974. Suicide had connections with the New York art world and the seedier club scene pre-CBGBs. Following in the footsteps of sixties futurists the Silver Apples, they made a minimalist sound but added their own darker mood and subject matter. Similarly seedy synthesizer bands like Soft Cell were clearly impressed with what they heard.

What to buy first: *Suicide* 1977

SUPER FURRY ANIMALS

Who knows where Super Furry Animals came up with their musical plan or if they even have one. Certainly, listening to their albums, it becomes obvious that they have many moments of revelation, where two or more sounds, styles or ideas suddenly gel together to produce something extraordinary, but the moments of genius are random. Maybe they couldn't do it again if they tried.

Their debut album was called *Fuzzy Logic*, a term used in maths to describe something that has no specific value of its own and only makes sense in context, a context is always shifting. That explains the sound of the Super Furry Animals in a nutshell. Listen to any one of their five albums and then try and describe it using general stylistic or generic terms. I can guarantee that it will keep changing. There's psychedelia obviously, and new wave, some folk, jazz and, of course, techno. Don't forget punk, acid house, ambient and on a couple of occasions calypso. Ultimately though it's all pop. Every track on every album has a hook or a melody, and the band is so good at creating these that they are even able to make the Welsh language, alien to most of their listeners, catchy. There's 'Torra Fy Ngwallt Yn Hir' on *Radiator* and a whole album full on *Mwng*. Super Furry Animals have had an impact inside Wales as well. The Welsh language is more widely taught in Welsh schools following the success of a scene which has been growing since the mid-eighties, the national party Plaid Cymru picked up youth votes it wouldn't have normally expected to get, with the national football team doing alright too.

The band was formed in 1993 out of the ashes of several bands that were crucial to the Welsh language scene centred around Bangor. Gruff Rhys and Dafydd Ieeuan were members of Ffa Coffi Bawb, a band which put out two albums of techno-inflected oddness and were signed to the Ankst label that later also had Catatonia and Gorkys Zygotic Mynci. Ankst helped Ffa Coffi Bawd get on in a scene which extended outside Wales to any country in Europe with a minority culture that could identify with the struggle for a voice. They sold records in the Basque region of Spain and in eastern Europe too. Super Furry Animals was an attempt to get their music to a wider audience, which effectively was their overarching big plan.

There were two singles on Ankst and then the debut *Fuzzy Logic*, which was a breath of fresh air following the increasingly predictable Britpop moment. Where Britpop bands, with a couple of notable exceptions, took one retro idea and did it to death, Super Furry Animals took 20 and twisted them together seamlessly. *Fuzzy Logic* is basically a fuzzed-up guitar album with analogue keyboard weirdness overlayed and then an array of various instruments slotted in wherever a particular texture or sound is required. The flute, played in the style of a mediaeval fool at the end of 'Fuzzy Birds' fits both the laid-back Canterbury folk-rock of the song and the fact that the subject of the song is a talking hamster whom Rhys is thanking for peddling the wheel that drives his electricity. Mad. 'Something 4 The Weekend' is a drug song with a glorious chorus, 'Hometown Unicorn' details an alien abduction and features one of the greatest throwaway guitar solos ever after the first verse, 'Hanging With Howard Marks' is a drug-runner song and 'Mario Man' hints at what's to come on the next album, it being one of those songs that's done in sections.

After a summer of festivals, which the band attended in their official armoured tank amid moaning from Rhys that the band were fed-up of playing rock stages when they felt a closer affinity to the dance tents, they issued *Radiator*, which is not a concept album as such but has the air of one. Where *Fuzzy Logic* was a collection of songs thrown together in no particular order, and fading away a little by the end, *Radiator*'s songs, although still stylistically very different, flow into one another. The songs all start and finish simply and often quietly, building and unravelling somewhere in the middle.

There's a nice rhythm to the collection as a whole, and by the time 'Demons', 'She's Got Spies' and 'Hermann Loves Pauline' have all arrived, exploded and left, everything is set for the final section of the album, four songs which together are the band's very own *Abbey Road* side two. After a glam Ziggy start with 'Bass Turned To D.E.A.D.' the band moves into its 'Golden Slumbers'/'Carry That Weight' section with 'Down A Different River', that shifts into 'Download', the calm before the storm, and finally 'Mountain People' celebrating 'hand-me-down culture' and peat-piling, a stirring acoustic anthem that gradually stirs in some Ennio Morricone cinemasonics, string sections and finally mindfuck techno to kill the classical beauty they have just created. Done live, 'Mountain People' was usually the cue for the band to leave the stage while keyboardist Cian Ciaran inflicted 20 minutes of hard techno beats and relentless knob-twiddling around a sample of Steely Dan's 'Show Biz Kids' – 'you know they don't give a fuck about anybody else'. It's something everyone should experience before they die, and if you're lucky the band will return to the stage dressed as odd aquatic-type aliens to stand stock still for the duration of the bleeps.

Guerilla expanded the techno dimension again and handed more textural control to Ciaran, but for the completely Welsh language *Mwng*, the band opted to record some of their earlier songs in a more straightforward style. It remains the biggest-selling Welsh-language album ever and got a mention in the new Welsh parliament. Having released their albums on Creation up to this point, in 2001 they moved to Sony and really went to town on the album *Rings Around The World*, mixing it in 5.1 surround sound. It was, once again, mind-blowing.

First team: Gruff Rhys (v, g), Dafydd Ieuan (d, v), Cian Ciaran (k, p, v), Guto Pryce (b), Huw Bunford (g, v)

Place, time, scene: Cardiff 1993. Super Furry Animals belonged to a well-established Welsh-language scene that cannot be pinned down musically, other than to say that it made the connections between organic folk, psychedelic head music and the developing techno form. From their first album it was clear that Super Furry Animals were here to shake up the complacency of Britpop and grunge that had held sway for the first part of the decade. Their musical eclecticism is typical of contemporary music-making but nobody does it as seamlessly and melodically as Super Furry Animals.

What to buy first: *Radiator* 1997

And then: *Fuzzy Logic* 1996, *Guerilla* 1999, *Rings Around The World* 2001

T

TALKING HEADS

Talking Heads were an experimental band with a difference. Most artists wanting to try something different are driven by a desire to create new sounds or ways of working so that they can hear their innovations in the finished product. Talking Heads were interested in that too, but they had another motive, or at least it seems that David Byrne had another motive for their experimentation. He wanted to adjust the sound of the band in order to explore an artistic idea. He wanted to make real music that sounded unreal, to conduct a study in postmodern art. Throughout the band's career, the theme of Byrne's writing focused on his detached observations about the world and people in it. He even made a film, *True Stories*, based on the same principle. With Brian Eno on board as fifth member of the band for three of its albums, Byrne had the perfect working partner, even if it did fragment the band with the other three members possibly feeling like hired hands at times. Still, they were all very mature about it, and simply got on with side-projects and returned to the band when it was time to reconvene. It's a sense of detachment that runs through a lot of Talking Heads' work, and Byrne in particular gained a reputation as one of the new breed of serious artists who was comfortable working solo, dabbling in a variety of genres and industry roles. For some he was perceived as a focus of new styles and ways of doing things from around the world, for others he was just plain pretentious. Now, as all good arguments tend to end up saying, it was probably a bit of both.

The band coalesced around Byrne, Tina Weymouth and Chris Frantz, who had all attended art school and CBGB's together, where they played their first gigs as a trio, Byrne upfront with 12-string acoustic guitar and singing. With the record label scramble of 1977 to sign any band playing the club, they soon had a deal with Sire Records, and a single 'Love Goes To Building On Fire'. Jerry Harrison, who had played with the Modern Lovers, joined for the album 1977 and their jerky-rhythm style that seemed to emanate from Byrne's off-kilter vocal and dance movements was introduced to a waiting world in songs like 'Psycho Killer' and 'Uh-Oh, Love Comes To Town'. For the second album, Brian Eno expressed an interest in working with the band, and was able to help Byrne realize the synthesis of the ideas in his songs and the way the band sounded.

By recording the band and feeding the result through his synthesizer, and then combining the original mix with the electronically enhanced one, Eno transformed the band's soulful groove, built around Weymouth's lead bass, into a soulful groove that sounded oddly removed from reality, and perfectly mirrored Byrne's songs and vocal performance, which were designed to question the role of the rock' n'roll singer as a spiritual channeller of ideas and energy. Byrne was taking the classic template of the rock shaman a la Jim Morrison, and turning it on its head, undermining the belief in the transcendence of the rock'n'roll experience by showing that the role of the enigmatic front-man could be hollow and one step removed from the purely spiritual connection that some might have believed. Clever punk, in a nutshell. *More Songs About Buildings And Food* was a suitably dour title for a collection of songs that Byrne was suggesting did exactly what it said on the tin. One of the tracks, a version of Al Green's 'Take Me To The River' was an American hit when released as a single in 1978, and spelt out the arrival of a new type of cold soul.

Eno and Byrne worked together to produce the next two Talking Heads albums, *Fear Of Music* and *Remain In Light* which continued with the detached, laboratory-clean sound, but emphasized all the more by the band's expanding understanding of complex rhythms. The Weymouth–Frantz backline was funky enough anyway – being married may have helped in some subconscious way – but when African drummers were added into the mix, along with a horn section and guest vocalists to add a gospel feel reminiscent of Fela Kuti's Africa 70 Afrobeat collective, the band were pushing the boundaries of what music should sound like, all the time drawing attention to the fact that an album of songs is an industrialized and manipulated product. They jammed in the studio and looped chosen sections together to create ever more complex underpinning rhythms, but kept the melodies and chord progressions very simple. Standout tracks of this period include 'Life During Wartime' and 'Cities' from *Fear Of Music* and *Houses In Motion*, and the breakthrough UK single 'Once In A Lifetime' from *Remain In Light*, although they did not fare so well in their home country where the single and album were judged too black for white radio and too white for black radio. What better evidence do you want that *Remain In Light* was the direction that music really should be taking?

It was the last Talking Heads album for three years however, as the band took the opportunity to get away from each other, relations having been strained during the recording for the last album due to Byrne's apparent dictatorial style. Weymouth and Frantz embarked on their punk, disco, rap hybrid project Tom Tom Club and had immediate commercial success with the single 'Wordy Rappinghood', Harrison made a solo album and Byrne immersed himself in an avant-garde ballet project and production work for the likes of Fun Boy Three and B-52s. When they reconvened in 1983 for the *Speaking In Tongues* album the mood and the in-

tention was much more straightforward. Eno was not involved and the band got down to the business of producing a less self-conscious set of uplifting pop songs. 'Burning Down The House', 'This Must Be The Place' and 'Swamp' were also included on the live *Stop Making Sense* album, which was released along with a video of the band in performance, during which Byrne, with assistance from some clever editing, finds himself in an ever-expanding suit, demonstrating a lighter, more visually appealing side to the band. In fact, their video for 'Road To Nowhere', a single from the band's most successful album *Little Creatures*, with its innovative look, synthesis of sound and vision, artistic message and humour, set the standard for 'serious' pop videos in the years to come.

In 1986, Byrne conceived and wrote the film *True Stories*, based around his usual preoccupation with showing America in all its mad glory, and a Talking Heads album was recorded as the soundtrack. After a two year break the band released a final album, *Naked*, which captured the band at their most relaxed and supremely confident. The song writing, playing and overall vibe is tip-top. A good one to go out on, for the band that changed the way that pop music was made.

First team: David Byrne (v, g, k, b), Tina Weymouth (b, k, v), Chris Frantz (d, k), Jerry Harrison (g, b, k), Brian Eno (k, b, v)

Place, time, scene: New York 1977. Talking Heads had an artistic agenda from the start, and with help from Brian Eno, who seized the opportunity to continue his aborted pop project of the seventies, they developed a new aesthetic and structural approach to music production which ultimately blurred the lines between pop, rock and soul forms and progressively undermined 'serious' pop music's claims to any kind of transcendental function. Clever bastards. Radiohead named themselves after a Talking Heads song, and REM have surely been inspired by many of the band's musical and philosophical practices.

What to buy first: *Remain In Light* 1980

And then: *1977* 1977, *More Songs About Buildings And Food* 1978, *Speaking In Tongues* 1983, *Naked* 1988

In retrospect: *Stop Making Sense* 1984

Teenage Fanclub

TEENAGE FANCLUB

While the US independent scene was busy dividing itself up into those seriously experimenting with the developing clash of metal and punk on one hand and those advocating lo-fi values and taking the piss on the other, Scotland's Teenage Fanclub breezed in and showed that you could have both. Their early grunge sound, which quickly gave way to something more harmonic and folk-based, had all the right muso credentials – years of involvement with a Glasgow scene that lionized the gentle psychedelia of the Beach Boys and Big Star saw to that – and their attitude was offhand and relaxed enough to connect with a new type of music fan that dabbled in the new self-reflexive irony of bands like Pavement. Scotland has a history of producing intellectual and rock/pop-educated musicians from the Rezillos to Orange Juice and beyond, and the

Belshill scene that was home to Teenage Fanclub was no different. BMX Bandits, Superstar, the Soup Dragons, 18 Wheeler and the Telstar Ponies all emerged from the Belshill scene, armed with impressive record collections and a knack for classic songwriting that must be standard issue when it comes to the Scottish genome. There are three songwriters in Teenage Fanclub and over the course of six albums they have developed the musical setting for their songs in a way that other bands from the late eighties have not managed. As the grunge bands and lo-fi bands of yore disappear or get stuck in a stylistic stalemate, Teenage Fanclub continue on their way unhindered.

The history of Teenage Fanclub begins with a band called Pretty Flowers in 1983 led by Duglas T. Stewart, Sean Dickson and Norman Blake and based in the Belshill area of Glasgow, not far from the scene that had launched Primal Scream and the Pastels. Those two bands had been thrust into the national spotlight due to their inclusion on the infamous *C86* tape together with 20 other bands from around the UK, which it was posited would save guitar-pop and provide a blockade against the all-conquering hip-hop enemy. The Belshill mob were well out of it at that point, and as Pretty Flowers splintered into the BMX Bandits, Boy Hairdressers and the Soup Dragons, the scene up north became more vibrant still, developing organically and crucially remaining in touch with a more regional audience and culture. As the hopefuls signed to Creation, 4AD and various major labels hoping for a return to guitar-based pop, foundered under the weight of expectation, the key players on the Belshill scene concentrated instead on having fun and perfecting their songcraft away from the public glare. There was plenty of cross-pollination. Norman Blake and Francis MacDonald divided their time between the Hairdressers and the Bandits between 1986 and 1988 before forming Teenage Fanclub in 1989, and both Gerard Love and Raymond McGinley had played with the Bandits and Hairdressers respectively before completing the new quartet. With local legend Brendan O'Hare replacing MacDonald before the band's first recording sessions, Teenage Fanclub effectively started as scene veterans with an impressive collective musical knowledge drawn from relentless record-buying and a good sense of where indie music was going to go next. When Stephen Pastel made a timely demo tape intervention in 1989, making sure that Alan McGee of Creation Records got a copy, it was immediately apparent to all who heard them that Teenage Fanclub were the first British band in years that had a potential connection with the American independent scene.

The debut album *A Catholic Education* was released on the independent Paperhouse label and was the British response to Dinosaur Jr's stoned classic, *You're Living All Over Me*, but with just a hint of retro psychedelic pop to make it something different. The Stone Roses had built their sound around a certain jangle that recalled bands like the Byrds and had thrown in one or two harmonies too. Teenage Fanclub did something similar but buried their sparkle in a form of lo-fi sludge that made sense to a wide cross-section of American fans. The single 'Everything Flows' was an instant hit in an underground scene which was slowly emerging into a new strand of mainstream alternative. Soon Nirvana and Sonic Youth were talking about Teenage Fanclub and Geffen were interested in signing them after their American deal with the fabulously cool Matador label was up. A throwaway album of instrumentals called *The King* confirmed the band's sense of the absurd, but when the second album proper, *Bandwagonesque*, was released in 1991 the output emphatically matched the hype.

At the behest of producer Don Fleming, Teenage Fanclub brought the guitar squall under control, took the tempo down and brought the words and harmonies to the fore. The opening track 'The Concept' demonstrated the new style, immaculate hooks were given extra oomph by well-timed power chord crashes and dead-on harmonies, and the lyrics revealed a sardonic humour based around characterizations drawn from the band's own social experience, 'she wears denim wherever she goes, she says she's gonna get some records by the Status Quo'. It was a stylistic trait not lost on the Brit poppers to come. Oh and the extended coda at the end of the song is the best blend of harmony singing and broken-down guitars you'll ever hear. The songs keep coming right across the album, most played at a relaxed pace that on some occasions seems almost stationary. The obsession with dancefloor rock and the importance of the groove was apparently lost on Teenage Fanclub who had more traditional concerns, for instance 'What You Do To Me' found the band at their most overtly reverential, perfecting a noise-guitar pastiche of one of their key influences, Big Star.

The *Thirteen* album which followed was a self-produced set which tightened up the musicianship another notch, and with songs entitled 'Gene Clark' and 'Commercial Alternative' a mature awareness of their chosen profession was clearly evident. 'Radio' was the key single taken from the album, a power-pop masterwork that was a definite move away from the guitar-scape sound of their earlier work towards something more defined and shaped. The *Grand Prix* album once again featured songs by Blake, Love and McGinley, although you wouldn't know there were three separate writers at work when the overall sound is so consistent and the standard so high. Songs like 'Sparky's Dream' and 'Mellow Doubt' displayed their west-coast influences proudly, at a time when retro American sounds had been surgically removed from most British music and harmonies were no-go areas for Britpop bands keen to affect a more individual shouty-punk or spoken Cockney style. The album's highlight 'Neil Jung' is still their best song, the sound of Crosby, Stills and Nash, had they joined Neil Young's Crazy Horse boys instead of Neil joining them.

Having left Creation after *Grand Prix*, Teenage Fanclub stripped away all of the electricity to record an EP of some of their earlier material for those who may not have realized that there were living breathing songs existing amidst the lashing guitars. Suitably inspired, they kept the noise down for the 1997 album *Songs From Northern Britain* (i.e. Scotland) and put the harmonies right upfront. 'I Don't Want Control Of You' and 'Ain't That Enough' are the best folk-rock songs since Buffalo Springfield and the Byrds, gentle, soothing moments of something real and entirely free from cynicism that sometimes only human voices in harmony can convey. In his most personal book yet, *31 Songs*, Nick Hornby writes that 'I need somewhere to run to, now more than ever, and songs like "Ain't That Enough" is where I run'.[62] 'Here is a song, my love, ain't that enough?'. Indeed. Teenage Fanclub have located the Holy Grail and, judging by *Howdy!* released in 2000 wherein the band take on classic pop a la Badfinger and Wings, they intend to keep it.

First team: Norman Blake (v, g), Raymond McGinley (g, v), Gerard Love (b, v), Brendan O'Hare (d)

Place, time, scene: Glasgow 1989. Teenage Fanclub were the latest in a tradition of Scottish bands who combined songcraft with an historical appreciation of American music. While the majority of British indie bands of the period were continuing in the tradition of the Smiths with a bright jangly sound and sensitive or political lyrics, or tinkering with new dance styles, Teenage Fanclub were more readily assimilated into the American independent tradition that had evolved into the Seattle-based sound of grunge. Via a gradual taming of their early guitar squall and focus on more traditional pop elements, Teenage Fanclub have ultimately emerged as something of a rarity among UK bands, a band that can still deal in irony when it wants to but isn't defined by adopting a self-consciously ironic position. They make real

music, refreshingly free of cynicism, which ain't easy in these postmodern times.

What to buy first: *Bandwagonesque* 1991

And then: *A Catholic Education* 1990, *Grand Prix* 1995, *Songs From Northern Britain* 1997

In retrospect: *Four Thousand Seven Hundred and Sixty-Six Seconds: A Short Cut To Teenage Fanclub* 2003

TELEVISION

The reaction to pop music's transition into rock complete with new electronic instrumentation, a variety of recording effects and out on stage Jim Marshall's stacked-up noise monsters, was for some a return to the smaller pub and club circuit where it was all a lot more basic. New bands had been thin on the ground since the studio took over from live gigs as the musician's new workplace. Of course when the story of punk gets told it's with all this in mind, but the emphasis is usually placed on punk's anti-musician philosophy where it became an unwritten law that musical skill contravened the very fundamentals of the new style. That way led to cynicism, pretentiousness and wizard costumes. But that could happen anyway, some of the biggest tosspots in music are resolutely non-musical. They're called managers.

The problem facing creative popular music in the mid-seventies was nothing to do with how you played or what you played, it was whether or not it meant anything to the listening audience. Was there some form of reciprocal communication between the stage and the floor, or was it all going one way, very loudly over people's heads? What if the bombast could be removed and the music left in tact, stripped down to only the parts that were necessary to get the point across? Television were the band that found a way to do that. Their music was complex and raw simultaneously. It had a visceral thrill but was clever as hell. Well no – Verlaine was probably cleverer than his old friend Richard when it came to music, and more driven too. That's why he sacked his old friend from Television when the music got beyond him, betraying a ruthlessness and a confidence that ultimately led to his downfall at the hands of those who had bought into the punk myth, which he and his band had always striven to avoid.

Tom Verlaine was born Tom Miller in New Jersey. Like his friend, Richard Myers who became Richard Hell, he was a keen reader and writer of poetry and literature. They moved to New York together in the late sixties and after setting up a publishing press for their work, they opted to start a band instead. The Neon Boys lasted all of a year before becoming Television at which point Hell departed. The line-up of Verlaine, drummer Billy Ficca, bassist Fred Smith and second guitarist Richard Lloyd were the first to play the newly-opened CBGBs club in the seedy Bowery district of New York. In fact they were the first new music band to play there ever.

The club had originally been set-up as a country, bluegrass and blues (CBGBs) venue but low turnout meant that owner Hilly Krystal started looking for other options. When Verlaine collared him in the street it was to ask for one gig, which became a Sunday night residency and then regular headline slots across the week, paving the way for the Ramones, Blondie and Talking Heads amongst others. Crucially, the residency gave the band an opportunity to experiment with their sound, pushing boundaries while having to always keep the audience entertained. Not since the Velvet Underground's shows at Café Bizarre and Max's Kansas City had a rock band really tried out innovative new ideas outside the studio environment. The club was key to Television's eventual sound. When Brian Eno was asked to record a studio session with the band for an Island Records demo, Verlaine was confident enough to tell the undisputed king of sonic capture that even he had got it wrong.

The self-produced and released single 'Little Johnny Jewel' was an epic start. The tense atmosphere of the track is rooted in its sparse interplay between bass and drums and builds towards a wide-ranging and inventive, but importantly thin sounding, guitar solo that was the sign of things to come. The track sparked a lot of interest in similar scenes beginning to emerge elsewhere in the US and over in Britain too where the record was a popular import purchase for a year or so after its release due to growing interest from nascent punks. Julian Cope writes in his *Head-On* book[63] that he bought the record in October 1976, two months before the release of 'Anarchy In The UK' and that 'It made the New York Dolls sound like Yes – the bass had no bass, the guitars had no power at all and the singing was awful. The whole record was awful. And epic. And completely brilliant.'

'Little Johnny Jewel' was followed by a deal with Elektra, and then the debut album *Marquee Moon* which blew the lid off punk and caused confusion amongst those who thought they knew what the new musical environment was about. The sound was suitably raw and the vocals clearly not in any way related to anything in the mainstream, but the scope was astonishing, the lyrics were surreal and poetic 'I remember how the darkness doubled, lightning struck itself', and the arrangements of the music and sheer skill of the musicians were awe-inspiring. They had a groove alright, but it was a million miles away from the angry heavy-metal head-banging rhythms of their contemporaries. Television inspired more of a head-nod than a head-bang, an energy-conserving move which has been *de rigueur* for those demonstrating appreciation for good music ever since. The guitar solos are the stars of the show of course: try Verlaine on 'Friction', Lloyd on 'Elevation' and both played against each other on the title track which, if you've never heard it, I guarantee will be ten minutes of your life well spent.

During promotional visits to support *Marquee Moon*, Verlaine who began as a hero of the British music press, soon incurred their wrath with his apparently elitist comments concerning British punk bands and the institutionalized nature of new wave, which he claimed played right into the hands of the corporate niche marketers. He was right of course, but he could have toned it down a little.

When the band released the follow-up *Adventure*, which was just as impressive as *Marquee Moon*, the reviews were unnecessarily critical. As punk mythology continued to become more entrenched, Television could now, it seems, be rightly adjudged to have become egotistical in their search for ever more musical innovation. Verlaine in particular felt the backlash, which has now become a standard cyclical technique of music journalists keen to demonstrate their stock of cultural capital amongst their peers. They split shortly after its release, probably fairly certain that their work would stand the test of time. And it has.

First team: Tom Verlaine (v, g), Richard Lloyd (g, v), Fred Smith (b, v), Billy Ficca (d)

Place, time, scene: New York 1974. Television instigated the CBGBs scene, which remains the exemplar of creativity in a live setting. Apart from the obvious influence on the attitude of those who came after the first wave of punk who wanted to retain the philosophy but experiment with the musical form, Television must also be given credit as a prime motivational influence on the no-wave bands that played at CBGBs and had an express intention to experiment but without recourse to traditional notions of musical ability.

What to buy first: *Marquee Moon* 1977

And then: *Adventure* 1978

13TH FLOOR ELEVATORS

In 1965 while a whole generation of American music-makers were turning on to the invading British bands led by the Beatles and developing a collective garage band scene that had access to power amps, electric basses and organs made by Vox and Farfisa, in Texas the 13th Floor Elevators were headed back to the source. Driven on by Roky Erickson's snarling blues voice and given substance by Tommy Hall's forthright and mature lyrics and idiosyncratic jug-playing, the band were a progressive blend of everything that was good about early folk and rhythm and blues which was itself a primal mix of jazz, country-blues, boogie-woogie and gospel. When you take into account their desire to experiment too, there's a case to be made for the 13th Floor Elevators as the true Texan heirs to Buddy Holly. Well, if he had got monged out on drugs and read Nietzsche at any rate.

The relationship between Erickson and Hall was not dissimilar to that which existed between Ray Manzarek and Jim Morrison in the Doors – the older teacher and the young impetuous wild student. However where Manzarek was a calming, earthing influence, Hall apparently felt no such responsibility towards Erickson. He turned him onto every drug imaginable, from magic mushrooms to DMT, a variety of LSD that was said to have effects that magnified the trip experience by five hundred, and provided reading lists that included the aforementioned Nietzsche along with Gurdjieff, Huxley and Timothy Leary. Where the Doors and other contemporaries such as the Mothers, the Velvets and the Magic Band were grounded, at least to some extent, the 13th Floor Elevators were always floating and drifting. As Hall's lyrics to 'Slip Inside This House' advised, 'lift your mind into the dance' – a call to arms that their Texan brethren, the Butthole Surfers paid some attention to.

The band was formed in September 1965 after the dissolution of Roky's previous band the Spades, a set of teenage musicians who had all been taught their chops by the multi-instrumentalist vocalist. With the Elevators he had more freedom to concentrate on his own contribution. He was backed by the innovative guitar-playing of Stacey Sutherland who may just have invented the acid-guitar sound copied by so many, and a solid backline of Ronnie Leatherman and John Ike Walton. Their first single was a re-recording of the Spades' 'You're Gonna Miss Me' which was not only a concise blast of proto-psychedelic punk but also introduced an odd new sound in Hall's jug-playing. He cooed and gobbled throughout the song, creating the deranged sounds by holding a microphone next to his prized ceramic jug while he blew into it. Some have said that by adding varying amounts of liquid or organic leafy material (ahem) he could create different pitches and textures while others have claimed that the jug itself was surplus to requirements and that Hall could make the music using his mouth alone. Whatever, it got people talking, especially as the bizarre sound cropped up on a high proportion of future recordings by the band.

The first album was called *The Psychedelic Sounds Of The 13th Floor Elevators* and sounded like nothing else released in 1966. always on the verge of falling apart, 'Fire Engine', a song about DMT, hurtled to its conclusion driven by vocalised sirens and Sutherland's Chuck Berry riffing and featured a blood-curdling scream that Paul Dianno of Iron Maiden would perfect over a decade later. 'Reverberation' was an aptly titled wobbler that featured dual vocals – Erickson's sturdy foreground and a ghostly shadow, and two songs written by Powell St John – 'Monkey Island' and 'The Kingdom Of Heaven' – feature strange monkey impersonations and plunging jug noises respectively.

By the time the band had released the second album *Easter Everywhere* in 1967 they had become public enemy number one in their home state of Texas. After relentless hassle by the squares and the law they had been lucky to escape a lengthy prison sentence with hard labour for possession of hashish but still they didn't hold back on the drug references in their songs. Anti-conservative ranting and both liberal and faintly fascist philosophy were still their stock in trade. 'Slip Inside This House' is the album's epic eight-minute highlight, a song groovy enough to be covered by Primal Scream some years later on their summation of psychedelia and dance music, *Scream-adelica* in 1991. The album also contains the melodic 'She Lives (In A Time Of Her Own)' and 'Earthquake' where Erickson really comes into his own as the creator of swirling psychedelic pop music. With Hall gone by the time the album was released Erickson had a clear run at making some truly wonderful music but unfortunately he only recorded three more songs with the band before his life irrevocably altered.

Once again arrested for possession he was offered prison or psychiatric confinement. He opted for the latter and pretty soon after, electro-shock therapy did for him. He has never fully recovered, another experimental mind destroyed by experimental science. The final album *Bulls Of The Woods* was released in 1909 containing one of his best songs, the ghostly 'May The Circle Remain Unbroken' featuring a thoroughly unique vocal performance. There have been a couple of attempts at reformation but Erickson's mental health has stood in the way of anything long-term. Hall remains an enigmatic historical figure in the footnotes of rock history and in 1978 Sutherland was shot dead by his wife. There's a film in it surely?

First team: Roky Erickson (v, g), Tommy Hall (jug, v), Stacey Sutherland (g), Dan Galindo (b), Danny Thomas (d)

Place, time, scene: Austin, Texas 1965. The 13th Floor Elevators were the first of the garage rock bands to try something different. They integrated folk, politics and raw rhythm and blues into their basic electric sound and from their very first album had created a more eclectic sound than their rivals. They were *the* nuggets band that influenced not just their sixties contemporaries but also the post-punk scenes around the world in the late seventies.

What to buy first: *Easter Everywhere* 1967

And then: *The Psychedelic Sounds Of The 13th Floor Elevators* 1966

In retrospect: *Absolutely The Best* 2002

THROBBING GRISTLE

Genesis P-Orridge was born in Manchester in 1949. His contribution to alternative music is significant, but it's not the full extent of his artistic work over the last 35 years. He describes himself as a cultural engineer. His most recent work is on a project called 'Breaking Sex' which promotes the use of body art and implants to fictionalize the body, to get away from the standard physical human form. That's not just messing with our perceptions of gender, it encourages a move away from looking human altogether if it can be achieved, adding horns, fangs, steel spikes and what he calls 'serial breasts'. He may have started by messing with people's perceptions of what constitutes music, but he's since moved on to the body itself as a site of experimentation.

Orridge took over where Captain Beefheart left off, at least in terms of music. Where Beefheart was keen to destabilize the accepted rules of popular music which relied on familiar rhythms, harmonies and melodies, and hopefully encourage a more critical process of listening, Orridge went further and manipulated the very sound that was the basis of rhythm, harmony and melody. Orridge was less concerned with waking people up from their pop music induced narcoleptic state, and more concerned with provoking the listener to a higher state of consciousness by using sound to evoke a far greater range of mental images and emotional feelings. He wrote a thesis known as the Splinter Test which claims that one sample, when it is heard, sets in train a whole series of cosmic conections: 'No matter how short, or apparently unrecognizable a sample might be in linear TIME perception, it must, inevitably, contain within it (and accessible through it) thee sum total ov absolutely everything its original context represented, communicated, or touched in any way. On top ov this it must implicitly also include thee sum

THE A TO X OF ALTERNATIVE MUSIC

total ov every individual in any way connected with its introduction and construction within thee original'[64].

OK, so it's a fairly straightforward idea and musicians and producers have been doing something similar for years now. But Orridge was doing it back in the early seventies when the manipulation was carried out by hand not computer, and when you listen to the work of his band, Throbbing Gristle, you realize that the splinters of sound are not there to add texture and flavour or to provide a groove, they're there to fuck with your brain and to mess with your emotions. Throbbing Gristle, as Orridge's disconcerting Aleister Crowley speak printed above and his experimental lifestyle attest, were there to scare the willies out of people.

In the early seventies Genesis P-Orridge was a performance artist working in London. By 1975 he had coined the term 'industrial music' and was working with his girlfriend Cozi Fanni Tutti and engineer and graphic designer Peter Christopherson on a series of soundscapes which bore little, if no resemblance at all, to traditional music. The idea for a band came when the three met Chris Carter, a musician who built his own synthesizers whose work included sound and visual production for the BBC. He brought with him a number of years' experience with sound and lighting that had initially been inspired by early Pink Floyd shows in the capital. He perhaps saw something of the Syd Barrett in Genesis P-Orridge.

The first show was on July 6th 1976 at Air in London and was followed later that year with a performance at an event entitled Prostitution held at the Institute of Contemporary Arts (ICA). Like the 30 or so other shows that the band played in the next five years, the performance was carefully prepared and presented to achieve maximum shock effect. The attitude was in keeping with the emerging punk scene, although Throbbing Gristle were never taken seriously by punks, the utter desolation and dark terror of their music somehow interpreted as some kind of ironic put-on. The names and the preoccupation with sex probably didn't help.

An early track, 'Hamburger Lady', is typical of the band's output. The synthesizers and guitar combine to produce a howling-wind effect complete with metallic creaking, evoking mental images of a disused tin mine

on a Cornish moor about 3 am. The vocals are barely audible which is probably just as well, as the story concerns the plight of a disfigured women sinking further into depression following a horrific burning. The track appears on the album *D.O.A. The Third And Final Report*, released on their own Industrial Records label which signed up Cabaret Voltaire and Clock DVA amongst others. It also put out records by the cut-up originator himself William S. Burroughs.

The third album *20 Jazz Funk Greats* is notable for its experimentation with dance rhythms and drum machines and is probably their most accessible, notably due to the production, carried out at the band's own Death Factory studio in Hackney. The album was a significant influence on 23 Skidoo who recorded their funk-inflected debut long-player at Death Factory with production from Orridge and Christopherson, and confirmed the new dancefloor direction that industrial music was taking, eventually being tagged Electronic Body Music (EBM).

Throbbing Gristle split in 1981. Carter and Tutti have worked together as a duo since then, and Orridge and Christopherson set up Psychic TV, knocking out at least 20 albums, many of which are live or released in serial form. Christopherson is also one half of the esoteric underground band Coil, while Orridge's role as the leader of Thee Temple ov Psychic Youth – an anti-cult who practice pro-sexual self liberation philosophies non-hierarchically – made him a natural cultural icon for the late-eighties rave scene which he embraced wholeheartedly.

First team: Genesis P-Orridge (v), Chris Carter (s, d), Cosey Fanni Tutti (g), Peter Christopherson (elec)

Place, time, scene: London 1976. Throbbing Gristle are the originators of industrial music along with Cabaret Voltaire who were developing similar methods in Sheffield at the same time. 23 Skidoo, Clock DVA, Thomas Leer and SPK took the form forward as did Einstürzende Neubauten in Germany, a band which made music with manufactured tools. Dance music of all types owe a great debt to the early industrial 'weird rhythms, no melodies' pioneers.

What to buy first: *D.O.A. The Third And Final Report* 1978

And then: *20 Jazz Funk Greats* 1979

THROWING MUSES

Boston band Throwing Muses were the first of their kind, an independent, underground band led by three women. The music was initially a mix of punk and country styles but soon settled into an idiosyncratic noise-guitar model that was influential during the late eighties. Kristin Hersh's lyrics are seemingly deeply personal and because of her prominent position within a male-dominated culture, are scrutinized for signs of feminist discourse. Hersh herself is disappointed that, in her words, 'men write about the world and women write about women'. Like Patti Smith before her and PJ Harvey after her, she is keen to simply be judged at face value with no specific feminist agenda.

Hersh formed the Throwing Muses with her half-sister Tanya Donnelly when they lived in Long Island. The drummer David Narcizo learned to play a borrowed kit that had no cymbals and this became a trademark of their early sound. The first mini-album is a truly original mix of chopping-changing guitar patterns, inventive drumming (straight, ska or polka) and Hersh's astonishing voice that has a decidedly Celtic/English folk lilt except when she is screaming like a petulant child. The combination with Donnelly at certain points makes for some unusual harmonies. Every track is infectious and refreshing with lyrics that are downright surreal sometimes. The album came out on the British 4AD label in 1986, a year before fellow Bostonians the Pixies made their breakthrough. It has to be up there as one of the best debuts by any band anywhere. That good!

But then, inexplicably, the next three albums just failed to deliver. The best songs are those featuring harsh guitar work, but this is rarely inspired. The lyrics are still interesting even if there is a growing

Throwing Muses

emphasis on the 'aren't men crap' theme. It may be true but you know, come on, Kristen. It wasn't until *The Real Ramona* in 1991 that the band pulled themselves back together again and, following Tanya Donnelly's departure to form Belly, the Muses finally delivered an album, *Red Heaven*, that had the twists and turns, hooks, and balls-out guitar that it was always clear they could manage given the right mindset. It's just great to hear Hersh and Narcizo banging out whatever feels good at the time.

Hersh's solo albums tend to be quieter, especially the debut *Hips And Makers* which followed the renaissance of *Red Heaven*. The track 'Your Ghost' may not be the most affecting lyric that she has written, but delivered against a sparse piano background with a controlled and deeply emotive voice, it might as well be. The Muses put out *University* in 1995 and *Limbo* in 1996 and there have been more solo albums since too. She's got her mojo working again. Hoorah!

First team: Kristin Hersh (v, g), David Narcizo (d, v), Tanya Donnelly (g, v), Leslie Langston (b)

Place, time, scene: Boston 1985. Wow, the Throwing Muses began in some style with an album out of nowhere, and then seemed to fall into indie mediocrity for the rest of the decade. The early playfulness in the Throwing Muses' output is detectable in the Pixies' early work and in bands like the Geraldine Fibbers and Babes In Toyland.

What to buy first: *Throwing Muses* 1986

And then: *Red Heaven* 1992, *University* 1995, *Kristen Hersh: Hips And Makers* 1994

TINDERSTICKS

Nobody was expecting Tindersticks – they came out of nowhere. In the early nineties independent music was still adhering to the principles set up by the punk and post-punk movements. On one hand, keep it simple and on the other, complicate the hell out of the simplicity. That meant rhythmic, textural and harmonic experimentation and on no account solos, arrangement, sweet singing or songs dealing exclusively with love and relationships. Personal songs had to have social significance, melodies clothed in noise and weird-ness, and vocals whined, screamed or affecting an air of disinterestedness. A few bands bucked the trend to an extent, but even Nick Cave and Robert Smith who were both hopeless romantics succumbed to harsh atmospheres and dense textures to evoke the required mood. The Cardiacs were masters of arrangement and Tim Smith knew a thing or two about key changes, but Tindersticks are more understated and subtle than all of them. They don't build songs, they grow them.

Vocalist Stuart Staples has admitted that he has problems with contemporary music, 'it's a distraction and that's supposed to be enough, but I find myself putting Al Green on again because I believe in it, it lets me think what I want to think, it let's me feel a certain way'.[65] His own songs, interpreted by a set of immensely talented musicians, are written from the heart, and avoid the one-dimensionality that comes from the focused stylistic branding that has become a natural part of music-making in the present day. The band is always happy to read wildly varying reviews of their music because it lets them know they are still on the right track. Jonathan Donahue of Mercury Rev bemoaned the death of the holistic song during the nineties, concerned that style and the self-conscious combination of styles was prioritized over substance. Tindersticks have it the right way round. They use Staples' songs and voice as a starting point and draw out the sincerity, beauty, intensity, sadness and humour in his lyrics. The songs are often uplifting and bleak at the same time, and even in full-tilt epic mode they retain an intimacy that comes from the musicians' connectivity to the source of the song.

The band moved from Nottingham to London in 1992. Staples, guitarist Neil Fraser and bassist Mark Colwill had all worked together at the independent record store Selectadisc in their home town – always a great opportunity for concerted listening to an eclectic range of music – and Staples in particular had a taste for open-hearted easy listening testifiers like Neil Diamond and Lee Hazelwood. Keyboardist Dave Boulter spotted this tendency early on and encouraged Staples to write with poignancy and melancholy as guiding principles. The first London gig was at the Islington Powerhaus in December 1992, two weeks after Radiohead had played the venue. By the end of the following year Radiohead had just about broken through in the UK with their single 'Creep' and Tindersticks had the *Melody Maker* album of the year with their debut double set that featured sumptuous string arrangements, discordant guitar jamming and every mood enhancing sound in-between. The songs avoid the 1993 production strategy of quiet-loud dynamic rushes and instead, evolve from minimal and delicate late-night bar songs where Staples' voice is accompanied by a simple piano or guitar shape, into something bigger and grander, often involving the type of string and horn arrangements that Ennio Morricone was so good at. Film noir and spaghetti western are just two of the cinematic devices Tindersticks use to give a visual dimension to their songs. On later albums they peddle soft-porn, art-house and even flirt with the chick-flick genre.

On the second album the band enlisted the assistance of fellow musical traveller Terry Edwards of Gallon Drunk, and got more sophisticated with their deployment of strings and brass. On the first track, 'Diablo En El Ojo', arranger Dickon Hinchcliffe keeps both restrained and distant in the background while Staples' doleful vocals are shadowed by a low-level distorted guitar. Mind you, hear it live on their album *Bloomsbury Theatre 12.3.95* and the potential power of those under-recorded guitars becomes immediately apparent. 'A Night In' comes on all dark but then has a pretty little refrain that marks it out as the closest thing that Tindersticks will ever get to pop music, and that's followed by 'My Sister' which jazzes along jauntily while a story is told about the life of a blind woman (the narrator's sister) who is left by her father, beaten by her husband and handicapped by a freak accident. Dead at 32, she has asked for a 'cheap coffin so the worms can get to her quicker', tragic and comic, and containing a throat-lumper moment about how she sees twinkling lights in the darkness. Throughout, Staples' voice is unaffected and plain, lacking in lyricism and at odds with the extraordinarily inspired free-form musical jazz that accompanies him. 'Tiny Tears' is an old song which tells the perennially

tragic tale of a relationship breakdown, while 'Travelling Light', which pairs Staples with Carla Torgerson from the Walkabouts, is maybe the band's finest moment. It's concise, catchy and teeming with pathos, especially the line about the hole in the roof where the rain falls through 'where you always decide to sit', a neat utilization of imagery and analogy that Cave or Cohen would be wholly satisfied with.

On the third album *Curtains* the mood is once again laid-back and brilliantly orchestrated, and even reflects on the political economy of the band's own existence. 'Ballad Of Tindersticks' tells a tale of fame and success which they have experienced and by that point, opted out of. With two more albums placing emphasis on the soul aspects of their sound in a way not dissimilar to American band Lambchop, Tindersticks took the opportunity to fade once again into the shadows, always there for anyone seeking something more than momentary distraction. They'll keep knocking this stuff out for as long as it feels right which is good news for everyone concerned.

First team: Stuart Staples (v), Dave Boulter (k), Neil Fraser (g), Mark Colwill (b), Dickon Hinchcliffe (v), Al McCauley (d)

Place, time, scene: Nottingham 1992. Tindersticks bucked the trend towards noisy dynamics and integrated styles in early-nineties music, and focused on the songs. The band's skills in creating evocative soundscapes for Staples' stories keep the songs intimate and personal but not too close that the listener feels intimidated or embarrassed by what they are hearing. In fact, the cinematic nature of the songs' construction make them seem like short vignettes told about characters and situations that seem familiar from more filmic settings.

What to buy first: *The Second Tindersticks Album* 1995

And then: *Tindersticks* 1993, *Curtains* 1997, *Simple Pleasures* 1999, *Waiting For The Moon* 2003

U

UNDERWORLD

Rick Smith and Karl Hyde didn't react immediately to the new minimalist electronic sounds that they began hearing in the mid-eighties. At that point they had just wrapped up the Freur project which had scored a UK hit and appearances on *Cheggers Plays Pop* with the single 'Doot Doot'. The track and accompanying album had a strong electronic dimension and this was carried over into the newly formed Underworld in 1987, a band made up of several ex-Freur members who had picked up a deal with the Sire label and were soon knocking out synth-pop albums and touring internationally. They were largely irrelevant. It was however, all good groundwork. When the rave scene exploded in the UK and the groove became the new god, Smith in particular was ready and desperate to embrace the new beat science. Underworld Mk 1 disintegrated and together with DJ Darren Emerson, Smith and 'beat poet' Hyde were poised to take rock music to the next stage. The new Underworld were still at heart a band that played live and made albums (with lyrics) to be listened to, which set them apart from the DJs and producers that were fast taking over. They also had an innate connection to and understanding of groove-based electronic music which many of their indie/rock/pop contemporaries could not match.

Hyde and Smith met at Cardiff College where they studied art and electronics respectively. Obvious really. They formed Screen Gems, then Freur and quickly found themselves out in Cologne recording with the legendary Holger Czukay of Can. In fact, the version of 'Doot Doot' that they recorded with Czukay was not released as a single as their record label opted for the band's own original demo in the end. With Freur and the first incarnation of Underworld, keyboards were a crucial part of the overall mix but it was the collaboration with Darren Emerson that convinced the duo that they should take centre-stage. As a jobbing club DJ, Emerson knew that a good

dance track paid careful attention to the beat and should be relatively free of traditional song elements – verse and chorus structure, multi-tracked instrumental elements and vocals – that made mixing difficult. Underworld began constructing what Smith has referred to as sound installations that could be deconstructed and reassembled with ease. The live show became legendary as Smith and Emerson mixed everything spontaneously, often with motifs running throughout. They thought nothing of returning to a particular song several times in one performance, reading the audience to determine in what order they should segue their sets. In 1992 following the release of their early singles 'Bigmouth' and 'Dirty', they played a 14-hour set in the Experimental Sound Field at Glastonbury Festival, a multimedia event that incorporated live musicians, DJ sets and screens around the perimeter of the field, showing images that complemented the sounds coming from the stage. They also toured with Orbital as part of the Midi Circus Roadshow where they demonstrated the increasingly integral midi system which fired out sounds at key moments during live performance.

The 13-minute track 'Mmm Skyscraper I Love You' was released in 1993 to universal acclaim. A mix of space-rock and techno that had a major impact on Orbital, Fluke, Leftfield and the Chemical Brothers, it combines at different moments, latin rhythms, Gilmour-style cosmic guitar, various bleeps and pulses, an array of odd transformed samples and Karl Hyde's cut-up lyrics that reference God, Elvis and 'a little whipped cream'. Hyde's lyrics apparently come as short bullet-point notes or 2000 word essays. They sometimes inspire a sound installation or are inspired by the sounds already laid down. The band keeps everything they work on and stores the tapes away for possible future use.

The first album with the new line-up was *Dubnobasswithmyheadman* which was released in 1994 before the debut albums by Leftfield and the Chemical Brothers, and more grounded than previous releases by Prodigy and Orbital. As well as the full-length version of 'Skyscraper', there's the trancey 'Cowgirl' which cropped up again as 'Rez' on the second album, 'Dark And Long' which is both dark and well, long. The track was used to great effect in the film *Trainspotting* along with 'Born Slippy', a song used to represent the character of Begbie, a violent drunk, which was driven by a stream of consciousness rant delivered by Hyde during which he exclaims 'lager, lager, lager' and refers to himself as a 'mega mega white thing'. It's less a call to hedonistic weekenderism, and more accurately a cathartic cry for help for the singer with a very real drink problem of his own.

Things get trippy for the follow-up *Second Toughest In The Infants* released in 1996, which foregoes the sweeping keyboard washes in favour of less textured more direct constructions that feature syncopated jungle rhythms and more defined sonic interventions. 'Pearl's Girl' is almost industrial sounding, 'Rowla' has acid synth scrawled all over it, 'Confusion The Waitress' is punctuated throughout by what sounds like a looped piano recorded on stretched C120 cassette, and 'Blueski' is a montage of lazily picked guitar parts with no keyboards involved at all and recalls tapes made at home by Nick Drake. Bloody marvellous stuff. On *Beaucoup Fish* the guitar is back again for 'Shudder' leading into 'King Of Snake', a high energy return to Georgio Moroder's 'I Feel Love' sung by Donna Summer which has provided Smith and Emerson with several moments of inspiration over the years. The dede-dede-dede-dede bass line is joined by Italian house piano and Hyde once again throws out nonsensical lyrics about Tom and Jerry and drinking ''til you go pink'. 'Push Upstairs' is a concise house-pop gem and 'Cups' is a journey through all that can be done with electronic music, a kind of 'now that's how you do it' to the new breed of commercially-minded 'producers' creating one-dimensional club fodder quickly and soullessly with relatively cheap new quantizing software.

Emerson left before the release of *A Hundred Days Off* in 2002 and speculation arose as to the ability of Smith and Hyde to continue without his crucial input. Of course that concern was not shared by those who had actually been listening properly for the previous ten years. *A Hundred Days Off* is probably their best album, 'Two Months Off' their best individual track, a hard electro-riff driven trance-trip built around the line 'You bring light in' and it's got bells on it too. As for the rest of the album, there's blues, tribal chanting, house, dub and techno aplenty and it sounds magnificent live. Underworld clearly won't miss Emerson. Smith's quest for sonic perfection and Hyde's ability to deliver the emotional goods lyrically and vocally to blend the crude with the precise, the human with the machine, the art and the science, has always been at the heart of the Underworld project and can be detected right back to their earliest work. And they're the only synth-pop band in this book. Well, kind of.

First team: Rick Smith (k, prog, g, b), Karl Hyde (v, g, b, k), Darren Emerson (t-t, k, prog)

Place, time, scene: Romford, UK. Underworld are almost unique as a rock band that fully embraced dance-based electronic music and reformulated the structure of their musical output. They have not merely flavoured their rock with beats or gone over to the other side and revisited rock clichés for effect. If anything, they have deconstructed their creative practice and sound and in so-doing furthered the progress of rock music as a self-reflective artform that is ever more aware of the textures, moods, rhythms and melodies that constitute it. And made it rock fucking hard with bleeps.

What to buy first: *Dubnobasswithmyheadman* 1994

And then: *Second Toughest In The Infants* 1996, *Beaucoup Fish* 1999, *A Hundred Days Off* 2003

In retrospect: *Everything, Everything* 2002, *Underworld 1992–2002* 2003

V

VELVET UNDERGROUND

The Velvet Underground was the band that brought art and rock'n'roll together. Before the Velvet Underground there was no alternative form of popular music. Let's face it, pop music was evolving so fast and in such interesting directions that there was no urgent need for an alternative. By the mid-sixties the self-contained band format was well established, lyrics had become meaningful and profound and were even showing signs of becoming poetic, and a healthy live scene was ensuring that bands were emerging with a tightness and focus which resulted in self-composed and arranged music shorts that rightfully remain among the best that pop music ever did. But it wasn't art, at least not the kind of art that reflects on itself and the wider world. There was technique. Pop musicians, engineers and producers had learnt how to paint with sound to create a form of entertainment that could make the listener feel emotion or dance the night away, but these were distinct projects, produced artefacts. They obviously meant something to the people who bought them, but it didn't matter to the producers if their work had no effect beyond the tangible physical act of buying the record. That was the purpose of pop music. In 1965 that changed, Bob Dylan crossed over from folk into pop with his *Bringing It All Back Home* album and towards the end of the year a British band, the Who, finally acknowledged and addressed their generation. By then the Velvet Underground had been in existence for just under a year and had already decided that pop music was dead and that they were going to replace it with something altogether different.

By the time the band formed, Lou Reed was a veteran of the pop industry. He had released records when he was just 13 years old and had spent several years as a jobbing songwriter for Pickwick Records. He was a professional, he knew how to knock out a pop song. The thing is, he spent his spare time listening to free-form jazz and writing songs about heroin use. He was the very embodiment of the dichotomy, a pragmatic mainstreamer and an idealistic free spirit. All it required was for someone to push him one way or the other.

Enter John Cale, a New York-based music student living it up on a Leonard Bernstein scholarship. Having grown up in Wales and attended music college in London, he has confessed that he was unaware of the whole R&B club-scene going at places like the Marquee, the Flamingo and Crawdaddy clubs where the Stones were embarking on their rock'n'roll crusade. The Beatles didn't interest him either. He was too involved in his studies. He was inspired by the experimentation of musicians like Lamonte Young, Stockhausen and of course, John Cage. These were artists concerned with the form, not the content of a musical piece. They dealt in textures, harmonics and headfuck, and Cale wanted in. When he got to New York he joined forces with Young and focused his attention on his viola. He wanted to make it drone like Indian instruments did, and was interested in the possibilities of its amplification. When he met Lou Reed, two worlds collided, and there was a helluva noise.

The first thing that Reed and Cale worked on together was an ironic stab at the empty physicality of the dance record. It was a song called 'The Ostrich' which featured lines like 'First you stand on your partner's head', and was based around the simplest of musical patterns. Let's call it an early deconstruction of the pop song. It was one of two recorded by the Primitives, a project which mutated into the Velvet Underground with the addition of Reed's college buddy, guitarist Sterling Morrison and mutual acquaintance and stand-up drummer Mo Tucker. The band began playing regularly at Café Bizarre where they were able to develop their techniques and arrangements of songs such as 'Waiting For The Man', 'Heroin' and 'Venus In Furs', all of which appeared on their debut album recorded in 1966 in a studio paid for by their manager Andy Warhol.

He had seen them play at Café Bizarre in late 1965 and had decided immediately to include them as the centrepiece of his multimedia stage show entitled The Exploding Plastic Inevitable. The Velvets played their songs as dancers interpreted the lyrics using whips and syringes and a selection of Warhol's films played on a screen at the back of the stage. The overall concept belonged to Warhol, and was based on cultural theorist Marshall McLuhan's belief that communications technology was updating the potential of everyday life. Many ideas could be expressed simultaneously, triggering new forms of understanding, and best of all, anybody could get involved and use anything they wanted for their artistic tools. Warhol's reiterative screen-printing was part of the same idea, and if crass marketing images could be used as art, rock'n'roll could be used too. The thing is, many of those who experienced The Exploding Plastic Inevitable which toured across the country after its initial run at Warhol's Dom club, were more interested in the sounds emanating from the four black-clad musicians bearing down on their instruments all the while wearing shades to protect them from the extravagant light show. It was the droning viola, long sustained notes, piercing guitars, monotonous rhythms and the coolest speak-singing that stole the show.

The debut album collected together the Velvets' live favourites and added a few songs written by Reed at Warhol's behest for German model Nico, who had been added to the band to give it visual focus. She sang 'Femme Fatale', 'I'll Be Your Mirror' and 'All Tomorrow's Parties', leaving the more socio-realist tracks like 'Waiting For The Man', 'Heroin' and 'Run Run Run' to Reed. She was supposed to sing 'Sunday Morning', the gentle folk nursery rhyme that opens the album, but Reed was too keen on the neat blend of whimsy and paranoia that he had created in the lyrics to give it up that easily. 'Venus In Furs' is the standout track, an off-kilter droner that features Reed holding a conversation with an absent demon, building to a sustained one-chord guitar climax, a style that wouldn't really become fashionable until about a decade later. And those lyrics, vividly detailing a scene of seedy sadomasochism, must have produced hitherto unfamiliar mental images in the minds of pre-permissive society listeners.

Musically, the whole album is controlled and artful. There are no loose hippy jams, and the sparseness that pervades the album neatly fits the subject matter of songs that are dealing with stark urban realities of drug addiction, specific sex (not universal love) and a general sense of alienation and loss of innocence. It's a good one. I'd recommend you buy it and play it to all your friends.

The album was released through MGM's Verve label a few months after labelmate Frank Zappa's debut album *Freak Out*. Best known as a jazz label, Verve were keen to get on board with the new psychedelia, although Reed was never keen to acknowledge the connections between what he and Zappa were doing. He considered the Mothers Of Invention to be hippies, and like their contemporaries, playing a cynical game that placed the communication of art and reality after the primary imperative of forging a corporate career. Most psychedelic bands were subject to the same criticism from Reed, and it didn't help that Verve, in Reed's opinion, seemed to be pushing the Mothers' album harder than the Velvets' debut. The tour that went with the album took in the hippy west coast and both Jim Morrison and proto-punk Iggy Pop attended the gigs, leaving suitably inspired. By the time it ended, Nico had opted for a solo career and the connection with Warhol became less high profile as the Velvets tried to tone down the art tag they had picked up during the previous year.

The *White Light/White Heat* album was recorded in New York in 1967, in the summer when all the hippies had left for California. It was recorded quickly in just a few sessions and, unlike the debut album, a lot of it was played spontaneously. According to Sterling Morrison, the band would practise the beginning and the end of songs and then go for a take. In an interview with Victor Bockris and Gerard Malanga for their book *Up-tight: The Velvet Underground Story*, Morrison provides an insight into the recording of perhaps their most important song: 'For "Sister Ray" which we knew was going to be a major effort we stared at each other and said "this is going to be one take, so whatever you want to do, you better do it now" ... There is a musical struggle ... think it's great the way the organ comes in. Cale starts to try and play a solo. He's totally buried, then there's a sort of surge and he's pulling out all the stops until he rises out of the pack.'[66] 'Sister Ray' is the band at their peak. After several years playing live together, developing and internalizing a focused philosophy of their musical approach, it all finally comes together in that one track. And there's no bass. Throughout the album the guitar sound is fuzzy and all of the instruments leak into one another because they are being played so loud. It makes for a wall of sound that becomes more than the sum of its parts. Band members have had their own differing opinions on the finished product, but what's clear is that it sounded like nothing else recorded that year and remains an important aesthetic statement calling into question the search, then just underway, for the perfect studio representation of live sound, a project which has continued ever since and has only really succeeded in producing sounds and technical arrangements that do not exist in reality and have very little to do with the musicians involved. *White Light/White Heat* is what electricity sounds like when it's flowing through real people with real instruments.

A few months after the release of the album, Cale left. The band continued with Doug Yule taking his place but they were never again as challenging or innovative as they had once been. They still made great records. The 1969 album *The Velvet Underground* has been called Lou Reed with a backing band due to the emphasis placed on songs rather than experimental sound work. It's a pop album. 'Sweet Jane', 'What Goes On' and 'Pale Blue Eyes' are all much more accessible and helped the band to a deal with Ahmet Ertegun at Atlantic Records. The band spent the summer of 1970 playing a series of residency shows at Max's Kansas City in New York and became quite prolific, recording enough songs for another album, *Loaded*, which was released after Lou Reed left at the end of the summer, and a host of compilations released over the years since the band split. With Tucker and Morrison gone by 1971 and the band virtually a Doug Yule solo vehicle, the writing quite clearly has to stop at this point.

Except to say that Reed and Cale both emerged as godfathers of difficult and cool music sometime around 1978, when those turned-on by punk began tracing the lines back to the origins of alternative music and realized that the bloke who sang about coloured girls going 'doo de doo de doo doo d'de doo de doo de doo' had once had this thing with the guy who produced the debut albums by the Stooges and Patti Smith. Without the Velvet Underground there would be no Iggy, no Bowie, no Pistols, Television or Sonic Youth, no Fall, no Jesus And Mary Chain and no White Stripes. Brian Eno once famously said that although hardly anybody bought the Velvet Underground's debut album, everyone that did started a band. Wise words, Mr Eno.

First team: Lou Reed (v, g), John Cale (viola, k, b, v), Sterling Morrison (g, b), Mo Tucker (d, v)

Place, time, scene: New York 1965. The Velvet Underground bore no resemblance to any other music in New York at the time. Their dark blend of classical and pop techniques was very different to the folk rock of the Fugs and the Holy Modal Rounders, who played early counter-cultural songs in Greenwich Village. Their adoption by the art community kept them isolated from other music-based scenes as they travelled around the US, and they only really received recognition as a rock band just before they split. Only a select group of fans knew their music at the time and their full influence was not apparent until those original fans formed their own bands and helped develop the punk scene several years after their demise.

What to buy first: *The Velvet Underground And Nico* 1967

And then: *White Light/White Heat* 1968, *The Velvet Underground* 1969

In retrospect: *The Very Best Of The Velvet Underground* 2003

W

WHITE STRIPES

The White Stripes are the most recent of an illustrious line of primal Detroit-based bands. Following in the tradition of the MC5 and the Stooges but operating at the time of Eminem and Kid Rock, the duo, allegedly once married, now divorced, are plugged in to the source of rock'n'roll.

Like Iggy before him, Jack White (real name: Gillis) began as a drummer in Detroit bands Goober And The Peas and The Go, although previous to that he had been half of another duo with his friend Brian Muldoon who was 16 years his senior and ran the upholstery firm that White worked at part-time.

They called themselves Two Part Resin – it was just drums and guitar. It was during this partnership that White developed his love of blues music, particularly Son House and Howlin' Wolf. All that other stuff like AC/DC and Led Zeppelin took a back-seat as he returned to the source. At his first gig with Goober And The Peas he ended the show with an Elvis Presley song and soon gained notoriety as the strange kid on the Detroit scene, especially when he began playing with Megan White as the White Stripes.

The story goes that she started playing drums one day at a rehearsal and immediately provided the rhythm that White needed for his unique 'over-the-top' guitar playing. Within two months they were

The White Stripes

playing the Detroit scene, often supporting other 'full' bands in which White as he was now calling himself, also featured. When the Go were offered a deal with Sub-Pop he made the conscious decision to stick with Meg in the White Stripes, who by now had released a couple of singles on Dave Buick's Italy label. Their own debut album *The White Stripes* was a triumph of simplicity where the key thing musically is what's left out rather than what's put in, a moment of quiet suddenly being disturbed by loud feedback guitar is exactly what attention-grabbing rock'n'roll is all about. 'Little People' is the standout track.

By the second album *De Stijl*, the Whites had supposedly split up, but on record they were sounding better than ever. There's slide, blues harp and some amazing blues-rock screaming that is somewhere between Robert Plant and Bon Scott. The subjects of marriage and relationships are raised again and again throughout the album, sometimes loudly and with angst ('Let's Build A Home'), other times like what the Violent Femmes would do ('You're Pretty Good Looking') and occasionally melancholic ('Apple Blossom'). Compared to the breakthrough *White Blood Cells*, *De Stijl* has the rawer blues power and the better songs.

But of course you can't knock an album that gets people interested in honest to goodness rock music again. *White Blood Cells* was recorded in a bigger, better studio and sounds bigger because of it. There's more variety, which isn't always a good thing, but the White Stripes manage to retain their simplicity. White's voice takes on different personas, so on 'Fell In Love With A Girl' he comes on like Leonard Phillips of cartoon-punks the Dickies, and by the end of the album he's almost crooning when he sings 'This Protector'. 'Dead Leaves And The Dirty Ground' is smothered in the best-sounding guitar for years, all serious and brooding, while 'Hotel Yorba' is a throwaway rag complete with loose drumming and the type of sing-a-long chorus that nobody does anymore.

The most recent album, *Elephant*, is currently being analysed for over-ambitious tendencies by some, and for others, is being criticized as just more of the same. It's a difficult one for a band based around a set-up so basic and an idea so pure when the rule of industrialized music is to progress and offer something different to the awaiting amassed international audience. Blues guys like Robert Johnson and Son House are retrospectively respected for their commitment to a style, and are judged on their voice, songs and playing skills. To assess the White Stripes in terms of their success in emulating Black Sabbath or the Stooges, or how well they've set up the studio and arranged the songs, is missing the point. They're still tapped into a period way before all that. OK, so they may have tried something a little more elaborate that is sometimes beyond their means and craft, but forget that. On *Elephant*, just like the albums previous to it, the White Stripes demonstrated once again, for example with the pure dirt of 'Ball And Biscuit' and the pure dirty bassline of 'Seven Nation Army' that they are making records for all the right reasons. The costumes are easily changed, the soul within remains the same.

First team: Jack White (v, g, b), Meg White (d, v)

Place, time, scene: Detroit 1996. Following in the footsteps of the great Detroit bands of the sixties, the White Stripes, along with bands such as the Go and the Von Bondies, are making a pure form of rock'n' roll again, although the White Stripes go that bit further back, attempting to connect with the spirit of the blues before it became rhythm'n'blues. It will be interesting to see if their stripped-down approach will inspire a new set of music-makers that draw inspiration from the availability of home recording technology, the minimalism of certain dance music forms and the spirit of electrified music existing before the Rolling Stones. The future of music is just around the corner?

What to buy first: *De Stijl* 1999

And then: *White Blood Cells* 2000, *Elephant* 2003

WIRE

Wire came from out of nowhere. They even took themselves by surprise. In 1976 they were a punk band that had secured gigs at the Roxy, and then when they got into a recording studio it all changed. Their earlier more straightforward songs were dropped and in their place, over the course of two years, emerged three albums worth of experimental songs that have inspired specific bands and general approaches to recording and song structure ever since. Along with the Fall, Gang Of Four and the Pop Group, Wire were a key post-punk band which revelled in the new freedom that they had been given as rock music threw up its hands and allowed the new set of bands carte blanche to do whatever they wanted, but unlike the other bands mentioned, they couldn't help making pop songs. No amount of buried vocals, abrupt riffs and staccato rhythms, it seemed, was going to stop Wire being a catchy and fascinating-sounding band. They ended it themselves in 1979, convinced that they had explored enough, only to reform in 1985 and embark on another trilogy of albums that confirmed their role as explorers in sound and texture who knew how to get the darkest sounds from the instruments at their disposal, as is to be expected from a punk band making progressive music.

Wire was originally a quintet of art school students with guitarist Bruce Gilbert at 30, considerably older than the optimum age for a punk-rocker. Having despatched George Gill and signed up soundman Mike Thorne as their producer, the band comprising Gilbert, vocalist and guitarist Colin Newman, bassist and lyricist Graham Lewis and drummer and best name in pop history, Robert Gotobed, recorded their debut album *Pink Flag* in a few manic sessions when they should have just been making a couple of tracks for a single. According to Newman, each of the 21 songs was originally intended as an homage/pastiche. The title track was apparently intended as 'Johnny B. Goode' without chords and 'Strange' took on the Velvet Underground. The songs dealt with media reporting, the futility of war, sexuality and people who used to be lion tamers – all the usual stuff really, and as mentioned earlier, dead catchy.

On the second album, *Chairs Missing*, the band sound even better and the songs are longer but still minimalist. Like Can and Captain Beefheart, and in line with contemporaries, Gang Of Four and the Fall, the strategy adopted is self-consciously artistic, sounds are placed exactly where they are required for the maximum effect, and Mike Thorne must take some credit for this, hence the band's acknowledgement of him as the mythological fifth member. 'Practice Makes Perfect' is the first and best track on the

album, Newman's guitar beating out the familiar football crowd pre-chant, duh, duh, d-d-d-duh, alongside Lewis' proto-Hooky bass, while lead guitar spiders along over the top. As the song builds, a dark keyboard drone and synthesized voices à la 'Blue Monday' are thrown into the mix, and for a moment the track might just be the root of all things electro-pop and goth-rock, which at that point were not due to happen for a few years yet. The vocals are still jerky but often dipped so that they operate as another constituent part of the mix rather than out there as the lead sound, while Bruce Gilbert is given the opportunity to sprinkle a little grated and grating guitar at key moments. The two singles taken from the album, 'I Am The Fly' and 'Outdoor Miner' both give voice to everyday entomological concerns, although the former may be metaphorical. Dead catchy too.

After the third album *154* in 1979, which included visits from a cor anglaise and a modernist viola player called Tim who contributed psychedelic drones to the otherwise feedback assault of 'A Touching Display', oh and the fast punk workout of 'Two People In A Room' with off-mic shouting, the band split. Various solo adventures ensued, notably Newman's *A–Z* which contained songs originally destined for a fourth Wire album that he followed with an instrumental set for 4AD and then the altogether more pop *Not To*, before the four reconvened in 1985 for Wire Mark II.

The three albums made between 1987 and 1990 tracked the band through new technology. They were sampling and sequencing with the best of them. *The Ideal Copy* is probably the best of the three and has been reissued with the preceding *Snakedrill* EP, which was the sound of the band hitting the ground running. Machine-like in sound and hypnotic at times, tracks 'Drill', 'Ambitious' and 'Over Theirs' are hard songs with a cold-funk underpinning that are not a million miles away from the sounds on the first Nine Inch Nails album. Gotobed left after *Manscape* in 1990, an album worth getting simply for the mighty 'Torch It!', and the other three opted to continue as Wir – geddit? That lasted one album, and the next thing that was heard about Wire was a brand new album in 2002 called *Send* which joined the dots between their early minimalist, pre-post-punk experimentation, acquired technological know-how and a mature understanding of all the wyas that the music industry sucks and how to avoid falling for any of it. It's a punk rock album by a punk rock band. Immediate, sharp and simple. God, Wire are good.

First team: Colin Newman (v, g), Bruce Gilbert (g), Graham Lewis (b, v), Robert Gotobed (d)

Place, time, scene: London 1976. Wire were the first post-punk band to embrace the possibilities of studio recording, and quickly learned how to get the best sounds out of over-amplified guitars amongst other things. They created song structures that undermined traditional rock practice but always kept hooks and melodies central to their work.

What to buy first: *Chairs Missing* 1978

And then: *Pink Flag* 1977, *154* 1979, *The Ideal Copy* 1987, *Send* 2002

In retrospect: *On Returning (1977–1979)* 1989 *Wire 1985–1990: The A List* 1993

X

X

X combined punk, rockabilly and blues at their early shows in Los Angeles in 1977 and in so-doing eventually set off a new scene in the area dubbed Paisley Underground. Steve Wynn of Dream Syndicate and Sid Griffin of the Long Ryders were both fans of X before they formed their respective bands, and may not have considered the possibilities of more traditional music otherwise. X made real music fun.

Led by John Doe and Exene Cervenka, X were one of the first hardcore punk bands in LA and, like their New York counterparts Bad Brains who used reggae as their foil, X's original formula for hard, fast punk was built around the specific musical style of rockabilly. Guitarist Billy Zoom played like Chuck Berry trying to get across a stateline, i.e. with some urgency. DJ Bonebrake supplied the pounding drums, while Joe and Exene traded vocal harmonies with one another. Ray Manzarek, keyboardist with the Doors produced the band's first four albums, and was perhaps their spiritual guru. You can bet that he talked them through the spiritual and shamanistic potential of what they were doing and maybe mentioned his friend Jim while he was at it.

Of the four albums, the second one *Wild Gift* was the one that got all of the attention and was made album of the year in the *LA Times* which didn't happen to punk albums that often in 1981. The songs are very cleverly written. 'White Girl' is a tale of a young girl shacked up with an older, abusive man, 'Back On The Base' is about Elvis – 'I'm the King of Rock'n'Roll, if you don't like it, lump it' – and 'We're Desperate' is a classic punk song about, well, being a punk and the trouble it causes some of the time. X are not a nihilistic punk band by any stretch of the imagination, their whole sound is uplifting.

By 1982, X were beginning to talk about new roots in their music and with their third album *Under the Big Black Sun* they started walking it like they talked it. Together with Wall of Voodoo, X were inventing what would become known as cowpunk, a blend of the two great blue-collar music forms that crossed the generations. It also allowed X to address more mature subject matter. The death of Exene's sister brought poignancy to several of the tracks on the album and her normally atonal vocals are visited by a real sense of sadness on 'Dancing With Tears In My Eyes'. Billy Zoom, the one-time guitarist with Gene Vincent's band, is on fire throughout and Doe's songs are amongst his best. Written with Exene, but more likely created in the first instance by Doe, most of them deal with relationships, one of the best being the saucy 'Motel Room In My Bed'.

The band's fourth album *More Fun In The New World* followed *Under The Big Black Sun* into the Billboard chart but the band were beginning to take on a more sophisticated country sound that suggested that they were looking to sustain a career. Doe and Exene divorced after its release, potentially providing endless material for a fully-fledged country band where the two divorcees still perform together, but with the departure of Billy Zoom before *Ain't Love Grand!*, the X factor had gone from the band. They finally split after two more studio albums, in 1995.

First team: John Doe (v, g), Exene Cervenka (v), Billy Zoom (g), DJ Bonebrake (d)

Place, time, scene: LA 1977. X were a hardcore band that integrated rockabilly and blues into the act from the beginning, thanks to the guitar work of Billy Zoom. Their more intelligent approach and adoption of a slight yearning country twang to their rockabilly punk, especially on the ballads, appealed directly to the Paisley Underground bands of the early- to mid-eighties.

What to buy first: *Wild Gift* 1980

And then: *Under The Big Black Sun* 1981

In retrospect: *Beyond & Back: The X Anthology* 1997

Y

YO LA TENGO

Yo La Tengo formed in 1985 when the fashion for shaping guitar noise and feedback into a usable pop sound was at its height. Following Glenn Branca's experiments with detuning and minimalist arrangements making maximum rock'n'roll by using six guitars instead of one, Sonic Youth set out on a career of music-making that put noise into a rock format. A couple of years later, Scotland's Jesus And Mary Chain, inspired by the Velvet Underground, were integrating droning noise and dark melodies on their *Psychocandy* album. Enter Yo La Tengo, a band set on a similar course, based in Hoboken, New Jersey, whose lead vocalist and guitarist Ira Kaplan had a much bigger record collection (as former music journalists do) and a dead-on Lou Reed vocal.

Together with his partner drummer Georgia Hubley playing the role of Mo Tucker, and assistance from various, spectacularly talented friends, Kaplan developed a band which combined the spirit of the Velvets with the unrestrained blast of Mission Of Burma, and later when James McNew joined on bass, a fully realized sense of groove too. Catch 'em live and you'll realize that this is a band full of music fans, and skilled ones at that. They think nothing of swapping instruments or taking requests from the audience for cover songs that they may not have ever played together before, and it's that sense of adventure and level of skill that has seen them progress where other bands have fallen by the wayside.

The first album, *Ride The Tiger*, was produced by Clint Conley, the bassist from Mission Of Burma; guitarist Dave Schramm who added some awesome guitar-work to an album that may not be the most representative of the band's staggering magnificence but does set-up the basic tenets of Yo La Tengo practice. There are two types of song, wistful, melancholy, quiet and well, noisy bastard rock. There are also a couple of obscure covers, of songs by the Kinks and Love, which fit right in there like they were songs the band had written themselves. Schramm is not on the follow-up, *New Wave Hot Dogs* or *President Yo La Tengo*, but that allows Kaplan and Hubley to develop a more direct style which focuses on melody and harmony, sometimes stripped down to utter simplicity and sometimes encased within droning guitar-works. *Fakebook* was an album of covers that Dave Schramm dropped by for. Again, they all sound like Yo La Tengo songs even though they are written by Ray Davies, John Cale, Cat Stevens and Gram Parsons. 'Painful' reveals an ever-developing understanding of song structure and with the addition of bassist James McNew, a solid and strong bass rhythm that keeps Kaplan's addiction for splaying feedback all over the walls in check. It was a good album, but *I Can Hear The Heart Beating As One* was better.

In fact, it could well be the defining album of everything good that's been going on in alternative guitar-based music for the last decade. Released in 1997, it has the feedback and harmonics of Sonic Youth, the vocal harmonies and krautrock/pop blend perfected by Stereolab, the lazy-ass irony and pastiche of Pavement and importantly, the melodic skills always associated with Yo La Tengo themselves. Kaplan is at his electric-lash best on 'We're An American Band' and 'Sugarcube', Hubley's voice is tragic on 'Shadows' and sounds like she could probably do with a big cuddle on 'My Little Corner Of the World', and McNew's bass does sterling work throughout, providing the ground from which layers of sound emerge and sonic sparks fly. Check 'Spec Bebop' for a lesson in controlled mayhem, and the album's centrepiece, 'Autumn Sweater' which is the exact sonic definition of what is meant by the phrase 'less is more', well until you listen properly at any rate, then it becomes apparent that the song which seemed so simple is actually layered with a complexity of rhythms and textures, none of which detract from the central melody. Genius.

The album that followed was snappily entitled *And Then Nothing Turned Itself Inside-Out*. It took the apparent minimalism of 'Autumn Sweater' and spread it out over an entire album. The vocals are often spoken, as on 'The Last Days Of Disco' and 'The Crying Of Lot G.' and the sound is muted with the exception of one song 'Cherry Chapstick' which seems out of place, although the fact that it is effectively a themed-concept album with most of the songs written by Kaplan and Hubley about the history of their relationship together might explain that. The cover version this time is George McCrae's 'You Can Have It All', a disco classic that is still dance-able the way Yo La Tengo do it – if you want to get arrested! – while the hub of the album is the final track 'Night Falls On Hoboken', a 17-minute guitar build and burn that will immediately have you reaching for the repeat button. Yo La Tengo are getting better and better and better. Watch out.

First team: Ira Kaplan (g, v, k, b, d), Georgia Hubley (d, v, g, k, b), James McNew (b, v, d, g, k)

Place, time, scene: Hoboken, New Jersey. Yo La Tengo were another band inspired by the Velvet Underground, formed at a time when noise-guitar bands were all the rage. They have transcended their early influences though and by continuing to listen to new styles and developments have internalized entire genres of music which can be selected and synthesized at will. The minimalist underpinning of their sound is a perfect grounding for sonic exploration on a grand scale.

What to buy first: *I Can Hear The Heart Beating As One* 1997

And then: *Ride The Tiger* 1986, *President Yo La Tengo* 1989, *Painful* 1993, *And Then Nothing Turned Itself Inside-Out* 2000

In retrospect: *Genius + Love = Yo La Tengo* 1996

NEIL YOUNG

Neil Young is an untouchable. Of course, he gets the occasional bad review, probably deservedly, but the point is no-one feels that they are in a position to criticize the work of an artist who has consistently broken the rules. He has transcended any scene that he has been involved with, or any musical style for that matter, because he takes risks. He's also a realist, not an idealist. His early career moves were partly dictated by pragmatism, he wanted to make money and set himself up for a life of making music. When he had more money than he could possibly need, following several massive-selling solo albums and a lucrative spin-off project with some hippy chums, he, in his own words, left the middle of the road and 'headed for the ditch' where he's been ever since. He was the hippy that the punks admired and the grungers imitated, the only artist to have been threatened with legal action for making uncommercial music, and possibly the guitarist of his generation (Hendrix was always too much of a showboater).

Young's early bands the Squires and the Mynah Birds were formed in Canada. The Squires did an early form of folk-rock, taking traditional songs and electrifying them just as Dylan was doing south of the border. They lasted a few years and took a shot at the big time in Toronto in 1965 but disbanded shortly afterwards. Young joined the Mynah Birds with bassist Bruce Palmer and Rick James in the days before he was a 'superfreak' funk star, and then just another young man AWOL from the US navy. James' arrest put paid to that band, and so Young and Palmer headed to California in Young's big black hearse where they were spotted by two old friends they had met from a previous visit to the US, Richie Furay and Stephen Stills. Ever since their first meeting, Stills had wanted Young in his band and now he had him. They called themselves Buffalo Springfield, got a manager, befriended the Byrds and were soon house band at the Whiskey-A-Go-Go club on Sunset Strip. After several false starts they finally scored a hit single, which was both Stills' and Young's driving ambition, with 'For What It's Worth', a sparse song written by Stills in reaction to a riot on the Strip which had been caused by police heavy-handedness in enforcing a controversial curfew. The song is basically Stills' voice and Young's simple but powerful guitar, backed-up with a kick-drum.

The band's first album was the only one that Stills and Young actually properly worked on together, and it was a disappointment to the band and their record label. The second one, *Buffalo Springfield Again*, released later the same year was much better but was in effect two half albums masquerading as one. Young's songs are amongst the best he has ever done, notably 'Mr Soul' and the Jack Nitzsche-arranged string songs 'Expecting To Fly' and 'Broken Arrow', proving that although Young was happiest on stage playing his guitar wildly until he blacked-out from one of his regular epileptic fits, he was no slouch in the studio either. 'Expecting To Fly' is a powerful orchestrated song, beautifully arranged and probably inspired by an acid trip, but when sung by Young in his high-pitched whine, comes off sounding like a song of loss and yearning.

Buffalo Springfield lasted one more album before splitting in 1968, and although Young would team up with Stills, together with David Crosby and Graham Nash, a couple of years later for Woodstock and an album entitle *Déjà vu*, he realized that the time was right for solo stars that laid their soul bare for a new

type of audience, searching for their own sense of self and identity – the post-war baby boomers that had got into rock'n'roll, the Beatles and the hippy dream, had grown up and wanted more grown-up answers. With *After The Goldrush* and *Harvest*, he played right into their hands with songs dealing with the environment, advancing age and racism in red-neck America. There was also the anti-heroin track 'The Needle And The Damage Done' on *Harvest* which, along with songs like 'Heart Of Gold' and the Jack Nitzsche-produced epic 'A Man Needs A Maid', portrayed Young as a man on a spiritual and personal quest to find himself, amid the tragedy of contemporary life. That was the middle of the road as far as he was concerned, and with *Harvest* in the bag in 1972, he set about three decades of wilful experimentation and hard rockin'.

Everybody Knows This Is Nowhere released back in 1969 had teamed Young with Danny Whitten, Ralph Molina and Billy Talbot, aka Crazy Horse, and introduced Young's party piece, the extended jam. 'Down By The River' is that album's highlight, but there were many more to come, especially when he worked with Crazy Horse. There's 'Like A Hurricane' on *American Stars N' Bars* and 'Cortez The Killer' on *Zuma* to name just two. Danny Whitten died of an overdose late in 1972, using heroin which he had bought with money given to him by Young as a pay-off after he had fired him. It provoked a dark night of the soul for Young that lasted for three albums. *On The Beach* was described by *Rolling Stone* as one of the most despairing albums of the decade. He had split from his wife, his son had been diagnosed with cerebral palsy and he was apparently obsessing about the state of a society that counted Charles Manson among its number. And then there was *Tonight's The Night* in 1973, recorded in a drunken blow-out with Molina, Talbot and guitarist Nils Lofgren. Young's microphone pops at various points and his voice seems wasted on several of the tracks. The songs deal with death and dark things, kicking-off with the title track which describes Danny Whitten's and roadie Bruce Berry's deaths 'out on the mainline', complete with ironic honky-tonk piano for added punch. There's a song on there sung by Whitten from beyond the grave too, all about going downtown to score some drugs. Heavy stuff. It's Young's best.

In 1979 he ended his contract with Reprise Records with *Rust Never Sleeps*, his own response to punk-rock which had effectively killed off the 'me' generation hippies. The title song claims to be 'the story of Johnny Rotten' and is a positive take on the changes taking place from a man who had been trying to make the hippies get real for a few years by that point. He signed with David Geffen next, having been assured that he could put out whatever type of music he liked, although Geffen was probably thinking that meant quiet *Harvest* albums or loud and caustic *Rust Never Sleeps* type albums. He wasn't ready for *Re-ac-tor* and *Trans*, two albums which were Young's response to his sons' cerebral palsy. Both his children were afflicted and the concepts behind the albums were based respectively on the repetitive physical manipulation patterning programme that his son Ben needed to undergo to encourage his crawling, and the push-button machine that his speechless son needed to communicate. *Re-ac-tor* was annoyingly repetitive and on *Trans*, Young's voice was delivered via a vocoder. Geffen charged Young with delivering non-commercial albums, threatened to sue and Young responded first with a country album and then with a metal album. They parted company in 1987.

'This Note's For You' in 1988 came with a video that parodied Michael Jackson's hair-burning incident while filming a commercial for Pepsi – 'nuff said – and was followed by another great trilogy of albums to mark Neil Young's take on the new rock mainstream. *Freedom* in 1989 was a mix of styles underpinned with occasional blasts of unfeasibly loud guitar, *Ragged Glory* was nine songs of feedback blow-out including

the not-so radio friendly 'Fuckin' Up', and *Weld* was a triple live album of immense power and volume that dedicated an entire disc to solid feedback. He toured with Sonic Youth in 1991, the year of *Nevermind*, and was well-placed to continue with his rejuvenated passion for noise. Of course he didn't. He made *Harvest Moon* instead, a follow-up to his classic 'middle of the road' money-spinner back in 1972.

I could go on, but you get the idea don't you? Neil Young does what he does. And there's a few more years left in the old dog yet.

Place, time, scene: San Francisco 1966. As a member of Buffalo Springfield, Neil Young was one of the founders of underground rock on the west coast of the USA, however unlike many of his contemporaries he kept a healthy distance from the culture that went along with the music, and was well-placed when the hippy dream died and a more reflective style of writing was called for. His decision to use his financial security as collateral for a series of uncompromisingly bleak, loud and experimental albums in the seventies, eighties and nineties is an inspiration to many determined to buck musical trends.

What to buy first: *Tonight's The Night* 1975

And then: Buffalo Springfield: *Buffalo Springfield Again* 1967, *Everybody Knows This Is Nowhere* 1969, *After The Goldrush* 1970, *Harvest* 1972, *On The Beach* 1974, *Rust Never Sleeps* 1979, *Freedom* 1989, *Ragged Glory* 1990

In retrospect: *Decade* 1977

Z

FRANK ZAPPA

Frank Zappa was a workaholic and, although it may not always have been obviously apparent, he took his work seriously right from the start. Like Lou Reed in New York, Zappa was driven by a need to shake-up a music

scene which, in his opinion, had set off on the wrong track entirely when Elvis arrived and sweetened up the social realism and barely-restrained sexuality of black R&B music. Both bands, Frank Zappa And The Mothers of Invention and the Velvet Underground were on a mission to make an art-form out of popular music, to make it matter aesthetically and socially. Both knew what was wrong with popular music and how it could be fixed. It was simple, they just had to open it up.

Jazz and avant-garde classical music had developed in intriguing new directions for most of the twentieth century and as far as Zappa could hear, and John Cale could demonstrate, pop music and so-called serious music went together just fine, it was just a case of getting it down on tape. Of course, there were crucial differences in the way that the two bands went about their projects. Reed, in particular, had little time for Zappa. He considered him too closely aligned with the hippies operating out on the west coast, and maybe didn't appreciate the cartoon buffoonery of the visual and lyrical aspects of the Mothers' early work. But then Zappa probably had some reservations about all that artistically clichéd New York angst too. Calling his band the Mothers, working with the Monkees and hanging out with freaks and organized groups of groupies was all part of Zappa's anti-art art. Just like the Velvets, he was keen not to be applauded for his cleverness and held up as a groundbreaking genius.

Author Ben Watson who appraised Zappa's life and work in the excellent *Negative Dialectics Of Poodle-Play*[67], has him down as a Situationist – an artist who makes his art accessible to a wider audience by turning it into a spectacle and so inspire others to make art of their own everyday lives. The sarcasm, the jokes, the crudity, the apparent sexism and the rumours about eating shit on stage all serve a purpose. Call it low culture, low art if you want, but don't dismiss the music in the same way. Zappa had the studio technique, the arrangements, the orchestrations and orchestras, and the on-stage live conducting that made each incarnation of his band seem like a spontaneous super-eclectic jukebox. For over three decades and over 40 albums, what Zappa said and the way he said it with his music was always important, always political and always for everyone, no matter what colour collar they were attributed with. Warhol and McLaren dabbled in ironic critique and music, Zappa brought both together and created an art-form.

Zappa began with drums. He learned how to keep time for a bagpipe band and pretty quickly had himself one

snare drum to work on at home. At the age of 14 he discovered the avant-garde rhythm music of Edgar Varese and as a birthday present was allowed to phone the artist to discuss his music with him. Throw in an obsession with Stravinsky's 'Rite Of Spring' and late nights hanging with high-school buddy Don Van Vliet, later to become Captain Beefheart, in the Mojave desert listening to black music, specifically west coast R&B, Chicago blues and street-corner doo-wop, and it was all abundantly clear. Frank Zappa's life would be made of music, outsider music.

By 1963 Zappa had his own Studio Z where he made regular recordings with various musicians, including a night session with a young girl where they simulated sex sounds for a bogus client who turned out to be a detective specializing in entrapment of undesirables with long hair and black friends. He did some time for that. He also scored a rockabilly film and spent hours building musical pieces out of rudimentary musical samples and found sounds and narration. In 1962 he recorded with Beefheart as the Soots and followed it up with a teen opera, but both projects failed to get financial backing. Zappa had by this point demonstrated his creative abilities as a composer. He saw his role as that of organizer, of sounds and people. And he had the confidence to do it on a large scale. Vocalist Ray Collins recognized this and convinced his band the Soul Giants that Zappa could be the driving force they needed to make the breakthrough. In 1965 they became the Mothers, adding . . . Of Invention at the behest of MGM who signed them in 1966, after a show at the Whiskey-A-Go-Go, and within the year had an album out.

The double *Freak Out* was released in July 1966, just before the Beatles put out *Revolver*. It covers a range of musical styles, each one nailed by Zappa, his band and a collection of session musicians hand-picked by Zappa to play key roles. The album was the next stage in Zappa's efforts to push commercial pop music into places it had never gone before. 'Who are the Brain Police?' is basic Kafka, a nightmare vision of a dystopian future complete with weird vocals that enter from unexpected sonic angles. 'Trouble Every Day' is a distorted blues stomp that relates the story of the Watts race riot through the medium of TV sports commentary, and 'Monster Magnet' is 'what freaks sound like when you turn them loose in a recording studio at one o'clock in the morning on $500 worth of rented percussion equipment.[68] Hardly anybody bought it.

Zappa followed it with *Absolutely Free*, another album of songs dealing with the key themes of uncritical consumerism, authoritarian government, individual repression and how vegetables keep you regular. Again the music defies genre, and taking inspiration from Varese and Stockhausen, builds the sonic backdrop out of shorter recorded passages. Holger Czukay and Can did something similar several years later. The fourth album *We're Only In It For The Money* is Zappa's overt attack on apparently innovative music that is simply serving a corporate purpose. The cover shot is a parody of the *Sgt Pepper's* cover and the songs are viciously ironic. 'Let's Make The Water Turn Black' is lilting folk-rock aimed squarely at the Byrds, and 'Who Needs The Peace Corps?' just about holds on to the parody style but seems to verge on out and out anger at times. The line 'I will love the police as they kick the shit out of me in the streets', which was removed from initial releases of the album, sums up Zappa's central concern with the evident conservative quietism of the hippy movement and its peaceful co-option into the political mainstream. Zappa fan John Lennon's rewording of the lyrics to 'Revolution' on the *White Album*, recorded a few months after the eventual release of *We're Only In It For The Money* marks the point at which Lennon changed his cultural position on such matters too. For the next four years Lennon pursued a directly political policy and eventually worked with the Mothers in 1972 on live tracks recorded at the Filmore East for the album *Sometime In New York City*. By then Zappa had become the definitive underground rock star. His blend of cynicism and musical experimentalism plus the long straggly hair, hippie moustache and sponsorship of Cynthia Plaster-Caster and the Girls Together Outrageously groupie organization gave him almost universal appeal amongst album-buyers who wanted to get to the root of new musical styles like glam-rock, progressive art-rock and the return-to-basics garage punk emerging out of Detroit. Zappa's albums in the period between 1968 and 1974 are all key to any collection.

Cruising With Ruben And The Jets is a pastiche of fifties doowop and romantic teen balladry, a perfectly executed exercise in contrariness. Zappa made it because he could and it had the added effect of annoying the revolutionaries with their heavy political music. *Uncle Meat* set the scene for art-rock as an extended form. Drawing on outside musicians, the album is a collection of instrumentals, extended solos and sampled speech. It's heavy stuff. *Hot Rats* is much lighter and contains another selection of instrumentals, kicking off with the pastoral beauty of 'Peaches En Regalia' and ending with the epic 'Willie The Pimp' featuring vocals from Captain Beefheart and Zappa at his wah-wah best. *Weasels Ripped My Flesh* is a set of live performances that demonstrate what Zappa calls his 'conductive' skills, and the ability for the musicians working alongside him to shift tempo and style instantly at their master's behest. *Chunga's Revenge* brings Mark Volman and Howard Kaylan into the Mothers' fold. Formerly members of perfect pop purveyors, the Turtles, and now calling themselves Flo and Eddie, they contributed harmonies to the next few albums and were key to the symphonic sound of *200 Motels* before making off with several members of Zappa's band in 1972. At that point Zappa was wheelchair-bound following an onstage attack which tumbled him off-stage and into hospital. He returned in 1973 with the LA groove funk-rock of *Overnite Sensation* which got him some radio-play with tracks like 'Dirty Love' and 'Montana', and pissed off all the art-rockers who listened to the album and found it too slick by half. It was neat and tidy and somehow seemed empty in its obvious commerciality. But then, that was the idea of course. The Z man strikes again. He followed it with a surreal pop music telling of *King Lear* and then went off to work with the London Symphony Orchestra.

OK, I have to stop now. There are just too many albums to talk about and virtually every one of them has a story attached and some form of musical or cultural significance going for it. Zappa knocked them out right up until his death from cancer in 1993 and even picked up a Grammy at one point for his innovative 1986 free-jazz album, *Jazz From Hell*. He didn't feel particularly honoured and no doubt saw the whole thing as a cynical exercise in media housekeeping. An artist with 50 groundbreaking albums to his name spanning the entirety of post-Elvis popular music history cannot continue to exist outside of the accepted institutionalised mainstream of American music. That would surely mean he had won?

First team: Mothers Of Invention 1966–68: Frank Zappa (g, v, k, d), Ian Underwood (p, fl, sx), Ray Collins (v), Bunk Gardner (d), Don Preston (p), Roy Estrada (b)

Place, time, scene: Los Angeles 1966. The Mothers Of Invention were part of the early psychedelic scene but soon turned on the movement as it became more institutionalized and tied in with the investment capitalism of the music industry. From that point on, Zappa set about distinct musical projects that seemed to purposely oppose current fashions. His production techniques, arrangement and virtuosity influenced many bands intent on making art-rock, and his insistent focus on controversial subject matter, particularly concerning sex and sexuality, probably inspired glam-rock and punk.

What to buy first: *Freak Out* 1966

And then: *Hot Rats* 1969, *Uncle Meat* 1968, *Apostrophe* 1974

In retrospect: *Strictly Commercial: Best Of Frank Zappa* 1995

New Alternatives?

And to finish, another exercise in trajectory-tracing but this time without the benefit of musical hindsight. The 15 acts listed below may be the future of alternative music, or perhaps not. At the time of publication they represent some of the most interesting attempts to do something honest, different and with the potential to get culturally connected, even if the culture they need to connect with has not given access just yet.

BASEMENT JAXX

First team: Felix Burton (t-t, prog, v), Simon Ratcliffe (t-t, prog, g)

Place, time, scene: London 1998. The clues were there on their debut album *Remedy* that Basement Jaxx were the duo most likely to successfully adapt when dance music inevitably got incorporated as another element in the perpetually diversifying supergenre of rock. Dance oriented singles will continue, but even the best dance albums were always exercises in form and texture when it came down to it. Basement Jaxx had melodies and hooks right from the start, and they were always itching to play live with a band; that much was obvious from the way they structured songs like 'Red Alert' (check the funk band introduction, nothing quantized about that). Since then the mood has got heavier, the rhythms less repetitive and guitars (plugged and unplugged) are central to the proceedings. The songs aren't just about partying either; there's some darker, relationship stuff on 2003's *Kish-Kash* with a vocal contribution from Siouxsie Sioux no less. Electro-clash, my arse. Basement Jaxx are plugged into the source.

What to buy first: *Kish-Kash* 2003

And then: *Remedy* 1999

BLACK REBEL MOTORCYCLE CLUB

First team: Peter Hayes (g, b, k, v), Robert Turner (b, g, k, v), Nick Jago (d)

Place, time, scene: San Francisco 1998. Black Rebel Motorcycle Club seem to have resurrected the guitar-noise aesthetic that went under with the advent of grunge and Britpop, and are here to offer a solid alternative to the guitar, sampler, laptop mash-up that has fused rock with hip-hop. The fascination with Jesus And Mary Chain is clear, but the bottom-end groove and heavy-fuzz motif that runs through their sound is entirely their own. Few new bands have so much input into their own technical production as Black Rebel Motorcycle Club and they've avoided clever branding ideas too.

What to buy first: *B.R.M.C.* 2001

And then: *Take Them On, On Your Own* 2003

THE CORAL

First team: James Skelly (v, g), Ian Skelly (d), Bill Ryder-Jones (g, tr), Nick Power (k), Paul Duffy (b, sx), Lee Southall (g, v)

Place, time, scene: Wirral 1997. A band inspired by the Oasis hegemony of the mid-nineties, whose members have since worked backwards through the readily available back-catalogue of the sixties and seventies to create a musical experience that resonates with the new eclectic approach to cultural consumption in the new millennium. How many other bands can you name that have brought together Mersey-beat and Beefheart influences, to name just two sources of inspiration? The Coral love their music and are discovering and mastering old styles and techniques at a breathtaking rate. They fall somewhere between progressive muso-ism and 'mad for it' no-brainer-ism. The perfect position.

Dizzee Rascal

What to buy first: *The Coral* 2002

And then: *Magic And Medicine* 2003

DIZZEE RASCAL

First team: Dizzee Rascal (v, prog), Wiley (prog)

Place, time, scene: London 2002. Dizzee Rascal makes uncomfortable music. The lyrics are stark and not romanticized in the least, the shootings, stabbings and teenage pregnancies are real. Dizzee's eerie vocal is joined by sinister chattering, the like of which has not been heard on record before and is made all the more disconcerting when teamed with electronic pulses in place of the more familiar beats, and an overall sound that is part electro-funk, part Kraftwerk and has splashes of early sparse and heavy Def Jam. Dizzee, who has learned much of his art from friend Wiley and the Roll Deep crew, assembles his music on

an iBook computer, somehow managing to summon up the filthiest bass-lines this side of hardcore ragga. Two-step if you want, it's just possible, but that's not really the idea at all.

What to buy first: *Boy In Da Corner* 2002

INTERPOL

First team: Paul Banks (v, g), Daniel Kessler (g, v), Carlos D. (b, k), Daniel Fogarino (d)

Place, time, scene: New York 1998. Interpol may be the New York band of the moment that outlasts all the competition. Theirs is not a haphazard project. Unlike most garage-punk bands who place a premium on recording live to capture the energy of the performance, Interpol's earliest recordings were built out of individual instruments recorded into an 8-track one at a time, and with access to a 24-track they haven't changed their approach. For Interpol, building a mood is crucial, and on *Turn On the Bright Lights*, that mood is severely claustrophobic. The reference points are Joy Division and the Cure in their heavier moments.

What to buy first: *Turn On The Bright Lights* 2002

LEMON JELLY

First team: Nick Fraglen (samp), Fred Deakin (t-t)

Place, time, scene: London 1998. Lemon Jelly specialize in music that makes people happy. It's built from samples and manipulated on cold, calculating machinery, but comes off sounding warm and soothing, and most importantly, not permanently linked with the post-rave chill-out scene that always had a slight air of cynicism about it. In fact, it might be impossible for anyone to dislike Lemon Jelly, perhaps because of their utter commitment to fantasy music where the lush sounds are perfectly teamed up with narrative samples and extraneous noises that evoke waking dream sequences. Their appeal amongst children and infants has been noted by the cooler end of the parent profession.

What to buy first: *Lemonjelly.ky* 2000

And then: *Lost Horizons* 2002

NEPTUNES (N.E.R.D.)

First team: Pharrell Williams (d, v, prog), Chad Hugo (prog)

Place, time, scene: Virginia 1997. OK so they're a production team, but haven't you heard, the beats are the key thing in the new millennium, and the Neptunes have got more beats than anyone else. After studying under Teddy Riley, their break came with the Ol' Dirty Bastard single 'Got Your Money'. Since then their loose and flappy kick-drum sound and patented bass licks have worked wonders making pop and R&B interesting, at least some of the time anyway. Their own N.E.R.D. project proved that they could rock too. Williams leads a band of tip-top musicians and rappers collectively known as Spymob, who regularly take R&B licks to hardcore punk hang-

outs while Hugo stays in the studio, devising ways of getting the cross-cultural mayhem down on tape.

What to buy first: *The Neptunes Present ... Clones* 2003

And then: N.E.R.D. *In Search Of ...* 2002

RADIO 4

First team: Greg Collins (d), Anthony Roman (b, v), Tommy Williams Jnr. (g, v), Gerard Garone (k), and P.J. O'Connor (perc)

Place, time, scene: New York 1999. Radio 4 are named after the PiL song that appears on their *Metal Box* album which, along with releases by Gang Of Four and no-wave New York band Liquid Liquid, made a good job of fusing disco, dub and funk with the harsh guitars and attitude of punk. Produced by The DFA, a production team made up of a veteran punk and a beat scientist, their first single 'Dance To The Underground' shook up the indie club scene, potentially inspiring a generation of non-dancers to shake booty in a way that entirely undermines the terpsichorean art as applied to more popular forms. Dance music gets its punk comeupppance. There's a whole scene going in New York right now. Try the Rapture, Playgroup, Electric 6 and The Faint for variety.

What to buy first: *Gotham* 2002

SEAFOOD

First team: David Line (v, g), Kevin Hendrick (b, v), Charles Macleod (g), Caroline Banks (d, v)

Place, time, scene: London 1998. Indie guitar music returns. Seafood write songs that are at heart delicate and gentle, and explode when the power chords crash in and the amps get cranked up really high, but do it at a much faster pace than the indie bands of yore, and with occasional bursts of shouting. 'Psychic Rainy Nights' is a masterclass in duelling Fenders and Gibsons as fed through Boss and Sansamp effects units.

What to buy first: *Messenger In The Camp* 1998

And then: *When Do We Start Fighting* 2001

SPEARMINT

First team: Shirley Lee (v, g), James Parsons (b, g), Ronan Larvor (k), Simon Calnan (d)

Place, time, scene: London 1996. For a moment in 1996 Spearmint were being touted as the next big thing by the British music press, but with no further support from the mainstream or specialist media the band's pop potential stalled. In the late nineties the official alternative categories became fixed, and catchy, passionate, indie soul-pop was not an available option. We did our bit at Xfm though. It was a moral issue. 'Sweeping The Nation' was played every hour in daylight hours for six weeks straight, it was after all their tribute to 'bands who never got played on the radio'. The most moving song of the last decade, bar none.

What to buy first: *A Week Away* 1998

And then: *My Missing Days* 2003

SPOON

First team: Britt Daniel (v, g), Jim Eno (d)

Place, time, scene: Austin, Texas 1999. Britt Daniel is a worthy successor to the lone-star state's finest; from Buddy Holly to the 13th Floor Elevators and Butthole Surfers. He combines impressive songwriting skills and oddball sounds that make his work across four albums stylistically impossible to clarify. The 2002 album *Kill The Moonlight* is built around minimal instrumental structures, setting off his amazing white soul voice and innate grasp of melody to stunning effect. The simplest most accurate pop music of current times.

What to buy first: *Kill The Moonlight* 2002

And then: *Girls Can Tell* 2001

THE STREETS

First team: Mike Skinner (v, samp)

Place, time, scene: Birmingham, UK 2000. The name refers to a new take on UK garage, reclaimed from the clubs and injected with a healthy dose of hip-hop attitude. The beats are slower and the rhymes relate directly to the garage and urban culture that Skinner sees around him, albeit delivered in his own seriously clued-up and sometimes downright hilarious patois. Less self-obsessed than So Solid Crew, more personal than Miss Dynami-tee-hee.

What to buy first: *Original Pirate Material* 2002

SYSTEM OF A DOWN

First team: Serj Tankian (v), Daron Malakian (g), Shavo Odadjian (b), John Dolmayan (d)

Place, time, scene: Los Angeles 1996. System Of A Down are a political band in the vein of later period Sepultura, but with Brazil exchanged for Armenia. The lyrics pull no punches, perhaps even more direct than Rage Against The Machine at times. Musically it's all about sudden and well-executed stylistic shifts, taking in thrash metal, eastern folk moves and pomp-rock. Puts Korn to shame.

What to buy first: *Toxicity* 2002

And then: *System Of A Down* 1998

2 MANY DJS

First team: David Dewaele (prog, t-t), Stephen Dewaele (prog, t-t)

Place, time, scene: Belgium 2000. The brothers Dewaele also operate under the name Soulwax as a fairly straightforward rock band, but the reason they are here is for their skills involving the technical manipulation of audio and inspired take on the science of juxtaposition. Fellow 'bootlegger' Richard X has made it clear that the art of slamming two existing songs together is more than just an exercise in musical one-upmanship, and the Dewaeles know exactly what to choose and how to edit, balance, loop and work the pitchshifter to get the mix just so. Without asking, they 'mashed up' the Stooges and Salt'n'Pepper and Nirvana and All Saints and inspired a new way of listening. The first time they did it was on their Belgian radio show, available as *As Heard On Radio Soulwax Part 2*, but now an album beloved of both dance-heads and rock critics. The Remix show on Xfm went bootleg crazy for at least six months in 2002, and now anyone with access to Pro-Tools and a CD-ripper is at it. If you want to do it legal, it involves a lot of letters, emails, faxes and phone calls to get that all important clearance, so 2 Many DJs deserve to be in just from the perspective of sheer administrative organization.

What to buy first: *As Heard On Radio Soulwax Part 2* 2002

YEAH YEAH YEAHS

First team: Karen O (v), Brain Chase (d), Nick Zinner (g)

Place, time, scene: New York 2000. Just as Patti Smith brought a different dimension to the first New York punk scene in the seventies with songs that audiences could relate to on a more personal level, Karen O puts herself into her songs and performances, and that means we get her intelligence, sense of fun and raw sexuality. The sound of the band is stripped bare – no bass, just like the Blues Explosion and Royal Trux before them – an electrified version of the folk songs that the band started out making before they succumbed to the rock'n'roll beast.

What to buy first: *Fever To Tell* 2003

Notes

1 The Country Bluegrass Blues Club (CBGBs) was opened by Hilly Kristal in December 1973. It was situated in the Bowery district of New York.

2 Ronald Sukenick, taken from an online article 'Avant PoMo Now'. 4 January 1996. www.altx.com

3 The Twisted Wheel was a northern soul club which opened on Whitworth Street in Manchester in 1966. It was notable for some of the first all-nighters.

4 The Hacienda opened on Whitworth Street in Manchester in 1982. It was owned by Factory Records with New Order retaining a financial interest. Its catalogue number was FAC 51.

5 Dave Lewis. Review of Hammersmith Odeon gig. *Sounds*. 1977.

6 The Roxy was situated in Neal Street in Covent Garden. It opened in December 1976 and closed four months later. Virtually every significant punk band of the period performed there.

7 Mark Eitzel, interviewed for *Chick Magnet*. 1994. www.exitproductions.com

8 Rakim, interviewed for thaformula.com. Posted 12 June 2003. www.thaformula.com

9 Lollapalooza was an idea realized by Perry Farrel of Jane's Addiction and Porno for Pyros who organized the first event – a travelling US rock festival – in 1990. The first year's line-up included Nine Inch Nails, Butthole Surfers, Ice-T, Henry Rollins and unsurprisingly, Jane's Addiction.

10 Greg Graffin. 'A Punk Synopsis'. 1997. www.spunk.org

11 Steve Albini. *Matter*. Vol 1, No 1. January 1983.

12 *River's Edge*. A film about small-town Generation X kids gone wrong. Directed by Tim Hunter, 1987.

13 *The Wire* is a British music magazine, launched in 1982. It had the original subtitle 'Jazz, Improvised Music And . . .'.

14 Middle Earth operated out of a basement in King Street in Covent Garden in 1967. It transferred to the Roundhouse in Camden in 1968. UFO was situated in the basement of 31 Tottenham Court Road. It opened in December 1966 and was a regular haunt for the Beatles, the Stones and the Who. Pink Floyd and Soft Machine were two of the key bands that played at the club.

15 Matt Groening. *Mojo* magazine, page 129. December 1993.

16 The Sunday Social was a club night organized by Heavenly Records. It was launched in the summer of 1994 in a pub called The Albany situated at the top of Great Portland Street in London, and is acknowledged to be the birthplace of Big Beat music.

17 Robin Guthrie, interviewed by Patrick Jennings for *The Guitar*, page 156. 2001. www.bellaunion.com

18 Max's Kansas City opened its doors for the first time in December 1965. It was situated at 213 Park Avenue South off Union Square in New York City. Mickey Ruskin was the club's owner, a music fan who gave the Velvet Underground a residency period at the venue in 1970. When punk broke in 1975 Max's, along with CBGBs was central to the Bohemian art scene, although it's rumoured that Patti Smith was initially turned away from the venue for being too 'grungey'.

19 Julian Cope. *Head-On*. Thorsons 1999. First published Magog Books Ltd 1994.

20 Greil Marcus, interviewed for *Rolling Stone*. 1982. From *The Rolling Stone Interviews – The 1980s*. St Martin's Press 1989.

21 The Whiskey-A-Go-Go was situated at 8901 Sunset Boulevard, on the corner of Clark and San Vicente in Los Angeles, an area known as the Sunset Strip. Elmer Valentine opened the club in 1964. The term 'go-go dancer' originated at the club, inspired by the resident female DJ

who danced in a cage at the side of the stage. House bands included Johnny Rivers, Frank Zappa and the Mothers of Invention, Love and the Doors who transferred to the Whiskey after a successful run as house band at the London Fog, a much smaller club situated next door.

22 From *Electric Dylan*, chapter entitled 'Highway 61 Revisited'. Originally featured in issues 7 and 8 of *The Bridge* magazine, now found at rdf.pwp. blueyonder.co.uk

23 Danny Rampling opened Shoom in 1987 after returning from Ibiza where, together with fellow DJs Paul Oakenfold, Nicky Holloway and Johnny Walker, he had discovered the smile-inducing culture driven by Balearic beats. The club, situated in the Southwark fitness centre in London, was a key factor in the popularization of house, techno and acid music in the UK. It closed in 1990.

24 Graham Massey, interviewed for *Melody Maker*. 6 June 1998.

25 Tony Fletcher. *Never Stop: The Echo And The Bunnymen Story*. Omnibus Press 1987.

26 Nick Cave. 'Thistles in the Soul'. *Nick Cave: King Ink*. Black Spring Press 1988.

27 Blix Bargeld, interview by Jason Goss for *Perfect Sound Forever*. December 1998.

28 Alec Empire, statement to accompany the blacklisting of Atari Teenage Riot back-catalogue. www.digitalhardcore.com

29 Alec Empire, interviewed by Todd Hanson for *The Onion a.v. Club* (online journal). 23 July 1997.

30 Brian Eno, interviewed by Lester Bangs for *Musician*. 1979.

31 The Fall, interviewed by Danny Baker for *Zig-Zag*. March 1978.

32 Mark E. Smith, interview in *Volume*. September 1992.

33 Wayne Coyne, interview in *Nude As The News*. 2003. www.nudeasthenews.com

34 The Electric Circus was situated on St Mark's Place on the Lower East Side of New York. It attracted high profile celebrities in the early sixties and after 1965 became a centre of bohemian society. The Dom was the name given to the bar located downstairs at the club, which was taken over by Andy Warhol and the Velvet Underground for their Exploding Plastic Inevitable

multimedia psychedelic music and theatre extravaganza in 1966.

35 Andy Gill, interviewed by Jason Goss for *Perfect Sound Forever*. January 2000. www.furious.com/ perfect

36 Greil Marcus. Review of Gang Of Four. July 1990. www.gillmusic.com

37 Michael Stipe, quoted on sleevenotes to reissued *Entertainment* album.

38 Howie Gelb, interview with *Bucketful Of Brains*. December 1992.

39 The *New Musical Express* (*NME*) compiled the *C86* cassette to be sold exclusively through the paper. The album was later released for sale. It was compiled as a follow-up to *C81* but unlike its predecessor it was roundly criticized for its poor production quality and generic nature. The aim had been to resurrect guitar-based pop to challenge the growth of hip-hop but it ended up becoming a derisive term and bands like Primal Scream, the Wedding Present and the Pastels were not served particularly well by their inclusion.

40 Eric's was situated on Matthew Street in Liverpool just down the road from The Cavern Club. It opened its doors in October 1976 and closed them in March 1980, just long enough to bring punk-rock to a bunch of teenagers, many of whom formed their own bands and created a vibrant post-punk scene to rival that of sixties Merseybeat. Echo And The Bunnymen, the Teardrop Explodes, Wah, OMD, KLF, Frankie Goes To Hollywood, Dead Or Alive and the Lightning Seeds can all trace their roots back to the club.

41 Nicky Wire, interviewed by Mark Lawson for BBC Radio 4. July 2003.

42 Wayne Kramer, in sleevenotes for *Big Bang: The Best Of The MC5*. Winter 2000.

43 Mercury Rev, interview with *Uncut* magazine. January 1999.

44 Mike Watt, in Michael Azzerad, *Our Band Could Be Your Life – Scenes From The American Indie Underground 1981–1991*, page 354. First Back Bay 2002.

45 Stuart Braithwaite, interview with dotmusic. com. April 2001.

46 Mudhoney interview with *Backlash*. December 1988.

47 David Cavanagh. *The Creation Records Story: My Magpie Eyes Are Hungry For The Prize*. Virgin Publishing 2000.

48 Kevin Shields, interview with KUCI. www.kuci.org

49 The Mercer Arts Centre was situated on the outskirts of Greenwich Village. It incorporated practice rooms, boutiques and two performance spaces, The Kitchen and The Oscar Wilde Room. The infrastructure for the building was based on the former Grand Hotel, and part of it collapsed some time in 1974 while Chris Stein of Blondie was practising there.

50 Stephen McRobbie, interview by Vanessa Hays and Carsten Wohlfeld. 1997. www.twee.net

51 David Thomas, included in Jon Allan's liner notes for *The Day The Earth Met Rocket From The Tombs* (Glitterhouse Records GRCD549).

52 David Cavanagh. *The Creation Records Story: My Magpie Eyes Are Hungry For The Prize*. Virgin Publishing 2000.

53 The Living Room was a live band night situated in the upstairs room at Adam's Arms on Conway Street in north London. The chief promoters were Alan McGee and Dick Green who began booking bands for the venue in 1983. The Television Personalites were one of the first acts to play there and the Living Room soon became one of the few London clubs willing to book unsigned bands. The Loft, the Pastels and a fledgeling Primal Scream all played there as the venue became a testing ground for bands later signed to Creation Records.

54 John Lydon. *No Blacks, No Irish, No Dogs: The Authorised Autobiography Of Johnny Rotten Of The Sex Pistols*. Picador 1995.

55 Marcus Gray. *It Crawled From The South*. Guiness 1992.

56 Mayo Thomas, interview by Richie Unterburger. 2002. www.richieunterburger.com

57 Lou Barlow, interview with Billy Bob Hargus. January 1997. www.furious.com

58 Dave Marsh, in *The Heart Of Rock And Soul*. Plume 1989.

59 Julia Stringer. *Popular Music* 11/1. January 1992.

60 Carla Bozulich, quoted in *Alternative Press*. 1996.

61 Sonic Boom 1997, from sleevenotes to *Forged Prescriptions*.

62 Nick Hornby. *31 Songs*, page 76. Penguin Books 2003.

63 Julian Cope. *Head-On*. Thorsons 1999. First published Magog Books Ltd 1994.

64 Genesis P. Orridge, in Richard Metzger (ed.), *Book Of Lies: The Disinformation Guide To Magick And The Occult*. Disinformation 2003.

65 Stuart Staples, interviewed by Nick Hasted for *The Independent*. 20 June 1996.

66 Sterling Morrison, in Victor Bockris and Gerard Malanga, *Up-tight: The Velvet Underground Story*. Omnibus Press 1983.

67 Ben Watson. *Negative Dialectics Of Poodle-Play*. St Martin's Press 1993.

68 Frank Zappa, unreferenced in Ben Watson, *Negative Dialectics Of Poodle-Play*, page 66. St Martin's Press 1993.

Index

Page entries in **bold** refer to main entries within the text whilst entries in *italic* numbers refer to photographs.